Precursors of Nelson

Sir George Rooke (see Chapter 2). Oil by Michael Dahl

Precursors of Nelson

BRITISH ADMIRALS
OF THE
EIGHTEENTH CENTURY

Edited by
PETER LE FEVRE & RICHARD HARDING

STACKPOLE
BOOKS

Contents

The Contributors

Dr David Aldridge was a lecturer in history at the University of Newcastle-upon-Tyne. He retired in 1993. He has published widely in dictionaries, encyclopædias and journals and contributed to *British Naval Documents, 1204-1960*, the Navy Records Society centenary volume published in 1993.

Professor Daniel A Baugh is Professor Emeritus of Modern British History, Cornell University. His principal works are *British Naval Administration in the Age of Walpole* (Princeton 1965) and *Naval Administration, 1715-1750*, NRS (1977). He has also written on government and society in England, 1660-1830, especially on relief of the poor. During the past two decades his articles and essays have been chiefly concerned with the maritime, colonial, and financial aspects of British defence policy and maritime geopolitics in the eighteenth century.

Kenneth Breen was head of the department of history at St Mary's College, Strawberry Hill from 1983 until his retirement in 1993. He has served on the Councils of the Navy Records Society and the Society for Nautical Research. Among other items, he has published on 'Graves and Hood at the Chesapeake' and 'Sir George Rodney and St Eustatius in the American War: A Commercial and Naval Distraction, 1775-1781', both in *The Mariner's Mirror* in 1980 and 1998 respectively.

Patricia K Crimmin was Senior Caird Fellow at the National Maritime Museum 1998-1999. From 1967 until her retirement in 1998 she was lecturer and then senior lecturer in history at the Royal Holloway College, University of London. She is a Fellow of the Royal Historical Society, Fellow of the Society of Antiquaries, Treasurer of the British Commission for Maritime History and a vice-president of the Navy Records Society and a councillor of the Society for Nautical Research

She is author of a number of articles on maritime and naval history and is currently engaged on a major study of prisoners held in Britain during the French Revolutionary and Napoleonic Wars.

Dr Michael Duffy is Director of the Centre for Maritime Historical Studies at the University. He is the author of many books and articles on naval subjects, including *Soldiers, Sugar and Seapower: The British Expeditions to the West Indies and the War against Revolutionary France* (1987). He is a Fellow of the Royal Historical Society and vice-president of the Navy Records Society. From 1991 until 2000 he was the Hon Editor of *The Mariner's Mirror, The Journal of the Society for Nautical Research*.

Professor Richard Harding is Professor of Organisational History at the University of Westminster. He is the author of *Amphibious Warfare in the Eighteenth Century* (1991), and has published studies on the development of the Royal Navy and seapower in the age of sail: *The Evolution of the Sailing Navy* (1995) and *Seapower and Naval Warfare* (1999). He is a Fellow of the Royal Historical Society, a councillor of the Navy Records Society, a member of the British Commission for Maritime History and, from the end of 2000, Hon Editor of *The Mariner's Mirror*.

Professor John Hattendorf is the Ernest B King Professor of Maritime History and Director of the Advanced Research Department at the US Naval War College, Newport, Rhode Island. He is the author of many books and articles on seapower and naval affairs, ranging from his doctoral research on Queen Anne's navy to collections of essays on contemporary maritime strategy. He has edited many collections of essays and documents for publications. He was also the general editor of 'Classics of Sea Power', the series which reprinted a number of important tracts on this subject.

Dr Roger Knight retired as Deputy Director of the National Maritime Museum in July 2000. He has published many articles and contributed to numerous collections of essays on the subject of naval administration. He edited the two-volume *Guide to the Manuscripts in the National Maritime Museum* (1977-1980) and the *Portsmouth Dockyard Papers, 1774-1783* (1987). He edited the eighteenth century section of the Navy Records Society centenary volume *British Naval Documents, 1204-1960* (1993). He is a Fellow of the Royal Historical Society and a councillor of the Navy Records Society.

Professor Andrew Lambert is Professor of Naval History at King's College, London. He is a Fellow of the Royal Historical Society, a vice-president of the British Commission for Maritime History, Hon Secretary of the Navy Records Society, and on the editorial board of the Society for Nautical Research. He has published extensively on naval subjects, including *The Crimean War: British Grand Strategy Against Russia, 1853-1856* (1990), *The Last Sailing Battlefleet: Maintaining Naval Mastery, 1815-1850* (1992) and *The Foundations of Naval History: John Knox Laughton and the Historical Profession* (1998).

Brian Lavery is Head of Ship Technology at the National Maritime Museum. He is the author of several major works on the ships of the sailing navy, including *Deane's Doctrine of Naval Architecture* (1981), *The Ship of the Line*, 2 vols (1983-1984), *Anatomy of the Ship: Bellona* (1985), *Nelson's Navy: The Ships, Men and Organisation, 1793-1815* (1989). He recently edited a wide range of documents for *Shipboard Life and Organisation, 1731-1815* (1998), published by the Navy Records Society.

Dr Peter Le Fevre is an independent scholar and freelance researcher. He has written a large number of articles on the late seventeenth century navy and naval officers of the period. He has done extensive research into the records of late seventeenth century administration at the Public Record Office and has spoken there and elsewhere upon the *Anne*, one of Charles II's Thirty New Ships, which now lies in the mud in off Rye. He is currently completing a full-length biography of Arthur Herbert, Earl of Torrington.

Dr Ruddock Mackay taught history at St Andrews University from 1965, becoming Reader in 1974. He retired in 1983. Apart from numerous articles on a variety of naval subjects, he has published *Admiral Hawke* (1965), *Fisher of Kilverstone* (1974) and *Balfour: The Intellectual Statesman* (1985). He edited selections from the Hawke Papers at the National Maritime Museum for the Navy Records Society, which were published in 1990.

Dr Roger Morriss is a freelance scholar and researcher. From 1979 until 1995 he held various positions at the National Maritime Museum, including a substantial time as Head of Manuscripts. He is author of *The Royal Dockyards during the Revolutionary and Napoleonic Wars* (1983). In 1992 he carried out research into the naval records held in United States archives for the National Maritime Museum, which was published as *Guide to British Naval Papers in North America* (1994). His latest work, *Cockburn and the British Navy in Transition: Admiral Sir George Cockburn, 1772-1853* was published in 1997.

Dr Nicholas Rodger is Professor of Naval History at the University of Exeter. He was Hon Secretary of the Naval Records Society from 1975 until 1992. He is author of a number of acclaimed works on naval history. His *Wooden World: An Anatomy of the Georgian Navy* (1986) has become a bestselling book. In 1998 the first volume of an intended multi-volume history of the Royal Navy, *The Safeguard of the Sea: A Naval History of Britain, 660-1649* (1997) received the Anderson Medal from the Society for Nautical Research. He is the author of many other books, articles and reviews on naval history, including *The Insatiable Earl: A Life of John Montagu, 4th Earl of Sandwich* (1993). He is a Fellow of the Royal Historical Society and a councillor of the Navy Records Society.

Christopher Ware joined the staff at the National Maritime Museum in 1977. In 1988 he was part of the project to list and number the oil painting collection and was involved in the production of the concise list of oil paintings. From 1990 to 1993 he worked on listing and cataloguing ships plans. He is the author of *The Bomb Vessel* (1995) and a forthcoming study of First Class Cruisers. He has contributed to seminars and conferences and has reviewed for *The Mariner's Mirror*. He left the National Maritime Museum in 1999 and is now a freelance researcher and writer.

List of Illustrations

The portrait of Arthur Herbert is in Normanby Hall Country Park, Scunthorpe, and the photograph was supplied by courtesy of the North Lincolnshire Museums Service. All other illustrations are from the National Maritime Museum, London, who provided the photographs [the order references are given in square brackets].

Preface

The impetus for this book was the start of the 'Nelson decade' in 1995: the start of ten years of Nelson celebrations. A comment was made that it was a shame that people did not often recognise the significance of the material, personnel and organisation of the Royal Navy that Nelson drew upon. From this comment came the present book.

The intention is to bring together a series of essays that will shed light upon the development of the Royal Navy during what has been called 'The Great Age of Sail'. Its purpose is to help understand why the navy was so effective in the hands of Britain's greatest sea officer, Horatio Nelson. It is not, however, a book about Nelson and there are serious questions about how far the subjects of these essays should be allowed to stand alone, distinct from their relationship to Nelson. There are the questions of who to leave out, who to put in, whether weight should be given to some individuals rather than others. While there will never be agreement on who should or should not be included in a volume such as this – there was even discussion as to whether Nelson himself should be included – we have tried to select naval officers who contributed across a range of aspects of naval development.

We do not believe that there was one type of officer or one contribution that was critical to the development of the navy which justifies a volume of 'heroes', 'politicians' or 'administrators'. It was the contributions in many fields across many decades that made the Royal Navy such a large, flexible and effective fighting organisation. This has led to the inclusion of some familiar names, but also some less familiar, who at first sight do not appear on the first rank of the naval pantheon. They are unique in their personal contributions, but also representative of many other officers who served. It was not for space alone that the decision was taken not to go back to the pre-1688 navy. The 1688-1815 period chosen – often labelled 'The Long Eighteenth Century' – is unified by the fact that England was at war for over sixty years against France and Spain. Nelson's victory at Trafalgar was the culmination of this struggle and ushered in a further sixty years of British naval hegemony.

The production of a volume such as this is fraught with dangers and therefore the following general editorial policy has been pursued. Each author has been asked to present their views of their subject's contribution to the development of the sailing navy. The structure of the essay has been left to them, with some minor rules regarding footnote conventions and essay length. Some of the contributors, particularly of those subjects who have not had full recent biographies, have been allowed greater leeway in the length of the essays. The introductory essay attempts to draw the readers' attention to the common threads of development, which have not been laboured in the texts. It is hoped that the result is a collection that does justice to the unifying theme and to the individual officers in their own right.

Many debts have been incurred in the production of this volume. We are grateful to Robert Gardiner of Chatham Publishing for accepting the proposal for the book, and for his encouragement, advice and patience. We would like to thank each of the authors who have had to endure additional requests and clarification of points at various times over the last few years from the two editors; they have done so good humouredly and without complaint. Professor David Syrrett has been a constant source of encouragement, help and suggestions. He gave us the benefit of some very good advice when he heard of the project and has taken a lively interest in the book over the years. We would like to thank Mr Alan Pearsall and Mr Colin White for their interest in the project and suggestions. We would also like to thank Dr J D Davies for reading all the essays and giving us much food for thought in his criticisms. We would also like to thank Mrs Margaret Le Fevre, Peter's mother, for the title. All the portraits and prints in this volume, except that of Arthur Herbert, Earl of Torrington, are courtesy of the National Maritime Museum. The Torrington portrait is reproduced by courtesy of the North Lincolnshire Museum. We are very grateful to these institutions for permission to reproduce the pictures in their care. Finally we should thank the admirals who are the subjects of this book, for without them and their contributions there would have been no book, and, possibly, no Nelson.

Introduction

At approximately 1.30pm on 21 October 1805 Horatio, Lord Nelson was shot on the deck of the *Victory* by a sharpshooter in the mizzen-top of the French battleship *Redoubtable*. Captain Thomas Hardy, his flag captain, had Nelson picked up and taken down to the surgeon in the cockpit whilst he continued pacing the quarterdeck as if nothing was amiss. On his way down, Nelson had his face covered with his handkerchief so that the crew of the *Victory* would not be discouraged as they saw their admiral gravely wounded.[1] Nelson spent the next few hours listening to the battle taking place around him until he died at 4.35 that afternoon, knowing that he had won the battle of annihilation he had so much desired.[2] He was already publicly applauded as a hero, and that battle off Cape Trafalgar was to immortalise his name. One hundred and fifty-two years earlier at the Battle at the Gabbard on 2 June 1653, General-at-Sea George Monck is supposed to have thrown a cloak over the body of his fellow general, Richard Deane to prevent news of his death discouraging the crew.[3] Thirty-nine years later, off Cape La Hogue on 12 May 1692, the *Plymouth,* flagship of Richard Carter, rear-admiral of the red, was heavily engaged with three French ships. At about 1pm Carter was struck by a cannon ball whilst on the quarterdeck. Carter's flag captain, William Wright, promptly covered Carter's face 'so that the crew would not be dispirited by the loss of their admiral'. Carter was carried below while the ship continued to fight the French. Carter died at 8.00pm 'much lamented by his crew who mourned the loss of the brave admiral'.[4] Nelson's death is much better known, thanks to the celebrity of his name during his lifetime and to the account by the *Victory's* surgeon, Dr Beatty. However, the reactions of Hardy, Monck and Wright to the loss of their admirals were so similar that one sees the human dimension of fighting a ship in battle had not changed much in one hundred and fifty years.

Nelson is by far the most famous admiral of the Royal Navy. During his lifetime and ever since he has epitomised the ideal of the fighting officer. His understanding of tactics, his aggressive determination and his charis-matic leadership singled him out as an example to be followed and a hero to be admired. His record of glorious actions, his heroic death in his hour of greatest triumph and the association of Trafalgar with the ending of Napoleon's threatened invasion of Britain, have all combined to give Nelson a place in the popular history of the Royal Navy that few could hope to equal. During the last quarter of the nineteenth century as technological change and the growth of other navies challenged Britain's naval supremacy, serious historical study of the Revolutionary and Napoleonic Wars sought to establish the essential principles of seapower.[5] The wars between 1793 and 1815 had confirmed Britain as the paramount maritime power. It was in these wars that historians believed they could isolate the strategy, tactics and other leadership attributes that constituted the key components of naval power. To replicate these, adapted to the massive changes in technology, would be to reconstitute maritime supremacy. Nelson, inevitably, featured prominently. He had fought the battles that were seen as the foundations of seapower. His leadership was examined in detail. His relationship with his fellow officers, his famous 'Band of Brothers' who fought at the Nile, became the model of professional communication and understanding. The confidence he placed in his subordinates was remarkable and his approach became the model for effective motivation and delegation.[6] His aggression in every action was admired by contemporaries and noted as an essential quality. His famous phrase before Trafalgar, 'No captain can do very wrong if he places his ship alongside that of an enemy', became common in the service within years. Vice-Admiral Codrington, who was at Trafalgar, incorporated the phrase into his instructions to the allied fleet before the battle of Navarino in 1827.

What was equally admired was his tactical vision. He knew his own fleet and that of his enemy. He understood their relative capabilities. The awesome sight of a line of battleships at anchor inshore at Aboukir Bay did not deter Nelson. Without reconnaissance or waiting to gather his full force he attacked the French fleet in the last hour of daylight. His leading ship, Captain Foley in the *Goliath*, found his way around the van of the French line and proceeded to batter the unprepared port side of the French ships. The rest of the van followed, until Nelson took his flagship, *Vanguard*, along the seaward side of the French. After the crushing victory, when Captain Saumarez criticised what he saw as a lack of order in the attack, Nelson retorted, 'Thank God there was no order'.[7] To catch the enemy between two fires was both possible and desirable. Caution and strict order were unnecessary. The audacity of the 'Nelson Touch', his plan to approach the Franco-Spanish fleet off Cape Trafalgar in two lines perpendicular to the enemy, contrary to perceived wisdom, 'was like an electric shock. Some shed tears, all approved – "It was new – it was singular – it was simple!"; and from Admirals downwards, it was repeated – It must succeed, if ever they will allow us to get at them'.[8] The drama that surrounded Nelson's approach to battle and leadership and his unparalleled success remains one of the most important foundations of the continuing popularity of the naval novel.[9]

Nelson was undoubtedly one of the most remarkable officers of the Royal Navy. Yet the emphasis upon Nelson the leader and hero, which appealed so much to nineteenth and twentieth century notions of personality and leadership, has obscured an understanding of how Nelson fitted into the navy of his time. There are many social and technical studies of the navy in this period.[10] The personalities are well known. Biographies of naval officers from Drake to Nelson were part of an extremely popular navalist *genre* of literature at the beginning of the twentieth century. More modern and generally less 'heroic' biographies of admirals such as Exmouth, Rodney and Hawke, and of Nelson's captains and colleagues, have developed our understanding of the men who commanded at sea in the age of sail.[11] The political leadership of the navy has been explored and presented in a number of Navy Records Society volumes. Recently, there have been studies of the administration of the navy.[12] In sum, more is now known and presented to the public about the Royal Navy than ever before. However, in sheer volume alone, the literature on Nelson continues to outstrip all other work on the sailing navy.[13]

Nelson was an officer in command of a fleet that was at the height of its effectiveness. Since 1796, when enemy battleships actually outnumbered the British fleet, the qualitative advantage of the Royal Navy whittled away enemy strength. By 1800 over 200,000 tons of enemy shipping had been captured, together with over 75,000 enemy seamen. In 1805 the Royal Navy outnumbered the battleships of France and Spain by over 40 per cent and their cruisers and frigates by 125 per cent.[14] British crews were better trained and armed with a tradition of victory. But the British fleet was not a weapon created in these short years. Navies were the most complex organisations of their time and the operational effectiveness of the Royal Navy was the result of decades of slow development. Nelson was both the product and the beneficiary of decades of investment and professional development.

The navy that Nelson led to three stunning victories between 1798 and 1805 had a capability that far outreached its rivals. Since 1793 the Royal Navy had experienced spectacular victories, such as the Glorious First of June (1794), Cape St Vincent (1797) and Camperdown (1797). Its cruisers

swept away enemy warships and commerce. After Nelson's death it continued to dominate the oceans of the world. It was able to prevent the
invasion and blockade of Great Britain. It could effectively disrupt trade to
and from parts of Europe dominated by Napoleon while breaching the
Continental System in the interest of British exports. It was able to react
effectively to new threats, such as the war with the United States in 1812.

The purpose of these essays is to explore the development of this naval
capability through the contributions of a selected group of naval officers.
The development of the Royal Navy required a range of skills and knowledge applied over many generations to achieve this overwhelming capability. No officer, not even Nelson, could encapsulate all these skills and
insights, and these essays are intended to show how individual officers
brought their particular talents to bear upon the complex organisation that
was the Royal Navy. This book is not a history of the navy, still less does it
pretend to provide definitive biographies of these officers. Furthermore, it
does not attempt to imply that these officers alone were responsible for the
development of the navy. Rather, each of these seamen demonstrates some
significant facets of command, administration, tactical or political acumen
which were central to the navy in which Nelson served. Some like Hawke,
Hood and St Vincent had a direct impact upon Nelson and the way in
which he perceived his duty. Others like Vernon, Anson, Cornwallis and
Barham established or operated the general strategic doctrine of the navy
that enabled Nelson aggressively to seek out the enemy secure in the
knowledge that there was a tried and tested structure of defence behind
him. Still others, by far the majority, had contributed to creating the
professional culture of the navy that served Nelson so well.

So often the seventeenth and eighteenth century navy is popularly perceived as being led by men who placed rigid formalism before victory and
private profit before decisive action. There were reasons why naval battles
in these years lacked the decisive edge of those between 1793 and 1815, but
they were seldom related to the quality of the officers and men who fought
the battles. Byng showed Nelsonic aggression at Cape Passaro in 1718.
Wager demonstrated a similar determination to come to grips with the
Spaniards in 1708. Shovell and Rooke conducted long campaigns to support the allied armies in Spain against enemies more formidable that those
faced by the navy between 1808 and 1814. As the eighteenth century
progressed, the Royal Navy's superior numbers and quality discouraged
enemies from seeking battle. During this period French naval operations
were usually aimed at achieving a specific objective, such as escorting
convoys or expeditionary forces. They did not seek battles of attrition or

annihilation to gain a permanent naval advantage over the Royal Navy. In these circumstances, to engage the enemy and hold him in order to inflict decisive defeat became the key problem. When, in February 1744 off Toulon, Admiral Mathews found himself in the unusual situation of bearing down on a combined Franco-Spanish fleet awaiting action, he and his fleet were ill-prepared. The movement of the fleet towards the enemy was extremely variable, but Captain Edward Hawke in the *Berwick,* who was in the van division, did all he could to get to grips with the enemy, temporarily taking the Spanish *Poder.* The prize was lost, but the impression Hawke made was extremely positive and contrasted noticeably with the recriminations that attended the conduct of so many other officers in the light of the general failure of the action. The need to inflict decisive damage upon the enemy by close action was clearly recognised and desired by naval officers, but there was seldom the chance to bring the enemy to battle in this way. At the two battles off Finisterre in May and October 1747 Anson and Hawke respectively won pursuit actions against French squadrons. In November 1759 Hawke won a spectacular pursuit action by chasing a French squadron into Quiberon Bay.

By the time the War of American Independence broke out the French navy had recovered from its collapse at the end of 1759. Still, its recovery was more quantitative than qualitative. Its ability to hold its own in battle depended upon maintaining the coherence of the line. The British admirals knew that they if they broke the French line the superior gunnery and training of their crews would be decisive in a *mêlée.* Rodney at the Saintes in 1782, Howe at the Glorious First of June in 1794 as well as Jervis against the Spanish at Cape St Vincent in 1797 achieved creditable victories by breaking the enemy line. Although Nelson considered Howe's victory incomplete, he recognised what Howe was trying to achieve and acknowledged his debt to the latter. Other officers, who did not have the opportunity to drive into the enemy line, understood the importance of an aggressive approach to their enemy. In smaller actions Hood frustrated the French in the West Indies. Hood, Keith and Cornwallis had to carry out unglamorous blockade duties. While Nelson's attitude to blockade was different, these officers carried out their duty in a manner that left the French in no doubt as to their intentions.

What were the steps that led to the establishment of the Royal Navy as the outstanding naval force of its day? There are many aspects to the development of the navy. They cannot be isolated or categorised to emphasise one element more than others. The British navy took its shape during the Civil War and Commonwealth.[15] It became politically entrenched in English society and achieved a remarkable degree of administrative maturity during the third quarter of the seventeenth century. During the next one hundred and fifty years the operational capability of the Royal Navy developed dramatically. The navy was built upon a dynamic and flourishing maritime economy, but it was money, administrative capability, manpower and a professional officer corps that converted these raw materials into formidable seapower.

Money and Administration

Money was an essential prerequisite of a force that relied so heavily on a large range of domestic and foreign raw materials. It was essential to maintain the effective payment of large numbers of seamen and artificers, for whom there was a fluctuating demand, but who could nonetheless find ready employment in the maritime economy. Although money was always in short supply and Parliament was unwilling in peacetime to maintain a large fleet in commission, the navy was never starved of funds. Retrenchments were more severe in the early part of the eighteenth century. The rise of rival naval forces from the 1760s and the loss of the American colonies in 1783 encouraged Parliament to maintain a large fleet in repair at the end of the century. Despite growing concerns about naval budgets after 1787, the crises with Spain in 1790 and Russia in 1791 helped to ensure that when war broke out in 1793, Britain had over 100 battleships and 115 frigates in good repair. This willingness to fund the navy was a primary consequence of the political acceptance of the navy as the principal military weapon of the state, which emerged largely from events during the Civil War and Protectorate. The rhetoric of 'Blue Water' policies developed strongly in the political battles of the 1690s and became an important element in British political propaganda during the first half of the eighteenth century.[16] By 1740 prints, pamphlets, ballads, pottery, medals and stories proclaimed British maritime dominion.[17] However, it is usually forgotten that during this period it was far from obvious that Britain's future lay in a maritime empire. It was only in the 1750s that the boasts and hopes began to be clearly realised. There was a critical period from 1739 to 1758 when the rhetoric was not matched by the results. It fell to officers such as Edward Vernon and George Anson to champion the political cause of the navy. In 1739 the outbreak of war with Spain was accompanied by public expectations of easy conquests in Spanish America and the rapid humbling of Spain. Vice-Admiral Vernon's capture of Porto Bello in March 1740 seemed to justify these expectations and was greeted with wild public rejoicing. Three years later, after a large expedition sent to extend

Vernon's victory had been destroyed by disease and Spanish resistance, the Blue Water hopes were in tatters. Yet Vernon remained a popular figure and he vigorously defended his role in the expedition. His claims that the navy alone could have forced Spain to sue for peace by pressure in the West Indies, and that the failure of the expedition was primarily the fault of the army, were generally well-received by the public. Whatever the justice of his claims, Vernon kept the idea of decisive naval power alive in the public mind at a time when the evidence of events did not seem to justify it.

While Vernon's popularity was brief, Commodore George Anson's arrival in England on 15 June 1744, after a circumnavigation of the globe, ushered in a man who was to be a professional and political champion of the navy until his death in 1762. Anson, famously taciturn as an individual, communicated a professional and political message so effectively to the world that his name is intimately associated with the realisation of the 'Blue Water' plan. From the details of uniform, professional expectations and pay, through the design of ships, to the deployment of squadrons and the global strategy for war, Anson played a part. His ability to work with politicians as mercurial as William Pitt and as established as the Old Corps Whigs, gave him a political authority that reinforced his professional vision. Officers like George Byng, Sir Charles Wager, Vernon, Anson and Barham were at home in the world of politics, but it could be dangerous territory, as Thomas Mathews, Edward Vernon, John Byng, Augustus Keppell, Henry Palliser and St Vincent all found out with varying degrees of pain. Political connection was extremely important to professional progress, but involvement in party politics at a time of instability was hazardous. Howe, Hawke, Hood, Rodney, Cornwallis and Keith were all careful and circumspect in combining political and professional careers.

While money was a vital prerequisite, buying the necessary materials, manpower and skills did not create a navy. The conversion of the materials into a fleet depended on a growing group of professional administrators. Dockyards had to be created and managed; ships built, supplied, victualled and manned. The growth of the professional administrators is a study that lies beyond the scope of this work. However, sea officers played an important role in the effective administration of the Royal Navy. Pre-eminent among these in the public mind was Charles Middleton, Lord Barham, who was Comptroller of the Navy from 1778 to 1790 and ultimately First Lord of the Admiralty between May 1805 and February 1806. Middleton's influence on the administration of the navy was substantial, but he was not alone. George Byng, Viscount Torrington, was a competent First Lord and he was succeeded in 1733 by Sir Charles Wager, a man whose knowledge of naval and colonial affairs was fundamental to the effective development of the navy and naval policy under Sir Robert Walpole. At a critical period, Anson was an excellent First Lord from 1751 to 1756 and from 1757 until his death. Hawke was an effective member of the Board of Admiralty from 1766 to 1771, preserving the fleet from drastic financial cuts and ensuring that basic repair work continued. Other sea officers also held some posts as dockyard commissioners. Serving sea officers advised upon matters great and small of naval administration.

Manning the Fleet

A recurrent problem was manpower. Britain probably had a more elastic supply of maritime labour than any other state. Yet when war broke out and the fleet had to be manned there was constant tension between the demands of the merchants and the needs of the Royal Navy. The attractiveness and rewards of service in the navy among the seafaring population is a matter of debate, but officers were aware that it was their duty to have their ships manned. In early 1708 Edward Vernon spent a great deal of his energy finding seamen from the maritime community of London and did not hesitate to invoke all due legal process in his quest of a good crew. It was not just junior captains like Vernon that needed to focus attention on manning. There were many aspects of life that discouraged service in the Royal Navy. The attractiveness of service in other navies, merchant ships or privateers were important factors, but the slow and irregular payment of wages was a major problem. The difficulties related to manning were of such importance that senior officers often found it necessary to address the concerns of individual seamen.

The popular image of the navy being manned by pressed men restrained only by harsh discipline has been substantially revised in recent decades. Officers knew the task they were facing and they also knew that a loyal crew of competent seamen was essential to the effective operation of their ships. In the worst case, loyal seamen could prevent disaster. Charles, Lord Berkeley, the captain of the *Tiger* in 1683, reported to the Navy Board that his purser's attempts to create mutiny had failed because 'my officers and men having a great love to discipline ... and loyalty to me'.[18] More usually the main benefit of loyalty was that seamen and officers would follow a commander whom they thought was fair and capable. The need for the commander to represent the interests of the men with the powers in London was, therefore, important. In 1703 Norris told the Admiralty that several seamen 'have complained to me and think it hard they should be obliged to sell their tickets at a great loss.'[19] John Leake wrote to the Navy

Board in October 1691 about a William Starr who was serving with him on the *Eagle* as a quartermaster. His previous ship had left him behind and Starr voluntarily offered to serve with Leake. Leake had known Starr for several years 'and do . . . believe he never had a design to desert the service' and he asked that the 'R' (for 'run', *ie* deserted) recorded against his name on his previous vessel, which would eliminate his right to any wages earned on that ship, be removed.[20] Some officers could rely on their local connections, but the key to recruitment was the officers' personal reputations.[21]

The need to treat men well was a common theme. Vernon spent some time after his last sea command preparing plans to encourage seamen to serve in the navy. Keith enjoined his officers to treat the seamen with respect. Even St Vincent, who has a reputation for iron discipline, was punctilious in enforcing fair treatment of seamen within the code of discipline and representing proper requests to higher authority. Self-interest and altruism combined to ensure that conscientious officers tried hard to support a loyal following on the lower deck. This could cause embarrassment. In 1756 Rodney wrote to the Admiralty on behalf of seven seamen who had deserted their ship in order to join his vessel. Their 'regard for their old Captain' was a sentiment Rodney had to defend.[22] Nelson went to sea with a fleet that was manned in much the same way as it had been for over one hundred years, by volunteers, pressed seamen and by landsmen. He gathered a following and a loyalty that reflected his professional standing. That he was able to develop this to create an unprecedented image of the naval hero is a tribute to his own personality and the circumstances in which Britain found herself. However, he was building on the professional foundation of loyalty and following that had been operated by generations of sea officers, as well as upon the crucial expansion of the pool of maritime labour.

Health and Hygiene

The health of seamen at sea was another factor in the effectiveness of British fleets. From the end of the seventeenth century officers were concerned about improving the health of seamen on ships. The Earl of Torrington had fresh vegetables delivered to his fleet while it sheltered in Torbay in 1689, while John Norris, as commander-in-chief in the Mediterranean in 1709, was ordered to test and report upon Dr Cockburn's medicine 'for the flux'.[23] Vernon, concerned about the harmful effects of drunkenness upon the health and discipline of his seamen, is now more famous for instituting 'grog', produced by watering down the rum ration, than for any other service he carried out. Norris's surviving papers contain many references to diet for sea service. As the eighteenth century progressed, other officers such as Boscawen, Hawke, Anson, Rodney and St Vincent improved shipboard hygiene by the internal organisation of the ship living space, discipline, victualling and introducing anti-scorbutics.[24] By the 1760s formal medical science was being applied to the problems of shipboard health. In the fifty years that followed the works of Dr James Lind, Sir Gilbert Blane, and Dr Thomas Trotter were applied by administrators and naval officers to reduce death and sickness on Royal Navy ships.[25] The overall effect was to enable British ships to remain healthy at sea over longer periods. At the beginning of the century it is quite probable that French ships arriving in the West Indies were healthier than their British counterparts, but by the end of the century the British contemplated their enemy's living conditions with considerable distaste.[26]

By the time Nelson began his independent command, the British had reduced the tension arising from improved efficiency created by extensive seatime and the damage done to efficiency and seamen's health from long incarceration on wooden warships. Nevertheless, Nelson fretted over the health of his men on long cruises. Nelson was above all a fighting admiral who cherished independent command at sea and was valued for this above all else,[27] but he, like all commanding officers, was compelled to spend a large part of his time on matters of fleet administration. Battles of annihilation depended on having the better ships and crews at the point of contact. The methods he used and the support he could rely upon were tried and tested by his predecessors, whose efforts ensured that the fleet was effectively manned as its role and responsibilities extended across the globe.

Shipbuilding, Design and Technology

Another important aspect of the Royal Navy was the development of the ships themselves. Ship design had been traditionally seen as a deficient area of British naval power. British ships, both battleships and frigates, were considered inferior to their French and Spanish counterparts. While there is some truth in this in so far as French designs were copied to produce some good frigates in the 1750s and 1790s, it can be overstated. The problem of design had been recognised from the earliest days of the sailing battleship. Some senior sea officers had always been interested in the matter of compromises between seakeeping and firepower. Their beliefs and recommendations were not always happy ones in the absence of detailed hydrodynamic knowledge, but marginal changes may have been made as a result of the work of admirals. Some like the Earl of Torrington took a lively interest in the minutiae of ship design. He recommended new ship designs in 1689 as well as having lanterns made from a new ground-glass technique and attending the trials of new gun carriages which he had fitted in the *Royal Sovereign*. When the Admiralty decided to introduce a new establishment for ordnance in 1703 they asked John Leake to act as an advisor because of his knowledge and experience gained by being deputy to his father, Richard Leake, Master Gunner of England.[28]

From 1719 the matter of ship design was neglected, but between 1739 and 1745 the shock of combat with new Spanish and French ships compelled the Admiralty to act. In June 1744 Vernon was asked to comment on the design and manning of British ships and in June 1745 a committee, chaired by Sir John Norris and assisted by flag officers like Vernon, was set up to revise the standard ship specifications, known as Establishments.[29] A new establishment was proposed and a compromise that suited the committee, the Admiralty and the Navy Board was accepted. It was not an adequate response to the threat posed by the new Bourbon warships and Anson, who had joined the Admiralty in 1744, continued to have doubts about ship design. He provided vital support to the Surveyor of the Navy, Thomas Slade, in his rise from Assistant Master Shipwright at Woolwich to become joint Surveyor of the Navy with William Bately in 1755. Slade was to design some of the most powerful and seaworthy classes of ships, ranging from three-decked battleships (including the famous *Victory),* the '74's that were to become the backbone of the line of battle, and the powerful 32-gun single-deck frigates.[30] Anson also ensured that experiments on shipboard artillery were carried out to maximise the effectiveness of the broadside. Howe wrote to the Secretary to the Admiralty Board, Philip Stephens in 1770 about the sail plan of the three-deckers.[31] Barham, whilst Comptroller of the Navy from 1778 to 1790, was a powerful supporter of new developments such as coppering and the introduction of the carronade. Towards the end of the century the profession of naval architect was beginning to emerge and separate the admirals from the design and building of ships. The technology itself was reaching its natural limits. Nonetheless, St Vincent was still consulted on the best designs for long blockade duties.

Navigational and general maritime matters also claimed the attention of senior naval officers. The Longitude Act of July 1714 established a board, with funds and a large financial prize, to encourage the discovery of a method of measuring longitude. The act was partly stimulated by the loss of Sir Cloudesley Shovell when his ship the *Association* and three others of his squadron foundered on the rocks off the Scillies on the night of 22 October 1707. John Norris's experiences in 1707, when he almost came to grief on the Gilstone Ledges in Scilly, gave him a great interest in solving

navigational difficulties. He and Wager reported to the Board of Longitude
on John Harrison's first chronometer. Hawke also served on the Board in
1763.

Signals and Combat

In the final analysis the test of any navy is how it performs as a fighting force
at sea. The preliminary task of design, building, maintenance, manning and
supply are critical prerequisites of naval effectiveness, but it is in the handling of the ships at sea that the naval officer comes into his own. Here,
Nelson was in his element. Courage, aggression and the desire to close with
the enemy were hallmarks of his leadership but he was, again, heir to a
strong tradition in the navy. The failure to engage with determination had
been the fatal mistake of two of Vice-Admiral Benbow's captains, Richard
Kirkby and Cooper Wade, who were executed in April 1703.[32] Vice-
Admiral John Byng suffered a similar fate on board the *Monarch* on 14
March 1757 after the indecisive battle with the French off Minorca. Determination to fight and beat the enemy was expected. Engaging at close
range, within pistol shot, was also an expressed objective of officers such as
Rooke at the Battle of Málaga, 13 August 1704.[33] The same determination
was demonstrated by Hawke at Toulon, Finisterre and Quiberon and by
Howe on the Glorious First of June. Traditionally, this is often overlooked.
The imperative of preserving the line of battle is presented as an *ideé fixe* for
the naval officer from the 1660s to the 1780s.

Since the 1930s a great deal of work has been done examining the
development of the sailing and fighting instructions, although much of this
has only recently been published.[34] Although the main principles of the
Permanent Sailing and Fighting Instructions were established by the Earl of
Torrington in April 1690 and were used from 1702, modifications or
additional signals were incorporated throughout the century. Standardisation was partly the result of co-operation with the Dutch fleet at sea. As the
fleets combined, captains who were originally serving in the rear-admiral of
the blue's squadron could find themselves moved to the vice-admiral of the
red's squadron and even to different positions within the squadron. These
changes meant that new lines of battle had to be issued. The old system of a
double-page ship plan bound into the fighting instructions would be inef-
fective. It was far easier to have standardised sailing instructions with specific flags laid down for specific tasks, while the admiral's clerk issued
separate lists of the line of battle as they altered.[35] Commanders retained the
power to amend the instructions as they saw fit. When he was commander-
in-chief in the Mediterranean, Norris issued eight signals for chasing, of

which the first four were added to the Permanent Instructions. Vernon, Anson, and Hawke, among others, added additional instructions to improve a commander's tactical control over his fleet. For the most part these additions were designed to make the admiral's intentions clearer so that the line could close with the enemy in a variety of circumstances to fight at close quarters.

By 1780 two distinct pathways had emerged. Officers such as Rodney and Hood developed the Permanent Instructions, while other officers were looking at different systems of signalling. The Channel Fleet became the centre for re-examination of the signalling system. After the indecisive battle off Ushant in July 1778 Richard Kempenfelt, Captain of the Fleet to Sir Charles Hardy, developed a numerical code system probably based upon earlier work by Admiral Lord Howe. It became a flexible tool covering both line of battle and reconnaissance activities. Howe's Signal Book, issued to the Channel Fleet in 1790, also based on a numerical signalling system, became the foundation of the Admiralty Signal Book of 1799 – the signals with which the Royal Navy fought for most of the Revolutionary and Napoleonic Wars. It provided the longer-range control and communication in use in Nelson's squadrons.[36]

Leadership and Discipline

While communication between ships was an important element in the fighting efficiency of a fleet, the morale, discipline and organisation on board ship were the foundations of the fighting strength of each vessel. Here, attention to the details of life aboard was an important matter. The confidence the crews reposed in their officers is an article of faith to those who seek the essence of Nelson's leadership. The confidence that the French would be beaten in an open battle was an important aspect of the willingness to close for battle. However, a similar confidence was expressed in 1690 and 1704. 'Tis a daring attempt of the French . . . To seek us in the Channel when both fleets are so powerful,' thought one commentator. As the fleets approached each other off Beachy Head on 30 June 1690, the seamen 'throughout the whole fleet showed an extraordinary joy and satisfaction, that they were going to engage the always hated enemy the French.'[37] When Richard Hill learnt in 1704 that the French fleet under the comte de Toulouse was in the Mediterranean he hoped 'he may come in the way of Sir George Rooke and be beaten well by him'.[38] A participant in the Battle of Málaga on 13 August 1704 told a friend, 'Tis impossible to express the universal cheerfulness our men showed when they found they should fight, and . . . They was as merry and cheerful in the midst of the Engagement as though they had been at one of their Chatham Land-ladies, joking with one another.'[39] It was equally evident thirty-six years later when Vernon expressed no doubt that his small force would soon deal with the 'Bully Don'. On 18 April 1780 one midshipman described the 'hearty good will' aboard the *Intrepid* as Rodney's squadron engaged the French under de Guichen off St Lucia.[40] The seamen's faith in Nelson was borne out by his great victories, but they had a faith in victory that was by then a tradition in the navy.

Victory was partly owing to the discipline and training that the men experienced at sea. Once again this training was a tradition long before Nelson's time. Exercises with small arms and the great guns were common. Since 1677 the practical seamanship and experience under sail demanded of every midshipman before he could receive his lieutenant's commission greatly stimulated the men's confidence in their junior officers. This re-form, carried through by Samuel Pepys, was framed with the advice of six sea officers, including Arthur Herbert. By the end of the eighteenth cen-tury a lot more published material could be discussed and analysed.[41] Of-ficers such as Vernon, Rodney, Jervis, Howe, Hood and Keith also paid great attention to the details of shipboard life and honed the discipline of their officers and crews. Indiscipline and misdemeanour could easily endan-ger the safety of a ship. The 'disorderly deportments' of the quartermaster of the *Phoenix* in 1681, 'keeping Candles lighted in the hold, smoking tobacco and drinking in excess at very unreasonable hours' created diffi-culties for her captain.[42] On 22 September 1742 the *Tilbury* caught fire and sank off Navassa Island in the West Indies as a result of a struggle with a Marine who had stolen rum from the purser's stores. Over one hundred men were lost.[43] The creation and preservation of discipline was the amal-gam of incentives, systems, routines, rituals, and retribution that had been developed over centuries to meet the expectations of officers and seamen. It was not universally benign but the reputation of the navy for unrelieved savage discipline is overdrawn. Nelson, like the officers mentioned above, demanded obedience, competence and personal loyalty from his crew. He received it because of the articles of war and *The Regulations and Instructions Relating to His Majesty's Service at Sea,* which since 1731 had governed the behaviour of officers and men; but, more importantly, he gave competence and personal loyalty to the crew. Neither lenient nor brutal, Nelson was the beneficiary of a social system within the fleet that had been fashioned over decades and developed in recent years. The mutinies of 1797 were a major shock to the authorities, but they did not signal a fundamental breakdown of the system that had preserved the navy in the past.

Last but not least there is the officer corps itself. The contrast between Nelson's 'Band of Brothers' and the fractious bickering that attended the early years of the War of Austrian Succession, or the War of American Independence, has been highlighted on many occasions.[44] Nelson's correspondence with his captains has survived from a number of different sources and testifies to the warmth and confidence that existed between them. Whether this was unusual is impossible to tell in the absence of similar evidence from other admirals. While some officers had powerful connections on land, such as Herbert, Vernon, Howe, Cornwallis and Keith, others, like Wager, Norris and Hood, carried very little social weight. It was connections made through service that became increasingly important.

The networks of patronage and mutual obligation, while not new, increasingly tied together the officer corps from the 1670s, when substantial English squadrons remained in the Mediterranean for prolonged periods.[45] Herbert as commander-in-chief of the Mediterranean squadron gathered around him a group of captains who were linked together by friendship, service and fighting. The networks can be easily seen in these essays and in the lives of other officers. Norris, Vernon, John Jennings and John Graydon all started in the navy serving as servants or volunteers with captains such as Cloudesley Shovell. They continued to serve together as lieutenants or captains under Sir George Rooke, Sir George Byng and Shovell.[46] Rodney owed a great deal to Admiral Henry Medley and Hawke. Jervis received the patronage of Boscawen and Saunders in his early career and the recommendation of Duncan at the critical point in career early in 1797. Initially, this increased the professional power of the commanding admiral in relation to the authorities in London. Informal meetings between officers, such as Herbert held when he was commander-in-chief in the Mediterranean, engendered loyalty to him but enraged Pepys, who reviled Herbert's 'creatures'.[47] In October 1688 John Berry consulted in private with the captains of his division over the steps to be taken to fight the Dutch invasion fleet.[48]

Very little evidence survives to tell how common these informal consultations were, but there are enough to suggest that professional dialogue may have been common.[49] Some like Hood are known to have made a point of consulting their officers. The council of war provided the forum for such discussion, as did dinners that might follow them. Mathews infamously did not consult prior to the battle off Toulon in 1744, which might be a clue to the expectations of his officers. Vernon certainly discussed matters with his second in command, Sir Chaloner Ogle, whilst in the West Indies. Peter Warren, commanding on the Leeward Station, also consulted his fellow captains before he decided to take ships to Boston to assist the attack upon Louisbourg in 1745. Others, like Rodney, were too imperious. The prestige and power of an officer partly depended on his ability to make good professional judgements about his colleagues. Anson, Hawke, Hood, and St Vincent excelled in this. Rodney and George Byng were less successful in this regard.

Another important element in this network of mutual trust was the court martial to restore trust that had been tarnished. On two occasions Herbert pressed for courts martial of officers under suspicion – Jones in 1689 and Norris in 1701. Despite his previous friendship with Mathews, Vernon argued for his court martial along with Vice-Admiral Lestock and some of the captains in the wake of the Battle of Toulon in 1744. The court martial was a blunt instrument that sowed anxiety and discord whilst in progress. The courts martial after the battles of Toulon, Minorca and Ushant are clear evidence of this, but they were also the means for resolving the disputes that emerged from disappointing naval actions and for establishing the expectations of the service. For an ambitious officer whose conduct had been called into question it was professionally impossible not to demand a court martial whatever the dangers inherent in the process. It operated imperfectly for many defendants, but it contributed to the naval network of personal obligation and professional expectations that was a fact of life by the time Nelson entered the service.[50]

In the final analysis Nelson's tactical genius and aggressive spirit provided the essential force at the heart of British strategy in the war against Revolutionary and Napoleonic France. That strategy was put in place and held together by other men. Vernon and Anson had evolved the Western Squadron that was the linchpin of British naval defence. In 1804–5 Barham and Jervis at the Admiralty and Cornwallis in the Channel provided the essential defensive structures that enabled Nelson to pursue his aggressive war against the enemy.

This collection of essays demonstrates the long development of professional capability in the Royal Navy. Apart from the debt Nelson owed to Captain William Locker, commander of the *Lowestoffe* when Nelson joined her as a lieutenant in 1777, too little is known about the precise influences upon Nelson's professional education. However, it is indisputable that the navy upon which Nelson relied was partly shaped by the men who are the subjects of these essays. They are also representative of the forces that evolved and developed the navy. The expectations Nelson had of the fleet were the expectations created by these officers. Nelson's great talent lay in exploiting a deep understanding of the tools with which he had been provided. He understood what was possible, he knew the techniques that had to be employed and he had the energy to convert his understanding into effective military action. This series of essays will not diminish Nelson's reputation, but demonstrate the variety and depth of skills and insights that made the navy and naval power the formidable weapon that it became in Nelson's hands.

Arthur Herbert, Earl of Torrington. Oil by John Closterman

1

Arthur Herbert, Earl of Torrington
1648-1716[1]

'A Fine Man . . . Both in Courage and Conduct'

PETER LE FEVRE

Arthur Herbert's name is well known because of the part he played in the events of the Glorious Revolution of 1688, when he was the commander-in-chief of William's Dutch invasion fleet. The conventional views of Herbert – his brutality, debauchery, immorality and neglect of duty – were put forward by his enemies, who hated him. These views are summed up by one of his leading detractors, Samuel Pepys: in his opinion, 'of all the worst men living, Herbert is the only man that I do not know to have any one virtue to compound for all his vices'; this view is echoed in John Ehrman's statement that Herbert was 'almost a professional badman'.[2] However, these black-and-white judgements should not be accepted as uncritically as they have been. Herbert certainly possessed virtues to compound for the vices he had; while the part he played in the development of the later eighteenth century navy has never been expounded until now.

Arthur Herbert was born between July and October 1648[3] and was the third son of Sir Edward Herbert of Aston in Montgomeryshire, Attorney General to Charles I, and Margaret Carey, the only daughter and sole heir of Sir Thomas Smith, James I's Master of Requests, and the widow of Thomas Carey, second son of Robert Carey, Earl of Monmouth. Sir Edward Herbert's close identification with Charles I's policies, and especially his role in the attempted arrest of the Five Members which led to Herbert's impeachment and expulsion from the House, meant that at the outbreak of war in 1642 the family joined the King in Oxford, where Arthur's two brothers, Charles and Edward, were born. After Oxford surrendered in 1646 the family left. Although Gilbert Burnet suggested that

Herbert was 'bred in Holland', the family lived in Brussels and Paris, where he was educated. Despite his later statement alleging 'the want of a better education than I could meet with at school', he seems to have learnt French, which he understood and used to answer William's queries in 1688.[4] Like other Royalist exiles the family lived a hand-to-mouth existence, dependant on gifts of money and fruit from old friends and other exiles such as Sir Ralph Verney at Blois.[5] By 1661 the Herbert family were living in Weybridge, Surrey in a large house of twenty-five hearths with 'six or 7 rooms on a floor and has meadows and pastures belonging to it'.[6]

Early Service

In 1663 Herbert, aged 15, 'pitched upon . . . sea service . . . to which it seems he had a more particular inclination than any other way of life.'[7] Herbert started his 'sea service' with the Irishman Sir Robert Holmes. It was probably through his mother that in 1663-4 Sir William Coventry, secretary to James, Duke of York, recommended Herbert to Holmes for the voyage he was undertaking to Guinea. Holmes was told not only to give the young boy 'accommodation and protection but such advice as he shall need'. Herbert probably learnt his forthright manner from Holmes, who had a reputation for speaking his mind.[8] Herbert returned to England with Holmes early in 1665 and was discharged from the ship on 3 January 1665.

After the Dutch declared war on England on 22 February Holmes was appointed to the command of the *Revenge*. It is more than likely that Herbert rejoined his old commander and consequently took part in the Battle of Lowestoft in June 1665. The following year Holmes was appointed captain of the *Defiance* on 26 March 1666 and two days later Herbert was appointed lieutenant of the ship.[9] Holmes was rear-admiral of the red squadron, which was commanded by George Monk, Duke of Albemarle. The *Defiance* was in the thick of the action and had her flag shot away and her sails and rigging shattered, so she was forced to anchor briefly while repairs were made. At the end of the Four Days' Battle Holmes had 40 men killed and 73 wounded on the *Defiance*, while the ship was so badly damaged she was sent to Yarmouth on 7 June to refit.[10] Among the *Defiance*'s wounded was another of Holmes's lieutenants, John Dawson, who was discharged on 13 July 1666. Herbert succeeded Dawson and oversaw the ship's repairs.[11]

Holmes was appointed to the command of the *Henry* on 12 June 1666. He recommended Herbert to James, Duke of York, 'who professed a more than ordinary kindness to him'. As a result, and possibly because James

Shovell immediately sailed for Plymouth, where he met up with Killigrew, but it was too late for them to participate and the presence of the French Fleet in the Channel prevented either of the detached squadrons from reinforcing the main fleet. In light of this, the King ordered Shovell to cruise in the Soundings to guard against any French attempt to attack Ireland.

In London, Torrington was brought to the Tower and a number of experienced flag officers were mentioned as possible candidates who might serve as joint admirals in command of the main fleet. During the discussion on this matter, Queen Mary wrote to the King in Holland that her advisors recommended Haddock, Ashby and Shovell. Although he was the junior of the three, she wrote, 'They tell me Shovell is the best officer of his age.'[31]

Meanwhile at sea, on reports that French frigates were at Kinsale, Shovell sailed there, where the port had just surrendered to English forces under Major-General Kirke. With Duncannon Castle still resisting, on 28 July Shovell immediately ordered in several frigates to bring about its reduction. From there he sailed for Plymouth, but was recalled to form a squadron to intercept a French squadron under d'Ambreville, reportedly covering the French evacuation of Galway and Limerick. Interrupting this operation in order to meet heavy demands for other duties, the Admiralty ordered Shovell to sail for the Downs. Having missed d'Ambreville on the Irish coast, Shovell returned to the Downs on 10 October, where he received new orders to take all available ships to Plymouth and to cruise for the protection of trade in the Soundings. On 3 December Shovell sailed for this duty, in which two of his ships took the 18-gun French warship *Frippon*. Once again, a printer sold a broadside recounting 'a great and bloody fight between the English Fleet commanded by Sir Clovesly Shovel and the French at sea.'[32] Dispersing units of his squadron to the Irish coast and to the Soundings, Shovell returned to the Downs in mid-January 1691, whereupon he joined the fleet under Sir George Rooke, escorting the King to Holland. On March 10 Shovell married Elizabeth Hill Narbrough, the widow of his patron, Admiral Sir John Narbrough, who had died in the West Indies in 1688. At the same time, Shovell also took up responsibility as an active step-father to Narbrough's three children.[33]

Meanwhile, at The Hague on 17 February 1691, the King appointed Shovell a major in the First Marine Regiment, commanded by Peregrine, Earl of Danby. Some time after hearing the news, Shovell wrote to the Earl of Nottingham to thank him for the unexpected honour and to request that he be made lieutenant-colonel of the Second Marine Regiment. Making a very rare direct reference to Rooke, as well as commenting on the

employment of a naval officer in such a role, Shovell wrote in his characteristically direct manner:

> I hear, my Lord, that 'tis designed that Rear Admiral Rooke shall have the lieut.
> collonellship; he is a gentleman I have no objection against, but humbly wish he
> had either been a major before me or I may be lieut. collonel before him.
>
> 'Tis argued he is an older flag. I confess it, but doe not se that should have any
> influence on the officers of them regiments, and further, my Lord, if my friends
> have been so good as my pretension I believe I might have the prehememence;
> for in King Charles time I commanded a squadron against Sally by comission
> and had power to hould court martialls and execute condemned men by my
> order, which power exceed the power of the admiral in these seas, and the trust
> farr greater the[n] that of a private flagg. A nother thing I must begg of your
> lordship's leave: that my humble opinion is that a major of these regiments
> ought to be an officer who very well understands the disipling, managing and
> fighting a regiment ashore, which at present I doe not understand.[34]

Shovell and Rooke remained with the main fleet until July 1691. At that
point, Shovell was sent to get intelligence of the French fleet at Brest. He
proceeded close inshore, flying the white flag of France on several of his
ships and no flag from the others, imitating the returning French fleet with
English prizes. By this ruse Shovell seized several French merchant vessels
loaded with money intending to purchase the prizes and also ascertained
that an unexpectedly powerful force of eighty-four ships of the line lay at
Brest.

At the end of the campaigning season ashore, Russell detached Shovell
to escort the King on his return from Holland to Margate, where William
landed on 19 October 1691. Before his departure, and while still at the
camp at Ath, the King granted Shovell's request to be lieutenant-colonel in
the Second Marine Regiment commanded by Henry Killegrew.

In January 1692 Shovell was promoted to rear-admiral of the red and
granted a coat of arms in commemoration of his earlier battles in the Mediterranean and his more recent conduct in action against the French.[35] At the
same time Rooke moved up to vice-admiral of the red and joined his father-
in-law, John Hill,[36] as an Extra Commissioner of the Navy Board. In March
Shovell again escorted the King back to Holland, accompanied by a squadron
of seven Third Rates and flying his flag in the newly rebuilt and renamed 100-
gun *Royal William* (ex-*Prince*). On his return, Shovell rejoined Russell's
fleet and was among the eighty ships with him on 19 May, when they
encountered Tourville's fleet of forty-four ships off Barfleur.

In that same fleet, Rooke flew his flag in the *Neptune* in command of the
van division of the rear or blue squadron in Admiral Edward Russell's

Anglo-Dutch fleet, nearly twice the size of the opposing French fleet. At the outset of the battle Russell ordered the blue squadron to close up, but a sudden calm prevented this manoeuvre and the French rear stayed out of gun range, leaving Rooke out of the initial action.

Shovell commanded the rear division of Russell's centre squadron and ordered his division to fill their topsails as soon as the engagement began. At 11am the opposing fleets opened fire in light west-southwesterly winds at such close, musket shot, range, that Shovell later remarked he had never before seen two fleets engage at such short distance. The first stage of the engagement came to an indecisive halt after fog and gun smoke precluded the admirals from directing their fleets.

After about two hours the wind shifted into the northwest and freshened slightly, giving Shovell the opportunity to luff up into the new breeze and break through the French line to the windward side and divide the French rear squadron by separating its van from its centre and rear divisions. Seven of Shovell's nine ships were able to follow his manoeuvre. The Dutch, in the allied van, made a similar tactical manoeuvre and forced the French line to turn. As the wind died and the fog began to develop again, the French doubled back on their own line. When the fog cleared momentarily, Shovell engaged Tourville's flagship and six others, but the wind quickly died again and, as the tide turned and began to sweep the opposing fleets to the east, Tourville anchored. Shovell followed suit, up-tide on Tourville's starboard bow, where the opposing ships could only exchange fire from their stern and bow guns.

Shovell immediately attempted to dislodge the French from this position by sending down fireships on the tide, but they did no direct damage and achieved little more than forcing the French to re-anchor further away. Shortly thereafter, Shovell faced nine French ships from Gabaret's and Pannetier's divisions coming down upon him with the tide. In the face of this new threat, he cut his anchor cables and Tourville's squadron then succeeded in heavily damaging Shovell's ships as they drifted past at close range. The wind rose by evening and, in a three-hour engagement, Rooke's ships supported Shovell's division, passing the French closely under heavy fire. By ten in the evening the engagement had ended, but the larger English force had not been able to destroy the smaller French fleet.

Shovell pursued the main body of the French fleet as it moved westward. About midnight the next day, with his flagship nearly disabled by the heavy fire it received, Shovell shifted his flag into the frigate *Kent*. Continuing westward, Shovell soon led the chase with ten ships in company with him. He came nearly within gunshot of the French off Cherbourg on 21 May, but withheld his fire while awaiting reinforcements. Shovell followed the French to the roadstead of La Hogue and anchored offshore. The following morning, Russell ordered Shovell to attack, but he was unable to carry this out due to little or no wind. At this point Shovell reported that he was suffering from a sudden and severe illness, probably caused by blood poisoning from the splinter wound that he had received during the fleet action.

On the 23rd Rooke quickly volunteered to take the wounded Shovell's place and carried on with the attack. With Russell's orders to do so, Rooke temporarily shifted his flag to the *Eagle* and pursued the French into the Bay of La Hogue. Standing in close to the shore, he sent in small boats, whose men boarded and burned twelve French ships of the line and a fireship in the shallow water off the island of Tatihou and the nearby Fort St Vaast. In an attempt to burn some of the transports that were aground at low water in the harbour, Rooke led the way for two fireships to follow him in his barge. Within sight of James II and his army at Morsailines, Rooke's very effective operation created a strategic turning point that the indecisive fleet action off Barfleur had not achieved. As a result, the French did not seek another fleet action in the war.

In the meantime, Shovell returned to the *Royal William* and proceeded to Portsmouth for repair, later going on to the dockyard at Chatham. Shovell went ashore on 28 May to recuperate at Fareham and, when he returned to the fleet, he hoisted his flag in the *Duke*. In early August he convoyed transports to the Downs. Paralleling this, Rooke's detachment rejoined the main fleet at Torbay and also returned to the Downs in October.

During the autumn and winter of 1692 the dispute that had arisen between Russell and Nottingham over the conduct of the fleet developed into a major political battle in Parliament as well as a contentious issue between the Commons and the Lords. As a result of this situation, it was difficult for the Admiralty to choose any one individual to command the fleet for the next season. As far as the King was concerned, the Admiralty was out of control as the leaders of the Tory party actively began to advocate their 'blue water' strategy as preferable to William's land campaigns.[37]

Because of this, it was 23 January 1693 before three flag officers could be appointed to jointly command the fleet. They were Killigrew and Delaval, two officers who had Tory political leanings, and Shovell, who was known to be a Whig. Shovell was the junior of the three and appointed admiral of the blue. Some weeks thereafter, on 20 February, William III visited

Portsmouth and, in recognition of Rooke's performance at the Battle of La Hogue, knighted him on board his flagship *Neptune*.

Up to this point the war situation at sea had prevented the Turkey Company from getting any escorts for its trade into the Mediterranean. Thwarted in attempts to make a direct attack on France, and with none of his earlier close naval advisors remaining in office, William III, for the first time, imposed his personal direction on English naval affairs. In an effort to get a squadron to the Mediterranean for his larger strategic purposes, the King insisted on priority for the Smyrna Convoy and that Rooke be appointed to command it.[38]

On 27 April Shovell was additionally appointed to join Rooke as one of the Extra Commissioners of the Navy Board, and on the following day the three joint admirals met in London to discuss the fleet's forthcoming operations. They agreed to attack Brest, before the French fleet could come out and before the Toulon squadron could arrive. In another meeting at Portsmouth on 15 May, the admirals considered Rooke's orders to escort the Smyrna Convoy. Although they incorrectly believed that the Brest squadron would remain in port, Rooke was apparently hesitant to sail before the whereabouts of the French Toulon squadron could be more carefully ascertained. Finally, on the Queen's command, the Admiralty directed that the Grand Fleet sail immediately with the merchant fleet.

On receipt of this order, the joint admirals decided to accompany Rooke and the merchant fleet to a position 90 miles west-southwest of Ushant and there leave Rooke to proceed on his own. Further delay prevented sailing until 30 May 1693, when Rooke departed in the *Royal Oak*, to protect the 400 ships in the outward-bound 'Smyrna' convoy that had waited nearly two years for the opportunity. The main fleet, commanded by joint admirals Killigrew, Shovell, and Delavall, accompanied Rooke, making 101 warships to escort the merchant ships into the Bay of Biscay.

Upon reaching their predetermined position, the admirals still had no information on the whereabouts of the French fleet and decided to stay with Rooke for an additional 60 miles. On 7 June the joint admirals turned to the north and Rooke, with twenty-one English and Dutch warships, continued on with their charges. The joint admirals, thinking that the longer they stayed with Rooke the more they were leaving England undefended, did not know that the Brest fleet had already sailed to the south. Their desire to protect home waters unwittingly left Rooke and his fleet to fall into the hands of the combined Brest-Toulon squadrons. With good intelligence of the English fleet's movements, the French fleet under Tourville, including seventy ships from Brest and another twenty from Toulon, lay in wait at Lagos Bay on the south coast of Portugal. The Admiralty had failed to warn Rooke and had made no suggestion of the possibility of such an attack from so large a force.

When Rooke rounded Cape St Vincent and sighted French warships, he, at first, underestimated the enemy's strength. Only after Rooke began to engage did he realise that he was far outnumbered. Quickly shifting tactics for the new situation, he fought a skillful defensive action, while simultaneously directing the merchant ships toward safe harbours. Two Dutch warships attempted to draw the French off and were captured. In addition, the French took or destroyed ninety-two merchant ships valued at £1 million, scattering the remainder into various ports where French cruisers prevented them from continuing on. After the action, Rooke could only locate fifty-four merchant vessels and took them to a rendezvous at Madeira, and then went to Cork, before rejoining the main fleet at Torbay on 16 August. In describing the action afterwards, Rooke commented, 'I will only add that I embarked myself in this unhappy expedition contrary to my own inclinations & reason, out of a passive obedience to the king's pleasure by which I exposed reputation and run the risk of ruining my fortune . . .'.[39]

News of the disastrous attack on the Smyrna Convoy reached London in mid-July and created a financial crisis that undercut the government's attempt to obtain credit for the war effort. Although the merchants had suffered severe losses, from this point of view, the reaction was wildly exaggerated.[40] The Admiralty, the ministers, and the joint admirals' conduct of the operation all came under tumultuous parliamentary criticism. Rooke, although he was publicly thought to be a Tory, was actually better described as merely 'not a Whig.'[41] In fact, whenever he could, he avoided party politics and tried to limit his conduct to professional naval matters. This was an attitude that William found attractive, and for this reason the King promoted Rooke to admiral of the blue in July 1693, just before news of the disaster had reached London. The three joint admirals, under criticism for their own conduct, were reluctant to see Rooke so easily cleared of blame, and they demurred for ten days before they forwarded notice to Rooke of his promotion, which took effect in August. In the end, the joint admirals escaped formal censure, but they were removed from their joint command. On 6 October 1693 the Queen vacated Shovell's commission as admiral and the others were also suspended from duties during the debates on their conduct. On the King's return later in the autumn, Shovell was momentarily named to command the small squadron that was expected to sail for the West Indies, but this plan was soon set aside.

In Rooke's case, the King appointed him deputy lieutenant of Kent in February 1694 and, shortly thereafter, ordered him to command the main fleet. As part of the general reorganisation at the Admiralty and Navy Board, the King recalled Russell to command the fleet in November, and to serve as First Lord of the newly reconstituted Admiralty Board. In connection with this, Rooke's patent as Extra Commissioner of the Navy Board was exchanged for one as an Admiralty commissioner.

In 1694 Shovell returned to sea as vice-admiral of the red in the main fleet under John, Lord Berkeley of Stratton. Under him, Shovell participated in the expedition to Camaret Bay, which carried the troops under Lieutenant-General Thomas Talmash and also included some of the experimental 'machine vessels', designed by William Meesters. These vessels of 20 to 100 tons were filled with explosives and were intended to be towed inshore just before a bombardment. Detonated by a preset firing mechanism, the explosions were to signal the main attack.[42] From the first, Shovell doubted they could be made to work effectively.[43] In the autumn of 1694 Shovell commanded the squadron off Dunkirk, where he again attempted to use Meester's vessels, but this attempt proved to be the fiasco that ended the experiment.

In November 1694 Shovell again was at the centre of public attention. In the Downs, he ordered the *Stirling Castle* to fire on the 56-gun Danish warship *Gyldenløve,* commanded by the future Danish admiral Captain Niels Lauritsen Barfoed, for failing to strike her pendant in salute to the Queen's flag in English home waters. Three men were killed and eighteen wounded in the action, which created a diplomatic tempest, yet earned him full support from the Admiralty as a sidelight in the navy's protracted attempt to control neutral shipping. At the same time, the incident resulted in English vessels becoming more punctilious in saluting the Danish flag flying over Kronborg Castle at Helsingør at the entrance to the Sound. In November Shovell was nearby, but did not enter Danish waters when he convoyed merchant ships from Göteborg to England.

In 1695 Shovell was in command of his flagship *Cambridge* as well as Berkeley's second flag officer[44] during the attacks on St Malo and Dunkirk. In August he was spoken of for commanding a small Mediterranean squadron, but eventually Russell was sent with a full fleet of fifty-six ships. In December he took command of the *Duchess* as his new flagship as vice admiral of the red.[45] Similarly, in April 1696, he commanded the *Victory* as well as being admiral of the blue[46] in command of the bombardment of Calais. After operating in the Bay of Biscay in July and August, Shovell was sent orders by the Admiralty to command the fleet in the Mediterranean,[47] but when the French Toulon squadron slipped into Brest that plan was not put into effect.

A year later, he was appointed to command the ships attending the King in his passage to Holland. While at The Hague, Rooke met with English and Dutch officials on plans for the coming campaign. In August 1695 Rooke was ordered to relieve Russell as commander-in-chief of the fleet in the Mediterranean. However, crossed orders between the King and the lord justices delayed Rooke's arrival at Cadiz until 16 October. Basing himself there with thirty ships of the line, Rooke sent out cruisers from Cadiz for intelligence, patrolled for trade protection, and maintained a show of force in the region to support the alliance with Spain. In February 1696 Rooke had orders to return to England, if there was no sign of the French fleet attempting to come out. As a ruse, he pretended he was moving the fleet into the Mediterranean, but, as ordered, returned to the Channel on 22 April.

Shortly after his return, Rooke was promoted to admiral of the fleet and took command in the Channel. Unable to prevent the Toulon squadron from reaching Brest, Rooke gathered a fleet of 115 English and Dutch ships, but was limited in what he could achieve due to their manning level. While wrestling with this problem, Rooke revealed an unusual amount about his personal views when he wrote to Sir William Trumbull at this time:

> I find you Ministers in great haste to have the Fleet at sea. I pray God it may answer your expectations, but we are most certainly in a miserable condition as to men; so that considering so much depends on the success of a battle, as my thoughts suggest to me there does, I must own to you I am very apprehensive of the consequence; for if the fleet be beaten, I do not see what can hinder the enemy from prosecuting their late intentions of invading us; but my great hopes are their fleet may be as ill manned as ours and then possibly our mob may prove the better of the two, but whether this is a sufficient ground to venture our all upon, I must submit to wiser men's determinations: for my own part I have composed my thoughts, and settled my resolution to venture my life cheerfully in the service of my country upon any terms, and I will rather choose to die in the defense of our liberty and religion than submit to Popery and Slavery; or retreat before persecution into the mountains of Wales and Scotland.[48]

On 27 May the King personally ordered Rooke to pass command to Admiral Lord John Berkeley and to return to the Admiralty, where his administrative skills were needed. Before leaving the fleet, Rooke proposed that it should blockade the French squadrons at Brest and attack French coastal towns, but after relieving Rooke on 3 June, Berkeley and his council of war thought this impractical. On his return to London, Rooke's request for half pay as admiral of the fleet was denied by the Admiralty Board, but the King granted him, at his pleasure, a pension of £3 per day for remaining on shore at the Admiralty.

In May 1697 Rooke returned to sea in command of the fleet in the First Rate *Britannia*. The continued scarcity of both seaman and provisions prevented fully manning the fleet, while the lack of frigates hindered intelligence collection. Although the French put to sea from Brest without opposition, Rooke's squadron later encountered a fleet of fifty-four merchantmen on the French coast under the Swedish flag. Discovering that most were carrying enemy goods, Rooke seized them. Despite the diplomatic protests that followed, Rooke's contention was proved in the High Court of Admiralty. Rooke returned to the administrative affairs at the Admiralty Office, while Shovell remained at sea as admiral of the blue and was appointed commander-in-chief in the Thames and Medway in August 1698.[49] In this role he provided escort for the King on his return from Holland in November.

After the Peace of Rijswijk both men stood for parliamentary election. Rooke was a political follower of the Tory statesman Daniel Finch, second Earl of Nottingham, as well as his nephew through marriage. The son of Charles II's chief law officer and later lord chancellor, Heneage Finch, Lord Nottingham had left office in the political dispute following the Smyrna Convoy disaster in 1693 and remained out of office until 1702, but the Finch family's political connections remained powerful and widespread.[50] With this backing, Rooke won the second parliamentary seat in the government borough of Portsmouth in the election of 1698. In the same election, Shovell was returned as second member for the government borough of Rochester and retained that seat for two years. In February 1699 Shovell participated in the debate over the Navy Estimates, noting that, in his view, it was useful to continue to recruit soldiers as Marines, as they 'would in due course turn into sailors.'[51]

In March 1699 Shovell exchanged his appointed position as an Extra Commissioner of the Navy Board to be a Principal Officer, as the Controller of Victualling Accounts. In that role during 1700 he joined with the other commissioners in defending themselves against the allegations of peculation and mismanagement from the former clerk of the Treasurer's accounts, Gilbert Wardlow,[52] who had been dismissed the previous year. Additionally during this period, both Rooke and Shovell supported John Graydon's successful petition to be reinstated in command at sea, after he had been ultimately cleared of malicious charges against him.[53]

In 1700 Rooke returned to sea, flying his flag in the Third Rate *Shrewsbury*. With William III's explicit instructions 'for preserving tranquility in the North'[54] on the basis of the 1689 Treaty of Altona and, thereby, to maintain stability in Europe, Rooke arrived on the Dutch coast in late May with eleven English ships of the line. After a meeting at The Hague with Dutch leaders, Rooke continued on to the Texel, where Lieutenant-Admiral Philips van Almonde's squadron joined him for the passage to Göteborg, Sweden. On 21 July 1700, and again on the night of 26–27 July, a combined force of some fifty-eight Dutch, English and Swedish ships fired on Copenhagen. While the allied fleet held the Danish navy at Copenhagen, Charles XII personally led the Swedish army across the Sound on 3 August. Denmark agreed to a truce and, in this precarious period, Rooke worked to disengage the opposing Swedish and Danish forces. After the re-establishment of the Altona settlement in the treaty of Travendahl, the Anglo-Dutch Squadron departed, having successfully prevented the first phase of the Great Northern War from further complicating the international tensions that were leading to war over the Spanish Succession.

In 1701 both Rooke and Shovell returned to sea duty. In the summer of 1701 Rooke commanded the fleet in the Channel. On news that the French fleet had put to sea from Brest, he strongly recommended to the Ministry that the country was not yet in a position to risk its navy in any major engagement. He should protect trade and husband its resources in the event that a major war broke out with France. At the general election in 1701, Rooke was again returned as MP for Portsmouth, but Captain William Bokenham of the Chatham Royal Dockyard succeeded Shovell in the second seat at Rochester.

The War of the Spanish Succession

With William III's appointment of the Earl of Pembroke as Lord High Admiral on 26 January 1702, the Admiralty Commission was dissolved. Although Pembroke considered commanding the fleet at sea in person, the King's death and Anne's succession to the throne in March brought in the new queen's consort, Prince George of Denmark, as Lord High Admiral in May 1702, coinciding with Anglo-Dutch entry into the War of the Spanish Succession. Unlike his predecessor, George established a Council with Rooke as the senior of four admirals to assist and advise him. Additionally, Rooke became Vice-Admiral of England with 20 shillings a day and the wages of 16 men. At the same time Shovell was promoted to admiral of the white in May 1702. Among his first duties was to preside over the controversial court martial of Rear-Admiral Sir John Munden, held on board the *Queen,* at Spithead, for failing to engage a French squadron in the opening days of the war. The court martial cleared him of the charges against him. Upon its completion, Shovell returned to sea as second in command to Rooke.

In these early months of Anne's reign, John Macky probably composed his posthumously published notes on both Rooke and Shovell. Of Shovell, Macky wrote, 'No man understands the Affairs of the Navy better, or is beloved of the Sailors so well as he. He loves the *Constitution* of his *Country* and serves it without *factious aim;* he . . . proves a very grateful Husband . . . hath very good Natural Parts; familiar and plain in his Conversation; dresses without affectation; is very large, fat, fair Man . . .'⁵⁵   In some contrast, he described Rooke in quite a different manner, as 'a Gentleman of very Good parts, speaks little, but to the Purpose. He always showed a Dislike to men of *Revolution Principles* and discouraged them all he could in the Navy . . . a Stern-Looked Man of Brown Complexion, well shaped and Sixty [*sic*] years Old.'⁵⁶

In the summer of 1702 Rooke again stood in the general election in Portsmouth and was returned, this time, in the first seat, which he held until 1705. In the same election Rooke's brother-in-law, Edward Knatchbull, newly appointed as sub-commissioner for prizes, was elected to the first seat in Rochester. Meanwhile at the Admiralty, as planning continued for an expedition to Cadiz in 1702, consideration was given for Prince George to command at sea. In the end, however, Rooke became its commander with orders that directed, if Cadiz proved impracticable, 'you are then to proceed to Gibraltar or take in your way home, Vigo, Ponta Vedra, Corunna, or any other place belonging to Spain or France.'⁵⁷ In preparation for the expedition, Rooke reissued in June the Fighting and Sailing Instructions for the fleet, based on those that Russell and Torrington had issued in the 1690s. Just as the expedition sailed in July, Rooke's wife Mary died in giving birth to his only child, a son named George.

Sailing with him, Rooke had three English and five Dutch flag officers, 160 Dutch and English vessels of all types, with the Duke of Ormonde commanding 9662 English troops and Major-General Baron de Sparre with 4000 Dutch troops. While Rooke sailed to attack Cadiz, he ordered Shovell to cruise further out in the Atlantic, in search of Châteaurenault's squadron returning with the Spanish silver *flota.*⁵⁸ It was at this point that Shovell shared some of his general thoughts about current naval strategy with Lord Nottingham, now back in office as secretary of state for the Southern Department:

> . . . the misfortune and vice of our Country is to believe ourselves better than other men, which I take to be the reason that generally we send too small a force to execute our designs; but experience has taught me that where men are equally inured and disciplined to war, 'tis without a miracle, number that gains the victory, for both in flesh, squadrons and single ships of near equal force, by the time one is beaten and ready to retreat the other is also beaten and glad the enemy has left him; To fight, beat and chase an enemy of the same strength I have sometime seen, but rarely have seen at sea any victory worth boasting, where the strength has been near equal.[59]

Ten days later Shovell repeated the sentiment when he commented, in regard to Châteaurenault, 'I wish I was stronger than he for equal numbers seldom make great victories at sea.'[60]

Just before the landing, Prince George of Hesse-Darmstadt arrived to join the commanders as imperial commissary, but, at that point, Rooke was reticent as he had received no instructions to accept him as such. The German prince soon joined Ormonde in criticising Rooke (who was repeatedly bothered by severe attacks of gout) and the entire naval side of the operation. On 15 August troops landed at the Bay of Bulls, but when it became clear that there was no local support for the allied effort, the troops re-embarked in mid-September. At the end of the campaigning season and with a shortage of supplies, the land and sea officers found that they could not agree on any alternative operation. At this juncture the King of Portugal offered Lisbon as a winter base, but Rooke decided returned to England to refit the fleet. En route, Rooke obtained intelligence that the French squadron under Châteaurenault had brought the long-awaited Spanish silver *flota* into port at Vigo, and he immediately sent orders for Shovell to rendezvous with the main fleet at Vigo.

Arriving off Vigo on 10 October in bad weather, Rooke's Anglo-Dutch fleet found the French warships anchored broadside, behind a heavy boom that was defended by a shore battery and a fort. With little room for the full fleet to manoeuvre, Rooke ordered fifteen English ships and ten Dutch ships of the line with all the available fireships to enter the harbour and take or destroy the enemy ships. Ordering the troops to land on the following day and to assault the forts, he also directed Vice-Admiral Sir Thomas Hopsonn, in his flagship *Torbay*, to break through the boom, which they succeeded in doing on 12 October. During this action Rooke took or destroyed fifteen French ships of the line, two frigates, one fireship, a corvette, three Spanish galleons and thirteen other Spanish ships. While this was a very successful military and naval operation, wildly inaccurate estimates were circulated as to the amount of silver captured. In fact, the Spanish had managed to unload the majority of the silver bullion before the attack. Spanish Treasury records show that, after expenses and losses, it still received from this convoy the largest sum ever obtained in one year from America, 6,994,293 pesos, while the English Treasury recorded an amount valued at £14,000.[61]

On receiving the news that Châteaurenault had arrived at Vigo with the galleons carrying their cargo of silver bullion, Shovell rushed to support Rooke, arriving on 16 October, four days after the initial attack. On the 19th, Rooke left Vigo for home with the main fleet, arriving at the Downs in early November. Under Rooke's orders, Shovell remained behind to manage the aftermath of the action, to repair and re-rig the captured vessels, and to supervise the care of disabled ships, destroying those that could not be taken to sea. In particular, Rooke ordered Shovell to prevent any embezzlement of prize goods. Shovell completed this work quickly and departed Vigo on 25 October, but was delayed in his return by bad weather in the Bay of Biscay.

The episode was hailed by Robert Harley as a 'most glorious expedition',[62] the House of Commons voted Rooke its thanks on 10 November 1702, and the Queen appointed him a member of the Privy Council. The Duke of Ormonde's public condemnation of Rooke's conduct, however, led to an inquiry, which soon became embroiled in party politics, as the Tories tried to discredit Marlborough and the Whigs criticised Ormonde and Rooke. During the questioning before Parliament, Torrington, as a member of the House of Lords' committee, repeatedly attacked Rooke.[63] In this ordeal Rooke narrowly escaped censure by showing that there had been such differences of professional opinion that the commanders could only agree to return home.

In March 1703 Rooke declined the Ministry's offer to him of the command of the Mediterranean fleet on the grounds that the planned force was not large enough for one of his rank; the Admiralty sent Shovell instead. From April through June 1703 Rooke was at sea in home waters in command of the main fleet. Flying the Union Flag in the First Rate *Royal Sovereign*, he cruised against enemy shipping in the Channel and the Bay of Biscay. In early May Rooke ordered the printing of his *Sailing and Fighting Instructions for Her Majesty's Fleet*. Reprinted with Rooke's name removed, they provided the basis for English fleet tactics for the remainder of the century, although Rooke's instructions lacked the index that facilitated tactical signalling. By May, however, Rooke had become seriously ill and he requested immediate relief. The Admiralty ordered Admiral George Churchill to take his place, but, by the time Churchill approached the fleet, Rooke stubbornly insisted that he had recovered enough to continue. He remained in command until his health forced him ashore on 30 June.

While Rooke was thus occupied, Shovell had become one of the advisors to the newly formed Ordnance establishment[64] and was also present to supervise the opening of the goods from Vigo, ensuring that an accurate account of them was made. With that duty accomplished, Shovell concentrated on preparing his fleet for the Mediterranean. Flying his flag in the *Triumph*, Shovell faced continued delays in preparation, and eventually departed St Helens on 1 July without all the assigned vessels, convoying a fleet of some two hundred merchant ships to Lisbon. Prevented by headwinds from leaving the Channel, he returned to Torbay to await the other English and Dutch vessels. He set sail again on 13 July, capturing several enemy vessels on his passage to the coast of Portugal. Joined there by Vice-Admiral Sir John Leake, Shovell formed a squadron of twelve Dutch and thirty-five English warships; he attempted to enter the Mediterranean on 4 August, but a strong Levant wind at the Straits continued to prevent his passage for a month. Finally able to enter, he sailed first to attempt to make contact with the Camisard rebels in the Cèvennes, but the French had learned of this plan and had taken effective precautions to prevent its success. Thereafter, Shovell carried out his orders to sail for Livorno, where he arrived on 19 September.

Admiral van Almonde had earlier advised Shovell that the Dutch squadron was required to return home by 20 November. Aware of this situation, Shovell and the English flag officers decided to accompany the Dutch back, since they had not received the expected information from the Austrians on how to proceed in supporting the war from that side. After sending several ships on missions to renew the peace agreements at Algiers, Tunis, Tripoli, and Morocco, as he had been instructed, Shovell's Anglo-Dutch fleet left the Mediterranean on 26 October and returned to England on 16 November.

On 27 November, shortly after his return, Shovell was anchored at the Gunfleet before proceeding up the Thames. Caught there by the Great Storm of 1703, *Triumph* broke her anchor and had her rudder torn off. Dragging her bower anchor and driving toward the Galloper sand, the flagship was personally saved by Shovell when he ordered the main mast cut away.

Meanwhile, Rooke had returned to London in August 1703, after his period of recuperation at Bath. Still in ill health and discontented, he thought of resigning, but several ministers persuaded him that he was needed to take command of the squadron to take Emperor Leopold I's second son, the Archduke Charles of Austria, to Spain. As he was the allies' central emblem in the war over the Spanish Succession, they intended to place him on the Spanish throne, having already declared him King Charles III. Delayed by the Great Storm of November 1703, Rooke brought Charles from Holland to Portsmouth on 26 December, where the dukes of Somerset and Marlborough welcomed the fleet on its arrival and invited the King to Windsor, where the Queen received him. In February 1704, carrying orders written in the queen's own hand, Rooke and the allied squadron had a thirteen-day passage to Lisbon, where Charles remained as a guest in the royal palace. There, the Dutch vessels left from the previous year joined Rooke's squadron.

On reports that the Spanish fleet was returning from the West Indies, Rooke soon took the squadron to sea, where a detached division under Sir Thomas Dilkes captured several 'galleons'. On Rooke's return to Lisbon, he found orders for him to continue into the Mediterranean, allowing him wide latitude for his operations. If needed, Rooke could choose to support the military operations of the Duke of Savoy, attack Toulon, encourage revolt of the Cèvennes, support the Catalans at Barcelona in their allegiance to Charles III, or do other serious damage to the French and their allies.

Selecting the best opportunity he saw available, Rooke chose to bombard Barcelona and land 1600 Marines, but this did not prove as opportune as it looked. When Bourbon forces prevented any local support for the Habsburg cause, Rooke had to break off the attack and re-embark the troops. At that point Rooke received news that the comte de Toulouse was heading toward the Mediterranean with the squadron from Brest. Shortly thereafter, Rooke sighted parts of the French squadron, but he felt that his forces were not strong enough to prevent them from reaching Toulon and decided, instead, to sail for Lisbon to rendezvous with reinforcements, instead of fighting.

When news of this reached England, Daniel Defoe embarked on a major campaign criticising Rooke's conduct. Although he later told Robert Harley that he carried no personal grudge against Rooke, Defoe believed that a Tory should not be allowed in such high offices as Rooke held. 'How can such a Man be trusted with the English Navy?' Defoe demanded. 'When People ask one another of the fleet,' he wrote,

> the common answer is how should we expect better with such an Admiral, A man that never fought since he was an Admiral, that always embrace'd the party that oppos'd the Government, and has constantly favored, Preferred and kept company with the high furious Jacobite Party and has filled the fleet with them.[65]

Defoe's repeated criticisms led several of Rooke's friends to challenge Defoe to a duel, an event that Defoe also used against Rooke in the press.[66] While this was going on in the political arena, the Admiralty had already ordered Shovell to take a large reinforcement of twenty-five ships to Rooke's assistance. Meeting Rooke's fleet as it was heading for Lisbon, Shovell joined forces with him on 16 June off Lagos Bay, bringing new orders for Rooke.

Now, with a total strength of sixty-three ships, Rooke's new orders required him to stay on the Spanish coast and obtain the approval of the kings of Spain and Portugal for any fleet operations. At this point Charles III proposed a new assault on Cadiz, but, when a council of war examined the issue on 17 July, the flag officers determined that, in the light of the experience from 1702, a large land army was necessary for any success in such an operation. The fort at Gibraltar, however, offered a more practical alternative and was reportedly in relatively weak condition. Both Rooke and Shovell knew the place well, as did several other English officers, who had often used that port with the Mediterranean fleet during the 1680s.

On 21 July Rooke, flying his flag in the Second Rate *Royal Katherine*, landed Hesse-Darmstadt at Gibraltar, in command of 1800 Dutch and English Marines, with several hundred Catalans who had accompanied the fleet from Barcelona. On the demand that Gibraltar surrender in the name of King Charles III of Spain, the garrison refused, as it had pledged its allegiance to the Bourbon candidate, Philip V. Rooke ordered sixteen English ships under Sir George Byng and six Dutch ships under Rear-Admiral Paulus van der Dussen to bombard the fort and other positions on the following day. On Sunday 23 July Rooke ordered boat landings on the Mole and at Rosia Bay. After three days the city council and the governor, Don Diego de Salinas, surrendered the 250-man garrison to Prince George of Hesse-Darmstadt and the inhabitants took an oath to Charles III as their legitimate king. When Rooke reported his action to London, the news was met with some puzzlement. Although Gibraltar had been mentioned as a possible target earlier, now that it was actually in allied hands Lord Godolphin remarked, 'I know not how far it is tenable or can be of use to us; those at Lisbon will be the best judges and directors of that matter.'[67]

Having taken control of Gibraltar for the allies, Rooke began immediate preparations to meet the French fleet, which he logically assumed would immediately move to recover Gibraltar. After obtaining water on the African coast, Rooke's fleet returned toward Gibraltar and, on 9 August, a scout sighted the French under Toulouse. The two opposing fleets both made preparations for battle, but did not encounter one another again until

13 August, when they formed opposing battle lines about 24 miles South of Cape Málaga.

The two fleets were equal in number with fifty-one ships in the battle line, but the Franco-Spanish Fleet had been more recently supplied and repaired, while the Anglo-Dutch had more frigates and the Franco-Spanish had galleys. Throughout the action in light winds, the Franco-Spanish ships stood between the Anglo-Dutch fleet and Gibraltar. In this action Shovell commanded the van of the Anglo-Dutch line, with only one flag officer, Sir John Leake, to support him, rather than the normal two. In the course of the battle, when many ships in the van were too damaged to manoeuvre, Shovell performed the difficult operation of sailing his flagship, *Barfleur,* astern under backed topsails to support Rooke. In this manoeuvre, *Namur,* Shovell's second ahead in the van, followed suit.

Despite heavy exchanges of gunfire, no vessel was sunk or taken on either side in the action, although a number were disabled and towed out of the line and 2768 English and Dutch officers and men were killed or wounded. During the battle, when two ships of the line were heavily damaged and low on ammunition, Rooke called in two of his 50-gun frigates to replace them in the line of battle. A commonplace event in the Dutch wars, this had became a rare event in the history of fleet battle tactics after 1689. Making repairs throughout the following day, Rooke distributed his limited ammunition equally throughout the fleet and decided to attempt to break the French line, but, before he could do so, the wind shifted and the Franco-Spanish fleet retired toward Toulon during the night of 15–16 August.

Strategically, the engagement settled the immediate future of Gibraltar and marked the last time in the war that the French attempted a major fleet action. At the tactical level, the engagement had been indecisive, but, nevertheless, proved to the next generation of English naval officers that the line of battle was the most effective means to engage a fleet of equal size. After ensuring that the Anglo-Spanish fleet was not going to attempt to go to westward of him, Rooke took his fleet to Gibraltar for repairs on 19 August. After providing for the further defence of Gibraltar, Rooke and Shovell both returned to England on 24 September.

By coincidence the Battle of Vélez-Málaga had occurred in the Mediterranean on the same day that the Duke of Marlborough had won his victory at Blenheim in Bavaria. This coincidence aroused the passions of party politics from the previous year and the Tories declared Rooke to be the equal of Marlborough,[68] while the duke's political friends were incensed to find Rooke raised to Marlborough's stature. When the Tories threatened to arrest Defoe for his political attacks on Rooke, Defoe complained to Harley, 'The Victory at sea they look upon as their victory over the Moderate Party and his health is now Drunk by those here, who won't Drink the Queen's nor yours.'[69] A popular ballad 'On the Sea Fight Between Sir G.R. and Toulouse, 1704' echoed the same view.[70]

Throughout this political campaign, Rooke was seriously ill and went to Bath for his health. There, in December, Charles Bernhard removed chalk from his joints,[71] but with little apparent improvement to his condition. On 8 January 1705 Rooke's secretary, Hugh Cory, recorded in his journal that the admiral had resigned his commission for reasons of his health, 'weakened and crippled by gout.'[72] Prince George accepted his resignation on 13 January and Rooke was paid as commander-in-chief of the fleet through that date and played no further role in naval affairs.

Coincidentally, Rooke's political patron, Nottingham, resigned and, with the dissolution of Anne's first Parliament in the spring of 1705, all Nottingham's leading supporters lost their offices. In very poor health, Rooke purchased a farm at Barham, Kent, and retired to his family home, St Lawrence House, near Canterbury. He no longer participated in naval affairs, although he continued to hold the honorary position of Vice-Admiral of England during the remaining four years of his life. After his death, that office remained vacant for nearly a decade. Even after his retirement from public life, Rooke's name came up in politics. For example, Marlborough noted that it was strange that Rooke, as member of the Privy Council, had not signed the Kentish petition. In another example, the Admiralty mistakenly included Rooke's name in the draft patent for members of the Lord High Admiral's Council, presented for signature in June 1705. Rooke's name was quickly removed by the Queen's order,[73] and some contemporary observers and historians have misinterpreted this and other post-retirement references to Rooke as evidence of his political dismissal from office. In fact, they merely document his physical disability in full retirement.

On 25 December 1704 Shovell left his position as Controller of Victualling Accounts and, on the following day, was appointed Rear-Admiral of England,[74] an office that had been vacant since the Revolution sixteen years before, and a member of the Lord High Admiral's Council. On 13 January 1705 he succeeded Rooke as admiral and commander-in-chief of the fleet, flying the union flag at the main mast of *Britannia* at the Nore. Shovell's promotion, at this juncture, reflects the decision that he was a less controversial appointment than either of the other leading contenders would have been: George Churchill or Torrington. In addition, the Dutch found Shovell fully acceptable, a key factor for allied naval operations. After a four-year hiatus from Parliament, Shovell was returned in the 1705 general election as Member of Parliament in the first seat for Rochester.

On 1 May the Lord High Admiral directed that 'the Chief Command of her Majesty's fleet should be exercised by joint commission, that the affairs thereof may be carried on by joint council and advice.'[75] Prince George appointed Shovell and Charles, Earl of Peterborough and Monmouth, to the joint command, for an expedition to the Mediterranean that had the seizure of Toulon as its original object.

The fleet of twenty-nine ships of the line sailed from St Helens on 23 May 1705, and reached Lisbon on 11 June. There they were joined by ships under Sir John Leake and a Dutch squadron under Lieutenant-Admiral Philips van Almonde, bringing the fleet's strength up to fifty-eight ships with additional frigates and other vessels. As the fleet was approaching the Mediterranean, the Duke of Savoy attempted to persuade the other allies to assist him in recovering Nice. However, at the express desire of King Charles III of Spain, the fleet sailed to Barcelona, settling the question as to where the fleet would be employed. There, Peterborough landed the troops without opposition on 12 August, accompanied by King Charles and the Prince of Hesse-Darmstadt. After considerable debate between the Dutch, King Charles's court, Shovell and Peterborough over the proper course of action, it was finally agreed to besiege Barcelona, which capitulated three weeks later on 23 September. With no appropriate winter base for the fleet in the Mediterranean, Shovell left Peterborough at Barcelona and, passing Gibraltar on 16 October, returned to England on 26 November 1705 with twenty-four warships and several other vessels.

On 10 March 1706 the commissions for Shovell and Peterborough as joint commanders-in-chief were renewed and the Dutch particularly requested that Shovell, not Leake, command the fleet. On 10 July Shovell received orders to make all haste in preparing the expedition to carry more than 9000 troops under Earl Rivers. At first, Shovell took the fleet with embarked troops to make a false attack on Normandy, drawing the French army away from the place of the real planned assault, but bad weather prevented the attack.

Shovell then sailed for Portugal with the troops on board, but his transports were scattered by a storm *en route*. Once the fleet was reconstituted at Lisbon, the original plan was to land the forces in Portugal for an overland attack on Madrid, but an English council of war objected to the Portuguese plan to divide English forces into two armies. Declining this, Shovell and Rivers proceeded to move the force by sea to Spain, landing them in February 1707 at Alicante. Ordering Sir George Byng to support operations at Alicante, Shovell returned to Lisbon for part of the fleet to refit.

Two months later Shovell returned to Alicante and went on to Barcelona, where Byng with Vice-Admiral Phillips van der Goes and the Dutch squadron rejoined on 20 May. While there, Shovell played an instrumental role in persuading Charles III and his court that the most valuable service in the war effort was to implement the allies' long-planned assault on the French naval base at Toulon. The key to this was to use the Anglo-Dutch fleet to support the armies under the Duke Victor Amadeus II of Savoy and Prince Eugene of Savoy.

Arriving on the French coast at the mouth of the Var, Shovell first reduced the enemy entrenchment near the sea. Then Prince Eugene and Victor Amadeus consulted with Shovell on board his flagship, *Association*, on 2 July, and, at that point, with Shovell's agreement to keep ships available for support throughout the following winter, the military commanders resolved to march the allied armies directly on Toulon. More than a hundred cannon were landed from the fleet, and allied forces were in such force that the French sank many of their warships in Toulon harbour. With the fleet based off Hyères, the siege continued until 4 August, when French troops rallied to their own defence. Two days later the allied generals became convinced that they could not prevail over the revitalised French and asked Shovell to embark the cannon, take on board the wounded, and raise the siege.

By 23 August the armies had dispersed and Shovell, deeply disappointed, sailed for Gibraltar, where he left a squadron under Sir Thomas Dilkes on 29 September. Continuing on with twenty-one ships in the main fleet, he reached the Soundings on the morning of 21 October. On the following day, while trying to confirm its position, the fleet lay-to in hazy weather from early in the afternoon until nightfall. Shovell detached three vessels for Plymouth, apparently thinking the fleet was further to the eastward than it was. Shortly after 6pm, still unable to confirm his position, Shovell ordered the fleet to continue up the Channel in fleet formation. At about 8, in dark and rainy weather, lookouts in several ships suddenly saw rocks and the loom of the St Agnes Light, and fired warning guns. The flagship also fired warning guns but, before she could change course, struck the Outer Gilstone Rock in the Scilly Isles and sank quickly.

Most of the nineteen vessels in the fleet escaped a similar fate, but the 54-gun *Romney* was also wrecked on the same rocks, while the 70-gun *Eagle* sank off the Tearing Ledge, just southeast of the Bishop and Clerks rocks.[76]

Of the 1315 men in these three ships, there was only one survivor, a quartermaster from the *Romney*. Vice-Admiral Sir George Byng's flagship *Royal Anne*, as well as the *St George*, narrowly escaped the Gilstone. The fireship *Firebrand* struck the same rocks, but managed to get into the relative safety of Smith Sound before sinking where her crew could get ashore. Bodies and wreckage floated ashore for some time.

Reputedly still alive, Shovell came ashore from the wreck on the south side of St Mary's Island at Porth Hellick Cove. The fact that Shovell's body washed up more than six miles from the wreck site, in close proximity to the bodies of his two step-sons (Sir John Narbrough and James Narbrough), his pet dog, and the flagship's captain, suggests that they had been able to leave the wreck together in a boat. Numerous legends and traditional stories surround these events. The most persistent is the alleged confession of a woman in the 1730s, who on her deathbed reported that she had found Shovell alive on the beach and, coveting the emerald ring on his finger, took his life. As her dying wish, the parish priest sent the ring to James, Earl of Berkeley. In 1879 a ring that matched the general description was reported to be in the possession of the Berkeley family, but has not been traced since.

Like others, Shovell's body was buried on the beach. Identified as Shovell's, it was taken and reburied higher up on the beach, before being taken up again, prepared by a naval surgeon and placed in a casket. Moved on board the *Salisbury*, the ship carried the body to Plymouth, where Dr James Younge embalmed it at the Naval Hospital. Shovell's death, with the loss of the *Association* and her consorts, was a great national disaster and accompanied by a great outpouring of grief. From Plymouth, Shovell's casket was taken overland in a cortege. *En route*, thousands paid their respects to the admiral as the casket passed though Okehampton and Exeter, then passing through all the towns along the main road to London. On arrival, the body lay in state at the Queen's expense at Shovell's home in Frith Street, Soho.

Two months after the accident, on 22 December 1707, most of the nation's leading admirals, George Churchill, Matthew Aylmer, Sir Stafford Fairborne, Sir John Leake, Sir George Byng, Sir John Jennings, Sir Thomas Hopsonn, Sir William Whetstone, Sir James Wishart, and Sir John Munden, accompanied the body as it was borne in an elaborate hearse from Shovell's home to Westminster Abbey. He was buried in the south choir aisle, near the east cloister door. In 1708 Queen Anne ordered Grinling Gibbons to carve a spectacular monument in marble, showing him lying recumbent under an inscription that noted he was 'lamented by all, But especially the Seafaring part of the Nation to whom he was a generous Patron and worthy example'. John Molesworth summarised Shovell's role as one of the leading naval figures of his time when he wrote to his mother on hearing the news of Shovell's death, 'He is universally regretted for his courage, capacity, and honesty, which it will be hard to parallel in another commander.'[77]

Shovell's death, among the 1314 men who died with him in the navigational accident in the Scilly Isles, was a disaster on a national scale. These circumstances have clearly influenced his reputation within history. Among the immediate consequences of his death, which is still actively remembered nearly three hundred years later, is the fact that it led to the determined effort to solve the problem of accurately finding one's position at sea, particularly in the quest to find longitude.[78] A former professor of mathematics at Cambridge, William Whitson, organised a campaign that capitalised on public knowledge about Shovell's death and led to Parliament enacting an Act for the Discovery of Longitude in 1714.

Both Sir George Rooke and Sir Cloudesley Shovell achieved the highest positions within the navy and had acquired rewards and titles that went with them, including considerable wealth. Although in naval history Rooke and Shovell are virtually inseparable characters as the leading seamen of their day, there were clear contrasts between them in terms of their private family lives as well as in their reputations in general history.

Shovell left his estate, May Place at Crayford, Kent, as well as other lands in Norfolk and Kent, his London townhouse and a considerable fortune.[79] Survived by his mother, who died in 1709, Shovell had married late and to the widow of his patron, Sir John Narbrough. Widowed again, she lived until April 1732. Her two sons by Narbrough had died with Shovell, but two daughters of his own marriage survived him, well-launched in social circles. Shortly after her father's death, the elder daughter, Elizabeth, married Sir Robert Marsham, who was created Lord Romney in 1716. After his death, she married John Carmichael, Earl of Hyndford, the English minister at Berlin 1741-4, St Petersburg 1744-9, and at The Hague, where she eventually died in 1750. Shovell's second daughter, Anne, married Hon Robert Mansell, and secondly, John Blackewell. In 1708 Lady Shovell was mentioned as one of three possible matches for Lord Pembroke. But, as Lady Marow gossiped to her daughter, 'she had lately married a daughter to Sir Something Masham, and had given her fifteen thousand pounds down and promised twenty thousand more at her death, therefore was disabled from marrying men, looking chiefly at fortune.'[80]

In contrast, Rooke married early and several times: first, to the daughter of Sir Thomas Howe of Cold Berwick in Wiltshire; second, to Mary, daughter of Colonel Francis Lutrell of Dunster Castle, Somerset; and third to Catherine, daughter of Sir Thomas Knatchbull of Mersham Hatch, Kent. With his second wife, he had one son, George (1702-1739), who died young, without children. Like Shovell, his mother survived him, and left the bulk of his estate and his properties in Kent to his surviving third wife, who lived until 1755.[81]

The reputations of Rooke and Shovell in general histories have been curiously different. In the case of Shovell, the politics of his time, the circumstances of his death, his prominent monument in Westminster Abbey, as well as the memorable and mirthful combination of his first and family names, have all combined to give him a positive image in general British history. Within a year of his death, three accounts of his life were published.[82] Even in his lifetime, Shovell repeatedly figured in the public press as a gallant fighter. No evidence has come to light to suggest whether Shovell personally had a hand in creating this public image of himself.

Shovell's public image contrasts starkly with Rooke's fate in the popular press, although a comparative narrative of their parallel naval careers shows remarkable similarity. With the higher reaches of the Government, Rooke was a man who seemed to want to avoid the public limelight and political controversy in attending to his duty. Writers such as Daniel Defoe were unwilling to accept this and created quite another image of him. Rooke's death in quiet retirement on 24 January 1709 led to no great public notice, and, indeed, the political attempts of the Tories during Rooke's lifetime to turn him into a popular hero during his active career had failed miserably. Tory writers such as William Pittis, who attempted to extol Rooke's 'immortal memory', were far less talented writers.[83] He was buried quietly at the parish Church of St Paul, Canterbury, and a rather conventional bust and tablet remains to mark his memory within Canterbury Cathedral. Omitting much, the inscription includes the Latin phrase: *Oh! Quantum est historiae in isto nomine!* Historians have interpreted Rooke's achievements harshly and sometimes inaccurately. Typical of them, G M Trevelyan wrote, 'Though highly competent to manage a fleet and to conduct any given operation, Rooke was cautious to a fault, sulky, and unimaginative.'[84]

Under newer light, Rooke and Shovell were certainly the most eminent English seamen in the last years of William III's reign and during the first years of Anne's. Among the naval officers of their day, both Rooke and Shovell stood out as a skilled seaman, successful captains of fighting ships, and effective fleet commanders. John Narbrough had initially recognised their early talents, and then Arthur Herbert had been their patron, leading on to higher success. In Rooke's case, successive sovereigns, from Charles II to Anne, had immediately and repeatedly recognised his talents. William III, in particular, valued Rooke's forthright honesty in his advice on naval policy, strategy, and tactics. For similar reasons, William was also attracted to Shovell's professional competence, as was Anne and her consort, Prince George of Denmark. These same characteristics were certainly features that made them both acceptable as key senior commanders over allied Dutch naval forces.

In terms of their contributions to the Royal Navy, both Rooke and Shovell are significant figures in the long and continuing tradition of admirals who are made from successful captains of fighting ships. With that initial training, they both became skilled flag officers who were willing to take aggressive risks in combat, in an age when it had become uncommon to do so. The rashness of individual commanders that had characterised naval actions during both Rooke's and Shovell's formative years during the Anglo-Dutch wars had largely disappeared. During the period when they had reached flag rank, the greater emphasis lay on creating the basic discipline necessary to forge individual ships into the larger weapon of a fleet. This was no easy task to achieve in practice, and the emphasis on discipline inadvertently created what many saw as over-cautiousness. Concern over this problem was one of the background issues involved in the courts martial of both Benbow's captains and Rear-Admiral Sir John Munden in 1702. As responsible fleet commanders, both Rooke and Shovell played important roles in trying to overcome this while also carrying forward the development of the fighting instructions for the fleet. With their experience drawn from their early training under Herbert, as well as their individual experiences in all the major fleet actions of the period, Bantry Bay, Beachy Head, Barfleur, and Vélez-Málaga, both men shared similar firm beliefs about fleet tactics. Both saw that, in facing a superior enemy, the key was to protect one's own force to fight another day; in facing an enemy fleet of equal size, to maintain the fleet line of battle and to concentrate firepower. Both believed that the only way to ensure a fleet victory was to have superiority in numbers. To their credit, both saw that a sea battle involved calculated risks and that its purpose was to damage an enemy's force sufficiently so that it was no longer an immediate threat to England's strategic position.

Their views on these issues consolidated the Royal Navy's battle experience from the second half of the seventeenth century and firmly established it as the basic tactical doctrine in the eighteenth century. Yet the battles that Rooke and Shovell fought were only stages in the evolutionary process that the Royal Navy used to develop effective methods by which one fleet in battle-line formation could meet and successfully fight an enemy arrayed in a similar formation. Both Rooke and Shovell stood out in showing that they were ready and able to fight the fleet, as well as showing themselves determined and skilled flag officers that led by personal example in combat. However, the battles they fought showed that these were not the only elements for naval success. An admiral in the 1690s and early 1700s was limited in battle by the fact that commanders of individual supporting ships, by and large, did not yet share similar skills and attitudes. They tended to lack the discipline necessary to make their individual ships parts of the larger tactical unit that comprises a fleet. Additionally, cumbersome tactical communications limited an admiral's ability to be flexible and the more general measures of strength found in manpower, physical condition of ships, ammunition, and the size and capabilities in the available weapons. Under these limitations, both Rooke and Shovell stressed heavy firing of large guns in a static line-of-battle as the most effective means of concentrating force and maintaining tactical cohesion to meet the broader ends of fighting.

Earlier generations made a great distinction between the professional capabilities of gentlemen officers and tarpaulin officers. These same terms were also applied to Rooke and Shovell, pointing to the differences in their very early years of naval service and in some of their personal characteristics. By the first decade of the eighteenth century, however, such terms had come to have no significance in differentiating the quality of an admiral's professional achievements.

George Byng, Viscount Torrington. Oil by Sir Godfrey Kneller

3

George Byng, Viscount Torrington
1663–1733

'He . . . left nothing to fortune that could be accomplished by foresight and application'

CHRIS WARE

George Byng's name was doubly damned by history. Elevated to a peerage as Viscount Torrington, Byng was thereby tainted by association with an earlier holder of the title, Arthur Herbert, whose reputation has been under a cloud for the three centuries since the unsatisfactory battle off Beachy Head (30 June 1690). This confusion in public, and to some extent academic, circles over his peerage and person[1] is compounded by his being the famous father of an infamous son – John Byng, who lost Minorca in 1756 and his life the following year. Byng junior was immortalised not just in naval history but more widely by Voltaire – mention the name Byng and it either elicits a blank look or the quotation from *Candide* about the English killing an admiral from time to time *'pour encourager les autres'*.[2] So why include George Byng, Viscount Torrington in a book on the precursors of Nelson? Put simply, Byng stands out as one of the most successful sea officers of his generation, perhaps of the whole of the eighteenth century. These are large claims; but Byng's greatest triumph came outside a major war – no matter that in terms of numbers of ships taken or destroyed it was the most complete victory the Royal Navy inflicted on an opponent until Nelson's day – so one can see the difficulties under which Byng's reputation labours. But to reveal Byng and his career in their true light is to uncover another major contributor to the fighting tradition that culminated with Nelson.

Early Years

George Byng was the son of John Byng of Wrotham in Kent; his mother
Philadelphia was the daughter of the Johnson family of Loans in Surrey.
Byng was born on 23 January 1663, and as with many others sea officers of
this period little is known of his early childhood or schooling, though it has
been suggested that he was brought up and educated by a friend of the
family, the Countess of Middleton. All that may be said of his education is
that in common with many others of his generation his spelling follows the
inconsistent phonetics widely practiced in those days. If he was part of the
Middleton household he possibly accompanied them to Tangier, as John
Lord Middleton was governor from 1669 to his death in 1674; if so, he
would have encountered many of the sea officers such as Arthur Herbert,
Cloudesley Shovell and George Rooke with whom he was to be associated
in later life.

Byng first went to sea in 1678 as a King's Letter Boy, or volunteer per
order, at the relatively advanced age of 15. Though one source says the
recommendation was at the behest of the Duke of York himself, it was
actually George Legge who was responsible for obtaining the letter.[3] In
this year there was the possibility of war with France, and Pepys's
memoirs list the number and state of ships in sea pay as eighty-three ships
and some 18,000 seaman; young Byng was one of that number. The first
ship that Byng served on as a volunteer was the *Swallow,* whose captain,
Joseph Haddock, was an amiable ex-merchant captain, who showed Byng
great encouragement and probably taught him basic seamanship. Byng was
discharged from the *Swallow* on 28 November 1678 and was entered on the
same day as a volunteer on the *Reserve,* Captain David Lloyd.[4] This was also
the period when England had an outpost on the African shore of the straits
of Gibraltar at Tangier; acquired as part of the dowry of Catherine of
Braganza, it was at best a mixed blessing for both the navy and the army,
giving as it did a foothold in the Mediterranean, whilst at the same time
being a drain on the exchequer, which was a sensitive subject for all Stuart
monarchs. Byng entered as a volunteer on the *Phoenix*, Captain William
Blagge, and when the ship arrived at Tangier on 10 May 1681 Byng was
discharged. Here he would probably have renewed his acquaintance with
Shovell and Rooke and come into contact with Arthur Herbert, the
commander-in-chief of the Mediterranean squadron.[5]

It was also while at Tangier that Byng became acquainted with Major-
General Percy Kirke, the Governor of Tangiers, and according to one
source he spent time as a cadet in the grenadiers as part of the garrison of

Tangier. At this point he was said to have left the sea service and decided to become a soldier. It must be stated that little evidence – outside near-contemporary printed sources – can be produced for this change of heart on the part of Byng. One account claims 'the general, who always patronised him with great friendship, made him ensign of his own company and soon after a lieutenant.'[6] This cuts across modern research which shows that Byng became a lieutenant in the Queen's Regiment in 1687, some four years after he is supposed to have gained a commission in Kirke's Regiment. This confusion, if such it is, shows the problems of studying sea service officers at this date. There was still no impermeable barrier between the land and sea service: although there was a growing professionalism among the sea officer corps, it was not seen as a conflict of interest to hold commissions in both land and sea services. The fact that Byng held such a dual commission was to have significance for Byng's career towards the end of the 1680s when he came into contact with Arthur Herbert, who had been sent out to the Mediterranean in command of a fleet to enforce peace with the Barbary States.

In 1684 Byng was appointed lieutenant of the *Oxford*, commanded by John Tyrrell,[7] and then moved with Tyrrell and the *Oxford*'s crew in 1685 to the *Phoenix*, which was to go to the East Indies. The *Phoenix* was a Fourth Rate and Byng was one of four lieutenants aboard and one of a select few of his generation who was to see service in the East Indies, an area which was not a theatre of regular warfare at sea until after Byng's death. In fact, in the War of the League of Augsburg there was an unofficial truce on the Indian subcontinent between the Companies des Indies and the English India Company. Byng's sojourn in the East Indies, whilst not coinciding with the outbreak of war, was not without incident. The *Phoenix* ran down and engaged a pirate vessel which had been annoying European shipping. Byng was detailed to command a boarding party, and in the fierce action that followed aboard the pirate vessel no quarter was given; most of Byng's companions were killed and the pirate vessel actually sank with Byng aboard. Despite being badly wounded and more than half drowned, he survived. Like Nelson, however, he was lucky in a time of comparative peace to have stayed employed, which, along with the events laid out below, gave him a head start at the outbreak of war in 1688. Unlike Nelson, Byng was reliant on the interest of no family members, but this does not invalidate the comparison. There are similarities in Byng's whole-hearted commitment to action, when joined, irrespective of the personal danger; a trait the young Nelson also displayed.

It was in 1685 when Byng was serving in the *Phoenix* that other events took place which would have a major effect on his early career. With the death in February of that year of Charles II, his brother James came to the throne, which in terms of the navy could only be seen as a good thing. Here at last was a monarch who had held active command at sea as well as exercising the role of Lord High Admiral during the Third Anglo-Dutch War. James's policy, in funding terms, greatly benefited the navy, Parliament voting extra sums which helped to relieve the financial stress the navy had been labouring under since 1679. As calculated by Pepys, the navy's debt in 1679, the year before Byng went to sea, was £3,305,000 with approximately seventy-six ships in sea pay manned by 12,040 men; in 1684, just before Charles's death, the debt had risen to £3,384,000 with just twenty-four ships in sea pay manned by 3070 men.[8] These figures make clear how fierce was the competition for appointments at sea, even at Byng's junior level at this stage in his career. His links with Arthur Herbert may well have been valuable here. Herbert was not only close to the pinnacle of naval command, but he was also an experienced courtier, both of which could have been beneficial to the young Byng. However, it was in the unfolding events around the King that Byng was to play a role which, according to his memoirs, was out of all proportion to his rank and standing in the navy.

James's accession did not go smoothly from the start. The illegitimate son of Charles II, the Protestant James, Duke of Monmouth, sought to foment rebellion. In an ironic anticipation of later events, he landed in the West County, hoping to gain support. However, his plan had none of the sophistication of William of Orange's successful invasion, either in terms of substantial internal or, more importantly, external help. However, it could not be, and was not, just dismissed by the new King. The navy's part was to bring forward several vessels for service to try and intercept either Monmouth or any support for him from seaward. This must have been a strain on the dockyards and the exchequer: one source estimates that it would have cost upwards of £3,120,000 to put the fleet in good repair; another, admittedly biased, source states that at the time ships were rotting at their moorings, with toadstools growing in the holds, so this might even be an underestimate.[9]

Whilst Byng was fighting for his life in eastern seas, a battle of a different kind was joined soon after James's accession. Arthur Herbert was the commander of a small fleet which provided support to James's army against Monmouth at sea. He was also engaged in a struggle with George Legge, Baron Dartmouth for the King's favour and the command of the fleet.

Byng was later to follow suit in assiduously cultivating William III, Queen Anne and George I for place and influence at court and, although absent at the start of what led to the revolution of 1688, his close contact with Arthur Herbert and Russell would give him ample opportunities to watch the perils and rewards of such struggles. The irony was that even though it was Dartmouth who had made him lieutenant in the *Oxford* in 1684, in the end, as the situation turned ever bleaker, Byng was to side with Herbert against Dartmouth despite this early favour from him. Initially, James did not move to install Catholics to prominent commands, nor did he seek straight away to circumvent the Test Acts of 1673, to allow Catholics once more to hold commissions in the navy. The first move came with the re-appointment of Sir Roger Strickland to command the fleet. This placed him in direct competition with Arthur Herbert for this important position. Furthermore, one of Strickland's friends, George Legge, Baron Dartmouth, had a brother at court who materially helped Strickland's cause and lent weight to his campaign for preferment.[10]

To all this Byng was oblivious, although Strickland's reinstatement threatened the position of Herbert. The latter was in a position to help Byng, who, so it was reported, 'had declared himself a Roman Catholic', possibly to curry favour with Strickland.[11] The real problems broke out over the winter of 1686–7, when it was known that Sir Roger Strickland had converted to Catholicism and that the King was seeking to gain support from prominent members of the court for the repeal of the Test Act. One of those taken into the King's confidence was Arthur Herbert, but he did not react in the way the King expected, refusing to countenance the repeal of the Act. For this he was removed from office, which gave Strickland and Dartmouth unfettered access to the King on naval matters and, more importantly, removed for the time being one of Byng's promoters.[12] However, Byng was not entirely out in the cold, as he gained in 1687 a captaincy in the Queen's Regiment of Foot. The colonel was Percy Kirke, the ex-governor of Tangiers.

In 1688 Byng was appointed first lieutenant to Sir John Ashby in the fleet which Dartmouth was to command and which was to watch out for and intercept any invasion attempts by William of Orange, or his adherents. However, history offers some clues as to where Byng's loyalties might lie. Most, if not all, of the officers of the Queen's Regiment defected to William almost as soon as he landed. Herbert commanded the invasion fleet and as the rewards for Herbert would be great, any benefit he gained would also trickle down to George Byng. However, Byng was not content to play a passive role in the affair. Byng and Captain Matthew Aylmer took a straw poll of the officers of Dartmouth's fleet, and although James had insufficient time to introduce many new Catholic officers into the fleet (they formed only about six per cent of the fleet), there was great resentment amongst the sea officers.[13] Pepys was also moved to remonstrate with the King over appointments of inexperienced sea officers to commands. Tension continued to rise throughout 1688 after the earlier defection of Edward Russell, with whom Byng had come into contact in Tangier. Russell was a leading conspirator with Arthur Herbert, who swayed many of the junior officers towards the Williamite camp. Unlike Nelson, Byng had to make a choice between two opposing camps and he chose William. The fact that he conveyed despatches between William and Dartmouth shows that he was not just carried on the tide of events, although, as J D Davies has shown, the circumstances are much more complicated than Byng's memoirs would have us believe.[14] What is true is that after Dartmouth's poor handling of the fleet he sent Captain Matthew Aylmer and Lieutenant George Byng with a submission to the new King, who by then had arrived at Windsor. Byng's baptism in court politics was over, or so he may have thought; with William on the throne war with France was inevitable.

Byng reaped the rewards of backing the winners as he was promoted to captain in December of 1688, and given command of the Fourth Rate ship *Constant Warwick* and a cornet's position in the Earl of Oxford's Regiment. The *Constant Warwick* was ordered by Herbert from Spithead to Torbay to act as convoy for vessels waiting there on voyage to Ostend and Rotterdam. The protection of English trade and the attack of the enemy's were to be a leifmotif throughout Byng's career. In April 1689 he was appointed to the *Reserve* and in May was appointed to command the *Dover*. Byng joined the Grand Fleet commanded by Herbert (now Earl of Torrington) in June 1689 and was part of the small force commanded by Sir Francis Wheeler that Torrington sent to cruise on and off before Brest for two weeks, where they adopted a policy of close and distant blockade.

In the spring of 1690 Byng was part of a squadron under Shovell off the coast of Ireland, and in May Byng was appointed to the Third Rate *Hope*. Byng's first taste of fleet action was to take place in June 1690 as the *Hope* was part of the Grand Fleet commanded by Torrington, who was surprised by the news that the French fleet was seeking to enter the Channel as French fleets by and large avoided fleet action unless it was necessary to carry out a particular operation. Byng was in the red squadron under Rooke. The action that took place off Beachy Head on 30 June 1690 is one of the most controversial, as the French defeated the combined Anglo-Dutch fleet.[15] The recriminations and courts martial that followed had an

important indirect effect on Byng. His first fleet action showed him the need for concentration of force, good intelligence of the enemy's where-abouts and intentions and aggressive action when battle was joined. All of these factors preoccupied Byng when later in his career he was to have sole command of a fleet. His correspondence is littered with references to the need for small ships for scouting (as well as for harrying the enemy's trade), to the need to keep his fleet concentrated, and his overwhelming desire to get at the enemy. All of these were later to be marked out as touchstones in the Nelson way of war, and were evident in Byng, even if at the time of Beachy Head he had little opportunity to display them. In October 1690 Byng was appointed to the *Royal Oak*, which had been Rooke's flagship at Beachy Head. The ship was paid off shortly afterwards and Byng was unemployed. Torrington was dismissed from all his posts in December 1690.

Early in 1691 Edward Russell was given the command of the fleet. It is possible that as Byng knew Russell he may have been more affected by his defection to William than by Herbert's. The change of command at the highest level did not impede Byng's career and Byng was to serve under Russell for most of the rest of the war. The year 1691 was an important point in Byng's life, as he married Margaret Master of Dover and was again appointed to the *Royal Oak*, in which he was to remain for the next two years. In November 1691 Russell, in his list of captains who had served with him, noted that Byng 'was a young man [he was 28] but good'.[16] He did not take part in the defeat of the French fleet at Barfleur and La Hogue in May 1692, but in March 1693 the three joint admirals, Sir Ralph De-lavall, Sir Henry Killegrew and Shovell, asked Byng to serve as their First Captain in the flagship, *Britannia*. However he refused, possibly out of regard for Russell, and resigned his commission and retired to Bedfordshire.

It was during this period that the naval war started to change in aspect. In the first year to eighteen months the main concern had been the possibility of invasion, or the reinforcement of James's army in Ireland by the French. The two abortive actions in which the Anglo–Dutch fleet had taken part, Bantry Bay and Beachy Head, were a product of this. France sought to undermine English participation in the war by destabilising England via James in Ireland. However, whilst England was a new participant, France had been at war for years and the strain on her finances was beginning to show; for the French fleet the years 1692–3 were a watershed. The con-tinued cost of the major land and sea war was draining the French treasury so fast that the Sun King's ministers could not contrive ways to fill it. The

effect was the slow change from the big battlefleet operations which had
started the war to smaller squadrons operating against the source of England's wealth, her trade. To that end increasing numbers of privateers were
sent out from the Channel ports, but these were backed by smaller French
men of war which were hired to businessmen to act as corsairs. This
method kept some ships of some force at sea but without drawing directly
on the over-stretched treasury.[17]

Whilst on the face of it this was an ideal solution, in effect it ceded
dominance of the sea to the Anglo–Dutch fleet; this did not become apparent immediately, and there would be misfortunes for English trade along
the way, but in the long run it did not redound to the benefit of the French.
The Smyrna Convoy disaster of 1693 was to be the worst incident in this
new phase of the campaign, when over ninety merchant ships bound for
the Mediterranean were lost, even though under the protection of a squadron commanded by Sir Cloudesley Shovell. For the Royal Navy this was to
become a recurring problem, and familiar to Nelson over a century later,
but also one Byng would have to deal with himself in the next war. To
counter this increasing threat to seaborne trade and to quell the protesting
voices of the City merchants, more ships and squadrons were assigned to
convoy duties. William also wanted to place a fleet in the Mediterranean on
a year-round basis, something that would be difficult without a dockyard
or, at the very least, a friendly port where the fleet could revictual and
repair. In the Nine Years' War Spain was, at least in theory, part of the
alliance against France, which meant that her ports were open to the fleet
for refitting and resupply. In November 1693 Sir Francis Wheeler was sent
to the Strait with a small squadron, arriving early the following January.
Wheeler looked in to Barcelona to see if the Spanish Plate Fleet had arrived
safely, which it had, he having orders to wait for it if it had not arrived.
While the Plate Fleet rode safely in port, Wheeler's squadron was hit by a
storm as it attempted to pass through the Straits into the Mediterranean and
several ships, including his flagship the *Sussex*, were lost with all hands. This
just underlined the difficulties of operating a major fleet all the year round
at distance from the major dockyards. This again was something Byng was
to face.

The joint admirals were replaced by Russell alone in 1694. Byng had not
gone unnoticed by Russell, who made him First Captain of his flagship, the
Britannia. Byng stayed with Russell and the fleet in the Mediterranean for
the rest of 1694 and 1695. As the war at sea slowly wound down Byng came
home with the fleet in 1696 and served in the Channel for the rest of that
year. Later in that same year Byng and his long-standing colleague,

Matthew Aylmer, were two of the men entrusted with overseeing the introduction of the Act of April 1696 to encourage seaman, the so called Seaman's Register.[18] In this he was taking his first steps as an administrator as well as an active sea officer, a dual role which Byng would maintain throughout the rest of his career. As Byng ended his first period of active service he had experienced a great deal and had been forced to make some hard choices. He had also seen the price of failure as well as success; and whilst limited in what he could achieve he had retained the powerful interest of Edward Russell. He even had some limited experience of independent command, having been put in charge of a detached squadron by Sir Francis Wheeler as early as late summer 1690.

The War of the Spanish Succession

Byng, by now a captain of fourteen years seniority, was to play a much greater part in the next war. Nevertheless, he was to receive a check at the start of the war in 1702. In view of his connections he might have thought that he would receive his flag. This did not happen; instead George Churchill was given a flag since he was senior to Byng on the captains' list. For this slight, amongst others, Byng was to nurse a grievance against Churchill for several years to come. Byng eventually gained his flag early in the new year, 1 March 1703; in the meantime he was given command of the *Nassau*, a Third Rate. The ship was one of Rooke's fleet that went out to the Mediterranean as part of the abortive attempt to land troops at Cadiz, which ended in fiasco. On Rooke's return with the fleet he was able to take, or destroy, much of the Spanish Plate Fleet, which had taken refuge in Vigo harbour. Its odyssey had begun in July 1702 when it left Havana harbour, a fleet of upward of sixty sail including fifteen line of battle ships. The greater part of this *flota* arrived off Spain in September and sailed into Vigo Bay. They had managed to slip past Sir Cloudesley Shovell, who had been cruising off Ushant as it was thought at first that the Plate Fleet was intended to go into Brest. Shovell then shifted south towards Corunna, but he missed them once again. When the Admiralty obtained intelligence of where the treasure fleet had gone, this news was passed on to both Shovell and Rooke. However, before the news had arrived from England Rooke had received his own intelligence of the whereabouts of the Plate Fleet from Captain Hardy of the *Pembroke*, which had been at Lagos. This allowed Rooke to beat Shovell to the prize; the attack was to be formed of fifteen English and ten Dutch ships of the line with ten fireships. Troops that were landed to attack this fleet were split up into small groups under the command of subordinate flag officers. The Spanish lost fifteen ships of the line, and the Royal Navy gained four ships for its own service.

Byng was next involved in a campaign that culminated in the attack and capture of Gibraltar. This was to follow on from an operation early in the year in which the fleet in the Mediterranean had sought to bring the Catalans over to Charles III's side, which involved an assault on Barcelona, where the fleet arrived on 17 May. After about 1500 troops and seaman had been landed, the town was bombarded, but the Catalans felt this was insufficient inducement to break with the Bourbon claimant to the throne. Rooke concluded that the whole thing had furthered Charles III's cause not one jot: in fact, it had done 'more hurt than the loss of a battle'.[19] Whilst on their way up the coast the fleet, including Byng, sighted the French, initially under Du Quesne-Mosnier, and a small squadron was detached to chase him. Later, news was received that the main Brest fleet under Toulouse had been seen off Lisbon. Rooke with the whole fleet put about and headed for the Straits, seeking either to engage Toulouse or, failing that, to go into Lisbon in search of stores before returning to the Mediterranean and continuing operations against the French.

On 27 May 1704 Rooke's fleet sighted Toulouse just off Minorca. The wind, however, died and the Anglo–Dutch fleet lay becalmed in sight of the French. The French and Anglo–Dutch ships were approximately equal with thirty-six ships in Rooke's fleet and thirty-two in the French. However, the Anglo–Dutch were in a poor state and it was agreed that they could no longer stay off the enemy coast without repair and reinforcement, so Rooke once again made sail towards Lisbon. On 16 June Rooke's fleet met up with Shovell's squadron that had been sent to join him in the Straits. The combined strength of the two fleets was now sixty-three ships of force, more than a match for any fleet the French could send out. Charles III's cause was not prospering, and Rooke and Shovell were under pressure to carry out a major demonstration, not unlike that which had been attempted at Barcelona. This they felt was impractical without troops, and the closest at hand would be in Portugal. Instead, they decided upon the seizure of Gibraltar. Rooke, Shovell and Byng had all served at Gibraltar when the English Mediterranean fleet commanded by Herbert had briefly used it in the 1680s.

Prince George of Hesse would command ashore and would be supported by sixteen ships of the fleet under the command of Rear-Admiral Byng, along with six Dutch ships. The fleet moved into Gibraltar Bay on 21 July and landed about 2000 Marines. Having summoned the garrison to surrender and the governor replying in the negative, the ships moved in to bombard the fortifications, but the lack of wind meant that it would take all day to get them into position to undertake the attack. The bombardment began at midday on Sunday the 23rd, and late in the day seamen landed, overran some of the batteries and shortly thereafter Gibraltar capitulated. As a fleet base, however, it left a lot to be desired: whilst there was a good harbour, the water supply was limited and there were no drydocks to take ships into for major repairs. (This was still the case when Nelson was in the Mediterranean some ninety years later.) After the fleet had helped to secure Gibraltar from attack, they sailed to the African coast to take on water. The French Fleet was sighted on 9 August and on Sunday the 13th the two fleets came to battle off Málaga.

The fleet of which Byng was a part was not the same force that it had been two months earlier: there had been detachments of ships on several services, reducing the number by ten to fifty-three. The Anglo–Dutch fleet was also low on ammunition, resulting from the prodigious expenditure of shot in the bombardment of Gibraltar. The French had gathered fifty ships, as well as the galley fleet, which itself numbered some twenty-four vessels. The battle started at around 10am, the French lying to leeward on a southerly course and awaiting the Anglo–Dutch fleet. The allies came down on to the French in line abreast, the English in the south with the Dutch to the north. The French sought to double the head of the allied line, but Leake saw what they were attempting to do and countered the French moves. There followed several hours of intense fighting between this part of the two lines, at the end of which the French drew off to leeward. In the centre things were not going so well for the Anglo–Dutch. The French sought to break the line ahead of Rooke's squadron, but when Leake asked permission to leave his position in the van and prevent this manoeuvre, he was refused. The *Monck* stopped the French advance and paid a heavy price for it, having to withdraw from the fight. In the same way Byng's squadron was also heavily engaged, but his squadron was one which was particularly short of ammunition, and several ships had to withdraw for want of shot or to stop leaks. The end of the battle saw the Anglo–Dutch fleet as having had the better of the action. Although they did not know it at the time, this was to be the last action between the French and Anglo–Dutch fleets during the war.[20] George Byng returned to England in October 1704 and was knighted by Queen Anne shortly afterwards.

In the next session Byng was promoted to vice-admiral of the blue on 28 January 1705 and for the first four months was involved in Channel cruising. In May he sailed with Shovell and Charles, Earl of Peterborough for an expedition to the Iberian peninsula. Byng's part in the operation was to take a squadron of ships to watch Brest. In the event of the French sailing he was to pursue and endeavour to stop them from entering the Straits. There was a concern that the Toulon and Brest squadrons would sail and seek to unite as they had the previous year. Shovell was concerned that Byng's squadron was insufficient for the task and pressed the government for reinforcements. In fact, the French were not preparing any kind of major operation with the fleet and those ships ready for sea were disarmed at the end of August. In the summer Byng was also elected as MP for Plymouth.

At the beginning of 1706 Byng attended a select committee of the House of Lords, chaired by his old friend the Earl of Torrington, in connection with the difficulties involved in manning the fleet. He was also commander-in-chief at Portsmouth, fitting, and hastening out, convoys and protecting trade until March, when he was ordered to join Sir John Leake at Lisbon and raise the siege of Barcelona. When Leake returned to England at the end of the year Byng was left at Lisbon, where he was joined by Shovell.

The next great project that the allies were to undertake was the attack on the French arsenal at Toulon, which was to take place in early 1707. Byng was not directly involved in the assault on Toulon as he left Shovell's fleet at Lisbon and carried out operations on the coast of Spain, one of which was to land powder and shot for General Galway's army. Byng's command consisted of twenty-one ships, nearly half of which were Dutch, while his second in command was Sir John Norris. Norris in turn left Byng's squadron to carry out separate instructions and then sail on to Turin, where he arrived in May 1707.[21] At Toulon the allied progress ashore was very slow as Prince Eugene's actions were very lethargic compared with those when he was acting in concert with the Duke of Marlborough. There was also a lack of powder and shot and engineers to construct the siege lines. The attack dragged on through July and into August, and Shovell recalled Byng from the coast of Spain to take part in the bombardment from seawards of the fortifications and harbour of Toulon. Byng arrived on 2 August in the *Royal Anne*, but the weather was so foul that when the ship tried to moor her cable parted and she ran aboard another ship in the fleet. Despite the poor weather, the big ships and bomb vessels were brought into action against the town and the fleet bombarded the harbour, damage being done to both. The attack from the landward side turned out to be a complete failure, despite seamen being landed to man some of the guns in the siege batteries. Byng's last task before he sailed from the Mediterranean at the end of this campaign was to protect the troops involved in the attack. He did this by threatening to burn the town if the French interfered with the withdrawal.

Following the collapse of the attack on Toulon, Shovell and Byng returned to England in October. It was on the voyage home that Shovell's flagship, the *Association*, was wrecked on the Isles of Scilly and he was drowned, while Byng in the *Royal Anne* managed to escape, partly by good luck and partly through the presence of mind of his officers. Byng attended lady Shovell at her house in Soho and was a pallbearer of Shovell's coffin to Westminster Abbey for burial.[22] The disaster left Byng the most senior admiral after Sir John Leake still actively employed. When he learnt that Leake was to be appointed commander-in-chief, but that he himself was not to get promotion from vice-admiral of the white, Byng wrote an angry letter to Sidney Godolphin attacking George Churchill. However, Byng's action proved premature as he was promoted to admiral of the blue on 26 January 1708.

The year saw Byng operating in home waters against the threat of invasion by the French and Jacobites. The news of a possible invasion in favour of the Pretender had come to the notice of the government, and with most of the land force operating on the continent, it was the navy which would have to forestall any attempt. Byng with half a dozen ships arrived in the Downs from Portsmouth on 25 February, where he was joined by Admiral John Baker. In all there were twenty-four ships of the line. Byng held a council of war the next day at which it was decided to go to Dunkirk to gain more information on the prospective expedition. The fleet anchored off Gravelines on 27 February and Byng carried out a personal reconnaissance and learnt that the French ships were inferior to his. So powerful was the British squadron, which made its appearance off Dunkirk on the 27th, that the French thought that it must have been a division from the main fleet. In fact it had been a great strain on the resources of the navy to get even this many ships to sea so early in the year.

Once Byng moved his ships from Dunkirk the French made preparations to sail for Scotland. What followed was a game of cat and mouse between Byng and Forbin, who was to carry the Pretender to Scotland. All the while Byng and his squadron were trying to cover all possible eventualities. The French managed to slip out from port and gain a head start on Byng up the East Coast. Not all Byng's ships were fast and he said as much in his despatches. Despite this, several of the French ships were brought to action. Byng himself nearly cornered Forbin off the Scottish coast, but only a partial action ensured. By 27 March the cold weather had got to even such a seasoned seaman as Byng: 'it near breaks my head'. Five days later Byng received the thanks of the House of Commons for preventing the invasion.[23] Byng returned from Scotland on 16 April. After a short stay in London, during which he wrote to Plymouth asking to be re-elected as an MP, an approach which was successful, on 7 May Byng was ordered to sea with a powerful squadron. His duties were to watch Brest and stop the Dunkirk squadron getting into the harbour as well as protecting trade, a role later of the 'Western Squadron'.

During the spring Byng and Sir John Jennings were approached to be the naval advisors on Prince George of Denmark's Council, which they turned down. Lord Treasurer Godolphin wrote to Byng of his refusal, 'nobody can ever build a house that won't be contented to lay the foundations by degrees.' From the end of June to mid-September Byng was involved in combined operations with Major-General Thomas Earle on the French coast. He then escorted the Queen of Portugal to Lisbon and while at Lisbon he heard of the capture of Minorca by Shovell and James Stanhope. He was ordered to transfer all the stores and dockyard equipment at Lisbon to Port Mahon. He sailed from Lisbon to Minorca on 27 December and this saw the development of Port Mahon as a naval base.[24]

In 1709 Byng returned to the Mediterranean as commander-in-chief, where he was concerned to annoy the enemy trade. However, like Nelson, he was short of small ships and even went to the length of buying in a prize, at the cost of £3900, to serve as a frigate.[25] He returned to England late in 1709 to find that his old friend Edward Russell, Earl of Orford since 1697, had been asked to be First Lord following the removal of the Earl of Pembroke. Orford was refusing to accept unless Jennings and Byng were added to the Commission and Queen Anne, remembering their refusal in 1708, was holding out. In the end a compromise was reached whereby she would accept one of them, and Byng was placed on the Admiralty Commission, the order being issued on 8 November 1709.[26] As he was then admiral of the white and still in sea pay, Byng obtained an agreement at the same time from Queen Anne that his attendance at the Admiralty Board would not prejudice his future service at sea. Byng and Sir John Leake were present at the first meeting on 9 November and then they attended nearly every session. When Orford resigned in 1710 Byng and Leake were both on the new Commission. When Orford had been there he had been First Lord, but Leake, although named first on the Commissions between 1710 and 1712, refused to act as such, and neither did Byng. The Minute Books also make it clear that Byng did not, as Leake's biographer alleged, act as the chairman of the Admiralty Board when Leake refused to do so. Byng remained a commissioner until March 1714 when he was dismissed. He was reinstated in October 1714 when Orford returned to the Admiralty and remained a commissioner until 1721. However, it was not until 1727 that Byng, now Viscount Torrington, became First Lord of the Admiralty, a post he continued to hold in the renewed Commissions until his death in 1733.[27]

After the end of the War of the Spanish Succession in 1713 the navy did not slip quietly into obscurity, and neither did Sir George Byng. During the war he had attended the Admiralty Board as often as his sea service might allow. However, he was not about to allow his administrative duties to interfere with the possibility of flying his flag at sea. There is tantalising evidence for this from the Board of Admiralty minutes soon after the death of Queen Anne: when discussing the renewal of the Board members' new commissions, there is a small entry referring to 'agreement with Sir George Byng concerning the keeping of his seniority on the list of active flag officers under her late majesty'.[28]

There is some evidence that Byng approached the exiled James III in 1715 offering his services, but why is not clear; possibly as a form of insurance or as an agent provocateur. In July 1715 Byng commanded the Channel fleet, which was intended to prevent a Jacobite invasion. In 1716 Byng was employed at the Admiralty, keeping an eye on Jacobite naval preparations and in providing an adequate fleet for the Baltic.

Baltic Service

In 1717 Byng hoisted his flag, but this time his destination was not the Mediterranean but the Baltic. The Baltic had been a source of serious concern to the navy for the better part of two decades. The clash of the two northern titans, Charles XII of Sweden and Peter I of Russia, had a destabilising effect on the whole region and, while no English territory was threatened, the essential naval supplies of timber, pitch and tar appeared to be. The accession of the Elector of Hanover to the throne as George I was to add a new dimension to the conflict. After the discovery of Swedish diplomatic intrigues, a bill was passed through the House of Commons in 1717 prohibiting commerce with Sweden. On 30 March, just twenty-eight days after the Bill's passage through Parliament, Sir George Byng sailed with twenty-one ships of the line for the Baltic. Upon his arrival he concerted his actions with those of the Danish fleet and sent out his smaller ships cruising to keep the Sound open for English commerce. In fact, the Swedish fleet made no attempt to interfere with the operation of Byng's squadron. As the year drew to a close he was in touch with the Admiralty concerning which ships might stay out in the Baltic and which were to

come home before the winter. As it turned out, Byng himself was ordered
home in November at the same time as some of his fleet. He was to have a
fresh command in the new year, one in which he would achieve a victory
only surpassed, and then only just, by Nelson at the height of his powers.[29]

To the Mediterranean

In March 1718 Sir George was appointed commander-in-chief in the Mediterranean, where he faced a complicated situation provoked by the diplomacy of the Quadruple Alliance (Britain, France, the Netherlands and the
Empire) which was attempting to settle some of the outstanding questions
of European power politics by the rearrangement of territories. Spain
strongly objected to many of the proposals, but particularly the transfer of
Sicily to the Emperor, in exchange for Sardinia, which would be ceded to
the House of Savoy. The disputes between Philip V of Spain and the Holy
Roman Emperor, Charles VI, also revolved around Charles's claim to the
Spanish throne, as well as the inheritance of Don Carlos, Philip's younger
son. The thought of a Bourbon swearing fealty to a Habsburg Emperor was
too much for Philip and his wife Elizabeth Farnese; they both wanted their
son to have the Duchies of Parma and Tuscany as of sovereign right and not
as a vassal of the Emperor. To make matters even more complicated for
Byng, technically there was no peace between the Emperor and Spain,
whilst there was between Spain and Britain. George I wanted to use the
navy as part of his diplomacy between the two, to bring pressure on Spain
by sending the fleet, and on Charles VI by holding back from action until
he could wring concessions from the Emperor on the question of territories. The die was cast when the new Spanish Grand Inquisitor was arrested
in Milan. Using this as a pretext Philip sent twenty-nine ships to Italy. The
fleet ranged in size from a 74-gun ship to an 18-gun sloop – the product of
the renaissance that the Spanish navy had recently undergone – but only
eight could be considered fit for the line of battle.

On 24 May Byng received his instructions: upon his arrival he was to
inform the King of Spain, the Viceroy of Naples, and the Governor of
Milan that he had been sent to promote all measures which would resolve
the differences between the Spain and the Empire and to prevent any
further hostilities. If, however, Spain sought to invade the Italian territories
of the Emperor, Byng was to hinder them in any and all ways possible. If
the Spanish had already landed, he was to try and induce them to give up
the project and even offer to help withdraw their forces. Byng sailed on 15
June 1718 with a fleet consisting of twenty-two ships of the line, two
fireships and two bomb vessels.

Throughout the period March to June 1718 the consuls in Italian and Spanish ports had sent a regular flow of despatches showing the increasing amount of military activity in Spanish territories. Complaints started to arrive of merchant ships of all nations being stopped and taken up by the Spanish; some under the threat of force. There was also news of preparation in the Spanish dockyards, of ships being brought forward for service, and troop movements were also monitored. Upwards of 12,500 troops were mentioned as being gathered in Spain's Mediterranean ports; though at first their destination was not identified, it soon became known to be Sicily.

On 30 June Byng's fleet arrived off Cadiz, where he detached the *Superbe* with a letter to the British minister at the Spanish court, James Stanhope. Entrusted with this letter was Byng's secretary, Thomas Corbett (the future Secretary to the Admiralty). In fact, Corbett did not catch up with Byng and the fleet again until after the Battle of Cape Passaro. Byng did not await the King of Spain's response but continued towards the Straits, reaching Cape Spartel on 8 July, where he was rejoined by the *Superbe* and *Rupert*, the latter having been sent into Lisbon for intelligence. Despite all the material which the consuls had sent back to the Secretary of State before Byng departed from Britain, it was only from these two vessels that he learnt that there had been great preparations for war and that a Spanish fleet had sailed from Barcelona on 18 June. Part of Byng's instructions allowed him to take under his command Vice-Admiral Sir Charles Cornwall, who had been operating off the coast of Tripoli with a small squadron. Byng added Cornwall's ships to his own, thus concentrating all possible forces in the area.

Meanwhile the Spanish had landed their troops on Sicily and in a short time had control of the majority of the island, except the citadel of Messina. The imperial troops that the Emperor had been gathering to counter the Spanish threat had been slow in working their way down the Italian littoral. Byng's assistance was sought by the Viceroy of Naples to convoy the hired German troops to relieve the citadel. Prior to his arrival at Naples, Byng had sailed to Port Mahon and landed troops; he sailed again on 25 July, having received news of the sighting of the Spanish fleet off Naples, and made haste to catch up with them. Byng arrived in the Bay of Naples on 1 August 1718 and having embarked the German troops he sailed on the 6th, arriving off Messina on the 9th. He sent ashore a letter to the commander of the Spanish land forces suggesting a cessation of hostilities for a period of two months. The Spanish commander said he could not do so owing to his 'having no power to treat with him' (Byng).

Byng disembarked the German troops and prepared to move the fleet before the citadel of Messina. Whilst standing in towards Messina on 10 August Byng's fleet came across two scouts for the Spanish fleet; he ordered his fleet to give chase. The Spanish fleet consisted in total of twenty-six warships, which sought to elude Byng's fleet, and a general chase ensued. Several of Byng's faster sailing ships were detached to try and remain in contact with the Spanish fleet in case the chase continued through night; the sternmost of them was ordered to carry three lights at the taffrail and one at the main mast head. It was on 11 August that the action between the two fleets was joined. Part of the Spanish fleet made for the shore and Byng detached Captain George Walton of the *Canterbury*, the *Argyle* and six other ships after them. As the *Argyle* came up with the Spanish, they opened fire, and it was only after she had been fired upon for the second time that the British ship returned fire. At the same time as these initial skirmishes all his flag officers were ordered, if they became separated, to rendezvous at Syracuse. The *Kent, Superbe, Grafton* and *Orford* were the first to come into action. The *Orford* attacked the *Santa Rosa*; the *San Carlos* was engaged and taken by the *Kent*. The *Grafton* first tackled the *Principe de Asturias* but seeing two other British ships coming up to her went on to chase a 60-gun vessel. At 1pm two of the leading ships of Byng's fleet engaged the Spanish admiral aboard the *Real San Felipe*, 74 guns. The *Kent* came up under her stern and fired a broadside and then fell away to the leeward of her; the *Superbe* then came up on the admiral's weather quarter. The *Real San Felipe* shifted her helm and avoided the *Superbe*, who fell away on to her lee quarter. Byng in his flagship, the *Barfleur*, chased after two Spanish vessels which had fired whilst she was closing with the Spanish flagship; he continued to chase the two vessels until nightfall. Meanwhile Rear-Admiral George Delavall in the *Royal Oak* chased two Spanish ships to leeward of the main body of the fleet.

The action was more of a general chase than anything else. Captain A T Mahan is niggardly in his praise of this battle, saying only that Byng acted within his orders and served Great Britain well. However, Byng's fleet took twelve major Spanish warships; to this tally must be added four minor warships, one storeship which was burnt and six others which were taken. In total, twenty ships were either captured or burnt including the transports and storeships.[30] This ranks as the most decisive British naval victory until Nelson's at the Nile in 1798.

From the time of his entry into the Mediterranean it is quite clear from Byng's correspondence that the Spanish fleet was his main objective. As soon as he had news of their whereabouts he sailed in force to seek to engage them; and once battle was joined he showed aggression in seeking to destroy as much of the enemy's fleet as possible, traits which would later be linked to the name of Nelson. Byng's task was not over with the destruction of the Spanish fleet; he remained in the Mediterranean until the end of 1718. The Spanish resorted to issuing letters of marque against British trade, and whilst Byng stayed out he made such provisions as he could to protect trade to and from Italy and the Levant. The local consuls, who hired ships to stand off the coast of Italy and warn British ships of the possible danger, aided him in this. It was something a grateful government took some time to recompense them for. On the victorious admiral's return from the Mediterranean, King George called on Byng to wait on him at Hanover, an honour which Byng found wore thin as time went on; in fact, he was moved to beg that 'the Secretary of State would soon come out and relieve me'.[31] Byng's reward was even longer in coming than his relief from court, but on 9 September 1721 Sir George was created Baron Byng of South Hill and Viscount Torrington. Byng probably took this title because of his early association with Herbert and because the title of Orford, which he might have considered, was unavailable, being held by Admiral Russell, who did not die until a year after Byng's elevation to the peerage.

George I died at Osnabruck on 11 June (old style) 1727. When the news reached England it precipitated considerable political anxiety and anticipation. It was expected that Sir Robert Walpole's days at the Treasury were numbered as the new King, George II, brought in his favourites. However, by the end of June Walpole had weathered the crisis of the accession. He had to make many compromises, but his clever distribution of the rewards of office dampened much resentment and consolidated the new political order. The Admiralty played its part. Walpole used the opportunity to remove the last remnants of the Earl of Sunderland's appointees. On 2 August 1727 a new Commission of Admiralty was issued. Lord Berkeley, who had been First Lord since April 1717, was dismissed and Torrington was appointed in his place. According to Lord Hervey, this was done to 'embitter Lord Berkeley's disgrace' rather than as a mark of particular confidence in Torrington.[32] Nevertheless, he held the post for the next four renewals.

Torrington seems to have been an active First Lord, attending and chairing nearly every meeting.[33] He was fortunate to have with him his old secretary, Thomas Corbett, who was Chief Clerk at the Admiralty when Torrington joined the new Commission. In September 1728 Corbett was made Deputy Secretary. He was a very able administrator, who remained at the Admiralty until his death in 1751, providing an important element of administrative continuity during a period of major challenge and change for the Royal Navy. The idea that towards the end of his life Torrington was too weak to attend the meetings and Sir Charles Wager was effectively running the Admiralty seems to be misplaced. The Minute Books show that between January and December 1732, part of the period in which he was said to be infirm, he acted as chairman at over one hundred meetings and that Wager was not present at all of them. At one meeting, on 7 December 1732, he was the only member present and had already dealt with four matters before Thomas Winnington joined him.[34] The challenges during Torrington's tenure were not extreme, but Daniel Baugh has described Torrington's period as First Lord as 'among the most innovative of the peacetime era'. Torrington chaired the session on 13 March 1730, at which Norris and Wager were both present, which considered the foundation of the Naval Academy at Portsmouth. On 26 November 1730 he chaired the meeting that considered Thomas Corbett's draft of the *Regulations and Instructions*. He was present at discussions about the establishment of permanent bases in the West Indies and, in January 1733, discussions about 'Rules . . . admitting old and disabled seamen to Greenwich Hospital'.[35] He attended his last meeting on Saturday 13 January 1733 and died at his house in the Admiralty buildings four days later on the 17th.

Conclusion

At the start of this chapter George Byng, Viscount Torrington's historical persona was said to be masked, primarily by his title and its association with the unfortunate Arthur Herbert; but as has been seen, Byng's association was a positive one in terms of his career. After Herbert's disgrace, his connection with Edward Russell, the other mainspring of the naval conspiracy against James II, promoted his career still further. The second factor in Byng's historical obscurity, the confusion with his infamous son, should be dispelled by wider knowledge of his victory at Cape Passaro. Great claims have been made for the boldness of the execution of the battle and the completeness of the destruction of the enemy. This determination to carry action through to a victorious conclusion was present throughout Byng's career, whether at Málaga or in the bombardment of the defences at Gibraltar, and not least in the eastern seas when the pirate ship which he boarded was sinking beneath him. Trust in his subordinates and single-minded focus on the destruction of the enemy: these surely are the qualities of a Nelson. Sir Isaac Newton's famous line that 'he stood on the shoulders of giants' may have been a gibe at his enemies in the Royal Society, but it is equally applicable to Nelson and all those who raised him so high. George Byng, Viscount Torrington was one of those Titans.

Sir Charles Wager. Mezzotint by Johan Faber

4

Sir Charles Wager
1666–1743

'a very good Admiral, but . . . likewise an able Minister'

DANIEL A BAUGH

Sir Charles Wager was one of the most remarkable and admired British admirals of the eighteenth century, but little notice was taken of him in the nineteenth, and in the twentieth his name is scarcely recognised.[1] The best remembered sea officers are generally those who commanded battlefleets in combat, and although as an admiral Wager was given command of large fleets on four separate occasions, three of them involving deployment with orders to destroy the enemy if confronted, no battles occurred. Before he became an admiral, however, he had made a great name for himself as a fighting officer. As commodore of a small squadron in the West Indies in 1708, he fought a fierce night battle off Cartagena in which he managed to sink one large Spanish galleon laden with silver and capture a second, almost single-handedly. The achievement made Wager rich and brought him fame in his time, but a century later it was seldom remembered, partly because Victorian Englishmen tended to have a lesser regard for heroic deeds involving monetary gain.

During the eighteenth century Wager's name was familiar for a second reason. He was First Lord of the Admiralty for nine years (1733 to 1742). In reality he exercised the authority of the office for almost twelve years because, beginning about 1730, his predecessor, Viscount Torrington, was often beset by ill health and trusted in Wager's competence. In this respect Wager's career bears a superficial resemblance to that of Lord Anson, whom leading ministers also recognised as the authority in sea affairs some years before he became First Lord. A difference was that Wager, from 1730 to 1733, was considered to be First Lord in all but name. In addition, Wager's career in naval administration was long and comprehensive. Before coming to the Admiralty Board in March 1718, he had been at the head of the Navy Board for three years, and his tenure on the Board of Admiralty – twenty-four consecutive years – was longer than anyone else's in the eighteenth century (Anson's total stood second at seventeen years). Thus, Sir Charles Wager was a key figure in British naval administration for over a quarter century, and the dominant figure from 1730 to 1742.

Wager's lengthy and influential role in naval administration has either been forgotten or dismissed. In the heyday of naval history a century ago, it was imagined that the British navy was in decay during Wager's quarter century, that the decay grew worse toward the end of the period, and that it was Lord Anson who rescued the navy from this degradation. The degradation being taken as a fact, it was further presumed that it must have in some way been the First Lord's fault, and it was easy to conclude that he was 'too old'. None of this was based on any historical research, and the notion that the British navy was decaying in Wager's time has been almost completely annihilated by recent studies.

Wager's years at the Admiralty coincided precisely with the period of Sir Robert Walpole's dominance of British government. There is not the slightest doubt that Wager was the 'seaman' whom Walpole trusted; they were personal friends as well as closely co-operating ministers of state. Yet this may be another reason why Wager's reputation has not fared well with historians: being trusted by Walpole is not something that has tended to evoke historical esteem. In spite of the tribute paid to Walpole's statesmanship by an older and wiser William Pitt in the 1750s, the discerning biography by the Liberal statesman John Morley, and the compelling scholarly re-examination by Sir John Plumb, Sir Robert Walpole remains in popular historical imagination the corrupt political manipulator and nothing else.[2] Not the least of Walpole's services to the British nation was his determination, when Lord Torrington died, that Sir Charles Wager should have the top position.

Determination was indeed required. Although Wager was widely regarded as the likely choice, there was an obstacle. The First Lord was expected to be a peer or to be made one, and land being the basis of ancestral rank, Wager was destitute of qualification. He was all too aware of the problem. When Lord Torrington became very ill in the summer of 1731, Wager wrote to Walpole (just prior to sailing for the Mediterranean), saying that he realised that it was considered 'necessary the head should be a lord, (not an Irish lord,) for which', as he recognised, 'I may be said not to be qualify'd'. He hastened to add, however: 'I think I may, without much vanity, look upon myselfe as well qualify'd as some' who had been made peers of the realm.[3] His best argument — aside from his personal achievements and services to the crown, of course — was his naval background (what he wrote to Walpole about this will be seen in a moment), but it is interesting that he also thought it necessary to say something about the landed status, however modest, of his paternal forbears.

It tells us something about him that he had foreseen the possible need for this years earlier. In 1710, when he had just returned from the West Indies and was at Bath to recover his health, he had asked a favour of a Gloucestershire man he met to make inquiries about the Wager family — Wager had often heard from his mother that his 'Grandfather came out of Glo'stershire'. The reply informed him that there was in the neighbourhood of Charleton King (near Cheltenham) a Mr Samuel Cooper, who had married a Jane Wager and could attest that her ancestors 'had been standing there for near 200 years'. In April 1732 Wager wrote again to Mr Cooper, hoping for more information, suggesting that 'if in your way . . . you should meet with any old People that have heard or remember anything more of the family, the Registers being deficient', he would like to be informed. His explanation of why he was asking this favour is of historical as well as personal interest:

> [Years earlier] I made it in my way to make you a Visit as I came to London, . . . not knowing what occasion I might have to say from what family I came: and last sum'er when Lord Torrington, who is at the head of this Board, was dangerously ill, I had reason to believe, that if he dy'd, I might succeed him, and I have the same reason to believe so still. But his Lordship is very well recover'd, and as like to live as I am: and as I am now in the 66th year of my age, ambition is wore out, if ever I had any, and my Inclination has been for many years to retire. But I have been sent on several expeditions (not by my own choice), wherein I have succeeded so well, as to have the King's approbation, and very like may be put, in case of a Vacancy, at the head of this Board without my desiring it, for as I said before, a Retirement is more suitable to my Age and Inclinations, having, I thank God, more than sufficient to carry me to the end of my Journey. But if it happens otherwise, and I should ever be first Commissioner (which I assure you I do not desire), I may probably be made a Peer, the first Commissioner being always so, and of the Council, for the more easy access to the King on all occasions; and tho' this may never happen, I was willing to be able to say that I was not altogether an Upstart, but descended from, an antient family, tho' they never had but a small estate.[4]

It was evidently important to have one's ancestors distinguished from totally unpropertied migrants.

Parentage and Upbringing

Sir Charles Wager's primary claim to being 'as well qualify'd as some' for a peerage was partly based on his naval lineage. When he wrote to Walpole in 1731 he dwelt on this:

> My . . . father became a captain in the navy, and dy'd at Deal, captain of his majesty's ship the Crown, then in the Downs, in the year 1666. My mother's father, whose name was Goodson, was a vice-admiral in the navy in the time of the parliament, and was a vice-admiral at the taking of Jamaica, and was left there with the command of those ships by Pen[n], who came home and was put in the Tower; that was in Oliver's time; so that on both sides I am related to the navy.[5]

Both of the men he mentioned were 'tarpaulins' (and Wager's grandfather, John, 'who came out of' Gloucestershire, may also have taken up a career at sea). Wager's father, Captain Charles Wager, was born at Chatham in 1630 and had been a boatswain's mate in the merchant service. He became a lieutenant, then a captain in the navy of the Commonwealth. A near relation, George Wager, advanced from boatswain to commander of an 18-gun warship in that navy. This man, when cornered by two Ostenders in 1656 and unable to prevent a hundred of the enemy from boarding his ship, went below to the powder room and blew it up, killing practically everyone including himself.[6] Wager's mother, Prudence, was the daughter of Vice-Admiral William Goodson, who had come into the navy as captain of a merchant ship converted to a warship; he led a naval battalion ashore at the futile attempt on Santo Domingo as well as during the conquest of Jamaica in 1655. And, to look ahead a bit, when Wager married in December 1691, his bride, Martha, was the daughter of Captain Anthony Earning of the Commonwealth navy. Although Earning eventually became commander of an East India Company ship – in which he was killed in an Indian Ocean sea battle with the Dutch in 1677 – he was plainly unsympathetic to the monarchy in 1660 and lost his commission.[7] Clearly, Wager's background was the Commonwealth navy.

His father, however, promptly accepted the Restoration in 1660 and was captain of the *Yarmouth* in the fleet that brought Charles II to England. He established a reputation in the Royal Navy as a highly capable, trustworthy, and well liked officer.[8] A notable instance of his competence came in December 1664 when half of Sir Thomas Allin's Straits squadron ran aground on sandy shoals near Gibraltar. Captain Wager's ship not only avoided grounding but sent a longboat which helped get the flagship safely off. A year later when he returned to England, Samuel Pepys met him over dinner and recorded his impression: 'A brave stout fellow this Captain is, and I think very honest.' He died shortly thereafter, but Pepys was reminded of him two years later when he heard a friend who had been to Tangier contrast Captain Wager's character with that of others who went to the Straits, remarking, as Pepys noted, 'that above all Englishmen that ever was there, there never was any man that behaved himself like poor Charles Wager, whom the very Moores do mention with teares sometimes.'[9]

Captain Wager's marriage to Prudence Goodson was registered at St Gregory by St Paul, London, on 30 January 1663; she was 25 years old. The future admiral was their second child, born in 1666, and although he seems not to have known his birth date, he had been told that it was after his father's death on 24 February. His place of birth was not West Looe, Cornwall, as is sometimes reported, but Rochester, Kent.[10] Obviously, although he was the son of a naval officer, young Wager had none of the professional advantages of that situation. Nor would he find them on his mother's side: the naval career of Vice-Admiral Goodson was abruptly terminated in 1660 by his fervent, indelible religious and political radicalism; the old Cromwellian stalwart refused to accept the monarchy. For the rest of his life – not without reason evidently – he was thought to be someone who would be happy to see the Restoration reversed.[11] Wager's mother was as solidly nonconformist in religion as her father, and she remarried a Quaker, Alexander Parker, a London merchant.

Young Charles already had an older sister, Prudence, and the remarriage produced six more children.[12] Under the circumstances it was to be expected that he would be placed out of the household at an early age and entrusted to a religious nonconformist. Wager was, in fact, placed in the hands of a Quaker merchant captain of New England named John Hull. This man was born in Barnstable (Cape Cod), Massachusetts in March 1654 and operated a transatlantic shipping service. He was the son of Tristram (or Trustrum) Hull, a sea captain and substantial citizen of Barnstable and Yarmouth, Massachusetts, and his wife Blanche, both of whom were Quakers. (He is not to be confused with the John Hull of Boston – silversmith, attorney, merchant and landowner – whose name turns up everywhere in New England colonial records.) In 1687 he settled in the colony of Rhode Island, buying 370 acres at the north end of Conanicut Island, across from Newport. Just prior to this he had lived in London for two or three years and had married, in the London Quaker Meeting on 23 October 1684, Alice Teddeman. Wager's mother was a witness at the marriage.[13]

Descendants of John Hull have long averred that he was the man who brought up the future admiral and provided his early apprenticeship at sea. The centrepiece of remembrance has been a fascinating tale. It is said that when a menacing French privateer hovered near John Hull's ship, he being a pacifist went below and left the conn to young Charles. But Hull could not resist taking a peek and noticed that the privateer had placed itself in a position where it might be rammed. Advising the youth that he might wish to alter course to that end, it was done, and the privateer was sunk with practically all hands.[14] Documentary validation of this story remains lacking, but there is strong evidence to support the claim that Captain John Hull brought up young Charles Wager. When Dr Teddeman Hull, John Hull's oldest son, who became a physician, visited London in 1742 he had a letter of introduction from Governor Richard Ward of Rhode Island which stated that he was 'the son of Captain John Hull, late of this colony, under whom Sir Charles Wager was educated'. Moreover, there is clear evidence that Wager knew and cared about the Hull family; he wrote to Sir Robert Walpole in 1730 and 1731 to recommend John Hull's youngest son to a vacant colonial Collectorship.[15] Still to be discovered are the age and circumstances in which the future admiral was placed under John Hull's care, and the times and places of his residence in New England.

After Sir Charles Wager's death, Arthur Onslow, a long-time Speaker of the House of Commons, remarked on the influence of the Quaker upbringing on the admiral's character:

> He was of the most gentle and humane disposition I ever knew, and spent almost the whole he got in generous acts of charity and compassion. I had a long and intimate acquaintance with him, and have seen where his temper has been tried by much provocation, but I never saw him discomposed. He had a very good understanding, great plainness of manners, and a steadiness of courage that no danger could daunt, with the same calmness in it that he shewed in the most ordinary acts of his life. He was indeed a person of most extraordinary worth, and the world bore him a respect that was due to it. His father was a captain of a man of war before the restoration, and very likely after that: but dying when this son was young, and the mother marrying a Quaker, he was bred up among that people; by which he acquired the simplicity of his manners, and had much of their fashion in his speech as well as carriage. And all this, with his particular roughness of countenance, made the softness of his nature still more pleasing, because unexpected at first.[16]

The mature Wager's religious disposition was as mild as his temperament, but his political inclinations strongly and consistently favoured the Whig cause, as could be expected of someone brought up in nonconformist circles. Although he tolerated the privileges of social rank, it is clear that, unlike some Whig gentlemen, he considered such privileges to be a nuisance. The temper of the family, as well as the times, is suggested by the fact that two of Wager's half-sisters (whose parents were both Quakers) married cathedral deans.[17]

Lieutenant, Captain and Commodore, 1689-1709

If Wager met the official requirement of at least a year of Royal Navy sea service before becoming a lieutenant, he must have entered the navy before the Revolution of 1688, because he is listed as lieutenant of the *Foresight* frigate on 1 August 1689 (the earliest surviving record of his naval service). Given the policy of James II, which accommodated Protestant nonconformists as well as Catholics, that possibility cannot be ruled out. On the other hand, the tumultuous year 1689, which began with the establishment of William and Mary on the throne and witnessed a rapid expansion of the navy in the spring (to defend the revolution against the forces of Louis XIV), saw quite a number of competent, literate young men who could be counted on as loyal to the new regime made lieutenants direct from the merchant service. It is quite possible that Wager was one of these. From the *Foresight* he was soon moved to the *Dreadnought*, 64 guns, and became her first lieutenant by 1691. In 1692 he was in the *Britannia*, Admiral Russell's flagship, and took part in the Battle of Barfleur, soon being made post (on 7 June 1692) when Russell appointed him to captain of the *Ruzee* fireship.[18]

The year 1693 saw him in command of the *Samuel and Henry*, 44 guns, in which he was assigned to convoy the New England trade. In 1694 he was captain of the *Newcastle*, 48. The following year, after a month as captain of the *Mary* he was re-assigned to the *Woolwich*, 54, which saw Channel service under Sir Cloudesley Shovell. In early March 1696 the *Woolwich* was part of the squadron assembled to watch Dunkirk and the Flemish coast against a supposed invasion threat.[19] A month later Wager was transferred to the *Greenwich*, 50 and toward the end of the year was ordered to America as commodore of a small squadron for convoying the tobacco trade from the Chesapeake; his homeward voyage was delayed: the masters of the vessels petitioned the Council of Maryland to ask 'Captain Charles Wager, the Commodore' to wait because the crop matured late and also because they were undermanned, so many of their seamen having deserted and gone to Pennsylvania.[20] After returning, Wager continued in command of the *Greenwich*, employed largely on Channel services, though he was ordered to sail to Rochefort in June 1698 to observe the state of the French navy at that base. At the end of 1699 the *Greenwich*, like most of the fleet, was paid off. Finally, Wager was on half pay. He lived at Kilminorth (he wrote 'Killmynorth') near West Looe in Cornwall, a place where he had already established his family by June 1699 when the ship was in drydock for repairs.[21]

Why he came to Kilminorth (he lived in the Watergate cottages near the river) is not known, but one possibility is that he had met James Kendall, a substantial West India merchant when Kendall was a member of the Admiralty Board in the later 1690s. Kendall was a landowner in the region, and Wager became a freeman of West Looe in 1699.[22] Also, as he informed the Admiralty in June 1700, his residence was only 'about ten miles from his Majesty's Yard at Plymouth'. He added that he could 'be at London in four or five days, if required'. Evidently he was eager for employment, and eight months later, in February 1701, he was appointed to the *Medway*, 64 and was moved the following January to the *Hampton Court*, 70, one of fifty-one ships commissioned the same day in anticipation of war. He remained captain of the *Hampton Court* for the next five years, and sometimes held command of a squadron on detached service. For example, in April 1703, 'there were on the French Coast, under Command of Captain Charles Wager one Third, three Fourths, one Fifth, and one Sixth'. They plied between Cape Barfleur and the Isle of Batz for intercepting the coastal trade of western France, but with scant success.[23]

Later that year he went out to the Mediterranean and in October came under the command of Admiral George Byng (later Lord Torrington). The occasion having arisen for renegotiating England's treaty with the Dey of Algiers, Captains Wager and John Baker were the men Byng sent ashore to carry out negotiations and witness the signing. Wager's return home coincided with the legendary storm that hit southeast England in late November; the *Hampton Court* barely survived and was severely damaged. After repairs she went out again to the Mediterranean, and Wager was with the fleet under Sir George Rooke that captured Gibraltar in 1704. Although some accounts of the famous sea battle off Málaga list the *Hampton Court* as a participant, it appears that Wager was away on detached service. He was present, however, at the capture of Barcelona in 1705 and wintered with Leake's squadron at Lisbon. In February 1706 Wager was sent ahead in company with Captain Stephen Martin to observe the *flota* ships preparing to leave Cadiz, to no avail. He was with Leake at the relief of Barcelona, then at Ibiza in September when the island surrendered to King Charles, and shortly afterwards at Majorca when that island did the same (after a brief bombardment the people rose and pressured the Bourbon party to surrender). On this occasion Wager was one of two captains sent ashore in the exchange of hostages while the articles of capitulation were being worked out. Soon after, he went home with Leake's squadron, making a quick passage to England.[24]

The foregoing record indicates that by the end of 1706 Wager was not only a senior captain but one who was experienced and successful in commanding detached squadrons as well as executing diplomatic duties that required nerve, care, and good judgment. It was not surprising that in January 1707 he was chosen to be commander-in-chief in the West Indies. After hoisting his pendant in the *Expedition* at Spithead on 28 March he proceeded slowly down the Channel to collect the trade, took departure on 11 April, and after stops at Madeira, Barbados, and Nevis anchored at Port Royal, Jamaica on 22 June. His predecessor, William Kerr, had concentrated on self-enrichment rather than shepherding the trade, so the islanders were pleased to see a new commodore. At this time they were also afraid of being attacked by a French squadron known to be on its way from Europe under the command of Admiral Ducasse.

Wager's initial deployments were designed to gain intelligence of the arrival of Ducasse and to protect trade. Yet even the worried Jamaicans realised how eager the British government was to capture the Cartagena galleons after they loaded Peruvian silver at Porto Bello. By the end of December the commodore learned two key facts: first, that Ducasse had indeed arrived in the Caribbean with a strong squadron (ten of the line) but had sailed on to Havana, thus indicating, as Wager correctly surmised, that his mission was simply to escort the combined galleon fleet, after it assembled, across the Atlantic; second, that the Cartagena galleons had finally gone to Porto Bello to load. Wager knew that from Havana, far to leeward, Ducasse could neither surprise Jamaica nor assist in shielding the galleons at Porto Bello, and if those galleons were to follow their usual pattern of returning to Cartagena before setting out for Havana, he would have a chance to intercept them. In early March 1708 he received a reliable report that the galleons would be ready to leave Porto Bello about 1 May. He sailed southward from Port Royal on 14 April and despite a severe thunderstorm that caused great damage to the *Expedition*'s rigging, his four-ship squadron (one merely a small fireship) was in the position he desired (about 36 miles west of Cartagena) when he learned on 23 May that the galleons were at sea.

Four days passed and he feared that they had gone straight to Havana, but on the morning of 28 May ships began to appear to the south and southwest; at length the count was seventeen. Most proved to be armed, three of them possessing broadsides that matched the strength of the

Expedition, 70, *Kingston*, 60 and *Portland*, 50. Wager resolved to attack. An afternoon calm gave way to a moderate wind from north-northeast and he bore down. The change of wind direction prevented the Spanish from weathering the Baru peninsula and its adjacent islands, so they tacked to the northward. But they did not try to flee; rather, they formed a loose line of battle under easy sail: the admiral in the 64-gun *San Josef* in the centre; the vice-admiral, also in a 64-gun ship, in the rear; and the rear-admiral in the *Santa Cruz*, 50 in the van, each spaced about half a mile from the admiral with armed merchant ships in between. Clearly, the Spanish admiral did not believe that the small British squadron would dare oppose his entry into Cartagena.

He seriously underestimated the resolve of the British commodore. Knowing 'the three Admirals . . . had all the Mony', Wager ordered Captain Timothy Bridges of the *Kingston*, which was close by, to attack the vice-admiral and sent a boat to Captain Edward Windsor of the *Portland* with orders to attack the rear-admiral.[25] The former showed no alacrity and the latter failed utterly to follow orders, but Wager did not hesitate to direct his flagship toward the *San Josef*. The *Expedition*'s guns roared just as the sun was setting and the fighting continued as darkness fell, and then, an hour and a half into the engagement, the *San Josef* blew up. She sank instantly, carrying the admiral, officers, passengers and crew – almost 700 in all – to the bottom along with most of the registered silver. Only eleven seamen survived to be rescued the next day. The *Expedition*, less than half a pistol shot away, was showered with large planks and fiery splinters, but the greatest hazard came from the wash of a blast which seemed to push outward rather than upward and forced great quantities of water through her gunports. As the British crew feverishly put out fires and worked the pumps, the Spanish squadron scattered, but, dark as it was, Wager could discern one large ship not far away. It proved to be the *Santa Cruz*. By 10 pm the *Expedition* managed to get close to her, a dark shape against the starry sky. Which way she was headed he could not tell, but his first broadside blasted through her stern and took down her mizzen yards. Substantially deprived of manoeuvre, and recognising the hopelessness – just before 2am the other British men of war, which had been drawn to the scene by the gunfire and shipboard lights, joined the fight – the Spanish rear-admiral surrendered. Total British losses in both engagements were 6 killed and 11 wounded, all in the *Expedition*. There was no registered silver on board the *Santa Cruz*, but she contained considerable treasure nonetheless – silver ingots and chests of pieces-of-eight belonging to passengers and private merchants.

The *Expedition* was much damaged aloft; there were 300 prisoners on board, and part of her crew had to be assigned to the prize. Wager was therefore in no position to go after the remaining *San Joachin*, but because the Spanish ships had tacked to the northward and might still try to turn back to Cartagena, there was a chance of intercepting them. Therefore the commodore remained on deck, and just before sunrise he spied a large ship and three smaller ones in the distance. He immediately made a signal to the *Kingston* and *Portland* to chase. They did so, but to Wager's astonishment they abandoned the chase in mid-afternoon and he had to signal them to resume. Eventually they got close enough to fire their broadsides but abandoned the pursuit when the Spanish vice-admiral took refuge in the Salmedina shoals. At this point the British warships were near the harbour entrance, from which a 40-gun galleon happened to be emerging. Seeing them, the galleon quickly turned around and deliberately drove ashore on the Baru, where the crew set her afire to prevent her falling into British hands.

Information from captured Spaniards and accounts from lieutenants and soldiers on board the *Kingston* and *Portland* amplified what Wager had seen with his own eyes: Captains Bridges and Windsor had failed to do their duty. The arrival of a small squadron from England provided enough officers to convene a court martial, and both captains were thereby deprived of their commands.[26]

Before he left Jamaica in the autumn of 1709 Wager became seriously ill – something to be expected sooner or later in the West Indies in those days – but survived. He arrived in England a rich man. He also came home a rear-admiral, the elevation in rank having occurred in November 1707 according to seniority, before the battle was fought. His wealth stemmed chiefly from the silver on board the captured galleon, its value estimated at over £60,000. (After his return to England he had to fight off a threatened prosecution by the Treasury Board which claimed a share.) But his wealth also derived from numerous other prizes, for as a commander-in-chief authorised to have a captain under him he was entitled to the flag officer's one-eighth share of all captures within the West Indies command, wherever they occurred. Some carried valuable cargoes of cacao and other commodities. Nevertheless, Wager gained the merchants' praise for his conduct in protecting their trade.[27] In England, his bravery and success against the galleons brought him immediate acclaim. He arrived a hero and was knighted by Queen Anne (8 December 1709). At Portsmouth he was nominated for a by-election to Parliament and was elected on 23 January 1710.

Later ages have tended to regard the battle which brought Wager wealth and fame as a personal but not a strategic or national achievement. At the time, however, it was unquestionably considered to be both. It provided a much-needed boost to the public image of the navy, and, above all, it inhibited the flow of treasure to the Bourbon powers. By this point the French and Spanish monarchies were desperate for precious metals to pay for campaigning. The sinking and burning of two silver galleons (more than the capture of a third) dealt them a sharp blow. But the quantity of silver thereby lost, considerable as it was, mattered less than the shock effect of the successful attack, which worked in combination with Spanish resentment of France's high-handed commandeering of bullion (when it was escorted to Europe by French squadrons) to prevent further sailings from Porto Bello and Cartagena.[28] For the rest of the war Peruvian silver had to be transported in more difficult ways.

Admiral and Diplomat

Upon his return to England, Wager went to Bath to recover his health and then settled into life ashore. He was re-elected at Portsmouth in 1710 notwithstanding the Tory landslide, but the Tory-dominated House soon overturned the result on petition and he had to quit his seat.

In 1710 Wager was 44 years of age. During the preceding twenty years his total time away from sea-duty assignments had amounted to about two years. He now possessed fame and fortune. From this time onward Sir Charles Wager was prepared to spend the rest of his life ashore. No doubt, if he had been asked to take command of a squadron while the War of the Spanish Succession still continued, he would have complied, but it is unlikely that he was ever asked since he was marked as being a strong Whig. During this time he probably resided once again at Kilminorth. He had become acquainted with Sir Jonathan Trelawny, Bishop of Winchester, who dominated politics in that part of Cornwall. By 1715, if not earlier, Wager was purchasing from bankers mortgage loans that Trelawny had contracted.[29] These were investments but also something else: the bishop controlled the parliamentary seats of both East and West Looe, and Wager served as MP for West Looe from 1713 to 1715.

When Queen Anne died on 1 August 1714 immediate steps were taken to secure the Hanoverian Succession. Wager was ordered on 3 August to go aboard the ships at Portsmouth and speed their readiness for sea. Toward the end of December he was ordered to go out to the Straits and take command of the Mediterranean fleet, relieving Vice-Admiral James Wishart, a staunch Tory. Since Wishart was the man who had been elected for

Wager's seat at Portsmouth in 1711 and Wager regained that seat in the general election of January 1715, there was a complete reversal of fortune, perfectly illustrative of the revolution in politics that had occurred. Wager was now positioned to be offered the most important sea commands.

Instead, he resigned the Mediterranean command (never leaving Spithead) and opted for civil employment ashore, the Comptrollership of the Navy. This important office of business (always held by an experienced sea officer) placed him at the head of the Navy Board, the board which for centuries had been charged with the upkeep and administration of the Royal Navy. Three years later, in March 1718, he moved to the Board of Admiralty, where he remained until almost the end of his life. Although he had deliberately chosen a career ashore, he did not cut himself off from the possibility of employment at sea: he remained on the list of admirals and over the years rose through the flag ranks in the usual way, according to seniority.

After some years he did go to sea again. The first call came in early December 1721 when he was suddenly ordered to Portsmouth to take command of ten ships and set out immediately for Lisbon. A Portuguese tribunal had sentenced two British merchants to death for violating the prohibition against exporting gold coin (a law that was commonly circumvented, as everyone knew). Wager's orders were to enter the Tagus and demand satisfaction, but he never sailed because the Portuguese court, aware of these naval preparations, overruled the judgment.

Five years passed before he again took command of a fleet, but now his service was to be intensive. The first mission was to the Baltic, where British battlefleets had been deployed regularly between 1715 and 1721. The chief adversary had formerly been Sweden; now it was Russia. The objects had been constant, however: preventing the Great Northern War from spreading, guarding the interests of Hanover, and protecting British trade, which was strategically important, the Baltic being an indispensable source of naval stores. Peace between Sweden and Russia was made in 1721, but within five years Russia mobilised a fleet; Sweden (dreadfully weak in the aftermath of Charles XII's exhausting campaigning) and Denmark were under threat. Wager left the Thames in mid-April 1726 and made a quick passage to Copenhagen, where he met with the court and completed arrangements for co-operation with the Danish navy. His report of 30 April evoked a glowing response from Secretary of State Townshend: 'his Majesty has commanded me to let you know from Him, that he was before persuaded you was a very good Admiral, but he now sees that you are likewise an able Minister. All the answers you gave to the questions

proposed to you at the Conference with the Danish Council were extremely right.' Proceeding to an anchorage near Stockholm, Wager met
with Swedish statesmen (who were wary of the British) and had an audience with the king. Stephen Poyntz, the envoy to Sweden, told undersecretary of state George Tilson in an informal letter: 'Sr. Cha. Wager is a
pure good man such as you describe him. His look struck terror, but his
smiles reconciled all they were bestowed on. His reception here was but
awkward, except from the K. of Sweden and C[ount] Horn, but he puts up
with all for the good of the service.'

The purpose of sending this fleet to the Baltic was to keep the Russian
fleet and troop transports confined while the Swedes made up their minds
to side with Britain and its allies; the navy of Denmark was to be ready to
assist. The Gulf of Finland was Wager's ultimate destination and he arrived
at Reval (Tallinn), the forward base of the Russian fleet, on 29 May. If the
Russian fleet came out, he was ordered to engage and destroy it, but
otherwise to avoid hostilities. The appearance of his fleet (twenty of the
line) caused consternation at Reval and rage at St Petersburg. Though
furious, the Tsarina nevertheless issued orders to halt all further fitting out
of warships and to unload ammunition and provisions at Reval. With over
700 men sick and a likely prospect of late-season storm damage or else
being hemmed in by contrary winds, Wager requested permission to withdraw, but he was ordered to remain so that the Swedish Rikstag would feel
more secure. Finally, he left Reval on 20 September. It took almost five
weeks to reach Copenhagen and he was not safely in the Thames estuary
until 1 November.[30]

Within two months Wager was ordered back to sea. Hoisting his flag on
board the *Kent* at Portsmouth on 24 December, he was ready to sail in four
days but was delayed by contrary winds until 19 January. His destination
was the bay of Gibraltar, which he reached on 2 February 1727. At this
time Europe was divided into two blocks and stood on the precipice of a
general war: an Austro-Spanish alliance was opposed by the Alliance of
Hanover (Britain, France, and Holland). Spain had pledged to pay subsidies
to the Emperor Charles VI (who chiefly wanted the money so that he
could subsidise German principalities supporting the Imperial cause); in
return he granted some long-standing Spanish claims in Italy. But Spain's
initial military goal was to recover Gibraltar. British strategy focused on
defending Gibraltar and starving the Spanish treasury by blocking the silver
ships from leaving Cartagena. The latter task was given to Admiral Francis
Hosier – a dreadful mission which, though it achieved its object, cost the
lives of over 2000 seamen, 60 officers, and two admirals (Hosier's successor,

Edward Hopson, died too) without a shot being fired. All were victims of tropical disease, chiefly yellow fever.

Wager's mission was to bolster the defence of Gibraltar. While he was *en route* the Spaniards broke off relations with Great Britain and, having built batteries on the bay shore, were ready to begin the siege. Wager brought out six ships of the line, two cruisers, two bomb vessels, and additional troops for the garrison. In mid-February hostilities began as the British ships and the Spanish shore batteries exchanged gunfire. On both sides, however, the range was too great for serious damage. The British navy helped to cover the land approaches (Wager ordered two frigates and a bomb vessel to 'the back of the Hill') and escorted troop reinforcements, ammunition and provisions to the beleaguered garrison. Great Britain and Spain were undoubtedly at war and at one point in early May there was a furious artillery exchange, but usually the actions were cautious and desultory. Wager was not only responsible for guarding Gibraltar, but also for cruising off Cadiz, looking out for rumoured incoming silver ships (without success), assigning convoy escorts, and preventing the Spanish warships at Corunna and Santander from joining those at Cadiz. Numerous ships joined and left Wager's command, but, as he complained to Walpole, he did not have enough cruisers to blockade Spanish privateers. No naval engagement occurred, but prizes were taken by both sides.[31]

Peace preliminaries were signed on 31 May because the Emperor despaired of success, partly because Spain was giving him so little subsidy money (a consequence of Hosier's achievement). Although hostilities ceased in mid-June, the King of Spain was extremely reluctant to let go. The batteries for besieging Gibraltar were maintained, Spanish men of war continued to be fitted out, Spanish privateers continued to pose a danger to British shipping, and a much contested South Sea Company ship captured by the Spanish and held in Vera Cruz was not given back. All this indicated no real inclination to peace and was exacerbated by the aid and comfort which the Spanish court was providing for exiled Jacobites. One result was virulent war fever in London. With rumours of war circulating everywhere it was necessary that Wager's fleet should stay in Iberian waters through the winter. Finally, the Spanish court, sensing its isolation, was forced to relent and signed a convention suitable to the British government on 6 March 1728. Among its provisions were immediate Spanish withdrawal from the siege works at Gibraltar and immediate departure of the British fleet.[32] And so at last Wager was ordered home; he arrived at Spithead on 9 April, after sixteen months' absence.

He resumed his regular attendance at the Admiralty Board. Thirteen months later, on 10 May 1729, he hoisted his flag in the *Cornwall* at Spithead in command of thirty-three warships. A month later fourteen Dutch joined him. This great fleet (twenty British and nine Dutch ships of 50 guns or more) did not move for six months, after which time the Dutch went home and twelve of the largest British ships were ordered laid up. It was ridiculed as the 'stay-at-home fleet', especially by those who wanted war. The expense seemed to be to no purpose.

Yet the British government really had no choice. The court of Spain had been acting as if the convention had never been signed: it continued to demand the return of Gibraltar and ignored British West Indian grievances. The French were supposed to pressure the Spanish into compliance and although the congress stipulated by the convention for the purpose met in and near Paris, they did nothing. Cardinal Fleury always sounded friendly and ready to help, but Britain's Spanish complaints were of no concern to the French; their thoughts were focused on opposing the Emperor, especially in Germany. George II had similar priorities, but any temptation he might have felt to settle the commercial and maritime quarrels with Spain by giving back Gibraltar was constrained by strong addresses by both Houses of Parliament against it. Matters were therefore at a stand, and when Parliament had opened in late January 1729, it was immediately clear that the opposition had lost patience. Britain had sustained all the costs of fitting out and deploying fleets, Admiral Hosier's men had done all the dying, and what, it was asked, had France contributed to the alliance? The King's ministers had lost patience, too. On 31 March their representatives at Paris were told to inform the French 'that it is high time one way or another to come to a decision, and not to spend in fruitless conferences the season that is proper for action'. On 5 May they were directed to ask Cardinal Fleury pointedly how France intended to 'act against Spain' if Spain failed to comply. Attached to this was a reminder: 'His Majesty is fitting out a strong squadron, which when compleat will consist of near twenty men of war, besides bomb-vessels and fireships, and is to be commanded by Sir Charles Wager.'[33] In short, the fleet's purpose was to inform all Europe as well as Parliament and public that time was running out and Great Britain would, if necessary, proceed to hostilities. Armed patience was rewarded: the court of Spain signed the Treaty of Seville on 9 November 1729.

The treaty, which silenced demands for the return of Gibraltar and would supposedly terminate Spanish depredations in the West Indies, was made possible by offering the Queen of Spain something which she greatly wanted that was of little account to the British – a promise that existing territorial rights of her son, Don Carlos, in Italy would be guaranteed by the Alliance of Hanover. The requisite garrisons to be placed in Parma and Tuscany would be Spanish, not neutral, troops – a concession from the Emperor that the British had finally gained by supporting his daughter's right to inherit in Germany. A British fleet was to co-operate with the Spanish navy in conveying the troops to Leghorn. The Spanish, however, remained apprehensive. If the French imposed last-minute obstacles, would the British hold firm?

At the moment when Wager was ordered to command this fleet (21 May 1731) he was ill and scarcely able to walk; two days later, however, he informed undersecretary of state Charles Delafaye that he had 'brought away the stone' and was recovering rapidly. In any case, his flagship, the impressive 90-gun *Namur*, was still in the dock at Chatham. By late June some alarming reports of French troops massing near Dunkirk for a possible embarkation caused a change of plan. Wager shifted his flag to the *Grafton* and went immediately to the Downs, but he quickly realised that it was a false alarm. There were no transports on that coast, not even many boats. In a letter to Delafaye he observed:

> If the ffrench can persuade us, to keep our ships at home, and not send the intended squadron, to joyn the Spaniards, will they not gain their point, and perhaps come out, . . . and so fright the Spaniards into joyning with them, next year? If there be any probability of the ffrench making warr upon us next year, will it not be better for us to make Warr upon them this year, before they are redy?

He added the next day: 'I am not for abating One Ship of Don Carlos his Squadron [*sic*]; fit out more if you want them.' He was glad to receive, on 6 July, prompt orders to move on to Spithead. There he raised the question of whether as a vice-admiral he might be outranked by Spanish admirals; his promotion to admiral of the blue on 10 July was quickly arranged.[34]

On 1 August the fleet entered Cadiz Bay and the round of invitations, warm welcomes, grand entertainments, and dinners at Cadiz and Seville began, followed by reciprocating invitations whereby Spanish naval officers and men of rank were entertained aboard the *Namur* and other British ships. There was also joint planning of the expedition. Wager's orders were to convey the Spanish troops to Leghorn, waiting there (British soldiers were to accompany the fleet) to see that they got ashore and took up their positions without incident. There was much delay; the Spanish fleet was not ready to sail, and the soldiers at Barcelona were sick with fevers and fluxes. The combined fleet did not reach Leghorn until October but, with British forces at the ready, all went peacefully. Finally, on 26 October Wager could write, 'It is pretty late in the Year, but we must take our chance for a short or a long passage.' He arrived at St Helen's on 10 December with five ships; the others, scattered by storms, straggled in. He was happy to inform the undersecretary that an officer he sent to Seville (Captain [Curtis] Barnett, 'a brisk young fellow') reported the success at Leghorn to Spanish ministers before they learned through their own channels; he also remarked on his own sense of 'pleasure to have a success where doubtful'.[35] Thus, for one brief moment this man who had blasted and captured Spanish galleons, whose long career had been and would continue to be devoted to figuring out ways to crush the Spanish, was cordially received by them. In a congenial spirit amidst uncertainty of success he had efficiently achieved what they needed.

Between April 1726 and December 1731 Sir Charles Wager spent as many months flying his flag as he spent ashore – an intensity of sea service uncommon for admirals even in wartime. He made no complaint and seems to have felt gratified by the successes. These were years when British seapower was much employed; often two or three large squadrons were simultaneously dispatched and admirals were scarce (partly because some died). It should be noted, however, that the missions for which Wager was chosen were ones upon which the policy of Great Britain greatly depended, and for which diplomatic discretion and strategic acumen were prime qualifications. Though scarcely noticed in the annals of naval history, their importance at the time to the king and the ministers whose political fate hung in the balance was enormous.

First Lord and Maritime Expert

When Lord Torrington died in January 1733, undersecretary Delafaye reported to a colleague:

> Every body looks upon sir Charles Wager as the person who will now be at the head of the affairs of the navy; as indeed I may say he has been for some time, for tho' lord Torrington had the name and the appearance of it, sir Charles, by giving way in some things not essential, and by suggesting matters in such a way that the other imagined the first thought was his own, kept all in order, without ever having any squabble.[36]

Wager was popular enough to be nominated and elected for Westminster in 1734. In addition to managerial talents, his appointment as First Lord of the Admiralty (officially 21 June 1733) brought three major benefits to the navy. One was the trust he inspired in the officer corps. A second was the energy he devoted to bolstering the government and defending the navy's conduct and performance in the House of Commons. The third was his direct experience and wide-ranging knowledge of naval and maritime matters.

Because the officer corps was governed essentially by patronage, most of it operating within the naval establishment, factional dissension was a constant threat. To have a First Lord who was an experienced sea officer prepared to insist on professional ability in matters of promotion was a great asset to the service. Moreover, the officers knew that Wager's reputation for tolerance did not extend to quarrelling. Although, like every First Lord, he politely accepted 'court' recommendations, he was selective in pushing them. For instance, in a letter of 1733 to Commodore Ogle he spoke of his prior letters as containing 'generally Recommendations which I could not avoid' and quickly turned to three cases that mattered (two of them professional, one 'court' but stemming from personal acquaintance). Under Wager, promotions to flag rank were carefully considered and quite a few senior captains were passed over (it is a mistake to believe that senior captains were not passed over before the institution of 'Yellow Admirals' in 1747). Those disappointed were upset, of course, but respect for the Admiralty was maintained. In the war that ensued three of those who had been bypassed were restored in rank, but only one by Wager and that was Vernon, who, from his conduct on the opposition benches had made himself thoroughly obnoxious to George II's ministers. But in December 1738, with a West Indian expedition in the offing, Wager pressed hard, writing to Newcastle: 'I wish the King could be persuaded to let Vernon have this command. He is certainly much properer than any officer we have to send . . . and is a very good sea officer, whatever he may be, or has been, in the House of Commons.' It set a strong example of professionalism over politics. (During the decade from Wager's resignation to the appointment of Anson as First Lord, there were disturbing conflicts which reverberated through the corps.)[37]

Since the First Lord of the Admiralty was a member of the Privy Council and participated in high-level discussions of naval policy and strategy, defending the navy's performance and the ministry's use of the fleet in Parliament was a logical extension of his duties. Not all First Lords of the eighteenth century were good at this. Wager was, and he was especially valuable because the King did not see fit to make him a peer. Thus, after 1733 (as well as before, if he was not at sea) his parliamentary attendance was frequent. To Walpole in 1732 he described himself as a 'Parliament man', adding that 'a constant attendance in Town' was a heavy burden on his income. Walpole knew this, and also knew that Wager was not only a staunch and loyal supporter but a man who was heard with great respect – a point of immense importance in the years following George II's accession because naval policy and strategy were objects of fierce and continual attacks from members of the opposition. Wager could effectively counter the misinformation, exaggerations, and false assumptions. In him the government side in the House of Commons had a well liked, well informed, trusted authority.

Sir Charles Wager was in fact a one-man bureau of intelligence. His competence reached beyond naval matters to maritime geography, navigation, seaborne commerce, and transatlantic colonies. Countless memoranda have survived, most of them drafted in his own hand.[38] It seems that when anyone in the cabinet had a question or needed a comment on some proposal touching these subjects, it was referred to Wager. From an advisory standpoint he resembled a French minister of marine and colonies, yet he did not presume that his expertise surpassed that of the Board of Trade. For instance, when asked (in 1735) to comment on Captain Thomas Coram's proposal for settling Nova Scotia under a scheme of trustees, his opinion was that civil government under an able governor selected and directed by the Board of Trade was the best guarantor of success. Wager could describe the differing political situations of Algiers, Ceuta, and Sallee. He understood the commercial effects of sugar duties. When shown a petition from a body of Jamaica merchants, he observed that not one 'considerable trader' had signed it. Did the French have a good reason to prohibit British shipping from using the bay at Cape Donna Maria (western Hispaniola) in peacetime, and how serious an inconvenience would prohibition pose? Wager gave a detailed, assured answer. His letter to Benjamin Keene, envoy at Madrid (whom he held in high regard), explaining why a *guarda costa* was bound to be a 'licens'd pyrat' and why recompense from Spain was so difficult to obtain, shows an intimate understanding of an intricate subject.[39] (It also reveals how his strung-out sentences could get tangled by complexities, a tendency that probably mirrored his speech and may have been the reason why listeners in Parliament and council meetings sometimes complained of not being able to understand him. But usually his writing and speech were plain and direct.)

The performance of the navy when war came in 1739 has been the ground on which he has been judged historically. Did his many capabilities fail to translate to performance? The question implies that a First Lord had substantial control. Yet he did not even control appointments of admirals to key commands. The Channel fleet was given to senior admirals, either Sir John Balchen or the elderly Sir John Norris, both good men, though the latter's lack of initiative as a fleet commander was disappointing. The most important command at this time was the West Indies. As noted above, Vernon was Wager's choice and Wager had to fight for it; there was none better to be made, though toward the end even Vernon's performance was disappointing.

The First Lord could try to influence strategy but could not determine it. Key decisions were made by a small circle of ministers; Wager and Norris were the 'seamen' experts. Wager's strategic ideas had been formed in what has been accurately termed an 'age of uncontested British supremacy'.[40] British naval policy aimed at overawing all possible opponents – not just to deter but to dishearten them from even contemplating a naval challenge. The policy was actively pursued. But Wager knew that, in war, a superior battlefleet could not of itself carry out anything quick and decisive against Spain: the enemy's fleets avoided confrontation; the galleons declined to sail; Spanish trade was placed with neutral shipping. Meanwhile, Spanish cruisers and privateers feasted on British shipping. This was happening in 1727 when Wager wrote to Walpole: 'You will I hope pardon my being so free; but I am very much afraid, that if you do not send ships every where, there will be great number of Merchant ships taken, tho' the squadron may be strong enough to defend themselves.'[41] Throughout his career he regarded the protection of British trade as a fundamental, not peripheral, object of seapower, not least because trade was a constant, serious political consideration in the House of Commons – as Wager himself thought it should be. In accord with this view he was a forceful advocate of the new and improved naval bases that Britain established in the early 1730s in the West Indies, the region where the richest trades of the time were centred.

From 1715 to 1739 every use of the British navy that Wager had witnessed was defensive, yet he often turned his thoughts to the problem of how Britain's naval force might be used offensively. Although he was aware of the emerging commercial challenge of France, the perennially troublesome adversary was Spain, and the way to defeat Spain in a war was to shut off its supply of silver from the New World. The ideal method would be to capture incoming galleons in European waters, but this, as he knew from direct experience, was extremely hard to do – in fact, never achieved – because they were too easily forewarned. An offensive enterprise against the Spanish overseas was therefore required; Wager compiled lists of the possibilities.

He preferred objectives that could be achieved rapidly with moderate force, for it apparently did not take much to deter the Spanish from attempting to ship the silver. Vernon's speedy conquest of Porto Bello suited Wager's criteria. The other major shipping point for silver that was weakly defended was Vera Cruz, but since it was far to leeward, he thought it should not be an early choice. The strategy that would perplex the Spanish the most, and do them the greatest harm in proportion to British effort, would be to threaten the Peruvian coast from the 'South Sea'. This was where the silver shipments to Panama and Porto Bello originated. Difficult as a voyage to the Pacific was, Wager had long believed that this enterprise would hurt Spain more profoundly and durably than anything done in the Caribbean. Anson's famous voyage round the world which left England in 1740 was a result of Wager's advocacy, but it was not given the level of resources he had thought necessary for effectively coercing the Peruvian ports, so the Manila galleon became its key objective.

The strategy actually chosen, which absorbed nearly all available resources, was the Duke of Newcastle's. To satisfy the parliamentary opposition the duke wanted something big done – an attack on Havana. Wager opposed this; he knew that Havana had become too strongly fortified in recent years, that the requirements of taking such a place were enormous (at least 8000 soldiers would have to be gathered and transported), and that sending so large a force with its accompanying fleet far to leeward would expose Jamaica and other British islands to enemy attack. He knew that big operations in the West Indies could easily end in big failures – a possibility to which Newcastle seemed oblivious – and that Britain had had no experience of transatlantic combined operations as large as this one would be. Wager therefore feared delays and was well aware that in the West Indies delays were fatal because tropical diseases would speedily decimate the forces. He had no doubt that Vernon, too, understood this. Even so, on 6 August 1740 Wager reminded Vernon (with heavy irony for emphasis): 'you know, as well as I, that whatever is determined to be put in Execution, must be immediately proceeded upon, for Soldiers, no more than other People, cannot do any thing when they are dead, and that will be their Fate if they stay too long at Jamaica.'[42]

The words 'whatever is determined to be put in Execution' signify Newcastle's dominance. Because the duke would not give up the idea of Havana, the joint commanders were left to decide when the army arrived in the Caribbean whether Havana or Cartagena should be the objective. As a result, Wager and Norris had to draw up plans for either possibility, which they did pretty well, but a clear focus on Cartagena (chosen without hesitation by the joint commanders), could have improved the planning. The story of failure at Cartagena is well known. What occurred in the aftermath is less familiar. Faced with a general European war in 1741, Wager urged Vernon either to achieve a lesser objective speedily or else send some ships of the line home.[43] Unfortunately, Vernon did neither.

The long-standing historical presumption that the navy was ill-prepared for war in 1739 has lacked specifics, but one point of criticism has been prominent: the comparative backwardness of British warship design. When all factors are considered a comprehensive indictment is unjustified, but certainly the class of three-decked 80-gun ships should have been drastically altered or else eliminated. Wager had heard complaints of the instability of some of these ships, but appears not to have considered the matter urgent. With respect to ships the truly serious and immediate problem, brought to the fore by Vernon's reluctance to send ships home, was the shortage of 60s and 70s. With so many of these in the West Indies the Admiralty was obliged to commission quite a few 'great ships' of 90 and 100 guns for the Channel squadron. Their firepower was not needed at this time; they were less versatile and their manning requirements were appalling. The conservatism of the 'navy list', which implied a fixed number of ships of each rate, was ultimately to blame. All-weather ships efficient for distant theatres were now the prime need, and too many of the largest classes had been maintained and rebuilt. Wager's Admiralty may be credited with two sensible, if relatively minor, steps: increasing the number of 60-gun ships and speedily ordering new frigates built in merchant yards when war broke out. Otherwise, it must be acknowledged, the conservatism of the navy list and established designs persisted.

Ships were not the main problem; manning them was, and Wager had long been aware of this fact. In May 1731 he remarked: '. . . we have no difficulty but in getting men; . . . our Country being such a free Country, that every man does what he pleases: by reason of which, this Nation will be lossd [*sic*] one time or other, if it wont admit of a remedy.' He favoured keeping guardships in commission through the winter to ease the manning problem. In a debate of 28 January 1734 he urged the House not to delay voting the sea service estimate, saying, 'seamen are long in getting, and now is the season'. Manning had not been easy even in the annual peacetime mobilisations of the 1730s, and soon after the outbreak of war Wager, strongly encouraged by Norris, pressed for legislative measures; the government introduced bills to facilitate manning, both in early 1740 and in 1741, and Walpole supported them, but Parliament would not pass anything meaningful.

The second year of the war, 1740, produced a disaster, not only because skilled seamen, now much in demand by the merchant marine at higher wages, desperately avoided impressment, but also because those recruited fell sick in great numbers. By a stroke of ill-fortune the winter of 1739-40 was one of the coldest in modern history, and when the men contrived to keep warm and were crowded together they transmitted typhus in epidemic proportion (lice were the agents). There were no naval hospitals, only hired sick quarters which were often inadequate and soon over-whelmed. At least ten per cent of the men died, more ran away, and while the others slowly recuperated the augmentation of 1740 reached a standstill – this at the moment when everyone was anxious for the departure of the fleet with the army for the West Indies. Opposition criticism reached its loudest pitch. Had it not been for the dreadful epidemic, the British navy's preparedness would surely have appeared more satisfactory to posterity.[44]

The purpose of the opposition 'Patriots' was not only to start a war that would 'humble Spain' (they presumed) but also to get rid of Walpole.[45] Wager defended his chief with all he had. Captain Thomas Smith, who witnessed the great debate in the House of Commons (13 February 1741) on the motion to petition the King to remove Sir Robert Walpole from office, reported to Admiral Richard Haddock:

> Sir Charles Wager is as Hearty as I ever knew Him, spoke in the motion . . . at four in the morning, tho He had been there from seven the morning before. He said that Sir Robert was called the Ruling Minister, & therefore was to answer for all mismanagements, in every office; He must say that if there had been any in the Office of Admiralty, He & the rest of the Board ought to answer it at their own peril, & not Sir Robert who He affirmed never interfered farther than pressing in the strongest terms for the Fleets being fitted from time to time with the greatest Dispatch.[46]

There are strong reasons to believe that Wager really meant this, though few First Lords of the eighteenth century were prepared to say the same.

On that February night Wager was almost 76 years of age. According to Smith, he had been twenty-one hours in the House when he rose to speak. He had been ill on a couple of occasions in the 1730s, but frailty was not the reason why he suggested to the King that Norris should convey him across to Hanover in May 1740, for at that moment Sir John Balchen's squadron, cruising off Ferrol, appeared to be in danger and the First Lord wanted to stay close to the Admiralty office. George II refused, saying, 'No, you shall go.' Certainly he trusted Wager's judgement as a seaman. There had arisen an instance in December 1736 where, halfway back from Hellevoetsluis, the wind had shifted during the night, bringing a violent storm, and Wager decided to turn back, which proved to be very wise. (Court gossip had it that while waiting at Hellevoetsluis the King was so impatient to sail that he had said to Sir Charles, 'Let it be what weather it will, I am not afraid,' to which Wager had replied, 'If you are not, I am.')[47] The King insisted again in May 1741 that Wager must be the admiral to convey him across, even though the timing fell in the midst of the Westminster election. As it happened, there was a surprise nomination of Vernon, and seeing the flow of voting go towards the hero of Porto Bello the bailiff peremptorily closed the poll, thus provoking a riot. Some men commented that Wager had been fortunate to be absent (his fellow candidate, Lord Sundon, feared for his life and hid in a church), but his absence was tremendously unfortunate for Walpole's ministry because if anyone could have, and would have, spoken to the crowd, it was Wager; he was still a popular admiral and the challenge might not even have been instigated if the King had not taken him away. Just before Christmas 1741 the House voided the election by a vote of 220 to 216 and Wager lost his Westminster seat. On 9 January 1742 he had an audience with the King and asked to resign, pleading age and infirmities. The King replied, 'I don't see that, and you shall serve me on.' But Walpole's hold on the House of Commons was slipping away and his fall triggered Wager's resignation as First Lord of the Admiralty, on 11 February (the new Board took office a month later).[48]

In December 1742 Wager was appointed Treasurer of the Navy, a handsome sinecure which served as a pension. He remained in Parliament, having been elected for West Looe in tandem with his old friend Benjamin Keene, recalled from Madrid in wartime. There is no indication that he visited Cornwall at this time, though he remained in touch with the borough's politics. Since 1720 Wager had leased Hollybush, a stately brick house, evidently rebuilt in the Queen Anne style (demolished 1884) and situated at the southeast corner of Parson's Green, Fulham. He was there often and seems to have loved the place. But he was reportedly living at Stanley House, Chelsea when he died, peacefully, on 23 May 1743, aged 77.[49]

His chief heir was Charles Bolton, son of his sister, Prudence. Wager's widow, Martha, was his executor. They had no children, but numerous relatives, many stemming from his half-sisters – all of whom he is said to have helped financially or by appropriate patronage recommendations. Yet Wager was also known for spreading his generosity very widely, to individuals in need as well as philanthropic organisations. Francis Gashry, long his right-hand man of business (and successor as resident of Hollybush House as well as an MP for East Looe) arranged the monument in Westminster Abbey. The core of the epitaph reads:

A man of great natural talents, improved by industry, and long experience, who bore the highest commands, and passed through the greatest employments with credit to himself and honour to his country. He was, in his private life, humane, temperate, just, and bountiful. In public station valiant, prudent, wise, and honest; easy of access to all; steady and resolute in his conduct; so remarkably happy in his presence of mind, that no danger ever discomposed him.

Epitaphs are of course a suspect genre, but every surviving scrap of evidence confirms the truth of this one. Lady Wager died in 1748 and was buried next to him, in the north cross.[50]

Sir John Norris. Oil by George Knapton

5

Sir John Norris
1660?-1749

'there never breathed a better seaman'

DAVID ALDRIDGE

Sir John Norris's parentage and date and place of birth remain unknown. Sir John Knox Laughton supposed that the future admiral was probably identical to a John Norris of Speke, Lancashire who was born in 1662, but a reference to *The Norris Papers*, published by the Chetham Society in 1846, would have immediately convinced Knox Laughton that such identification was erroneous. He also seems not to have given credence to John Campbell's early nineteenth century statement in the *Lives of the Admirals* that Norris came of a 'respectable' family in Ireland, perhaps because Campbell cited no authority for it. In fact, both on the basis of his marriage in 1699, at the age of 29, to Elizabeth Aylmer of Balrath, County Meath, which was followed by frequent Norris–Aylmer intermarriages well into the eighteenth century, and of substantial evidence of property dealings in Dublin and Newcastle, County Down, in which Norris was involved in the 1720s and 1730s, it seems that Campbell's statement can probably be upheld. Norris's grant of arms, which came with his knighthood in 1705, involved a blazon in which the arms of Aylmer and Norris of Speke were impaled. There is no evidence that the adoption of the latter was contested, and this in turn suggests that a branch of the Norris of Speke family had been earlier 'planted' in Ireland. The admiral may, therefore, have been a relative, though perhaps a distant one, of his namesake born some eight years earlier.[1]

On 14 September 1680 while the *Gloucester Hulk* was victualling at Woolwich Norris was entered on the ship as a servant to Richard Borthwick, the ship's captain. It is perhaps possible that Norris had already served at sea as the ship's paybook records a ticket number beside Norris's name.[2] The *Gloucester Hulk* arrived in Tangier at the end of December 1680 and in January 1681 was sent to Gibraltar and cut down to become a careening hulk. The ship's crew was discharged and Norris joined the *Sapphire,* commanded by Cloudesley Shovell, on 19 February 1681. Shovell was to become Norris's patron and friend. Through Shovell the adolescent Norris had an early introduction to diplomatic niceties when dealing with North African potentates.[3]

Norris was entered as a midshipman on the Third Rate *Anne* on 2 June 1687. The *Anne* was the flagship of Henry, Duke of Grafton, and Shovell was Grafton's flag captain. Grafton carried the new Queen of Portugal, Princess Marie Sofia Isabel of Neuberg, to Lisbon – a contact that Norris probably found useful in later years. The *Anne* sailed on into the Mediterranean to make sure that the Barbary states pirates were not breaking the treaty.[4] When the *Anne* returned to England in 1688 Shovell and Norris moved to the *Duke*, and served as part of the fleet under George Legge, Baron Dartmouth at the time of William's invasion.

On 27 March 1689 Norris was entered as a midshipman on the *Edgar*, commanded by Shovell, and took part in the Battle of Bantry Bay on 1 May 1689, where the ship was immediately ahead of the *Elizabeth*, the flagship of Arthur Herbert. The *Edgar* was badly damaged and had 13 men killed and 42 wounded. Norris was present at Portsmouth when William of Orange visited the fleet and knighted Shovell. In August 1689 he was promoted to lieutenant on the *Edgar*. Norris moved in October 1689 to the *Monck*, which took part in the abortive attempt on Kinsale. Shovell was rear-admiral of the blue in 1690 and commanded a small force on the Irish coast. Norris took part in Shovell's recapture of the *Pelican* fireship in Dublin Bay. On 11 June 1690 Shovell escorted William of Orange to Belfast.[5]

It was Shovell who appointed Norris to the command of the *Pelican* fireship on July 1690. Norris served on the courts martial which tried and acquitted Arthur, Earl of Torrington for his conduct on 30 June 1690.[6] In January 1691 Norris returned to the Straits in the *Pelican*, but by October he was back in Irish waters. He was stationed in the Shannon following the surrender of Jacobite forces in Limerick. Recommended by Shovell, Norris commanded the *Spy* fireship in February 1692. The appointment proved profitable for Norris as he took two French frigates, which gave him £1000 or more in prize money, although, on the basis of the number of brass guns taken, he claimed six times that sum. Norris, as part of the red squadron commanded by Edward Russell, was present La Hogue in May 1692.[7]

Shortly afterwards he made his first Atlantic passage to Newfoundland. In February 1693 Norris was appointed to the Sixth Rate *Sheerness*, and in June took part in the convoy action off Lagos with the combined Brest and Toulon fleet during which almost a third of the valuable 300-strong Smyrna Convoy was taken. The *Sheerness* became separated from Rooke but managed to avoid capture by the French, while at the same time protecting vulnerable merchantmen. Because of this conduct, Norris was promoted to the command of the Third Rate *Royal Oak* from September to December 1693. In 1694 Norris was appointed Admiral Thomas Hopsonn's second captain in the Third Rate *Russell* but was paid as the captain of a Second Rate.

The Mediterranean and Newfoundland

In May 1694 Norris's career entered a new stage. He was despatched with the fleet under Edward Russell to the western Mediterranean. Russell, the victor of La Hogue, was one of the most contentious and acerbic senior naval officers of his day. A major figure in Whig politics and the executant of William III's naval strategy, Russell was both First Lord of the Admiralty and Treasurer of the Navy. His operational purpose in the Mediterranean was exceptional – to keep Spain and Savoy at the side of the allies against France. This demanded that the fleet stay out in the Mediterranean over winter, which in turn imposed new logistical requirements. Russell returned to England in October 1695. For eighteen months Norris served with this fleet, laying the foundations for an advantageous association with Russell and gaining more experience in the management of large naval forces in distant waters.

Norris commanded the Fourth Rate *Carlisle* in 1695 and was part of the small squadron of five ships under James Killigrew which met the two French ships *Content* and *Trident* between Pantellaria and the Tunisian coast on 18/19 January 1694/5. After a long chase and fight, during which Killigrew was killed and the captain of the *Southampton*, Richard Kirkby, was seen to fall out of the fleet, Norris and the other two ships captured the badly damaged *Content* and shared in the prize money.[8] It was a feat of seamanship as well as accurate gunnery since not only were all the *Content*'s masts severely damaged, but the main mast of the *Carlisle* herself had to be secured before the pursuit could begin. Russell immediately recognised Norris's quality, and the *Content*, converted to a 70-gun ship at Woolwich in 1696, served as Norris's ship from 1696 to February 1697, when he was appointed commodore of a squadron going to Newfoundland and transferred to the *Monck*.

With the possible exception of the Admiralty's role in George I's British ministerial crisis over the winter of 1716/17, the Newfoundland command of 1697 and its aftermath constituted the most serious threat to Norris's career. Newfoundland had never been an object of conquest and occupation by England; but a French decision not to occupy St John's had appeared to provide an opening for British intervention, and the port was taken by the English in June. The island was famed for its fisheries and prized in mercantilist literature as a nursery of seamen. Furthermore, the war was drawing to a close and the successful occupation of Newfoundland would strengthen the English position at the imminent peace negotiations. The French were established at Placentia, over one hundred miles to the southwest of St John's across trackless terrain. They were numerically superior in ships and were known to have a further force at Carbonear on Conception Bay, only twenty miles west of St John's. Norris's instructions warned him that success in Newfoundland would depend on maintaining 'a good agreement' with Colonel John Gibson, the commander of the 750 troops that accompanied him. Ensuing events revealed not only that this command was a collective one, but that Gibson had rather more power in decision making than Norris. This was compounded by the generality of the instructions, later 'disapproved' by a House of Lords committee in June 1699.

While on the passage to Newfoundland, and in the course of two cruises when the fleet had arrived, Norris's ships had taken a number of prizes, worth over £40,000, or so it was later claimed. A decision on 24 July to concentrate the prizes and the squadrons alike behind a boom in St John's harbour appeared to reflect a greater concern to protect the prizes than attack the French. A further decision taken on the same day, 24 July, proved to have much greater consequences. Captain Charles Desborow, who commanded the fast-sailing *Mary Galley*, was ordered to discover French strength. During Desborow's five-day absence news was received in St John's of a weak French force carrying Spanish treasure from Cartagena. Desborow seems to have sighted the French briefly before he returned. Almost immediately on his return Norris sent Desborow out again to cruise south and west of Placentia. This instruction seems to have been given because Norris failed to obtain a majority vote in favour of the entire naval force at St John's sailing in pursuit of the French. However, the reports of Spanish treasure and the vote against moving out of St John's, which would have divided the naval forces and the army, probably caused an increasing mutual suspicion among the officers. Desborow returned after almost ten days' cruising and reported that he had been north to Conception Bay where he had found a large French force bound for Quebec. His disobedience in regard to his orders and his imprecise reporting, despite two prolonged absences, may have rendered Desborow a convenient scapegoat. Desborow was found guilty by a majority verdict at a court martial and was 'broken'. This set in train a bitter wrangle, leading to the Lord's committee of enquiry in March 1699.

Norris returned to England with his squadron in October 1697. Russell, by now Lord Orford, refused to countenance Desborow's complaints early in 1698 and Norris moved to the Fourth Rate *Winchester*. He was sent to Genoa, where he was visited by the Grand Duke and Duchess of Tuscany.[9] Norris returned to England in October 1699 to find that in his absence Desborow had accused Norris of embezzling the prize money and that he had been suspended. The war was now over and the Commons was increasingly antagonistic towards the 'Whig Junto', hounding Orford for his 'negligence, mismanagement and malversation'. The Lords committee which examined the 1697 Newfoundland expedition found the structure and scope of the command to be at fault and that Desborow's breaking was wrongful. Under Desborow's accusation of embezzlement, Norris was suspended in April 1699. A month later, on 13 May, Orford finally resigned as First Lord of the Admiralty and Treasurer of the Navy.

It was probably during this period that Norris married Elizabeth, eldest daughter of Admiral Mathew Aylmer. He lay under suspension until March 1701. During this phase of his career, Norris had gained a reputation for cupidity beyond accepted practice, although he was, in part, the victim of circumstance. The last year of the war had involved huge expenditure on the navy – 34 per cent of government expenditure. However justifiable this may have been, profits were evidently being made by well-placed individuals such as Orford. Prize money disputes were hard to separate from the hot political issue of taxation and wartime expenditure. The hostility of the Commons to Orford and the Whig Junto was reflected in the financial peculation that Norris's case seemed to represent. The crisis over the Spanish Succession appeared for a time to threaten the Junto further, but it survived a snap election in the autumn of 1700. From June 1701 William's propaganda, and the disinclination of the Lords to pursue the impeachment of Somers, Orford and Portland over their formal implication in the King's secret diplomacy, led to a stabilisation of the Whig position.

Norris petitioned the House of Lords in 1701 to have the suspension lifted. The Lords agreed to hear the case. When Norris learnt of the Lords' decision he wrote to Josiah Burchett, the Admiralty secretary, asking if the Admiralty Board would allow seven captains 'that they may be in town to be present at the said hearing' and also that various warrant officers could attend the hearing. In his defence before the Lords Norris pleaded that 'he was highly sensible of misfortune in lying under the displeasure of the House'.[10] Norris's appeal to the House of Lords was successful as the Lords voted to approach King William to have his suspension lifted. Twelve Lords, among them the Earl of Torrington, entered a protest against the outcome on the grounds that Norris's suspension could not be removed as long as he did not face a court martial. The protest remained a stigma on Norris, and a potentially dangerous one with Tory fortunes waxing. While impeachment processes were dropped in mid-June 1701, an attempt was made to revive them in the following year. Not until October 1709 would Whig fortunes be revived to the point where Russell would accept a second term as First Lord.

Command Again: Cadiz and the Mediterranean, 1702–1708

Following his reinstatement, Norris was appointed captain of the *Russell* in April 1701, and three months later he informed Josiah Burchett that 'yesterday the vessel was discharged and when their lordships shall have any further Sarvis for me I shall be ready to receive them'. He also told Burchett, 'I do believe I am one that has bin least imployed since the peace and have not received my wages since it . . . Since I see gentellman continewed in pay that have bin much longer in commission since the Peace than my selfe, I am in hope my discharge is not ment of their Lordships displeasure.'[11] Norris did not have to worry, as in December he was appointed captain of the *Orford* and ordered to join Rooke and Shovell at Cadiz. Shortly before he left Portsmouth Norris was involved in a dispute with the Dockyard Commissioner, Henry Greenhill. Norris had pressed one George Watmore who had then offered to serve as a volunteer. He asked leave to go on shore and get what he needed and Norris agreed. When the ship was ready to sail Norris sent his lieutenant on shore to get Watmore. Norris's lieutenant had to use force, as he found that Watmore had persuaded Greenhill to issue him a protection, dated 14 February 'to fetch fire faggotts, but . . . I am credibly informed he has not . . . been employed in that service, but I am told his usual employment is smuggling to the coast of France.' Norris also informed Burchett that Greenhill was likely to write to get Watmore's impressment overturned, as Greenhill's attitude was 'we ought not to impress any man'.[12] Norris joined Rooke's fleet on 8 August 1702 and was assigned to the blue squadron, commanded by Shovell. On 22 August, when Norris came on board Rooke's ship, the Newfoundland episode came back to haunt him. Captain Lord Archibald Hamilton,

Thomas Ley, James Wishart and Captain Trevor were gathered on the quarterdeck. Hamilton asked Norris if he had taken any more wine or brandy, and Norris answered no: upon which Captain Trevor asked the price of his claret, whether he might have any at 41 shillings a hogshead. Norris said he would have £6 or saltwater, and Captain Ley told Norris 'he would rather the prizes were ashore' than he would give £6 a hogshead. At this retort Norris told Ley 'he was a rascal that wished his prizes ashore; the other replied he was a rascal if he called him so'. Norris then struck Ley 'and threw him over the gun'. When Rooke found out what had happened he ordered Norris to be confined, 'upon which Captain Norris drew his sword and offered to stab Captain Ley'. Hopsonn held Norris's arm and ordered him to be disarmed and confined. The next day, 23 August, Rooke suspended Norris 'for the affront, insolence and indignity offerd to her Majesty's service and flag'. Norris was replaced as captain of the *Orford* and confined on the *Prince George* until 29 August, when his suspension was taken off 'upon his own submission and being sorry for his fault, and the application of his Grace the Duke of Ormonde'.[13]

Norris commanded the small flotilla of boats taking the soundings of Cadiz harbour during the nights of 3 and 4 September which revealed that the only passage ran within pistol shot of Puntales Castle. Consequently it was decided at a Council of War that if both the forts were taken then the fleet could force a passage and destroy the enemy ships and galleys. However, it was decided not to attempt it and the fleet left Cadiz. Rooke learnt that the Spanish silver fleet was unloading at Vigo bay and stood away for Vigo. While a council of war was being held, Norris, who was near the boom, came on board the *Royal Sovereign* and gave Rooke 'a pretty near account of the batteries and position of the boom'; Norris's was one of the ships that took part in the attack, landing soldiers.[14] Norris remained in the Mediterranean, serving under Shovell and Rooke in 1703 and in 1704. It was at this point that Norris met Edward Vernon, who was serving as fifth lieutenant on the *Barfleur*, Shovell's flagship. Vernon and Norris became friends.[15] Norris was Shovell's second in the line of battle at Málaga on 13 August 1704, having 6 killed and 9 wounded. In January 1705 he moved from the *Orford* to become Shovell's flag captain on the *Britannia*, where he remained until October 1706.

An attack on Toulon had been a long-standing objective of the Duke of Marlborough, both as a means of destroying French naval power in the Mediterranean and as a step towards stimulating unrest in Provence among the Protestant Cevennois. Charles Mordaunt, Earl of Peterborough, and Shovell were appointed joint admirals of the fleet. Owen described Norris

as serving as 'chief of staff to the joint admirals'.[16] This was clearly resented
by Peterborough, who complained to Sidney Godolphin that Shovell was
'entirely governed by one Norris . . . a man of whom I can say no good
. . . This gentleman, who thinks himself fit to govern the world, has been
meddling in all things, and by accident and circumstances, has been prevailing in many matters, much to my dissatisfaction.' Norris acted as 'the
mouthpiece' between Shovell and Prince George of Hesse-Darmstadt over
making a last push against Barcelona. Peterborough decided to attack Fort
Monjuich, the fortress on top of the hill which dominated Barcelona.
Shovell lent seamen and cannons to attack the vital fort. Norris played his
part by preparing scaling ladders and the Marine regiments to accompany
Captain Philip Cavendish of the *Antelope*. He also collected arms for Cata-
lan auxiliaries. In September 1705 the allies captured Barcelona. When in
November Norris returned to England to convey the good news to the
queen, she knighted him.[17] It is possible that Norris's knighthood was as
much in recognition of his services at Barcelona as for being the bearer of
the good news to the queen.

Norris returned to Lisbon early in 1706 and transferred to the *Torbay*.
When Norris heard he had been made rear-admiral of the blue in March
1707 he wrote from Lisbon to Burchett, 'I pray of you to give my humble
dutyfull thanks to his Royal Hiness for the grate favors he has bin pleased to
be Stow upon me. I shall Ever, with all duty youse my utmost deligence to
obay all his Royal Hiness is Command.'[18] The plan to attack Toulon was
revived in 1707. Shovell warmly supported the plan, but the magazines
were short of stores and it was uncertain how far a mortar bombardment
would damage the port's facilities. Shovell was also unable to raise adequate
credit at Genoa or Leghorn to provide the Imperialists with the powder,
munitions and grain that they had been promised in London. Shortages in
siege ordnance were the more serious since Victor Amadeus of Savoy,
Eugene's confederate, considered that Monaco, Antibes and Villefranche,
all strong places, should be taken on the march to Toulon. Shovell believed
these places could and should be by-passed, so an envoy to the court at
Savoy was required and Norris was Shovell's choice. Norris arrived at
Turin in May, where he had to deal with ordnance and commissariat
problems and the competing appeal by the Imperialists for an attack upon
Naples. The force available, more north German mercenary than Savoyard,
amounted to about 45,000. In six weeks, apart from transmitting Shovell's
assurances against a background of consistent scepticism, Norris successfully
negotiated ordnance and grain supplies. He rejoined Shovell off Finale at
the end of June. On 30 June Norris led a force of over 500 seamen to storm

the French works at the Var crossing in advance of the army marching west from Ventimiglia. The later abandonment of the siege of Toulon was not owing to the navy. Despite capricious weather and the tactics of the French galleys, the bombardment of the port was sufficiently effective to prevent the Toulon fleet, much of which had been deliberately semi-submerged by the French, from appearing as a force again during the war.

Norris narrowly escaped the disaster off the Scillies in which Shovell drowned on the night of 22/23 October 1707. It stunned the navy and personally affected Norris. It was probably for this reason that he became interested in the search for the discovery of longitude and one of the Commissioners of the Board from 1714. Norris was elected as Rye's MP in 1708, possibly through the influence of John Lord Somers, and he also bought Hempstead Park at Benenden, Kent from the Guldeford family. Norris was appointed as rear-admiral of the white on 8 January 1708, hoisting his flag on the *Ranelagh* on 8 March 1708.

During 1708 Norris served in the Mediterranean under Sir John Leake. He took no part in the capture of Minorca, but briefly returned to Turin to conduct Charles III's consort to Genoa, whence she sailed for Spain. Norris was appointed vice-admiral of the red on 18 December 1708 and three days later was appointed admiral of the blue. In 1709 Norris succeeded Aylmer as captain of Deal Castle and served under Leake again. While Leake watched Dunkirk and Nieuport, Norris cruised off the Dutch coast, and in June Norris was sent to the Sound to intercept grain shipments from the Baltic to famine-stricken France. Norris wrote from the Sound that he was 'master in those seas, and shall be able to stop at least 100 sail of ships, most neutral and some Dutch, laden with corn for France'. Norris 'having stopped all the neuter ships laden with corn in the Sound' in fact let the Dutch ships go, even though he suspected that they carried corn for France and only took some Swedish merchantmen. Norris was thanked by the Dutch representatives in Copenhagen for his discretion over the Dutch ships.[19] This was Norris's introduction to the complex nature of Baltic trading and its accompanying subterfuges. He met the long-serving British representative at Elsinore, Robert Tigh, always a valuable source of intelligence and a skilful moderator between British mercantile masters and Sound Toll officialdom.

Norris was appointed commander-in-chief in the Mediterranean. Although his old patron, Orford, was back at the Admiralty, relations between the two men had cooled, particularly over Norris's criticisms of Sir George Byng's failure to trap Forbin's expedition off the east coast of Scotland in 1708. Hence it is probable that Norris received this

appointment more by rotation than the particular favour of Orford. Norris
arrived at Minorca on 13 March 1710 to supply the allied army in Cata-
lonia, in preparation for Stanhope's drive on Madrid, but this ended when
Stanhope surrendered at Brihuega in December. In July 1710 Norris had
carried 1000 troops commanded by Colonel Seissan to Cette in Languedoc
to assist a revolt in the Cevennes. The town was successfully taken on 13
July, but the Duke de Noailles retook the town on 19 July, when the army
re-embarked. In 1710 Norris also issued eight chasing signals which were
later incorporated into the eighteenth century sailing instructions.[20] In June
1711 Sir John Jennings, who was senior to Norris, came out to strengthen
the fleet in the Mediterranean. He did not supersede Norris but worked
jointly with him. The allied cause in Spain was by now defunct: the new
Tory administration had no desire to support Charles III after he had
succeeded his brother Joseph I as the Emperor Charles VI. Shortly before
Charles left for Vienna he conferred a Neapolitan dukedom on Norris
worth 4000 ducats a year. Norris did not use the title and probably did not
receive the pension, though he did leave it to his two sons John and
Henry.[21] Overall the command may have been work-a-day, but as for all
his fellow officers, experience of Dutch unwillingness to shoulder with
Britain the burden of maintaining an effective naval presence in the Mediterranean left Norris with no illusions about the nature of the Anglo–Dutch
partnership; and their concerns about Vienna's ambitions in the southern
Netherlands were well known. Norris made no secret of his distaste for the
timorousness of their naval commanders regarding Genoa's support for
Franco–Spanish designs on Sardinia in 1711.[22]

The Baltic, 1715-1716

Norris returned to England in 1712 and did not serve again until 1715. The
Tory domination at home precluded Norris from office. He was secure in
his seat at Rye, with his long-serving fellow member, Phillips Gybbon, and
he retained his captainship of Deal Castle, however unremunerative that
post might be. Abroad, the energies of the Tory administration were directed towards the pacific resolution of outstanding issues in western and
southern Europe, in indispensable collaboration with France. In so far as
the ministry comprehended the complexities of the Great Northern War as
it stood in 1714, it hoped that, with Sweden's traditional ally France,
Britain would be able sufficiently to honour her 1700 treaty obligations to
Charles XII. This policy must not, however, so imperil relations with
Russia as to shelve the prospects of the coveted commercial treaty, hopes of
which were supported by the knowledge that Britain was by far Russia's

most profitable trading partner. In the years to come Norris was to exercise command in the Baltic and he never let this over-riding commercial objective slip from his view.

By the time the Elector of Hanover, as George I, assumed the British crown in 1714, the strains of the Great Northern War were drastically eroding Swedish strength in northwest Germany. By 1710 Danish privateers were seizing neutral vessels trading with Sweden, including British ships. In the same year Swedish privateers were encouraged to attack neutrals, to deny Russia any commercial advantage from the east Baltic ports she had wrested from Sweden. Hanoverian plans to eject the Danes from Bremen, which the Danes had taken in August 1712, punctuated much Hanoverian policy until they evacuated the duchy in October 1715, following a Hanoverian payment and an electoral declaration of war on Sweden. Hence after George I's accession Hanover would be especially guarded in any naval undertaking Britain might give Denmark, even though Charles XII's privateering policy, made yet more severe by his edict of February 1715, rendered a British convoying presence in the Baltic that year inevitable.

In March 1715 Norris was appointed to command the Channel squadron. On 10 May the Admiralty Board, with Orford in the chair, drew up Norris's instructions for 'his proceeding to and from the Baltic'. It is not known if Norris nurtured a particular interest in the Baltic after his visit to the Sound in 1709, or if his seniors in flag rank, Byng and Jennings, had in turn rejected taking the command. Its significance should not be underestimated – it was to be the first time that a British squadron was to venture into the Baltic. The Baltic had a vital place in the maritime economy. It was the primary source of naval stores – tar, pitch, hemp and timber for the Royal Navy and merchant marine. Since the mid-sixteenth century the navies of Sweden and Denmark-Norway had dominated the Baltic, but the broad balance of power between them had permitted a trade in naval stores that was generally stable. In the seventeenth century the Swedish-Danish wars threatened to undermine the stablity of the Baltic trades, which stimulated some direct Dutch intervention in the Baltic, and English squadrons had tried to influence events from the Sound. The decision to send a squadron to the Baltic was a significant extension of British naval power into a new area, with all the attendant logistical and diplomatic novelties that this entailed.[23] Norris chose as his flag captain William Faulkner, who had served as his lieutenant in the 1690s. With his flag in the *Cumberland* Norris with seventeen ships escorted 106 merchantmen to Reval.[24] Primarily, it was a convoying command, which together with 200 Dutch merchantmen, under Dutch convoy, comprised the largest group of merchant ships to pass the Sound in under a week in any year between 1700 and 1729. The Baltic squadrons Norris commanded between 1715 and 1721 averaged twenty-six ships in each season, almost all of them over 50 guns, the *Cumberland* being 80 guns. Lighter draughted frigates and sloops, especially needed for channels and shoals, were increasingly added, and both in 1720 and 1721 supplementary armament included swivel guns and mortars. With the renewal of the Anglo-Swedish alliance in 1719 it was possible that engagements with Russian forces might ensue.

In 1715 it was the Swedes that posed the greatest concern to Norris. Their privateers were unrelenting and garrisons under the direct command of Charles XII held out at Stralsund and Wismar. Such were Hanoverian hopes, with clamouring Danish, Prussian and Russian allies, that British naval power could be exerted against Sweden in the south Baltic, that George I's leading Hanoverian councillor, Bernstorff, secretly asked Norris, once initial convoy work was completed, to place his ships across the vital Swedish supply lines between Karlskrona and Stralsund/Wismar – a request that was both illicit and contrary to British interests. Norris was warned by Orford that naval co-operation with the Danes against Sweden could not be countenanced by Parliament.

In the event convoying tasks in 1715 precluded hostilities against the elusive Swedish privateers. When Norris arrived at Reval the Tsar was at Kronstadt but, hearing of the British visit and that Norris would return, Peter hurried to Reval. When Norris returned he found Peter with nineteen Russian ships of the line. Norris stayed for three weeks while the admiral and captains of the two fleets entertained each other and Tsarina Catharine and most of Peter's court dined with Norris on his flagship. During the visit Peter inspected the English ships and Norris was allowed to freely inspect the Russian vessels. Norris described three new 60-gun ships built in St Petersburg 'as in every way equal to the best of that rank in our country and more handsomely furnished'. At the end of the visit Peter offered Norris the command of the Russian navy, which he declined, but despite Norris's refusal Peter gave him his royal portrait set in diamonds. Among the gifts Norris gave Peter was 'a clock I had of Tompion, made to bear the motion of the sea, also the chairs of my cabin which he afterwards used in his own ship.'[25] In October Norris sent eight of his 50 gun ships to assist the Danes in the localised waters of the south Baltic. This operation was authorised by Hanover and aroused concern and anger at the Admiralty: the detachment must assist Danish operations against the Swedes in Stralsund, but any consequent parliamentary enquiry was avoided because the ships' movements could not be distinguished from convoy work. In the same month Hanover declared war on Sweden, but Britain remained strictly neutral. Even before this, Norris's Baltic command had revealed to the admiral that British and Hanoverian interests were dangerously divergent.

In 1716, with the Swedes defeated in Germany, George I, as Elector of Hanover, was under less pressure from his allies. Nevertheless, Norris was sent out to the Baltic again in 1716 with a squadron of seventeen ships, once more flying his flag in the *Cumberland*, with Faulkner his flag captain. Relations between Norris and Orford were becoming increasingly acerbic and Norris was denied a junior flag officer and the customary provision of a spare set of topmasts. At Copenhagen, under instructions from the King, Norris was to wait with the convoy until an answer was received from Charles XII to renewed protests over British trade dislocation. With the Dutch refusing to convoy without Norris, the admiral was finally released from waiting for a reply from Charles XII (which can hardly have been expected) by intelligence from London of Swedish links to the Jacobite cause. Norris was now free to act against the Swedes if necessary and could send a detachment with the Dutch to convoy the merchant fleet now straining to reach its destinations in the Baltic. A crisis arose, however, when Tsar Peter, at Copenhagen, abandoned the plan to invade southern Sweden and moved his 50,000 troops to winter quarters in Mecklenburg, adjacent to Hanover. Norris could not persuade the Tsar to proceed with the invasion of Sweden. He also treated as it deserved a Hanoverian plan to take drastic action against Russian forces there which included the kidnapping of Tsar Peter himself.[26] When Norris returned to England in November 1716 he found himself censured by Orford for the way he had handled his command, and Orford blocked Norris's admission to the Admiralty. At the same time Norris refused to act as Sir George Byng's second flag during the 1717 Baltic season.[27] In April 1717 Orford resigned from the Admiralty, one feature of the collapse of George I's first British ministry which Orford had done much to bring about.

At the Admiralty and back to the Baltic, 1718-1721

Norris's perceptions of Russian motives were naive, and this was proved to him in 1717 during a mission to Peter the Great, who was in Holland. George I hoped to exploit Norris's cordial relations with Peter, and his mission was shared with Charles Whitworth, Britain's uniquely informed representative in Russia from 1705-1711 and an authority on her naval potential. The Tsar's refusal to discuss a draft commercial treaty with Norris revealed to Norris and Whitworth what they had suspected, that Peter believed that Hanover's connection with Britain had irredeemably subverted her former friendship towards Russia.[28]

In March 1718 Norris was appointed to the new Admiralty Board, now under the Earl of Berkeley, which also included his seniors, Sir George Byng and Sir John Jennings. Sir Charles Wager was the fifth naval officer on this Board. Norris was again sent to the Baltic command with another flag officer as his second. Norris's squadron consisted of fourteen English ships, and there was also a substantial Dutch squadron. The embargo on all trade with Sweden, which Britain had imposed in February 1717 with the intention of starving Sweden into submission, was unpopular with British importers who were now starved of Swedish iron. The Navigation Act was temporarily suspended to permit the importation of iron from Dutch ports, where it was stockpiled by Dutch Baltic merchants, who shipped the iron out of Sweden into Königsberg. This invidious situation made Norris's position in 1718 much harder, and there were also diplomatic reasons why he could not chide his Dutch confederate over his permitting Dutch merchantmen in his charge to trade into and out of Swedish ports. In any case, Norris had too few ships to send into the east Baltic because of a perceived need to blockade Karlskrona: in the summer it seemed likely that there might be a Russo-Swedish accommodation which would lead to a junction of the two fleets to enforce a fresh condominium in the Baltic. Norris, still smarting under the Russian prevarication of 1717, avoided being sent on another mission to Russia after he returned to Copenhagen, since, as he told James Stanhope, he might as well 'be frozen in the sea' as have any prospects of success in talks with Russia. The 1718 campaign was both wearisome and fruitless as far as Norris was concerned. Meanwhile, in the Mediterranean, his professional colleague and rival Sir George Byng had won the dramatic chase action against the Spanish fleet off Cape Passaro. The Baltic would continue to be the scene of Norris's attentions, but in the coming years he did not relish the prospect and had to be continually convinced by Stanhope that he could be 'sure of all the support the King can give you'.

The death of Charles XII in action in Norway on 30 November 1718 brought radical changes in Sweden. Peace settlements with Hanover, Prussia and Denmark could now be worked out under the auspices of Britain and France. The new monarch, Ulrica Eleonora, had always deprecated her brother's privateering war and willingly terminated it in March 1719. Within a month Britain reciprocally lifted the embargo on trade with Sweden. Norris returned once more to the Baltic in June 1719 with only twelve ships under his command, as he had to await reinforcements from the Mediterranean. Queen Ulrica of Sweden and Lord Carteret, the British envoy at Stockholm, hoped that Norris's ships would be used to defend Sweden against the attacks being made on it by Russia. However, unknown to Carteret, Stanhope was not prepared to let Norris's fleet be used unless Sweden ceded the port of Stettin and a substantial part of Western Pomerania to Prussia. Sweden agreed to Stanhope's demands and in early August Stanhope released Norris to join Sweden's naval forces. Norris could now expect hostilities with the Russian navy in the eastern Baltic, which at least in galley strength considerably outnumbered the combined Anglo–Swedish fleet and could have inflicted heavy damages in any conflict that season with Norris's fleet. However, Peter withdrew his fleet and any chance of a clash was avoided.[29] In 1720 Norris was again sent to the Baltic with twenty-eight ships to act with the Swedes in a spoiling attack on Reval. However, a reconnoitre of the base's defences confirmed the impracticality of the plan. In 1721 Norris returned to the Baltic. This time his flagship was the Second Rate *Sandwich*, and he was careful to ensure against any real possibility of hostilities with Russia, especially when it became clear that a Swedish–Russian peace, on Russia's terms, might soon take place. Only under pressure from the Swedes would Norris agree to risk action with the Russians by taking his ships up to the northern end of the Stockholm archipelago, within 50 miles of the Russian forces at Åland. But once at this station he was well placed in July and August to follow the progress of the Swedish–Russian peace negotiations at Nystad. Over the winter of 1721–2 ministerial strength mustered by Walpole and Townshend proved sufficient to withstand pertinent questions and protests in the Lords arising from the size of the Navy debt, which, it was argued, could only have been escalated by Baltic squadrons that had obviously failed to succour Sweden. At the same time these questions raised legitimate questions concerning George I's constitutional propriety in using British forces for Hanoverian ends. While Sir George Byng, enobled as Viscount Torrington, was called upon to justify the expenditure in the upper house, Norris himself escaped censure.

The 1721 expedition was Norris's last trip to the Baltic. His Baltic commands brought out qualities in Norris which hitherto he had been unable to exploit – adamantine resistance to plausible requests, measured judgement, a capacity to grasp diplomatic complexities. The place of these Baltic expeditions in the record of the eighteenth century navy is difficult to assess. While the diplomatic source material is voluminous, the naval material is thin and virtually nothing is known beyond what can be deduced from Norris's own reportage of just how Baltic service became feared by the men who carried it out. In April 1721 the Swedish represent-ative in London reported home that Baltic service was 'exceedingly feared' and on the evidence above all of the climate and poor supply, many seaman had every reason to 'run'. In 1727 Norris made a brief and unremarkable return to Copenhagen in consequence of the Anglo-French guarantee of Schleswig to Denmark being currently threatened by Russia.

Admiral of the Fleet

In 1722 Norris was elected an Elder Brother of Trinity House.[30] He was also elected MP for Portsmouth in the same year. In 1723 Norris published *Maps of the Baltic and North Sea* which contained a dedication to George I, 'Your Majesty having been graciously pleased during the Troubles in the North to send into the Baltic for the protection of your subjects trading thither a squadron of your ships'. Norris's book of maps was, for the English seaman, a notable advance upon John Seller's popular *The English Pilot*, and it was probably because of this book that Norris was appointed Master of Trinity House on 24 May 1723 and to which he was re-elected in 1726 until 1733 when Sir Charles Wager replaced him.[31]

Norris was dismissed from the Admiralty in May 1730 after he and his son John attacked the government in the Dunkirk debate on 27 February. Norris voted against the government on the Army Bill in 1732 and the Excise Bill in 1733. While Walpole's ministry steadied itself and began the recovery that was to secure it until 1739, Norris was in danger of terminat-ing his naval career. In June 1733 Viscount Torrington died and Sir Charles Wager became First Lord of the Admiralty. Whether this played any part in subsequent events is unknown, but in February 1734 Norris made his peace with the government and he was appointed Admiral of the Fleet. He wrote to Walpole to thank him and also told him that the city of Rochester had offered to elect him as their member at the forthcoming general election, but he declined the offer and told Walpole he intended to stand at his old seat of Rye, where he was duly elected.

He hoisted his flag in the *Britannia* and was sent to Lisbon in 1735 with a squadron to support Portugal against Spanish threats to the Portuguese crown. Norris's diplomatic skills were again recognised, as he was ap-pointed minister plenipotentiary to act jointly with the envoy extraordinary at Lisbon, James O'Hara, Baron Tyrawley.[32] Norris worked not always harmoniously with Tyrawley to present George II's position to the King of Portugal. The king was extremely reassured by the presence of Norris's squadron, but had to be told firmly that it was not provided to support a

Portuguese attack upon Spain. Norris's past experience in dealing with Hanoverian, Danish, Swedish and Russian schemes to embroil his ships in actions contrary to British interests enabled him to tread the difficult path of supporting allies without being diverted by them. The Baltic experience also enabled him to judge the logistical limits of a squadron. From his anchorage in the Tagus he had to juggle the need to defend Portuguese trade, watch Cadiz and gauge the stores and victuals he needed for his journey home. Norris's papers show he was a stickler for all shipboard measures for battle-readiness, 'which every officer knows but may sometimes neglect'. Apart from his own journals and correspondence, his papers contain the data that one would expect of a man deeply interested in the effectiveness of the navy. He kept recipes for curing victuals, various sets of regulations and instructions, lists of artificers, lists of rates of pay and descriptions of different parts of the world. Whilst Norris's squadron lay at Lisbon, the *Centurion* arrived carrying John Harrison and his first chronometer. Norris was a member of the Board of Longitude, and when he returned to London in 1737 he was present at the first meeting of the Board to discuss the chronometer's trials.[33]

With the outbreak of war with Spain in 1739 Norris was called upon to attend meetings of ministers to prepare for the new conflict. His journal provides one of the best accounts of how ministerial thinking developed over the critical period from June to December 1739. Although he resented Wager's right to attend Cabinet as First Lord and he was irritated by Wager's changes to his plans for the winter guard, Norris actively contributed to discussions to which he was summoned. He advised on the flag officers to command the mobilised fleet, and he worked well with Wager during the early autumn of 1739 to examine various proposals to attack the Spanish Indies. Unlike Wager, Norris had never served in the West Indies, but he considered plans ranging from speculative operations in the South Seas to major attacks upon Havana. His journal shows that he had a keen understanding of the logistical and operational issues raised by these plans. The South Sea operation emerged as a small expedition under Captain George Anson, which led to his famous circumnavigation of the globe. The West Indian plan was eventually couched in general terms and formed the basis of the great expedition to the West Indies of 1740-2. Ultimately neither operation yielded the results hoped of it. Nevertheless, Anson's navigational feat and capture of the galleon *Nuestra Senora de Covadonga* became celebrated achievements that made up for other disappointments in the war. The expedition to the West Indies ended in failure and the death of about 10,000 soldiers and seamen; yet its naval commander, Edward

Vernon, was to be lauded as a hero and did much to preserve popular support for the naval war.

As Admiral of the Fleet, Norris did not have responsibility for the disposition of the fleet: this lay with the ministry and the Admiralty. However, he was kept busy in other ways. He was also appointed a Commissioner for Prize Appeals in 1739 and between 1742 and 1748 attended twenty-four meetings of the Prize Court.[34] One of the critical issues in 1739 was the need to get the fleet seaworthy and manned quickly. In September he addressed the needs for 1740. He suggested to ministers that troops and Marines should be used to make up the number of men on board the ships. Norris replied to Walpole's comment that George II would not be happy about the use of troops that their business was 'to give the King the best advice . . . and not consider what advice he would like best'. In 1740 he and Sir Charles Wager introduced a seaman's registration bill into the Commons but the bill was so severely criticised that it was withdrawn.[35]

While Norris was undertaking this work, his formal duty as Admiral of the Fleet was to command the Channel squadron, and he hoisted his flag in the *Buckingham* at Chatham on 14 June 1739. However, war was not declared until 19 October and Chatham was conveniently close to London to enable him to attend meetings with ministers during the year. During the early part of 1740 he remained in London. He attended councils of flag officers on manning the fleet in January 1740, just as he had done over thirty-five years before.[36] However, as the West Indian expedition prepared to depart, rumours arrived of the Spanish preparations at Ferrol and Cadiz. The intentions of the French at Brest were also unknown. Norris was ordered to sea with the Channel squadron. His orders were to take twenty of the line and go to Galicia to watch Spanish movements there. For most of the summer his fleet was embayed in Torbay, but as concern about the French fleet at Brest grew, so his instructions became more difficult to carry out – he could not go to Galicia and watch Brest at the same time. The position was not helped by the ministry asking him to attack St Sebastian in Guipuzgoa, inside the Bay of Biscay.[37] By September Norris was still struggling in and out of Torbay, while the French and Spanish squadrons had got out to the West Indies. The escape of the Bourbon squadrons was an immense disappointment. In June 1741 Norris was instructed to cruise between the mouth of the Channel and Finisterre. This marked an improvement on 1740 and a step towards the policy of a Western Squadron. If the French came out of Brest to go to the Mediterranean, the same wind would enable Norris to bear down on them or follow them. If they went up-Channel the westerly would allow Norris to follow as well. He was still ordered to try to attack St Sebastian if possible. It is not known who was responsible for revising the orders, but Norris keenly felt the impact of the 1740 operation. In 1741, when Pulteney claimed that the fleet had done nothing, Norris offered to fight him, but was stopped by Walpole.[38] The 1741 campaign was rather more successful, although winds and provisioning still kept the fleet at Spithead for long periods.

In February 1742 Walpole finally fell from office and Wager resigned from the Admiralty at the same time. Norris was offered the second seat on the new Admiralty Board under Lord Winchelsea. He firmly believed that he should head the Board and indignantly refused the offer.[39] Norris was extremely angry and disappointed at this turn of events. Not only had he fifty-two years' service as a captain, he had nobility from the late Holy Roman Emperor, but also, as Admiral of the Fleet, he should have access to the Cabinet and head the Admiralty. He refused the command of the Mediterranean fleet when Haddock's health broke down, and Norris warned the Duke of Newcastle that it would not do to have him as an enemy. On 4 March 1742 he had a private audience with George II to press his point but got nowhere.

For the next year Norris was in retirement, but in February 1744 he was recalled to take command of the fleet assembled to deal with a threatened French invasion. He arrived at Portsmouth on 5 February. Fourteen ships were in good condition and ready to sail. Norris remained convinced the Brest squadron would not try to pass east of him but would remain off the Lizard. He believed that the invasion threat came, not from the Brest fleet, but from the small ships assembling in the Channel ports. The years of feeling slighted had not helped. On 11 February he told Newcastle that he had long argued that Dunkirk ought to be embargoed, but he was not listened to, despite basing his views on those of his one-time patron, Orford. However, he was shocked to hear from London on the following day that large men of war had been seen off Calais. He prepared for sea immediately. Stormy weather accompanied his progress towards the Downs as he fulminated against those who had neglected the possibility of an invasion attempt that did not rely on the Brest fleet. On 24 February, whilst in the Downs, news arrived of the French off Dungeness and Norris put to sea again. On 25 February a great storm divided the two fleets and when Norris surveyed the scene on the following day the French had gone. Their invasion flotilla in the Channel ports had been badly damaged and the threat had receded. Norris remained at the Downs and requested leave to retire, 'being convinced in my conscience that my obtaining it is as necessary for His Majesty's service under the present[?] management of the Admiralty, as for my own reputation and safety'.[40]

Norris was not left entirely in retirement. In December 1744 Winchelsea resigned and a new Admiralty Board, headed by the Duke of Bedford and including George Anson, brought renewed energy to some of the problems that had beset the navy. In June 1745 Norris chaired a committee set up to investigate the ships of the Royal Navy. The 'Establishment' of 1719, which laid down the general dimensions and armament of ships, had been considered inadequate since the beginning of the war. The committee's report, which was not accepted in its entirety by the Admiralty, went some way to incorporating improved dimensions and design, proved by foreign vessels, into Royal Navy building practice. The new Establishment of November 1745 was a step towards the new designs that were to prove so important during the latter stages of the Seven Years War.[41]

The war ended with the navy having achieved two magnificent chase victories off Cape Finisterre in May and October 1747. Yet the stresses faced by the navy throughout the war had not passed without political repercussions. Discipline and valour within the officer corps had been questioned on more than one occasion since 1739 and the desire of the Admiralty to tighten control over the officers led to the Navy Bill. On 24 February 1749, five months before he died, Norris the 'naval oracle of Britain' presented a petition to the House of Commons signed by five admirals and fifty-two captains against this bill making half-pay officers subject to trial by court martial.[42] Norris died at Hempstead Park 13 June 1749 and was buried in Benenden Church, where he is commemorated by a magisterial bust by Scheemakers, erected in 1750. The epitaph mentions Norris as attaining 'supreme command with the rank of Admiral of the Fleet and Vice-Admiral of England. It is but bare justice to his Memory, to say . . . that there never breathed a better seaman, a greater officer, a braver man, a more Zealous Wellwisher to the present Establishment, nor conse-quently a truer Englishman.'[43]

In such a long career at the centre of naval affairs it was difficult for Norris not to have had a great influence on the navy that entered the War of 1739. He fought no dramatic fleet actions, but his activities represent the growing diplomatic and organisational capabilities of the navy. He repres-ented what the professional sea officer had to become as Britain's naval power developed. His abilities as diplomat, recognising the power of naval force and its impact upon allies as well as enemies, was important in developing confidence in Britain that navies possessed potentially large diplomatic power. Norris clearly recognised the limitations of sailing warships in the shallow waters of the Baltic when faced by galleys and he never underestimated the power of Russian naval forces. It is possible that for the public at large Norris's successes helped exaggerate the ability of British naval power not only to defend but to impose upon other powers. As such, the first forays of the Royal Navy into the Baltic were an important element in the development of British foreign policy in the first half of the eighteenth century. Norris's experience in the long-range diplomatic mission gave him insights into logistics, manning and ship capability that made him a valuable advisor to the Walpole ministry. Throughout his life he seems to have felt slighted by colleagues and politicians, perhaps stemming from his suspension in 1699. This may have made him at times an uneasy partner, but despite this, he was, until the end of his life, highly regarded by those same people. His claim that he had 'served the crown longer as an admiral than any man ever did, and as zealously and faithfully as any man ever can do' was a credo as well as a cause for pride.[44]

Edward Vernon. Oil by Charles Philips

6

Edward Vernon
1684–1757

Blue Water Advocate

RICHARD HARDING[1]

There are few naval officers whose reputations have fluctuated as much as
that of Edward Vernon. Lauded as a hero and patriot in the early 1740s, he
died largely forgotten by his contemporaries. In the early nineteenth century he was neglected, and with the publication of Horace Walpole's
Memoirs in 1847 he was cast as a 'silly noisy admiral' whose lust for self-
advertisement was destructive to the public good. With the development of
professional naval history from the 1870s Vernon's reputation began to rise.
Vernon's many pamphlets were seized upon as the reflections of a conscientious naval officer who offered solutions to the serious problems faced
by the navy of the 1740s. His interpretation of the disastrous expedition to
the West Indies of 1740-1742, presented in his own pamphlets and other
contemporary publications, became the accepted view of events by the
early twentieth century. By 1907 Vernon had been raised to the status of a
hero whose counsel was ignored by corrupt and incompetent politicians,
administrators and soldiers.[2] Eventually, when he had the opportunity to
exercise command in the West Indies, he was thwarted by these same
people. Today, Vernon's reputation lies somewhere between the two extremes. His violent temper is acknowledged. He never fought the great sea
battles that would have placed him in the first rank of naval heroes. Nor did
he hold high office in naval administration. Yet his pamphlets, his parliamentary speeches and his correspondence while commander in the
Channel do give him an important place in the development of the navy.
To scholars of the navy his significance has usually lain in his contribution
to manning, signalling, the development of the Western Squadron, and

discipline. These were real achievements of a highly professional officer. Recently, scholars of popular culture have linked Vernon and Nelson together as representatives of the values that fashioned British identity during the eighteenth century.[3] Whatever Vernon's long-term influence on British political culture, it is possibly in that area of his life that generated most contemporary heat – his parliamentary career – that the navy owes most to him. The naval and colonial power that underpinned Nelson's navy was not the inevitable trajectory of British history in the 1740s. For a short but significant time, Vernon was the most prominent public face of maritime war, arguing for its utility and the means by which it could be waged. He helped hold public confidence until the victories won by Anson and Hawke in 1747 consolidated maritime warfare at the heart of British politics and diplomacy.

Family Connections and Education

Edward Vernon was born on 12 November 1684, the second son of James Vernon, editor of the *London Gazette*. The Vernon family were Cheshire gentry, but this branch were men of business who had prospered during and after the Civil War, as the demands for efficient administrators grew from the state and an expanding mercantile economy. Edward's grandfather, Francis Vernon, had settled in Westminster. He was a merchant captain, who had been a victualler to the navy in 1628, and Parliament's deputy treasurer at war between 1642 and 1645. Francis married Anne Welby, daughter of a London goldsmith, and their eldest son, also Francis Vernon, continued the combination of commercial and administrative activities, before being murdered in 1677 on his way to Persia overland on a commercial venture.[4] Edward's father, James Vernon, the second son, had the benefit of a solid education at Oxford before entering secretarial service. He served Sir Joseph Williamson in Europe, sending news back of the Dutch during the first year of the Anglo-Dutch War. In 1673 Francis Vernon became private secretary to the Duke of Monmouth, the natural son of Charles II. Clearly, in Francis, the family successfully bridged the gap between their City and Parliamentary origins and the Court. James was an industrious and effective administrator and in 1679 he was elected MP for the University of Cambridge, under Monmouth's patronage. Although now integrated into the court environment, James Vernon's origins and attachment to Monmouth made him fearful of the impending succession of James, Duke of York, and he voted for the Exclusion Bill. With Monmouth's exile, Vernon's political fortunes declined. He had left Monmouth's service in 1679 to become clerk and editor of the *London Gazette*.[5]

He was not re-elected for the University, but he continued to be close to the Duke, urging a reconciliation with the King, and a warrant was issued for his arrest during Monmouth's rebellion in 1685. James was not arrested and his brother's death had at least given him an independent fortune to fall back upon if his employment was terminated.

As the plot against James II developed during 1688, Vernon allied himself with William of Orange and his fortunes revived. He was appointed private secretary to the Earl of Shrewsbury, Secretary of State, and continued to serve his successor, Sir John Trenchard. During the first half of the 1690s James Vernon played a central part in establishing the new regime and became secretary of state himself in 1697. Identified as a staunch Whig, he lost the post in 1702, with the revival of Tory power after the accession of Queen Anne. In 1695 James Vernon was elected as MP for Penryn, a seat which he exchanged for Westminster in the 1701 election, but returned to hold it again in both the 1705 and 1708 elections.

While these events absorbed James Vernon's time and energies, almost nothing is known of Edward's development, other than that he was sent to Westminster School in 1692 and left in 1700. His elder brother, James, followed his father into administrative and court service, becoming groom to the Duke of Gloucester in 1698. After Gloucester's death in 1700, James Vernon junior became clerk of the council extraordinary and embarked on a career that was to span diplomatic and administrative appointments.[6] James also followed his father into Parliament, being elected member for Cricklade in Wiltshire in 1708.

It is unclear why Edward should have been sent into the navy. A family connection existed through his grandfather, Francis Vernon. Edward's formal education gave him a good grasp of mathematics and French. His informal education and background probably gave him confidence to move easily in politics and diplomacy.[7] The recent war with France (1689-1697) had been fought across a greater portion of the globe than any previous conflict and it had involved a sustained attack upon enemy commerce. With tension over the Spanish Succession and in the Baltic, Edward's father understood the opportunities this presented for a young man.

A Professional Education, 1700-1706

The appointment of James Vernon as secretary of state positioned the father to assist the son. By early 1700 Swedish-Danish relations were rapidly deteriorating and war in the Baltic seemed extremely likely. On 9 May 1700 James Vernon prepared the instructions and final orders to Admiral Sir George Rooke. Rooke was to take an Anglo-Dutch squadron to the

Sound. He was to support the Swedes, but to try to bring about a peaceful conclusion to the confrontation if he could. On 10 May Rooke, accompanied by James Vernon, boarded the *Katherine* yacht to take him to his squadron in the Downs.[8] On the same day, Edward Vernon was entered as a Volunteer on Rooke's flagship, the *Shrewsbury*, commanded by Captain Benjamin Hoskins. On 8 June 1700 the combined fleet dropped anchor at Gothenburg and on 6 July it joined the Swedish fleet inside the Sound. The Danes retreated to the defences of Copenhagen harbour and refused to negotiate, despite a long-range bombardment by the allies. At the end of July a Swedish army landed to besiege the city, which finally convinced the Danes that they ought to negotiate and peace was agreed on 18 August. This was Vernon's first experience of war at sea and of its diplomatic impact ashore. The warships had not been able to force the Danes to treat, but an amphibious army had settled the matter.

On 4 March 1701 Vernon moved to the *Ipswich* and shortly afterwards to the *Boyne*. By mid-summer of 1701 a large fleet was assembled at Spithead under Rooke as tension between France and the maritime powers increased in the wake of the death of Charles II of Spain. The *Boyne* became flagship of Rear-Admiral Sir John Munden. While Rooke's fleet cruised in the Channel during August, Munden was detached with a strong force to escort Vice-Admiral Benbow out of the Channel on his way to the West Indies. The whole fleet returned to winter at the Downs and Spithead. On 4 May 1702 war was finally declared. The *Boyne* was part of an expeditionary force under the Duke of Ormonde and Rooke sent to capture Cadiz in 1702. The force consisted of thirty English and twenty Dutch ships of the line, plus cruisers, bombs and fireships. They escorted an army of over 13,500 Anglo-Dutch troops. The fleet arrived off Cadiz on 12 August and, after a series of councils of war, Ormonde landed his army on 15 August in the Bay of Bulls, on the far western extremity, across the bay from the town of Cadiz itself. Progress by the army was very slow, and the behaviour of ill-disciplined troops and seamen after the capture of the town of Santa Maria stimulated fierce Spanish resistance. The Dutch attempt to take Fort Matagorda, which dominated the waters between the Bay of Cadiz and Puntales Roads, was a failure. The commanders now considered further advance on the city to be impossible and on 15 September the allied army re-embarked. On the day after the re-embarkation, 16 September 1702, Rooke gave Vernon his first commission – third lieutenant on the *Lennox*.

While the allied fleet made its way up to Vigo in pursuit of the treasure fleet rumoured to have arrived at that port, the *Lennox* convoyed ships back to England. What Vernon learned from this expedition is impossible to establish, but it formed an interesting collection of events. Vernon had again experienced an amphibious operation. However, unlike the determined Swedes who moved to invest Copenhagen, the allied army had advanced slowly. Again, the ships alone had been unable to take the city, but this time the army had failed in its duty. The reaction in England to the failure was extremely hostile, and it was only the good news of the capture of part of the treasure from the Spanish *flota* at Vigo bay on 12 October 1702 that deflected a major political attack upon Rooke. Nonetheless, the House of Lords set up an enquiry into the failure at Cadiz and Rooke was forced to defend himself against hostile questioning.[9] By the time Vernon was enjoying his first commission, he had experienced amphibious operations in some detail. He had seen both the successful and unsuccessful employment of seaborne armies. He had seen the limitations of naval forces against major objectives ashore. He had seen the diplomatic results of a successful operation and the political repercussions of failure. Although no evidence remains of Vernon's views at this time, he was to become an intensely political man and it is quite likely that he drew many lessons for his service and behaviour from these early experiences.

Vernon stayed with the *Lennox* on a variety of convoy duties during 1703, including a visit to Smyrna with the Levant trade. His father was now out of office and he had to look to his own professional reputation to sustain him. On his return to England in March 1704 Vernon took up a commission as fifth lieutenant on Admiral Sir Cloudesley Shovell's flagship, the *Barfleur*, in which he sailed to the Mediterranean. Vernon remained with Shovell throughout 1704, being with him on the *Barfleur* at the Battle of Málaga (13 August). No information has survived of his conduct in this action, but in his general service he appears to have pleased Shovell. He returned to England with Shovell and when Shovell succeeded Rooke as Admiral of the Fleet, Vernon stayed with him as fourth and then third lieutenant on Shovell's new flagship, the *Britannia*, in December 1704. Shovell returned to the Mediterranean in the summer of 1705 and Vernon was present at the capture of Barcelona (28 September), another successful amphibious operation.

Early Command Experience, 1707-1712

On 22 January 1707 Vernon was given his first command, the *Dolphin*, a small Fifth Rate of 28 guns then at Sheerness under orders for the West Indies. The achievement of post rank was a critical point in any officer's career and in later life Vernon wrote that he was guided by Shovell on taking his first command. He was still only a third lieutenant, with no experience of higher office. He indicates that he could have taken a command in the Mediterranean, perhaps of a small vessel to get experience of independent command, but Shovell advised him to return to England where he could more easily get a post ship.[10] Whether Shovell was behind Vernon's appointment is unknown, but his prediction proved to be accurate and it was a useful step to give him seniority over some of his contemporaries. Before Vernon could get the *Dolphin* rigged and stored, he was transferred to the *Rye* (32 guns) at Portsmouth on 2 February. On 20 February Vernon was ordered to Lisbon with despatches for Shovell and the Earl Rivers and he sailed the same day. When Vernon reached Lisbon he found that Shovell and Rivers had sailed into the Mediterranean to join the allied force under Galway in Valencia. Vice-Admiral Sir George Byng was in command at Lisbon and Vernon was sent cruising down to Gibraltar. When Shovell returned to Lisbon and decided to take the fleet back into the Mediterranean to execute Marlborough's plan to attack Toulon, Vernon was left at Lisbon, but in May he joined the allied fleet at Alicante and sailed with it towards Toulon. On 30 June the *Rye* was one of the ships ordered to assist the allied crossing of the River Var by bombarding the French positions on the west bank. On the following day, Vernon was present at the landings intended to distract the French from the main crossing. He continued cruising and escort duties until the autumn of 1707, when he was ordered back to England. The passage was marred by catastrophe. On the night of 22 October the fleet passed too close to the Scillies and Shovell's flagship, the *Association*, and several other ships were lost.

On 7 November 1707 Vernon was given command of the *Jersey*, 50 at Woolwich, which he prepared for sea. In January he had the first of a number of disputes with civil authorities over seamen. One of his seamen, George Anderson, had been taken up by the constables of Westminster to be pressed into the army. Vernon immediately objected and had Prince George of Denmark, the Lord High Admiral, write to the Westminster justices. The justices refused Vernon's objections on the grounds that they had no evidence that Anderson was a seaman, that he had been taken up on the evidence of an army officer, and that he had taken the shilling. Whether the Prince of Denmark's intervention made any difference is impossible to know, but at the petty sessions the justices did not enlist Anderson and left him to Vernon. It was a victory over the army, but Vernon feared that the sea service would be ruined 'by the obstinate opposition of some of the justices'.[11] Vernon's commission was for the West Indies and he was well aware of the unpopularity of this station among seamen. Vernon had to mix coercion with persuasion and he, like many of his colleagues, encouraged a personal following. His crew was largely volunteers who had followed him from the *Rye*; sixty more enlisted from the *Sunderland*, on Vernon promising to give them shore leave until the end of January; forty more from the *Experiment* were prepared to join the *Jersey* if the Admiralty agreed to pay the wages owed them before they sailed. Vernon had press gangs out in London and down river to the Nore to complete his manning, but while at Woolwich the lure of London caused Vernon to fear that he would quickly loose his pressed men. He tried to get the ship moved to Long Reach before the men came aboard.

By the end of January the *Jersey* was fully manned, but instead of proceeding to the West Indies Vernon sailed in February 1708 with Sir George Byng's squadron to the French coast. They were to watch a large French force at Dunkirk, thought to be preparing for an expedition to Scotland. In March Vernon was with the fleet that pursued Forbin's expeditionary force to Scotland and, although he took no part in the battle, he helped secure the only prize of that affair, the French warship *Salisbury*, 50. After this action Vernon was sent south with some of the French prisoners. He resumed preparations to proceed to Jamaica to augment Commodore Wager's squadron and he was ordered to take as many supernumeraries as he could to reinforce Wager. Vernon arrived at Port Royal on 6 September 1708 and spent the next year with Wager's squadron, cruising. He observed the Spaniards' failure to challenge the British at sea and in October 1708 he had his first sight of Cartagena de las Indias, the great city of the *galeones*, the treasure ships, where Wager had won a spectacular victory back in May. There he saw where the Spaniards had run ashore their warships and galleons, fearing an attack from the British.

In September 1709 Vernon sailed for England, and he delivered the *Jersey* to the Deptford dockyard officers on 17 December. Back in command of the ship early in the new year, Vernon spent the first half of 1710 on a range of duties in the Channel and then went back to the West Indies, arriving at Port Royal in December. Vernon remained on that station until March 1712, when we was ordered home again. When he arrived home he was not given a new command. His father and brother had lost their seats in the Tory general election victory of 1710 and deprived of their offices.[12] The prospect of peace, and his Whig credentials, kept him unemployed for over two years.

A Naval Diplomat: The Mediterranean 1716–1717

The accession of George I on 1 August 1714 and the new Whig-dominated Parliament ushered in the revival of Vernon family fortunes. On 2 March

1715 Edward was given command of the *Assistance*, a two-year-old 50-gun ship, then at Sheerness. Manning again proved tiresome. As before, Vernon appears to have been a popular officer, always capable of attracting a large number of volunteers, His view of the seaman was typical of contemporary patrician paternalism. He understood the habits of the seaman. He believed the slowness of men returning from shore 'is occasioned by the men growing every day more abundantly profligate'. They lived on credit in London and had to lie low or abscond until their creditors grew tired of pursuing them.[13] Combating the seaman's inability to resist the temptations of port life with moral and administrative weapons for the good of the navy was to be one of Vernon's lifelong tasks.

With the Jacobite rebellion still unconquered, competition with the army for manpower continued to worry Vernon. One of his men applied for a discharge to enlist in Lumley's Horse, but Vernon rejected the request, 'as I find seamen are as scarce to be got as souldiers [sic]'.[14] After fitting and manning his ship in the spring, Vernon spent the summer on duties in the Channel and the North Sea. By early in 1716 Vernon was the most senior captain in the Downs and had command of that station in the absence of a flag officer. In July 1716 Vernon was ordered to take the new British ambassador's equipage to Constantinople. The ambassador, Edward Wortley-Montagu, was then at Vienna. He was to join Vernon at Leghorn for the final stage of the journey. The departing ambassador, Sir Robert Sutton, would return with Vernon from Constantinople. The voyage involved a number of diplomatic complexities regarding the status of British warships in Ottoman waters, and a further difficulty was caused by the ministry taking the opportunity to carry the envoy from Tripoli back to Port Mahon. After a few diplomatic exchanges, partly arising from the fact that the envoy did not want a long sea passage but wished to travel by land across France, Vernon finally sailed in late October. During a terrible storm in the Straits the sea broke through the stern, drove in the bulkhead of the stateroom and smashed all the windows. Three days later, on 6 March 1717, the envoy was finally put ashore at Port Mahon, no doubt to his great relief. Vernon sailed on to Genoa, where he learned that Wortley-Montagu would go to Constantinople by land.

While at Leghorn, concerting plans to proceed to the Dardanelles, Vernon also took up the matter of Venetian impressment of British sailors. On the voyage out, Vernon had tangled with the Spanish authorities in Cadiz over British sailors being admitted into Spanish service. Here, Vernon had been unable to do much, as he could not prove the nationality of the seamen, who seemed not to want to recognise former shipmates, but at Leghorn the seamen were being held against their wishes. After a long argument with the governor of Leghorn, Vernon got two British sailors released, but the Venetians took many more. Vernon was convinced that

> the seamen are more corrupted and debauched in this port into foreign service, than in any other port in the world, besides and in my opinion, nothing contributes more to the debauching them, than the great number of Public tippling houses kept in the town by His Majesty's subjects, there being said to be forty to fifty of them, who are a great many employed as crimps by forreigners [*sic*] to debauch the English seamen into other services.

The seamen were either kept drunk until taken away or owed so much that they were sold into foreign service. Vernon was determined to do what he could and travelled to Pisa for an audience with the Grand Duke of Tuscany. During this interview Vernon and the Grand Duke conducted their discussions in French. He got an English resident's son released, but seems to have achieved little else.[15]

Vernon's diplomatic skills were also needed to ensure that the voyage to Constantinople went smoothly. The protocols for mutual recognition between warships and the Turkish forts that held the Narrows of the Dardanelles had not been established. Vernon was determined that he would receive no less dignity than the French received. The services of a dragoman were arranged for Vernon's arrival at the upper forts. The dragomans were interpreters and expert advisors on Ottoman affairs employed by western diplomats.[16] In this case, the dragoman was faced with a problem – nothing could be found of the precedents established by the French, but when the *Assistance* arrived at the lower forts it was discovered that the French had paid a toll of £50. Vernon decided to pass without ceremony or payment. The event was ignored at Constantinople, but when Vernon prepared to depart with the ambassador, Sir Robert Sutton, he was aware of a potential hazard. The Turkish fleet of twenty-five line of battle ships had left Constantinople and preceded him down towards the Narrows. He and Sutton decided to settle on a salute with the captain of the fort before they arrived. They agreed on nine guns, with the fleet firing three for the passage of an ambassador. He landed Sutton at Toulon to continue his journey overland. Vernon sailed to Port Mahon to reinforce the island at the request of the governor, Lord Forbes, who feared a Spanish attack. When it was discovered that the Spanish armament was intended for Sardinia, Vernon sailed on to Cadiz, where once more he took up the matter of detained British seamen with the local authorities.

The West Indies Command: Professional and Political Success, 1718-1727

War with Spain broke out in December 1718, and Vernon's next commission, on 11 March 1719, was to the 60-gun *Mary*, attached to the Earl of Berkeley's squadron at Portsmouth. On 15 May Vernon was appointed commander-in-chief of His Majesty's ships at Jamaica and he hoisted his broad pendant on 24 July. On 4 October 1719 he arrived at Port Royal. With a small squadron of two 40-gun ships, two 32s, a 20 and two sloops, Vernon distributed his forces to cruise around the north coast of Jamaica and the Windward Passage, protecting the trade from Spanish privateers and pirates. He was already familiar with the problems of West Indian service – manpower shortages, lack of naval stores, poor careening facilities, merchant collusion with straggling seamen and illegal trading. This command gave him his first experience of having to manage these problems.[17] In March 1720 Vernon cruised up to Havana with the *Ludlow Castle*, hoping to thwart a Spanish expedition to the Bahamas. On 18 April he sighted three Spanish sail in line, which turned out to be a 64, a 54 and a frigate. Having manoeuvred overnight to cut them off from Havana, he sighted them again the next day and, followed closely by the *Ludlow Castle*, bore down to meet them. With a strong breeze and the weather gage, he found that he could not use his lower tier of guns effectively in his first pass and tacked to pass again to leeward, intending to push between the Spanish ships. Very close action followed as the Spaniards prevented Vernon's movement, but in the encounter the *Ludlow Castle* lost her fore-top and fell out to leeward. Vernon followed to protect her stern as the Spaniards prepared to attack. Vernon took in sail to meet them and this display induced the Spaniards to break off and make a course for Havana.[18]

By June notice of the cessation of hostilities arrived, but Vernon continued to operate against pirates and Spanish privateers whose commissions continued to issued after the announcement of peace. He was ordered home in June 1721. Throughout Vernon's time in the West Indies the Spaniards had shown little appetite for a fight. The larger Spanish Barlovento Squadron at Havana had not ventured leeward nor sought him out. Their privateers attacked commerce and had instructions to raid isolated plantations. All his experiences both of conditions on Jamaica and of his enemy confirmed his belief that although seapower was a fragile instrument, the Royal Navy possessed a general superiority over the 'Bully Don'.

Vernon arrived back in England in August 1721. While neither his father nor his brother resumed their parliamentary careers, they had official posts and his family appears to have stood well in the favour of Sir Robert

Walpole. Vernon stood for one of the parliamentary seats at Penryn, Cornwall, in the general election. The precise relationship between the Vernons
and Penryn is unclear. His father James had stood for this small borough,
and won the seat three times in 1695, 1705 and 1708. The chief political
interest was held by Hugh Boscawen, first Viscount Falmouth, who was
the government's main political manager in Cornwall. With this support,
Vernon was returned unopposed on 12 April 1722.

Vernon's political and professional star seemed to be reaching its zenith.
He had come from a strong Whig background that had primed his career in
the navy. He had received the patronage of Rooke and Shovell and had
served with the senior officers in the fleet, Sir John Norris, Wager and
Byng. His own behaviour as a captain had proved his capability and,
equally important, he was articulate and confident in pressing his views
with seamen, the Admiralty, the civil powers, the army, foreign officials
and courts. He had extensive professional experience, a high regard from
his peers and political support. Now in Parliament, with a powerful new
administration, he stood to reap personal and professional rewards. These
attributes did, however, have a negative side, which was less welcome to
the Walpole administration – professional credibility combined with independent views and an extremely low tolerance of being opposed. He also
expressed himself in terms bordering on outrageous invective. Vernon's
early interventions in Parliament were innocuous, but on 20 April 1725 he
demonstrated the unpredictability of his approach. Lord Bolingbroke petitioned the house for restitution of his lands and titles, something to which
the administration was not averse, but Vernon denounced him as 'a complicated villain, and if acts of infamy were the way to recommend him to
the king he had done it effectually'[19].

Vernon's stand for Hanoverian Whig principles did him no harm in this
instance. In April 1726 Vernon was appointed to command the new 70-
gun Third Rate *Grafton,* in a squadron under Admiral Sir Charles Wager
sailing for the Baltic to counter a potential Russian threat to the peace
there. He remained in command of the *Grafton* when the squadron returned to Britain, and in 1727 he was sent back to the Baltic with another
squadron under Sir John Norris. On 19 June, at Copenhagen, news arrived
of the death of George I. Vernon received the honour of going back to
England with a loyal address from the fleet.[20]

Blue Water and Whig Patriotism, 1727-1739

Vernon was placed on half pay at his own request, and at the general
election he was re-elected for Penryn. Very soon, however, his interven-

tions in committee and on the floor of the house grew increasingly hostile to the ministry. It is difficult to identify the precise reasons for his disenchantment. There is evidence of growing tension during 1726, when his brother was omitted from the new Excise Commission.[21] Further tension occurred in January 1727/8 when Viscount Townshend amended the obituary to James Vernon senior in the *London Gazette*, despite the protests of the Vernon brothers.[22] However, perhaps the underlying cause of tension was Vernon's conviction that Walpole's ministry was increasingly at odds with Britain's domestic and foreign interests. The association of domestic liberty, maritime trade, and defence by a strong navy against the despotic land powers of Europe was long-standing in British political rhetoric. There was an attractive simplicity to the idea that standing armies were a threat to domestic liberty and trade by their need for taxation revenues to support them and their armed capability to collect taxes. Land wars demand large armies and thus entailed high domestic taxation and increasing threats to liberty. Naval forces, on the other hand, supported overseas trade that generated additional wealth and taxation revenues. This additional income from trade was garnered at the expense of Britain's enemies, thus impoverishing them while enriching Britain. Therefore, war at sea conducted by a strong navy could not threaten political liberties, but generated the resources for higher taxation and stimulated trade. As a whole, these ideas made up 'Blue Water' policy. Both Whig and Tory had employed elements of it at various times in the previous forty years. However, it was only by 1729 that the confluence of Walpole's domination of domestic politics, the revival of French maritime commerce and the foreign policy difficulties created by alliance politics all combined to give 'Blue Water' a coherence and credibility that it had never possessed before. Vernon had more reason than most to be convinced by 'Blue Water'. His professional experiences at home and abroad had shown him the power of the Royal Navy. In the West Indies the Spaniards had never shown the will to resist Britain. Naval power projected ashore by a competent landing force had proved its ability to influence powers such as Denmark and Spain. From his upbringing, he knew the value of trade and the importance of political liberty. He had seen the despotic powers of Europe and the Near East and as a humble captain had negotiated with them with reasonable success. Vernon became the most articulate and committed spokesman for the 'Blue Water' policy of Country Whiggism.

Since 1716 British foreign policy had rested upon an alliance with France. This alliance had allowed Britain to concentrate her military efforts in her navy, whilst, in theory, having the diplomatic leverage of a powerful

French army. It neatly fitted the political attractiveness of naval defence whilst neutralising the French threat to Britain and the Hanoverian Succession, and even providing land forces for extended influence within Europe. In practice, the French alliance seldom met British expectations. This was particularly the case in the long-running disputes with Spain over the searching of British merchant vessels in the Caribbean. Spain, reliant as she was on the treasure from South America, seemed particularly vulnerable to naval power. When, in 1726, war seemed likely between Austria, Spain and their allies of the treaty of Vienna on the one hand, and the signatories of the Alliance of Hanover (including Britain and France) on the other, British squadrons were sent to blockade the two ends of the Spanish treasure route. One force under Sir John Jennings was to cruise off Spain, whilst another, under Vice Admiral Hosier, went to the Caribbean to blockade the Spanish treasure fleet ports. Peace preliminaries were signed in May 1727 and it was believed by some in the opposition that Hosier's blockade had played an important part. Over the next eighteen months negotiations dragged on, with France acting more like a broker between Britain and Spain rather than an ally. The Spanish difficulty was only one of a number of diplomatic problems facing Walpole, but to the opposition it appeared that his failure to exert naval force more vigorously was symptomatic of his subservience to French policy objectives.[23]

In January 1729, during the debate on the Address, Vernon made his famous, heated, denunciation of the ministry's foreign policy. It encapsulated the essence of 'Blue Water' ideology. Vernon suggested that the ministry corruptly produced edited documents to lay before the Commons. However, even if the copies of the instructions to Hosier in 1726 were accurate, his death and the decimation of his fleet in the West Indies during 1726–7 could have been avoided had the ministry not ordered Hosier to blockade the Spanish treasure fleet.[24] His experience of the Spaniards indicated that a blockade was unnecessary. Conciliation would achieve nothing, while force would be irresistible. Porto Bello, the staging post of Spanish silver from Panama to Havana, could have been taken easily with three hundred men. His strong views, passionate speech and accusatory style became a feature of his parliamentary work. According to the Earl of Egmont, Vernon was so passionate in his views about the French fortifications at Dunkirk during the debate on 12 February 1730 that 'He brought up the Pope, the Devil, the Jesuits, the seamen, etc, so that the House had not patience to attend him, though he was not taken down. He quite lost his temper and made himself hoarse again'.[25] In 1732 his inflammatory rhetoric earned him a rebuke from the Speaker and an accusation from one of his victims, Sir John Eyles, that he hid behind parliamentary privilege.[26] His headstrong approach had earned him an earlier rebuke in 1728 when he removed papers from the table to copy them whilst the house was sitting and he failed to desist when challenged.[27] Whilst between 1729 and 1734 Vernon's style unnerved and irritated the political situation – frustration with Spanish behaviour in the West Indies, the threat of French commercial and military power and concerns about Walpole's domestic ambitions – made his simple and vigorous message very attractive: any attacks upon liberty and extension of domestic taxation only assisted the Pretender, and behind the Pretender stood France. Failure to defend trade and the plantations to the utmost was to surrender to France. In 1729 he warned against French competition in the woollen industry. He amused the house by claiming that the French would deal with the British sheep and Pretender in one go. Once the Pretender was installed 'they could afterwards remove the animal and then they would give him a kick and tell him "get you out for you're the son of a whore, we are the lawful heir".'[28] In 1730 he spoke unsuccessfully for printing the transcript of a trial that appeared unfair. He moved for Byng's instructions of 1718 to enlighten the debate on relations with Spain. He supported the King's claim to St Lucia. In February 1732 he used 'several hot and indiscreet expressions' against the Salt Duty.

In July 1729 Vernon married Sarah Best, daughter of the prosperous Rochester brewer, Thomas Best, which gave him opportunities in local Kent politics and secured his financial position.[29] He had purchased an estate at Nacton, near Ipswich in Suffolk. However, his political position at Penryn was looking increasingly fragile. Matters with Walpole's ministry were coming to a head over the Excise Bill. In the critical vote of 14 March 1732/3 Vernon, like Hugh Boscawen, voted against the Excise. Boscawen lost his role as government election manager in Cornwall and in the 1734 election Vernon lost Penryn. He was also defeated in his local borough, Ipswich. Like other opponents of the Excise, Vernon was soon to feel the King's resentment. He wrote to his father-in-law on 9 May 1734, 'I find you have had the advice as early as I could of Lord Forbes being made the fflagg over my head which Mrs Vernon and I are both very easy under; and I hope I shall always take a greater pleasure in being a Martyr for the good of my Country; than a prosperous slave in contributing to betray its liberty and prosperity.'[30] He took comfort from the fact that the 'Country Party' had exerted itself well in Essex. For the foreseeable future Vernon had to expect to play the role of a Suffolk country gentleman, concerning himself with his estate and supporting the cause of the Tory candidate, Sir Cordell Firebrace, prospective MP for Long Melford, as the only one who 'has to[o] much honour to be ever capable of Betraying the trust reposed in him by bartering away the property or liberty of his constituents for pensions, ribbons, titles or places'.[31]

While on the surface Vernon's naval and political career seemed over, there were still factors that gave him hope for the future. His reputation as the spokesman for the Blue Water policy was not forgotten. The rhetoric that Vernon had practised 1728 to 1734 was repeated consistently as the dispute with Spain developed from the winter of 1737. He still exercised some political influence in Rochester, one of the Admiralty boroughs, through his wife's family and through his friendship with officers like the Commissioner at Chatham, Thomas Mathews. Furthermore, he was well respected within the navy. If a crisis occurred, he would not be ignored.

That crisis seemed to be approaching in December 1738 as war with Spain over the depredations of the *garda costas* began to appear more likely. By early June 1739 the ministry had agreed that a squadron should be sent to the West Indies to destroy Spanish shipping. Vernon heard about this and visited 'his steady friend' Sir Charles Wager, the First Lord of the Admiralty, to solicit this command.[32] The ministry's naval advisors, Wager and Norris, had a high regard for Vernon and they easily convinced their ministerial colleagues that he was a good man to appoint. The Duke of Newcastle reported to the Duke of Devonshire: 'I hope we shall soon despatch our five ships to the West Indies, who will command them is yet uncertain, your friend, My Lord Granard, has absolutely refused. We are all for Capt Vernon, who in that case would be made a vice admiral and restored to his rank. Our master is a little averse to it, but we hope it will do.'[33] The arguments used by Wager and others when they met the King on the following day are unknown, but to Wager Vernon was 'much properer than any officer we have to send, being very well acquainted in all that part of the West Indies and is a very good sea officer, whatever he may be, or has been, in the House of Commons.'[34] Vernon's long-standing public commitment to effective action against Spain and the fact that no serving senior officer could be induced to take the appointment were probably also significant factors. After Philip Cavendish refused the post, George II gave up his objections and Vernon kissed hands on 10 July as vice-admiral of the blue and commander of the West Indies squadron.

The West Indies, 1739-42

Vernon sailed for Jamaica in July and arrived at Port Royal in October. His instructions were to destroy Spanish shipping and possessions in the West Indies: 'Pray God Grant me a happy meeting with the Spaniards.'[35] He knew the West Indies and the Spaniards well, but it was the first time that he commanded a small squadron of battleships. He quickly proved that he had lost none of his professional acumen. Within days of assuming command he issued two additional instructions to his squadron. The first of these instructions was for specified captains to fall out of the line of battle if Vernon's force was superior to the enemy. These officers were then to consider themselves a *corps de reserve,* which was to support any vessels in the line which were in difficulty. While they had to pay particular attention to the flagship, these captains were given freedom to position themselves as they saw fit. The defensive power of the line was further reinforced by instructions to fireship and bomb tender commanders to act in a similar fashion. Further additional instructions ordered captains to engage the enemy more closely, following the position of the flagship. At later points additional instructions were designed to further strengthen the line. Bomb ketches were to place themselves in front and astern of the flagship in the line of battle to destroy the enemy admiral's masts and rigging. A series of night signals were introduced in case action should occur after dark.[36]

The origins and implications of these additional instructions are difficult to establish. There is no evidence as to where and how Vernon developed these ideas, but they were introduced at stages over a period of months, which suggests a maturing of ideas as the campaign unfolded. The initial instructions of July and August 1739 seem to be distinctly defensive in nature. Whereas the usual way of exploiting a numerical superiority would be to extend the line of battle to double the enemy, Vernon appears to have wanted to strengthen his centre and provide a reserve to support threatened ships. It does not seem that he intended to use the reserve to break through the enemy line. His additions certainly gave the admiral greater control over his line at the beginning of day and night actions. He was also aware that the smoke of battery fire soon obscured signals and the admiral's control diminished rapidly in action. In this case it was vital that individual captains acted with initiative at critical points in the line. These were important changes, but Vernon never had occasion to test his innovations. They were not the basis of aggressive decisive action, but they did provide a step towards greater flexibility based upon the responsibility and initiative of individual captains. The importance Vernon attached to individual initiative and understanding in the confusion of action is clear. He was determined that his captains understand his intentions and he met his captains to explain his demands clearly to them.[37] Before the attack upon Porto Bello, Vernon issued orders outlining the general plan of attack 'as the weather may not serve for calling you together before the attack nor time permit it'.

The instructions covered a number of matters related to behaviour and dispositions expected in the attack, but the decision to 'give my general plan of attack to each of you [is] that you might not be misled by the motions of other ships of the squadron'.[38] Like Nelson before the Battle of the Nile, but unlike Mathews and Lestock at Toulon, Vernon and his officers shared a vision of what they should do when they came to grips with the enemy.

Vernon was probably most relaxed where his authority was unchallenged. He was an untiring writer and there is no reason to doubt that he forcefully expressed his views to his officers to mould them to his tactical vision. He enforced a discipline and training on his crews that spared no one. He struggled with the colonial authorities to preserve his precious pool of seamen. This was uppermost in his mind in his crusade against 'the formidable Dragon, drunkenness'.[39] Drink was at the root of desertions, straggling, indiscipline, accidents and sickness. Keeping men out of the punch houses and away from raw, new rum occupied a significant part of Vernon's orders. The introduction of 'Grog', rum watered down in the ratio of 1:8, is probably Vernon's most famous contribution, but his efforts to use all administrative means at his disposal – confinement, corporal punishment, the careful application of clemency, the development of hospitals, injunctions against swearing and the reinstitution of daily prayers – formed part of Vernon's plan to preserve the fundamentally solid but naïve seamen for service to the crown.[40] In doing this, Vernon helped develop this public image of the seaman. How this public image contributed to the political development of the navy in the critical period up to 1763 still needs a great deal of research, but in parliamentary debates about the navy and its performance the recruitment and treatment of the seaman as an honest free man necessarily undertaking forced labour formed a significant theme.

Whilst Vernon was at home in command of his squadron, he was not to have such control over the wider conduct of the campaign in the West Indies. He had a clear idea of how he wished to conduct operations. Nineteen days after arriving at Port Royal he wrote to the secretary of state, the Duke of Newcastle, about the prospect of capturing Spanish colonies. He knew Havana would be a great prize, but his best advice was to 'lay aside all thoughts of such expensive land expeditions as all the advantages may be better and cheaper procured by keeping a strong superiority at Sea in these seas'. Porto Bello, 'the only mart for all the Wealth of Peru to come to Europe,' was his objective and 5 November 1739 he sailed to attack the little town.[41] On 20 November he attacked the forts with his six warships and by the next day the town was in his hands. Vernon had left England as expectations of an easy victory against Spain were growing. War had been declared on 19 October and news of Vernon's victory arrived in March 1740 as a confirmation of public expectations. The rejoicing went far beyond the usual celebrations of victory. Vernon was transformed from a knowledgeable and articulate spokesman for 'Blue Water' to national hero almost overnight. Addresses of congratulations came to the King from across the country. His popular appeal was immense. Medals, pottery, road names, and public house signs bore the name Vernon or Porto Bello, and his birthday became a day of celebration across the country. Both Houses of Parliament voted their thanks and the City of London made him a freeman. The ministry shared the delight at Vernon's success and had already decided that a major expedition would be sent to the West Indies to bring Spain to peace by taking and holding some of her important colonies. The ministry hoped that Havana, the 'key to all America', would be the objective, but left the final decision to the council of war under the joint command of Vernon and the army commander, Lord Cathcart.[42]

Meanwhile, Vernon did not seek the destruction of Spanish facilities, but the opening of Spanish ports to British trade. It was a policy that he had pursued between 1719 and 1721. He destroyed the fortifications at Porto Bello, but otherwise left the town unharmed and open to British merchants. During March 1740 Vernon went to Cartagena de las Indias. He bombarded the city, but found it impossible to assault with his ships. He conceded to Newcastle that 3000 troops would have enabled him to capture the place and he would be prepared for the future, as he informed Newcastle, 'I know now as much of the avenues to their harbours as they do themselves.'[43] Vernon had also learned that the rolling seas and poor ground made the waters off Cartagena a dangerous anchorage. He sailed up to Porto Bello for repairs, then on to the little fortified port of Chagres. After two days the fort surrendered. It was destroyed and the town was left open to trade. Whilst he was at Porto Bello news reached Vernon that the intended expedition was definitely coming out.

Over the summer of 1740 Vernon's concerns grew. He was convinced that land forces would soon die, to no real advantage. He was short of naval stores and seamen. News that Spanish and French squadrons were on their way to the West Indies was worrying. Although France was neutral, the behaviour of the French governor on St Domingue suggested to Vernon that France was bent on assisting the Spaniards. He decided to husband his forces at Port Royal, refusing to risk damage or to be drawn to leeward. Vernon's experience of the Caribbean and his concerns made him determined that the expeditionary force would serve as he intended. It would not go to Havana, but to Cartagena, which he believed the troops could rapidly take before they were reduced by disease. The city lay to windward of Jamaica so that they could return rapidly to the island if it was threatened by Spanish or French attacks.[44]

The expeditionary force arrived in January 1741. Cathcart had died on the voyage and the army of about 8500 British and American troops was commanded by Major General Thomas Wentworth. The naval escort, commanded by Vice-Admiral Ogle, brought Vernon's squadron up to thirty-three ships of the line. Although this fleet made the Franco-Spanish threat less worrying, Vernon was saddled with another serious problem. The Caribbean provided barely enough seamen to replace losses on his small squadron. This vast fleet would soon be losing seamen by disease and desertion that could not be replaced. The army was the only adequate source of manpower.

Although nominally equals in command, Wentworth deferred to Vernon's experience in the opening months of operations. He provided troops to help man the ships and concurred in the attack upon Cartagena. During the attack upon Cartagena, relations became strained as Vernon pressed Wentworth forward, making ill-considered accusations about the inaction and incompetence within the army. When the army finally reached San Lazar, the final fortification before Cartagena, Vernon again urged Wentworth to press on and, contrary to the opinion of his council of war, Wentworth accepted Vernon's demand to assault the fort. The action on 10 April 1741 was a disaster. Both officers realised that a reduction of this last obstacle was impossible before disease, which was beginning to take a hold, reduced the army's capability. Vernon would not put his seamen ashore to suffer the same fate. The reports that were sent to London glossed over many of the issues raised by this operation, as the expeditionary force quietly returned to Jamaica.[45]

The next objective was to be Santiago on the southern coast of Cuba. Vernon knew a direct attack from the sea was difficult and was determined to land the army to the east. Unfortunately, he did not tell Wentworth and from the beginning relations between the two services deteriorated. As Vernon urged the army to push on through difficult terrain and manipulated the information he allowed Wentworth to have, he was also acutely aware of how the news of failure would be received in London. His despatches to London had always been very full and he started to enclose carefully selected items of his correspondence with Wentworth. The despatches themselves began to contain complaints and criticisms of the

general. Wentworth's correspondence was, by comparison, brief and sometimes ambiguous. It was not until much later that Wentworth's enclosures
began to shed much light on the campaign. Verses defending Vernon's
behaviour were circulating in London during 1741. Vernon also asked his
brother James to publish an account of Wentworth's incompetence, and in
the summer of 1741 Captain Charles Knowles, a close colleague of Vernon's, was sent home. Knowles was probably the author of a pamphlet, *An
Account of the Expedition to Cartagena*, which circulated in London during
the summer, which was extremely hostile to the army. The campaign on
Cuba ended in December 1741 with relations between the two services at
an extremely low ebb.

A final attempt was made to attack Panama with a reinforcement of 2000
troops that arrived. Given the rumours of French squadrons coming to the
West Indies, Vernon was unenthusiastic, but it was a favourite scheme of
the governor of Jamaica, Edward Trelawney, and Wentworth was determined to do something significant with the reinforcements before they
wasted with disease. Trelawney and Wentworth forced the operation on
Vernon with the same disastrous effect as Vernon's earlier pressure had
created. Vernon did not follow the agreed plan, so news got through to the
Spaniards to defend the inland passes. He refused to allow the transports to
concentrate before appearing off the town. With the army spread out across
the sea from Cartagena to Porto Bello, the operation was called off. The last
weeks of the operation were spent with minor expeditions to the island of
Roatan and to Georgia. By September the army had ceased to exist as a
military force and the troops were largely split up on the warships. Vernon
was, at last, effectively commander-in-chief, but on 23 September orders
arrived to return to England. Vernon sailed on 19 October, arriving off St
David's Head on 26 December 1742.

In Defence of Blue Water, 1743-1745

Vernon found his public popularity intact. In the 1741 general election he
had been chosen for Penryn, Rochester and Ipswich. He had also been put
up at London, Westminster and Portsmouth, but ministerial disquiet over
such numerous nominations led to support being withheld in these seats.
Vernon chose to sit for Ipswich, a seat that he held from then until his
death. He had a half-hour audience with George II, during which he
pressed the King not to rely on land forces, but keep a force superior to the
enemy at sea. According to his brother James, 'the King bore the lecture
pretty well', but Vernon found his reward was not what he might have
hoped.[46] Unlike Wentworth, who was despatched to Flanders to

command a division, Vernon found himself unemployed and passed over in promotion. Vernon's hostility was directed at the First Lord, the Earl of Winchelsea, although it is most likely that the ministry as a whole were aware of the distorted picture of the expedition that Vernon had been encouraging. According to his brother James, there was pressure from Trelawney to have Vernon's behaviour examined in Parliament, but the ministry would not permit it while he was so popular. Ministerial unity, not professional regard, protected him.[47]

Whilst there was no official enquiry into the failure of the expedition, pamphlets appeared in the squabble between the army and the navy. During 1743 Vernon fell back upon organising his correspondence for publication. The background to this war in print was a growing disquiet with both the land and sea war since 1740. The war in the Mediterranean had been inconclusive and disappointing even before war broke out with France in February 1744. The battle off Toulon on 11 February spread discord in the navy as Lestock and Mathews tried to justify their behaviour. Norris had only just managed to deter a French invasion attempt that winter, assisted more by atrocious weather than good seamanship. On land the disputes over the neutrality of Hanover in the autumn of 1741 and the employment of Hanoverian and Hessian troops during 1742–3 had raised questions about the purpose of the war. The King's preference for his Hanoverian troops at the Battle of Dettingen in June 1743 had thrown further fat on to the fire.

During this period it was far from certain how the war should be fought. The land campaigns were achieving very little and the naval campaigns had thrown up disappointments and suspicions that the naval officers were neither capable nor courageous. It was against this background that Vernon stood out as the champion for a powerful and competent naval war. On 16 April 1744 he seconded Lord Granard's motion for a committee to investigate the war at sea. He published his correspondence relating to the West Indian expedition, together with the selected enclosures. He also published his first plan regarding the more effective manning of the fleet.[48] He was certainly not disinterested, but he was undeniably a competent commentator upon events. He could not be excluded indefinitely and on 9 August 1743 he was promoted vice-admiral of the red. However, putting his expertise before the public probably did not endear him to the Admiralty or Navy Board. They were struggling with a war that was not going well, particularly the consequences of the failure at Toulon. Vernon was a respected officer whose opinion on naval matters was valued, but he took the opportunity of a request from the Admiralty for his advice on British ships to launch an attack upon Sir Jacob Acworth, the Surveyor of the Navy, which he promptly published.[49] He claimed that this publication led to his omission from the promotions that occurred during the summer of 1744, but his public profile, his acknowledged experience, his outspoken country stance and his invective made him a powerful advocate of the 'Blue Water' policies at a time when the results of any strategy seemed remarkably thin.

During the first half of 1745 debate over the conduct of the war was coming to a head. In December 1744 the Duke of Bedford replaced Winchelsea as First Lord of the Admiralty. Bedford had been very impressed with Vernon's message and was to correspond with him on a number of naval and strategic matters. On 19 March the parliamentary enquiry opened regarding the miscarriage at Toulon.[50] Vernon played an important part as an expert witness. He was sure of his ground, and his interventions appeared for the most part measured and even-handed. Vernon's rejection of Robert Vyner's motion to exclude Mathews from the list of officers to be court-martialled was probably decisive. His motives are unclear, but despite his long-term friendship with Mathews, he would not be seen to compromise the service. One particular incident raised Vernon's ire more than any other. In January a small British squadron had sighted some French vessels. The commander, Captain Griffin, set off in chase of a small vessel that broke away from the French force. Captain Mostyn, who led the chase of the French, identified the force as two large men of war. He hauled his wind on two occasions to wait for his colleagues rather than engaging the two Frenchmen. Vernon was outraged and stunned by Mostyn's acquittal by court martial. During the Toulon enquiry Vernon was so perplexed by these events that in one speech he drifted off the subject on to Mostyn's behaviour.[51] He published his opinions on the matter, taking the opportunity to set out his views on the inadequacy of the officer corps.[52] It sent a shudder through his colleagues, but encapsulated public views on the professional obligations of naval officers. He also published *An Infallible Project for the More Effectual, Speedy and Easy Manning of the Navy of England* in the same year. It was a subject Vernon knew well, combining humanity and stern discipline for the seaman. Good pay and conditions, fair treatment for the seaman and his dependents, combined with firm discipline would end the 'cruelty unparalleled by the despotism of Louis XV'. On 23 April 1745 Vernon was promoted admiral of the white. His habit of corresponding freely and clearly played an important part in bringing him to the peak of his career, but it was soon to prove his undoing.

The Channel, August–December 1745

On 25 July the Pretender's son landed in Scotland and measures to prevent a French invasion had to be revived with urgency. The allied position in Flanders had deteriorated badly since the defeat at Fontenoy in May. Vernon had already been suggested to command the three-deckers concentrated in the Downs in case of a French invasion. Fears that the Brest fleet might be coming north led to Vernon's appointment to command all the Channel forces. Vernon went down to Portsmouth on 4 August 1745 and busied himself with manning his vessels and establishing good relations with his Dutch allies. Again, his views were forcefully and clearly put:

> I have always looked upon squadrons in port as neither a defence for the kingdom, nor a security for our commerce, and that the surest means for the [preservation] of both, was keeping a strong squadron in the Soundings, which may answer both these purposes, as covering both Channels and Ireland and at the same time secures our commerce.[53]

This disposition of the Western Squadron was to be put to good effect by Anson during 1746-7, but Vernon had no time to implement it. On 15 August, as his force assembled at Spithead, he was ordered to the Downs where the latest intelligence suggested French invasion forces were assembling to support the Jacobite rising in Scotland.[54] Vernon was opposed to this move. Blockade duty in shallow waters with insecure anchorages around the North Sea coast was not appropriate for large battleships. This was a constant theme in his correspondence during the late summer and autumn. By October he believed there was no longer any threat of the Brest squadron coming up the Channel and the defence against invasion was an affair of small ships. His frustration at command of such a force of small ships and the reduction of the force and its manpower for other duties mounted during the autumn. He kept a close watch on the Flanders coast throughout the period, but became involved in a frustrating correspondence with Admiralty over the size of his squadron and the limits of his command. In late November this became heated over Vernon's right of appointing warrant officers and on 1 December Vernon threatened to resign.[55] The dispute rumbled on through December as Vernon made dispositions to resist a possible French invasion. Finally, on 26 December 1745, Vernon was ordered to hand over command to Vice-Admiral Martin, who had come up from Plymouth to join Vernon's squadron.

By mid-March 1746 copies of Vernon's correspondence with the Admiralty during the previous year were in print under the titles *Seasonable Advice from an Honest Sailor* and *A Specimen of the Naked Truth from a British Sailor.*

When called before the Admiralty for a meeting under Bedford's chairman-ship on 9 April, he refused to confirm or deny that he was responsible for the publication of the correspondence. He asserted that he had been badly treated and that the publication was a private matter on which he was not obliged to answer. Bedford laid the matter before the King, who ordered that Vernon be struck off the flag list on 11 April. This time there was no recovery.

Final Years 1746-1757

Vernon remained politically active although increasingly marginalised. He spoke in February 1749 on the naval officers' petition against making half pay officers subject to martial law, and in the Address of Thanks in Novem-ber of that year. His subjects were the traditional ones. He spoke violently for habeas corpus and against the arrest of Alexander Murray in 1751, being called to order several times by the Speaker. He spoke against the Three Shilling Land Tax and, in 1754, against the amendment of the Naturalisa-tion Act. He chaired the parliamentary committee on the Herring Fishery and helped establish the Society of Free British Fishery. By this time his fiery rhetoric bored the House and the waspish Horace Walpole composed verse on his 'rule o'er Billingsgate and fish'.[56] During the Address of Thanks on 13 November 1755 Vernon argued to remove the words relat-ing to European treaties against France, but 'The attention of the House was entirely put at an end, as it generally was, by Admiral Vernon.'[57] Vernon's professional credibility was also spent. During 1746-7 Vernon conducted a dispute with his old second in command from the West Indies, Sir Chaloner Ogle, over the distribution of prize money. It was to be referred to a council of sea officers to avoid the expense and delay of litigation. His nephew, the lawyer Francis Vernon, had to advise his uncle that he could find no one in the service that would stand disinterestedly for him.[58] In January 1748 Vernon published *Original Letters to an Honest Sailor*, being copies of several letters from political figures to him since 1739. It caused his enemies a little concern at first, but passed without serious repercussions.

By 1756 Vernon had largely retired from public life. His three children had all died and his wife died during the year. He himself died on 30 October 1757 at Nacton and was buried in St Martin's Church, Nacton on 6 November. Vernon's great contribution was as an enthusiastic advocate for the maritime economy and defence. Throughout his pamphlets and speeches ran the theme of an overwhelmingly powerful navy, based on good ship design, the humane encouragement of seamen to man the fleet, and the development of the maritime economy. His impeccable Whig credentials, country politics and 'Blue Water' strategy were a neat encapsulation of Whig patriotism. At a time when it was far from obvious that a maritime strategy would be successful, his advocacy provided professional support to the political message and helped embed it at this critical point in British political culture. His influence was based partly on his flamboyant style, but largely on the professional respect in which he was held. Until the fall of Louisbourg in the summer of 1745 Vernon had achieved the greatest maritime victories of the war. Although he never tested his ideas in a fleet engagement, his additional signal commands in 1739 helped create greater tactical flexibility in the line of battle. His view of the Western Squadron cruising on station in the Approaches was successfully applied by Anson and Hawke in coming years. As a trenchant critic of naval officers who failed in their duty, whether disinterested or not, he was in tune with current public concern, and he was not prepared to put long-standing friendship before a strict enquiry, as Admiral Mathews found to his cost. In doing this he helped shape public and professional expectations of behaviour that were to be the foundation of performance in the next half-century. On the other hand, his performance on the West Indian expedition was a major factor in its dramatic defeat. His behaviour in 1745 was highly questionable and his personality destroyed any long-term political weight he might have exercised. As early as 1744 Anson overshadowed Vernon's achievements by his circumnavigation (1740-1744) and his family connections with Lord Chancellor Hardwicke. Anson's great victory off Finisterre in May 1747 entirely eclipsed the disgraced admiral and before the war ended a new generation were emerging under the eyes of Anson, Hawke and Boscawen.

George, Lord Anson. Oil by unknown artist

7

George, Lord Anson
1697-1762

'Political and professional head of the navy'

N A M RODGER

As the younger son of a minor country gentleman, Anson came from a background typical of many sea officers, but his career was shaped by two distinctive factors. Unusually in Staffordshire, most Jacobite of English counties, his family were firm Hanoverians; and his uncle Lord Macclesfield was Lord Chief Justice from 1710, then Lord Chancellor from 1718 to 1725. These factors ensured that the young officer's merit was not overlooked (in spite of the misfortune of losing his first patron, Captain Peter Chamberlain, who was drowned in 1720), and that he was continuously employed during a long peace when the navy was largely demobilised. In May 1716 he was made a lieutenant by Sir John Norris; two years later he went to the Mediterranean in Sir George Byng's fleet, fought in the Battle of Cape Passaro, and later joined the flagship. In June 1722 he was made master and commander of the sloop *Weasel* cruising in the North Sea, and in 1724 he became captain of the frigate *Scarborough*, appointed as station ship in South Carolina. His duties there were to suppress piracy, a recent memory on that coast, and to protect British trade (much of it illegal, from the Spanish point of view) against the Spaniards in Florida. The work was undemanding, and left time to move in Charleston society, where he was popular with the settlers, and was remembered for his generosity and good nature.

Mr Anson . . . is far from being an anchorite, though not what we call a modern pretty fellow, because he is really so old-fashioned as to make some profession of religion: moreover, he never dances, nor swears, nor talks nonsense. As he greatly admires a fine woman, so he is passionately fond of music . . .[1]

He remained in Carolina for six years, investing in local property and shipping and becoming a substantial figure in Carolina society, to which he returned as captain of the frigate *Squirrel* in 1732.[2] When she paid off in June 1735 Anson went on half pay for the first time in his career. In December 1737 he was appointed captain of the 60-gun *Centurion*, and sent to protect British trade in West Africa. From there he crossed to the West Indies, and returned to England in the autumn of 1739.

Anglo-Spanish relations were by then in crisis, as Sir Robert Walpole's government struggled to preserve peace while the opposition inside and outside Parliament noisily demanded war, loudly proclaiming that naval operations against so effete and wealthy an enemy as Spain could not fail to be easy, glorious and profitable. Neither Walpole nor the First Lord of the Admiralty, Sir Charles Wager, thought victory would be so swift and painless, but if war came it had necessarily to be a war by sea, and they shared with the opposition a strong awareness of a national history (to a considerable extent, a national myth) of naval triumphs over Spain, going back to Sir Francis Drake. Moreover, contemporaries were acutely aware of Britain's need of bullion to balance its overseas trade accounts, and greatly exaggerated the quantity of gold and silver still being returned from Spanish America. The ministry's strategy was therefore based on amphibious expeditions against Spanish colonies. The main force was to go to the Caribbean, while two smaller squadrons attempted the remote but ill-defended Philippines and the Pacific coast of Spanish America. Anson, with his existing ship the *Centurion*, was initially destined to command the expedition against Manila. When that was cancelled, he took over the Pacific plan. He seems to have been the personal choice of Wager, a shrewd judge of men, though Anson's only obvious qualifications were plenty of recent sea time, and long experience outside home waters. His orders were to raid and plunder the Pacific coast of South America, to attack Panama if in the meanwhile the Caribbean expedition had gained a foothold on the opposite side of the isthmus, and if possible to capture the annual 'galleon' which linked Mexico and the Philippines. In addition he was to encourage rebellion by the Indians against the Spaniards, or by the Spanish colonists against their king; either or both of whom, it was confidently hoped, would be aroused by the exciting prospect of Protestantism and English liberty.[3]

The Circumnavigation, 1740–1744

Preparations for the expedition, in a hard and sickly winter, and during the first general mobilisation after many years of peace, were slow and frustrat-

ing. The squadron did not finally sail until 18 September 1740, and
although it seems to have been moderately well manned with seamen,[4] the
promised landing force of 500 regular infantry had been replaced with
newly-raised Marines, and 'invalids', or garrison troops, recruited from the
pensioners of Chelsea Hospital. Some of these unfortunates were carried
aboard on stretchers.[5] The delay had given the Spaniards good time to learn
the objectives of the expedition, and warn their colonial governors. Anson's squadron consisted of the *Centurion*, 60, *Gloucester*, 50, *Severn*, 50,
Pearl, 40, *Wager*, 28, the little sloop *Tryal*, 8, and two storeships. Less than a
month after he finally left Portsmouth, Don José Pizarro with five Spanish
ships of the line sailed from Santander to intercept him. Pizarro narrowly
missed Anson's squadron on the coast of what is now Argentina. Soon after,
on 7 March 1741, Anson passed through the Straits of Le Maire and began
to beat westward round the Horn. Thanks to their delayed departure it was
now the worst season of the year, in the worst waters of the world.

> The weather was still stormy with huge deep, hollow seas that frequently broke
> quite over us, with constant rain, frost or snow. Our decks were always full of
> water, and our men constantly falling ill with the scurvy; and the allowance of
> water being but small reduced us to a most deplorable condition.[6]

Unaware that they were fighting an eastward current as well as the gales,
they were very nearly wrecked on the coast of Tierra de Fuego on 13 April.
Soon after, another gale scattered them. When the squadron finally assembled at Mas-a-Tierra in the Juan Fernández Islands in mid-June, all but
the *Centurion* and *Tryal* had disappeared. Next month the *Gloucester* struggled in, and in August the storeship *Anna* arrived, her crew of sixteen in
reasonable health. Of the remainder it was later known that the *Wager* had
been wrecked, and the *Severn* and *Pearl* forced back into the Atlantic. Anson
was lucky that Pizarro's squadron had been even more completely shattered
than his own, while other Spanish ships sent from Chile to watch this very
island had left before he arrived; in every other respect the rounding of the
Horn, though an epic of endurance, was a military disaster. Of 961 men
who had sailed in the three surviving warships, scurvy, cold and privation
had killed all but 335, barely enough to handle the ships, and too few to
man fully the guns of the *Centurion* alone.

Virtually none of the objectives in Anson's orders were now feasible, but
he determined nevertheless to do what he could. Leaving the island in
September, the squadron moved northward up the coast, taking some
prizes and burning the small town of Paita. At the end of the year Anson

arrived off Acapulco, hoping to intercept the inward-bound galleon from Manila, but she had arrived already, and the Spaniards were forewarned of his coming. As there was nothing more to be gained on that coast, Anson decided to return home as Drake had done, across the Pacific. The *Tryal* had been scuttled as unseaworthy, so the squadron was now reduced to two ships, the *Centurion* and *Gloucester*.

On the long passage westwards scurvy broke out again, the sinking *Gloucester* had to be burnt for want of men to save her, and before the *Centurion* reached Tinian in the Marianas Islands on 28 August 1742 she too was reduced to a desperate condition, leaky and almost sinking, with few but the officers left to work the ship. Fresh fruit and rest ashore soon restored the survivors, but on 21 September another crisis arose when the *Centurion*, still not repaired, disappeared one night during a storm. Assuming she was lost, Anson and the survivors ashore set to work to enlarge a small Spanish vessel they had captured, the commodore and other officers as usual working with the men. On 10 October, however, the *Centurion*, which had been blown out to sea with only a handful of men aboard, reappeared. She now made her way without incident to Canton, where with much difficulty Anson was able to have the ship properly repaired, and to find a few more men. In April 1743, still with little more than half the *Centurion*'s normal complement, Anson sailed, ostensibly for England, but actually meaning to make one last attempt to retrieve success from the ruins of the expedition by intercepting the westbound Manila galleon. Now at last his endurance was rewarded: on 20 June off Cape Espíritu Santo the *Centurion* met and took the *Nuestra Señora de Covadonga*, carrying 1,313,843 pieces of eight and 35,682 ounces of virgin silver. The Spanish ship, essentially an armed merchantman, made a good defence but stood little chance against even a short-handed 60-gun ship. Anson now returned to Canton, where he sold his prize, and thence to England, where the *Centurion* arrived without further incident in June 1744. More than 1300 members of the original expedition had perished, and 145 completed the circumnavigation to see England again.[7]

Anson's voyage is remembered as a classic tale of fortitude and leadership in the face of fearful disasters, but to the British public of 1744 it was the treasure of the galleon, triumphantly paraded through the streets of London, which mattered. The war against Spain had yielded few of the expected easy victories, and now France had entered the war. Anson's triumph showed that the heirs of Drake were not altogether unworthy of him. The commodore himself was the hero of the hour, and every political group was anxious to recruit him.

The Admiralty and the Western Squadron

By this time Walpole was out of office, and the Earl of Winchelsea was First Lord of the Admiralty in an administration headed by the Duke of Newcastle and his brother Henry Pelham. Winchelsea was not a success; a battle off Toulon in February had been badly mismanaged, and it was already becoming clear that the aftermath was going to reflect still less credit on the navy and the ministry. Winchelsea's refusal to confirm one of Anson's promotions caused an immediate rift between them, and led to Anson refusing his promotion to rear-admiral. He must have realised the strength of his position, and the weakness of Winchelsea's. He had acute political instincts, and he was certainly in touch with his uncle's old friend Lord Hardwicke, Lord Chancellor since 1737.[8] Almost immediately Anson joined the group of opposition Whigs led by the Duke of Bedford, a group which had lately recruited the Duke's father-in-law, and Anson's Staffordshire neighbour, Lord Gower, who may have formed the initial connection. When the ministry was strengthened in December 1744 by incorporating a part of the Whig opposition, Bedford became First Lord of the Admiralty, accompanied by his colleague the Earl of Sandwich, and by Captain George Anson. The very first act of the new Board was to confirm the disputed promotion.[9]

Anson was now a politician as well as a public figure, but high society found him a curiosity and something of a disappointment. He had always been equable and self-possessed; the unfailing calmness and confidence with which he had faced every disaster and emergency on the famous voyage depended on iron self-control. Uncommunicative except with close friends, an indifferent conversationalist and a notoriously bad correspondent, he had no taste for the frivolities of the fashionable world, and no need to make any concessions to it, since he already possessed independent wealth and political consequence. Contemporaries were puzzled or envious, and less successful politicians deployed their wit at his expense: 'Lord Anson was reserved and proud, and so ignorant of the world, that Sir Charles Williams said he had been round it, but never in it.'[10] Anson was now rising as fast in the political world as in the navy. Already he had entered Parliament as MP for Hedon. Though by no means a figurehead, Bedford was not by temperament a working head of the Admiralty Board. His attendance, which was good for his first few months in office, had declined by June 1745 to Wednesdays and Thursday mornings, which constituted the Duke's normal wartime working week.[11] Otherwise he stayed at Woburn, though he expected to be fully informed by letter of business of importance. The working members of the Board were Sandwich, who as an earl stood second on the Board patent and acted as Bedford's deputy; Anson, almost the junior member of the Board and still only a captain until April 1745, but the only sea officer of real weight; and (from April 1745) the able young politician Henry Legge.

Bedford, Sandwich, Legge and Anson were aged 35, 26, 37 and 47 respectively when they took office, and Anson was almost the oldest member of the Board. These young men fully shared the prevailing mood of disappointment with the navy, and were determined to change many things. Anson, as we shall see, was deeply involved in many of the reforms which followed, but he did not cease to serve at sea. A rear-admiral in April 1745, vice-admiral in July 1746, he almost at once took command of important squadrons in the Channel. During 1745 and 1746 he and his colleagues were responsible for the most important single development in British naval strategy during the eighteenth century: the creation of the Western Squadron. The principle of amalgamating the main squadrons in home waters into a single fleet, cruising in the Western Approaches to the Channel, was simple and not completely original. For most of the year the prevailing winds over the British Isles blow from the southwest, up the Channel. Neither France nor Spain had a naval base in the Channel, so any enemy fleet had to come from the westward. An invasion force might sail from the ports of Normandy or Brittany, but it would sail without naval escort unless a fleet came up the Channel to cover it. Most of Britain's foreign trade (the Baltic trade excepted) came up and down the Channel. If the main fleet cruised to the westward, off the mouth of the Channel, it was well placed to cover convoys outward and homeward bound, to watch the main French naval base at Brest and intercept fleets coming and going from it, to guard against any attempt to invade Ireland, and to block, or at least pursue an enemy fleet entering the Channel. One single fleet, held within easy reach of home where it could be effectually controlled and maintained, was able to satisfy all the most essential British strategic requirements at once. The development of the Western Squadron was the result of a debate in which Anson, Sandwich, Bedford and Admiral Edward Vernon all played significant parts, but it was Anson who made the actual proposal to unite several squadrons in July 1746, and he who became commander-in-chief of the new force, with the responsibility of putting the idea into practice.[12]

The immediate spur to the creation of the squadron was Vice-Admiral William Martin's failure to intercept the French expedition to Canada which sailed in June 1746, and Anson's first task was to cruise to catch the same force on its return, which he narrowly failed to do. Next spring Anson was at sea again, cruising to intercept a large convoy known to be about to sail for the East Indies. Unlike Martin the previous year, he had a number of frigates, carefully disposed, and freedom to vary his movements according to the intelligence he received. On 3 May, north of Cape Orte-gal, he was rewarded by meeting what was in fact two French convoys, for India and America, combined. Anson had a large superiority, and in spite of a gallant defence all the French men-of-war and many of the merchantmen were taken. The victory was all the more welcome after seven disappoint-ing years of war. Anson was rewarded with a peerage, and returned to the Admiralty leaving his second, Sir Peter Warren, to command the squadron. When Warren fell ill, the newly-promoted Rear-Admiral Edward Hawke took command, and on 14 October, not far from the position of Anson's victory, he too intercepted and defeated a French convoy, taking six out of eight ships of the line of the escort.[13]

The value of the Western Squadron was now beyond any dispute, and in fact it formed the basis of British naval strategy for most of the next century. Anson's contribution to it was not only at the strategic level. He initiated, and both Warren and Hawke further developed, new signals designed to allow a fleeing enemy to be engaged without the delay of forming a formal line of battle.[14] Anson rigorously trained his captains in manoeuvres and signals so that they were thoroughly accustomed to what they might have to do in action, and he took pains to keep them informed of his intentions. These were not commonplace habits of command. His officers had great admiration and confidence in their commander-in-chief. According to Warren,

> no service had ever been so agreeable to him as this cruize under Anson, & that with respect to action he had learned more from him than in all the time he had been at sea before; adding that tho' the ship-captains in their squadron were very good officers, yet he did not think they would have done so well under any other commander, Mr Anson having called them all on board him the morning before the action, & given them directions what he believed would be right for them to do, supposing they should not be able to see, or he to change his signals.[15]

When Warren took over command, he assured Anson that, 'I will follow your advice, and be very communicative with the Captns of our squadron, I always thought it very necessary to be so and a thing that woud be very much for the Kings service to lett them know ones scheme, or plan of opperation.'[16] Anson also insisted on engaging at close range. 'I am glad you told his Majesty that you and I had recommended the Engaging the Enemy close on all occasions,' Warren wrote, 'I dare say where we happen to be we shall show such an Example as all officers must follow that have spirit or any regard to Honour or reputation.'[17] Long after the details of Anson's victories were forgotten, 'the good old discipline of the Western Squadron' remained an inspiration for future generations.[18]

The 1744 Admiralty Board and Naval Reform

Meanwhile, at the Admiralty, Bedford, Sandwich and Anson were deeply involved in a series of reforms, both of the seagoing navy and of its administration ashore. Much of this work was conducted by correspondence, for all three were often absent from the Board: Bedford because he preferred Woburn to his desk, Anson because he was at sea much of each summer, and Sandwich because in August 1746 he was appointed British plenipotentiary at the peace negotiations at Breda, and subsequently at Aix-la-Chapelle, which eventually concluded the war at the end of 1748. 'Custom', Anson believed,

> . . . is usually a power too mighty for reason to grapple with; and is the most terrible to those who oppose it, as it has much of superstition in its nature, and pursues all those who question its authority with unrelenting vehemence. However, in these later ages of the world, some lucky encroachments have been made upon its prerogative; and it may be reasonably hoped, that the Gentlemen of the Navy, whose particular profession hath of late been considerably improved by a number of new inventions, will of all others be the readiest to give up those practices, which have nothing to plead but prescription . . .[19]

Anson represented a rising generation of sea officers who were dissatisfied with the navy's condition and performance. 'You Sir', wrote his friend Commodore Curtis Barnett,

> have nothing to ask and less to fear; I therefore expect a great deal from you; and if I am deceived will never again hope to see the grievances of the sea-officers redressed, or any real improvements made, but conclude we are to go on in the old stupid Tracts of our Predecessors, leave all to chance and blunder on ad infinitum; without any regular system of discipline.[20]

Discipline, in the broadest sense, was one focus of Anson's interests. It embraced not only training, tactics and signalling, but the enhancing and settling of sea officers' rank and status. In 1746 the new Admiralty Board received a deputation of officers asking for their ranks to be officially

defined and distinguished by a uniform, which would put them on a par
with the army, and with foreign navies. Anson anticipated opposition from
more senior admirals, and had perhaps privately encouraged the movement. He certainly used his followers to promote the idea, and had them
design trial uniforms. The result was the adoption in 1748 of a formal
scheme of ranks, and the first officers' uniform.[21]

Behind many of Anson's reforms was the lamentable performance of the
navy in the Battle of Toulon in February 1744, on which occasion the
commander-in-chief, Admiral Thomas Mathews, had shown himself brave
but destitute of tactical experience; his second, Rear-Admiral Richard
Lestock, had refused to fight at all; and few of the captains had displayed
either ability or initiative. This was followed by courts martial on all of
them which were subjected to naked political interference (leading to the
entire acquittal of Lestock), while at the same time the House of Commons
mounted its own, still more partisan, enquiry. To complete the confusion,
in the middle of these trials a Lieutenant Fry of the Marines, who had been
court-martialled and cashiered at Jamaica, won a civil action (and £1000 in
damages) in the Court of Common Pleas against the president of the court
martial, Admiral Sir Chaloner Ogle, and was encouraged by Lord Chief
Justice Willes to proceed against each member of the court in turn. This he
did, beginning with Rear-Admiral Perry Mayne. Ogle was at this point
(May 1746) presiding over the courts martial of Mathews and Lestock, with
Mayne acting as his deputy while he was ill. Incensed by this interference
from the common lawyers, the members of the court suspended their
sittings, and were with difficulty restrained from trying to impeach the
Chief Justice, who in turn threatened to imprison them. The Admiralty
now feared that it would become impossible to hold courts martial at all,

> which coming once to be known among the Common Seamen and Marines, it
> is easy to forsee, what Scenes of Riot and Disorder His Majesty's Ships of War
> may come to be, and what fatal Consequences may be apprehended from such a
> Failure of Discipline and Government over His Majt.'s Forces by Sea.[22]

It was urgently necessary to establish the powers and independence of
naval courts martial, and to limit as far as possible their latitude to vary or
avoid the penalties prescribed in the Articles of War, which they had so
openly abused in some of the recent trials; 'led away by their private
prejudices or narrow principles, to the discredit of themselves, & to the ruin
of their profession'.[23] Thus was born what became the 1749 Navy Bill,
which among other changes to the Articles of War greatly reduced a court

martial's discretion to vary the prescribed sentences for various offences, and aimed to make officers on half pay subject to court martial. Unfortunately for Anson and Sandwich, the bill came into Parliament at the same time as the 1749 Mutiny Act, whose similar proposal in respect of half pay army officers was presented as an example of the dictatorial ambitions of the unpopular Duke of Cumberland, Captain-General of the army. This drew the 'Leicester House' opposition centred round the Prince of Wales into opposition to both bills, and especially the alleged design to 'make so many brave men slaves' by preventing them from resigning their commissions to avoid court martial. Many sea officers were connected with the opposition or persuaded by its arguments, and in the end this part of the bill was dropped. Most of the changes, however, were adopted. Among them the charge of 'cowardice, negligence or disaffection' now carried the death penalty without the alternative of 'such other penalty as the court may determine', which had hitherto provided the well-connected with an easy escape route.[24]

The performance of Mathews and Lestock had highlighted another of the Admiralty's difficulties: the choice of flag officers. There were three aspects to the problem. Firstly, there were too few admirals. There had been only one in each of the nine ranks until December 1743, and though George II had been persuaded to increase the number, he was reluctant to increase it by very much. Secondly, admirals were chosen only from the head of the captains' list, that is, from officers most of whom were elderly and many of whom were otherwise unsuitable. Lastly, the captains themselves claimed (though the Admiralty had never formally conceded) that those who survived to reach the head of the list had an established right to promotion. The new Admiralty Board planned to tackle this situation by instituting compulsory retirement schemes for both admirals and captains. This was a radical idea in an age when all sorts of rank and office still partook of the nature of private property, and when superannuation or retirement pensions were available (on application) only to a tiny minority of officers. Forcing admirals to retire proved to be too radical an idea to be accepted, but in 1747 the Admiralty successfully instituted the rank of 'Rear-Admiral without distinction of Squadron'. This neatly subverted the captains' pretensions by creating what was in effect a compulsory retirement scheme for senior captains, in the form of promotion to a notional rank which carried the title and the half pay of rear-admiral, but no claim to employment. It was now possible for the Admiralty to reach as far down the captains' list as it desired, selecting the able candidates for active flag rank, and retiring the rest as 'yellow admirals'.[25]

Another of the navy's most intractable difficulties was manning. Since the fleet was largely demobilised in peacetime, there was always an acute shortage of skilled seamen in wartime, especially in the opening months of a war as the fleet recommissioned. As no eighteenth century British Parliament was prepared to contemplate anything so redolent of tyranny as conscription, the navy was forced to rely on the inefficient and blatantly unfair system of impressment. The French, however, applying the resources and traditions of an absolute monarchy, had a system of conscription of the seafaring populations which (though it did nothing to increase France's inadequate stock of seamen) permitted the French navy to move faster in the early stages of mobilisation. To counter this initial advantage, and perhaps to establish a precedent which might in time have been built upon to reform the whole manning system, the Admiralty in April 1749 proposed a small reserve of 3000 seamen retained on 'half pay' of £10 a year. This modest proposal, however, was immediately denounced as a scheme of ministerial despotism, and had to be dropped as politically impossible.[26]

The Admiralty had more success with its attempts to reform the Marine regiments. As they were part of the army and not subject to the Admiralty, their discipline when afloat caused constant disputes, while the military structure of proprietary regiments, managed as private businesses by their colonels, was quite unsuitable for forces which served at sea in small detachments borne on the books of ships. The result was that by 1746 the Marines' financial affairs were in chaos. A committee of the House of Commons investigated, and at its recommendation the Marine regiments were transferred to Admiralty control in February 1747. Two years later the Admiralty floated the idea of replacing the unsatisfactory regimental structure with a permanent corps of Marines, but the end of the war was a bad moment to propose a new military establishment, and the Marine regiments were simply disbanded as they had been at the end of previous wars.[27]

While all these reforms and attempted reforms were going on, in the years 1745 to 1749, Anson and his colleagues were as concerned with ships as with officers and men. British ships of the line were generally believed to be too small to bear the weight of armament they were given, to carry their lower tier of guns sufficiently high out of the water for the ports to be opened in a seaway, and to sail well. Experience of war with Spain and then

France brought British officers into contact with ships which were larger and better than their own, and aroused vocal discontent. In particular the two battles of Finisterre in 1747 provided a large number of handsome new French ships of the line which were much larger than their British contemporaries. French frigates also were often faster and better adapted to their purpose than their British counterparts.[28] With hindsight it is clear that the differences between British and foreign battleships were as much of philosophy as quality. The big French ships were very expensive to build and maintain, which implied a limited fleet much of which would be out of service at one time. The relatively compact but economical, durable and powerful British ships were better suited to British strategy. What was needed was not a slavish copying of foreign designs, but some increase in size and some borrowing of French or Spanish features to produce more seaworthy and better balanced ships. This in effect was what the Admiralty eventually achieved, but its initial efforts were not very successful. Bedford's Board started by ordering a halt to all existing construction while a committee of admirals met to recommend a new 'Establishment' of guns and dimensions for each rate, while another committee of master shipwrights prepared new standard designs.[29] These committees moved cautiously some way in the direction Anson and his colleagues wanted, but they proved to be more a brake than a spur to progress. The greatest obstacle was Sir Jacob Acworth, Surveyor of the Navy since 1715, who was now serving his seventh sovereign and did not take well to being taught how to design a ship by amateurs half his age. Anson and Sandwich agreed

> in wishing that Sir Jacob should retire with every Circumstance that can make his old age easy & happy, but retain no influence in Naval Architecture. For it is high time Ships began to have bottoms to them, & more Expedition as well as better Oeconomy prevail'd in the Dock Yards. This cannot happen whilst he has any Influence, for whilst he has any he will have all.[30]

Unfortunately, Acworth could not be shifted and would not retire, while Joseph Allin, put in as Joint Surveyor in 1746, proved to be much less adventurous a designer than Anson had hoped. When Sir Jacob finally died in March 1749 after sixty-four years' unbroken service, only limited progress had been made in improving the design of British battleships.

With frigates the new Board had more success. Relatively small, cheap and rapidly built, they were often designed by the master shipwrights of the yards or by private builders, rather than by the Surveyor, so new influences could be more easily and swiftly assimilated. Unlike line of battle ships, frigates had more or less direct competitors in privateers with which they could be compared, and enemy prizes of rival design were relatively common.[31] An important part in developing rival designs was played by Benjamin Slade, Master Shipwright of Plymouth Yard, who seems to have been the favourite designer of Anson and his naval followers, and the one they most came into contact with in these years when the Western Squadron was operating from Plymouth. The French privateer *Tigre*, taken in 1747, was entrusted to his hands. 'As all our Frigates sail wretchedly,' Anson wrote to Bedford from his flagship off Ushant,

> I intreat your Grace that an order may be immediately sent from your Board to the Navy Board to direct Mr Slade the Builder at Plymouth to take off the Body of the French *Tyger* with the utmost exactness, and that two Frigates may be order'd to be built with all possible dispatch; of her dimensions and as similar to her as the Builders Art will allow; let Slade have the building of one of them.[32]

Slade investigated the designs of other French prizes, sending Anson plans, models and proposals. None of the prizes was copied exactly, for the French ships for all their speed were cramped, unseaworthy and weakly built, but the British designers, including Slade, Allin and others, worked with considerable success to adapt the best aspects of foreign designs to their own requirements.[33]

Ship design was not the only responsibility of the Navy Board which aroused the dissatisfaction of the 1744 Admiralty. Bedford and his colleagues had been rebuffed in their efforts to promote change, or simply to acquire information, on a wide variety of matters.[34] Acworth's death, and the retirement the same month of the elderly Captain Richard Haddock, the Comptroller of the Navy, opened the way for another attempt to improve the management of the dockyards. To this end the Board decided on a simple but revolutionary move. On 9 June 1749 their Lordships,

> taking into their consideration the number of Men Borne in the several Dock and Ropeyards, the great Expence Attending the same, And that the Works are not carried on with the Expedition that might be expected from them, which must arise from the remisness of the Officers, or Insufficiency of the Workmen, or both,[35]

decided to visit the dockyards themselves. Since even the Navy Board never visited the yards as a body, and seldom went further than Deptford or Woolwich as individuals, this gave the Admiralty the opportunity to outflank the Navy Board's superior experience with first-hand knowledge. It might be thought that on a pre-arranged visit they would have seen only what they were supposed to see, but in fact they met widespread evidence of idleness, waste and mismanagement, while in several yards the senior officers were either too old and ill to work, or had not been sighted at all for long periods. All this offered ample scope for improved management of the existing system, but the Lords of the Admiralty were especially interested in an important innovation. Everywhere they discussed with the yard officers the extension of 'task' or piece-work in place of the day wages by which most work was done in the yards. Nevertheless the Admiralty limited itself to imposing task-work on certain groups of workmen, and both this order, and its other efforts to tighten up the efficiency of the yards, met with obstruction or blank refusal from the Navy Board.[36]

Hitherto we have been considering the work of the 1744 Admiralty Board as a whole, with Anson implicitly accorded a leading role. It has long been traditional among naval historians to regard him as the real head of the Board, with Bedford too idle and Sandwich too inexperienced to play a significant part. In reality they formed an effective team. Bedford took the final decisions on matters of importance, and provided the essential political weight to back his colleagues. Anson contributed his unequalled professional experience and his rising political consequence. Sandwich applied his first-class mind and ferocious energy to mastering his new brief. Sandwich and Anson had a genuine esteem for one another, and though they must early have realised that in the long run they were rivals to succeed the Duke as First Lord, in the meanwhile they had strong reasons to work closely together. Since both were often absent, especially after Sandwich went to Breda in 1746, they needed to cover for each other. Moreover, they had a common rival on the Board, whose ambitions they both feared. Captain Lord Vere Beauclerk had none of Anson's claims to naval distinction, but he was the senior of the two, both on the Board patent and on the captains' list, and the son of a duke could never be a negligible factor in politics.[37] Anson and Sandwich therefore worked together to keep the reluctant Bedford in harness until Sandwich could decently replace him.

> Tho I have long known that your Grace intended to leave Ld Sandwich your Successor I must own that he is the only Person after your Grace that I would act with and cannot help declaring that ever since your Grace made me acquainted with him I have had the greatest esteem and friendship for him, not so much for his Parts, which are equalled by very few but from a thorough conviction that he will upon all occasions act upon the same honest Principles for the good of his Country that your Grace has ever acted, and therefore being

no great Politician myself, shall take him for my Pilot and be wholly directed by him.[38]

In February 1748 Sandwich duly succeeded the Duke as First Lord of the Admiralty, but he and Anson were closer than ever. While he was absent on the Continent, Sandwich needed Anson to run the Admiralty and watch his political flanks, while Anson needed all Sandwich's support against Beauclerk, who seized the opportunity to make another push for power.[39] This is the context of a letter from Sandwich which has sometimes been quoted to demonstrate that he was a mere nonentity who allowed Anson to control the Admiralty completely:

> I would not lose a moment to desire that you would consider yourself as in effect the head of the Admiralty; that you would not only write to me your sentiments, as to any measures you would wish to have executed, and where my assistance is necessary, but that you would always make use of my name wherever it may be necessary; and, if you would have anything deferred, desire time to write to me about it, and you may always depend on the decision that you tell me is agreeable to your opinion. I shall beg you would suffer everything I do to go through your hands, as it is my meaning to throw my share of the power, and the direction of the whole, as much as possible, into your hands.[40]

The two continued to work closely together in 1749, when Anson was home from the sea and Sandwich from the Continent, and in November of that year the baffled Beauclerk finally resigned from the Admiralty.

It is not possible to make a simple division of responsibility for the reforms attempted and achieved by the Admiralty during these years, for they were the product of a team which worked harmoniously together. It is clear, however, that Anson took the lead in professional naval questions. In tactics and training, rank and discipline, and in ship design, his colleagues deferred to his knowledge. In strategy (including the creation of the Western Squadron), in the legal and political question of the authority of the Admiralty and of courts martial, the Board acted together. The civil administration of the navy and the management of the dockyards was Sandwich's special subject, to which he later devoted a substantial part of his long career.

1749–1756: Admiral and First Lord

As a full admiral in May 1749, and Vice-Admiral of Great Britain the following year, Anson was already at the head of his profession. His career in another sense was crowned in April 1748 by his marriage to the Hon

Elizabeth Yorke, eldest daughter of his political mentor Lord Hardwicke, the Lord Chancellor. Since Hardwicke was not only the leading jurist of his generation, but the anchor of successive Cabinets for over twenty years, the marriage secured Anson's situation at the heart of the political Establishment. Lady Anson was a striking contrast to her husband: pretty, vivacious, fond of dancing and society, and twenty-eight years his junior, but she was an intelligent woman who took a close interest in his political career and in naval affairs, and the apparently ill-matched couple were happy together. Their only sorrow was that they never had children, and Anson was deeply affected by her death in June 1760.[41]

In most respects Anson's political weight now exceeded Sandwich's, and for several reasons the young earl had enemies. He added to them by the vigour with which he argued for higher Navy Estimates. In November 1750 a Cabinet meeting broke up in uproar over this issue. At the same time the Pelhams were disenchanted with the Duke of Bedford, who had been secretary of state since leaving the Admiralty, and who tactlessly insisted that Sandwich succeed him in that office too. The result was a political coup in June 1751 which ejected them both from office.[42] Anson was the obvious successor as First Lord of the Admiralty, where he was to remain for most of the rest of his life. It was an implicit condition of his appointment that he was not expected to trouble his colleagues as Sandwich had done. During the next four years the Navy Estimates fell to levels not seen since the years of profound peace and French alliance in the 1720s and early 1730s. Moreover, Anson abandoned Sandwich's attempts to reform the dockyards. No further Admiralty visitations took place, and the subject of task work was allowed to sleep.[43]

In the 1750s, however, the French were not allies and the diplomatic situation was not stable. Few of the signatories of the Peace of Aix-la-Chapelle were happy with it, while undefined frontiers and unquenched ambitions in North America provided a source of mounting tension between Britain and France. In the course of 1754 there was fighting in the Ohio valley. In the same year Henry Pelham, the leader of the administration, died, and was succeeded by his brother the Duke of Newcastle. The Newcastle ministry decided to reinforce North America with troops under Major-General Braddock. When the French countered with a larger reinforcement, a squadron under Vice-Admiral Boscawen was despatched to intercept and turn back the French warships carrying the troops. Boscawen was authorised to use force, but the Cabinet seems to have hoped that his mission could be carried out without provoking a general war. Both moves misfired: Braddock was heavily defeated by the French and their Indian allies, while on 10 June 1755 Boscawen met the French squadron already dispersed by fog off Newfoundland, and captured only two ships – enough to provoke a war, but not much to win it. Convinced (prematurely, in fact) that general war was now unavoidable, the ministry ordered the Western Squadron, again at sea under Hawke, and other forces in home waters, to capture as many French merchantmen as possible. In the autumn a large fraction of French overseas trade was coming home, not suspecting its danger, and the resulting manpower losses severely hampered French naval preparations.[44]

Having mobilised early, and struck in peacetime against an unprepared and reluctant enemy, the British had secured what might have been a decisive advantage. In the spring of 1756, however, Britain's own naval difficulties forced her on to the defensive at sea. Partly because of the perennial problem of manpower, but also (in Newcastle's opinion, at least) because of the Admiralty's failure to keep the navy in readiness, it was acutely difficult to find sufficient ships to face two widely separated threats.[45] France was known to be preparing a large force for the invasion of Britain, and another, smaller, to attack the British Mediterranean colony and naval base of Minorca. It was obvious that either might be a feint to cover the other, and that the French ministry was not obliged to make a final choice until the last minute. In this dilemma Anson, his Cabinet colleagues and the King were clear that the threat in the Channel was by far the more serious, and that the Western Squadron under Hawke had first priority. Not until 6 April did Vice-Admiral John Byng sail with a squadron to cover Minorca. Arriving at Gibraltar on 2 May, he learned that the French had already landed and were besieging the British garrison in Fort St Philip. By then, if not long before, Byng had clearly convinced himself that success was impossible. Off Mahon on 18 May he fought an indecisive action with the French Toulon squadron, of roughly equal strength to his own, then hastened to return home, leaving Minorca to its fate. Though the French army ashore, dependent for all its supplies on shipping from Toulon, was extremely exposed to naval action, Byng did not even leave his frigates to harrass the enemy.[46]

Even before the news of the battle reached England, the deafeatist tone of Byng's letters had convinced the Cabinet that he must be replaced, and Hawke was on his way to relieve him. By the time Byng reached England on 26 July he was the subject of public execration. Sea officers were furious that the navy's honour had again been betrayed by what many assumed to be simple cowardice. The ministry, of course, preferred that the admiral should take responsibility for the disaster rather than themselves. In this they failed, for the public blamed both, and in November the government was replaced by one formed by William Pitt, and consisting largely of his relations. Anson was succeeded by Pitt's brother-in-law Lord Temple. Pitt had obvious reasons to blame his predecessors rather than Byng for the disaster. Though a court martial was unavoidable, a friendly president was chosen, and Byng himself looked forward to a complete acquittal. Nevertheless, he was convicted under the twelfth Article of War of failing to do his utmost to defeat the enemy 'through cowardice, negligence, or disaffection', and though the court explicitly exonerated him of cowardice or disaffection, they could hardly avoid negligence. This was one of the articles reworded in 1749 to leave no alternative to the death penalty, and so the court reluctantly condemned him to death. Even now no-one expected the sentence to be carried out, and the government had no desire that it should be, but the admiral's fate was sealed by a combination of accidents, including the King's implacable hatred of cowardice, and the extraordinarily tactless interventions of Voltaire and Temple.[47]

Anson cannot escape all responsibility for the loss of Minorca. With hindsight it is clear that he erred on the side of caution in concentrating on the Western Squadron, though he was obviously right that the defence of Britain was the essential priority. He must take some blame for the relative slowness of mobilisation, and he was chiefly responsible for the choice of admiral – though Byng was virtually the only officer available of suitable seniority and long experience in the Mediterranean. Anson cannot reasonably be blamed (though he sometimes is) for Byng's trial, which was unavoidable, nor for his execution, which took place while Anson was out of office.

Anson and the Seven Years War

Anson was not popular after the fall of Minorca, and only the insistence of his father-in-law returned him to the Admiralty in July 1757 when the ministry was reconstructed as a coalition of Newcastle and Pitt.[48] He thus became one of the key Cabinet ministers who directed the Seven Years War, and an architect of an unparalleled series of victories. No one would now claim, as was once the fashion, that William Pitt alone deserves credit for the succesful strategy of the war. On the contrary, it is clear that Anson was an influential, at times a dominant voice, as he had to be when so much depended on the navy. When naval affairs or overseas expeditions were discussed in Cabinet, Anson took the lead.[49] He therefore deserves full credit for the strategy which led to the conquests of Louisbourg in 1758 and Quebec in 1759, and the great naval victories of Lagos and Quiberon Bay in 1759. The 1762 Havana expedition was his scheme from the beginning.[50] He had not lost his habit of trusting subordinates, and privately consulted commanders-in-chief overseas on what strategy they would propose (going so far as to write in his own hand to preserve secrecy).[51]

Anson was much more than a strategist and a Cabinet minister, however. He was the working head of the Admiralty, the chief who (very unlike Temple) ensured that 'the business was done well, quick, and as it ought to be'.[52] He was the head of the seagoing navy, whose austere ideal of duty and high standards of conduct were spread throughout the service – not least by his own followers like Charles Saunders, Augustus Keppel and Lord Howe, all of whom reached high rank during this war. Under Anson's leadership, officers were ill advised to plead sickness or any other excuse to get out of disagreeable or unhealthy assignments. Devotion to duty and courage in action were the principal recommendations for promotion. 'My constant method', he wrote,

> since I have had the honour of serving the King in the station I am in, has been to promote the lieutenants to command whose ships have been successfully engaged upon equal terms with the enemy, without having any friend or recommendation, and in preference to all others, and this I would recommend to my successors if they would have a fleet to depend on.[53]

Nor was his care limited to officers: at the height of the war he was still taking an interest in the careers of individual ratings.[54]

Even after many years at the Admiralty, Anson preferred the quarterdeck to the desk, and longed to command at sea again. Viewing the Western Squadron in 1755,

> it gave me great pleasure to see them at Spithead and would have given me much more to have gone to sea with them; but when I mentioned it to the Duke of Newcastle, he asked me what was then to become of the Admiralty, I cannot say I think it would be the better for my absence, but I am certain I sacrifice the thing that would give me the greatest pleasure by being obliged to continue at it.[55]

He had his chance in 1758, when the sensitive Hawke resigned his command of the Western Squadron in protest at a fancied slight.[56] This considerably embarrassed the Admiralty, which could neither spare the services of

so talented an officer, nor overlook the glaring breach of duty: 'this step of
Sir E Hawke has spread a very improper spirit of discontent in the fleet at
Spithead.'[57] The only solution was for Anson himself, at the age of 61, to
leave the Admiralty and take command for the summer, with Hawke as his
second, until he presently fell ill, 'a good deal occasioned by the uneasiness
of his mind from his own late conduct.'[58] 'I don't think the affairs of the
Admiralty go on the better for my absence', Anson told his father-in-law,
but, 'I do assure your Lordship when I began to exercise my fleet I never
saw such an awkwardness in going thro' the common manoeuvres necessary to make an attack upon an Enemy's Fleet at all, what we now do in an
hour, in the beginning took us eight . . .'[59]

This summer was Anson's last experience of commanding a fleet at sea,
but he continued to be deeply concerned with the practicalities of naval
operations. The great victory of Quiberon Bay in November 1759 was
made possible by the adoption, for almost the first time, of a sustained close
blockade of Brest, in all weathers. This demanded not only seamanship,
perseverence and courage from Hawke (once more in command) and his
captains, but new administrative arrangements to keep the ships at sea for
long periods. Anson had always been keen on fresh food and vegetables to
keep men healthy, and he had been seriously worried by scurvy in his fleet
in 1758.[60] Now, in the face of great expence and difficulty, the Admiralty
set up a system of supplying the Western Squadron at sea with fresh meat
and vegetables. The result was that on the day of the battle there were
fewer than twenty men sick in a squadron of twenty sail.[61]

Another of the reforms begun in the 1740s which Anson was able to
complete during this war was in the formation of the Marines. When they
were reformed in 1755, as usual on the outbreak of war, they adopted a
non-regimental structure under complete Admiralty control, and at the end
of the war they were allowed to remain as a permanent corps.[62] In ship
design, also, Anson was able to complete the efforts which had earlier been
frustrated. The retirement of Sir Joseph Allin in 1755 at last allowed Anson
to appoint a Surveyor of the Navy who shared his ideas. Thomas Slade was
the outstanding British naval architect of the century, the designer of what
later generations regarded as the classic classes of 74-gun ship and frigates, as
well as the fastest and most famous of all First Rates, the *Victory*. He
achieved the harmonious synthesis of British and foreign design elements
which Anson had looked for ten years before.[63]

The choice of flag officers was primarily Anson's, and notably the bold
use of the rank of commodore to appoint able young officers to high

command long before they became eligible by seniority for promotion to flag rank. The extreme example of this was Keppel, who in 1761, aged 36, was commanding a fleet of sixty-three sail, with two junior commodores under him. When he first hoisted his flag the following year he was a captain of eighteen years' seniority, and had been a commander-in-chief, off and on, for thirteen of them.[64] No other First Lord of the Admiralty so boldly circumvented the limitations of promotion by seniority.

It used to be argued[65] that Anson sternly resisted the attempts of Newcastle and other politicians to interefere in the promotion and appointment of officers. This is true, but it is not true that Anson objected to political considerations as such. On the contrary, he was a leading politician himself, accustomed to mingling his political and naval activities, and he did not object to other admirals doing the same. Civilians like Newcastle were dangerous because they did not necessarily understand the paramount importance of professional merit in naval appointments, and because they represented a leakage of patronage, and hence of power, out of the hands of the Admiralty and the admirals. Political influence in their hands was safe because it supported their authority; naval patronage in outsiders' hands was dangerous.[66] Even the King was sharply rebuffed; Anson threatened to resign if George III carried out his plan to make his brother a rear-admiral.[67] Sea officers of undoubted talent, like Augustus Hervey, who recklessly involved themselves in opposition politics and even attacked the First Lord in person, were steadily protected by Anson from the consequences of their own imprudence.[68]

As a wartime First Lord of the Admiralty Anson was able to display most of his greatest qualities. He did not devote great attention to the dockyards, and the navy attained the necessary numbers chiefly by letting numerous contracts to private shipbuilders to build ships, many of which subsequently had short working lives and laid up trouble for his successors.[69]

Perhaps had he lived into another long period of peace he might have tackled these problems, but the precedent of 1751–55 suggests not. In the event, Anson died on 6 June 1762, at the height of a victorious war for whose success he could take a large part of the credit. Even at his death, though sufficiently famous, he was a private man not well known to his contemporaries, and in high society there were spiteful or envious observers who dismissed his abilities.[70]

Outside the navy he was appreciated best among the small circle of kinsmen who knew him well. 'He had a very extensive knowledge,' his brother-in-law wrote,

acquired more by practice than study of his own profession; he could explain it
to others clearly & pointedly without parade or affectation. He was in himself
shy & reserved, but where he was once free or admitted others to be so with
him, no man could be more agreeable & communicative. He thought deeper
about Men & things than a Stranger would have imagined who had only seen
him in mixed companies. He had high notions of sincerity & honor & practised
them without deviation in all parts of his life. He loved reading little, & writing,
or dictating his own letters less, & that seeming negligence in an office which
must be attended with frequent applications to the first Lord in person, to
which answers are always expected & are often proper, drew upon him the ill
will of many. He had a remarkable quickness in making dispositions of ships, &
appointing them to the services for which they were fittest, and without making
a bustle, or *raising* the daily Newspaper & Coffeehouse Ruffs, conducted the
business of a very complicated department with uncommon vigor & dispatch.
He had a natural partiality to a good Sea officer, & raised the greatest part of
those who distinguished themselves in that service during the last war. He
withstood recommendations of interest or favour more than any first Lord of
the Admiralty was ever known to do.[71]

'Patience & Perseverance are two of the Vertues your Lordship is so
remarkable for', as one of his followers told him.[72] They were the fruits of
self-mastery. Anson was very far from insensible, however well he concealed his feelings.[73] In December 1746, at sea off Ushant, having just learnt
that he had failed to intercept the French squadron returning from Canada,
he admitted to Bedford that, 'From what I have felt this last fortnight I
think whoever happens to have success at Sea cannot be too well rewarded,
for I would not suffer the same anguish of mind, that I have done upon this
disappointment for all the honours riches and pleasures this world can
afford.'[74]

Both as a sea commander and as a statesman, Anson triumphed over
adversity by courage and determination. Flexible and pragmatic at a tactical
level both at sea and ashore, he kept his ultimate goal clearly in view. He
was an outstanding judge of men, which served him well both in the navy
and in politics. His professional legacy was above all a tradition of devotion
to duty, of aggressive attack and of taking his subordinates into his confidence which was transmitted through his followers to future generations.
Hawke learnt it from him, and the young Nelson learnt it from Hawke's
follower, Captain William Locker.[75] Anson was certainly lucky in passing
his career in a period in which political tension, so destructive to the navy
both earlier and later in the century, was at a relatively low ebb. He was
lucky too, as well as skilful, in building up the political strength which

allowed him to buttress his authority in the navy and push through many of his intended reforms. No one else ever so successfully combined the roles of political and professional head of the navy, for no politician ever knew so much about the service, and no admiral ever made so outstanding a political career, or turned it so much to the navy's advantage.

Edward, Lord Hawke. Oil by Francis Cotes

8

Edward, Lord Hawke
1705–1781

'. . . so brilliant an officer . . .'

RUDDOCK MACKAY

Hawke's barrister father was of Cornish stock. His mother stemmed from the Yorkshire gentry. For patronage, after his father's death in 1718, Hawke depended on his uncle, Colonel Martin Bladen, who was a Commissioner of Trade and Plantations from 1717. In 1720 the future winner of two major conclusive victories was appointed by warrant to enter the navy as a volunteer, aged 15. However, his uncle's death in 1746 left Hawke without any important political connections. While sheer merit sufficed in a number of cases to advance officers to high rank in the eighteenth century navy, there was always a considerable chance that it would not. It will be seen that in 1747 Hawke was nearly excluded from promotion to flag rank through his lack of political influence.

In February 1720, when Hawke joined the *Seahorse* (of 20 guns) Britain happened to be at war with Spain – a fleeting boost for those seeking naval employment. Five years of trade protection, mostly in the West Indies, followed. Having done time as a midshipman and reached the age of 20, Hawke was due to take his lieutenant's examination. The *Seahorse* was back in the Thames at Galleons Reach when, on 2 June 1725, he passed this important test. This date may well be the best surviving indication of the month, or possibly the day, of Hawke's date of birth. An Anson or an Honourable Edward Boscawen, with their strongly influential connections, might be allowed to pass the examination at 19, but Hawke could hardly expect to break the rule. If Boscawen, after passing, had to wait for only seventeen days before being commissioned, Hawke's immediate reward was a spell as an able seaman, firstly on the African coast and then in the pestilential West Indies! Nevertheless, he remained a 'young gentleman' destined to be an officer. Having reverted to midshipman, he was discharged at Woolwich on the decommissioning of the *Kinsale*, 40. He was apparently unemployed until April 1729 when, at the age of 24, he was finally appointed a lieutenant in the *Portland*, 50.

The ensuing decade of peace was, from Hawke's point of view, notable for the bulge of officers left over from the War of the Spanish Succession. This helps to explain his spells ashore on half pay from January 1730 to May 1731 and again, when a post captain, from September 1735 to July 1739. Late in 1729, however, he spent a month of much relevance to his subsequent career on board the *Leopard*, 50 at Spithead. Peter Warren, who in 1747 would take over the Western Squadron from Anson but, when suffering from scurvy, recommend Rear-Admiral Hawke as his temporary replacement, commanded the ship. Meanwhile, from May 1731 Hawke was fourth lieutenant of the *Edinburgh*, 64 and in November he had an initial experience of storm damage in the Bay of Biscay when returning to England with Admiral Wager's squadron. Continuing Spanish hostility to British trade, together with Colonel Bladen's valuable support, brought employment for Hawke in the West Indies. There, service under Commodore Sir Chaloner Ogle led to Hawke's promotion in 1733 to master and commander and in 1734 to post captain. During these early commands (in 1733–5) of the *Wolf*, 10 and the *Flamborough*, 24, Hawke learnt much about coping with the extraordinary threats to shipboard health experienced on that station, to say nothing of tempestuous weather and consequent damage to the ships.

Hawke paid off the *Flamborough* at Spithead in September 1735. In 1737 he married his uncle Bladen's niece, Catharine Brooke, an heiress aged 17. They had four children who survived beyond infancy. Hawke proved to be an affectionate father and, in due course, grandfather. His marriage was a happy one until it ended with Catharine's early death in 1756. Hawke remembered her as 'the best wife, the best mother, and the best of friends'.

The Battle of Toulon, 1744

In 1739 the onset of war with Spain saw Hawke appointed to take the *Portland*, by now almost unfit for the sea, to the West Indies for further protection of trade. The fact that he, unlike so many others, did not succumb to the fevers rampant on the station testifies to the strength of his constitution. In January 1743, after much repairing of storm damage, he got the decrepit *Portland* back into the Thames, where she was soon broken up. In June he was given command of the *Berwick*, a new ship of 70 guns. He was to join Admiral Thomas Mathews in the Mediterranean, where the French were expected soon to enter the war on the side of Spain.

When Hawke took command of the *Berwick* at Deptford he experienced great difficulty in manning the ship. He reported to the Admiralty that he had to take a number of 'very little, puny, weakly fellows' who had never been to sea. 'I beg their Lordships' pardon for mentioning this affair, but I thought it my duty to do it, for when a ship is so very badly manned, she can be of very little or no service.'[1] Yet in the course of five months he would have a crew fit to fight against odds.

On 11 February Mathews fought his famously discreditable battle against a Franco-Spanish fleet off Toulon and Hawke showed how, in the future, he would expect individual captains to conduct themselves in a fleet action. Breaking away from Mathews's ineffectively engaged line, he bore down on the Spanish *Poder*, 64. Notwithstanding the severe health problems suffered by his 'puny' and inexperienced men on the outward voyage, he could rely on superior gunnery and seamanship in his brave interpretation of the Printed Sailing and Fighting Instructions. He disregarded the risk of being outnumbered and subsequently court-martialled.

Why did no other captain likewise bear down to leeward and clinch matters with a ship edging away? The reason was that Mathews continued to fly his original signal for the line of battle *after* he (later) hoisted that for engaging, despite the fact that a close general engagement had still not resulted. Displaying outstanding moral courage and fine tactical judgement, Hawke decided to obey Mathews's *second* signal only.

Before falling away to leeward the *Poder* had suffered casualties from the fire of Mathews's centre division, but those inflicted by the *Berwick,* from very close range, were extremely heavy. At the courts martial afterwards held on various participants in the battle, an officer of the *Norfolk* (of the centre division) was asked whether the *Berwick* had engaged 'nearer than the *Princessa* and *Somerset* had done?' He replied, 'the *Berwick* engaged the *Poder* some time after the *Norfolk* had left off firing. The *Berwick* went down to the leeward of the *Poder* and went close under her stern, and went up again on his lee side and hauled his wind upon her lee bow, and there engaged her till her main mast fell and her fore topmast, I believe.' The master of the *Norfolk* said of the *Berwick*: 'She engaged nearer than the *Princessa* and *Somerset* had done, for she engaged her close on board that a stone might be thrown from the one to the other.'² Having resisted bravely, the *Poder* struck to the *Berwick*.

In sum, Hawke had shown by example how individual captains should interpret the oft-reprinted Sailing and Fighting Instructions in a battle. As an admiral, he would expect all his captains to contrive to engage 'at pistol shot', whatever the form of engagement. Meanwhile the series of courts martial following the Battle of Toulon generated a spirit of reappraisal and tactical innovation in the British navy and Hawke's example became well known to a generation of officers. Lord St Vincent (born in 1735) told his eventual biographer Edward Brenton how accounts of Hawke's bold initiative had sickened him of line-bound tactical pedantry.

From July 1744 onwards Hawke derived useful experience of higher command through acting as commodore, on three successive occasions, of squadrons detached for service against the French and Spanish in the Mediterranean. He had three years to wait before his seniority as a post captain would make him eligible for a flag.

By early 1747 the Duke of Bedford's Board of Admiralty, of which Anson was a crucially influential member, had instituted a badly needed reform of the system of promotions to flag rank. Without this, the fixed establishment of admirals would have continued to be filled by captains of the greatest seniority and the British service would have resembled the French with its succession of elderly and defensively-minded admirals. However, the reform of 1747 happened to come one year after death had removed Colonel Bladen, Hawke's sole source of political patronage, from the scene. By 1747 Hawke had the requisite seniority as a captain, together with indisputable merit, but this did not mean that he was safe from being compulsorily retired as a 'yellow admiral'. With three vacancies to fill, the Admiralty rated the influential claims of three 'honourables and good men' – Knowles, Forbes, and Boscawen – ahead of Hawke who lacked indisputable social status. King George II, however, roundly declared that he would not have Hawke 'yellowed'! Consequently, Hawke, in accord with his seniority, was promoted on 15 July 1747 – like Knowles – to rear-admiral of the white, while Forbes and Boscawen became rear-admirals of the blue.

The Western Squadron, 1747

There is no sign or likelihood that the Admiralty saw in Hawke a future commander of the Western Squadron. After Anson's chase victory of 3 May, that command was handed on to Vice-Admiral Warren, while

Hawke became the port admiral at Plymouth. However, the continuing development of this westerly base during the French wars did prove relevant to Hawke's prospects. For when, early in August, Warren had to seek relief from scurvy, it was to Plymouth that he first went. Warren reported to the Admiralty – two days' ride away by 'express'– that there seemed to be 'no immediate service of great importance'. He recommended that Hawke be appointed as his second-in-command and that he should cruise with the squadron until he himself was fit to go out again. Anson was uneasy about putting the squadron under 'so young an officer'.[3] Finally Hawke was ordered to report his proceedings directly to Warren rather than to the Admiralty. This not only emphasised the temporary nature of Hawke's command; it also, as weeks passed without Warren's reappearance, proved an inefficient and time-wasting arrangement. However, Hawke allowed none of this to detract from the aggressive intent with which the squadron approached the growing possibility of a major engagement.

Anson evidently knew little of Hawke before August 1747. However, Hawke did owe much to Anson on account of the state of the Western Squadron. During Anson's time in command (1745-7) a fresh intensity was brought to training and manoeuvres. Anson also issued Additional Instructions refining the conduct of a general chase. This option had for long been included in the General Printed Sailing and Fighting Instructions for use especially, but not exclusively, when the enemy was running away. Basically, Anson imbued that sense of aggressive purpose lacking in the British performance off Toulon in February 1744. Before Hawke sailed from Plymouth on 10 August 1747, he was supplied by Warren with copious instructions emanating from Anson.

At that time the enemy's intentions were unclear. The French evidently wished to revive their West Indian trade, which had suffered grievously from British blockades underpinned by the Western Squadron. Hawke was ordered by Warren to destroy enemy commerce, whether inward or outward bound. He could change his rendezvous if he wished, but if he did he was to leave a sloop or frigate on his current rendezvous 'between the latitudes of Belle Isle and Ushant from ten to thirty or forty leagues to the westward'. This did indeed prove to be the focal area of Hawke's cruise. However, he was given discretion – which he used – to cruise as far south as Capes Ortegal and Finisterre to collect intelligence from intercepted vessels.

By early September the Admiralty realised that Hawke was facing a situation of major importance. On the 8th the lords therefore issued instructions appointing him to command the Western Squadron. They also directed him 'to cruise with the said squadron or the major part thereof between Ushant and Cape Finisterre, keeping twenty leagues to the westward of each cape, and to make the land every fourteen days'. However, Hawke meanwhile relied on his own intelligence and it was this that led him to intercept the huge French convoy and its considerable escort some two hundred miles west of Ushant on 14 October (almost in the *meridian* of Cape Finisterre). It was not until the day following the battle that Captain Arthur Scott of the *Lion*, 60, who had joined Hawke as part of a large reinforcement on 27 September, got round to giving Hawke the Admiralty's instructions of 8 September, together with his commission for command of the Western Squadron. According to Hawke's dispatch of 17 October, Scott had 'mislaid' these items![4] This may therefore be deemed one of the more fortunate miscarriages in British naval history. No disciplinary action seems to have been taken against Scott. Not only did he fight well on 14 October but, thanks to him, Hawke was admirably well located on that date!

To recapitulate, Hawke sailed from Plymouth in the *Windsor*, 60, together with the *Monmouth*, 64, on 10 August. On the 12th he found four ships on the rendezvous near Brest. By the 21st he had correctly concluded that the French warships at Brest were preparing to escort merchantmen, collecting at, or near Rochefort. Meanwhile, even though he would soon have to send in a ship afflicted with scurvy, his appeals to Warren for reinforcements had, by 10 September, brought his strength up to nine of the line (all except the *Monmouth* of only 50 or 60 guns), together with two sluggish frigates – 'a tolerable force', according to Hawke. He informed Warren that there was 'a large fleet of merchant vessels and ships making up at Rochelle, bound to the West Indies'. He thought that 'the most effectual method to intercept them would be by cruising with a squadron (if we can't have two) between the latitudes of 48.00 and 44.00 N, at a tolerable distance to the westward. By taking this measure, they could never know how to avoid us.' He had taken pains to feed the enemy with reports of his whereabouts when cruising near Cape Ortegal.[5]

On 26 September Hawke was joined off Cape Finisterre by Captain Thomas Fox with seven of the line, including three more 64s and the *Devonshire* of 66 guns, together with six smaller vessels. Hawke now heard from Warren that he was definitely unfit to come back to sea. On the 27th Hawke issued a fresh 'Line of Battle', comprising as many as sixteen ships of the line and miscellaneous frigates. Water and beer had been turning foul and he sent word to Warren that the squadron would have to go into port by the end of October. Hawke shifted his flag to the *Devonshire*, taking with him as his flag captain John Moore, who had come out with him in the *Windsor*. Warren had given Hawke intelligence of galleons returning to Spain – a famous source of prize money from which Warren himself had reaped enormous benefit. However, on 6 October Hawke replied in his own hand:

> With respect to the intelligence you sent me relating to the galleons, as it's uncertain when they will come home, and likewise impossible for me to divide my force in the present necessitous condition of the ships under my command, I must lay aside all thoughts of them during this cruise which cannot be of long continuance . . . I am in great hopes the station I am going to will throw us in the way of the enemy . . . With regard to lying in wait for them, all that any man can do is to put the most reasonable supposition into practice . . .[6]

Hawke mentioned that he had now been told to report directly to the Admiralty, but he also continued to keep Warren well posted.

By the 11th (as he told Warren) Hawke had received news originating – as was often the case – from a neutral Dutch vessel that 'eight sail of ships of war and near two hundred sail of merchant ships and vessels' were waiting at Rochelle. This piece of intelligence proved very accurate. Persisting westerly winds suggested to Hawke that the convoy would push well to the northward to get out of the Bay of Biscay. But he now had to send two of his 50-gun ships into Plymouth, leaving him with only fourteen quite small ships of the line. To Hawke's irritation, all of these, including those recently joined, were short of water and in need of cleaning.

However, at 7am on 14 October, with Ushant some two hundred miles to the eastward (and Cape Finisterre far to the south), and with the wind moderate at south-southeast, a signal was made for seven sail to the southeast. Hawke was cruising in extended order several miles to the northeast, and thus to leeward, of what turned out to be a strong French squadron escorting more than two hundred merchantmen. Clarity and simplicity characterised Hawke's signals during his approach. In his dispatch of 17 October he reported:

> I immediately made the signal for all the fleet to chase. About 8, saw a great number of ships, but so crowded together that we could not count them. At 10, made the signal for the line of battle ahead. The *Louisa* being the headmost and weathermost ship, made the signal for discovering eleven sail of the enemy's line of battle ships. Half an hour after, Captain Fox in the *Kent* hailed us and said

they counted twelve very large ships. Soon after, I perceived the enemy's
convoy to crowd away with all the sail they could set, while their ships of war
were endeavouring to form a line astern of them, and hauled the wind [thus
heading approximately southwest] . . . Finding we lost time in forming our line
while the enemy was standing from us, at 11 made the signal for the whole
squadron to chase. Half an hour after, observing our headmost ships to be
within proper distance, I made the signal to engage which was immediately
obeyed. The *Lion* [of only 50 guns] and the *Princess Louisa* [60] began the
engagement and were followed by the rest of the squadron as they could come
up, and went from rear to van.[7]

Hawke's reference to a 'proper distance' for engaging is best understood by
looking back to his personal example at Toulon, of which no captain
involved on 14 October 1747 can have been unaware. Bearing in mind that
Hawke fought his 'Finisterre' battle as a mere stand-in for Warren, expect-
ing to be superseded at any moment, the lack of recorded signals for 'all
captains' (indicating joint verbal discussion of tactics) is hardly surprising,
but the effect of Hawke's earlier example is reflected in some of the captains' logs. From what has already been said about Arthur Scott of the *Lion*,
the absence from his log of the range at which he opened fire occasions no
astonishment; but the log's general drift and his ship's high casualties imply
close action. However, Charles Watson of the *Princess Louisa* is explicit.
According to his log, the French began by firing at the *Lion*. Then, 'a few
minutes after, I got within pistol shot of the enemy's sternmost ship of 70
guns' and a hot engagement ensued.[8] According to a witness at Captain
Fox's subsequent court martial, the *Eagle* (of 60 guns) came up in her turn
and engaged the 70-gun *Neptune* 'at the distance of pistol shot'.[9] It will be
seen that, as a well-established admiral, Hawke would, in 1757, issue explicit instructions that all captains were, in any form of battle, to close to
pistol shot before opening fire.

Watson notes that he was quickly supported by that redoubtable veteran,
Captain Henry Harrison, in the *Monmouth*, 64. 'The *Monmouth*', Watson
continues, 'came up and seconded me with great bravery, and as I found
the rest of our ships coming up, I stretched ahead to engage the other ships.'
It was not to be expected that Hawke's ships could engage closely with a
series of more powerful opponents without incurring quite heavy casualties, but this cost could be more than justified by annihilation of the
French squadron. Although the marquis de l'Etanduère turned out to have
only eight of the line against Hawke's fourteen, two of Hawke's were only
50-gun ships and seven more were 60s. Hawke's most powerful ship, the

Devonshire, was outgunned by the French 74s, namely *Intrépide*, *Terrible*, and *Monarque*, and by the *Neptune*, 70, all with very large complements, to say nothing of the mighty flagship, the *Tonnant*, 80.

Harrison succeeded in getting to windward of the French line and exchanged broadsides with the *Tonnant* before finally reaching the *Intrépide* in the van. Hawke's flagship, the *Devonshire*, was not a fast sailer, but at about 1.30pm she finished off the rear French ship, the unfortunate *Severne* of only 50 guns. She was then driven twice to leeward by Rodney's *Eagle*, which had been rendered ungovernable by the *Neptune*. Having worked free, Hawke closed in on the *Tonnant* but was mortified by the breeching of his lower deck guns, which put him out of action for a time. Having subsequently got 'almost alongside' the *Trident*, 64, he soon silenced her. By nightfall the *Terrible* also had struck to the *Devonshire*. As already indicated, Hawke's use of the general chase had elicited an admirable response from his individual captains in terms of effective gunnery, manoeuvre, and mutual support. Besides those already mentioned, Charles Saunders and Philip Saumarez certainly needed no further signals after the flags for the chase and engaging had been displayed long before the light began to fade. At the end of the battle they saw the *Intrépide* and *Tonnant*, the only French ships not yet captured, breaking away into the night. Despite much damage aloft, Saunders in the *Yarmouth*, 64 and Saumarez in the *Nottingham*, at the cost of his life, pursued the two also damaged, but much more powerful ships. Saunders continued to fire at the *Tonnant* until about 10pm.[10]

No masts, other than two fore masts, were left standing on the six captured ships of the line. The recorded British losses amounted to 747 (170 killed and 577 wounded). With prisoners included, the French losses came to about 4000 – a crippling blow to the French navy. British mastery at sea over France and Spain had been conclusively established and lasted until peace was signed in October 1748.

Hawke himself had been severely burnt by exploding gunpowder, but he remained with the squadron off Brest until its limits of endurance had been reached. On 29 October he triumphantly brought the six captured ships of the line into Portsmouth harbour: *Monarque*, *Terrible*, *Neptune*, *Trident*, *Fougueux*, and *Severne*. In November he was made a Knight of the Bath and in the following May he progressed to vice-admiral of the blue.

He had shown at the (so-called) Second Battle of Cape Finisterre what an admiral of good tactical judgement and great aggressive intent could make of the persistently printed Fighting Instructions, especially when supplemented by Anson's Additional Instructions (reissued by Hawke on

12 August). Anson's article 10 clearly influenced the captains. Although l'Etanduère, to shield his convoy, stood to fight in a line on 14 October, Hawke, in his above-quoted dispatch, found it legitimate to hoist the general chase because the French were 'standing from us'. He does not refer to his advantage in numbers because, when hoisting the chase signal, he thought that the numbers might be nearly equal. Indeed some of the French looked – and were – of superior power. Essentially, he liberated his captains, confiding in the superior gunnery, seamanship, and fighting spirit that he had himself exemplified at Toulon. Five of his captains had been at Anson's (more one-sided) action in May. Mutual support, certainly, was a feature of Hawke's battle in October.

On 15 October Hawke had called a council of ten senior captains on board the *Devonshire* to decide whether, in view of the shattered state of many of his ships, further pursuit of the *Tonnant* and *Intrépide* was practicable. Before agreeing that it was not, all but one of them objected 'to ranking with Captain Fox', because he had not engaged closely with due persistence. This testifies to their understanding of what their admiral required. The evidence given at Fox's consequent court martial strongly implies that the captains were imbued with Hawke's expectation of a very close engagement and persistent mutual support.[11] As a well-established admiral in the Seven Years War, Hawke would formalise his 'pistol shot' requirement in stark terms, whence it was transmitted through a new generation of officers as far as Horatio Nelson.

The Seven Years War

Having become a vice-admiral of the blue in 1748 while cruising under Warren's restored command, Hawke, with the advent of peace in October, became commander-in-chief at Portsmouth. In 1752 he went on half pay. Before very long, however, a new war with France, arising principally in North America, began to seem inevitable; and in 1755 Hawke was reappointed to the Portsmouth command with the enhanced rank of admiral of the white. Although by dint of Admiralty patronage he had been adopted as an MP for Portsmouth in December 1747, he was certainly no politician and he never aspired to the degree of political influence and standing acquired by Anson. However, within purely professional confines, he showed administrative competence and good sense at Portsmouth. In 1755 he carried overall responsibility for the manning and fitting of as many as three squadrons, together with the expansion of Haslar Hospital, a wing of which had been built in 1754.

Before the renewal of war with France was formalised in May 1756, Hawke had himself gone twice to sea with a squadron to cruise in the Bay of Biscay. When the successful French landing on Minorca and Byng's retreat to Gibraltar became known in England, Hawke was sent out with Rear-Admiral Saunders to supply the Mediterranean fleet, as the wits said, with a 'little cargo of courage'. On arriving at Gibraltar on 4 July, Hawke superseded Byng and hoisted his flag in the *Ramillies*, 90, which remained his flagship until November 1759. His immediate aim was to relieve Mahon which, for all he knew, might still be holding out against the besieging French. (In fact, the garrison had surrendered on 27 June.) Hawke hurried his fleet to sea. Among the captains whom he had inherited from Byng was Augustus Hervey, a spirited officer devoted to Byng. When, in the late 1760s, Hervey wrote up his entertaining *Journal* from his early records of service, he was intent on discrediting Hawke, who by then was First Lord of the Admiralty. This accounts for much of his belittling of Hawke's strategy when the admiral was frustrated by the refusal of the French to come out again to fight. However, he fully accepts that Hawke 'certainly had the heart to gain an engagement' and, if with a touch of derision, he has left the only known account of how Hawke was wont to encourage his assembled captains. On 3 August Hawke, with Saunders present, told his captains he had intelligence of the French preparing to sail from Toulon. According to Hervey, the admiral 'made us a fine speech'. He would 'run up to them'. The 'honour of our country required we should do our very utmost to destroy these ships and he did not doubt we should'. So here we have a foretaste of the 'Nelson touch' some forty years before Nelson's heyday.[12]

Having persisted with his fruitless cruising, punctuated by much exercising in lines of battle, Hawke finally left Saunders in command at Gibraltar in December. In 1757 Hawke, by now an admiral of the blue, experienced further frustration. He was appointed to command the naval side of an expedition, promoted by the elder Pitt, to land an army at Rochefort. Despite the navy's capture of the key fortification on the island of Aix and much other co-operation, the army declined to land. General Mordaunt faced a court martial after the fleet, with its numerous transports, returned to Portsmouth early in October to a derisive welcome.

On a more positive note, however, before sailing again to cruise in the Bay of Biscay, Hawke decided to guard against any possibility that his captains might interpret the Printed Fighting Instructions (as at Toulon) in a defensive manner. These instructions, supplied to commanders-in-chief at their request, contained a fundamental article XIII. This said that, on the admiral signalling to engage, 'every ship in the fleet' was 'to use' its 'utmost endeavour to engage the enemy in the order the Admiral' had 'prescribed unto them'. For this injunction Hawke substituted the order that 'every ship in the fleet is to use' its 'utmost endeavour to engage the enemy as close as possible, and therefore on no account to fire until' it is 'within pistol shot'.[13] The fact that the oft-printed Instructions became effective only when signed by a commanding admiral and could be amended by him, and therefore should never have been described as 'permanent', is virtually endorsed by Boscawen's (previously intimated) arrival at Portsmouth on 20 October 1757. Currently a Lord of the Admiralty under Anson, he came as Hawke's second-in-command, and it was on that day that Hawke issued his Instructions. Far from raising any question about Hawke's fundamental amendment, he himself on 27 April 1759 issued an Additional Instruction of similar significance. Anson also embodied much of the substance of Hawke's amendment in an Additional Instruction of 30 August 1758.[14]

However, Hawke's cruise with Boscawen was uneventful. It was not until March 1758 that he was again employed on a specific operation. With six ships of the line, but to his annoyance without frigates, he descended on some forty merchantmen and five ships of the line preparing in Basque Roads outside Rochefort to sail for the relief of Louisbourg. Although none of the hurriedly lightened warships or beached merchantmen were captured, disruption was complete.

Two months later Hawke was still sensitive on the subject of Rochefort when, without any private explanation from the Admiralty, he was ordered to equip Commodore Howe for an amphibious operation. Believing that Howe was going to Rochefort (when in fact St Malo was the target), Hawke angrily struck his flag at Portsmouth. To rectify this serious situation, Anson himself took command of the Western Squadron with Hawke as his second in command. This unfortunate affair was much regretted by Hawke. It was the only blemish on his long record of fine professional example. However, by the spring of 1759 there arose the major threat of a French invasion of Britain. In such a crisis Hawke, as commander-in-chief, was found to be indispensable.

The Blockade of Brest

On 9 May Hawke was ordered 'to repair without loss of time to Portsmouth' and hoist his flag on board a ship of his choice. Once again he chose the *Ramillies*. On 14 May he issued copies of the General Sailing and Fighting Instructions with article XIII duly amended. As on 20 October 1757, the substituted words were inscribed by clerks. His captains were 'on no account' to fire until 'within pistol shot'.[15]

On 16 July Hawke, when blockading Brest, supplemented the aforesaid amendment with an Additional Instruction. This elaborated on conduct in a line of battle. Following the drift of Anson's above-mentioned instruction of August 1758, he might, when ready to engage, haul down the signal for the line of battle while still flying that for engaging (thus avoiding the paralysis induced by Mathews in 1744). With a view to very close action, Hawke explains: 'You are to observe that as soon as I shall have led on the Squadron, so as to be within the distance I shall think proper to engage at, I will haul down the signal for the line; when you are hereby required to continue engaging the ship of the enemy that shall be immediately opposed to you, in such close manner . . . as will enable you to take, sink, or destroy her.'[16]

The Admiralty was now providing for an exceptionally protracted blockade of Brest and other French ports. When Hawke sailed from Torbay on 20 May he had twenty-five ships of the line and fourteen smaller ships. His line of battle ships contrasted with those he had commanded in 1747. He had three flagships, two (including the *Ramillies*) being of 90 guns, and the other having the increasingly favoured armament of 74 guns. The *Royal George*, 100, was regarded as rather unwieldy and was commanded by a private captain. Otherwise, there were six more 74s, four 70s, four 64s, and seven 60s listed in Hawke's initial 'Line of Battle'. He had two 50s, now used as cruisers and especially useful for detached blockading duties. Hawke decided on a closer blockade of Brest than any attempted in the past, but even in June the weather proved adverse. Thick fog was followed by westerly gales which, although they prevented any significant egress by the French, forced Hawke to take the main body of the fleet back to Torbay, while Robert Duff in the *Rochester*, 50 remained off Brest with the *Melampe*, 36 and a cutter. Torbay was not an established base, but it gave admirable shelter to a large fleet. The Admiralty and its supply services largely overcame the unprecedented problems that arose, whether in Torbay or in the open sea.

By 20 June Hawke and the fleet were again off Ushant. Duff reported having seen seventeen sail in Brest Roads. This officer continued to make a valuable contribution throughout the campaign. From the outset it was recognised that Lorient and Port Louis, both situated in the Blavet estuary north of Belle Isle, were important for supplies going northbound to Brest or southbound to Vannes and Auray. There, in the northerly recesses of Quiberon Bay, the French expeditionary army was assembling for transportation to Scotland. Hawke soon extended his system of control down the Biscay coast as far as Quiberon Bay, where he put Duff in command, and later reached down to Nantes.

For five months Hawke remained with the battle squadron near Ushant. In July he placed Augustus Hervey – a perceptive choice – in command of a strengthened inshore squadron. By then Hawke knew with reasonable certainty that the French planned to wait till the British fleet was again forced by inevitable westerly gales to seek shelter on the coast of Devon. Then, on the wind coming easterly, the comte de Conflans would hasten from Brest to Quiberon Bay, about 130 miles to the southeast, where the transports would be ready in the Morbihan (an almost land-locked estuary).

Hawke meanwhile kept up a high standard of battle-readiness by exercising the fleet in manoeuvres and gunnery. In any case, the lee shore of Brittany provided a constant test of seamanship and Hawke could count on British superiority in this regard when the day of supreme trial arrived. But during the protracted blockade his abiding concern was the maintenance of good health, at a time when disease by far exceeded any other cause of death at sea. In retrospect it has been amply confirmed that the supply of fresh food, including much in the way of root vegetables but also some fruit, explains the remarkable extent to which the dreaded scurvy was kept at bay. The contemporary naval physician James Lind (1716-94) regarded the health of 'the grand fleet of England, commanded by Sir Edward Hawke', as 'perfect and unparalleled'. There were 'fourteen thousand persons pent up in ships' for a period of six months. Yet (as Lind observed) at the battle in November only one man in Hawke's flagship was unfit for duty and fewer than twenty in the whole fleet. Lind's distinguished successor, Sir Gilbert Blane, was able to build on the experiences of Lind and James Cook in promoting the good standard of health that made Nelson's exploits possible.[17]

Although Hawke's close blockade effectively cut off the French from their possessions in Canada and India, and led on to the conclusive battle in Quiberon Bay, it had a controversial sequel. During the American War the question of an open or close blockade remained hypothetical, because Britain faced exceptional world-wide naval commitments and challenges. The margin of naval superiority required to sustain a close blockade did not exist. In 1793 the position was different. The blow dealt to the French navy by the Revolution went far to restore a substantial measure of British operational superiority. Nevertheless, Lord Howe, who had been one of Hawke's most resolute captains, believed that open blockade was preferable, once wear and tear on the ships and men had been given due emphasis. His view prevailed for some years but the results were hardly commensurate with Britain's evident capability. At the turn of the century John Jervis, Earl of St Vincent, an admirer of Hawke and his methods, came to the fore. As mentioned above, he particularly admired Hawke's bold and successful initiative at the Battle of Toulon. Likewise, he immediately approved Nelson's spectacular departure from his own line off Cape St Vincent in 1797, appreciating that Nelson was fulfilling the admiral's own tactical intentions. Likewise, from 1800 to 1805, when Britain once again faced the threat of a French invasion, St Vincent reinstituted a continuous close blockade of Brest (for which see the essay on John Jervis below). As late in Hawke's life as August 1780, when serving under Geary, Jervis was sending his 'best respects' to Hawke and he obviously remained conscious of his famous example in the matter of close blockade. Hawke's influence on St Vincent must be deemed lasting and profound.

On 10 October 1759 Hawke was able to report to the Admiralty that all the ships' companies, excepting that of the *Foudroyant*, 80, which he soon sent in, were 'in very good health'. He would 'give their Lordships timely notice' should he need to be relieved, 'which, thank God, there is not the least appearance of at present'. Hawke drew strength from his unostentatious but genuine Christianity. Partly by discouraging profanity of language on board ship, and partly by promoting a humane outlook amongst his captains, he exerted a civilising influence. Tall and dignified, he was affable rather than familiar with his officers. As a disciplinarian he tempered firmness with compassion. He was consistently sympathetic to the needs of all manner of deserving officers and ratings, their families not excepted. While taking quiet pride in his own professional performance, he was not a showman.

On 11 October a hard gale arose from the west-southwest. To avoid being forced too far eastward, Hawke bore up for Plymouth, where reprovisioning was anyhow easier than in Torbay. On the 18th, with 'very little wind', the fleet got to sea with the help of boats. Already by noon the next day fresh easterly gales had carried him down to Ushant. Captain Hervey, now nearing the limit of his endurance in command of the battered inshore squadron, reported that the French had not stirred from Brest. But autumnal weather was now governing the situation. By 7 November the fleet was driven to seek refuge in Torbay. The (ill-fated) *Ramillies*, 'having for some time complained greatly and been waterlogged whenever it blowed hard', Hawke decided to shift his flag on board the *Royal George* (100 guns and 880 men). Several ships suffered further damage as the fleet struggled to put to sea. The ponderous *Royal George* was commanded by John Campbell, a Scot of much character, who apparently accepted without demur what, by that date, might have well been deemed a loss of standing by becoming an admiral's flag captain. Various damaged ships had to be left behind, including another flagship, that of Rear-Admiral Francis Geary. Meanwhile James Young of the 74-gun *Mars* became commodore in command of the rear division. That these sudden rearrangements were swiftly made without discernible friction or loss of efficiency testifies to the quality of Hawke's leadership.

Quiberon Bay, 1759

Hawke soon learnt that Conflans had emerged from Brest with an easterly breeze on 14 November – the day on which Hawke himself had finally got out of Torbay. The French quickly came almost in sight of Belle Isle, but then the easterly breeze strengthened to a gale. Both fleets were blown away to westward and thus, crucially, Hawke was able to benefit from his fleet's superior seamanship. On the 17th he wrote to the Admiralty: 'I have carried a pressure of sail all night, with a hard gale at SSE, in pursuit of the enemy and make no doubt of coming up with them either at sea or in Quiberon Bay.'

By 18 November, with the wind still easterly, Conflans again drew near Belle Isle. Now aged 64, he was a competent, if uninspired, commander. He had twenty-one ships of the line with larger complements than British counterparts, but he knew that their training, restricted by the closeness of Hawke's blockade, was patchy. He aimed simply to get his fleet safely into Quiberon Bay and destroy Duff's light squadron. At 11pm on the 19th he noted that the wind had turned westerly. Meanwhile at noon on the same day, Hawke, with twenty-three of the line, had reckoned that he was about seventy miles west of Belle Isle. With the wind veering westerly, he soon drew near that island. In the small hours of 20 November he hove to and waited for daybreak. By then the wind had strengthened to gale force, blowing from the west–northwest.

At 7am the frigate *Maidstone*, posted ahead of the fleet, let fly her topgallant sheets, indicating a fleet ahead. Pending confirmation that it was indeed the French battlefleet, Hawke concentrated his force by sig-

nalling a line abreast. At 9.45 Howe in the *Magnanime* signalled in confirmation. Hawke now hoisted a white flag with a red cross at his main
topmasthead and fired three guns, bringing into effect an Additional
Fighting Instruction first issued by Anson in 1746-7 to enhance a general
chase. In his dispatch of 24 November Hawke reported: 'Observing, on
my discovering them, that they made off, I threw out the signal for the
seven ships nearest to them to chase and draw into a line of battle ahead of
me and endeavour to stop them till the rest of the squadron should come
up, who were also to form as they chased, that no time should be lost in
the pursuit.'[18]

By 10am Conflans was aware of Hawke's fleet a good distance behind
him to the westward. He was then chasing Duff's frigates which, forewarned, had escaped from Quiberon Bay overnight by the difficult Teig-
neuse Passage. Conflans now gave up the chase but, fatally, he assumed
that, with a large fleet and a westerly gale, Hawke would not dare to follow
him beyond the entrance into a turbulent Quiberon Bay, begirt by hidden
shoals.[19] If the French were in the bay by 3pm, Hawke would be left with
only two hours of indifferent daylight in which to fight.

In a standard French manoeuvre, Conflans placed his flagship the *Soleil
Royal* (80 guns and 1000 men) at the head of his single, gradually forming
line. At 2pm he rounded the Cardinals Rocks which marked the western
edge of the entrance to the Bay. Hawke meanwhile kept his chase signal
flying, as he did for the rest of the day. He trusted the French to pilot him
past the hidden dangers. This heroic assessment would be triumphantly
vindicated. It was only during the night, when no French 'pilots' were
available, that two British ships of the line drove aground on fringes of the
extensive, largely concealed, Four Shoal that guarded the easterly side of
the Bay's entrance. As for the French, they did avoid all the hazards on
what Hawke would call 'that dark November day'.

Despite the 40-knot gale blowing at west-northwest, the pursuing British, to Conflans's astonishment, continued to carry a great crowd of sail.
With fingers chilled to the bone, the British topmen worked far aloft on the
plunging, juddering masts. Even the *Royal George*, according to her master
Thomas Conway, was achieving 8 or 9 knots. Meanwhile British observers
noted the French steering in a close-hauled but irregular line 'under an easy
sail'. Differing standards of seamanship had never mattered more.

By 2.45pm Hawke could see that several of his leading ships were close
to the three rearmost ships of the enemy and, needing no further order,
were opening fire (by implication at pistol shot). For the benefit of the fleet

as a whole he hoisted the red flag for a general engagement. It was seen flying below the chase signal as long as the light permitted.

Captain Nightingale of the frigate *Vengeance* (whose warning had permitted Duff's frigates to escape from Quiberon Bay) made a precise note at 3.17pm of a sudden, heavy, northerly squall. Every ship present was affected. As Conflans afterwards reported, with the wind reverting afterwards only to northwest (not to west-northwest), his already imperfect line was thrown into great disorder and he had to abandon his intended series of tacks up to the Morbihan. With the British persistently overhauling and engaging his ships, he soon had to look for some other route to safety. Meanwhile, as the French were engaging from windward and heeling over towards their opponents, they risked foundering if they opened the ports shielding their lower-deck main armament.

Before the advent of the northerly rain squall, the *Formidable* (80 guns and 1000 men), flagship of the French rear division, had already received a hammering from successive British ships. These ranged in strength from Augustus Keppel's favourite *Torbay* and Howe's *Magnanime*, each of 74 guns and 700 men, down to the *Defiance* of only 60 guns and 420 men. Like the rest of the frigates (of which there were ten in attendance during the fighting on the 20th), the *Coventry* was to leeward of Hawke's line of battle ships and was well placed to observe the British onslaught on the *Formidable*. Her surgeon (quoted by Geoffrey Marcus in his book *Quiberon Bay*) described her as 'pierced like a cullender'. Finally, at about 4pm, with all her more senior officers and many others dead, the *Formidable* struck to the *Resolution*, 74, which had come up with the ships of Hawke's rear division.

The superior seamanship of Hawke's ships, the closeness with which they engaged, and their high rate of fire, were much in evidence before, at 3.55pm, the *Royal George* hauled round the Cardinals. Now Hawke was left with an hour of daylight to show how he himself would put his 'pistol shot' amendment into effect. At that time Conflans was about to abandon his advance into the Bay where he was still standing close-hauled to the northeast. He was well into the Bay, probably about six miles northwest of the dim, low-lying shape of Dumet Island. He decided to bear up and, running before the wind, lead his fleet back towards the entrance and the open sea. He therefore hoisted the signal for the countermarch – another established French tactical manoeuvre. Seven of his ships fell away to leeward through having to wear and found themselves trapped to the north of Dumet Island. They had finally to seek refuge in the River Vilaine. Conflans, however, was still followed by about a dozen ships. Meanwhile, soon after 4pm, the

Thésée (74 guns and 815 men), in trying to use her lower-deck guns against the *Torbay*, suddenly foundered. Keppel (as Hawke reported) 'immediately hoisted out' his boats, despite the appalling conditions, and they saved twenty-two French sailors.

Hawke meanwhile kept urging Conway the master: 'I say, lay me alongside the French admiral.' Conway reminded the admiral that they might run aground. Hawke made the legendary reply: 'You have now done your duty in apprising me of the danger. Let us now see how well you can comply with my orders.' With some variation, the exchange passed into naval tradition.

The two flagships now drew quite rapidly closed on convergent courses. As he ran southwards, Conflans fired at British ships that were dealing out severe punishment to the *Juste* (70 guns and 800 men). He was followed by Bauffremont, wearing his chef d'escadre's flag in l'Etanduère's former flagship, the *Tonnant*, and by a dozen other ships. At 4.35, with Hawke imminently closing, the *Soleil Royal* and a number of her followers wore towards Dumet Island and fired their broadsides at the *Royal George*. Still intent on pursuing Conflans, Hawke came close alongside the following *Superbe* (70 guns and 800 men) and returned her fire. Then, at 4.41, he delivered a second broadside, whereupon the *Superbe* abruptly sank with all hands. Such a sinking by gunfire was a rare event in the days of sail. At Ushant, for example, Palliser's flagship was holed five times below the waterline, but did not sink. Hawke pressed ahead to rake the *Soleil Royal*, but was frustrated by the brave interposition of the *Intrépide*. This was the ship that assisted the escape of the *Tonnant* on 14 October 1747. According to Conway, Conflans and various French captains 'starboarded their helms and hauled their wind to the northward to get clear of us.' The *Royal George* hauled her wind to the southward to avoid 'being ashore on the island Dumet'. Conflans, like the captain of the *Héros*, again ran towards the entrance, but he had fallen away too far eastward to be able to weather the Four Shoal before dark. He therefore anchored not far northwest of le Croisic. Under threat early the next day, both French ships ran for the little fishing port, there being no navigable alternative. With the wind still blowing hard from the northwest, both ships missed the narrow, twisting channel and ran on to the rocks just south of le Croisic.

Altogether the British captured, or caused the destruction of, seven French ships of the line: the *Formidable*, the *Thésée*, and the *Superbe* on the 20th; and on the 21st, the *Soleil Royal* and the *Héros*, which were driven ashore (both being burnt on 22 November); the already-shattered *Juste* which was wrecked on a rock near the Loire; and the *Inflexible*, 64 which, having failed to emulate her six companions by getting into the Vilaine, was lost on the bar.

It remains to follow Bauffrement and his contingent. Near 5pm on the 20th, when it fell dark, he avoided being embayed like Conflans by hauling his wind and *weathering* the Four Shoal. The hardy version (found in W L Clowes's third volume published in 1898 and in some much later authorities), that his group escaped by passing between the Four Shoal and le Croisic, is decisively contradicted by Bauffrement's own dispatch (quoted in editions of 1902 and 1910 by Lacour-Gayet). Altogether eight French ships of the line reached Rochefort where, like the six in the Vilaine, they were soon neutralised by Hawke.

Having at last returned to England in January 1760, Hawke received the thanks of the House of Commons and an annual pension of £2000 for two lives. He seems at that date to have lacked the wealth to sustain a peerage.

In sum, it was a truly annihilating victory. Despite Choiseul's efforts to promote a French recovery, Britain maintained an unchallenged supremacy in French and, later, in Spanish waters until the war ended in 1763. In 1760 Hawke tightened the blockade of the Biscay ports. Although questioning the strategical value of the project, he obeyed Pitt's directions to prepare for the capture of Belle Isle. In 1762 he completed his final term in command of the Western Squadron. Meanwhile, on becoming French navy minister in 1761, Choiseul found the service 'in a state of degradation . . . The ships were left to rot, the stores empty.' The navy 'had not a *sous* of credit', and 'the morale of the fighting and civil officers was at the lowest ebb.'

Hawke and the Navy

By the end of his seagoing career Hawke had made a deep and lasting impression on the navy and on many in the country. King George II, until he died at the end of 1760, continued to hold the admiral in high regard; and in 1778, when the Bourbon powers, being better prepared than usual, took advantage of Britain's American predicament, George III sought to encourage Sandwich, the First Lord, by conveying Hawke's praise of the condition and personnel of the fleet: 'I thought the testimony of so brilliant an officer must afford pleasure to Lord Sandwich, and therefore have sent him this account.'

In the service itself the memory of Hawke's inspired conduct at Quiberon Bay outlived the disappointments of the American War. Edward Pellew, after winning early distinction in that war, rose to fame as a frigate commander in the French Revolutionary War. In January 1797, with a gale at southwest, he risked the loss of his two frigates in driving a 74-gun French ship on to the rocks north of Lorient. Referring to the loss of the smaller frigate, Pellew afterwards wrote to the First Lord of the day: 'What can be done if the enemy's coast is always to frighten us and give them protection as safely as their ports? If Lord Hawke had no fears from a lee shore with a large fleet under his charge, could I for a moment think of two inconsiderable frigates?'[20]

As for battle tactics, by dint of personal example supplemented by his simple, but very forceful version of the Printed Fighting Instructions, Hawke had continued to rely, to a Nelsonic degree, on his individual captains and ships. He expected them to provide, ship for ship, superior effectiveness of fire and timely mutual support when engaging the enemy. He did much himself to promote that readiness, as has been seen. Like all admirals, he also relied on prior decades of administrative and material preparation which, together with prescriptive regular training, went far to produce a reliable British ship-for-ship superiority until, in 1778, a French fleet emerged with something of an edge in gunnery and manoeuvre.

Hawke's influence on battle tactics can be traced down the years to Horatio Nelson. This influence was transmitted by William Locker, who served as a lieutenant in the frigate *Sapphire* during Hawke's blockade of Brest and also at Quiberon Bay. Hawke had originally commissioned Locker in 1756, and he had him in his flagship in 1760 and 1762; and in his *Memoirs of Celebrated Naval Commanders* (1831) E H Locker records the encouragement which his father derived from Hawke. In 1777 Captain William Locker commissioned the frigate *Lowestoft* and Nelson, aged 19, was appointed as her second lieutenant. Nelson later testified to Locker's inspiring influence. On 9 February 1799 the victor of the Nile wrote to Locker: 'It is you who always said, "Lay a Frenchman close, and you will beat him", and my only merit in my profession is being a good scholar.'[21]

In October 1762, when active warfare was coming to an end, Hawke progressed by dint of seniority to admiral of the white. At the apex there remained the still solitary eminence of admiral of the fleet, then occupied by Sir William Rowley. Hawke succeeded him in 1768. Meanwhile, in June 1762, Lord Anson died and it was mooted that Hawke would replace him. However, Lord Halifax, a politician popular with the merchants, was appointed. Hawke thus missed his most timely opportunity. Anson had wanted to put him on the Board of Admiralty in 1757 but, by the end of the war in 1763, Hawke's usual good health showed signs of decline. A quick succession of political First Lords led to the appointment in September 1766 of Sir Charles Saunders, who had attached himself to the Rockingham faction. In December he resigned for party-political reasons and Lord Chatham turned to Hawke. Remaining unattached to any political group, Hawke could expect to continue as First Lord until removed by illness or death.

Hawke stayed in office until January 1771. At the end of his term he was criticised for the unreadiness of some of the guardships when the dispute over the Falkland Islands threatened war with the Bourbon powers. However, it was ill health alone that forced Hawke's resignation. He was succeeded by Lord Sandwich, and Nicholas Rodger, in his book *The Insatiable Earl*, has amply confirmed what had been supposed about Sandwich's superior administrative flair. Sandwich was the greatest reformer of naval administration in that century and Hawke's own generous tribute to the state of the fleet in April 1778 has already been mentioned. Yet his own record as First Lord was more respectable than has sometimes been thought.

The admiral was assiduous in attending the Admiralty Board. According to the minutes,[22] he presided in 1767 at 118 meetings and missed 13; in 1768 the figures were 126 and 18; in 1769, 118 and 28; and in 1770, despite a painful illness, 156 and 30. At the meetings he presided with humanity and good sense, commissioning and dispatching James Cook on his first voyage of exploration and also ordering investigation of many suggestions for technical improvement. As a professional First Lord, Hawke was, like Anson, in a better position than a politician to fend off politically-inspired claims for naval appointments. With regard to the problem of maintaining in peacetime a sufficient number of wooden ships to meet the exigency of a new war, the simple answer was an adequate building programme. Of course, dockyard provision and efficiency were also a fundamental concern and Hawke achieved no great advance there. However, he did better in the critical matter of shipbuilding. Dr Rodger shows that, from 1763 to 1770 (with Hawke in office for half that time), as many as 31 ships of the line were *completed* – an average of 3.87 a year. By way of comparison, Sandwich, with all his political skills and administrative flair, could *lay down* no more than 26 of the line – an annual average of only 2 – for the years 1770 to 1782 (thus including those laid down in Hawke's final year).[23]

In January 1771 a worsening urinary complaint called the gravel, common among seamen of that time, finally compelled Hawke to resign as First Lord. King George expressed his sorrow at 'the loss of so able and gallant an officer' and 'he regretted very much' his 'bad state' of health. On 20 May 1776 he raised the admiral to the peerage as Baron Hawke of Towton in Yorkshire, where his wife's forebears had been lords of the manor.

The admiral died at Sunbury on 17 October 1781 and his son Martin Bladen Hawke succeeded him in the peerage. He has not, in the long term, been adequately remembered by the general public, but the deep impression which he left on his immediate successors is splendidly conveyed in a letter written to Mann on 18 October by Horace Walpole: 'Lord Hawke is dead and does not seem to have bequeathed his mantle to anybody.'

George, Lord Rodney. Stipple engraving by Charles Knight

9

George Bridges, Lord Rodney
1718?–1792

'no one before you can boast of having taken or destroyed 16 ships of the line in the space of two years and a half and have captured the commanding admiral of each of the nations with which we are at war'

KENNETH BREEN

The esteem in which Rodney was held by his contemporaries may be gauged from remarks made in letters and speeches by supporters as influential as Lord Sandwich and by opponents as articulate as Fox and Burke. From the time he entered the navy in 1732, though influence played a part, Rodney had impressed his superiors by his efficiency and his understanding of naval principles; by his vigour, determination and aggression when opposing the enemy; and by those qualities of leadership which led him to care for the welfare of his men. Consequently he had risen to post and then flag rank very much on these merits. To enter the navy, though, wealth, family connection and interest were almost indispensable pre-requisites and Rodney, in his own immediate family circle, had no direct access to any of these. In a curious way it was the misfortunes suffered by his family that opened for Rodney the path to his naval preferment.

George Bridges Rodney was born at the end of 1717 or the beginning of 1718 and was baptised on 13 February 1718 in the church of St Giles in the Fields in the county of Middlesex. The family into which George was born had clear links to Stuart and Tudor times. Anthony, his grandfather, had served as a cornet with Charles II, as a Captain in the Tangier garrison and in 1695 was at the siege and capture of Namur with William III. Rodney's father, Harry, had served first as a cornet with his father in Leigh's Dragoons and subsequently as captain in Holt's Regiment of Marines during the War of the Spanish Succession. Father and son continued to serve together in the War of the Spanish Succession and were present at the siege of Barcelona. Here Colonel Anthony Rodney's career came to an untimely end when he was killed in a duel with a brother officer in 1705. It is likely that this, in its turn, blighted the career of Harry Rodney who, in the remaining years of the war, advanced no further than the rank of captain. With the war's end he retired to Walton-on-Thames and married Mary Newton, daughter of Sir Henry Newton, a distinguished diplomat and judge of the High Court of Admiralty. This connection was potentially fruitful for the Rodney family in providing access to the world of affairs and influence for, though the family was one of strong traditions, it was by no means wealthy.

Harry Rodney and his wife Mary Newton had five children, of whom George was the fourth. Harry, never rich, appeared unable to manage his finances in a businesslike way and speculated in the South Sea Company at a time when the majority of investors were already selling their stock as swiftly as possible. The result was financial ruin, the loss of the property at Walton, the involvement of the family with money lenders and lawyers and debts still unpaid at the time of his death. The wealthier relatives of the family undertook responsibility for the children and George came into the immediate care of his godfather, George Bridges of Avington after whom it is probable he had been named. In his upbringing, therefore, George was spared from the dulling effects of poverty and grew in the more spacious world of Avington, near Winchester, in Hampshire. The Bridges family had, as head, the immensely wealthy and influential Duke of Chandos, who was an occasional visitor to his cousin George Bridges. Where the family home in Walton had nothing to offer George in comfort or influence, vital to any advancement in society and career, at Avington he had access to all those privileges which wealth and influence could give him.

In due time Rodney went to school at Harrow. It was common for boys to start at 7 or 8 years old and so it is possible that he went there in 1725 and stayed until 1732 when, on 7 July, he was entered on the books of the *Sunderland*, 60 guns, as a volunteer per order. At Harrow Rodney had learned something of the vicissitudes of life at a time when public schools had a measure of fighting and bullying, flogging and drinking, as a daily part of school routine, and this must have prepared him to some degree for life on board one of His Majesty's ships. Rodney's career in the navy, to end in triumph some fifty years later, began on the orlop deck of a guardship at the Nore.

In May 1733 Rodney was moved to the *Dreadnought*, another 60, a guardship at Portsmouth under the command of Captain Alexander

Geddes. In November of 1734 Geddes was replaced by Captain Henry Medley, who immediately advanced Rodney to midshipman. The *Dreadnought* sailed to Lisbon with Sir John Norris in May 1733 and while there was detached on missions to Minorca, Gibraltar and Cadiz. Rodney, on this first cruise, was lucky to be on a ship which gave exceptional opportunities for him to learn his craft as a seaman and to mingle in a variety of societies. The British Minister in Lisbon was the Hon Charles Compton, brother of the fifth Earl of Northampton, so that his position in the English community was pre-eminent both from his official post and from his family and social connections. The presence of the English fleet was of great importance to the community and it was commonplace for the officers to be welcomed and entertained by the various families. In this Compton was outstanding and Rodney, junior though he was, was warmly allowed the freedom of the family home and built a particular friendship with two of the Compton daughters, Jane and Kitty, a friendship which gave him some anguish of heart when, years later in 1752, he wrestled with the hard decision as to which of them to marry.

Rodney returned to England on 3 September 1737. His homecoming from this first cruise was saddened by the death, the previous year, of his elder brother Henry, followed by that of his mother Mary in January 1737. The family circle at Walton was further reduced by the death of his father towards the end of 1737. In 1738 Rodney was recalled to the *Romney*, 50, which had been given to his old captain, Henry Medley, and was posted to Newfoundland for fishery protection duties. This posting gave Rodney experience of the intricacies of coastal navigation in difficult waters and the special problems arising from fog and freezing conditions. With Rodney in the midshipmen's berth were John Byron and George Edgecumbe, who became his lifelong friends and who established their own reputations as flag officers in the years to come. The *Romney* returned to Spithead on 26 December 1738. Medley returned to Newfoundland the following year as Governor but without Rodney who, though, was to find himself in Newfoundland again, a number of years later, as Governor and commanding his own squadron.

The move from the *Romney* came about because the young midshipman was chosen by his uncle, Lord Aubrey Beauclerck, commanding the frigate *Dolphin*, 24 in the Mediterranean, and in July 1739 Rodney sailed on the *Somerset,* flagship of Rear-Admiral Nicholas Haddock, to join Beauclerck, for whom he acted as lieutenant. The dispute with Spain with the evocative name of the War of Jenkin's Ear started in December 1739 and the *Dolphin* was ordered home. Beauclerck was replaced by Captain Francis Holburne on 18 February 1740, the day on which Rodney became lieutenant. With Holburne, he was involved in one of the worst gales of the century while on passage to Leith in October of the same year. Holburne later commented that he had never been in such a storm of wind and reports from all along the East Coast spoke of many casualties among seamen and on shore and the foundering of many ships. For Rodney, a young lieutenant of 22, this was an experience of seamanship in the most adverse of conditions that would remain with him for much of his seagoing life.

Rodney was next appointed as fifth lieutenant to the *Namur*, 90, Thomas Mathews' flagship, in March 1742, an appointment that was a valuable route for further promotion. As the dispute with Spain intensified, a task for Admiral Mathews, commanding the Mediterranean fleet, was to prevent reinforcements from Spain feeding the campaign against Britain's allies in Italy. French neutrality was crumbling fast in favour of Spain and Spanish troops were in Provence, with transports for them assembling at Antibes. The transports being vulnerable to the British fleet, it was likely that the Spanish force would go overland through Genoa. There the merchant community saw prosperity in the stockpiling of essential supplies for the use of the Spanish force, including magazines of fodder and grain. The Genoese ignored the remonstrations of Mathews and he determined to destroy the magazines but wished to do so without provoking the Genoese into open hostility. Within months of his appointment to the *Namur* Rodney had climbed to being the first lieutenant and as such he was detached by Mathews to undertake this delicate task. His success in this earned Rodney a mention in Mathews' despatch and shortly afterwards he was appointed captain of the *Plymouth*, 60, to take her home for repairs in an English dockyard. On arrival at Spithead, on 31 March 1743, his commission as captain was confirmed so that, at the young age of 25, Rodney had achieved a place on the coveted list of post captains.

Post Captain, 1743-1759

In September 1743 Rodney was appointed to the *Sheerness*, a new 24-gun frigate, and spent twelve months in the Western Approaches, mostly on escort duties. During this time he was sent Midshipman Samuel Hood, who then moved with him to the *Ludlow Castle* in September 1744 for work in the North Sea under the command of Admiral Vernon. This brief encounter with Hood was later recalled by the First Lord, Lord Sandwich, when he was having problems in finding a suitable second in command for Rodney during his service in the West Indies in 1780. While refitting the *Ludlow Castle* at Sheerness after extensive storm damage, Rodney moved to the *Eagle*, 60, which was building at Harwich. *Eagle* became part of a new Western Squadron with Anson and benefited from constant exercises in tactics, formation sailing and gunnery. In the *Eagle*, also, Rodney gained both fame and fortune. A notable prize encountered in late October 1746 was the French privateer *Shoreham*, which tried a variety of stratagems to avoid capture until, thirty hours into the chase, she fired a final broadside at the *Eagle* for the honour of her flag and then struck her colours. Early in the new year the *Eagle* fell in with and captured the *Grand Comte,* a privateer from Rochefort, to be followed in February by the capture of the *Bellone* with the help of the *Nottingham* and the *Edinburgh*. The *Bellone* had an ill reputation, as Rodney and Philip Saumarez of the *Nottingham* reported in their letter to the Admiralty when they described what effectively was the murder of the crew of a merchant vessel which had surrendered to the *Bellone* as their own vessel was in danger of foundering.

On 21 April 1747 the *Eagle* was ordered to cruise independently for fourteen days and her luck continued in the taking of prizes. During this detachment Rodney fell in with Commodore Fox, who was leading a small reinforcement to join Anson and the Western Squadron, and he took Rodney under his command. Though he missed the action of 3 May in which Anson won a decisive victory over de la Jonquière, Rodney had the good fortune while with Fox to come up with a great French convoy from Santo Domingo. The *Eagle*'s share was six prizes which produced something more than £8000 in prize money for Rodney, a handsome foundation for his personal fortune.

Rodney was with the Western Squadron, now commanded by Hawke, when it sighted the French West India convoy on 14 October off Cape Finisterre with an escort of eight ships commanded by the French admiral de l'Etenduère. Though heavily outnumbered, Etenduère prepared to stand between the British fleet and his convoy. Hawke, finding he was not gaining on the French while in line of battle, gave the order for the chase and the battle that ensued became a series of individual combats. Near the rear of the English squadron, the *Eagle* and the *Kent,* commanded by Captain Fox, were closing with the *Neptune*, 70, a formidable opponent for an English 60-gun ship. It was Rodney's hope that his *Eagle* and the *Kent* would come up on either side of the *Neptune* and fire into her until she struck. Instead, Rodney found that he was on the quarter of the *Neptune* in a fierce action and that a French 64, the *Fougueux,* had come up on his disengaged side and started firing into him. The *Kent,* with mizzen topsail aback, appeared to be deliberately reluctant to join the engagement. Damaged and uncontrollable, Rodney's *Eagle* drifted clear of the *Neptune* and fell foul of Hawke's *Devonshire*, which was coming to her aid, while the *Kent* continued to be the reluctant onlooker. Six of the French line ships were captured and, under the escort of the Western Squadron, they sailed into Plymouth. Pocock, in the Leeward Islands, was warned of Etenduère's now unescorted convoy and most of it fell into his hands a month later. The euphoria of the return of the squadron to Plymouth with the prizes was marred by the inadequate performance of the *Kent* under Fox, who was court-martialled at Portsmouth in November and found guilty of misconduct. Rodney's part in the action off Finisterre was praised by Anson; the prizes added to his fortune and he was able to invest much of the money in land around Alresford near the Avington of his upbringing.

On 3 March 1749 Rodney 's commission for the *Rainbow*, 50 was signed, and on 7 April he was made Governor of Newfoundland. Under his command, also, were the *Mercury* and the *Saltash,* allowing him to fly the broad pendant of a commodore. He was warned in a private letter from Sandwich of the delicate situation arising from increasing French activity, which included the taking of much of Nova Scotia adjacent to the Bay of Fundy. Negotiations were in progress between the French and British courts but Sandwich told him that any help which he might give to Cornwallis, at his request, would be supported by the government. Sandwich was unable to make any public order to this effect but trusted to Rodney's prudence not to abuse the confidential information given to him. Requiring equal finesse in their handling were the Boston merchants trading with Newfoundland, who openly expressed republican sentiments at his table. In a letter to Lord George Germain, Rodney looked back on this period as governor when he wrote that the Boston merchants 'had the insolence at my table to avow such principles which gave me such disgust that I never permitted them to have the least connection with me further than as my duty as Governor Obliged me.'[1] Cod fishing was the main source of wealth for Newfoundland, and Rodney found that many abuses existed either from neglect of the more remote settlements or from the active favouring of certain individuals with the grant of monopolies of various kinds. To reach the more inaccessible groups, Rodney hired small vessels and manned them with his own officers and men and this, with the overturning of the monopolies and other abuses, gained Rodney the respect and support of the Newfoundlanders.

After wintering in England, Rodney returned to Newfoundland in 1750. Much of his work remained the same, but he also built a hospital and created a market garden to provide fresh vegetables for his crews, which had the double effect of keeping them healthy and keeping them occupied.

During his third summer in Newfoundland he was entrusted with the care and testing of a new compass designed by Dr Knight. His return home at the end of his commission was delayed in Lisbon at the request, supported by a letter from the secretary of state, of the local British community, which was embroiled in a quarrel with the Portuguese government. Thus Rodney and the *Rainbow* stayed in the Tagus, in the middle of a possibly explosive international situation, until the end of February. He reached Spithead on 18 March 1752, expressing feelings of exhaustion and ill health, a pattern that was to repeat itself for the remainder of his seagoing life.

While his ship was in London between his summer duties in New-foundland, Rodney renewed his acquaintance with the Compton family whom he had first met in Lisbon as a young midshipman. His dilemma was which of the daughters, Jenny or Kitty, to choose for his wife and he sought the advice of his aunt, Lady Beauclerck. Her choice coincided with Rodney's own preference and he set his heart on marrying Jenny Compton, an aim which he brought to a successful conclusion on 31 January 1753 in the Oxford Chapel, St Marylebone. During this time, too, he had embarked upon the building of a house on his land at Al-resford, made possible by prize money and now made more lavish to receive his new bride. Another indication of the changes occurring in his life, and the increasingly favourable view of him held by the Admiralty, was his election in 1751 to the safe Admiralty seat of Saltash in Cornwall. By way of further pleasure in the month in which he married, Rodney was made captain of the *Kent,* the ill-starred ship at the Second Battle of Finisterre and now a guardship at Portsmouth. This enabled him to spend much time enjoying the life of a country gentleman at Alresford, or to be in London to attend to parliamentary business, or to enjoy the social life that revolved around the Compton family in Grosvenor Street and, doubtless less pleasing to his wife, to develop his addiction to the gaming tables with some of his naval friends and other members of White's club. His first son, George, was born on Christmas day 1753. In 1754 Rodney faced two setbacks, first when the *Kent* was sent to the East Indies with a new captain and then, on the dissolution of Parliament, he was offered no safe parliamentary seat. Anxious to remain a Member of Parliament and with the help of the Duke of Bedford, he fought but lost Camelford in a contested and costly election. Some consolation came in May when he was given the Portsmouth guardship *Fougueux*, which returned him to full pay but allowed him to continue to enjoy the warmth of his family life in Alresford and in London. In the autumn his second son, James, was born.

The threat of war in Canada triggered the bringing forward of ships for active service, including the *Fougueux*, which went to Spithead in early February. Meanwhile, Rodney had successfully asked for the larger *Prince George*, 90 in the hope of giving himself more time with Jenny before the inevitable posting to sea. The *Prince George* joined Hawke in the Channel and off the coast of Spain and shared in the capture of numerous prizes. On his return home on 29 September 1755 Rodney learnt that his father-in-law, Charles Compton, was seriously ill. He died on 20 November and Rodney found himself executor of Compton's considerable estate, nominated as guardian of Compton's sons Charles and Spencer and proposed as his successor as MP for Northampton. In the event, his opportunity to be returned for this seat did not come until the election of 1768 and, though successful, it proved to be a costly contest which contributed to his indebtedness and financial insecurity.

Relations with France were on a knife edge and when news was received of Boscawen's abortive action off Newfoundland against the French it was clear, as Sandwich wrote, that Boscawen had done too little or had done too much. He had not effectively attacked the French but he had done sufficient to provoke the hostilities between England and France which opened in 1756. With ships being brought forward for war, Rodney was given the *Monarch* in June 1756 in Plymouth. In addition to preparing her for sea, Rodney was responsible for the whole business of the dockyard and the several ships in various stages of preparation for active service. The efficiency and verve with which he pursued this new responsibility indicated a man of competence, energy and ability. The *Monarch* was ready to join Boscawen and the Channel fleet early in July, a fleet described by Rodney as sufficiently strong to cope with the whole naval power of France. The *Monarch,* though, had many defects and she was forced to sail to Spithead and be docked for the rest of the year. In the autumn of 1756 his third child, Jane, was born but survived only for eighteen months.

The opening year of the Seven Years War had included the disastrous loss of Minorca which brought about a change of ministry and the recall of Admiral Byng to stand trial. This was to be on the *Monarch* in December and Rodney was to be a member of the court. He pleaded his own ill health and that of his wife Jenny and was excused by the Admiralty from any part, though later he was to join with Hervey and others in an attempt to overturn what he regarded as the unjust and excessive capital sentence. Rodney's wife Jenny, suffering deteriorating health made worse by childbirth, died on 29 January 1757. In one of her last letters to Rodney, hearing that he was sick in their Hill Street house, she wrote pleading to come to

London to look after him: 'for I never can be easy when the Dearest Person to me on earth is ill and I from him, he nursed by a Common Housemaid or man-servant . . .'[2] The devotion of wife for husband is manifest in this letter from the dying Jenny.

On 4 April 1757 Rodney was given the *Dublin*, 74, building at Deptford. After taking part in the abortive expedition to Rochefort, the *Dublin* was chosen to transport General Amherst and his staff on the expedition to Louisbourg, sailing in mid-March 1758 and reaching Halifax at the end of May, having captured a French Indiaman *en route*. Rodney stayed in Halifax while, to the northeast, the successful attack on the immensely strong fortress of Louisbourg had begun. In July Rodney joined Hardy's squadron in Gabarus Bay, and then on 15 August he sailed for home in charge of the escort and convoy which transported the French Governor of Louisbourg and prisoners of war, arriving off Plymouth on 14 September. As now seemed habitual, he asked for leave for a month for the recovery of his health.

Flag Rank, 1759-1778

Rodney achieved flag rank on 19 May 1759 when he was promoted rear-admiral of the blue and flew his flag in the *Achilles*, 60. His appointment was to command a force, including bomb ketches, to attack Le Havre, where it was known the French were building and assembling barges suitable for an invasion force. The planning of the attack was undertaken in great secrecy and included the leaking of false orders indicating that the squadron was destined for Gibraltar. Significant damage was done to the harbour and to many of the barges, but not enough to remove all threats of invasion. A second bombardment was prepared, but this still did not achieve a sufficient destruction of the potential invasion force, and finally Rodney's squadron maintained a blockade of the port until November, when the French struck camp and removed the barges up river. On 20 November 1759 Hawke destroyed the French fleet in Quiberon Bay and ended any further danger of invasion. During his service off Le Havre Rodney received the promise of the safe seat of Okehampton and was elected, unopposed, on 24 November 1759.

With the accession of George III in 1760, early 1761 saw the calling of elections and to Rodney's distress Newcastle did not choose him to continue as member for Okehampton. Instead, he was chosen for Penryn, but this was a contested seat with costly opposition. However, Rodney managed to scrape in and the seat gave him a platform from which to seek a good posting. Rodney looked for this to the West Indies, where

Martinique remained a threat to the British islands and there was risk of Spanish intervention, and so he was pleased to be given command of the Leeward Islands and the *Marlborough*, 60 as his flagship. In combination with a large military force under General Robert Monckton, he captured Martinique in February 1762, to be followed by St Lucia, Grenada and St Vincent. In March news was received that the French were out of Brest and *en route* for the West Indies. Rodney took decisive action to protect Jamaica but found his hopes of bringing the French to action dashed by orders appointing Sir George Pocock to chief command with a brief for an attack on Cuba. Rodney's command was stripped by demands for ships of the line, for transports and for soldiers, as all other objects had to yield to Havana. The outcome of the Havana campaign was success and fabulous wealth for those with Pocock, and routine cruising for those left with Rodney.

Back at Spithead, Rodney struck his flag on 15 August 1763. In the previous months he had been embroiled in quarrels with the army over trade from St Kitts against the terms of the peace treaty; he had experienced the way British merchants were using St Eustatius as an entrepôt; he had written exhaustively to Lord Grenville for preferment and for the grant of land on St Vincent and claimed that the operations in Martinique had put him out of pocket. Grenville refused him the lands he asked for but Rodney was created a baronet and promised Greenwich Hospital. In picking up the threads of life at Alresford, he determined to remarry and made Henrietta [Henny] Clies his wife in 1764. Their son, John, was born on 10 May 1765 and in December Rodney was given his warrant as Governor of Greenwich Hospital, which became his base for the coming five years.

With the general election looming in April 1768 and his patrons unable to give him a seat, Rodney had to look to his own resources and, calling on the influence of his brother-in-law, the Earl of Northampton, he was nominated for the borough of Northampton. In the event the election was vigorously contested and was said to have ruined three noble families. It was certainly the ruin of Rodney, whom it cost £30,000. This, added to mounting gambling debts, led him to an absurd arrangement with two notorious money lenders, Lowther and Mackreth, to repay them £800 pa for an unspecified number of years in return for a loan to pay some of his debts. His friends, though willing to help him sort his muddled finances, found themselves handicapped by a reluctance on the part of Rodney to discuss the true nature and extent of his indebtedness.

In 1771, with his personal fortunes at their lowest ebb, news came of a Spanish incursion into the Falklands. The Jamaica squadron was to be reinforced and Rodney gladly accepted the appointment as commander-in-chief. After a successful stewardship of his command he was due home in 1774, but a return to England meant also the problem of his return to his indebtedness and Sandwich gave him permission to stay in Jamaica when his successor had arrived to replace him. This was unacceptable to Rodney, who returned to England with his family to outface his creditors, protected by his parliamentary seat at Northampton. This fragile shield was snatched from him by the dissolution of Parliament within days of his return from Jamaica. To avoid arrest, Rodney applied for leave of absence and by 4 October 1774 he was in France.

When the accord between the French and the Americans was signed in 1778 war between England and France was inevitable. Rodney was still in France, his affairs unresolved and with a further burden of debt acquired during his exile. Rodney's zeal to be employed was well known, but he was likely to be arrested for debt if he attempted to leave France and he was sure to be arrested for debt if he returned to England. Some of his financial problems could have been solved had he been paid his salary as rear-admiral but the Navy Board refused to release this money until a dispute over unauthorised dockyard expenditure had been resolved. For this Rodney blamed Sandwich and relationships between the two were put under considerable strain. It was the chivalrous generosity of the duc de Biron in lending him 1000 louis that freed Rodney to return to London and to take a significant role in the war now developing. At a Cabinet meeting on 16 September Rodney was appointed commander-in-chief in the Leeward Islands with a first charge to deliver a relief convoy to Gibraltar on his way to the West Indies. He remained commander-in-chief until his recall with the change of ministry on the resignation of Lord North in 1782.

The Years of Distinction, 1779-1782

The Battle of the Saintes in 1782 was the jewel in the crown of Rodney's reputation as a naval commander, and 1779-1782 was a period in which Rodney showed those qualities which distinguished him as a naval commander and in which he achieved great distinction and was regarded by Lord Sandwich as the most able of the officers at his disposal. In some eyes, however, his time as commander-in-chief in the West Indies was flawed. It was argued that the period was not marked by good relationships with his fellow officers, by fruitful co-operation between the Leeward Islands and the North American stations, or by an imaginative appraisal of the likely moves of his opponent de Grasse when the seasonal move of ships to the north took place. He was accused, too, of being diverted from his main task of opposing the French by the lure of the wealth captured in the island of St Eustatius. Something of these relationships and questionable decisions will emerge in the course of the narrative of his command.

The relief of Gibraltar was an outstanding success. On 7 January 1780, off Finisterre, he captured a convoy of sixteen Spanish ships and a few days later, off Cape St Vincent, he met and, in the famous Moonlight Battle, comprehensively defeated Admiral Langara, the Spanish commander. Rodney's force was much superior to that of Langara but the nature of the battle, a night attack in heavy seas with an immediate order by Rodney to chase, marked the aggressive approach that Rodney habitually brought to his actions. Six of the nine Spanish ships were captured and one blown up. With Gibraltar relieved, the bulk of the fleet and merchantmen returned to England and Rodney sailed to the West Indies with the *Sandwich, Ajax, Montagu* and *Terrible,* reaching St Lucia on 22 March, where Rear-Admirals Hyde Parker and Rowley were awaiting him with a further seventeen of the line. Soon afterwards the French Admiral de Guichen arrived, bringing the enemy strength to twenty-three of the line.

On 7 April 1780 the two fleets were off Martinique, sailing towards each other. In giving thought to ways in which the use of the line of battle could be more effective, Rodney had expressed his intention of concentrating on the enemy van or rear, should opportunity offer. When it came, many of Rodney's ships failed to grasp his intention and clung to the hallowed progression of the line, particular offenders being Captain Carkett in the leading ship and Hyde Parker, commander of the van. The action was an inconclusive one in which damage and casualties were caused to each side but without advantage to either. In his despatch Rodney referred to the British flag not being supported and, in more private correspondence, to the 'barefaced disobedience to orders and signals'.[3] Rodney made clear his opinions of the action, issued an Additional Fighting Instruction to make more explicit his intention and drilled the fleet rigorously until on 15 May and then on 19 May, Rodney and de Guichen faced each other again. Neither engagement reached a conclusion, partly due to windshifts and partly due to a reluctance on the part of de Guichen to engage, but clearly Rodney had achieved greater co-ordination and understanding of his ideas in the squadron and the outcome was to prevent the French landing soldiers on any of the British islands. De Guichen returned to France, broken by the burden of responsibility and the loss of his son in one of the engagements.

Rodney had earlier been congratulated by Sandwich for expressing support for the principle of inter-station co-operation, which had long been

seen by the Admiralty as necessary for the best deployment of naval resources. Now, worried lest de Guichen should reinforce the North American theatre, he put his own precepts of mutual support into action and
sailed for New York with a squadron of ten ships of the line, arriving at
Sandy Hook on 14 September 1780. The commander in North America
was Vice-Admiral Marriot Arbuthnot, whose ability to co-operate had
lessened with advancing years and he was not pleased with Rodney's order
to put himself under Rodney's command. Arbuthnot complained that
Rodney changed the dispositions of his ships, that he promoted his own
nominees into Arbuthnot's squadron, and that he would take the
commander-in-chief's share of prize money. The outcome was that an
exhaustive correspondence was opened between Arbuthnot and Sandwich,
and between Rodney and the Admiralty. An immense task in sorting out
promotion problems faced Sandwich, who rebuked Rodney by writing, 'I
acknowledge your right but you will allow me to say that I wish you had
not exercised that right'[4] and he urged him not do so again. Rodney
probably thought that he had good reason for taking over the command,
being more senior than Arbuthnot, but his manner of doing so was calculated to inflame resentment. It is arguable that the failure to establish a
harmonious relationship prompted the inadequate exchange of intelligence
between the West Indies and North America and the diminished reinforcement that was to mar the campaigns of 1781.

Prompted by the acrimonious exchanges with Vice-Admiral Arbuthnot
that occurred during this autumn visit to the North American station,
Rodney wrote to Lord George Germain to suggest the appointment of a
supreme commander for the war in America and every part of the West
Indies. This would remove, Rodney suggested, all the difficulties of making different commanders-in-chief agree and prevent them questioning
whether or not to obey the orders of a superior officer because they had a
commission as a commander-in-chief on a particular station.[5] The theory
had much merit but the practicalities of implementing it carried insuperable
difficulties. It is doubtful if a man acceptable to the different senior officers
could have been found; indeed Lord Sandwich made no secret of the
difficulties he faced in finding officers who would work with one another.
As importantly, such a supremo would have needed a sophisticated communications systems to undertake the office efficiently and this facility was
not to be available until well into the twentieth century.

The implication of Rodney's suggestion was that he should have become
that supreme commander, and he frequently acted as though he had been
so appointed. Yet much that went wrong in personal relations when he

took his squadron to North America where Marriot Arbuthnot commanded can be attributed to Rodney. Arbuthnot stated that he was quite
prepared to co-operate with Rodney but that he was an independent
commander of an important station whom Rodney should have supported
and not arrogated supreme powers to himself.

A similar failure to understand the situation of a fellow commander
occurred during Rodney's return to the West Indies from New York. Sir
Peter Parker's squadron and his dockyard facilities in Jamaica had been
severely damaged by the hurricanes of October 1780. During Rodney's
return voyage his own squadron, too, had been scattered and damaged by
worse than usual gales, and both admirals thought that they should have
priority in repairing and reinforcing their squadrons. Of the two it would
seem that Rodney was the more unreasonable when the correspondence
showed how little it was possible for Parker to do to meet Rodney's
demands. The correspondence, too, reveals much about Rodney's attitude to the commanders of other stations – in his view their main task was
to comply with his requests for stores, for repairs or for reinforcements.
Rodney was fully aware of the damage to Jamaica, which had, he wrote,
'the appearance of a country laid waste by fire and sword' and that the
naval institutions had suffered from the 'dire effects of this hurricane'.[6]
Even so, Rodney expected Parker to provide facilities to repair the
damage to his squadron and to send him reinforcements, and his letters
refer to Parker's *duty* to hasten the reinforcements 'I shall *demand*'.
Rodney knew the problems in Jamaica but seemed blind to the implications of the storm damage and couched his demands in a somewhat
arrogant manner. The correspondence shows clearly why Parker was
unable to help Rodney in the way he expected and it indicates, too, a
coolness in the relations between the two men which may have underlain
the retention in Jamaica of the *Prince William* and *Torbay* when they
should have been speeding after the reinforcements sailing to New York
prior to the battle of the Chesapeake.

Rodney and Hood

In the West Indies relationships between Rodney and his second in command, Samuel Hood, appeared no better, though here much of the blame
must rest with Hood. Both were self-opinionated men and neither was
reluctant to record his views about the capabilities of the other. It is evident
that, despite protestations of good relations made by both admirals, Rodney
and Hood did not work at all well together. During the whole period of his
service with Rodney in the West Indies, Hood clearly felt that he was

subject to an incompetent commander and freely said so, readily finding new occasions for criticism. Immediately after the arrival of de Grasse in the West Indies and the action of 29 April 1781, Hood was writing to Sandwich, 'Never was a squadron more unmeaningly stationed and what Sir George Rodney's motive for it could be I cannot conceive.'[7] In a later letter to Jackson, deputy secretary to the Admiralty, he implied that the booty of St Eustatius was at the root of the decision.[8] In contrast to his views of almost every other officer, Hood saw himself as superior in understanding and ability. After the action against de Grasse on 29 April in which Hood and his division barely took part, he could smugly write, 'I am perfectly conscious of no one omission in the whole of my conduct and of having done everything that was in my power for the support of the honour of the British flag . . . I have no neglect to charge myself with and on that account I feel quite at ease . . .'[9] When, in the summer of 1781, Rodney delayed his decision as to whether he should go with the fleet to North America or to return home because of ill health, Hood wrote to Jackson, 'It is quite impossible from the unsteadiness of the commander-in-chief to know what he means three days together . . .'[10]

He even regarded the great victory of the Saintes as a battle mismanaged and, with the guns hardly silent, was expressing his views in letters to England. A whole catalogue of his criticisms is to be found in his letter to Jackson of 16 April 1782, from the failure of Rodney to order a general chase into the night of the 12 April to the way Rodney's flagship was run where all was 'confusion on board the *Formidable* and not the least degree of attention to a regularity of system and order'. 'Sir George Rodney,' he continued, 'requires a monitor constantly at his elbow, as much as a froward child . . .' In short: 'What can we expect under such blundering conduct in matters of highest importance to the welfare of our country without the all powerful hand of Providence aids us?'[11] Even after the Saintes, having been highly critical of his superior, Hood could write that had he 'had the honour of commanding His Majesty's noble fleet on the 12th, I may, without the imputation of much vanity, say the flag of England should now have graced the stems of upwards of twenty sail of the enemy's line.'[12] It is not surprising that the view of a perfect Hood, held by Hood, was by no means shared by Rodney. Rodney's letterbook has numbers of examples of later annotations against letters and instructions to Hood – 'Neglected by Hood' or 'Grossly neglected by Hood'.[13] Where Rodney had every right to expect supportive help from his second in command, he was subject to constant open and covert criticism from Hood. Such an atmosphere was not directly of his making but it was not one which best suited the efficient prosecution of the war against the French and the Americans.

Rodney had been joined on 7 January 1781 by Sir Samuel Hood to be his second in command and with a reinforcement of four ships of the line and the 50-gun *Panther*. This was a controversial appointment. Sandwich explained that he had difficulty in finding a suitable second for Rodney. 'It has been difficult,' Sandwich wrote, 'to find out proper flag officers to serve under you, some are rendered unfit through their factious connections, others from infirmity or insufficiency and we have at last been obliged to make a promotion in order to do the thing properly, Sir Samuel Hood is to have his flag.'[14] Those admirals first approached had declined. Hood, in his post as Commissioner at Portsmouth, had also at first refused, but within two days decided to accept the appointment. Sandwich thought Hood might be acceptable to Rodney on the basis of their previous service together. In terms of personality, Hood was not a good choice for Rodney. It was said that 'Hood carried no oil for troubled waters in his locker', that 'his pen was acid and constantly to hand'.[15]

A sequence of events now began which was to have an undoubted effect on the campaigning in the West Indies, was to mark Rodney's reputation and, ultimately, to expose him again to financial difficulty. For long, Rodney had been angered by the trading centred on the Dutch island of St Eustatius. Many of the cargoes traded to America were owned or, at least, handled by British merchants. While the island remained neutral there was little that Rodney could do to stop the trade. All changed dramatically when relations between Britain and Holland were severed on 20 December 1780: immediate orders were sent to Rodney and to General Vaughan, the army commander, to attack the Dutch possessions in the West Indies. Rodney and Vaughan acted promptly and St Eustatius was taken on 3 February 1781.

The capture of the island and the ending of the trade had been a priority of the Cabinet. Shining success that it seemed to be, the capture quickly soured the relationships of Rodney and Hood, and Rodney was accused of losing all sense of the strategic priorities of his command in the dazzle of the wealth that had been captured. The burden of Hood's argument centred on the stationing of ships – Hood's squadron – to intercept any French reinforcement from Europe. Hood wanted to be far to windward; Rodney wanted to keep Fort Royal blockaded to prevent any attack on the homeward convoy of booty from the island. In the event, the blockade proved illusory, for much of the wealth that Rodney acquired in the West Indies was lost to the French when the convoy on which it was shipped was intercepted by La Motte Picquet in the Western Approaches. Such fortune as did escape La Motte Picquet was to drain away from Rodney in the years after the war as he lost many of the cases brought against him in the High Court by the merchants seeking compensation for their lost cargoes. Claims appeared to an amount exceeding the whole of the captured property and his son-in-law claimed that, in settling them, Rodney 'died in honourable poverty'.

The anticipated French reinforcement of twenty sail of the line arrived in the West Indies under François de Grasse and was met on off Martinique on 29 April by Hood, who failed to fight more than a long-shot engagement. Both Hood and de Grasse were subsequently blamed for not fighting a damaging and decisive action, and both claimed that the enemy was sailing away from them and could not be brought to action. For the British this failure was of great consequence because it could be argued that a decisive and destructive action would have brought an end to French activity in the West Indies and prevented them from moving to North America in any strength. This action on 29 April and one other on 5 June off Tobago were the only two occasions when the English and French squadrons faced each other during the whole period that de Grasse was in the West Indies, and both were ineffectual.

This failure was compounded by three major errors of judgement. While it was common practice to remove ships from the Caribbean with the approach of the hurricane season and it was known that de Grasse intended to send a force to North America, Rodney failed to send adequate and timely intelligence to Thomas Graves, the naval commander in North America. Second was a singular failure to anticipate de Grasse's move or to make an informed estimate as to the force he would take, despite reports that a significant number of Chesapeake pilots were reaching de Grasse. Finally, the reinforcement eventually sent to North America was small in number and late in despatch. Twenty-two ships of the line were potentially available but this number was dissipated to fourteen.

Rodney, again failing in health, sailed for England on 1 August 1781 in the *Gibraltar,* leaving Hood in command and with instructions to reinforce the North American station. Rodney went to Bath to convalesce and soon became involved in the recriminations that spread as the news of the Chesapeake and the surrender of Yorktown reached London. His claims to ill health as the cause for his return were not well received – 'had it come about,' wrote the *Public Advertiser,* 'thru action then every man would have regretted the impaired health of the Admiral; but none finds himself interested in the fate of the storekeeper.'[16] Rodney, in England, was able to promote a version of what had happened safe from contradiction by his fellow commanders. His famous Bath letter of 19 October 1781 to Jackson at the Admiralty offered a distinctly slanted view of the instructions and intelligence Rodney claimed to have sent to Graves in North America. It was against this background of depressing news from North America and mistrust of the 'storekeeper' of St Eustatius that Rodney was recalled to his command in the Leeward Islands for whatever eventuality might emerge in 1782.

The Battle of the Saintes

When, in the final months of 1781, it became evident that the French were preparing a massive reinforcement for the West Indies, Rodney received letters from Sandwich enquiring when he would be able to resume his command in the Leeward Islands – 'our loss,' he wrote, 'will be great if we are deprived of your assistance'[17] – and, ever anxious to do his duty, Rodney abandoned the cure for the stone and the gout he was taking in Bath and set in train preparations to join his squadron of reinforcement at Plymouth. Gales prevented his departure until 8 January 1782 and gales haunted the first part of his passage. His letters home even suggest that, in his response to the pressure of the French threat to the islands, he risked his ships in a way that in less urgent times would have been regarded as imprudent. 'Ushant,' he wrote in a letter to his wife, 'we weathered in a storm but two leagues [about six miles], the sea mountains high.'[18]

Rodney reached St Lucia in mid-February and he was depressed by the reports which greeted him. St Eustatius had fallen to de Grasse in November and Demerara, together with six frigates, surrendered in early January. St Christopher (St Kitt's) fell to the French on 12 February, quickly followed by Montserrat. His mood was not made lighter when he met Hood on 25 February and learnt that the ships of Hood's squadron were in a poor state of repair and were low in provisions, especially bread, and lacked anchors, having abandoned them at St Christopher.

The major task facing Rodney on his arrival was to decide the best deployment for his squadron of thirty-six ships to counter the French threat to the islands. Intelligence made it clear that the French intended an attack on Jamaica and Rodney's plans were made accordingly. Hood was ordered to cruise to windward of Point Salines and Drake, his third in command, to patrol between Point Salines and St Lucia. Drake was also to keep watch on the French in Fort Royal. Hood, characteristically, was unhappy with these dispositions and thought that 'nothing short of a miracle can now retrieve the affairs of the nation'.[19] By 28 March it was learnt that three French sail of the line with three frigates and 6000 soldiers had managed to slip un-detected into Fort Royal, though this did not deter Rodney, who had written to Parker in Jamaica of his conviction that 'an end is now put to the Enemy's conquests'.[20]

Rodney had news of the sailing of de Grasse on 8 April and at once ordered a general chase, which continued into the night until the French were caught in the early hours of 9 April, when a desultory action caused damage to ships in Hood's leading division. With strengthening winds, the fleets disengaged and set about repairing damage. By daylight on 11 April the French had worked their way to windward and, in gale force winds, Rodney again ordered a chase. By evening the British were approaching a French straggler and to protect her de Grasse bore down with his whole fleet. This brought the French so near that Rodney at last felt confident that he could bring them to action next day. In the dawn light of 12 April the fleets were revealed a mere four leagues [12 miles] from each other between the northern end of Dominica and the Saintes.

Rodney at once hoisted the signal for line ahead at two cables lengths asunder and, with Drake's division in the van, heading north–northeast. The British line was led by the *Marlborough,* Captain Taylor Penny, and fire was opened on the French centre at 8.00am. Rodney, in *Formidable,* en-tered the action also towards the centre of the French line at some 8 minutes past 8. The *Formidable* backed her topsails as she passed the *Ville de Paris,* enabling a longer exchange of fire between the flagships. As the *Formidable* continued her progress along the French line and was approach-ing the rear, it became evident that the wind, shifting into the south, was preventing the French from holding their orderly line and large gaps appeared in it. The *Formidable*'s log has the laconic entry '. . . stopt our firing having cut through the Enemy's line. Bore up and raked four of the Enemy's ships which had got foul of each other . . .'[21] Two other breaks in the line completed the confusion in the French fleet, which fell away to the southwest in disorganised groups. As the breeze strengthened in the after-noon, so Rodney pursued the French. By the evening the last of the French to surrender that day, the *Ville de Paris,* hauled down her flag and Rodney ordered the fleet to bring to for the ships to attend to their wounded men and damaged masts and hulls. Altogether Rodney's fleet captured seven French ships of the line, a frigate and a sloop.

Sadly, this bright and glorious success was tarnished by criticism of Rodney under two heads. There were those who questioned whether it was Rodney who saw and seized the opportunity to break the line, sug-gesting the credit should have gone to his captain of the fleet, Charles

Douglas. Some argued that it was unwise for Rodney to have changed course to take him through the French line, claiming that, had the British fleet maintained its line, even more damage would have been inflicted on the French as they were forced to sail towards their opponents. This debate was reopened following the publication of Mundy's *Life of Rodney* in 1826, in which mention is made of those who claimed that the manoeuvre was inspired by a landsman, Clerk of Eldin. Clerk's followers supported their view by referring to the fact that Rodney owned and had annotated a copy of Clerk's *Essay on Naval Tactics* in which he detailed the manner and value of breaking through a line of battle. Much of the heat was taken out of the various arguments as to who was responsible for the breaking of the line by the intervention of the veteran Captain Thomas White, who was present at the battle in the *Barfleur* and whose well informed *Naval Researches* was published in 1830. It was White who posed the view that breaking the line had not been the best action to have taken. The debate continues, but it is clear that Rodney had given much thought to ways in which he could concentrate his force against a part of the enemy line to achieve decisive results, and his contemporaries recalled conversations in which Rodney claimed he would break de Grasse's line when conditions permitted.

After the battle Hood had written to Sandwich about a 'beating as no great fleet ever had before' but he saw no illogicality in adding, in the same letter, 'I was most exceedingly disappointed in our commander-in-chief'. Hood contended that he should have ordered a general chase to continue into the night of 12 April and that it would have enabled him to take almost every French ship. There is some force in this argument, but it does not take into account the damage to the ships in Rodney's fleet and the dangers of collision inherent in a night chase involving ships weakened by battle damage. In any event, honour and courtesy should have kept Hood and his fellow critics silent to allow all in the British fleet to enjoy to the full this moment of triumph. Rodney, by contrast, singled out for the highest praise Samuel Hood, Francis Drake, Edmund Affleck and Charles Douglas for their roles in the battle and ended, 'I want words to express how sensible I am of the Meritorious Conduct of all the Captains, Officers and Men who had a share in this Glorious Victory obtained by their Gallant Exertions.'[22]

The triumphant climax to Rodney's long and frequently distinguished career had come with his outstanding victory over the French Admiral François de Grasse at the Battle of the Saintes. By the evening of the battle the French had scattered in disorderly groups and the last ship to surrender was the French flagship, the *Ville de Paris*. The fruits of this action were both tangible and immediate in the prizes taken and of longer term diplomatic value. By any standards the Saintes was a magnificent victory in which the French were comprehensively beaten. The islands, including Jamaica, had been protected; an end was brought to the succession of failures that had followed Yorktown; and the battle restored in no small degree the tarnished British naval and military reputation among the European powers. It enabled Britain to take part in the peace negotiations which brought the American war to an end in a position of equality and strength, and Fox moved a vote of thanks in the Commons in May 1782 for 'the most brilliant victory that this country had seen this century'.

While Rodney was so successfully opposing the French in the West Indies in the spring of 1782, Lord North felt obliged to resign his ministry in the face of mounting opposition at home and the apparently unending news of disaster abroad. Keppel, who replaced Sandwich as First Lord, found himself forced by his political colleagues to dismiss his friend Rodney from chief command in the Leeward Islands. This was clearly repugnant to him, and his letter of 2 May 1782 started: 'The task of writing disagreeable information to you falls to my lot . . . for reasons of State that Admiral Pigot should immediately proceed to the West Indies . . . resigning the command to him and returning with as little loss of time as possible to England.'[23] When the victory of the Saintes was known in London, unsuccessful attempts were made to recall Pigot and leave Rodney in post. Instead, Rodney landed at Bristol on 15 September 1782 and this, effectively, was the end of his active naval career. To make partial amends Rodney was given an English barony, a pension of £2000 and much praise in the Commons from one-time inveterate critics Fox and Burke. Many cities honoured Rodney with their Freedom, including Huntingdon, at which ceremony Sandwich made reference to the fact that Rodney's record was unsurpassed in that he had taken or destroyed sixteen ships of the line and captured the commanding admiral of each of the nations with which England was at war.

However, Rodney's return was not unalloyed happiness. His son, George, had brought order to his chaotic financial affairs but he was still in debt to the money lenders Lowther and Mackreth. What should have been an illustrious retirement was blemished, too, by financial distractions relating to claims brought against him in the High Court of Admiralty by many merchants seeking compensation for the loss of their cargoes and ships in the capture of St Eustatius. Many of the papers which Rodney claimed would have justified his seizures of goods traded with the enemy had disappeared and judgement after judgement went against him. The rich prize of St Eustatius which might have given him financial security into his old age instead remained to haunt him through the courts in London.[24]

Rodney's private and public correspondence shows him to have been a man of curious contradictions. A loving family man devoted to his wife and children, yet one who risked ruin by his addiction to gambling. An officer who was careful of the welfare and health of his men, yet one who seemed unable to establish harmonious relations with those senior officers with whom he had to work. Highly successful in many of his actions and aware of the need to modify the employment of the hallowed line of battle, he nevertheless rejected signalling experiments and reform initiated in the Channel fleet. Rodney died in London on 24 May 1792, his illustrious retirement having been marred by financial distractions and saddened by the break up of his family. After years of unity and devotion to each other apparent in their letters, Rodney and Henny agreed to separate, even though their younger son, Edward, was born less than ten years earlier in 1783. Lady Rodney survived her husband by many years and died in 1829.

Samuel, Viscount Hood. Oil by James Northcote

10

Samuel Hood, First Viscount Hood
1724-1816

'Lord Hood is equally great in all situations which an Admiral can be placed in'

MICHAEL DUFFY

Samuel Hood was the son of Samuel Hood, Vicar of Butleigh in Somerset, a younger son of Dorset lesser gentry stock, and his wife Mary Hoskins from the same county.[1] The family had no direct connection with the navy, and family tradition has it that the opening came when in 1740 the carriage of Captain Thomas Smith broke down at Butleigh en route from Plymouth to London. Hood's father offered hospitality for the night, and in return Smith offered to take one the vicar's sons to sea with him. It may not have been quite so accidental, since the principal landowner of Butleigh was James Grenville, whose brother Thomas was Smith's first lieutenant, and who was related to George Lyttelton, of whom Smith was the bastard half-brother. At all events it was Samuel's younger brother, Alexander, who hastened to take up the offer and in January 1741 was entered in the books of Smith's *Romney*, 50 as captain's servant. Samuel, the eldest son, originally refused, but quickly succumbed to his brother's example, and followed into the *Romney* on 6 May 1741.[2]

It may be significant for the path of Samuel Hood's particular career and subsequent reputation that he entered the navy at the late age of 16, whereas his brother, who entered at 13, was closer to the normal pattern that set great emphasis on sea training at the expense of broader education. Samuel's greater education perhaps gave him an extra edge over others who, like him, lacked the advantages of an aristocratic upbringing and pedigree. He had 'manners and conversation . . . both of a superior order' to many of his naval contemporaries,[3] and a more thoughtful approach to his profession.

From Smith's *Romney*, Hood followed Thomas Grenville when he be-came captain of the *Garland* fireship, in which Hood was mustered as able seaman. In 1743 he moved as a tall, gangling midshipman into the *Sheerness*, 24, commanded by George Bridges Rodney, with whom his path was destined repeatedly to cross in their distinguished careers. In September 1744 he chose to follow Rodney, still as a midshipman, into the *Ludlow Castle*, 40, continuing to serve in the Channel and North Sea. In January 1746 he rejoined his first patron, now Commodore Thomas Smith, com-manding on the coast of Scotland to prevent help reaching the '45 Highland Rebellion. From Smith's *Exeter*, his patron appointed him acting-lieutenant of the *Winchelsea*, 20 (17 May 1746), whose captain, Henry Dyve, recommended confirmation of his lieutenant's commission, which was done on 17 June 1746. Still employed in home waters, Hood had his first fight and first wound (in the hand) in November 1746 when *Winchelsea* chased, engaged and, with the belated assistance of the *Portland*, captured the French 26-gun frigate *Subtile* off the Isles of Scilly.

Although one useful connection was lost when Thomas Grenville was killed in action in 1747, the patronage of Smith and Grenville's brothers continued. After a few months in the *Greenwich*, 50 with Captain John Montagu in 1748, Smith used his good offices with Rear-Admiral Charles Watson, who agreed to take him with him to North America as the third officer of his flagship, the *Lyon*, 60. Hood's zeal undoubtedly impressed Watson, and four years later he asked the Admiralty again for Hood as his lieutenant, 'being a very active good officer'.[4]

When Hood returned from America with Watson in November 1748, peace had been signed and he was placed on half pay. With the fleet demobilised, Smith's ability to help him was neutralised. Equally, although the 'cousinhood' of the Grenvilles, Lytteltons and William Pitt were now part of Henry Pelham's coalition ministry, and James Grenville was an MP, there were stronger claims on them for the limited naval patronage avail-able than those of the sons of the Vicar of Butleigh. Samuel Hood strength-ened his political 'interest' in 1749, however, when he married Susannah Linzee, daughter of the Portsmouth surgeon and apothecary Edward Linzee. Linzee was rising into a leading position in Portsmouth politics and was to be nine times mayor, while the corporation was strong enough to challenge Admiralty nomination of the borough's MPs, so that the First Lord was consequently obliged to give consideration to the patronage interests of the aldermen.[5]

Judging from the fact that his brother Alexander was not employed until 1755, it was this Portsmouth 'interest' that was crucial to Samuel. In

January 1753, the year in which his father-in-law became mayor for the second time, he was appointed to the Portsmouth guardship, the *Invincible*, 74, turning over to the *Terrible*, 74 in May. After the death of the Premier, Pelham, in March 1754, Hood looked to Smith's 'cousinhood' relatives being brought 'more into play', and one of them, George Grenville, became Treasurer of the Navy. However, again it seems to have been his Portsmouth interest, with a general election looming, that got him despatched in June 1754 to North America to command the sloop *Jamaica*. His marriage had eventually paid dividends, but there was more to it than self-interest. He confided to Smith that he found the parting from his wife 'very severe, I did not think it would have affected me so much but I find I love my sweet wench better than I thought for.'[6]

On the North American coast in 1756, under Commodore Holmes, he distinguished himself in the action with the French squadron off Louisbourg on 27 July. Unbeknown to him, he had been posted captain of the *Lively*, 20 five days before, but Holmes appointed him as his own captain in the *Grafton*, 70, and he returned home in her with Holmes towards the end of that year.

Post Captain, 1756-1780

From a relatively disadvantaged start, Samuel Hood had achieved the rank of post captain at the age of 32, and the formative influences on his career were all in place. Speaking of Smith, Watson and Holmes, Hood's biographer in the *Naval Chronicle* for 1799 (probably his secretary, John McArthur) declared that 'Few men have had the advantage of forming themselves after such models as Captain Hood enjoyed.' He ascribed gallantry and integrity to Smith. Watson was 'everything that would adorn the navy; being in the confidence of such a man, must have early installed those principles in the mind of our young officer which he afterwards so rigidly adopted as the rule of his conduct towards others.'[7] More recently Daniel Baugh has placed particular emphasis on the lessons from Smith's lack of concern for prize money, from his focus on duty and on performing good and faithful service irrespective of party political considerations (though well understanding the importance of powerful friends and connections), and from his kindness: 'Well educated, unaffected, generous, and honest, he made scarcely any enemies.'[8]

Hood's political connections in Parliament now came to the fore when the head of the Grenville family, Lord Temple, became First Lord of the Admiralty in 1756-7 and Lord Privy Seal from 1758 to 1761, while William Pitt, to whom Hood's brother Alexander became distantly related by marriage in 1758, became Secretary of State in the same period and the victorious director of the Seven Years War. Samuel Hood availed himself of the opportunity, offering his services to take command of any ship whose captain was absent on the court martial of Admiral Byng. He told Lord Temple that he was 'no ways inclined to be idle ashore while anything can be got to employ me.'⁹ In consequence, he received successive short commands in the *Torbay*, *Tartar*, and *Antelope*, but he now needed an opportunity to prove himself in command if he was to get any further. The chance came his way in the *Antelope*, 50 on 14 May 1757 when he encountered three sail off Brittany. Pursuing the largest, the *Aquilon*, 50, he chased, engaged and drove her on to rocks in Audierne Bay, where she became a total wreck. A week later he captured a 'small snow' bound from Bordeaux to Canada with wine, brandy and flour, and on the 25th a 16-gun privateer.¹⁰ The Admiralty communicated the Board's approval of his conduct and rewarded him on 14 July with a permanent posting to the frigate *Bideford*, 20, attached to Hawke's squadron cruising in the Bay of Biscay.

Next year he was commissioned to command the frigate *Vestal*, 32, and took part in Hawke's second visitation of the Basque Roads and the destruction of the fortifications on the Isle of Aix. In 1759 *Vestal* was appointed to Commodore Holmes's squadron for North America, but on the way out, on 21 February off Cape Finisterre, Hood chased and engaged the French frigate *Bellona*, 32. After a running fight of more than three hours, he reduced her to a wreck with only her fore mast standing, and she struck. *Vestal* too was badly damaged and forced to return to Spithead with her prize, but the action led to the victorious captain being presented to the King by the First Lord, Anson.¹¹

After refitting, *Vestal* patrolled off Havre, where flat-bottomed invasion boats had been collected, and she then formed part of the bombardment squadron assembled under Rodney to destroy that concentration. Rodney supervised the attack from the *Vestal*, complaining that the pilots provided for him had proved useless, and praising the captains of the *Deptford*, *Vestal* and *Juno* and the first lieutenant of the *Dolphin* for their efforts in anchoring the bomb vessels properly in position during the night to bombard the invasion flotilla effectively between 4 and 6 July.¹²

Hood's capacity was now recognised sufficiently by the Admiralty to grant his request in the next year to be sent to the Mediterranean. He explained that 'For ten years past, I have been afflicted more or less with a bilious disorder, which has been very severe within these nine months as to confine me to my cabin for many days together.' He hoped to get relief by service in a milder climate.[13] This brought him under the command of another distinguished admiral, Sir Charles Saunders, who, after Hood had executed his orders to scour the Spanish coast to his satisfaction, despatched him to the Levant, where he was engaged in convoy service until the end of the war in 1763.[14]

All Hood's earlier naval patrons were now dead: Watson in 1757, Holmes in 1761, and the one with whom he was most intimate, Admiral Smith in 1762. However, Hood was now far enough advanced in the service, in reputation and in his connections not to be kicking his heels idly at the peace. In September 1763 he was appointed to the *Thunderer* guardship at Portsmouth, in which in the summer of 1765 he carried a foot regiment to North America. He had become adept at the game of keeping his connections sweet, sending back to James Grenville a canister of the latest medical *nostrum*, spruce tops, and in the following years sending seeds to the two leading Grenville brothers, George (Premier from 1763 to 1765) and Lord Temple.[15] James Grenville of Butleigh broke with his brothers to stand by Pitt when the later returned to power as Premier and Earl of Chatham in 1766. This 'interest' and especially the political situation in Portsmouth, where Linzee was mayor for the fifth time in 1766 and the new First Lord of the Admiralty, Lord Hawke, was one of the borough's MPs (1747-76) with a general election only a year away, helped Hood into appointment in April 1767 as commodore and commander-in-chief of the North America station in the *Romney*, based at Halifax. It proved a turbulent three years' command as the notorious 'Townshend [revenue] duties' on the colonies aroused a storm of resistance and brought Hood repeatedly to the main trouble-centre, Boston.[16]

Hood returned to Portsmouth in 1770, just as the fortunes of his former political patrons collapsed. Chatham resigned office in 1768, a semi-invalid; George Grenville died in 1770; and thereafter Chatham and the remaining Grenvilles spasmodically raged in impotent opposition until Chatham's death in 1778, followed by that of Temple a year later. Fortunately, Hood had never committed himself partisanly to the Chathamite faction. His Portsmouth connections had become more important. During this decade his father-in-law, Edward Linzee, was mayor in 1771, 1777, 1779 and 1780, and his brother-in-law, Thomas Monday, was mayor in 1775.[17] The successful mode of operation of his Portsmouth connections was to do business with whichever was the government of the day, and this may have constrained and schooled him against partisan politics, but his professional dedication also played a strong part. He told the Second Secretary at the Admiralty, George Jackson, in January 1783, that

I shall ever most carefully and studiously steer clear, as far as I am able, of all suspicion of being a *party man*, for if once I show myself of that complexion, whether for or against a Minister, unbecoming a military servant to my Royal master, I must from that moment expect to lose every degree of consideration in the line of my profession, which ever has been, and ever will be, the first and greatest object of my wishes.[18]

In consequence he was given command of successive Portsmouth guard-ships, the *Royal William* from 1771 to 1773, followed by the *Marlborough* until July 1776, when, in his absence, she was severely damaged by an explosion while being cleared to go into dock, whereupon he and his crew were turned over to the *Courageux*, 74. It was a pleasant life on full pay. When the guardships were not exercising, he was as often as possible at his home, Catherington House, near Horndean, where his sister-in-law de-scribed his family as living 'in comfort and with a proper degree of ele-gance', and he rode into Portsmouth for the day.[19]

What he relished, however, was the prospect of 'real service', and with the American colonies in revolt in 1776 and Britain's French and Spanish rivals likely to be interested in their success, real service was at last a possibility. This had led him to take the *Courageux* despite the fact that, as he confessed to Lady Chatham, he was not partial to French-built ships. But what he was offered by the First Lord of the Admiralty, Lord Sand-wich, was the shore-based administrative post of Admiralty Commissioner at Portsmouth and Governor of the Naval Academy. He told Lady Chatham that he had hoped for something else, but his health would not permit. He was now 53 and the post was usually regarded as a final one, terminating an active career, but he negotiated with Sandwich that it would not preclude him from accepting a flag post when it was his turn. He also loyally pressed for his unemployed brother, Alexander, to succeed him in command of the *Courageux*, particularly since, as he explained, many people were 'sent from the sea coast by our family friends and followers of both of us'. Like his own former naval patrons, he now had an 'interest' of his own to manage and advance. Among those sent to him for a naval education was Chatham's third son, James Pitt, whose career was to be cut short by an untimely death in the West Indies in 1781. The *Naval Chronicle* for 1799 reported that four of *Courageux*'s lieutenants under Hood went on to reach the rank of rear-admiral.[20]

Hood took up his new post on 10 February 1778 and was soon involved in mobilising the fleet for war with France, which at last broke out that summer. The preparations brought a visit from George III in May, which proved significant for both of them. Under Hood's guidance the King at last completed his education in the complexities of running a navy and was clearly impressed by the businesslike Commissioner. George discussed the entry into the navy of his third son, Prince William, and wrote subsequently for further advice on fitting him out, adding that 'I cannot conclude without expressing my approbation at the Activity with which you forward the business of the dock Yard'. He showed his approbation by creating Hood a baronet.[21] Hood himself was now in the royal eye and favour, and his professional zeal to perform the King's service was further enhanced. In June, on the outbreak of war with France, he reminded the Premier, Lord North, that he was still available for sea service and was not a tool of Chatham and Temple, having supported the ministry's efforts both in public business and 'as a private man'.[22] As the leading government official in his locality, a Dockyard Commissioner had a political as well as an administrative role to play in the eighteenth century. At a Hampshire county by-election of 1779 Hood was described as 'armed "with the insolence of office"', commanding 'the attendance of every dependent of government' to vote for the government candidate.[23]

His sense of duty must, however, have been tested by the government's unwillingness to move him, and by its treatment of his brother, who was sidelined in the political fall-out following the unsuccessful attempt to court-martial the popular Admiral Keppel for his conduct of the Battle of Ushant. Alexander Hood incurred much public odium when it was revealed that he had made corrections to his ship's logbook which favoured the case of Keppel's accuser, Admiral Palliser. Political feuds over the Keppel affair split the navy as Keppel and other officers connected with the Whig Opposition declined to serve any further. Alexander Hood was caught in the middle between government and opposition and his career ground to a halt as Sandwich kept him back in a bid to restore harmony within the fleet. Sir Samuel Hood loyally supported his brother by urging Sandwich to bestow ships and postings upon him, but he refused his brother's suggestions that he use his influence in Portsmouth in opposition to the First Lord and the government in the 1780 general election. He had taken the line of supporting the government in the war crisis and some degree of consistency was 'requisite for every man to observe'.[24]

The reward for his consistency came at last at the end of that year. In March he again reminded Sandwich of his desire to hoist his flag and serve 'in the military line' and that he had accepted the post of Commissioner, not from inclination, but from a desire to accommodate the government. In September, as he struggled to find a second in command for Sir George Rodney on the West Indies station with his choice restricted by the defection of the Opposition Whig officers and by a reluctance of others to serve under the demanding, irascible Rodney, Sandwich remembered Hood. He had served with Rodney twice before and they had got on well. Hood initially declined on health grounds but in two days he announced a wonderful recovery and expressed his willingness to serve if it was not too late, repeating two days later that he was 'so much better and stouter these few days'.[25]

Perhaps the initial refusal was a further attempt to push Sandwich into looking after his brother, for whom he pointedly requested the First Lord's protection. There are also indications that Portsmouth politics were involved. The 1770s saw a power struggle for control of the corporation between Linzee's connection of Admiralty supporters and an independent Dissenter connection led by John Carter. Between Hood's original refusal and his second letter of acceptance his father-in-law was again elected mayor, as he then told Sandwich, and perhaps there was less need for Hood's local political presence as Commissioner in Portsmouth. In these circumstances, and on reflection, ambition and duty prevailed – he had been offered a chance that might not come again. Some years later, when a protégé, William Hotham, was thinking of rejecting a posting as lieutenant to the Newfoundland station, Hood advised him strongly to take it, declaring:

> The performance of your duty and your obedience to your Officer's orders will always ensure you approbation and, what is more to your purpose, *respect*, for no commanding officer, however overbearing he may be, dare take any liberty with an inferior who does his duty like an officer and a gentleman.[26]

On 26 September 1780 an extensive promotion of admirals enabled Hood to be given his flag as rear-admiral of the blue, which he hoisted in the *Barfleur*, 98. On 19 November he took out a squadron of eight of the line, escorting the trade, to reinforce Rodney. Hitherto, Hood's career had shown just how much a capable man of modest rank, no fortune and no direct family 'interest' could achieve in the navy by finding the most advantageous political connections for himself. Now began a two and a half years' tour of duty that ensured Hood's reputation and, through his prowess as an admiral, took his career and social position on to an altogether higher plane.

Hood and Rodney, 1780-1782

The initial omens were not auspicious. He was going to serve under a commander-in-chief who had told one of his predecessors that 'the painful task of thinking belonged to me, to him *obedience* to signals and orders', and who is alleged to have declared when he learned of Hood's appointment that 'They might as well have sent me an old apple-woman.'[27] He had not served in the Caribbean before, and had much to learn of its currents and windshifts among the islands. He was going to the main battle theatre of the American War, but had never taken part in a fleet action before. Indeed, he had little experience of serving in a squadron of ships of the line, except when the guardships had exercised, since most of his operational experience had been in frigates.

His first service with Rodney was leading an advanced division in the expedition against St Eustatius in January 1781. Deprived of the chance of independent naval command of a further expedition against Curaçao when Rodney lost interest (Hood alleged that he became dazzled by his mammoth prize-haul at St Eustatius), he was then despatched to windward of Martinique in response to a false report of the imminent arrival of a French fleet. For five weeks Hood stayed out to windward. To his disgust he was then directed to bring his ships to leeward to blockade the small French squadron in Fort Royal, Martinique – again, he alleged, to safeguard the departure of the St Eustatius prize convoy. He protested the disadvantage this would place him under, in trying to prevent the arrival of French reinforcements at Martinique, though he declared he would 'most readily submit to your superior knowledge and experience, and shall cheerfully obey your commands on all occasions with the utmost fidelity'.[28]

A case can be made for Rodney's instructions,[29] but when Admiral de Grasse appeared with twenty sail of the line and 150 merchantmen on 28 April, events confirmed Hood's warning to his commander-in-chief on the 1st that 'I do not feel myself at all pleasant in being to leeward; for should an enemy's fleet attempt to get into Martinique, and the commander of it inclines to avoid battle, nothing but a *skirmish* will probably happen, which in its consequences may operate as a defeat to the British squadron, though not a ship is lost and the enemy suffer most.'[30]

Despite his subsequent attempts to vindicate himself, Hood, in his first independent operational command, was not entirely blameless. Eager to keep his ships together for a fight, he neglected Rodney's instructions to send his ships to neighbouring St Lucia one by one for replenishment (to his commander's subsequent fury). The opportunity for a collective replenishment never arrived, and his crews were in poor shape when the French appeared. Moreover, he was caught out by local conditions when half his squadron became becalmed in the lee of Martinique, so that despite a day's warning he was unable to tack up in time to get between de Grasse

and Fort Royal. He was reduced to fighting a '*longshot* action' at about a
mile's distance, while de Grasse was joined by the four French ships from
Fort Royal, giving him twenty-four of the line against Hood's eighteen. In
frustration Hood hove-to his squadron under their topsails and invited the
French to come to him, but de Grasse's main object was to shepherd his
convoy safely into port. One of Hood's ships had to be sent off to Antigua
for repair, and two more days of indecisive skirmishing damaged five more.
With such damages and 2000 sick on his hands, Hood then bore up to find
Rodney.[31]

The experience was profoundly disillusioning for Hood, whose confidence in his commander was fast diminishing. Their relationship was further strained when Rodney annulled Hood's promotion of his first
lieutenant to fill a vacancy after the action and substituted a nominee of his
own. Hood now began writing home to his friends (and he was a prolific
writer), vindicating his own conduct and criticising that of Rodney.[32]

With the initiative lost, the French captured Tobago and an ailing
Rodney failed to bring de Grasse to battle. When the hurricane season
approached, de Grasse sailed for St Domingue with twenty-six of the line
and nearly 200 merchant ships bound for France. Rodney decided to return
home to repair his health and, on 23 July 1781, ordered Hood with fourteen of the line to reinforce Rear-Admiral Graves on the coast of North
America, whither he expected de Grasse to make a large detachment also.
What neither realised was that de Grasse would leave his convoy at St
Domingue and, on 5 August, sail with twenty-four of the line, almost his
entire fleet, and 3000 troops to the Chesapeake, where a Franco-American
army under Washington had Lord Cornwallis's British army trapped at
Yorktown.

Hood left St John's Road, Antigua, on 10 August, eager to catch any
French force on the American coast and bring it to action. In his haste he
overtook de Grasse, and failing to find him at the Chesapeake, hastened on
to Graves at New York. Reaching Sandy Hook on 28 August, he refused
Graves's invitation to bring his ships into harbour to replenish, instead
urging Graves to bring out his five of the line to join in finding either the
French squadron from the West Indies or de Barras's seven of the line at
Newport before they could unite. On 5 September their combined nineteen of the line surprised de Grasse in Chesapeake Bay, struggling to get his
twenty-four out to meet them.

In the ensuing battle Hood with the rear division never got into action,
and the only chance of defeating the French fleet was missed. In consequence
the navy was unable to rescue Cornwallis, who surrendered on 19 October.

What went wrong at the Chesapeake has been matter for violent debate. Hood himself began it by telling his confidants that Graves was 'unequal to the conducting of a great squadron'. He blamed his commander for not bringing his fleet into action quicker by signalling for a general chase to attack the isolated French van as it straggled out past Cape Henry, and, thereafter, for not concentrating a tightly formed line to destroy their van. Graves's own intention – to bring his fleet into action together – was thwarted by the failure of the West Indies squadron to interpret and act upon his signals as he wanted. It had been drilled to obedience in a different system and signals, and there had been insufficient time to work it up into Graves's more flexible system. Approaching at an angle, Hood felt constrained by Graves's line ahead signal which seemed to negate his simultaneous signal for close action, and so he did not follow his own instinct to get his division into the fight.[33]

In consequence, Hood still had much to prove when he returned to the West Indies towards the end of the year. But he was about to enter his *annus mirabilis*. He pressed Graves's successor, Admiral Digby, to release to him his own battleships, offering to share all prize money equally with Digby until he returned them in the spring.[34] Digby provided four, which Hood integrated into his experienced West Indies squadron by frequent exercises on the voyage to the Caribbean. On his arrival he learned that de Grasse too had returned, with thirty of the line, but when, in January, the French made their play by attacking St Kitt's (St Christopher), he was confident enough of his captains to take out his twenty-two of the line, begging the Admiralty secretary, Philip Stephens, to 'assure their Lordships I will seek and give battle to the Count De Grasse, be his numbers as they may.'[35]

The logbook of William Cornwallis's *Canada*, one of the ships donated by Digby, shows the extent to which Hood sought to keep his officers informed of his intentions. On the morning of 21 January he signalled for each ship to send a lieutenant to the flagship, and later for all flag officers. On the morning of the 23rd he summoned all ships to send a midshipman, all flag officers, the captains of *Alcide* and *Centaur*, and all to send a lieutenant. In the afternoon his flag officers signalled for the captains of their divisions, and when they sailed Hood signalled for all cruisers.[36]

At daylight on 24 January 1782 Hood was off the southern tip of Nevis, intending to surprise the French fleet in their anchorage at Basseterre, St Kitt's, and attack in succession the three rear ships of the French line. He was thwarted by a collision between his lead battleship and a frigate, and had to stand off to repair damages. This enabled de Grasse, who had twenty-eight of the line with him, to stand out to sea to bar his passage northward. Next morning, 25 January, seeing the French fleet had strayed to leeward, Hood decided that the best chance to save the island was to seize de Grasse's anchorage. A feint to attack the French admiral drew de Grasse further seaward, whereupon Hood hauled to the wind and 'pushed for it'. Belatedly de Grasse sought to overhaul him, but Hood sent one of his repeating frigates with precise instructions to his van ships to tack into and anchor in line in Frigate Bay from a point as close as possible to the headland at Green Point, with the rest of the fleet swinging around to anchor successively behind them after passing along the line of anchored ships. Lord Robert Manners, commanding the *Resolution* in the rear division, wrote that 'The van and centre divisions brought to an anchor under the [protecting] fire of the rear, which was engaged with the enemy's centre, and then, the centre being at anchor and properly placed, covered us while we anchored, making, I think, the most masterly manoeuvre I ever saw.'[37]

Over the next two days de Grasse attacked Hood's line, but by then he had drawn it as tight as possible and had his ships put out springs on their cables to enable a wider arc of fire from their broadsides, so that the attacks were driven off. After a feint on the 30th, the frustrated de Grasse stood off to await events.

Hood had successfully interposed himself between the French fleet and their army, besieging the British garrison on Brimstone Hill. But though he landed the few troops he had scraped together, they were too few and too remote to help, and, to Hood's chagrin, he received no assistance from the island's planters. The troops were re-embarked, but he hung on in the hope of reinforcement from Britain until Brimstone Hill surrendered on the 13th. He then took steps to get away quickly, before his fleet became trapped between de Grasse, now reinforced to thirty-two of the line, and the shore batteries he could now expect the victorious besiegers to bring to bear. All was prepared with great care and instruction. During 14 February Hood summoned all flag officers to the flagship, followed by lieutenants at 11am, 4pm, and finally at 9pm, when he had them synchronise their watches by his chronometer, ready to have his ships cut their cables together at 11 that night without any signal which might alert the enemy. This early use of such a ploy worked. Lord Robert Manners wrote that they 'sailed out in a line with so little noise or confusion that the enemy did not miss us for four hours after. Nothing could have been more fortunately executed, as not one accident happened from it.'[38]

Although Rodney subsequently criticised Hood for not sailing out boldly to seek combat with de Grasse, the episode was the making of

Hood's reputation. '[I]f you give him half the credit the enemy does, Sir Samuel Hood will stand very high in the public estimation,' wrote Manners.[39] Mahan has described the three-week operation as 'the most brilliant military effort of the whole war'.[40] Among the admiring opponents in de Grasse's fleet was a lieutenant on the *Zélé*, François Paul de Brueys d'Aigalliers. Sixteen years later his memory of Hood's successful repulse of de Grasse's attacks encouraged him to anchor the French Mediterranean fleet in Aboukir Bay. Unfortunately for him he faced not a de Grasse, but one of Hood's later protégés, Horatio Nelson.[41]

The Saintes, and the End of the War

The arrival at Barbados of Rodney with twelve of the line to resume his command on 19 February, followed by further reinforcements, changed the strategic situation. De Grasse withdrew to Fort Royal to await reinforcement and a convoy from France with troops and stores for a Franco-Spanish assault on Jamaica. Again Hood disagreed with Rodney on the best way to intercept the convoy. He urged that the fleet, now grown to thirty-six ships, should be split into two, with half to windward of Point Salines at the southern tip of Martinique (de Grasse's landfall the previous year), and the other half to windward of Guadeloupe, in case the French sought a landfall further north and tried to slip down the island chain to Fort Royal. Rodney insisted on keeping his fleet to windward of Martinique. Again Hood proved correct when the French took the unguarded northern route and got into Fort Royal before Rodney was aware of their arrival.

On 8 April de Grasse slipped out of Fort Royal with thirty-six of the line and a vast convoy of troops and trade bound for St Domingue. Rodney pursued with thirty-seven of the line, with Hood leading the van. Next day, however, Hood pressing on found himself isolated when the British centre and rear became temporarily becalmed in the lee of Dominica. For 'above an hour' Hood with eight ships had to withstand the attack of fourteen of de Grasse's centre and rear, with *Barfleur* taking the fire of five French ships, until more British ships came into action. De Grasse, focussing on protecting his convoy, drew off and shepherded it, together with battle-damaged warships, into Guadeloupe. Finally, on 12 April 1782 he was caught off Les Saintes with his fleet reduced to thirty against the British thirty-six. Because of the damage received in the action on the 9th, Hood's division had been transferred to the rear, but this put him in a position to follow Rodney's example by breaking through the French line when a shift in the wind threw it into confusion. He then became becalmed in the lee of Dominica, but when he got his division back into action in the late afternoon he found de Grasse's shattered flagship, the 110-gun *Ville de Paris*, looking to challenge him in order to have a flag officer to whom to surrender with honour. Hood hastened to oblige, and, after a brief but bloody ten minutes fire from *Barfleur*, he had the honour of receiving the surrender of both the French commander-in-chief and the only French three-decker ever taken in battle. It was perhaps a fitting triumph since Hood had been engaged in every action in which de Grasse had fought since his arrival on the western side of the Atlantic.[42]

Five French ships were captured, while the rest of the fleet fled in disarray. Hood pressed Rodney for a vigorous pursuit and raged in frustration when this was denied him. Exhausted after four sleepless nights since making contact with the enemy, Rodney opted for caution, being more concerned with the damage to his own ships, their shortage of powder, the safety of his prizes and the dangers of identifying friend from foe in a night action.[43] Not until the 17th did he finally give Hood permission to go ahead with ten of the line. Hood made all sail for the Mona Passage between Puerto Rico and St Domingo, which he reached on the 19th, only a day after the French fleet, but in time to capture two more ships of the line from Guadeloupe, as well as a frigate and a sloop.

To Hood this was little satisfaction, nor was the fact that Jamaica had been saved. In his eyes a wonderful opportunity had been lost to win the war. After initial rejoicing that 'His Majesty's fleet has given such a beating to that of France, as no great fleet ever had before', he was soon raging that 'Surely there never was an instance before of a great fleet being so *completely beaten* and *routed* and *not pursued*.' Twenty ships might have been taken before dark. The capricious Rodney required 'a monitor perpetually at his elbow, as much as a froward child', and his Fleet Captain and advisor, Sir Charles Douglas, was so very weak and irresolute that 'he is no more fit for the station he fills than I am to be archbishop.' 'My feelings are so strong', he wrote to Jackson at the Admiralty, 'that I must express myself so *to you* . . . to give vent to the perturbation and anguish of my mind; and sooner than undergo for a continuance of what I have so very painfully done for several weeks past, I would be content to be placed on a Welsh mountain to gather *buttons* as they drop from a goat's tail.'[44]

Hood was left to watch the French survivors at Cap François until the end of May, when he went to Jamaica and was set by Rodney to get the fleet refitted from its damages at the Saintes. His experience as Portsmouth Commissioner stood him in good stead in work which was 'heavy and arduous in the extreme. . . . I am regularly in the yard every morning as soon as a man can see to use a tool, where I tarry some hours, and return again after dinner till the day is fairly closed; and I can venture to say that more work was never done in the time by the same number of men in any yard in England.' By 21 June he was hopeful that all but one of those in the battle would be ready for sea in three days time.[45]

In July Rodney was superseded by Admiral Pigot, and Hood set himself to serve a new master. But pity for the plight of this political nominee of a new government, who had 'been so long on land and never hoisted his flag or commanded a squadron before', soon gave way to outbursts in his letters at Pigot's dilatoriness and neglect. Hood was a man frustrated with subordination in 1782. He dutifully obeyed orders,[46] but he let his correspondents at home know that he would have behaved differently had he been in command. His friends advised him to tone down his letters, but he declared himself 'too open and honest-hearted to live in the present times, and my mind often tells me I express my thoughts too freely; but I cannot help it, particularly when I am writing to one I flatter myself has a real regard for and will not commit me.'[47]

Hood's angry letters home did much to tarnish Rodney's laurels, but his own reputation stood high. In September 1782 he was given an Irish peerage as Baron Hood of Catherington, Hampshire. The City of London presented him with its freedom in a gold box. The King entrusted the further naval education of his midshipman son to Hood's care, writing in August that 'I shall be happy if William can be witness to as brilliant actions as have attended the *Barfleur* ever since she has left our Island.' Six months later George declared Hood to be 'the most brilliant Officer of this War'.[48] Among those climbing the sides of *Barfleur* to seek Hood's patronage, when the West Indies fleet moved to New York for the 1782 hurricane season, was the 24-year-old captain of the frigate *Albemarle*, Horatio Nelson, looking for a battleship and transfer to the West Indian station as 'the station of honour'. Hood promised his friendship, impressed by Nelson's zeal, and out of regard for Nelson's lately deceased uncle and patron, Captain Maurice Suckling, who had been MP for Portsmouth. He persuaded Admiral Digby to release *Albemarle* to accompany him back to the West Indies, and three months later her captain was writing that 'My situation in Lord Hood's Fleet must be in the highest degree flattering to any young man. He treats me as if I were his son, and will, I am convinced, give me anything I can ask of him . . .'[49]

Hood spent the last Caribbean campaigning season of the war in semi-independent command off Jamaica, trying to intercept and bring to battle French and Spanish squadrons that had no wish to meet him, finally returning to Britain in the summer of 1783. He continued to look after his

following, from greatest to least. He presented Nelson to the King at a
levee at St James's in July, and at the end of the year invited the unemployed young captain to dine at his London house, 12 Wimpole Street,
which he declared always open to him and the oftener Nelson came the
happier it would make him.[50] Next year Hood helped get him command
of the *Boreas*, 28 on the West India station. At the other end of the scale, he
advised the father of Jeffrey Raigersfeld in 1786 that he should remove his
son from the sea where he had already acquired three and a half years' sea
time, and place him in a private school to learn mathematics for a year.
After four months Hood found the young Raigersfeld a private tutor in
Portsmouth, recently retired from the Greenwich Observatory, and
brought him thither for a further year, entering him on the books of his
Portsmouth flagship, *Triumph*, while being taught. He then recommended
Raigersfeld to Sir Richard Strachan, who took him into the *Vestal*.[51]

By then Hood was a celebrity for other reasons. As the constitutional
crisis of late 1783 and early 1784 moved to a climax in a general election,
the King and his new Prime Minister, Chatham's son William Pitt the
younger, needed a popular naval hero as a candidate to help defeat Charles
Fox, leader of the factious Fox–North Coalition, in his Westminster constituency, and they turned to Hood. Although a year previously Hood had
blessed his luck that his son had withdrawn his name when an attempt had
been made to put him forward for Westminster, this time he allowed
himself to be pressed 'into one of the most disagreeable situations an officer
could be placed' out of duty to the King and his long friendship with Pitt's
family. He later described it as 'the most arduous and unpleasant business I
ever took in hand'.[52] There were advantages to him, nevertheless, in shifting to a new political power-base, since the death of his father-in-law in
1782 destroyed his long-reliable Portsmouth connection through the triumph of the opposing Carter party.[53] Hood was remarkably fortunate, or
skilful, in repeatedly finding influential new patrons or connections just as
the old ones disappeared. In one of the most famously expensive, riotous
and controversial elections of the century, Hood topped the poll, though
the close battle between Hood's running mate, Wray, and Fox took the
result to a parliamentary scrutiny, and he did not finally take his seat until
March 1785.

The parliamentary world was not one in which Hood was at ease,
though he made periodic sallies into debates in typically robust and impet-
uous fashion. Despite a government subsidy of £9000 towards the expenses
of the election, political life also exhausted the finances of a man who had
never set out to make a fortune. In January 1786 he told the Premier:

The situation of my finances (which the King is fully apprized of) stands in great need of assistance, as the being so much in town the last two years and the consequences of my election for Westminster have embarrassed me much, and unless Government does something for me I shall be obliged from dire necessity to retire and take a final leave of London at the close of the next sessions of Parliament.[54]

He did not get the major-generalship of the Marines that he asked for, but was shortly appointed commander-in-chief at Portsmouth during 1786-88 and again in 1791-93.

Hood's credit with the King was shaken in 1787 when the 'minder' he placed on the *Pegasus* as first lieutenant when Prince William became her captain, Isaac Schomberg, became involved in a dispute with his charge and demanded a court martial, while Hood's protégé Nelson, the senior naval officer at Antigua, exacerbated the incident by ordering Schomberg's arrest. Thereafter Hood was unable to do anything for Nelson for five years and temporarily dropped him, but he took the risk of offending Prince William by taking Schomberg, 'a deserving officer with no prospect of promotion but by him', as first lieutenant of his flagship.[55] Nevertheless, in September 1787, Hood became vice-admiral of the blue, and he appears to have been intended for commander-in-chief in the West Indies had the Dutch crisis of that year developed into war with France.[56] When the First Lord of the Admiralty, Earl Howe, resigned in the following year, Hood was briefly considered to replace him. However, a confidant of Pitt described him as 'very far from being popular in the house of Commons; and what is worse, he has spoken there . . . with a degree of indiscretion which has been distressing, . . . but which would be absolutely intolerable if he was to answer for the execution of so responsible an office', one likely to be an object of attack by the Opposition. He would have to be removed to the Lords, 'for which he has neither fortune nor calibre sufficient'.[57] Instead he was appointed to the Admiralty Board as principal naval adviser to Pitt's brother, Lord Chatham, who became First Lord. He remained a Lord of the Admiralty from 1788 to 1795. His appointment resulted in another expensive and turbulent Westminster election, in which he was defeated by a protest vote against Pitt's unpopular shop tax, and had to find election at Reigate until being returned again for Westminster in the 1790 general election. Two years later he told his brother that office had left him 'beggared and thereby broken hearted'.[58]

He yearned for an active naval command, but was again thwarted in 1791 when a fleet for the Baltic, which he was to command, was demobilised after Parliament refused to back Pitt's confrontation with Russia. At last, when war finally broke out with Revolutionary France in February 1793, he was given command of the Mediterranean Fleet. He left Portsmouth on 22 May in the *Victory*. Among the talented group of protégés he took with him went Nelson, who soon re-established himself in Hood's favour.

Mediterranean Commander-in-Chief

Hood was now sailing into a different kind of command and a different kind of war than any he had experienced in the past. The post of Commander-in-Chief of the Mediterranean Fleet was the most demanding in the British naval service. His Secret Instructions, dated 18 May, stated his leading objects as to give battle to the French fleet and to secure the free and uninterrupted navigation of the Mediterranean for the King's subjects and those of his allies.[59] It was unlikely, however, that the French fleet would come out to seek combat in a way that would solve his problems, which meant that he had both to establish a blockade of the French base at Toulon and at the same time exert supremacy over a vast command which extended from Gibraltar to Smyrna. Moreover, this had to be done in waters lacking in British bases and a long way from any help from the Admiralty or its dockyards. Nor was his task exclusively naval. The Mediterranean was ringed by states, great and small, all requiring careful diplomatic handling. Although he could correspond with the local British ministers and consuls, he was far removed from Foreign Office advice. Hood was particularly instructed to open 'an intimate and confidential intercourse' with the commanders of the fleets and armies of Britain's allies in the theatre – Portugal, Spain, Sardinia and Naples. Each had problems: Piedmont-Sardinia and Naples were cordial but hesitant to act offensively, while Spain was suspicious and hostile to any establishment of British naval supremacy in the Mediterranean.[60] There were also neutral states along each shore of the Mediterranean, where French warships could find refuge and from which France was still receiving essential grain supplies, which had to be persuaded into a greater sympathy with British war aims and methods. Hood was soon complaining that he had been made almost blind by writing to so many ministers and other correspondents.[61]

It is perhaps not surprising, therefore, that when the chance suddenly came to solve many of these difficult tasks at one blow, he resolved to take it irrespective of any untoward consequences. He had scarcely arrived off Toulon when he was approached by envoys first from the moderate federalist revolutionaries of Marseilles and then from the naval base, seeking his protection from the advancing armies of the central Jacobin republican regime at Paris. In return they were prepared to declare for a monarchy on the former constitution established between 1789 and 1791 and to place the forts and fleet at Toulon in British hands in trust, to be restored after the war. Although such terms were way beyond anything authorised by his government and he had no troops at hand beyond the Marines of his fleet, Hood accepted. On 23 August he issued a declaration that Britain and its allies were fighting to re-establish monarchy in France, and agreeing to the 1791 Constitution and to return the French warships after the war. Marseilles fell two days later, and there was some resistance within the French fleet, but Hood took the risk and on 27th landed 1500 men from his ships and took possession of the forts commanding the Toulon roadstead, buying off Breton dissidents in the fleet by undertaking to transport them home.

Hood was not a man to let opportunities pass him by. He recognised the dangers but felt he 'should be justified in running some risque' in view of the great importance of taking possession of Toulon and its forts towards shortening the war. When the war minister, Henry Dundas, gently reprimanded him for wrongly representing Britain's war aims – it had gone to war to resist French aggression, not to restore the French monarchy – Hood replied that he was aware his proclamation might not be perfectly correct, but, in a critical situation where 'all might be lost by the delay of a few hours', he accepted the conditions proposed in support of monarchical government.[62]

The political terms of the agreement may have embarrassed his government, and perhaps influenced its decision to send out a political commissioner to join him in the administration of the base, but all recognised the military opportunities opened by his readiness to take responsibility in difficult circumstances. In Nelson's words, he had secured that 'the strongest place in Europe and twenty-two sail of the line, etc should be given up without firing a shot'. The fortified base provided a bridgehead into the south of France where Britain and its allies might assemble an army to co-operate with the internal opponents of the revolutionary regime. The Prime Minister, Pitt, hailed it as 'in every view the most important which could be struck towards the final success of the war'.[63]

The problem, however, and the extent of the risk that Hood had taken, was that the opportunity had come too early. It was in Dundas's plans for the following year when troops became available from other operations. Presently Ministers had few troops to send and were dependent on help from their allies, while Hood was too optimistic that Toulon could be held in the meantime. Although a Spanish fleet arrived as he was completing his negotiations with the Toulonese, and may have strengthened his determination to press ahead, the allies could scrape together a polyglot force of only just over 17,000 British, Spanish, Sardinians, Neapolitans, Albanians and French royalists by December, instead of the 54,000 planned by Pitt, while the French concentrated over 30,000 against them.

Hood's incursion into the war on land thus led to him being quickly bottled up in Toulon and struggling to hold on until reinforcement arrived. To all his other tasks as naval commander were now added those of joint supervision, in a three-man commission, of military operations on land and political administration of Toulon, as well as more direct relations with touchy and suspicious allies than he had originally intended (he had projected concerted but separate roles for them[64]). When his fellow commissioner, Sir Gilbert Elliot, arrived in November, he found that Hood had 'so much more to do than a man can accomplish, and there is a great deal of it so much of the sort that he is not accustomed to, that I believe he really feels my arrival a relief.'[65]

If the pressure frayed his temper and led to the same sort of acerbic criticisms of inadequate military colleagues as in the previous war, it did not slow his activity. Nelson was shortly to write admiringly that 'His zeal, activity for the honour and benefit of his King and Country are not abated. Upwards of seventy he possesses the mind of forty years of age. He has not a thought separated from Honour and Glory.'[66] Within a fortnight of the occupation of Toulon he sent his brother-in-law, Commodore Robert Linzee, with news of the terms to try to win over a small French squadron at Villafranca and the French garrisons in Corsica. He was unsuccessful in both, and Linzee, attempting to execute Hood's alternative orders for an aggressive blockade of Corsica, had his ships badly mauled by a fort at the entrance to San Fiorenzo Bay. Hood declared himself misled by assurances from Corsican nationalists, but again accepted responsibility. He admitted to Dundas that he had received no instructions about Corsica and that 'my sending the squadron there was a spontaneous action of my own'.[67]

Hood's Secret Instructions of 18 May told him to 'neglect no opportunity . . . of impressing on the States bordering on the Mediterranean an Idea of the strength and Power of Great Britain.'[68] He applied this vigorously to neutrals sheltering French warships and trading grain to France. Initially he hoped to solve the problem by a ruse, deliberately sending two frigates to ports on the North African coast where he expected the presence of superior French forces, which might attack them and thus provide him with the justification to sweep every French ship out of the neutral ports of the Mediterranean. The ruse failed when the senior frigate commander, ignorant of Hood's object – which it was inexpedient to avow in advance –

avoided contact with the French and was in consequence placed before a court martial by his thwarted commander-in-chief.[69]

Instead, he availed himself of French insults hurled at a British frigate calling at Genoa, and on 26 September sent a force under Rear-Admiral Gell thither to secure the surrender of the French frigate *Modeste* and other French ships, as well as to exact satisfactory assurances that the French would be kept out in future. Gell cleared the port of the French, but the Genoese retaliated, under French pressure, by expelling all other foreigners and blocking the use of that port for sending troops and food to besieged Toulon. Gell was more successful in a similar visit to Leghorn, when the Grand Duchy of Tuscany expelled French republicans, but a further demonstration at Tunis by Linzee failed to move the Bey and, for fear of alienating him, Hood ordered Linzee to refrain from attacking a French 74 there.[70]

The final unfortunate consequence of this offensive policy came in December when the French launched their major attack on Toulon. Hood had only a third of his fleet present to resist the attack or to remove the French warships and refugee royalists when resistance crumbled. Throughout the siege his determination to think positively led him to reject the pessimistic view of the military commanders that they could not hold on. To the last he opposed evacuation, clinging to the hope that Austrian reinforcements from the Milanese and British troops from Gibraltar were about to arrive.[71] Perhaps to avoid creating defeatism, he ignored advice from both the British and Spanish governments to begin preparations for carrying off the French fleet. In consequence the final evacuation on 17 December was a hastily improvised affair: only three French battleships were removed, and attempts to burn the rest were botched, with only nine of the line, three frigates and two sloops being destroyed.[72]

Despite the final failure of the occupation and the inability to eliminate the entire French battlefleet of some thirty ships at Toulon, the operation nevertheless can be seen as a great naval victory that was decisive for the course of the ensuing naval war. Together with a further 74 removed earlier, the final French losses at Toulon amounted to thirteen ships of the line, a major diminution of the sixty-five with which they started the war, and which, combined with the damage inflicted on the Toulon arsenal, reduced them to the defensive and to isolated raids thereafter.[73]

Hood himself refused to be deflated by the setback. Once he had disembarked the refugees from Toulon at Italian ports, he set about seeking another base for himself through the occupation of Corsica, which would enable him to maintain a central position off the French coast. Further negotiations with the Corsican independence movement cleared the way for their acceptance of protective British suzerainty, but even before this was approved by the government,[74] Hood had landed troops at Mortella Bay on 7 February 1794, and with naval assistance by land and sea captured the port of San Fiorenzo on 19 February. Hood was for pushing on to attack Bastia. When the army commander, General Dundas, demurred, he first tried to deal directly with Dundas's subordinates, and when this failed, recalled troops loaned from their service as Marines in his fleet and landed them with seamen, 1200 strong, to attack the fortress port while he maintained a close blockade by sea.

Hood's arbitrary action wrecked relations with the army and led Dundas to throw up his command and return home. Elliot explained the dispute as resulting from the fact that

> Lord Hood is extremely sanguine and enterprising, and General Dundas has the opposite qualities of caution and backwardness. He seems always ready to throw the game up, and has not vigour and animation enough for an active command. Lord Hood may possibly err on the other side; may either not see difficulties, or may underrate them; but it seems to me that this is a fault on the right side of war, where activity and enterprise are generally so well seconded by the fears of the enemy, as to succeed beyond a reasonable calculation.[75]

Hood had made such a calculation at Toulon, but had been wrong. This time he was proved right, for his small force penned in a superior French garrison of 4500 from 4 April until its surrender on 22 May. By then another army commander had resigned at Hood's imperious attitude. Only one French garrison remained, at Calvi, and on 19 June this was besieged by General Stuart, a leader as active but as touchy as Hood, so that naval-military relations did not improve despite the emollient efforts of Nelson, to whom Hood entrusted the naval share of the land operations at both Bastia and Calvi. The latter finally fell on 10 August.

Hood was distracted from the Calvi operation by a foray of seven survivors of the Toulon battlefleet and had a last fleeting chance to achieve the crushing naval victory he still lacked. He sighted and chased the French squadron on 10 June with thirteen of the line. The French commander, Martin, however, got his ships into the shelter of Gourjean Bay next day. Hood planned their annihilation by anchoring two ships alongside each French vessel, but was then becalmed for two days, giving Martin the chance to strengthen his position by forming shore batteries and assembling a screen of gunboats, so that Hood withdrew, thwarted of his prey.

Hood went home in early November 1794, intending to return next spring. In recognition of his services, in March 1795, he was elected an Elder Brother of Trinity House and his wife given a British peerage as Baroness Hood of Catherington, and on 4 April he was made admiral of the blue. However, he became warmly involved in a dispute with the new First Lord of the Admiralty, Earl Spencer, over the size of his fleet. Spencer, with world-wide commitments increased after the French gained control of the Dutch fleet, and with a major expedition to the West Indies to prepare, would not give Hood the reinforcements he felt necessary. Unable to get his way, he protested to the Premier and demanded that the Secretary of the Admiralty place on record his conviction that his force 'will be very unequal to that of the enemy, and the various Services committed to my charge, but although I have not the shadow of prospect of being able to add Lustre to the Arms of His Majesty I entreat to have credit, for doing my utmost, that they are not disgraced.' Spencer thought this conduct injurious to naval discipline, and, with the King's approval, dismissed him from his command.[76]

It was an unfortunate end to an active naval career, though he was allowed an honourable retirement in the following year when he was appointed Governor of Greenwich Hospital, and, on vacating his Westminster parliamentary seat at the general election, he was elevated to the British peerage in June as Viscount Hood of Catherington. In 1800 he was granted a pension of £2000 a year for three lives to sustain his peerage. He was spoken of as a candidate to fill the unexpected vacancy as First Lord of the Admiralty in 1805, but his friend Sir Charles Middleton, two years his junior at 79, got it instead.[77] He finally died, aged 91 and still Governor of Greenwich, in January 1816.

Hood's Character and Influence

How did Hood acquire his immense and influential stature with the able officers who commanded the Royal Navy to victory in the Revolutionary and Napoleonic Wars? Unlike his almost equally long-lived brother, Alexander, who rose to the command of the Channel Fleet and to a peerage as Lord Bridport, he did not have chief command in a naval victory. He missed his chance in 1794, and his dismissal in 1795 robbed him of a better opportunity – his friend and successor, Lord Hotham, commanded the Mediterranean Fleet in the actions of 13-14 March and 13 July. Yet Hood's reputation stood far higher than either of these. Some commentators have regarded it as excessively inflated. John Tilley has asserted that 'Among eighteenth-century admirals, Sir Samuel Hood was a remarkable character:

he made his name one of the most famous in British naval history not by commanding a fleet in a great sea fight, but by convincing the historians that he had been cheated out of the opportunity to do so.'[78] But Hood has not simply convinced historians by his letters, he convinced the ablest of his naval contemporaries by his actions. Nelson described him as 'the greatest Sea-officer I ever knew'.[79]

What stands out above all is his sheer professionalism. He set high standards for himself and despised indolence or negligence in his superiors and subordinates. One of the latter in 1793–94 wrote that

> Without the least disposition to severity, there was something about him which made his inferior Officers stand in awe of him. He was so watchful upon his Post himself that those who acted with him were afraid to slumber; and his advanced age at the time he was last employed appears neither to have impaired the vigour of his understanding nor in any way cooled the ardour of his zeal.[80]

His standards were beyond the reach of many of the officers of the American War when the fleet was riven by political divisions. As Commissioner at Portsmouth he protested at the lack of proper exertions by the officers to preserve discipline and good order, complaining that 'The neglect of the Officers in general is really astonishing.' In the Caribbean he raged that 'To see things go so very *slack* and *untoward* cannot but affect a man in this country in the highest health, and it is impossible for *one* afflicted as I am with strong bodily complaints to bear up against them.'[81] Incompetence received short shrift. The officers of the watch of the ships whose collision wrecked his surprise attack at St Kitt's in 1782 were immediately suspended and ordered to be tried by court martial. The captain, first lieutenant and master whose ineptitude caused the *Berwick*, 74 to be dismasted and reduced to 'a most complete wreck', when Hood needed every ship following the evacuation of Toulon, were likewise court-martialled and sentenced to be dismissed their ship.[82]

He believed in keeping the fleet well-exercised, complaining of Pigot in 1782 that he had kept his command six weeks 'loitering' at sea while 'not one single manoeuvre has been practised – no, not even spreading in a line abreast . . . and closing a little at night,' by way of exercising the fleet.[83] When he had independent command of part of the same fleet on its return to the Caribbean in 1783, he was continually practising forming the line, exercising and chasing. In the summers of 1791 and 1792 he took out and exercised those ships remaining mobilised at Spithead to a level of fleet training not practised before the American War, which helped put the fleet in greater readiness for the French War that broke out in the following year. On the voyage out to the Mediterranean in 1793, Nelson noted that 'We do not keep in so compact an order as we ought, and the Lord does not spare signals.'[84]

Among the most significant traits of Hood's professionalism was his willingness to think ahead on active service. This was indeed a compulsive urge resulting from his temperament. He once confided to Jackson that while some men's minds were perfectly cool, tranquil, and indifferent, his was among those 'full of anxiety, impatience, and apprehension'. After urging Pigot to send ahead to have fresh meat and spruce beer ready for his arrival in New York in 1782, he commented that 'If the commander-in-chief of a great fleet does not upon every occasion look forward, the crews of it will be often deprived of what they stand in need of, are entitled to, and might have.'[85] This forethought made him one of the ablest naval strategists of his time. Daniel Baugh describes him as 'unquestionably brilliant. Time and again he grasped the situation, or guessed correctly the enemy's intentions.' But this was not just guesswork. He told Pigot in August 1782 that he 'had been thinking a good deal of the enemy's probable designs, and what was most likely to check them.' He made it his business to be informed, questioning officers with previous experience of station conditions, employing ruses such as prisoner cartels to penetrate enemy bases to ascertain the state and condition of their fleet. Then he worried through the possibilities and produced reasoned appreciations.[86] He was indeed uncannily accurate in forecasting French moves in the Caribbean in 1781–3, often to an unreceptive superior. 'As I feared, foretold, and laboured to prevent,' he lamented in March 1782, 'the French armament got safe to Fort Royal by making Deseada and running down between Dominica and Martinique.'[87]

Thinking ahead also involved an attention to detail. At St Kitt's he was careful to mask his damages by ordering his captains to shift topmasts and topsails after sunset and take care that their ships should appear perfect at daylight. Nelson appreciated the care Hood took to show confidence in his handling of the siege of Bastia by never visiting him in company with a more senior captain, who would take over command. It also made for clarity of orders. Hood, wrote Nelson, was 'certainly the best officer I ever saw. Everything from him is so clear it is impossible to misunderstand him.'[88]

As significant in his influence on the culture of the officers of the 1793–1815 wars was his perpetual offensive spirit. He was active and could not abide 'indolence and dilatoriness', and he was decisive. 'I never knew good to come from procrastination', he once told his friend Middleton.[89]

These were perhaps habits natural to a man who had spent most of his operational experience before gaining his flag as a frigate commander, and who had never been restrained by the discipline of commanding a ship of the line in a squadron during a long blockade. He was not afraid of responsibility and revelled in difficulty. William Hotham later recalled that 'I never saw an officer of more intrepid courage or warmer zeal; no difficulties stood in his way, and he was a stranger to any feeling of nervous diffidence of himself.'[90] When in 1768 he took steps against the dissident Boston colonists, he declared himself ready to face the consequences. To do his duty properly, he wrote, an officer 'should be a stranger' to fear, 'and he will ever be so, as long as he is conscious of acting with integrity and to the best of his judgement.'[91] 'Never, my dear sir, was a man in command in more trying situations than I have been,' Hood wrote to Middleton after St Kitt's, 'but, I trust, I have not disgraced the British flag in either, and it is in points of difficulty only an officer can show what he is made of and equal to.'[92] Hood was never short of confidence, always ready to act, always looking to get at his enemy, confident that, as at St Kitt's, his determination and quick thinking could get him out of scrapes. This was inspirational leadership, infectious to his naval subordinates. However, on land, where he lacked military knowledge, it seemed irresponsible and dangerous to less convinced army colleagues, who considered him opinionated and dogmatic, and he left a legacy of soured relations between the two services.

At St Kitt's Hood demonstrated that he had tactical ability. His letters after the Chesapeake and the Saintes battles at least show a willingness to analyse and learn from the tactical mistakes of others, and he was quick to add a signal for breaking the line when he commanded the West Indies fleet after the Saintes. The authority on signalling innovations declares his position as tactician and signaller as 'difficult to determine', and, after noting that he was as much a stickler for fleet discipline and station keeping as Rodney and Howe, concludes that 'It is doubtful . . . if he was really interested in advanced tactical ideas.' Indeed, Hood was too practical to think in theories, though his initial plan of attack at St Kitt's and that for Gourjean Bay in 1794 show a preference for a directed concentration of firepower which might be seen to presage British tactics at the Nile. He was sufficiently interested in improvements in signalling to seek, unsuccessfully, to take a new flag scheme to the West Indies in the 1787 mobilisation, and again in 1790 he unsuccessfully pressed his secretary John McArthur's signalling system on the Admiralty. Hood's support then helped carry through McArthur's re-arrangement of Howe's 1790 signalling system, improving its presentation and incorporating all relevant and necessary instructions in a single book in ways continued in the first official Admiralty signalling books in 1799.[93]

Part of Hood's professionalism that was not always shared by his admirers (including Nelson) was his relative indifference to prize money. He was prepared to share his prize money with Digby to get more ships in 1781. He declared he would rather have sunk the *Ville de Paris* at the Saintes if it would have ended Rodney's preoccupation with his prize and led him to chase the fleeing enemy. Wealth was never a preoccupation with him. 'He was exceedingly liberal, and never was, or would have been, a rich man', wrote Hotham. When he demanded from Pitt a public pension to enable him to support his peerage, he told the Premier that 'the greatest part of my income arises from the governorship I hold; and when I drop, Lady Hood, possessing every shilling I am worth, will not have more than £800 a year to maintain her.'[94]

Finally, he set an example to his followers by combining discipline with humanity. His secretary, McArthur, wrote in 1799 that:

> . . . no one possessed in greater perfection than himself, the art of preserving a strict authority when on board, with the talent of at the same time gaining the steady attachment of those who were under his command. He displays the sternness of the old school, and preserves a strict regard for implicit obedience; but then, the whole is tempered by a tenderness and urbanity, that prevents its ever being oppressive, or tyrannical.[95]

He seems to have loaned money to his men while commanding the *Jamaica* sloop in the mid-1750s. He was still deploring ways in which seamen were starved of their wages in 1780.[96] When during the St Kitt's operation he was obliged to supplement his crews' scarce flour provisions with yams, he requested that the Admiralty treat them as a present since 'it will show the poor fellows that they are attended to, and will, I am persuaded, be productive of very happy effects.' His concern to have scurvy preventatives ready when the fleet arrived at New York in 1782 has already been mentioned above.[97]

Hood's final positive legacy to the Royal Navy was the talented following he nurtured. One of them, later Admiral Sir William Hotham, declared that 'On the Publick Service, as well as in private life, I always found him a steady friend; and I am persuaded he never forsook anybody he was once disposed to serve, as long as that attention to duty was paid which everyone with feelings of honour will perform.'[98] He set his wife's brothers, Robert and John Linzee, on their way, the one to becoming an admiral,[99] the other a captain. Above all from among his relatives, he and his brother took under their protection their namesakes, sons of their first cousin, Samuel Hood, a one-time purser in the navy. Hood took the 9½-year-old Alexander to North America with him in the *Romney* in 1767, but especially he brought on Samuel, who entered *Courageux* with him in 1776, and was with him as a lieutenant on *Barfleur* from 1780 to 1782, when Hood made him a master and commander. It was probably Hood, while on the Admiralty Board, who ensured that the young Samuel came to the King's notice as captain of the frigate *Juno* in attendance as royal guardship at Weymouth in 1791-2. Hood then took him to the Mediterranean with him, detaching his protégé to a lucrative independent command at Smyrna before he returned home. The young Samuel Hood's distinguished career in the Revolutionary and Napoleonic Wars was only ended by his untimely death while vice-admiral and Commander-in-Chief of the East Indies station in 1814.

Outside the family circle, the American War brought three future major figures under Hood's influence. Nelson has already been seen. A year previously Hood took William Cornwallis back with him to the Caribbean where he served as captain of the *Canada*, playing a distinguished part at St Kitts on 25 January, and the Saintes. The two became firm friends, and when Cornwallis took the trade home in 1782, Hood recommended him to Jackson as 'That gallant, good officer, Captain Cornwallis'. They remained in correspondence thereafter, and Cornwallis, when commanding the Channel Fleet in 1801, praised Hood, 'of whom I had the highest opinion and whose conduct when I served under him I very much admired'.[100] James Saumarez also was with Hood at St Kitt's and the Saintes. He had brought out dispatches as master and commander of the fireship *Tisiphone* and was on the point of returning home when Hood gave him his chance by exchanging him into captaincy of the *Russell*, 74 on the eve of St Kitt's. At the Saintes, *Russell* shared with *Barfleur* in the final attack on the *Ville de Paris*, and when he returned home as post captain Hood recommended him as 'that excellent young man, Captain Saumarez'.[101]

The crop of young men that Hood took with him to the Mediterranean in 1793 extended his influence on the navy into the 1840s. Thomas Byam Martin was the son of Hood's successor at Portsmouth in 1780 and Comptroller of the Navy from 1790 to 1794, and himself became Comptroller from 1815 to 1831. He had been lieutenant to the younger Samuel Hood on the *Juno*. Lord Hood promoted him to the command of *Tisiphone*, and then to the *Modeste*, captured at Genoa. In 1794 he was praised by Hood for showing judgement and skill in conducting a convoy past a waiting French squadron.[102] George Cockburn attracted Hood's favour on the Mediterranean station when he took him as tenth lieutenant of the *Victory*, rising in two months to first lieutenant, and then appointed him to command a sloop, followed temporarily by the frigate *Inconstant*, and finally made him post captain of the 32-gun *Meleager* at the age of 21. Admiral Sir George Cockburn finally resigned from his post as senior Sea Lord at the Admiralty in 1846.[103]

All these men owed something of their distinguished subsequent careers to Hood, and the final judgement must go to the greatest of them all, Nelson, who, when he learned that Hood would not be returning to his Mediterranean command, wrote that 'This fleet must regret the loss of Lord Hood, the best Officer, take him altogether, that England has to boast of. Lord Howe certainly is a great Officer in the management of a Fleet, but that is all. Lord Hood is equally great in all situations which an Admiral can be placed in.'[104]

Richard, Earl Howe. Oil by John Singleton Copley

11

Richard, Earl Howe
1726-1799

'a scientific officer'

ROGER KNIGHT

Character and Career

> It was only at this moment that I had the invaluable approbation of the great,
> the immortal Earl Howe – an honour the most flattering a Sea-officer could
> receive, as it comes from the first and greatest Sea-officer the world has ever
> produced. [Nelson to Howe, Palermo, 8 January 1799]

Richard Howe was an active and professional seaman for sixty years. After a
brilliant early period, a flag captain at 24 and a commodore at 37, it was his
ship which fired the first shots of the Seven Years' War, and on that dark
November afternoon in 1759 it was the *Magnanime* under his command
which was the first into Quiberon Bay. He commanded the Channel Fleet
when it won the Glorious First of June, the first fleet action of the Revolutionary War, and he brought six French ships of the line home as prizes. His
reputation for personal courage was second to none.

In spite of these achievements, however, Howe's reputation then and
now has never been the epitome of British naval aggression, for his fleet
handling was seen as cautious by the next generation of naval officers,
fighting an absolute war. Howe himself fed this contradictory reputation,
for he had one of the most complex and contradictory characters in the
Georgian navy. For extended periods he was not popular with many sec-
tions of his fellow officers and he was pilloried in the press. His long career,
from 1735 to 1795, was interspersed by periods ashore when he took on
roles in politics and administration which were largely unsuccessful. As

commander-in-chief in North America between 1776 and 1778 he mixed politics and seamanship with a complete lack of political or strategic success. In the 1780s he was First Lord for five years at a time when the navy went through great change and improvement, but he lacked political touch so much that one is forced to the conclusion that improvements were effected in spite of him rather than because of him. At the same time, as a seaman and commander of fleets, with significant fleet successes in 1782 and 1794, no naval officer had more influence on the enormous changes in the later eighteenth century navy than Richard Howe, and none had more part in laying the foundations for the success of the navy of Nelson.

At first sight it is surprising that a figure of such dominance should not have had more attention from historians. Only Sir John Barrow's *The Life of Richard Earl Howe KG Admiral of the Fleet and General of Marines*, published in 1838, attempts to tell the whole story. To our eyes this book appears over-diplomatic, and at times unctuous, and it reveals more of Barrow than of Howe. Though there are some modern accounts of him in relation to parts of his life, notably in Professor Gruber's detailed and perceptive sketch of him written in 1972, the admiral, as he was when alive, remains elusive. Howe's reticence was famous: Frances Nelson, writing to her husband in 1794, described him 'the most silent man I ever knew'. His austere character allowed no expression of feelings in his letters, and certainly not explanation, while his secretiveness led him to large-scale destruction of his own correspondence late in his career. Sadly, the family papers were burnt at Westport House in Ireland at the beginning of the nineteenth century, so that little evidence remains from others close to him. The young Commodore Howe and his wife were painted by Gainsborough in 1766, a pair of pictures which now hang at Kenwood. By this time he was significantly rich, with a quite evidently supportive wife of great character, and his confidence and status are well portrayed. But Gainsborough captures that elusive and wary gaze; from his painting, Howe, faintly mocking, seems as confident now as he was then that his privacy will not be successfully invaded.[1]

Perhaps the most marked contradiction in this career was the extent of his influence set against his inability to express himself. Members of both Houses were often bewildered as to the exact meaning of a prepared speech from Howe at all stages in his career. The letters that remain are, for the most part, obscure and guarded, and thus unrewarding. Nelson described one he received from Howe as 'a jumble of nonsense', while there are many anecdotes about the lack of clarity of of his orders and expression.[2]

Even the uncritical Barrow quoted a sentence, in what can only have been exasperation, which must be the most convoluted in the history of the Royal Navy. Sir Roger Curtis, who had explained why he had disobeyed a signal from his admiral, received in reply from Howe:

> Your conduct, with regard to the despatches, testified so correct a judgement in every part, that, if my concurrence in opinion with you on the propriety of it will convey all the satisfaction you do me the favour to intimate, you are free to indulge yourself in the enjoyment of that consciousness to the fullest extent.[3]

It was little wonder that Howe went through long periods of being misunderstood.

Part of this clumsiness must have had its origins in an uprooted childhood and an incomplete education. He was the second son of an Irish peer, Emanuel Scrope Howe, who had married the daughter of Baroness Kilmansegge, the mistress of George I. Because of this family connection, Howe was close to the Royal Family all his life, with all the advantages and disadvantages this brought to his career in public life. His father, however, presumably because of lack of money, had to accept the Governorship of Barbadoes, where he died when young Richard was only 8. He had only a short time at Westminster School and seems, although there is only hearsay evidence for it, to have then gone to Eton for an even shorter time. Some mystery surrounds the exact sequence of these early years. The archivist at Eton has no documentary evidence of Howe's attendance, while J K Laughton could not conceive, writing in 1891 in the *Dictionary of National Biography*, that Howe could not have gone to Eton and that he ever went to sea, effectively as a gentleman apprentice, in a merchant vessel. Howe's lieutenant's passing certificate, although some of it is torn and missing, states the exact year and months of his time on the *Thames*, William Merchant, master.[4] Howe's connection to the King and his friendship with the Royal Family would hardly have encouraged the reticent admiral to reminisce on these early years. It must have been a solitary time for a young boy, who might have been less than 10 years old; and this period must have contributed to his life-long reticence and, allowing for the lack of family money at this time, his driving ambition. Had he mixed with his contemporaries and learnt the logic of classical languages, these years might have given some structure to his restless mind, dwelling as it did on every detail, 'his precision in minute matters' as Barrow calls it. His penchant for the minutiae of business, so useful in the running of a ship, was much criticised by his political opponents when First Lord of the Admiralty.[5] A more strategic, pragmatic view of life would have made it easier for him and, indeed, for those around him.

Howe's first years in the navy were, in modern parlance, on the fast track. In July 1739 he was entered into the *Pearl* under the captaincy of Edward Legge, sailing with Vernon's squadron to Lisbon. He transferred with Legge to the *Severn*, which accompanied Anson to the Pacific, but the ship failed to weather Cape Horn and it came home home via Barbadoes, reaching England in 1742. Howe thus just failed to become one of Anson's protégés. He then served under Sir Charles Knowles in the West Indies, coming into contact with Knowles's original mind and under whom he passed his lieutenant's examination. He was present at the unsuccessful attacks on Spanish bases on the South American mainland, returning to England in August 1745. After a short time in Vernon's flagship, he was given his first command, the *Baltimore* sloop, cruising in West of Scotland waters in operations against the Jacobites. Here he came up against two French privateers of greater gunpower in a loch off the Sound of Arisaig, had to break off the attack and was wounded in the head. He was now made post captain, appointed to the *Triton*, 24 and escorted a convoy to Lisbon. Here he transferred to the *Ripon*, 60, since her captain was unwell, and sailed to the west coast of Africa. Though he lost men from fever, it was an uneventful cruise up and down the Guinea coast, inspecting slaving posts and resolving a dispute between British and Dutch merchants. Howe then went to Barbadoes to join Knowles again and on 29 October 1748 Knowles made him his flag captain. At the end of the war, therefore, at the age of 24, Howe was a flag captain.

Howe used his connections to secure commands in the years of peace. In March 1751 he was appointed to the *Glory*, 44, in which he returned to the West African coast. He again crossed to the West Indies, calling at Barbadoes and Jamaica, arriving back at Spithead in April 1752. Three months later he commissioned the *Dolphin*, 24, cruising in the Mediterranean from October of that year to August 1754. A description of this quiet period is stylishly described in *Augustus Hervey's Journal,* for Hervey was on the same station, and Howe is particularly mentioned in various disagreements between the two officers.[6]

In early 1755 Howe was appointed to the *Dunkirk*, 60, sailing with Boscawen to North America. On 7 June the British squadron found the French in the fog off the mouth of the St Lawrence and three days later, the *Dunkirk*, coming up with the *Alcide*, fired the first shots of the Seven Years War. The French ship, being unprepared, surrendered swiftly. Howe and his ship returned soon after to England and he spent the rest of the war, as one of the most promising young captains, in the Channel Fleet. Still in the *Dunkirk*, he had a number of successes, removing a small French force from the Isle de Chaussy and capturing a 36-gun privateer. In July 1757 he and his ship's company then moved into his most successful ship, the 74-gun *Magnanime*. In September he was in Hawke's fleet against Rochfort, where he distinguished himself in the bombardment of the Isle d'Aix. Howe then commanded the ships and the transports against St Malo, unsuccessfully, and later against Cherbourg, successfully. In the latter raid the piers and harbour were thoroughly destroyed and Cherbourg ceased to be a naval base of significance for the rest of the Anglo-French wars. Another expedition against St Malo was not a success and there were no further coastal expeditions until 1761.[7] For nearly all the rest of the war, Howe was engaged in the remorseless blockading of Brest and the French coast. The *Magananime*, one of the swiftest sailers in the fleet, was always in the thick of the action. At Quiberon Bay he forced the *Héros* to surrender, but he did not put a prize crew on board because of dangerous seas; the French ship was wrecked the next day. After blockading for the next two years, during which time he was Commodore of the Basque Roads, in June 1762 he moved into the *Princess Amelia*, 80 as flag captain to the Duke of York. At the peace in February 1763 Commodore Howe struck his broad pendant. He had had a good war.

Howe devoted the next period of his life to building a political career and was ashore for twelve years. Had the Falklands crisis in 1770 not been resolved, he would have sailed as Commander-in-Chief, Mediterranean, an appointment which carried the seniority of rear-admiral to which he was promoted on 18 October 1770. Nearly five years later his next command was, however, his most controversial and certainly the one most picked over by historians.[8] There were complicated and ill-managed circumstances by which Howe was made commander-in-chief in America, alongside his younger brother, Sir William, the army commander. He also had wide powers of discretion as peace commisioner when he sailed on 11 May 1776 in the *Eagle*, 64. The burden of being able to make peace or war was to prove too much for him, although he had tactical successes. Critically, he arrived in New York on 12 July, just after the Declaration of Independence, the crucial psychological moment. Throughout his command he had to balance which ships should support the army and which should implement the coastal blockade against the colonists. He did not really have enough ships to starve the colonists of arms and powder and by

1777, after the critical battle of Trenton on 26 December 1776, Sir William Howe was losing the initiative on land. By now, Continental frigates began to make real inroads into British shipping in European waters and naval failure was an active political issue in London. From the middle of 1777 both brothers began to lose any semblance of a political and military strategy. They both moved against Philadelphia, which was eventually taken, although it hardly made any impact on the course of the war. On 31 October Burgoyne surrendered at Saratoga and the entire nature of the war changed; both brothers asked to be relieved of their commands.

For the next six months there was little activity until orders came from London that Philadelphia was to be evacuated, which was achieved on 18 June 1778, and Richard Howe, having received the first reverse in his career, was to be allowed home on the grounds of ill-health. It was at this point that he fought the most successful naval campaign, according to some, in his career. Against the French, who in March had declared for the colonists, and with conventional tactics, Howe did well. The short campaign against d'Estaing will be analysed later. Having neutralised this threat by seeing the French fleet in Boston harbour, with its topmasts struck, ready for the winter, he sailed for home, reaching St Helens on 25 October. Howe, now 52 and at the height of his powers, was not to have an active command for three and a half years and spent most of the time trying to defend his conduct in America. In spite of the fact that he was considered by Lord North's ministry as a replacement for Lord Sandwich in early 1779, he was a bystander for much of the war. However, when North finally fell in March 1782, the Rockingham ministry appointed him as Commander-in-Chief of the Channel Fleet on 2 April, a full admiral on 8 April and a British peer on 20 April 1782. Together with the appointment of his brother as Lieutenant-General of the Ordnance, this was Howe's price to the new ministry. The rest of his career will be outlined below.

Even Howe's few friends could not deny that he was a difficult man. Neither popularity nor public opinion were seemingly of consequence to him. He had very few friendships, Sir Roger Curtis apart, among his fellow officers and he held most politicians in contempt. At the same time, his private life was very happy and those in his immediate circle were very close. Codrington wrote, 'There was a shyness and awkwardness in Lord Howe's manner which made him apparently difficult of approach, and gave him a quality of austerity which did not belong to him.' He was extremely sensitive to honour. Although there were several points in his career when he carried matters to extremes, none illustrates this better than the incident after the

relief of Gibraltar in 1782, when the brash Augustus Hervey publicly criticised Howe: 'if we had been led with the same spirit with which we should
have followed, it would have been a glorious day for England'. Howe
challenged him to a duel; the two men, both nearer 60 than 50, met, with
their seconds, and the unfortunate Hervey had to make a humiliating apol-
ogy. Howe was not a man to be crossed.[9]

Perhaps it was this quality which appealed to the crews under him, who
were loyal to a man and appreciated the toughness and professionalism of
'Black Dick'. His care for them was well known and, though he could be
faulted for lack of decisiveness and communication in his part in the 1797
mutiny, the seamen's trust in his word diffused the worst at Spithead. He
was best at sea, when the enemy was near at hand. He was the sort of man
who was at his best when the odds were against him, and who, as Horace
Walpole observed, 'never made a friendship but at the mouth of a cannon'.[10] His political interludes were clouded by suspicion and lack of trust.
Little wonder that he shone in the ordered hierarchy of a man of war, when
the realities of life were simple if harsh, when his word was unquestioned
and other people's feelings were of little consequence.

Politician and Administrator

'Many things have happened, and they have neither approved, not otherwise, of
my conduct. That Lord Howe is a strange character . . .' [Nelson to William
Locker, 9 February 1787]

Yet for over thirty years Howe pursued a political career, starting as an
MP in 1757 and ending as First Lord of Admiralty in 1788. A number of
ambitious sea officers threw themselves into politics; Howe seems to have
done so from a sense of duty and to keep his back covered in the event of
military failure. Considered without his sea achievements, his political
career can be described at best as ordinary and at worst as a failure. He did
not mix easily with politicians and for some he had a particular contempt,
the elder Pitt excepted, and he was generally distant from them
throughout these thirty years. As an MP he was broadly independent and
was of no particular grouping, accepting a post on the Board of Admiralty
at the end of the Seven Years War from the Grenville administration, and
soon after that the Treasurership of the Navy from Rockingham on the
change of government. In spite of Barrow's apologist views, he was no
better or honest a Treasurer than the next one. As was the custom, he saw
a good deal of public money through his account. The Commissioners of

Public Accounts showed the balance in the hands of Lord Howe at the time of his leaving office in 1770 as £45,939 and ten years later the sum was still as high as £18,133.[11]

It was his attempt to play the conciliatory statesman on the world stage at the beginning of the American War that has attracted most attention from historians. For a man with no sense of political strategy it was a hopeless task. He had a strong and instinctive sympathy for the colonists at the same time as being out of sympathy with Lord North's government; he thus consistently underestimated the strength of American political feeling against Britain. By the time he reached America it was probably too late to effect a compromise, in any case; there were too many contradictions in his task. The general view of contemporaries of the Howe brothers was summed up by Walpole's acid pen: '[they] had accepted the American command against their principles, and against all their inclinations but one of interest, who had conducted it treacherously as many thought, impotently as everyone knew, who had returned hostile to the Ministries, yet so far from joining Opposition, had distressed it by counteracting it.'[12]

There is a greater sense of political and personal frustration through his period as First Lord of the Admiralty from 1783 to 1788. There were, fortunately, no naval crises, which would have exposed the distance of Howe from his colleagues in Cabinet and, more significantly, from the rest of the naval administration represented by Charles Middleton, the Comptroller of the Navy and in charge of the Navy Office. Middleton, exactly the same age and with a not dissimilar character, had been in post since 1778 and had established a formidable reputation. The two men, wary at first, saw the relationship as a struggle for supremacy. After the naval humiliations of the American War the younger Pitt ensured that naval estimates remained high, but he worked through Middleton rather than Howe. Much was achieved and fleet efficiency came to new heights, but between Howe and Middleton there were constant squabbles and the feeling of lost opportunity is strong. Middleton had long been used to being consulted on appointments, but soon after taking office Howe appointed a joint Surveyor without any reference to the Comptroller. In September 1784 Howe paid a surprise visit to Portsmouth Dockyard and found many faults; this was a direct invasion of Middleton's territory. In another fruitless contest Middleton wanted to roof over all ships on the stocks in the King's and merchant yards to give protection against damp and rot, a measure which would have had far-reaching consequences in lengthening the life of ships. Howe cancelled all these arrangements and ordered the ships to be launched.[13] Had two high-handed men joined together, much more could have been achieved. It was a squabble over Middleton's promotion, in which Pitt, not surprisingly, did not support Howe, which led to the First Lord's resignation. Howe's unpopularity went far beyond the service. 'On the whole', commented William Grenville in May 1788, 'I think it infinitely better, considering his great unpopularity in the Navy and in the House of Commons, that he should withdraw himself.'[14] Howe went at the end of July.

Howe's close and impenetrable personality was also responsible for his other great difficulty while in office, which was the mismatch between the promotions available and the number of officers who expected advancement. The same problem had faced Lord Sandwich in the 1770s. Howe's restrictions on promotion in the brevet of 1787 provoked an outcry and personal attacks in the press, and in caricatures which stressed his close relationship with the King. In January and February 1788 there were three stormy debates in both Houses. Howe's position was difficult; he took what he saw as the common sense view of the situation but lacked the political touch to see it through: 'he assured their Lordships that patronage was not so desirable as might be imagined, and that he was sure, out of twenty candidates for an appointment, to disappoint nineteen, and by no means certain of pleasing the twentieth.'[15]

Howe's System and Order

> This Fleet must regret the loss of Lord Hood, the best Officer, take him altogether, that England has to boast of. Lord Howe is certainly a great officer in the management of a fleet, but that is all. Lord Hood is equally great in all situations which as Admiral can be placed in. Our present is a worthy, good man, but not by any means equal to either Lord Hood or Lord Howe. [Nelson to the Revd Dixon Hoste, off Minorca, 22 June 1795]

In contrast to the subtle demands of national politics, Howe's grasp of and aptitude for detail contributed to the deepest foundation which Howe put into the navy which Nelson was to inherit. This was the system and order which he brought to everything he did as commander of a ship and of a fleet. His drive to regularise practice never wavered during all the decades that he was at sea, and in this he was at his most influential. Of all the British aristocratic naval officers of the eighteenth century, none was more the antithesis of the stereotype French officer than Howe. He thoroughly imbued himself in the ways of ships, fleets and seamen; contrast the lament of a modern authority on Louis XV's navy:

Several prequisites for professionalisation of the officer corps were present in the mid-century navy, notably a system of recruitment, training, and advancement and hierarchal order. But these were weakly established, insufficient in themselves, and inadequate when applied. The companies of *gardes* need not be criticised for trying to make sailors out of aristocrats; there is nothing logically impossible about the task.[16]

For Howe, an earl and intimate of the King, seamanship and the proper functioning of the officer corps were the very centre of his professional life.

Firstly, he was prominent in the standardisation of the organisation and discipline of the officers and men on board ship. Although it now seems difficult to imagine, in the first half of the eighteenth century the Admiralty was reluctant to lay down any regulations which threatened the independence of the captain of the ship, and the running of the ship was entirely his business; any change in this practice needed some strong-willed and influential officers to see them through. This was certainly needed by the time of the Seven Years War, when ships were becoming appreciably bigger. A 70-gun ship of the line at the beginning of the 1739-48 war had a complement of 480 men; its replacement, the 74, such as the *Magnanime* which Howe commanded for much of the war, had an establishment of 700 men. As the crew was divided into watches, gun crews and messes, it led to the crew being out of touch with the officers and the welfare of the men neglected. It was even more important to keep such a large body of men clean and healthy. Howe was one of the first, though probably not *the* first, protagonists of the divisional system which solved many of the problems of ship management. The principle of a division was defined by Howe in his later orders of 1776, by this time entitled, 'Instructions and Standing Orders for the General Government and Discipline of Ships of War':

> The petty officers and seamen of the ships companies are to be formed into two or three divisions, according to the complements and classes of the ship, each division to be under the inspection of a lieutenant, and subdivided into squads with a midshipman appointed to each, who are respectively to be responsible for the good order and discipline of the men entrusted to their care.[17]

The order book which Howe issued in 1759 for the *Magnanime* is the earliest ship's order book which survives today and is now in the National Maritime Museum. It lays down the duties of the officers. Although Howe had intended it to be systematic, it fell short, but 'it was pioneering work, written under active service conditions'. His 1776 instructions are much better, more logically organised and more lucidly expressed, and he undoubtedly worked on them during his time ashore during the peace; these he issued to all the ships under his command – not a popular move with his captains. He repeated these orders to the ships in the Channel Fleet in 1782. They were unquestionably influential; Brian Lavery's recent study finds that 'echoes of them are to be found in most of the captains' orders in the next thirty years'.[18]

As commodore in the *Magnanime* he also made innovations in signalling which was the start of a thirty-year effort to improve the command and control of large fleets. On 24 July 1758 he was the first person to issue a printed signal book with his own signals, 'Additional Signals & Instructions to be Observed by the Ships of War'. He had already begun to experiment with signal orders at the beginning of the war, distinguishing those ships on the starboard and larboard tacks. Earlier, in orders issued in manuscript in 1756, using existing schemes, he had had to hoist sails up and down, as well as signal flags, to transmit instructions; off the Brittany coast this was hardly advisable and he set about finding better combinations of signal flags.[19]

After four years of experience in the Western Approaches and off the Brittany coast, in 1762 he issued another revised printed book of 'Additional Signals & Instructions to be observed by Ships of War' to his squadron in the Basque Roads. It provides the link between his first changes and the more far-reaching changes he was to make at the beginning of the American War. Still, his convoluted language makes it as difficult for the historian to understand as it was for his captains. In Tunstall's opinion, 'his signal no. 59, for instance, is dangerously ambiguous, considering that it was intended for use in a sudden emergency':

> When the Commander-in-Chief upon making the Signal for Line-ahead or abreast, though meaning to form on the Starboard Tack, would nevertheless have the Ship appointed to lead on the Larboard Tack, and that Division then to lead: Or on the contrary the Ships of the Starboard Division to lead though forming on the Larboard Tack. The same change of Divisions is meant to be made when this Signal is shewn with the Signal for forming in two separate Lines of Battle.

Nevertheless, his thinking was going forward. Except for the instructional orders, the book was for the first time laid out in tabular form and there was no differentiation between sailing and fighting instructions. 'There were no startling innovations,' Tunstall comments, 'Howe's main purpose was to increase the efficiency with which his squadron could carry out his immediate task . . . for this he needed flexibility and simplicity of manoeuvres.'

He made provision for an *ad hoc* line of battle, which gave his captains more room for initiative; he reduced the number of times that signal guns should be used; he enabled privateers to send signals to the fleet; above all, to judge from his orders for battle issued slightly later, he was beginning to demonstrate his determination to concentrate or disperse his line. He was thus beginning to think on a far more sophistocated tactical level than hitherto. For instance, he observed that, in the event of being outnumbered by the enemy, 'I may perhaps attempt by studied delays to conceal from them my purpose of bringing them to action, until later in the day, and that opportunity offers of doing more to advantage.'[20]

It was at the beginning of his period in America, however, that Howe started to develop the new thinking which was to alter the systems of command and control of fleets, though characteristically it was a slow process rather than a sharp change. What was fundamental was that fleets should not be operated in battle by the traditional, prescribed 'Fighting Instructions', but that the fleet commander should control the fleet by signal. In 1776, the first year of his command, he issued instructions that the fleet be organised in two or three divisions according to its strength, which was a step forward. However, it was on 1 July 1777 that he made the real difference, by issuing 'Additional Instructions respecting the conduct of the Fleet preparative to and in action with the enemy', together with a regular printed signal book; together they were to supersede the signals provided in the regular Fighting Instructions. 'All signals', ran an accompanying note, 'contained in the General Printed Signal Book which are likely to be needful on the present occasion being provided in this signal book, the signals in the General Printed Signal Book will only be made in conformity to the practice of some senior officer.' To Sir Julian Corbett, 'Both in scope and arrangement they differed entirely from anything that had yet appeared . . . it was a direct blow at the old system, and that so long as he had a free hand and no senior officer arrived on the station he meant to rely for the tactical handling of his fleet on a signal book and not on a set of regular tactical instructions.'[21]

Howe was by no means the only senior officer in the push to improve the signalling system and the management of fleets. Rodney, Kempenfelt and the younger Knowles, for instance, were hard at work on signalling and tactics. Howe's thinking, however, led them all, proved by the final development of his system of numerical signals contained in the 'Signal Book for the Ships of War' issued in 1790. To Brian Tunstall, 'It was the long-delayed masterpiece for which the more progressive British sea officers had been waiting . . . all inhibitions were cast away and a true numerical system established.' It remained the standard form for the navy until 1799, when signals and instructions were amalgamated into the first official Admiralty signal book, which remained in use until 1816. The numerical break-through, with its infinite possibilities, enabled the real advances of the first years of the nineteenth century, including the developments by Home Popham. That it was achieved so quickly is a mark of Howe's influence and because, in this respect at least, he was that rare thing – a reformer at the very top of the profession.[22]

It was one thing, however, to issue new and better signal systems; it was quite another to get captains to understand and obey them, and Howe was never satisfied with the tactical efficiency of the captains who served under him. He was constantly issuing further instructions on sailing formations and battle orders, and even relating to ships' sailing ability. In the thirty years that Howe was in command of squadrons and fleets, he had seen the the size of ships and fleets grow and the demands on them increase. He constantly tried to improve them and saw the need for captains to enlarge their vision. This was appreciated by the King, who wrote to his son, Prince William: 'Lord Howe, who is certainly a scientific officer, assures me that he thinks in our service the attention is carried so long alone to seamanship that few Officers are formed, and that a knowledge of the military is necessary to open the ideas of the directing of large fleets.'[23] This was Howe's most important contribution to the professionalism of the Royal Navy: hence the epigraph to this chapter.

Howe's Defensive Legacy

What object they [the French] may have in view no-one can tell, but if it is in Italy, no Action will take place here before February, for before their Army can risk being cut off, there must be a Sea Action to force us into Port, when if we are not completely victorious – I mean, able to remain at sea whilst the enemy must retire into port – if we only make a Lord Howe's victory, take a part, and retire into port, Italy is lost. [Nelson to his brother Revd Nelson, 26 October 1794]

Nelson's view of Howe and the warfare that he waged is important. But how did the dashing captain and commodore of the 1740s and 1750s turn into the defensive admiral, which was and is Howe's reputation? There is no question that this reputation was current in the latter part of his career, and it has been reinforced by Victorian writers. Alfred Thayer Mahan

wrote disparagingly: 'Howe sees the defence of the empire in the preservation of his own fleet; Jervis in the destruction of the enemy. The one view
is local, narrow, and negative; the other general, broad and positive.'[24] Is
this a simplification?

An insight into Howe's approach can be seen from a minor action against
the Isle d'Aix, scarcely mentioned by Barrow but much admired by contemporaries, during the unsuccessful Rochefort campaign in 1757. From this one
can see the way in which Howe assessed risk. On 23 September Hawke sent
in five ships on a flooding tide to bombard the considerable fortifications on
the island; only the *Magnanime* managed to get to the fortifications, which
outgunned the ship many times. According to an eyewitness:

> Before the attack began, Captain Howe received the fire of the garrison with
> with great intrepidity, ordered all his men to lay down upon the decks, turned
> all his live cattle, fowls, and unnecessaries overboard; himself only with his
> speaking trumpet in hand, the pilot and a man at the helm appearing upon deck,
> till he came within sixty yards of the bastions of the garrison, when he began so
> furious a fire that the Monsieurs said that something more than a man must be
> on board that ship; the men in the garrison were so much terrified that most of
> them clapped themselves down under the works of the garrison and in the
> ditches, nor could be prevailed to stand to their guns, which obliged the
> governor to strike the colours, than was no sooner done than they all jumped
> up, taking snuff, dancing and rejoicing, as if they had gained a victory.

According to Hawke, Howe anchored within forty yards of his target and
'kept an incessant fire for about thirty-five minutes'. Howe lost two men
and eleven wounded; out of a French garrison of five hundred, one was
killed.[25] His seamanship was impeccable; on a windless day, with a strong
tide, he would have to anchor to deliver his broadside. While it was never
possible that the guns of one ship would make a breach in the walls, he
calculated correctly that the morale and calibre of the gunners in a distant
fort could be faced down by inferior firepower if that fire was concentrated;
and to achieve that he held his fire, which further unnerved the French. It
is the most marked of many calculated risks that Howe took in his career.

Another part of Howe's defensive reputation has come from the idea that
he was best in a defensive situation. In the opinion of Mahan, Howe's
campaign against d'Estaing in the summer of 1778 was his finest achievement. Although this campaign was obscured from public view by the
political commotion over their political direction of the war when the
Howes arrived back in London, this was a masterly defence when he was
heavily outgunned by the French. D'Estaing had a fleet of eleven heavier

ships, and was better manned; Howe had seven ships, most of which had been in American waters for two or more years, and he was poorly manned. Yet in two and a half months continuous manoeuvering, d'Estaing never managed to take the initiative.

Planning to leave for Britain when Byron came to relieve him, Howe was leaving the Delaware river for New York when on 29 June he first had warning from the Admiralty of the approach of the French. Calculating that the French would go for New York, he immediately placed cruisers along the American coast and stationed troops on Sandy Hook, and dug them in. He placed his ships inside Sandy Hook, anchoring them meticulously. By 11 July d'Estaing appeared off Sandy Hook. For ten days only a mile separated the fleets, with the dunes of Sandy Hook between them. D'Estaing's ships, however, though heavier, also had deeper draughts and he decided not to attempt the bar, nor challenge Howe's well positioned ships. On 22 July he sailed south. Eight days later the first of the British relieving ships from Byron's squadron limped in after their storm-tossed crossing. It was clear to Howe that French naval superiority would continue, so he continued to play his defensive game.

The French had, in fact, doubled back to the north to Rhode Island to aid the American forces besieging the British army there, a situation which was beginning to be critical for the British. Howe again correctly anticipated d'Estaing's destination, refitted his worn-out fleet hurriedly and arrived off Rhode Island on 9 August. He anchored off Point Judith. D'Estaing could have stayed in Narragansett Bay to see the British army defeated, but he decided to chase Howe. For the next two days Howe outmanoeuvred d'Estaing, reversing the French windward advantage, and at all times keeping the initiative. On 11 August there was a fierce two-day storm, badly damaging the rigging of both fleets; the British went back to New York, and the French retreated north to Boston. In spite of one more attempt to get to Rhode Island, during which Howe again threatened the French fleet, d'Estaing again played for safety by retreating to Boston, thereby enraging his American allies, who were closing in on the British army. Howe, by now beginning to receive significant reinforcements, was gaining the upper hand. Although arguably he missed the chance of cutting off the Continental army in Rhode Island, and he resisted Clinton's urging to attack the French in Boston, he pursued d'Estaing to Boston, although when he reached Boston he found d'Estaing safely inside. Correctly calculating that the French would not come out again so late in the season, Howe sailed for New York and turned over his command.[26] It was a perfect situation for Howe's cast of mind. No overall strategy was needed, just sound tactics; one problem after another had to be solved, preparations made, risks assessed.

To the last year of the American War, Howe brought his methodical talents as commander of the Channel Fleet. There was no other choice for the new government after the fall of Lord North in 1782 for the command to go to anyone except Richard Howe. The political heavyweight who had waited in the wings came back from his political exile to a striking success – the lifting of the siege of Gibraltar. After hoisting his flag on 20 April, for the next month he watched the Dutch fleet off the Texel in the southern North Sea, although that threat died away after the Dutch fleet returned to port. In early July he heard that the combined Franco-Spanish fleet was in Brest, while he had to escort a West Indies convoy home. With twenty-five of the line he met the combined fleet of thirty-six off Land's End; while the French and Spanish formed a line, Howe took the considerable risk of taking his fleet between Land's End and the Scillies, trying as always to get to windward, but in the night the two fleets parted. He missed the convoy, which arrived safely anyway, and the enemy fleet left the Western Approaches, having achieved nothing. By the end of August the Admiralty began to issue orders for the resupply of Gibraltar and on 11 September the Channel Fleet of thirty-five of the line, the supply ships for Gibraltar and three trade convoys left Spithead. Winds from the south delayed progress so that the voyage took nearly a month, the convoy not arriving off Cape St Vincent until 9 October. This was extremely fortunate for Howe, since the next day a storm scattered the combined fleet under Cordova, forcing it out of Gibraltar Bay. The British convoy thus came in unopposed, although most of the storeships were swept past by the current into the Mediterranean. Howe sent the storeships to an anchorage off the African coast. On 13 October the Channel Fleet was fifty miles off the Spanish coast, but a shift of wind from the east, again fortunate, gave them the opportunity of getting into Rosia Bay. The storeships followed soon and quickly discharged their cargoes. Gibraltar had again been relieved, although the Franco-Spanish fleet came into contact again when Howe left Gibraltar on 19 October. On the next day there was some long-range fire between them from which there were 68 men killed and 208 wounded. Short of water and with ten ships less than the enemy, Howe assessed the risk and decided to withdraw and return to England.[27]

It was to be nearly twelve years before Howe was to come within striking distance of an enemy fleet again. He was the only choice for the government as commander-in-chief of the Channel Fleet in 1790 at the Nootka Sound crisis, when he and a fleet of thirty-five of the line cruised for a month looking fruitlessly for the Spanish fleet. Eighteen months later, with relations with France deteriorating, he was again appointed commander-in-chief. He was by now 67 and was suffering from what he called his 'gouty infirmity'; he sailed from St Helens with twenty-three ships of the line, with Vice-Admiral Graves and Alexander Hood as his flag officers, to his final campaign which was to lead to his victory at the Glorious First of June. The fleet started the long blockade of the French fleet in Brest, but not the close blockade favoured by his old commander, Lord Hawke. Howe's cautious nature led him to a policy of 'open blockade', when he left only frigates to watch the French port and withdrew the main fleet to Torbay or Spithead. As a result there was little action, for which he was much criticised, until the spring of 1794, when the Channel Fleet combined the task of escorting the East and West Indies and Newfoundland convoys out of the Western Approaches, together with intercepting the incoming French grain convoy. Under Admiral Vanstabel, this convoy was gathering in Chesapeake Bay and was desperately needed by the Paris authorities, for the city was short of food. Howe sailed on 2 May from Spithead with thirty-two ships of the line and, having detached eight off the Lizard to escort the outgoing convoy, went to Brest to discover the French fleet was still there. He then sailed westwards hoping to find the grain convoy, leaving Rear-Admiral Montagu with six ships to cruise between Cape Ortegal and the latitude of Belle Isle. Howe returned from his westward cruise to Brest on 19 May to find that the French fleet of twenty-six of the line, under Villaret-Joyeuse, had escaped. Howe searched for both convoy and fleet until 28 May when 400 miles west of Ushant, in very fresh weather, the French fleet was seen to windward. Villaret-Joyeuse's main objective was to lead the British fleet away from the grain convoy. With both fleets close-hauled trying to get to windward of each other, Howe pursued the French for nearly two days. A thick mist then came down on both fleets when they were very close. For a further two days, in thick weather, the fleets sailed to the west.

On the First of June, with the weather moderating to a stiff breeze and the visibility clear, the French were four miles to leeward and Howe was able to pick his moment. He formed his line with his usual care. Each British vessel was to cut through under the stern of its opposite number. In the event, only seven ships broke through the line, while the remainder hauled up to windward and opened fire. The fight became very general and fierce, with Howe's flagship, the *Queen Charlotte*, in the thick of it. All ships, setting maximum canvas in a strong breeze, suffered heavy damage to masts and spars, and each ship's manoeuvrability depended upon the seamanship and training of its crew. Several ships on both sides were completely dismasted. The French, not as trained or experienced as the British, were inferior in seamanship and gunnery. Several French ships took very heavy casualties; allowing for prisoners, British killed and wounded amounted to 1148, while French losses were estimated to be over 7000. The *Vengeur de Peuple*, 74 sank in the course of the battle. In less than an hour after the close action began, Howe reported, 'the French admiral engaged by the *Queen Charlotte* crowded off, and was followed by most of the ships in his van, in condition to carry sail after him: leaving with us, about ten or twelve of his crippled or totally dismasted ships exclusive of one sunk in the engagement.'[28] However, several of the French ships managed to creep back to their main fleet under their spritsails and were taken in tow by French frigates. Failure to follow up such a clear-cut victory was to blight Howe's reputation, especially among the next generation of fleet commanders; his orders to recall the *Thunderer* and the *Queen,* when they were just about to take possession of two of the dismasted French ships, was particularly remembered. His age and health after several days of unremitting strain must have inhibited his decision-making; he is said to have been on deck almost continuously for five days. In the meantime, Montagu failed to find the convoy and put back into Plymouth, thus missing Vanstabel and the grain convoy, who with great skill had steered south and had come up the French coast to Brest through the Raz du Sein.

Though a great strategic opportunity to strike at the French republican regime was missed, the Glorious First of June was a considerable tactical and psychological victory, and the British public saw it as such. Within the navy, however, there was discord over those captains mentioned in despatches, and Howe found himself again unpopular with a large section of his fellow officers. In his first despatch after the battle Howe omitted an honourable mention of a number of captains and there was much illfeeling. The responsiveness of several ships to his signals disappointed Howe and he felt that their general performance was below standard. One captain, Molloy of the *Caesar*, mentioned by Howe in an unfavourable light, demanded a court martial. He was dismissed his ship. Howe was never likely to have 'a Band of Brothers'.

Though by now Howe was asking to be relieved, neither the King nor Pitt wanted him to go, and on 22 August Howe again left St Helens with a fleet of thirty-seven British and five Portuguese ships of the line, cruising between Ushant and the Scillies until October, when he took shelter in Torbay. By the end of November the fleet was back in Spithead. Howe spent the winter ashore, but in February 1795, on hearing that the French were at sea, set out again. This was the disastrous winter cruise by the French fleet, when four ships of the line were lost and the rest battered by the weather. By mid-February Howe and his thirty-six ships were again in Torbay, when the weather on the 13th and 14th swung around to the southeast at gale force. Nine ships parted their cables and were fortunately brought up again; it is claimed by some that the experience, in which Howe faced the prospect of losing British naval superiority in an afternoon, finally broke his nerve. 'Lord Howe', notes Brenton, '. . . was much too partial to that miserable anchorage Torbay . . . The fate of England now depended on our anchors and cables. The aged and gallant Admiral, incapable of sustaining the anxiety of his charge, soon afterwards resigned the command, and was succeeded by Lord Bridport.'[29] After a short cruise in which he saw the outward convoys off safely, he finally came ashore, but he was nominally commander-in-chief until May 1797.

Conclusion

> . . . our great Master in Naval tactics and bravery [Nelson to Howe, 8 January 1799]

There was one more passage in Howe's extraordinary career for which he has been remembered, although in truth his role in the Spithead mutiny was symbolic: he did not negotiate with the mutineers, but merely acceded to their demands; others took the decisions. Howe was at Bath when in early March 1797 he received eleven petitions for more pay from the fleet. Although he made informal enquiries as to whether this was a serious matter, he was inclined to disregard them and significantly he did not send this information to Bridport on board the flagship at Spithead. It was not until 22 March that he went to London to present them to Lord Spencer, the First Lord of the Admiralty, by which time the situation had deteriorated. By 7 May there had been some bloodshed, unpopular officers were ashore and the fleet was in open mutiny. After hesitation on the part of the government and a short debate in the House of Lords, in which Howe spoke briefly, and which worsened the situation at Spithead, a bill for a supplementary estimate to pay the men was brought forward, as well as a royal pardon for the mutineers. It was at the request of the King that Howe was sent down to talk to the men, without any official powers, for he had finally had his resignation accepted some days before. On 11 May Howe arrived at Portsmouth and was rowed out immediately to the *Royal George* to win the confidence of the men. Through the following days he visited every ship, explaining the Admiralty's position, taking opinion on the wording of the final pardon. On 13 May on board the guardship *Royal William* he received petitions from all the ships on individual grievances against oppressive officers. He had little alternative but to agree to the dismissal of fifty-nine officers and warrant officers, including one admiral and four captains. Once the royal pardon had arrived from London the mutiny at Spithead was over and Howe was the focus of the reconciliation. He was trusted as much by the ordinary seamen as by the King. A month late, Bridport put to sea with the Channel Fleet. The mutiny at the Nore had yet to happen.

Though throughout the mutiny Howe represented the image of the tough but caring officer of the mid-eighteenth century navy, it is misleading to think that this tradition was his main legacy to Nelson's navy. Indeed, by his character, he was an unlikely reformer; but through his influence and efforts no single naval officer did more to change the navy from its state in the mid-century, which has been described as 'the disordered cohesion . . . which owed little to the bonds of authority'.[30] He brought system to shipboard life and professionalism to seamanship; by steady hard work he improved the command and control of the fleet to a height which was unrecognisable forty years before. The impulses which drove him and the service hard in this direction also brought a tradition of caution and defensiveness. When Howe was in command there was an open, less risky blockade. This was not the aggressive, close style of Hawke, or after Howe, that of Cornwallis, and so admired by late Victorian commentators. He made it clear (for once) when he spoke in Parliament during the American War where he stood on the question of blockade:

> The ships, particularly the large ones, were liable to receive great damage, the crews get sickly, and if a strong southerly gale, or south east, or even south wester, should spring up, the fleet would be in great danger, particularly if it lay in with the French shore off Brest . . . He could affirm from his own knowledge that a station off Brest was a dangerous station, and should never be taken but upon great emergencies.[31]

According to the shrewdest of the late Victorians, A T Mahan, Howe had,

> none of the irritability attributed to genius, as he gives no sign of its inspiration – of originality. He is seen at his strongest in dealing stage by stage with difficult

situations created for him, following step by step, and step by step checking, the lead of another; his action being elicited by successive circumstances, not deriving from some creative, far-reaching conception of his own.[32]

This tradition of caution had to be abandoned in the absolute warfare against Napoleon. There was no room for Howe's style: for his career was a triumph of sustained risk assessment.

Charles Middleton, Lord Barham. Engraving by T Cadell & W Davies

12

Charles Middleton, Lord Barham
1726–1813

'He has very great official talents and merit, but he is a little difficult to act with'

ROGER MORRISS

An Administrator Reassessed

The very presence of this reappraisal among essays on the contribution of admirals to the development of the British navy is an apt reflection of the changing values that inform naval history. A century ago, in his monumental history, William Laird Clowes included only one textual reference to the activities of Charles Middleton, Lord Barham, and that in connection with the campaign of Trafalgar.[1] By the end of the twentieth century, according to the foremost historian of naval logistics during the American War of Independence, Middleton was 'one of the greatest naval administrators of the eighteenth century, perhaps second only in importance to Lord Anson'.[2] As we shall see, this essay will enlarge his importance also to the nineteenth century.

Such a radical reassessment of Middleton derives from the relatively recent growth in awareness of the importance of administration in naval history. Middleton's fame rests on his management of the Admiralty as First Lord between May 1805 and February 1806. Less known is his simultaneous direction of the Commission for Revising and Digesting the Civil Affairs of the Navy, instituted in 1805, and his service as first naval commissioner at the Admiralty between May 1794 and November 1795. But it is his role as Comptroller of the Navy between 1778 and 1790 that has been the subject of most revisionary writing. In 1894 John Knox Laughton, in his entry on Middleton for the *Dictionary of National Biography*, could pass over his Comptrollership without any reference to his administrative achievements during the American War. Now we acknowledge

Middleton's role as vital not only to the navy during the war, but to its physical and administrative strength at the beginning of the French Revolutionary War.

Reassessment of Middleton's career is facilitated by the survival of his papers, now in the National Maritime Museum. However, they are almost entirely administrative and present a highly partial picture of their author. The core consists of copies of Middleton's own writings, preserved through the care and selection of John Deas Thompson, their author's friend and would-be biographer. The danger of basing judgements on them has been braved throughout the twentieth century by all who have used the three volumes of Middleton's papers published by the Navy Records Society between 1906 and 1910.[3] Selected and edited by Sir John Knox Laughton, these printed papers depict a man striving against alleged inertia and political indifference for reforms and innovation that he claimed would make a significant difference to the efficiency of the British navy. Yet Laughton's selection from the papers naturally echoes naval affairs in his own time. The parallel of Middleton with Laughton's contemporary, Fisher, is unmistakable. This double process of selection has enhanced Middleton's reputation, especially as he, like Fisher, had a particular talent for self-promotion. Middleton's writings are replete with disarming declarations of his personal disinterest. His piety and membership of the evangelical set are now well known. He wore his religion like a badge, claiming that 'where there is no religion there can be no public principle'. But it would be unwise to take Middleton's declarations at face value, for they cloaked a palpable determination to advance himself. 'He was nakedly ambitious . . . a bureaucratic imperialist.'[4]

His ambition was harnessed to causes advocated ostensibly for the benefit of the navy and the British public, but his advocacy often had other ulterior personal purposes. For Middleton hated being controlled, resented being overruled by superiors, and seized opportunities for reform or innovation to advance himself in the struggle for control within the civil departments of the navy. Middleton's claims for what he could and had achieved must thus be treated with caution. Indeed any reassessment of Middleton's influence on the development of the British navy depends on distinguishing between claims made to recommend himself and the actual effect of his schemes on the efficiency of the navy. He was, for example, principally associated with introduction of coppering and of the carronade. With an eye for detail that suggested commanding knowledge, and an advocate's pen that appealed to the layman, Middleton argued that these innovations would compensate for Britain's shortage of warships at sea. Yet neither innovation was an immediate or a certain success and their author's claims for them were never fully proved. Even so, later Middleton would overlook their deficiencies and assert their importance to the war effort. In the same way, Middleton seized the opportunity of the movement for economical reform to advance reorganisation in the Navy Office and dockyards, including in his proposals the necessity for the Comptroller to have a seat at the Board of Admiralty. Significantly, though other recommendations were eventually adopted, this last partly self-serving proposal was not taken up.

To distinguish between his claims and the actual effect of policies is no easy matter, for Middleton's longevity as an administrator ensured that his opinions considerably influenced contemporary views, sometimes many years after innovations or reforms were first proposed or adopted. Indeed an 'obstinate persistence' contributed to Middleton's reputation. A dogged attachment to the same ideas runs the length of his career, and long-term circumstances favoured him. Thus, at the end of long administrative life, Middleton was able to carry into effect some of his own principal schemes. Yet the ascendancy of his ideas defeated rival programmes, by which some comparison of the merit or otherwise of Middleton's proposals might have been measured. Thus his influence can be seen clearly in the suppression of Samuel Bentham's nascent scheme for reform of dockyard administration, advocated on principles quite opposed to those to which Middleton adhered. Furthermore, Middleton's Commission of Naval Revision removed Bentham from influence at the Admiralty as Inspector General of Naval Works to a seat at the Navy Board as a junior commissioner. The early effect of Benthamism in the civil departments of the navy was thus swiftly squashed, while more conventional principles sustained by Middleton prevailed to last a few more decades.[5]

This ability to make innovations and effect reform in the long term was the product of long-lasting relationships with three particular politicians, Lord Sandwich, the younger Pitt and Henry Dundas. They appreciated him for his grasp of contemporary need and recognised that the interests of the navy and Middleton's ambition at some points coincided. His ambition ensured that he was industrious in the extreme, both in the routine day to day management of the navy and in the work of keeping his superiors informed. At a time when politicians knew little of the demands of shipping, dockyards and the practical task of building, fitting and repairing ships distant from London, Middleton provided a bridge between the political forum and naval contingencies. In the short term these relationships did not guarantee that Middleton's proposals for reform were effected in the way he anticipated; on the contrary, he was so often disappointed that he grew cynical in old age: 'politics mix with everything and therefore nothing is done as it ought to'.[6]

Nevertheless, in the long term the ascendancy of his patrons ensured that he too was given opportunities to return to office. He was not, however, an easy colleague. The burdens of work he bore, the frustrations of naval bureaucracy, and government politics bred in Middleton an irritability of temper. For all his Christian declarations, in personal relationships he could be impatient, aggressive, short-tempered, patronising of peers and oppressive of subordinates. At times, he could be cruelly judgmental and brutally tactless. He consequently made enemies as well as allies. Yet for all that, and indeed partly because of it, within the parameters of the navy he made a formidable administrator. He possessed a bureaucrat's obsession with efficiency. Moreover, regardless of his audience, he was prepared to articulate the goals to which he thought naval administrators should strive, and to impose those objectives on others.

Personality, high connections and longevity gave Middleton his influence as an administrator. His qualities appear the greater because, unlike Anson and Fisher for example, before being appointed to the Navy Board Middleton was neither distinguished, highly connected nor exceptionally experienced as a sea officer. The contrast is striking. Indeed the comparison of his earlier with his later years highlights both the paradoxes in Middleton's own character and the disparate demands of operational service and shore administration. Middleton manages adequately at sea but did not excel in a ship's environment. Yet on shore at the Navy Board he was in his element, both physically and temperamentally. Though focussing on Middleton, this essay thus reveals something of the demands of those different environments, a contrast which can only continue to enhance an appreciation of the importance of administrators to the navy in the late eighteenth century.

The Unremarkable Seaman, 1741–1778

Although he was the last of twelve children, both his parents, through their respective professional and personal lives, had influence. His mother, Helen Dundas, was part of the Scots clan of lawyers and politicians; her youngest son would later benefit from the partnership of Henry Dundas with the younger Pitt. His father, Robert Middleton, as Collector of Customs at Dundee, had connections both at sea and throughout the Scottish customs service. Even before Charles entered the navy, his father was able to secure him 'sea time' through entry in the books of a merchantman; Middleton actually entered the Royal Navy in April 1741 as captain's servant to Samuel Mead, who commanded in turn the 90-gun ships *Sandwich* and *Duke*. When Mead was approaching superannuation, Middleton was smoothly transferred to the *Flamborough*, a 20-gun frigate, the first command as captain of Joseph Hamar, with whom Middleton was to serve as servant, midshipman and master's mate for four years. He obtained his certificate for lieutenant on 4 October 1745 and the following day was appointed lieutenant to the *Chesterfield* of 40 guns, in which he served for four years, mainly in the Channel until 1748 and then on the west coast of Africa. There, while the officers were on shore in Sierra Leone, the *Chesterfield* was seized by mutineers; at sea by good fortune she was regained for the Crown and taken to the West Indies where the officers, including Middleton, rejoined the ship. He was placed on half pay in July 1749 and, though credited with six months' service in a guardship in 1752, not until the following year was he again commissioned for service at sea.[7]

From January 1753 Middleton had almost ten years continuous service. Initially this consisted of voyages from Portsmouth to Gibraltar, but when the Seven Years War developed in 1755 he was present on board the 60-gun *Anson* at Boscawen's interception of three, and capture of two, French 64-gun ships attempting to get into Louisbourg. Though war had not yet then been declared, it was 'the nearest approach to war service, on the grand scale, that fell to Middleton's lot to see'.[8] The remainder of the war was spent mainly in the Leeward Islands. During this period, one incident on board the *Anson* was significant in revealing Middleton's ability at man-management. He was not popular, and clearly not patient. The attitude of the crew to him was revealed in an incident on 30 January 1757 when a seaman, John Dunbar, suddenly entered the wardroom to complain that his rum ration had been stopped. On Middleton referring his complaint to the quarterdeck, Dunbar retorted, 'who am I to make it to but to you'. His manner put Middleton 'in some state' and he took up a stick and hit Dunbar with it; he then reached for a pike, but was prevented from taking hold of it by a crowd of men behind Dunbar thrusting him forward. One of the other seamen later testified that Middleton claimed that if he 'had a pike in my hand I would take your life'. Instead Middleton ordered Dunbar into irons to be court-martialled. The seaman was condemned by the court to sixty lashes for contempt, insolence, 'reproachful and provoking speeches tending to make a disturbance in the ship'. In his own defence, Middleton elicited a statement from another lieutenant that his 'constant rule' was 'to do as much justice as ever was in his power'.[9] Whether there was any connection or not, however, Middleton left the *Anson* within a month. In

February 1757 he was elevated to command the sloop *Speaker*, then the *Barbados*, and in 1759 achieved post rank in the frigate *Arundel*. A quarrel, this time with the latter's carpenter, resulting in another court martial, again affords insight into the tenor of Middleton's management. On New Year's Day 1760, after ordering his crew to cease work, he went below to order the carpenter, Thomas Slater, to clear the deck of oakum. Slater first said he would at dusk, and later, after it had rained, that he could not without breaking off from other work. After finishing work, Slater reported to Middleton on the quarterdeck, where words were exchanged terminating with Middleton hitting the carpenter with his open hand and kicking him. With this, Slater walked off, Middleton calling after him 'not a syllable more, Sir, for if you do I will knock you down'. However, Slater then retorted, 'you may as often as you think proper', upon which Middleton ordered him to be confined. Slater was found guilty of treating Middleton with contempt and mulcted of his personal pay and that of his servant for the space of one year.[10]

In July 1760 Middleton transferred into the 28-gun *Emerald*. His main task in her was to protect British trade in the Leeward Islands, escorting local convoys between the islands and homeward merchantmen out into the Atlantic beyond the reach of French privateers. Unlike some contemporaries, and possibly on account of his origins, he evinced little frustration with the needs of merchantmen and evidently found satisfaction in calculating how best to defeat the objects of enemy privateers using an increased number of frigates, brigs and sloops. But his correspondence holds one clue to his later readiness to go on shore: seasickness that made even writing difficult.[11] Over a period of nine months in 1760–61 the *Emerald* took sixteen prizes: five privateers and eleven merchantmen carrying sugar, coffee, timber and wine. His efforts were appreciated by the merchant community of Barbados who voted him a gold-hilted sword.[12] More important, the captures provided him with prize money.

In October 1761 the *Emerald* was paid off. He obtained the 32-gun *Adventure* in March 1762 and spent a year off the Normandy coast, but in April 1763, on being offered the *Pearl*, fatigue, scurvy and the attractions of life on shore prompted him to decline the offer. One may assume that the financial benefits of cruising in the West Indies permitted him to decline further service. Moreover, he was by then 36 and in December 1761 had married Margaret Gambier, whom he had met over twenty years before on board the *Sandwich*. She was the niece of Captain Mead and, according to John Deas Thompson, had declined another marriage and defied her father in order to wait for Middleton.[13] From 1763 until 1775 Middleton led the life of a country gentleman. On falling out with her father, Margaret Gambier had gone to live with her friend Elizabeth Bouverie. In 1763 Middleton moved in too, and took to farming the Bouverie farm at Teston in Kent. It was a life to which after 1778 he would regularly return. Like the Gambiers, he also became committed to evangelical religion, which would influence his attitudes after 1778. Until then, however, his preoccupations were anything but naval. In 1775 he obtained command of a guardship at the Nore, conveniently close to Teston; in 1776 he was given a larger one; and early in 1778 he was appointed to a 50-gun ship still building.[14] Yet neither his achievements at sea nor his interests on shore presaged the appointment and career that was to follow.

Comptroller of the Navy, 1778–1790

On 14 July 1778 Maurice Suckling, Comptroller of the Navy since April 1775, died after over a year of ill health. On 7 August 1778 Middleton was appointed in his place.[15] The appointment has always proved perplexing, principally because the grounds upon which Lord Sandwich, First Lord of the Admiralty, made the appointment are unclear. As Sandwich's most recent biographer has observed,

> Middleton was an obscure Scotsman with an undistinguished career behind him. His recent dealings with Sandwich had not obviously recommended him. As a captain of a guardship he had figured among Sandwich's correspondents asking for leave rather more often than was decent, and with some curious excuses . . . He had tried to get his brother appointed his purser in a highly irregular fashion, and had been rebuffed. His interest in agriculture, his involvement in the 'Clapham Sect' and the nascent Evangelical movement . . . all seemed to mark him as an officer busy in retirement.[16]

What then prompted the appointment? Certainly it was not his reputation as a naval officer; rather, it seems to have been a combination of personal and political connections. He was connected to the Dundas clan, dominant in Scottish politics; his wife brought him another connection with the Pitts; he was a proprietor of East India Company stock, with which Sandwich had an interest; and also, like Sandwich, he subscribed to the organisation of Concerts of Ancient Music, at one of which they probably met.[17] From these occasions Sandwich, a discerning judge of character, no doubt realised Middleton's potential for the post he had to fill. The latter's brother-in-law, Captain James Gambier, had already fulfilled Sandwich's expectations as an administrator, having been appointed in 1773 first briefly to the Navy Board as Comptroller of Victualling Accounts, then, until he obtained his flag in January 1778, as Commissioner in Portsmouth dockyard.[18] In March Sandwich employed Gambier to sound Middleton out on his readiness to accept the Comptroller's post. It was an office Middleton himself realised in which his 'turn to business and application' would make him useful. It was an offer he could not resist.[19]

Middleton took his seat at the Navy Board at a critical point in the American War of Independence. France had declared war on Britain in March 1778; Spain was to ally herself with France in 1779, Holland in 1780. Not only did the entry of these European powers signal a need to further disperse British troops to defend territories in the North American continent and West Indies, but also an overwhelming need to mobilise fully Britain's navy and employ her shipbuilding capacity to meet the logistical superiority of the Bourbon powers. While Britain during the first two years of the American War had exercised economy in the financing of her navy, France had taken the opportunity to further reinforce her restored navy by completing new ships of the line.[20] Between 1776 and 1778 France launched eighteen new battleships; after Spain entered the war in 1779 the Bourbon powers had a 44 per cent superiority in ships of the line over Britain.[21] The main initiatives Middleton was to urge in improving the British fleet during the course of the war were aimed at reducing this superiority. His first objective, however, was to establish his grasp on Navy Board business.

The board, descended from a Council of the Marine established in 1546, was the principal naval board subordinate to the Admiralty and had responsibility for managing the royal dockyards, for building, equipping and repairing all ships, for manning the fleet, forming the naval estimates, and overseeing the accounts of the other subordinate boards. For these purposes it commanded an office staff of about a hundred and maintained correspondence with the Board of Admiralty, the Treasury, the Victualling and Ordnance Boards, the dockyards and naval officers. It was situated on Tower Hill, in buildings on the corner of Crutched Friars and Seething Lane, so correspondence formed the main means of communication with the different branches of naval administration. It was, however, a means by which it was almost overwhelmed. The Navy Board had been reinstituted under new instructions in 1662, but since then, as Middleton himself recorded, the number of members had doubled, and

> its business increased an hundred fold and all continues to be transacted at one
> table with the same irregularity as matters come by chance before them. There
> is no division of business, no providing for dispatch. The consequence are hasty

decisions, confusion, accounts passed without examination, a perplexing variety of opinion, professional matters submitted to landsmen and mere clerks, some members overloaded with business, others having little to do but to interrupt or confound the rest, while distraction and irresolution from this indigested heap is the portion of him who must bring things to some conclusion in the day, be it right or be it wrong.[22]

For this purpose Middleton had been placed in his element. Robert Gregson, a clerk in the Navy Office since 1748, who assisted the Clerk of the Acts, effectively the secretary of the Navy Board, reported Middleton to be 'the most indefatigable and able' Comptroller he had known.

The load of business he goes through at the Board, at the Treasury, Admiralty and his own house, is astonishing, and what I am confident no other man will be able to execute . . . Upon the whole the weight of business falls upon a few, and of those few, chiefly upon the Comptroller and Secretary, who have piles of papers before them a foot high, to digest and minute, while two or three at the board are looking on or reading newspapers, who if they were to assist, the business would go on smoother and easier.[23]

Middleton's appetite for paperwork was voracious. Nonetheless, with his other duties, he found his post both exhausting and beyond him.

His duty as Comptroller includes not only the conducting all the public correspondence and business of the board, but charge of three great offices within the Navy Office. He visits the yards of Deptford and Woolwich weekly, controls the payment of them and of all ships paid off at them. The correspondence is so much increased as to have required during the whole of the . . . war, his attendance from 10 in the morning till 4 or 6 in the evening, for every day in the week, and to employ the greatest part of his time in other ways.

A key function was to go to the Admiralty Office three or four times a week to receive from the First Lord, the Secretary and other commissioners 'such information and orders as were necessary for providing without discovery the various preparations for expeditions of a secret nature'. These briefings permitted Middleton to arrange the hire of transports and victuallers without the 'publicity' of communication through the official correspondence, so pre-empting the escalation of contract prices under the prospect of demand for tonnage.[24]

The management of transports considerably added to the business of the Comptroller. When Middleton came to the Navy Office, ships to serve as transports were hired by four government boards: the Navy Board to carry stores out to foreign yards and the squadrons in North America, and to carry soldiers wherever they were required in the world;

the Victualling Board to supply the fleet with provisions; the Ordnance Board to ship ordnance trains and supplies; and the Treasury to ship victuals for British armies serving abroad. All four boards entered the market together and bid for ships against one another. The inefficiency was striking. Moreover, the Treasury in particular lacked the expertise to ensure the ships it hired were suitable or seaworthy. In consequence, Middleton proposed that the Navy Board hire ships for all the boards, and indeed assumed control of the supply of army victuallers in 1779. With a large-scale war being waged across the Atlantic, the transport service represented a major section of the war effort. In November 1780 there were eighty troop transports deployed in North America. The transports were inspected for hire in the royal dockyards, while the paperwork was performed in the Navy Office. In February 1780 23 per cent of all Navy Bills in circulation represented expenditure on transports. The Navy Board task was made difficult by the shortage of shipping, especially towards the end of the war, because tonnage was retained overseas. Also, difficulties of communication within government bureaucracy, the inter-ference of impressment, and the repeated demands of the customs service to unload victuallers at transshipment ports compounded the problem. Nevertheless, overseen by Middleton, the management of transports for both the movement and the supply of troops represented a significant improvement in the efficiency of managing the logistics of war in North America.[25]

Increasing the Power of the British Navy, 1778–1783

The demands of these duties, so he claimed, the correspondence in particu-lar, nearly turned Middleton's brain. After the war, he would propose reforms to the structure of the Navy Board aimed at reducing the burden on the Comptroller. In the meantime, however, his burden was enhanced by a succession of initiatives aimed at increasing the power and efficiency of the British navy. The parity of France in ships of the line in 1778 and the superiority of the combined Bourbon powers from 1779 made this of paramount importance. As Middleton prepared to succeed Suckling, the Battle of Ushant on 27 July 1778 demonstrated the capability of the French navy to inflict damage on the British fleet while itself surviving as a potent force. Between them, in July 1779 the French and Spanish were able to put together a force of sixty-six ships of the line to cover their intended inva-sion of Britain. Subsequently, in 1781 the Bourbon powers were able to enter the English Channel with forty-nine of the line. On both occasions Britain's own battlefleet in home waters was outmatched. Middleton's priorities were thus to increase the strength of the ships available at sea, and to increase that number with all expedition.

The first initiative was aimed at reducing the time ships in commission spent off station sailing to the dockyards and being refitted there. Half the British dockyards were up the rivers Thames and Medway in southeastern England, distant from the main theatres of operation in the Western Approaches and across the Atlantic. Only Sheerness, Portsmouth and Plymouth were directly accessible from the sea, but the first of these was small and even the two western yards struggled against numerous physical difficulties when it came to working on ships.[26] Such handicaps encouraged a degree of specialisation. In wartime the seaboard yards took the brunt of the refitting and minor repairs, while the inland yards tended to perform the heavier repairs and some new construction.

To reduce the need for ships to refit so often, and to reduce the cumulated time spent in dock, Middleton in 1778 revived the idea of coppering the British fleet. Fir-clad ships of the line had to be cleaned of their weed and have their sheathing repaired three or four times a year. Copper sheathing had been under trial since the Seven Years War, when its resistance to weed, to the *teredo navalis*, and to wear and tear had been acclaimed. Nevertheless, its corrosive effects on adjacent iron bolts and nails fastening the timbers of the hull, keel and rudder had created alarm. The challenge was to eliminate the electrolytic action. Between the wars, economy had militated against experiments, the principal of which involved altering all the metal fastenings below water level to copper. By 1775 only about a dozen frigates and sloops had copper bottoms. Nevertheless, Middleton had a particular interest in them and in 1778, as he awaited the Comptrollership, he asked for a coppered ship. The *Jupiter*, the 50-gun ship building at Deptford to which he was assigned, was to become on being launched the largest coppered ship in the navy.

On entering office Middleton maintained his enthusiasm for the innovation, and in the autumn of 1778 he learned from a Liverpool shipbuilder the technique of insulating the iron from the copper (which was also coated with white lead) by the means of thick tarred paper. Although the process later proved to be less than totally effective, Middleton had, by February 1779, persuaded the Admiralty to try the new technique on two ships of the line; by late May all ships of the line were ordered to be coppered as they came in for refitting or repair. In July the innovation was extended to frigates. With Britain threatened by the combined naval power of France and Spain, Middleton maintained in September 1779 that coppering was 'more than doubling our number of ships' and that by sheathing the

Western Squadron 'it may defy the power of France and Spain'.[27] By the end of the year the whole Western Squadron was ordered to be metal sheathed. Two years later 313 ships had been coppered, including 82 ships of the line.

The new sheathing of the fleet was a remarkable logistical achievement. But what did it achieve in operational terms? One authority in the period has maintained that the process 'contributed enormously to restoring or even reversing the balance of power at sea'.[28] The innovation certainly had a reputation for increasing the sailing speed of ships. In 1780 Rodney attributed much of his success at the 'Moonlight Battle' to his coppered ships. Sandwich and Middleton did not neglect to claim that other successes at sea were owing to speed derived from coppering.[29] However, the assertion was politically convenient and in 1783 the failure of the insulation of the iron from the copper came to light.[30] By electrolytic action, the copper seriously impaired the strength of the iron fastenings binding the hull timbers of ships together. Nevertheless, coppering had a significant effect on the logistics of dockyard operations in the later stages of the war. Because coppered ships were relatively resilient to the adherent qualities of molluscs and weed, those in need of refitting did not always have to enter dock to have their hulls cleaned and could be turned around within weeks rather than months. The spare dock capacity could thus be turned to the repair of ships. In consequence, more ships could keep the sea in operational use.[31]

Middleton was also very interested in the armament of ships. In July 1779 he seized upon the report of trials of carronades by the Ordnance Board at Woolwich to advance the proposal of arming all ships with these new weapons. The weapon was new, bored with the newly developed cannon lathe, and had been fitted in 1779 in the privateer *Success* of Liverpool, which lived up to her name in several actions using them. Middleton attended the Woolwich trials, thought them 'decisive', and recommended carronades be fitted 'on the poops of all ships, and the quarterdecks of others'. The Navy Board took up his recommendation, which the Admiralty accepted. The carronades were fitted in frigates which had unoccupied spaces on their quarterdecks. However, by December 1779, following numerous negative reports from naval officers, partly because the weapons endangered rigging, the Navy Board agreed to fit them only where they were wanted by commanding officers. Further trials by the Ordnance Board in the summer and autumn of 1780, because they matched carronades against cannon at long range, also produced unfavourable reports and their expense was questioned. However, during 1780 naval opinion began to turn in their favour, a shift which increased as actions at sea emphasised their power at short range.[32] Their cause was much helped by the early conversion of Lord Sandwich to a belief in their utility, but it was not until after February 1782 that he, with Middleton's assistance, persuaded the naval members of the Board of Admiralty of their value.[33] Indeed, the impact they made on the enemy was only fully realised in September 1782 when the *Rainbow*, completely armed with carronades at Middleton's suggestion, induced a French 40-gun frigate to surrender by firing a single forecastle gun.[34]

By this time great numbers of new ships, ordered from 1778, were being launched and equipped. Orders had been placed for the construction of thirty-two 74-gun ships and thirteen of 64 guns.[35] Between 1778 and 1783 thirty-three ships of the line and 131 ships of 50 guns or less were launched. Middleton was at the centre of this building boom, which was to flow over into the peace. He supervised the structuring of the estimates that were to bring forth this massive investment in the navy. Furthermore, his opinion partly determined where the building should take place. The dockyards were preoccupied with refitting, repairs and new coppering. Only the inland yards had labour for new building, but that was still insufficient for the number of ships wanted. Only 14 ships of the line and 18 smaller vessels were thus launched from the dockyards, whereas 19 ships of the line and 113 others were launched from the merchant yards.[36]

The construction of ships in the merchant yards was not popular with naval officers. During the American War, however, this prejudice had to be subordinated to sheer necessity. Moreover, in Middleton's view the disadvantages of merchant building in expedient haste – use of unseasoned or poor materials, and poor workmanship – could be overcome by proper supervision by dockyard officers specifically deputed to the task. A great growth in contract building had begun in the previous war, using contractors close to the royal yards, mainly along the Thames, Medway and Solent.[37] Proper supervisors could be selected from the inferior dockyard officers, the foremen and quartermen, who were in the patronage of the Navy Board. Needless to say, however, the provision for new building, as well as refitting and repairs, encompassing the provision of adequate quantities of materials and stores, demanded management in the dockyards of the best quality. It was an attempt to control that quality which brought him directly into conflict with Lord Sandwich.

The power of appointment to the senior yard posts was vested in the Admiralty, which received nominations, many politically motivated, from disparate sources. It was a system of patronage open to abuse and, through the appointment of incapable men, liable to weaken the navy, especially as officers allegedly knew that 'a proper vote would cover a corrupt practice'.[38] Middleton maintained that the Navy Board knew best from overseeing the dockyards who were the most suitable men available; he drew up lists of officers not only according to their professional abilities but according to their moral character.[39] In 1781, driven by frustration, Middleton began a determined contest with Lord Sandwich for control of dockyard appointments.[40] It was a contest he was to loose. Politics, he believed, had 'got too great a hold on this branch of the service' for him to withstand it. Yet, as Sandwich justly claimed, the Admiralty had good reasons for receiving recommendations from sources other than the Navy Board. Of fundamental importance, moreover, the authority of the Admiralty depended on the retention of patronage in the upper echelons of dockyard management.[41]

This dispute revealed Middleton in his worst light: blinkered, dogmatic and persistent. Sandwich remained urbane and courteous, though he had much to tolerate. But he seems to have accepted the abrasive side of his Comptroller as the complement of his administrative efficiency. Sandwich indeed had tolerated worse. As early as 1779 Middleton had rebuked the First Lord for the disabled state of the dockyards from want of attention to appointments, for lack of system in the disposition of the fleet, for the loss of discipline in the navy, and for not himself working longer hours. Middleton claimed that the Admiralty and the Navy Office were 'so nearly connected that I must be wilfully blind not to see the sad management that prevails at present'; 'unless a new plan is adopted, and your lordship gives your whole time to the business of the Admiralty, the misapplication of the fleet will bring ruin upon this country.'[42]

In April 1782 Sandwich was forced to resign from the Admiralty for the navy's role in the impending loss of the American colonies. Since then, and until Sandwich's recent vindication, Middleton's criticism's have been thought just. Nevertheless, experience of Sandwich's successors at the Admiralty led Middleton to make 'a proper sense of distinction' between their respective capabilities, and in 1789 he was unreserved in encouraging Sandwich to return as First Lord.[43] For his part, Sandwich can only have respected Middleton's role in increasing the effectiveness of British naval power, both by his labours to maintain the efficiency of the civil departments of the navy, so far as established procedures permitted, and by technical innovations that reduced the logistical advantage of the Bourbon combination. The respect accorded British naval power after the Battle of the Saintes in 1782 reflected the growth in strength generated by measures in which Middleton had a great part.

Reform and Reconstruction, 1783–1790

Peace in 1783 brought relief from the burden of wartime administration. Even before the war had ended, however, Middleton had embarked on a new campaign, for the reform of management in the Navy Office, that he would pursue until disillusion with the political process and fatigue would induce him to resign in 1790. He was encouraged to take up this campaign at the end of 1782 after Lord Shelburne became First Lord of the Treasury and Prime Minister. Shelburne entered office on the back of a movement for economical reform, and that autumn Middleton's proposals to Shelburne included the abolition of alleged sinecures and the funding of fees, which might partly finance increased salaries.[44] His proposals included the necessity for the Comptroller of the Navy to become a member of the Board of Admiralty, a recommendation that in Middleton's mind, in the wake of the American War, took high priority, both for the benefit of the navy and his own advancement. Yet, in the interest of this last proposal, he seems to have disregarded the potential consequences of prohibiting the receipt of fees. Shelburne's positive response to fee funding (though he made no commitment to immediate reform) forced Middleton suddenly into reverse. For the first time, no doubt prompted by discussion at the Navy Board, Middleton appears to have realised the potentially damaging repercussions. He had under-estimated the demoralisation, discontent and envy, especially among the middling and junior members of staff, who had paid premiums to enter office which the senior staff had no obligation to return. Middleton's reversal best indicates his interest in advancing his own ambitions rather than his sensitivity to the administrative fabric within which he worked.[45]

Nevertheless, Middleton continued to advocate a reorganisation at the Admiralty and Navy Boards which would include him as Comptroller becoming a member of the senior board. Lord Howe, who succeeded Keppel as First Lord in January 1783, was sympathetic neither to the idea of change nor to Middleton making them an issue. Indeed, he wrote to him in February 1783 quite bluntly:

> As you do not particularise the alterations in the constitution of the admiralty and navy boards which you have in contemplation, I see no cause to change my present sentiments upon them; nor to think a personal explanation of an arrangement consisting of many parts (and first proposed to take immediate effect, though afterwards found to be imperfect in its construction) may not tend to promote rather than delay the execution of the plan.[46]

With the end of the war and the necessity to defend Navy Office staffing and dockyard establishments, it was not the time to take on Howe. Middleton turned to the administrative problems of the Navy Board one by one himself. In July 1783 he was busy arranging into a system the 'multiplicity of accounts belonging to the separate branches' of the Navy Office, 'a monster of such magnitude and extent'. In October, taking advantage of the termination in the artificers' wartime powers of leverage, he turned to the abuse of chips. By then, the dockyards' standing and occasional orders, collected in the yards since the seventeenth century but in no digested order, were also under review, revised to 1767 by May 1785.[47] Consistent with contemporary concerns, Middleton continued to campaign against the fees received in the naval departments. He argued in September 1784 that they were inseparable from premiums paid on entry into every office, allowances for houses, poundage on monies handled, even the sale of old dockyard stores and the management of the Chatham Chest.[48] In short, he maintained that the whole fabric of employment in the naval departments demanded examination.

As he expected, he found a ready listener in William Pitt, Chancellor of the Exchequer.[49] No doubt his family relationship to Henry Dundas, Pitt's lieutenant, helped. Pitt was committed to the principle of abolishing fees and in August 1785 successfully passed through Parliament a bill for a Commission of Inquiry into Fees, Gratuites, Perquisites and Emoluments in the Public Offices.[50] Upon this Commission, Middleton pinned his hopes. However, there were only three commissioners and in their first two years of work the Commission on Fees produced only two reports, on the offices of the Secretaries of State and of the Treasury. In 1787 their commission was extended so that they might examine the offices of the Post Office, Admiralty, Treasurer of the Navy, the Commissioners of the Navy, the Dockyards and the Victualling Office. Reflecting the importance of the navy as an element in central government, five out of the seven departments they would examine would be naval.[51] For Middleton, the new commission provided a vehicle by which his recommendations might gain approval without going through the Admiralty where Howe resided until 1788. Such representations had to be kept secret. As he suggested to Francis Baring in December 1786, when he was not officially called upon for information, the commissioners would 'reap most benefit from my assistance by not otherwise openly bringing me forward', thereby avoiding either jealousy or contradiction at the Navy or Admiralty Boards. Rather, by his 'ready acquiescence in your regulations', he would be 'an example of willing obedience to them'.[52]

The fifth and sixth reports of the Commission, on the Navy Office and dockyards, signed in February and March 1788, reiterated Middleton's arguments for the Comptroller to superintend the whole office. It also called for a Deputy Comptroller to assist in presiding at the board, for the Clerk of the Acts to become board secretary, for an increase in the number of board commissioners from seven to ten, for the organisation of the commissioners into committees, and for the revision of the board's standing orders to the yards. Middleton was also able to advance questions like that for the appointment of a civil architect to manage building works in the yards, in which he was opposed by the Howe at the Admiralty.[53] His proposal for the Comptroller to become a member of the Admiralty Board was not included in the reports, possibly because Howe opposed it.

Throughout these years, Howe and Middleton, two equally determined men, did not get on. Howe was aware of Middleton's representations to the Commission on Fees – indeed he anticipated that the commissioners would 'be exactly of the opinion of Sir Charles' – and objected to the Comptroller receiving any more authority. Rather, he proposed Middleton be transferred to a yard commissioner's post and subsequently refused his promotion with other post captains to rear-admiral. To be fair to Howe, Comptrollers of the Navy were not normally of flag rank.[54] However, Middleton had the ear and favour of Pitt, and in September 1787 he was raised to rear-admiral, while in July 1788 Howe was asked to resign, to be succeeded by the Earl of Chatham, Pitt's own elder brother.[55]

The relationship of Middleton with Pitt offset the distance between the Comptroller and Howe. Pitt enjoyed working with experienced departmental managers and Middleton did not neglect the opportunity both to indulge his passion for providing advice, and to instil in Pitt the necessity for repair and enlargement of the fleet.[56] The First Lord of the Treasury received dockyard targets for the duration of the peace and proposed policies for enhancing British naval power once a new war began. The result was an unprecedented scale of peacetime investment in the navy. Between 1783 and 1789 twelve new ships of the line were built and sixty-five repaired.[57] 'It was no uncommon thing for Mr Pitt to visit the Navy Office to discuss naval matters with the Comptroller, and to see the returns made from the yards of the progress in building and repairing the ships of the line.'[58] Middleton aimed at ninety battleships and ninety frigates fit for service by the end of 1786. Such strength permitted diplomacy by deterrence during the Dutch and Spanish alarms of 1787 and 1790, and when war did break out in 1793 Britain had the capability of mobilising ninety-three ships of the line.

Middleton played a key role in the strengthening of the British fleet
before 1793. However, he was tired and frustrated by the failure of politicians to implement the reforms he had recommended to the Commission
of Fees. In hopes of relief, he had continued to manage the civil affairs of
the navy without the assistance of a deputy or the division of the Navy
Board into committees. He had premised economy on an alteration in
executive management, arguing that without it, 'like a defect in the first
spring of the machine, it will be universally felt'.[59] Over the winter of
1788–9 he attended Pitt and Chatham to prepare the reports of the Commission on Fees for an Order in Council, but 'the King's illness' intervened.
The illness and death of the Navy Board's secretary added to his difficulties.
Joshua Thomas, the assistant to the Clerk of the Acts, functioned as Middleton's secretary.[60] By December 1789 he wanted only a competent secretary and a sea officer next to him. By February 1790 he could feel a
'jealousy' against him within the Navy Office where, for want of official
prohibition, fees appeared to be 'countenanced by government itself'.[61]

His opponents included George Jackson, Judge Advocate of the Fleet at
the Admiralty since 1768. Jackson had begun his career as a clerk in the
Navy Office in 1743 and resented Middleton's 'importunity' in speaking
alone for the those who worked beneath him. He maintained that the
receipt of unofficial emoluments did not automatically imply abuse:

> the assertion should not stand on insinuation. Instances to prove the abuse
> should be adduced and openly brought to light or men of the most unblemished
> conduct and character stand condemned, without an opportunity of doing
> themselves justice.

As regards the proposed changes at the Navy Board, he 'doubted too much
of the good effect of the alterations to be hasty in his approval'. With
respect to the management of accounts, he suspected that an increase in the
influence of sea officers in committees would generate partiality through
the 'bias in the mind of one sea officer in favour of another' and warned
that to disturb existing management (which the new system will infallibly
do) would be dangerous and beget confusion, worse than any difficulty that
can now exist'.[62] In despair, Middleton resigned in March 1790. By contrast, the strength of confidence in Jackson was marked in 1791 by his
knighthood. He was to continue in office until his death in 1822.[63]

The Admiralty during the French Revolutionary War, 1794–1795

Though out of office, Middleton remained in communication with Pitt
and Chatham in 1790. During the Nootka Sound crisis with Spain he

offered advice on how best to prepare for an expedition, and even offered to serve on one if needed. In October 1793, after the outbreak of the French Revolutionary War, he wrote to Chatham, advising him how to maintain the fleet during hostilities, what information about French resources ought to be procured while Toulon lay in British hands, and how the British fleet ought to be managed from the Admiralty.[64] Though his advice seems to have been unsolicited, his knowledge was demonstrable, and in May 1794 he was recalled, this time to the Admiralty, to serve under Lord Chatham (and Lord Spencer from December 1794) as third naval commissioner (first from March 1795).[65] Recommending him to Spencer at the change in First Lord in December 1794, Dundas acknowledged that Middleton was 'a little difficult to act with from an anxiety, I had almost said an irritability of temper, and he requires to have a great deal of his own way of doing business in order to do it well'; yet he defended his 'great official talents and merit' and claimed that his retirement from the Admiralty at that time 'would be an irreparable loss'.[66] Middleton thus stayed on. Here, much as he had done in the Navy Office, he promptly set out rules for the management of business.[67] His long memory of the organisation of the blockade strategy practised in the Seven Years War helped to place thinking about the disposition of the British fleet on a logistical basis. Middleton's scheme weighted the British squadrons on each station according to the strength of the French opposition and the numbers of ships necessary to be away victualling and refitting.[68]

His relation, Henry Dundas, was now Secretary for War, and Middleton addressed him on matters such as the preservation of seamen and the protection of trade by the organisation of convoys.[69] The relative backwardness of the dockyards compared to the advances in steam technology was now evident even to members of Parliament, and in 1795 Middleton proposed 'an intermediate Sea Board . . . qualified to inspect and report on all plans of improvement relative to naval matters'. Samuel Bentham, brother to Jeremy, was at this time canvassing the Admiralty to consider his proposals for dockyard improvements and in June 1795, after meeting Bentham, Middleton altered his recommendation in favour of an arrangement put forward by Bentham, for an individually responsible Surveyor General attached to the Admiralty. The title was subsequently altered and the office of the Inspector of General of Naval Works was established in March.[70] Middleton had achieved a position at the Admiralty where he had a major influence on the management of both the fleet at sea and the shore establishment. He had risen to vice-admiral in February 1793 and full admiral in June 1795. However, in November 1795, quite suddenly, he resigned his post over the recall of an old friend, Sir John Laforey, from the command of the Leeward Islands station.[71]

There was more to it than sentiment. Lord Spencer had agreed that Hugh Cloberry Christian, just promoted rear-admiral in June 1795 but with a year of experience at the Transport Board, would command the naval element of the forthcoming expedition against the French West Indian islands of Guadeloupe, St Lucia and Saint-Domingue. With an intended 25,000 to 30,000 men, this was to be the biggest overseas expedition ever mounted from Britain. However, to avoid conflicting authorities in the Leeward Islands, Spencer planned that, once out there, Christian would succeed Laforey, who would shift his flag to Jamaica and become the overall commander in the Caribbean, while Rear-Admiral William Parker at Jamaica would remove to command the naval forces off Saint-Domingue. Middleton objected that the shuffling of senior officers to suit a junior was a breach of naval etiquette. He was deeply conscious of the importance of the authority attaching to flag ranks and had been forward in representing to Dundas the lack of discipline in the navy. He resigned because he refused to become an adjunct to the dissipation of respect for flag appointments.[72]

First Lord of the Admiralty, 1805–1806

Middleton returned to farming at Teston for eight years. When Pitt returned to office in 1804, and Dundas, now first Viscount Melville, became First Lord of the Admiralty in May 1804, he renewed his habit of despatching memoranda of advice to his relative. Moreover, he suggested that if Melville would care to have the revision of the dockyards' standing orders completed, the task begun in the 1780s could be resumed with the help of the digest still in his possession. By September 1804 Middleton's friend, John Deas Thompson, the naval officer for Leith, was installed at the Admiralty, concentrating into one list all the standing orders issued by the Navy Board since 1793, then abstracting them under various heads into one of the digest books brought from Teston.[73] By November Middleton maintained that he had reached the stage at which it was also desirable to revise the orders under which sea officers acted. Accounts and procedures would all be included.

The scope of the project was deemed sufficient for a Commission for Revising and Digesting the Civil Affairs of the Navy. This was established by letters patent under the Great Seal in January 1805 with Middleton as chairman.[74] For Middleton, his new post was a final attempt to create order in the navy. His recommendations to the Commissioners on Fees for reform in the Navy Office had largely been effected in 1796. However, the Fees report for the dockyards had been revised before it was adopted in 1801 by Samuel Bentham, the Inspector General, and by Evan Nepean, Admiralty Secretary. Middleton believed it had been 'sadly garbled' and altered 'to the views of interested individuals; whoever . . . will follow their progress . . . must see that the whole was a political job.'[75] For Pitt and Melville, the new Commission of Revision represented a happy replacement for St Vincent's Commission appointed in 1802 to inquire into Irregularities, Frauds and Abuses practised in the Naval Departments. The reports of this commission were proving an embarrassment. Indeed, its tenth report on the office of Treasurer of the Navy obliged Melville to resign as First Lord early in April 1805. Melville was eventually impeached for failing to prevent the Paymaster of the Navy mixing public funds with his own money in a private account in contravention of an Act of 1782.

On Melville's resignation, Middleton, though now aged 79, was asked to replace him. Rewarded with a peerage on 1 May 1805, the new Baron Barham of Teston turned his mind once more to the direction of sea operations. As First Lord of the Admiralty he continued the policies of his predecessor. His management of board affairs, his relations with his board colleagues and with officers at sea have been examined elsewhere.[76] Justly, he has been credited with orchestrating the campaign of Trafalgar. The editor of his printed correspondence, John Knox Laughton, claims he was 'the master mind and director of the whole campaign', a view with which subsequent historians have not disagreed.[77] His most recent biographer, who examined the Admiralty minutes, found him 'immersed in the details of strategy and tactics . . . His hurried scawl is everywhere.'[78] Annotations on letters received indicate a grasp of the logistics at individual ship level. The painstaking thoroughness he brought to administration and the discipline he demanded in the despatch and execution of orders was complemented by the easy grasp of a seaman for the demands of ship management. It was appropriate that on 26 October Collingwood's congratulations for 'the most complete victory that ever was obtained over an enemy' went to Barham. It was a fitting culmination to a career at the centre of the naval administration.

Pitt died on 3 February 1806. Barham resigned with the rest of the government on 10 February. He was worn out. Since becoming First Lord he had taken a back seat in the work of the Commission for Revising the Civil Affairs of the Navy. In this work he was content to be organised by John Fordyce, one of the other commissioners, who aimed to permit Britain to 'provide for a much greater navy than it ever had before', one 'on which our existence depends, more absolutely if possible than it ever did before'.[79] Fordyce and J D Thompson, overseen by Barham, eventually generated thirteen reports, eleven of which were adopted by the end of 1809, the year in which the Royal Navy reached its greatest numerical scale. Although the reports adhered generally to traditional principles, the eighth report on the dockyards contained directions for alterations that amounted, as the Navy Board acknowledged, to 'a total change of system'.[80] They formed the platform upon which the Royal Navy entered the nineteenth century, for much would remain as Barham directed for many decades.

Retrospect

Barham died in 1813. But he lived to see his reports adopted. Through their implementation he became the most influential naval administrator of the late eighteenth and early nineteenth centuries. As First Lord of the Admiralty and as first sea commissioner, both during challenging periods, he had already made his mark. The orderly management of the Trafalgar campaign bore the imprint of his meticulous organisation. The logistics of the campaign echoed his recommendations for the distribution of forces during the French Revolutionary war. On both occasions he brought to bear knowledge of the capabilities of the civil departments of the navy that was unrivalled. Even when out of office during the Revolutionary War, his confident advice to Pitt and Dundas made his an ever-present guiding hand.

Yet his greatest contribution was as Comptroller of the Navy between 1778 and 1790. In spite of delays in the reform of administration, he maintained control of the civil business of the navy through a period of danger and of expansion in the scale of operations. During the American War he foresaw the need to increase the power of the British navy by technological means as well as a building programme. Though the coppering of the fleet had its technological limitations, and the carronade was introduced too late in the war to make a significant impact in operations, both innovations affected morale and confidence in the British navy. At the same time, having unified under the Navy Board the supply and movement of troops by sea, Middleton was able to optimise Britain's capability of defending its empire overseas. So strengthened, the achievements of the navy made a significant contribution to the peace terms that were negotiated in 1783. If this was not enough, under his direction, the fleet was then thoroughly rebuilt by 1790 in preparation for war on an even greater scale.

His contemporaries found him a difficult character, one who never failed to speak his mind. His self–righteousness was trying. Nevertheless, he expressed in religious terms a standard of probity and efficiency that, partly through his work, became incorporated in the ethics of administration in the naval departments. In an age when the public service was struggling to free itself from the corrosive influence of private interest, Barham's qualities as an administrator and reformer were invaluable to the management of a bureaucracy demanding discipline, direction and adaptation to a growing scale of operations. His scruples were difficult to live with, even for himself. On the occasions of both his resignations in 1790 and 1795, he refused to remain in post when the disciplines of office were being undermined by politicians. Yet it was this attention to the punctilios of administration, combined with the breadth of his logistical understanding, that gave him his strength as a administrator.

He himself was not averse to playing politics to advance himself and his causes, but the latter were aimed in principle at benefiting the navy. For this purpose he always looked ahead. His epitaph might be 'forethought and preparation', terms he repeatedly dinned into the politicians with whom he had to work. Through his pursuit of this principle, his influence survived far longer than his actual service. The administrative machine he worked to improve between 1778 and his death in 1813 was the basis of British naval power well into the nineteenth century. It is too much to accord to Middleton alone an administration that permitted the British navy the capability of dominating the seas of the world after he died. Nevertheless, his contribution to the organisational foundation of that ascendancy was greater than that of any other single man.

John Jervis, Earl of St Vincent. Oil in the style of John Hoppner

13

John Jervis, Earl of St Vincent
1735-1823

'the very ablest Sea-Officer his Majesty has'

P K CRIMMIN

The Formation of a Naval Officer, 1748-1783

Although the Earl St Vincent became one of the foremost seamen and fleet organisers of his day, and helped shape the Victorian navy, Jervis had no familial connection with the service. His family, steadfast Whigs, were Staffordshire gentry. His father, Swynfen Jervis, a moderately successful lawyer, was appointed counsel to the Admiralty and auditor of Greenwich Hospital in 1747, possibly through a family connection with Lord Anson, then First Lord of the Admiralty. The move to Greenwich marked Jervis's first encounter with the navy. The impression on a boy of 13 was instant and irremovable. He had been intended for his father's profession but while Swynfen Jervis was absent from Greenwich on the northern circuit, the boy ran away from school, with a friend, and hid aboard a ship at Woolwich. After three days the hungry boys returned home but the young John refused to return to school. His mother's protests were undermined by the encouragement of the wife of the Governor of the Hospital, Lady Archibald Hamilton, who offered to get the boy entered in the Royal Navy, and by Lady Burlington, who recommended him to the Hon George Townshend, recently appointed commodore and naval commander-in-chief at Jamaica. In January 1749, with his uncle John Parker, Jervis saw Townshend, who agreed to take him on his flagship, the *Gloucester*, 50 guns, then at Portsmouth. He was entered on her muster book, as an able seaman, on 4 January and joined her on the 17th.[1]

When he returned to England in 1754 he was a midshipman and, within a year, lieutenant. In later life he often referred to this early period in the

West Indies as one of great hardship. His father, after an initial gift of £20, refused to help further and rejected a bill drawn on him by his son. The experience, which an ageing memory may have exaggerated, left Jervis with an ingrained dislike of debt and with habits of strict economy which he carried into command. Short of money and forced to live very simply, Jervis devoted himself to learning seamanship and navigation from the warrant officers of the ships in which he served.[2] These years developed self-reliance, a virtue he frequently commended in others, and a sympathy for those who possessed merit and ability but little money or influence; it was such men, often the sons of deserving officers, whom he sought to promote when he assumed command.

In his early career Jervis served under several capable, colourful and outspoken captains: Edward Wheeler in the *Sphinx*, 24 guns, between July and November 1754; and John Campbell, in the *Mary* yacht, then moored at Greenwich, from December 1754 to February 1755.[3] Later that year Jervis was third lieutenant in the *Nottingham*, 60 guns, sent to North America with Admiral Boscawen. He was impressed by Boscawen's humane concern for the health of his crews in the typhus epidemic that ravaged the fleet at Halifax; by the admiral's insistence on hygiene, on an adequate diet of fresh food, especially vegetables whenever possible, and with Boscawen's stern maintenance of firm discipline at that dispiriting time. In 1756 he served in the Mediterranean under Admiral Hawke's overall command, as fourth lieutenant in the *Prince*, 90 guns. He must have heard of Hawke's action, off Finisterre, in 1747, whilst he served in the *Gloucester*, since she had taken part in the battle only fifteen months before he joined her.[4] Within three years the victory of Quiberon Bay in November 1759 had made Hawke a national hero. His close blockade of Brest set the pattern for later blockades of that port, while his care of his men; his persistent demands for regular, plentiful supplies of fresh vegetables and good beer, was something Jervis imitated when blockading Brest between 1799 and 1801. The resolution and fighting spirit of Boscawen and Hawke, their successful methods, coupled with their humanity and attention to the health and welfare of their men, their discipline and the professional respect in which they were held, deeply impressed the young Jervis. All this taught him valuable lessons which he was to pass on to his protégés.

Jervis's career began to blossom with his appointment to the *Prince* in August 1756. Sir Charles Saunders, Treasurer of Greenwich Hospital in 1754-1766, and thus a colleague of Swyfen Jervis, was Comptroller of the Navy Board between November 1755 and June 1756 and later a member of the Board of Admiralty. He was promoted rear-admiral and sent to the

Mediterranean in 1756 as second in command to Hawke. When he hoisted his flag in the *Prince* in October, he promoted Jervis to third and, within a month, to second lieutenant. According to Horace Walpole, Saunders was 'a pattern of the most sturdy bravery united with the most unaffected modesty',[5] and an ideal patron for an able, ambitious young officer. When Saunders went to the *Culloden*, 74 in November 1756 he took Jervis with him as his second lieutenant and in June 1757, when he moved to the *St George*, 90, Jervis moved with him. Two years later Jervis was the admiral's first lieutenant in the *Neptune*, 90 in North America, where he was appointed commander of the sloop *Porcupine* in May 1759. During this time the British were assembling an army to attack Quebec and Jervis met General James Wolfe, who had command of the army. Jervis's promptness and decision impressed Wolfe, though the story of Jervis delivering Wolfe's last letters and keepsake to his betrothed is apocryphal. Jervis's contribution to the final assault on Quebec was to lead the advanced squadron guarding the transports past the fortress – a difficult and testing task. His successful exertions brought him promotion to post captain on 13 October 1760, when he was appointed to the command of the *Gosport*, 44 guns. For the remainder of the war he was engaged in the North Sea and on convoy duties to North America and the West Indies.

Peace inevitably brought unemployment, but in February 1769 Jervis dined with the King's brother, HRH the Duke of Gloucester. He learned that Sir Charles Saunders had told a mutual friend, Colonel Barré, that he had the greatest affection and regard for Jervis and thought there was 'no better Officer in the King's Naval Service'.[6] So it is unsurprising that in the same month Jervis was given command of the *Alarm* frigate, 32 guns. This was clearly a mark of Admiralty esteem. The *Alarm* was the first coppered warship and was under orders to carry bullion out to the Mediterranean for the English merchants at Genoa. Between 1771 and 1772 he again commanded the *Alarm* when the Duke of Gloucester cruised in her in the Mediterranean for his health. From both these expeditions Jervis learned a good deal about Mediterranean waters, which proved useful when he commanded there in the 1790s.

In 1772 he spent a year in France learning the language thoroughly and in 1773, with his friend Captain Samuel Barrington, he visited Russia, more particularly the dockyards and naval arsenal at Cronstadt to study the main Baltic ports, correcting and amplifying his own charts of the Baltic. In 1775 the two friends made a similar cruise to the west coast of France, from Brest to Bordeaux, gaining information about that area which again proved invaluable when Jervis commanded there in

1800-1801, though he then regretted not having also studied the land-ward approach to Brest.[7]

On 1 September 1775 Jervis was appointed to the *Foudroyant* of 80 guns, a French prize, taken in 1758, which he had helped to bring home from the Mediterranean that year. Still the largest two-decked ship in the navy, she was now a guardship at Portsmouth and here Jervis was based until 1778. In that year France joined the American colonies in their war for independence and this provided naval officers with fresh opportunities for employment. Jervis had brought the *Foudroyant* to a high pitch of efficiency and discipline. The Duke of Richmond, writing to Jervis in 1780 on behalf of a young relative he wished trained by him, declared 'if you will have the best education for young men on board your ship, you must expect to be plagued with requests of this nature'.[8]

Jervis served in Admiral Keppel's Channel Fleet in 1778 and took part in the indecisive battle of Ushant on 27 July. He was a firm supporter of Keppel in service and political matters, and his evidence at the latter's court martial in 1779, strongly in Keppel's favour, helped to acquit the admiral.[9] Unlike other officers at that time, Jervis did not refuse to serve while Lord Sandwich was head of the Admiralty, though he was very critical of Sandwich's administration in letters to friends. He was mortified at having to retreat before the Franco-Spanish fleet's attempted invasion of 1779,[10] but on 19 April 1782, when off Brest in Admiral Barrington's squadron, he took the *Pégase* (74 guns), part of an escort to a French convoy, in a single-ship action of under an hour. Only five men were wounded in *Foudroyant*, one of them Jervis himself, while *Pégase*, under-manned and newly commissioned, suffered heavy casualties. For this action he was rewarded with a KB in May and became more widely known outside the service.[11]

Parliament and Connections, 1783-1793

With peace in 1783 he entered Parliament, for the pocket borough of Launceston, Cornwall, on the Duke of Northumberland's interest. This was through the influence of his friend and political patron, the Earl of Shelburne.[12] His friendship with Shelburne, one of the subtlest political minds of the day, casts an interesting light on Jervis. He shared both the earl's political opinions and his preoccupation with eliminating inefficiency and waste from government. Like Shelburne, Jervis believed in moderate parliamentary reform; he supported William Pitt the younger's proposals of May 1783 and 1785 and those of the opposition in May 1793, all of them unsuccessful. He also believed in religious toleration, supported an unsuccessful attempt to repeal the Test Act in 1791 and believed in granting a measure of political emancipation to Roman Catholics.[13] But Jervis, like Nelson, did not believe in the abolition of the slave trade. Although, when at Genoa, he had defended two Turkish slaves forcibly removed from the *Alarm*'s boat, where they had taken sanctuary, and by his threats of retaliation against the city had them released and freed, it was the insult to the British flag he had resented, not the institution of slavery.[14]

Jervis gave his support to Pitt on several important issues in the 1780s. He voted against Fox's East India Bill in November 1783 and was reckoned a Pittite in the general election of 1784, when he was returned for Great Yarmouth as a government candidate. He again supported Pitt over the Regency crisis in 1788. He spoke infrequently in the Commons, chiefly on naval matters, and championed the navy as the supreme defender of the nation. In February 1786 he voted against the Duke of Richmond's expensive fortification plans, which he had already opposed when a member of the commission of enquiry on them. In March 1786 he inveighed against the inefficiency of naval administration, declaring himself anxious to 'root up and totally prevent the growth of evils so enormous and alarming'.[15] In 1787 he supported the claims of Captain David Brodie (1709-1787) to the promotion to which his seniority seemed to entitle him but which the current rules refused because Brodie had not served during the previous war. The case led to a modification of such rules, and from thenceforward captains who were not eligible for promotion when their turn arrived were distinctly placed on a superannuated list.[16] In December 1792 he introduced and obtained government support for a scheme to relieve distressed superannuated seamen and in February 1793 urged the Commons to consider the hardship suffered by newly commissioned officers on the late payment of their subsistence money. But Jervis did not support Pitt's warlike policies and though promoted to rear-admiral of the blue on 24 September 1787, and of the white on 21 September 1790, hoisting his flag during both the Dutch and Spanish armaments, in 1787 and 1790, he did not agree with them. In 1790 he had accepted a seat at Chipping Wycombe from Shelburne, now Marquess of Lansdowne. Like many in opposition in 1793, he believed Pitt was provoking war with France and he did not attend the debates in February 1793 on the outbreak of war. Rumours of Lansdowne's political influence on him and 'narrow prejudice' on account of Jervis's known opposition to the war, led him to resign his seat in January 1794 and he did not stand for Parliament again.[17] Given his attitude towards the war, Jervis's appointment to the command of a joint expedition against the French West Indies in the autumn of 1793 was, at first sight, surprising. However, he had offered his services to government and the choice of suitable officers was not extensive. Moreover, Jervis had served in the West Indies. He was a highly competent officer with a proven record, and a friend and political ally of the army commander Sir Charles Grey, who had been appointed in August.

The West Indies and the Mediterranean, 1794–1797

Since 1 February 1793 Jervis had been vice-admiral of the blue. He hoisted his flag on the *Boyne*, 98, with George Grey, Sir Charles's son, as his flag captain and arrived at Barbadoes in January 1794. At first all went well. Relations between the army and navy were cordial, and Martinique, Guadeloupe and St Lucia were taken during March and April 1794. But then French reinforcements recaptured Guadeloupe from British forces, which were seriously reduced by fever, and the British were soon on the defensive. Jervis's own health suffered and in November 1794 he was relieved by Vice-Admiral Caldwell and returned home in February 1795. It was a flawed homecoming. The reputations of both Jervis and Grey were damaged by their behaviour as captors of the French sugar islands and their rapacious attitude to the resulting prize money and appointments which followed their first success. They alienated French royalist support in the islands and made it easier for a republican counter-attack to succeed. Their conduct towards neutrals, particularly the Americans trading in the Caribbean, roused strong diplomatic protests. Although both commanders defended their conduct, and a motion of censure against them in the Commons in May 1795 was defeated, neither Jervis nor Grey got the peerages they might have expected.[18] Though Jervis was promoted admiral of the blue on 1 June 1795, the West Indian campaign might well have been the end of his career. In fact, the most significant part lay ahead, and with it the conjunction with Nelson with its momentous consequences for both.

Even if the government had been reluctant to re-employ Jervis, events at the Admiralty and in the Mediterranean forced their hand. In the summer of 1794 Pitt strengthened his government by a coalition with the major part of the opposition. Cabinet posts were found for several of them, including Earl Spencer, who replaced Lord Chatham, Pitt's brother, as First Lord of the Admiralty in December. His relations with Admiral Hood, commander-in-chief in the Mediterranean, became increasingly strained. Hood resigned his command in May 1795. The state of health of Vice-Admiral Hotham, his successor, led to his recall in the summer of 1795. The command was thereupon first offered to Admiral Duncan, who refused but recommended Jervis, a friend and officer he had admired since their service together between 1778-9. Lord Hugh Seymour, a member of Spencer's Board of Admiralty, also recommended Jervis to Spencer as 'an officer of rare merit' who would bring credit on the minister who employed him.[19] This was no small consideration to a minister, new to office, who had already alienated part of the service by his treatment of Lord Hood. Spencer told George III that Jervis was generally thought the admiral best able to deal with the difficult situation in the Mediterranean.[20] This prediction proved correct.

Jervis left England in the frigate *Lively* on 11 November and joined the fleet on 30 November 1795 at San Fiorenzo Bay, Corsica. It is often said that no sooner had the smoke from the salute to the flag cleared than the admiral gave the signal to unmoor,[21] but there was much to do before he did so. On 4 December he transferred to the *Victory*, 100 and it was not until 13 December that the signal to unmoor was made. It was a fleet which contained a number of junior captains soon to be famous; not only Nelson but Collingwood, Troubridge, Sam Hood, Fremantle and others, though Jervis knew few of them at that time.[22] Expelled from their temporary occupation of Toulon at the end of 1793, the British had occupied Corsica since 1794, basing the fleet at San Fiorenzo. During 1795 French squadrons from Toulon had evaded Hotham's loose blockade and played havoc with British trade throughout the Mediterranean. The French were preparing to carry the war to the rich Italian states the following year, opposed by a supine and under-equipped Austrian army. Jervis's first task was to mount an effective blockade of Toulon, where there were fifteen French sail of the line. He could never spare more than thirteen of his own ships for this task, sometimes only eleven because of the numerous calls on them. An inshore squadron under Captain Troubridge was set to attacking shore batteries and cruising some three miles off the harbour mouth. Another squadron, under Nelson, was sent to help the Austrians in their attempt to deny the Ligurian coast road to the French. Jervis had also to defend Corsica, co-operating with Sir Gilbert Elliot, the viceroy. Furthermore, he had to protect British trade throughout the Mediterranean and the Levant, as well as Austria's Adriatic possessions. He had to cover Leghorn and its supplies of naval stores and food. To do this he had to maintain and refit his fleet – a difficult task when the nearest British naval base was at Gibraltar, which was itself ill supplied. Moreover, Spain had made peace with France in August 1795 and was shortly expected to join her against Britain. If so, Gibraltar would be threatened.

When Jervis reached the fleet he realised that it could no longer remain passive at San Fiorenzo or Leghorn. Jervis began drilling and reforming it at once, cruising off Toulon, Corsica or in the gulf of Genoa. In the first month ships were constantly reminded to exercise in different evolutions, to form their order of sailing correctly, keep in close order, making more sail and to exercise at least five of their guns every day.[23] A second cruise between 19 February and 24 March 1796 continued this routine; ordering ships to preserve a proper distance between each other while in sailing order, ensuring all officers were at their stations, day or night, while wearing or tacking the ship.[24] Sprinkled throughout the record of these events and the weekly routine of the fleet were the phrases 'with utmost dispatch', 'without a moment's loss of time', and 'with the utmost expedition'. From now on repairs were made at sea[25] and stores delivered to ships to prevent them leaving their station and missing the enemy. Shortage of stores was a most serious problem, so a general order to captains in January 1796 urged the 'utmost frugality' in their use. In July the same frugality in the use of coal and candles was demanded.[26] In August 1796, in the eighteenth week of a cruise, Jervis asked the Navy Board for nails, timber, leather, lead and twine, for want of which threads were drawn from new canvas or from the breeching and tackle of guns in the great cabins of three-deckers, converted into oakum and spun into twine. He continued, in a tone which foreshadowed his later relations with the Board, 'We desire credit, though we have not found it from a Board where in former times much narrowness of Principle obtained but which in this more enlightened Age we conceived liberality of Sentiment would have produced praise for our Industry, Resources and Frugality'.[27] To avoid going into port, the whole fleet was caulked at sea in this period, a considerable feat.[28]

Since the fleet was 2000 men under strength when Jervis joined it, he determined sickness should not reduce it further. On 7 December 1795, only a week after he arrived at San Fiorenzo, he made the signal for the Physician of the Fleet. Further signals for him on 17 January, 6 and 18 February 1796 indicated health was to be a priority.[29] Surgeons were ordered to pay the strictest attention to the sick on board ship, and to visit them every day if sent to hospital, weather permitting.[30] Regular supplies of fresh food, including onions and lemons as anti-scorbutics, were ordered from Leghorn, Genoa and Barcelona. This was expensive but 'no price is too great to preserve the health of the fleet'.[31] Soap was issued, first to the sick berths, then generally from September 1796. The establishment and inspection of hospitals at Leghorn and Ajaccio, and improvements to the hospital at Gibraltar, raised morale and cut the sick list. Jervis harried the Navy and Victualling Boards to send adequate supplies of bedding and slop clothing, especially flannel drawers and waistcoats, jackets and hats.[32] He pressed the Sick and Hurt Board to send sufficient medicines, and when the latter were not forthcoming, wrote to William Cookworthy, a druggist at Plymouth to supply them.[33] Such a regime enabled him to blockade Toulon for twenty-seven weeks and he prided himself, justly, on this achievement.[34] But Britain's position in the Mediterranean was becoming untenable. The French army under Bonaparte proved unstoppable. In April 1796 Sardinia was forced to leave the allied coalition and cede Savoy and Nice to France. Bonaparte outflanked the Austrians, entered Milan on 15 May, and occupied Piedmont and Lombardy. Naples was forced to leave the allied coalition, withdrawing her troops and ships. The French then invaded Tuscany and captured the port of Leghorn on 27 June. Though Captain Fremantle swiftly evacuated British shipping, stores and people there, a source of fresh food and other supplies was closed and Corsica was directly threatened. Nelson's tiny squadron was directed to blockade Leghorn and seized Elba on 10 July 1796 to use Porto Ferrajo as a base.

The Battle of Cape St Vincent, February 1797

Jervis was already concentrating his forces to meet the increasing likelihood of a threat from a combined Franco-Spanish fleet. In July 1796 the admiral had ordered Rear-Admiral Man, then blockading Cadiz with seven sail of the line, to join him. However, Man, already in the throes of a nervous collapse, did not take on stores at Gibraltar, so his arrival at Corsica, far from being a welcome relief, made the situation worse in the main fleet. Jervis sent Man back to recover this mistake, but on 1 October Man met the Spanish admiral de Langara and his Cadiz squadron, heading for Car-thagena. Man was chased into Gibraltar. A total prey to nervous fears, he called his captains to a council of war and, despite Jervis's orders to rejoin him, Man sailed for England. Unaware of this, Jervis's position was very hazardous. The Cabinet had decided in late August to evacuate Corsica and orders to that effect reached Jervis on 25 September. Spain declared war on Britain on 8 October and de Langara, with a force of twenty-six sail, now made for Toulon to join the French. Jervis was completely outnumbered. For a fortnight he waited for Man at San Fiorenzo, with British merchant ships from the Levant. On 2 November, taking the merchantmen in tow, he sailed for Gibraltar. From 27 September, because of shortages, the fleet had been on one-third allowance of biscuit and flour, two-thirds allowance of all other food except wine, but despite the cold and tempestuous weather 'the People have been much pinched but have not complained'.[35] In fact, though storms and head winds lengthened the voyage, the fleet's confidence was high. 'They at home', Nelson wrote to his wife, 'do not

know what this fleet is capable of performing; anything and everything
. . . of all the fleets I ever saw, I never saw one, in point of officers and
men, equal to Sir John Jervis's, who is a commander able to lead them to
glory.'[36]

The fleet reached Gibraltar on 1 December and was immediately victualled and put on full allowance. A few days later a severe gale hit them,
wrecking the *Courageux*, and seriously damaging the *Zealous* and *Gibraltar*.
But the dockyard at Gibraltar offered few facilities for repair or supply and
by the end of the month Jervis, his force reduced to ten sail of the line, had
withdrawn to Lisbon. Based here, it was hoped he could prevent a conjunction of the Spanish and French fleets in any projected invasion attempts
on Britain, protect the Portuguese trade and defend Gibraltar. In Britain
public confidence in the navy had been shaken. French success in Italy; the
consequent evacuation of the Mediterranean; the attempted French invasion of Ireland in December 1796, frustrated by the weather rather than the
Channel Fleet, contributed to an invasion scare early in 1797, which produced a run on the Bank of England and a suspension of cash payments.
Jervis's remark just before the battle of St Vincent, 'A victory is very
essential to England at this moment', was a just appreciation of the
situation.[37]

The combined Franco–Spanish fleet left Toulon in December 1796. The
French pushed through the Straits, blown by the gale which damaged
Jervis's ships, but the Spaniards put into Carthagena. Their freedom of
manoeuvre was limited by having to escort to Cadiz four ships carrying
mercury (essential to the refining of silver), and when, after passing the
Straits, they were blown further into the Atlantic than they wished, they
were forced to beat back towards Cadiz. Jervis, cruising off Cape St Vincent, had been reinforced by five ships under Rear-Admiral Sir William
Parker, which brought his numbers up to fifteen. Nelson, coming from the
evacuation of Elba in the *Minerve* frigate, sailed through the Spanish fleet
unobserved on the night of 11 February and joined the British fleet on the
13th with news of the nearness of the Spaniards. The British anticipated a
successful action. On the eve of battle the toast at dinner on the flagship
was, 'Victory over the Dons, in the battle from which they cannot escape
tomorrow'.[38]

As the number of Spanish ships were revealed the following morning,
through the dissolving mist, it became obvious that Jervis faced a force almost
double his own. But his opponent's ships were seriously short of stores of all
sorts and poorly manned. The Spanish admiral de Cordoba's flagship, the
Santisíma Trinidad of 136 guns, was reputed to have only 60 experienced

seamen out of a crew of 900. Jervis's fleet, though numerically inferior, was infinitely more experienced and confident and he refused to be daunted by mere numbers. When the total enemy force reported to him reached twenty-seven ships, he declared, 'Enough sir, no more of that: the die is cast, and if there are fifty sail I will go through them.'[39] During the opening moves of the battle a gap opened in the Spanish line, separating the main body of ships from the convoy and escort. 'Like a hawk to his prey', according to Collingwood, the British made for this gap. *Culloden*, 74, Captain Troubridge, reached it before the Spaniards could close it and enabled the following ships to divide the Spanish fleet in two.

As the battle developed, Jervis signalled his ships to close with the larger of these divisions. Close-range fighting took place as Admiral Moreno tried to frustrate this manoeuvre by engaging the British centre, and though beaten off, a gap now opened in the British line which the shifting wind widened. Jervis altered course to the northwest, perhaps with the aim of doubling the main Spanish division, catching them between his centre and van. At the same time he wished his rear division to get into action quickly, in support of his leading ships, now about to engage the enemy. However, gunsmoke was obscuring the view, naval signals were not able to convey the admiral's exact intentions and some of the rear division, led by Vice-Admiral Sir Charles Thompson, did not respond. The mutual confidence and understanding between Jervis and Nelson, which had steadily developed through 1796, now enabled Nelson to divine Jervis's intentions, and, 'in an act of inspired initiative that has rightly won him universal praise',[40] Nelson wore out of the line and joined his colleagues in the van attacking the Spanish centre.

His courageous action turned the scale and forced de Cordoba to abandon his move towards the British rear. A mêlée developed, as the British ships overtook and engaged the Spaniards in a series of very close engagements, often at pistol shot length, and when it was broken off in the late afternoon four Spanish ships had been taken. Two, the *San Josef* and the *San Nicolas*, having been heavily engaged by five British ships, were finally boarded and subdued by Nelson; four others were badly damaged. Neither side chose to renew the action the following day. When, at the end of the action, Nelson visited the flagship, his face still streaked with powder and sweat, his clothes in tatters, the admiral hugged him and 'said he could not sufficiently thank me and used every expression to make me happy'.[41] It was an unusually demonstrative gesture on Jervis's part but fully expressed his satisfaction. Calder's criticism, that Nelson's behaviour had been contrary to orders, missed the essential point, for though Jervis valued obedience, he also valued initiative. Calder received a sharp snub: 'It certainly was so and if you ever commit such a breach of orders I will forgive you also.'⁴²

For the British navy the victory was 'a psychological triumph; for the Spanish a psychological defeat',⁴³ for though the Spanish fleet was not destroyed, Jervis declared them 'palsied from that hour'.⁴⁴ Earlier in February it was intended to grant Jervis a peerage, in recognition of his achievements in the Mediterranean. Now he was created Baron Jervis of Meaford in Staffordshire, and Earl of St Vincent on 23 June 1797. He had modestly suggested he should bear the title Yarmouth, 'wishing to avoid an appearance of arrogance in naming the action as my title', but the King himself chose that of St Vincent. In addition, he was granted a pension of £3000 and a gold medal. The City of London awarded him a fine sword and its freedom, both Houses of Parliament gave him their thanks, and addresses and thanks poured in from major ports.⁴⁵

St Vincent and the Naval Mutinies

The fleet's battle damage was repaired, first at Lagos and then, more fully, at Lisbon. Ships were ordered to refit completely for sea without loss of time,⁴⁶ to bottle up the shattered Spanish fleet in Cadiz. Here St Vincent instituted a close blockade, the main body of the fleet cruising off Cape St Vincent, before Cadiz or at Gibraltar, while an inshore squadron of seven ships was always before the port.⁴⁷ But the strain on men and ships was considerable and made worse by the effects of the fleet mutinies at home, in April and May 1797, which began to spread to the Mediterranean Fleet.

St Vincent was warned by the Admiralty to look out for mutiny in his own ships⁴⁸ and took immediate steps. He believed that idleness and boredom encouraged mutiny, so there was no relaxation in port. Ships' companies were kept occupied, bombarding Cadiz nightly from launches and gunboats. 'We are carrying on a desultory kind of warfare to divert the animal.'⁴⁹ At the same time Nelson, with a squadron of seven ships, was sent to attack Santa Cruz at Tenerife in July 1797. He was to carry the war to Spain, capture a homeward bound galleon, and thus divert men with action and the opportunity for prize money. There were disturbances and mutinous outbreaks on individual ships, the best known on the *St George* in July, quelled by her captain, Shuldham Peard, and his first lieutenant. The ringleaders, tried and sentenced on Saturday the 8th, were not hanged until the following day, because of the lateness of the proceedings. Executions on a Sunday were against custom and St Vincent was publicly rebuked by Rear-Admiral Sir Charles Thompson for ordering them. For this St

Vincent insisted Thompson either be sent home or he himself recalled, and the Admiralty chose the former course.[50]

Nevertheless, the situation worsened in 1798. News of a large French expedition, destination unknown, preparing at Toulon, decided the government to send a squadron into the Mediterranean to discover what the French were about. Lord Spencer and St Vincent, independently, thought Nelson fittest to command it.[51] Nelson, fully recovered from the loss of his arm at Tenerife, joined the fleet off Cadiz on 30 April, bringing new life to St Vincent. But Nelson was a very junior rear-admiral and his appointment to command an independent squadron sent on such a significant mission aroused violent protests and resentments amongst his seniors, chiefly Rear-Admiral Sir John Orde. This led to Orde being sent home by St Vincent, without Admiralty sanction, an action that earned him a rebuke from the Board, which offended him deeply.[52] Orde retained his resentment and when St Vincent returned home in 1799 challenged him to a duel, only prevented by George III forbidding St Vincent to accept.[53]

While Nelson disappeared into the Mediterranean, the commander-in-chief dealt with the serious disaffection which had spread to his ships. He had reduced his own strength to provide Nelson with a squadron of ten ships, 'the elite of the fleet'. They were replaced on 25 May by reinforcements under Sir Roger Curtis, many of which had been involved in mutinies at home, while some had broken out into fresh disturbances *en route*. St Vincent once declared responsibility to be the test of a man's courage and he now refused to appear afraid or overwhelmed by the situation. He insisted on the prompt delivery of letters from home, some of them known to be from the mutineers at the Nore, and when Captain Dacres of the *Barfleur* suggested they be withheld he refused, saying 'I dare say the Commander in Chief will know how to support his own authority.'[54] This proved to be the case in succeeding months.

St Vincent forbade all communication between his ships and those newly arrived from Britain, without his express permission. Where necessary, one of the captains trained by him in the Mediterranean was transferred to a newly arrived ship to bring it back to good order. Punishment quickly followed breaches of discipline for all ranks. Not even divisional commanders were exempt from public reprimand if they disobeyed the flagship's orders. In July he publicly censured officers whose misconduct, in command of boats of the fleet, resulted in the capture of a British launch by Spanish gunboats, and threatened court martial for future lapses. Lieutenants and inferior officers were reminded that the drum, beating to quarters, applied to them as well as to the men and that in future the only excuse tolerated for non-attendance would be a duly certified sick note.[55] The admiral had always insisted on traditional dress and modes of behaviour. He imposed these standards on joining the fleet in 1795. He reimposed it now on the newly joined ships. At daily mustering crews were to be properly dressed; hats were to be removed while the National Anthem was played and the flag raised, or when men were formally punished. Officers were always to salute the quarterdeck on coming aboard, and to remove their hats when speaking to a superior, not merely touching it 'in a negligent way'. They were to appear in full uniform at musterings and be properly dressed at all times. A standing order of November 1797 rebuked officers for wearing coloured clothes and round hats and threatened them with arrest and confinement to their ships on a second offence.[56] St Vincent himself always wore his star of the Order of the Bath and stood with his hat raised above his head when speaking or listening to anyone on his quarter-deck. For the admiral recognised the importance of outward, visible signs of respect for traditional forms and behaviour and knew that dress 'makes a statement'. If mutiny was to be crushed, officers must also respect authority.

Those ships, like the *Marlborough*, which appeared unwilling to hang their condemned mutineers, were surrounded by launches armed with carronades, and orders given to fire into the mutinous ships until all resistance ceased, if need be.[57] St Vincent also relied on the loyalty of the Marines. In May 1798 he called the Marine captains to the flagship, ordered them to watch their men, forbid the speaking of Irish, visit them at meals, call the roll twice a day and encourage the men to take pride in their regimental traditions and achievements. In July all captains were ordered to support the Marines, and separate them from the seamen. In three-decked ships they were to be berthed in the after part of the middle deck, and in two-deckers close to the bulkhead of the gunroom or officers' cabins.[58] While St Vincent never overlooked crimes or breaches of discipline, he never punished for trifles and forbade the harassing of men with those illicit punishments, like starting, which were a major grievance of seamen. There is evidence that he disliked his role. 'Do they think that I will be hangman to the fleet?' he once exclaimed.[59] But he maintained it and was prepared, in this crisis, to punish with the utmost rigour. In 1799 Sir Edward Pellew joined St Vincent from the Channel Fleet. There his ship, the *Impetueux*, had mutinied; Pellew asked for a court martial but the commander-in-chief, Lord Bridport, refused it and sent him to join St Vincent's command. When he arrived Pellew again requested a court martial on the mutineers. This was held, the men found guilty, and sentenced to death. One disclosed further evidence of mutiny planned in Bridport's fleet and Pellew pleaded for this man's reprieve, on the basis of his previous good character. But St Vincent was adamant, declaring that he would convince seamen 'that no character however good shall save a man who is guilty of mutiny',[60] and the man was hanged.

In the modern climate of opinion which emphasises 'concern' at the cost of 'respect', especially for authority, such accounts make grim, even repulsive reading. But some of the officers under St Vincent's command were unable to control their crews, either through weakness, fear or a desire not to proceed to extremes, and while some officers felt seamen had grievances, all had been shaken by the mutinies. Acts of mutiny were not uncommon in ships, often being little more than disobedience brought about by drunkenness or by feelings of injustice over particular issues. Captains often dealt with these in an *ad hoc* way and punishments were generally not unduly severe. But the 1797-9 mutinies were more serious because more widespread and seemingly co-ordinated. In such a situation those with strong nerves, determination and an absolute belief in complete obedience to traditional naval discipline fared best.

Not all senior officers were so blessed. Mutinous crews were not St Vincent's sole problem. 'Factious discontents' in some officers, like Thompson or Orde, and incompetence, or loss of nerve, were also problems. Sir Robert Calder, though an efficient seaman and an economical captain of the fleet, had no *'fortiter in re'* according to St Vincent and 'shrank from the audacity of the United Irishmen . . . and sacrificed discipline to the popularity of the moment'.[61] Captain Darby of the *Bellerophon* spoilt his crew intolerably and had annoyed St Vincent 'by his weak conduct towards them, and is laughed at by his own and all other People'. Sir Charles Knowles's 'imbecility' was responsible for the disorder in the *Britannia*.[62] Such comments reveal an officer corps not whole-hearted in its response to mutiny or to the responsibilities of command. The behaviour and character of the commander-in-chief was therefore all important. In a real sense, St Vincent was reimposing traditional values on his officers, as well as their crews. Hence his enthusiasm for those junior officers, Nelson, Troubridge and others, who met his own high standards. Their virtues appealed to the admiral; attention to duty, a professionalism honed by uncomplaining hard work and a stoic, cheerful acceptance of danger.

However, St Vincent's attitude towards the suppression of mutiny was not merely punitive. He was concerned to improve the conditions of seamen, and while this concern did not spring from affection, it was effective. Thus he had sick bays specially fitted up in each ship and surgeons were ordered to attend the sick regularly. He insisted on the regular issue of clean clothing, particularly warm flannel next the skin, and adequate bedding, regularly aired. When a shortage of tobacco raised the price beyond what pursers could afford, St Vincent made good the gap from his own pocket and at times he gave sums of money to deserving, needy seamen.[63] To try and counteract excessive drinking and gambling while ashore, he subscribed towards a library at Gibraltar and pushed hard for its building.[64] Throughout this difficult period, work to improve Gibraltar dockyard also went forward actively. It was forced to play a major role in refitting Nelson's squadron after the battle of the Nile, since St Vincent had no intention of sending ships home unless absolutely necessary. Existing watering arrangements at the Ragged Staff were improved; the approach was deepened and commanders of vessels there ordered to attend in order of seniority to maintain order and method. New water tanks were begun in 1799. The careening pits were repaired. Each battleship sent an experienced shipwright to work in the yard, who remained there till work was completed. On Nelson's strong recommendation a Portuguese shipwright, Joaquim, later anglicised to Joe King, knowing the language and methods of the yard artificers, was made boatswain of the yard. St Vincent himself was often in the yard before dawn, seeing which crews were most diligent at their work, whether the artificers were punctual and a proper watch kept, and he gave orders that the guards were not to salute him, so that he might watch the work of the yard unobserved.[65]

Amidst all this hard driving there were great successes. Nelson found and defeated the French fleet at the Battle of the Nile on 1 August 1798 and thwarted Napoleon's plans for India. In November 1798 Commodore Duckworth captured Minorca and thus gave Britain the Mediterranean naval base she had lacked since 1796. But St Vincent's health finally broke down under the strain; he was plagued with rheumatism, dropsy and a violent cough. There was an unsatisfactory period when Vice-Admiral Lord Keith, coming out with reinforcements as his probable successor, was in charge of active operations, while St Vincent tried to control events from Gibraltar and Minorca. But he finally resigned the command on 21 June 1799. On 31 July he left for England, in the *Argo*, arriving there on 16 August and striking his flag on the 19th in strong gales and squally rain.[66]

In Command of the Channel Fleet, 1800

A few months in the peace of Rochetts, his Essex home, and at Bath, saw an improvement in his health, and emboldened Lord Spencer to make a personal visit to Bath to ask him to take command of the Channel Fleet.

Despite the objections of his personal physician, Dr Andrew Baird, St Vincent accepted. 'The King and Government require it, and the discipline of the British Navy demands it. It is of no consequence to me whether I die afloat or ashore: the die is cast.'[67] George Grey was again appointed his flag captain, Troubridge his captain of the fleet. The admiral left England in the *Namur* on 26 April 1800 and, arriving off Ushant, hoisted his flag at first in the *Royal George* until the *Ville de Paris* joined in October.[68]

He was inevitably unpopular in a fleet still simmering with mutiny and in which officers had become accustomed to the milder rule of Lord Bridport. Almost at once Admiral Sir Alan Gardner expressed his annoyance at not being given the command, having served most of his career on that station. St Vincent asked for Gardner's removal and in August Gardner struck his flag.[69]

So it was with a distinct sense of *déjà vu* that St Vincent resumed the task of reintroducing acceptable standards and traditional values. The problem he faced was summed up in the toast drunk, without rebuke, at Admiral Lord Bridport's table, by the officers of that fleet: 'May the discipline of the Mediterranean Fleet never be introduced into the Channel Fleet'. Little support could be hoped for from such officers, though St Vincent wrote to all his admirals and captains requesting their co-operation.[70] He also re-issued every order he had introduced into the Mediterranean Fleet to enforce discipline and good ship management. It was an uphill task and he asked Spencer for some of his old Mediterranean captains, 'instead of the old women, some of them in the shape of young men, I am burthened with'.[71]

The dilatoriness of frigate captains in port annoyed him greatly, but senior officers too were guilty. The fleet had often left Torbay to cruise without some of the captains and in the early days of St Vincent's command one admiral was left ashore after attending a ball in the neighbourhood.[72] This resulted in a general order forbidding any officer going further than three miles from shore and no boat being allowed on shore after sunset. Captains who had the guard were to be present at all times during the watering of the fleet, not to leave their post till relieved and be accompanied by a Marine officer to prevent straggling or the bringing of liquor into boats.[73] Ships sent in to port, to be re-victualled and paid, were not permitted to remain more than a week, but even this proved too long and all officers were forbidden to sleep on shore. All this was deeply unpopular with officers' wives. The familiar story of one of them giving 'in full coterie' a 'bumper toast, "May his [St Vincent's] next glass of wine choke the wretch!" ', expressed their resentment.[74]

But as well as inducing a more professional approach to their duties amongst the officers, a serious problem of desertion of seamen was checked by this order. Some captains had given indiscriminate leave. This had caused resentment amongst those not so favoured and wholesale desertion in certain ships. To those captains who protested, St Vincent replied that if they could not bear to be parted from their wives in wartime they should retire. Some senior officers wrote to Lord Spencer to complain of the admiral's harshness and Spencer urged moderation. But St Vincent replied, 'I have great confidence in your judgement but the *suaviter in modo* will not do here. I have tried it in vain.'[75]

St Vincent also restored the close blockade of Brest instituted by Hawke and it was now to be invested with the same rigour Cadiz had experienced. Instead of a rendezvous at Torbay, the fleet was now to be 'well in with Ushant with an easterly wind'.[76] The main British force, between twenty-four to thirty-four ships, was stationed there. A squadron of approximately five ships was stationed between the Black Rocks and the Parquette shoal, an area full of hidden rocks and reefs, and exposed to the prevailing south-westerly winds. They were supported by three more, between Ushant and the Black Rocks. Frigates and cutters cruised between the advanced squadron and the Goulet, or were stationed at key points to prevent supplies reaching the port, and other frigates and sloops were placed along the coast of the Bay of Biscay from Isle Dieu to Cape Finisterre.[77] St Vincent's object was to seal Brest and ensure the inshore squadron was not driven off station without bringing on a general action with the French fleet. On 17–18 May 1800 a hurricane scattered the fleet from this dangerous station. Orders were instantly issued to refit and water with all possible speed, and the fleet returned shortly, to maintain its station for an unbroken 121 days.

Such a strict blockade would have been impossible without healthy ships. These were supervised by Dr Baird, who acted as unofficial Physician of the Fleet, and who assiduously visited all ships, enforcing the regular issue of lemon juice to eliminate outbreaks of scurvy. Cleanliness also played a large part in the maintenance of health. Hog sties were removed from the upper decks of ships and the space used as a sick bay, for the surgeon to see patients and issue medicines. Dry scrubbing with hot sand, rather than washing the lower decks, helped to eliminate damp, and bedding was aired weekly, weather permitting, the frequency being entered in the log. When he became First Lord of the Admiralty St Vincent ordered the substitution of hair mattresses for the lumpy, often mouldy, cotton flock ones then issued.[78] He urged that flannel be worn next the skin to mitigate rheumatism. Vaccination was offered to all who wished it.

Surgeons and their mates were to be attentive to their duties, carrying their pocket instruments with them at all times, afloat or ashore.[79] When he had commanded in the Mediterranean the admiral had deplored 'the passion for amputation which pervades all our Hospitals', urging 'a little more patience and perseverance might save some limbs and ulcerous complaints'.[80] Now there were sharp rebukes for those who did not measure up to this standard. The surgeon of the *Pompee* 'is a butcher of men and I impute the deaths of all who have been lost to the King's service in the *Pompee* to him.'[81] St Vincent had always considered the care of the sick one of the first duties of a commander-in-chief and his efforts produced tangible results.[82] In November 1800, when the fleet came into Torbay, the Sick and Hurt Board made their customary extra preparations to receive the large numbers of sick expected after extended cruising. It was thought Plymouth hospital would be overwhelmed and quarters were rented in the vicinity to accommodate the sick. But there were only 16 hospital cases out of 23,000 men.[83] The young officer who had seen fleets in which he served ravaged by sickness and disease, as admiral had helped to effect a revolution in seamen's health of which he was justly proud, and had given an example which pupils like Nelson whole-heartedly followed.

These measures contained the disaffection in the fleet and to some extent subdued it. But the price was eternal vigilance. Once more St Vincent placed his trust in the Marines and their Mediterranean orders were re-issued.[84] Moreover, because he thought staying in port destructive of confidence and order, the fleet now cruised regularly. 'My maxim is to keep the squadron in constant movement. We never bring to.'[85] Incessant manoeuvring off a dangerous coast, against tides, currents and winds, meant a need for good seamanship at all times. Captains were expected to be on deck when these manoeuvres were performed and St Vincent's presence with the fleet allowed him to see how the fleet behaved and correct any faults. In such circumstances he was once found by his secretary in the flagship's stern galley, on a wild night, clad only in a flannel dressing gown and cocked hat, watching the fleet tacking in succession. When Tucker begged him to return to his cabin, for the sake of his health, the admiral replied, 'Hush, sir, Hush! I want to see how the evolution is performed in such a night of weather and to know whether Jemmy [Captain Vashon of the *Neptune* next astern] is on deck,' and hearing Vashon's shrill voice giving the order, he said, 'Aye, that will do' and retired.[86]

Spithead he considered too far to go for supplies and Plymouth was substituted, but most repairs were effected at sea. No ship was allowed into port unless for dire emergency, and even then only for a limited time.

Under such rigorous training seamanship and health improved, so that, as Edward Pellew wrote to his brother in 1801, 'We make nothing now of a six month cruise. We have only been six days in port for the last six months.'[87] Nelson rightly claimed that St Vincent had 'taught us to keep the seamen healthy without going into port and to stay at sea for years without a refit.'[88] But once more, this work took its toll of the admiral's health and he was forced to live ashore, within the three-mile limit, at Torre Abbey during the winter of 1800–1801.

St Vincent as First Lord of the Admiralty

The resignation of William Pitt early in 1801, partly over the issue of Roman Catholic emancipation, led to the formation of a new ministry under Henry Addington, opposed to the issue, on 5 February. St Vincent's support for emancipation was well known, but a private interview with the King convinced him that he could serve in Addington's administration without sacrificing this principle. He therefore accepted office as First Lord of the Admiralty on 20 February, though not without some misgivings. 'I have known many a good Admiral make a wretched First Lord of the Admiralty,' he wrote to Lord Keith.[89] He is said to have consulted Lansdowne, who urged him to accept office though to attend Cabinets only when naval matters were discussed.[90] These were to be his main concern and the succeeding years were the most controversial of his career. He came to the Board with fixed ideas on the inefficiency and essential corruption of naval civilian administration, already expressed in Parliament in the 1780s and reinforced by experiences in the Mediterranean and Channel fleets. He was strongly supported by his naval colleagues, Sir Thomas Troubridge and Captain John Markham.

St Vincent was immediately confronted with a strike in the royal dockyards, which threatened the preparation of the fleet then being sent to defeat an alliance of Baltic states, led by Russia, which threatened Britain's trade in naval stores from that region. A pre-emptive strike was planned, with Denmark as the first objective. The yard delegates demanded a major pay increase to combat high food prices. Fourteen sail of the line, drawn from the Channel Fleet, were being repaired and equipped for the Baltic. Fourteen replacements needed to be brought forward in the yards. The strikers thus held a commanding position and refused the offer of a pay increase during the period of scarcity only, insisting on pay being permanently doubled. The Cabinet was willing to give in, anxious for the preparation of the fleet. But the First Lord and his naval colleagues were adamant. When the delegates returned for their answer they were all discharged from the service, as were those in the yards who had supported them. This broke up the strike and preparations for the Baltic campaign proceeded. However, it left ill feeling in the yards and confirmed St Vincent in his opinion that they were ripe for reform.[91] Nelson's victory at Copenhagen on 2 April 1801, and the death of the Tsar, dismantled the northern coalition and for the following months a threatened French invasion from a flotilla of boats at Boulogne occupied attention. But peace preliminaries with France were negotiated on 1 October 1801, the definitive peace was signed at Amiens on 27 March 1802 and the way was now clear for a reform of the royal dockyards.

St Vincent was deeply concerned with the heavy burden of taxation he thought was ruining the country and believed naval corruption added to this and must be eliminated. But he was not the first to desire wholesale reform. The failure of the American War produced pressure for greater efficiency and economy in public departments. Sir Charles Middleton, later Lord Barham, when Comptroller of the Navy Board (1778-1790), had tried to modernise working practices and procedures, with only partial success. The reluctance of the naval departments to admit change and the outbreak of war in 1793 had frustrated the recommendations of the Commission on Fees in the 1780s and the reports of the Select Committee on Finance in the 1790s. The growth in the size of the navy between 1793 and 1802 (the fleet almost doubled in size), and the accompanying increase in business, meant the Navy Board had 'lost control of administrative practice in the yards'.[92] Many irregularities and abuses occurred because officials were over-burdened with work. Before he left office, Lord Spencer authorised the abolition of many traditional practices and perquisites, including fees, and the reorganisation of yard management, which was put into effect by an Order in Council of 21 May 1801. St Vincent, conscious that public opinion was with him, was prepared to use politics to achieve his ends and to over-rule the traditional authority of the Navy Board.[93]

Between commissioned naval officers and civilian administrators there was often little sympathy. The naval officer felt impatience with the chairborne administrator; the administrator considered the serving officer willfully ignorant of administrative problems. Inevitable clashes were exacerbated by entrenched attitudes. Unaccustomed to the accommodations of political life, St Vincent tended to treat his Admiralty Board as junior officers, bound to obey, and the Navy Board and other civilian boards as recalcitrant defaulters. Even the Cabinet was not always immune from such treatment. In any case, the relationship between the Admiralty and the civilian administrative boards was potentially difficult. The Admiralty had superior authority, but was often ignorant of working practices at the civil boards, and even more in the yards. It was composed of politicians and naval officers, whose tenure of office was generally shorter than that of officials at the civilian boards, and it could rarely argue with the Navy Board on details. Administrative harmony was thus dependant on good relations between the First Lord and the Comptroller. When this broke down, as it did between 1801 and 1804, there could be chaos. St Vincent did not appreciate the working methods, the expertise or the difficulties of the Navy Board. He thought their failures sprang from inattention to duty and from slackness, and determined to eliminate these faults.

So, believing the peace to be more lasting than it proved, in July 1802 the St Vincent Board instigated a series of visits to the yards, beginning with Plymouth. It seemed to confirm the First Lord's worst fears. Writing to Addington in August, he declared they had found abuses which would take 'many months to go thoroughly into'. In September he declared Chatham 'a viler sink of corruption than my imagination ever formed'.[94] As a result the Navy Board was officially censured by the Admiralty for neglect of duty and allowing the public to be defrauded, and a Royal Commission of Naval Enquiry was appointed in December to investigate the whole civil establishment of the navy. St Vincent had difficulties persuading his Cabinet colleagues to approve the establishment of a commission. At first they rejected the idea and St Vincent angrily declared the Cabinet had mutinied.[95] St Vincent, who nominated the commissioners, pressed for them to have power to examine witnesses under oath. Since officials in the navy's civil departments were appointed by letters patent under the Great Seal they could not be summarily dismissed. But if that power had been granted it would have been possible to collect evidence against them, resulting in criminal prosecutions. St Vincent could then have replaced them with his own nominees and carried out his plans for reform unhindered. But an amendment, introduced in the House of Lords, allowed those giving evidence to refuse to answer questions which might incriminate them.[96]

After the publication of the Commission's first report, in May 1803, the Navy Board tried to present its case to the House of Commons. St Vincent refused to allow them to do so, but he could not prevent the Comptroller, Sir Andrew Hamond, MP for Ipswich (1796-1806), from declaring in the House in June 1803 that since St Vincent had taken office 'there had been so strong a prejudice that it was impossible to go on as things now stood'.[97] Informal communication between the Admiralty and Navy Board had already been broken off in January 1803 on the issue of contract shipbuilding, and formal contact alone was maintained thereafter[98]. St Vincent may have intended to force officials at the civil boards to resign or to abolish the offices completely. However, the conflict between the Admiralty and Navy Board provoked a campaign against St Vincent in the press, and in Parliament, from a 'new opposition' which included Lord Spencer.

Renewed war with France, from May 1803, increased these attacks. The First Lord's economies began to affect naval mobilisation; he cancelled contracts for ships with private builders, believing that work could be done more quickly and cheaply in the royal yards, and he reduced the prices paid to timber contractors so that supplies of timber dried up.[99] His treatment of the civilian boards caused morale to collapse and there were accusations of 'a system of terror' sustained by informers. Even Evan Nepean, his one-time secretary in the *Foudroyant*, a friend and political confidant, became irritated by the Commission's manner of collecting evidence, and resigned as Admiralty Secretary in January 1804. Naval officers too, like Nelson and Collingwood, were worried about naval defence and this gave added weight to criticisms of St Vincent's administration. Pitt, who wished to return to power, led these attacks from March 1804. St Vincent had been regarded as 'the shield and backbone' of Addington's ministry and if he could be discredited and the defence policy impugned, Addington's government would fall apart.[100] In a Commons speech on 15 March Pitt declared St Vincent 'less brilliant and less able in a civil capacity than in that of a warlike one'. Pitt accused the First Lord of preparing insufficient numbers of ships to defend the country from invasion and of being less well prepared, in building ships and raising men, than previous administrations had been at the outbreak of war.[101] These attacks were defeated in Parliament but Addington's government resigned on 10 May 1804 and St Vincent left office on 15 May.

Retirement and Legacy

The command of the Channel Fleet was offered to him in the summer of 1805. He indignantly refused unless Pitt should withdraw his allegations and apologise for them. In an interview with the King he explained that after Pitt's treatment he could not trust his personal honour with the prime minister. Votes of censure continued to be brought against St Vincent in the Commons by Jeffrey, the undistinguished MP for Poole. They were finally defeated on 14 May 1806, when Jeffrey's allegations of incompetence and mismanagement were lost without a division, and a vote of thanks to the admiral, proposed by Charles James Fox, unanimously agreed.[102]

In the short term St Vincent's period of office was detrimental to the navy. The conflict with the Navy Board caused low morale and a serious problem in the supply of stores in the dockyards. In the medium term two acts, passed in July and August 1803, one to regulate the administration of the naval charity, the Chatham Chest, the other the distribution of prize money, had a beneficial effect on all seamen. In the long term the Commission's fourteen reports provided a mass of information on which future administrations built. St Vincent's tough, often savage, approach ensured that officials realised the need for self-discipline in public affairs. His dismissal of seven yard officers for inattention to duty, his enhancement of the powers of individual yard commissioners, and his insistence that individual commissioners at the Navy Board be given specific areas of business to oversee, forced all officials to accept the principle of individual responsibility. It was a process which was not fully achieved until the Whig reforms of 1830s completely reorganised naval administration and centralised control under the Admiralty.[103]

After Pitt's death, in January 1806, and with his political friends, the Whig 'Ministry of All the Talents' now in power, St Vincent once more accepted the command of the Channel Fleet in March, resuming his blockade of Brest, despite indifferent health. In his last command he continued the same discipline and concern for economy and efficiency that he had shown earlier. Another change of administration, in March 1807, saw him resign on 24 April. This was the end of his active career. He lived another sixteen years and spoke on naval questions on his occasional appearances in the House of Lords, though he ceased to attend regularly from 1812. These were not years of undiluted happiness. He lost many of his protégés. He felt pride in the victory of Trafalgar and had been 'prepared for anything great from Nelson, but not for his loss'.[104] The disappearance of Troubridge in the *Blenheim* in 1807, returning from the East Indies, greatly upset him; Alexander Ball died in 1809, Collingwood in 1810, Sam Hood in 1815. His wife's last years – she died in 1816 – were marked by illness and confusion which sometimes made it embarrassing to entertain visitors. Yet he had a circle of younger friends and relations and remained interested in local, national and international politics until his death, on 13 March 1823.

Posterity has regarded St Vincent as the founder of a school of seamanship. But St Vincent himself denied it. In reminiscences he declared himself glad that Napoleon had seen such specimens of British naval officers as Sir Henry Hotham, Sir George Cockburn and Sir Frederick Maitland. When his secretary, Tucker, remarked that they all arose from the admiral's school, St Vincent declared, 'No, that is too much. They would have been as great anywhere; it was <u>with</u> such men that I formed a school.'[105] Yet allowing for the modesty of the admiral, St Vincent achieved a great deal. He reinstituted the close blockade of enemy fleets, which Hawke had used so effectively in the 1750s. So doing, he set new standards of 'keeping the sea' which his pupils transmitted in turn. Under his leadership a more active and aggressive pressure was imposed on the enemy, calculated to give him no respite, though often at great cost. The determination to succeed made St Vincent indifferent to criticism, to danger and his own well-being. He was sustained by whole-hearted devotion to the service. His motto might have been Sir John Fisher's 'Be in earnest, be terribly in earnest.' His willingness to take responsibility in the many difficult situations he faced, and maintain his decisions in the face of unpopularity, are the mark of a great commander. His approbation was gained by those who showed similar zeal, courage and activity, and were equally undaunted by difficulties. His contempt for those who were not so motivated or were half-hearted was equally direct. He rewarded proven subordinates with trust and loyalty which they returned, in Nelson's case with devotion. 'We look up to you, as we have always found you, as to our Father, under whose fostering care we have been led to fame'.[106] St Vincent's determination to promote on merit was not always easy to sustain in the eighteenth century, when political 'interest' and aristocratic patronage were frequently more important to advancement.[107] In the post-war navy the attitude to promotion was against him, but his emphasis on forwarding ability could never be wholly superseded.

St Vincent's abilities lay in the organisation and command of fleets. His patient, unremitting attention to detail set new standards of professionalism and efficiency. These were adapted to meet a new style of warfare after Trafalgar, when there were no more great actions but wearisome blockade. No more exciting to chronicle than it was to experience, and difficult to trace through regular issues of lemon juice, soap and fresh food, success could not be achieved without such detailed observance of the health and well-being of seamen. Here too St Vincent set new standards. Although his attitude to seamen was often harsh, his discipline savage, his humour occasionally cruel and his language sometimes unbridled and rough, his letters are full of warm and generous praise for officers and men, and his kindness to individuals was considerable and frequently secret. Civil administrators suffered from his over-enthusiastic zeal, but here too he set new and higher standards of accountability and responsibility, which the nineteenth century navy inherited as the norm. Nelson once declared St Vincent to be 'the very ablest Sea-Officer his Majesty has, and as the best and truest friend that can be in this world'.[108] It was a typically warm-hearted response at a particular point in Nelson's career, and the friendship between the two men later suffered. But it is a judgement many others have endorsed and it confirms St Vincent's own belief that 'the real character of sea officers cannot be masked from each other; and I ask to be judged by that test'.[109] By that test he succeeds.

Sir William Cornwallis. Stipple engraving by J Birchal

14

Sir William Cornwallis
1744-1819

The sheet anchor of British strategy

ANDREW LAMBERT

Although largely forgotten by historians because he never fought a major battle, Admiral Sir William Cornwallis commanded the main British fleet during the critical years of the Revolutionary and Napoleonic Wars, 1800-1805. His appointment as the senior admiral afloat was entirely appropriate, for he possessed that rare combination of professional skill and enduring temperament required for high command. While he was an old and close friend of Nelson, the two men could hardly have been more dissimilar in character. Mahan characterised him thus:

> Cornwallis, familiarly known as 'Billy Blue' to the seamen of his day, never won a victory, nor had a chance of winning one; but in command both of ships and of divisions, he repeatedly distinguished himself by successfully facing odds which he could not overcome.[1]

This study will consider the professional development and career experience that led Earl St Vincent to entrust him with command of the Channel, or Grand, Fleet in 1801 and re-appoint him in 1803. St Vincent, who had preceded him, and would succeed him, knew that the Western Approaches were the pivot of British strategy. Insular security, economic well-being, colonies and the development of British offensive strategies were all ultimately dependent on the maintenance of command at the entrance to the English Channel. While Cornwallis's principal task was to deny the French any opportunity to move their main fleet, based at Brest, into *la Manche*, where Napoleon had collected a large army and invasion shipping around Boulogne, he was also responsible for squadrons off Rochefort, Lorient and

Ferrol. The valuable convoys that frequently passed through his station were almost equally significant. While St Vincent selected the dynamic, aggressive and impulsive Nelson to command in the Mediterranean, where risks could and, in the event, were run, St Vincent wanted an altogether different man for the Channel. Cornwallis had built a peerless reputation as a tactician, on the defensive against superior forces. While Nelson might annihilate the enemy, Cornwallis was the admiral who would not be defeated, and possessed the temperament and resilience for a monotonous, dreary and yet dangerous task. His selection was inspired.

In 1805, after St Vincent had left office, Cornwallis and Nelson played out their roles almost exactly as the Earl had anticipated. Cornwallis anchored Barham's strategy, providing the central position on which all other fleets could fall back. Because Cornwallis pinned Admiral Ganteaume and his twenty-one sail inside Brest, Nelson was able to pursue Villeneuve to the West Indies, while Cornwallis and Barham could detach squadrons to escort convoys and regain the initiative in all theatres. In 1805 the Channel Fleet was all that stood between Napoleon and European hegemony. Ultimately Cornwallis's career revolved around the decisions he took in August 1805. He, rather than Nelson, denied the French an opportunity to invade England. His decisions ensured that when Trafalgar was fought Napoleon was miles from the Channel, and Villeneuve was heading for Sicily.

'You can always beat a Frenchman if you fight him long enough'

William Cornwallis was born on 20 February 1744, the fourth son of Charles, fifth Lord and first Earl Cornwallis, and his wife the Hon Elizabeth Townshend, daughter of Charles, second Viscount Townshend. Educated at Eton between 1753 and 1755, he entered the navy in 1755 under the patronage of the Duke of Newcastle, with whom his father was closely connected. His first service was aboard the *Newark*, part of the fleet sent to North America under Admiral Boscawen to intercept the French reinforcement of Canada. Moved into the *Kingston*, he was present at the capture of Louisbourg in 1758, and at the Battle of Quiberon Bay in the *Dunkirk*. The *Dunkirk* was shortly afterwards sent to the Mediterranean, where in December 1760 Cornwallis moved into the *Neptune*, flagship of Rear-Admiral Sir Charles Saunders. On 5 April 1761 Saunders appointed him lieutenant of the *Thunder*, Captain Proby, and on 17 July he was present at the capture of the French 64 *Achille* off Cadiz.

After the death of his father, in June 1762, and the retirement from office of his father's patron Newcastle, Cornwallis's mother and elder brother expressed some anxiety about his career. His mother pressed his claims for the command of a sloop, and a promotion, on Lord Halifax, the First Lord, and Admiral Burnaby, the Commander-in-Chief in North America. Earl Cornwallis, being a soldier, was anxious to buy a captaincy, 'for I have heard there are sometimes bargains of that sort'.[2] Evidently the earl believed that an officer might be 'persuaded' to vacate a command, to create a promotion opportunity. These rather irregular efforts, and the link with Burnaby, an officer of no particular merit, were probably counter-productive.[3]

As William had already given ample evidence of ability, and presence of mind under fire, the efforts of the Cornwallis family proved adequate to the difficult task of securing peacetime employment and promotion. In July 1764 he was promoted commander of the sloop *Wasp*; moving to the *Swift* in October and continuing in her until 20 April 1765, when he was made post captain into the *Prince Edward*. He owed this vital step to the new Rockingham ministry, with whom his brother had thrown in his political fortunes. He paid off this ship, which was immediately broken up, the following May. Cornwallis was an early convert to the 'Divisional System' which he introduced aboard his first captain's command.[4] Shortly afterwards he took command of the 28-gun frigate *Guadeloupe*, which operated on the Home and Mediterranean stations until 1773.

In politics Cornwallis was, by instinct and upbringing, a Whig. While he was never an active politician he, like any ambitious officer of the age, knew the value of his political friends. Most of his naval friends were of the same persuasion, and his criticism of some contemporaries was tinged by politics. His career had been greatly assisted by influence, and he knew how to work the machine. In 1768 he was returned as MP for the local constituency of Eye in Suffolk by his elder brother, and he retained the seat until March 1774. Eye, only two miles from the family home at Brome Hall, had an electorate of 200, and although never entirely safe, rarely forced the family to suffer the expense of a contest. In 1769 Cornwallis voted with the Opposition over the Wilkes affair, and in 1773 with the ministers over the Royal Marriage Act. It would appear that he never spoke in the House. He was returned again in 1782, while on active service in the West Indies, and managed to vote for the peace preliminaries in 1783. In the following year he was pressed by Lord Howe, then First Lord of the Admiralty, to stand for the government borough of Portsmouth. His name and reputation made him attractive to a naval constituency and, backed by the full weight of Admiralty influence, he secured the seat without a poll. After Howe left the Admiralty Cornwallis appears to have lost his enthusiasm for the seat, and being ordered to command in the East Indies, was persuaded by his brother to return to Eye in 1790.[5]

Thereafter Cornwallis remained in Parliament, eventually as a follower of Pitt, to whom his brother had attached his political fortunes. His final retirement in January 1807 followed the deaths of Pitt and his elder brother, the end of his own active career and a more distant relationship with his nephew. Throughout the period after 1790 Cornwallis attended infrequently, often being at sea, rarely voted and never spoke. Despite this, he took considerable pleasure from attending his own election in 1801. He did consider using his seat to criticise the Admiralty over his court martial in 1796, but chose not to break his impeccable silence.[6] His true vocation was the sea service, as he would realise during the national emergency of the late 1770s.

Despite his political opposition to the Ministry of Lord North, Cornwallis had been appointed to the 36-gun *Pallas* in 1774, operating on the west coast of Africa until 1776. Here he arrested several rebel American vessels which were loading gunpowder from European vessels in the African rivers. He also showed the darker side of his character in an unedifying factional correspondence with the First Lord, Lord Sandwich. Fortunately for him Sandwich appreciated his merits, and was prepared to overlook his faults at a time of national need when many Whigs refused to serve. Subsequently Sandwich would reward his services, while Cornwallis learnt that the navy was better served by patriots that politicians.[7] The *Pallas* moved to the West Indies, and then sailed from Jamaica with a convoy of 104 ships. Partly from bad weather but mostly due to the carelessness of the merchant ship masters, the convoy separated and by the time it reached the English Channel only eight or ten ships remained in company. Although Cornwallis was blamed for the dispersal of the convoy by the shipowners, his evidence demonstrated that the fault lay with the ship masters.

In early 1777 he was appointed to the 50-gun *Isis* on the North American Station, under Admiral Lord Howe, who shortly afterwards transferred him into the *Bristol*, and then sent him home in command of another 50, the *Chatham*, in March 1778. Moving to the 64-gun *Lion* in August 1778, Cornwallis returned to the West Indies escorting another convoy, and arrived at St Lucia in April 1779. Here he joined the fleet of Vice-Admiral Byron, taking a major role in the Battle of Grenada on 6 July 1779. As Byron rushed into action without trying to form a line, the leading ships, particularly the *Lion*, suffered severely from French fire before they could be supported. Almost entirely dismasted, and out of control, *Lion* drifted to leeward, and was cut off when the French fleet tacked to re-enter St

George's Bay. However, Admiral d'Estaing was too cautious to risk another engagement with Byron for the sake of a single prize, and Cornwallis managed to get some canvas spread on the stumps of his masts and make sail before the wind to Jamaica. While the *Lion* was refitting at Jamaica Cornwallis met Nelson, providing him with a maxim that summed up the Cornwallis approach to sea-fighting: 'You can always beat a Frenchman if you fight him long enough'. A shared commitment to the highest professional standards, and a dynamic approach to tactical problems, cemented a warm personal relationship that would last for the rest of their lives.[8] Subsequently the two men would develop the insight and judgement required for the highest commands. While Nelson was just embarking on the career of a captain, Cornwallis was about to take his first significant step as a squadron commander.

In the following March Cornwallis took the refitted *Lion,* the *Bristol* and the *Janus* to cruise in the Windward Passage. Off Monte Christi on the 20th he encountered a French convoy escorted by four ships of the line and a frigate, which chased the squadron, exploiting the light and inconsistent winds to bring it to action on the 21st. Although heavily outnumbered Cornwallis kept up a running fight at intervals throughout the day; but when the 64-gun *Ruby* and two frigates reinforced him the following morning the French broke off to cover their convoy. Three months later Cornwallis was detached with a small squadron to escort the homeward bound shipping through the Gulf. On 20 June, close to Bermuda, he sighted a convoy, which was carrying Rochambeau's small French army to America, escorted by nine battleships. The French, as was usual, reckoned their ulterior object, the safe and timely arrival of the troops, was more important than any naval action. Consequently they allowed Cornwallis's two 64s, two 50s and a frigate to pass with only a desultory exchange of fire. At the end of the year Cornwallis returned to England, with his friend Nelson, more dead than alive after the expedition to Nicaragua, as a passenger. Nelson generously attributed his survival to the kindness of his friends, especially Cornwallis.

In the spring the *Lion* was part of Admiral Darby's fleet for the second relief of Gibraltar. Cornwallis was then appointed to the 74-gun *Canada,* sailing for North America in August under Admiral Digby. The attempt to relieve Yorktown, where his brother was in command, proving futile, Digby detached the *Canada* and other ships to serve under Sir Samuel Hood in the West Indies. Consequently Cornwallis took a prominent part in the three major battles of 1782, St Kitts on 26 January, and on 9 and 12 April, to the leeward of Dominica. At St Kitts Cornwallis demonstrated his tactical acumen, and seamanship of a high order. The poor sailing of his next astern had allowed a gap to open in the British line, and de Grasse, attempted to push through in his flagship, the three-decker *Ville de Paris*, but the move was thwarted by Cornwallis throwing back his sails to close down the gap. On the 12th Rodney caught de Grasse with his fleet badly formed, and then used a shift in the wind to break through his line and impose a close action. Although he took the enemy flagship and the admiral, Rodney's hesitant conduct of the latter stages of the battle, when he restrained Cornwallis from pursuing the broken, fleeing enemy, excited the derision of a young captain, already predisposed to find fault with a Tory officer.

Cornwallis saw nothing in Rodney's conduct to excite admiration, sharing the view of his friend Hood that the pursuit should have been more vigorous during, as well as after, the battle. He was, from this time on, a member of Hood's school, a distinction he shared with his friend Nelson. For both men the Saintes was the definitive example of a victory that was not followed up. The day after the battle he turned down Rodney's offer of the *Ville de Paris*, the greatest prize yet taken by any British fleet. He spent enough time with Rodney after the battle to recognise that Sir George realised he had not done enough, and was unsure how his conduct would be viewed at home. He believed Hood would have taken twenty-five of the enemy fleet. In August the *Canada* was ordered home with the squadron under Rear-Admiral Graves, which was largely overwhelmed by a hurricane on 16-17 September; the *Ville de Paris* was among those lost. By contrast the *Canada* escaped with only minor damage to her rigging and reached Spithead in October.

By this time Cornwallis's reputation stood very high, and his old friends, notably Admiral Keppel as First Lord, were in office. In January 1783 he was appointed to the new 74 *Ganges*, and in March moved to the *Royal Charlotte* yacht, a largely honorary command that he held until October 1787. His election as MP for Portsmouth in 1783 confirmed his standing in the service, and a new political alignment for the family. In September 1787 he received a useful supplement to his income as a Colonel of Marines. He was then appointed to the 74 *Robust*. This succession of commands and rewards in peacetime reflected the steady support given by the family to the ministers. His particular connection was with Lord Lansdowne, who was also the patron of John Jervis. His next post was secured through more direct family influence.

As the earl was going to be Governor General of India, Cornwallis was moved into the 74 *Crown* with a commodore's broad pendant as

Commander-in-Chief in the East Indies in October 1788. He did not ask Nelson to be one of his captains, considering married officers unsuited to the work of distant stations. He arrived at Madras in September 1789, after a voyage of six months. His command was small, given the size of the theatre and the value of the interests at stake. Even so the French commodore protested that it was larger than agreed under convention, but Cornwallis disclaimed all knowledge of any convention. As part of his brother's policy to expand the frontiers of Indian territory across the Bay of Bengal, Cornwallis seized the Andaman Islands, where he developed a harbour, and supported the occupation of Penang.[9]

Although a fragile peace existed between Britain and France, the war between Britain and Tipu Sultan's Mysore exposed the ambition of France to re-enter the politics of the sub-continent. It was widely reported that Tipu was supplied with munitions by French merchant ships, in addition to having French advisors. In November 1791 Cornwallis learned that two French merchant ships were leaving Mahé escorted by the frigate *Resolue*. He detached two of his own frigates, each more powerful than the French warship, to search the merchant ships for contraband of war. When the *Resolue* refused to permit the search, and fired into one of the British frigates, she was forced to surrender after a sharp action in which 25 Frenchmen were killed and 40 wounded. Meanwhile the other British frigate had searched the merchant ships and, finding nothing suspicious, sent them on their way. The *Resolue* insisted on being considered a prize and brought in for adjudication. Cornwallis, lying at Tellicherry, merely sent her back to Mahé. The French commodore protested but made no further effort to hamper the exercise of the belligerent right of search.

When the Revolutionary War broke out, Cornwallis, who received the news before the French, quickly seized all the French ships within reach, captured the French trading post at Chandernagore, and supported the capture of Pondicherry. With the war in the east effectively over he left India in October 1793, reaching England the following April.[10] It is to this phase of his career that one must look for the source of his wealth, operating far from home, under the orders of his own brother, in a target-rich environment. He also formed some important professional links, recruiting and promoting John Whitby, who became his long-term flag captain, and Richard Strachan.

'The utmost firmness and coolness'[11]

Having been promoted rear-admiral on 1 February 1793, Cornwallis hoisted his flag aboard the 74-gun *Excellent* in the Channel Fleet in May 1794. He missed 'The Glorious First of June' while on convoy duty. On 4 July he became a vice-admiral, moving into the 80-gun *Caesar* and finally in December into the new 100-gun three-decker *Royal Sovereign*. He was already considered among the best flag officers in the service, the King even suggested him as a replacement for the ailing Howe as Commander-in-Chief of the Grand Fleet, rather than Lord Bridport.[12] In the event Cornwallis soon found an opportunity to enhance his reputation, although he remained a divisional commander. In June 1795 Cornwallis was commanding a squadron sent to cruise off Ushant and watch Brest. He had his flagship, four 74-gun ships and two frigates in company: *Royal Sovereign*, 100 (flag), Captain John Whitby; *Mars*, 74, Sir Charles Cotton; *Triumph*, 74, Sir Erasmus Gower; *Brunswick*, 74, Lord Charles Fitzgerald; *Bellerophon*, 74, Lord Cranstoun; frigates *Phaeton*, 38, Hon Robert Stopford, and *Pallas*, 32, Hon Henry Curzon.

On 8 June the squadron made land near the Penmarcks, took some prizes and drove a heavily escorted French convoy under the shelter of the batteries on Belle Isle. The French fleet at Brest then sent out a powerful force, which had been preparing for distant service, to relieve the convoy. Although the French sea officers knew the convoy would be safe, the Minister decided to send the squadron to sea. On the 12th nine battleships, two 50-gun *rasées*, seven frigates and two corvettes went out under Vice-Admiral Villaret-Joyeuse: *Peuple Souverain*, 120; *Alexandre, Droits de l'Homme, Formidable, Fougueux, Jean-Bart, Mucius, Nestor, Redoutable, Tigre, Wattigny, Zélé* 74s; *Brave, Scévola* 50-gun *rasées*; *Virginie, Proserpine, Insurgente, Driade, Fraternité, Fidèle, Cocarde, Régénerée* and one other frigate.[13]

At approximately 10.30 on the 16th Villaret caught up with Cornwallis near the Penmarcks. Because *Phaeton* held on towards the enemy rather longer than she should have, without signalling that they were French and in considerable strength, Cornwallis came closer than he would have done with better information. Once he recognised the disparity of force, Cornwallis hauled off and formed in line ahead. The French gave chase. At 14.00 the French force divided, exploiting the land breeze to come up with the British. The *Bellerophon* and *Brunswick*, being badly stowed, were out of trim and sailed badly. During the night they lightened ship, by starting their water, cutting away their anchors and throwing over board quantities of shot. Despite this the French continued to gain.

At daylight on the 17th the French were coming up fast in three divisions, one directly astern and one on each quarter of the British. At 09.00 a French battleship and frigate got into range and began firing on Cornwallis's stern-most ship, the *Mars*, which replied with her stern chasers. Recognising that his two slow-sailing ships could not afford the loss of a single spar, Cornwallis signalled the *Bellerophon* to move ahead of the *Royal Sovereign* and take station astern of the *Brunswick*, which was leading the squadron. By midday all the British ships were firing. By 13.00 a second French battleship was in action, but half an hour later the first dropped back, her main topgallant mast shot away by the *Mars*. For the next three to four hours the French ships kept up a harassing fire, inflicting considerable damage on the rigging of *Mars*; when Cornwallis recognised that she was falling to leeward and might be cut off, he wore round to her support in his powerful three-decker flagship, with the *Triumph* in support, and ran down to engage the enemy. This bold move caused four French ships steering to attack the *Mars* to pause, enabling her to regain the line of battle. Desultory firing continued until 18.00; shortly after 18.30 the French ships shortened sail, ended the chase and eventually stood to the east. They had been fought off, and now fell victim to a classic *ruse de guerre*. Earlier that day Cornwallis had detached the *Phaeton* to run ahead of the squadron. Captain Stopford skilfully built up the impression that he was in communication with the main British fleet, taking time to ascertain that they were 'friends' using signals that were known to the French. They had finally been convinced when strange sails were actually seen in the area to which *Phaeton* was signalling just after 18.00. Despite the weight of numbers the sovereign people had proved unequal to the constitutional monarchy.

While the *Triumph* had suffered some damage aloft, the *Mars*, which had borne the brunt of the fighting, had been hit on her main mast, fore yard and main yard, with a considerable amount of cut rigging and twelve men wounded. All of the British ships were damaged by the sustained firing of their own guns through their stern galleries, with the stern frames, galleries and bulkheads damaged or destroyed. The squadron put in to Plymouth, providing intelligence of the French fleet which enabled the main British force under Lord Bridport to bring Villaret to action off Île de Groix, taking three sail of the line, and driving him into Lorient.

The eventual outcome of these two actions was particularly unfortunate. The ministers had not informed the flag officers that a force of French royalist emigrés was at sea, heading for la Vendée. As Brest was not subject to a close blockade, Cornwallis's activities had produced the very effect those in London least wanted: he brought the French fleet to sea just as the invasion convoy was passing. Only his resolute and skilful defence, and Bridport's timely arrival, avoided a disaster at sea.[14] Instead the émigrés were wiped out ashore by Republican troops.

Cornwallis's report was typically understated and modest. He gave full credit to the good conduct and spirit of the officers and men. Both Houses of Parliament voted their thanks to the admiral and his ships.[15] This defensive success, crowned by the bold handling of his flagship, gave Cornwallis a tremendous reputation. Those familiar with his earlier career were not surprised by his dogged defence against a greatly superior force, and the determination to preserve his whole squadron. Despite this he refused the Order of the Bath, offered by Lord Spencer, as he considered he had hardly done enough to warrant the award. He wanted to defeat the enemy, not avoid defeat himself. His standing at the Admiralty could not have been higher, the Senior Naval Lord, Admiral Sir Charles Middleton (later Lord Barham), had his log specially bound up as 'Cornwallis's Retreat'.[16] Even so, had the French attacked with determination the squadron must have been taken, for it is highly improbable that Cornwallis would have abandoned his slower ships. As Sir John Laughton observed, the failure of Villaret-Joyeuse was more cause for censure than Cornwallis's retreat was for praise, sentiments echoed by Mahan, although he credited Cornwallis with 'the utmost firmness and coolness'.[17] As ever, such opinions could not be applied to his relations with politicians.

In October Cornwallis was one of the leaders of the so-called 'Admiral's Revolt', when a number of senior officers protested vehemently against a new set of regulations which removed soldiers serving in a permanent capacity as Marines on board warships from naval discipline. The occasion for this change in the Articles of War, promulgated by the Duke of York and meekly acquiesced in by Earl Spencer, was the imminent departure of yet another combined expedition to the West Indies. When Middleton resigned from office at the same time, on a related issue, Spencer replaced him with Admiral Sir James Gambier, an officer at once ignorant of many aspects of the sea service and significantly more compliant. Where Middleton would have resisted the new Articles, Gambier followed the First Lord. Cornwallis always believed that his role in the 'Admirals' Revolt' led to strained relations with the First Lord, Earl Spencer, and prejudiced him to find fault in the following year. By the same token Spencer's willingness to override the opinions of senior officers on matters of service discipline at the behest of the Cabinet and the Horse Guards further undermined his standing.[18] Spencer had already sacked Hood, the one man in the service that Cornwallis looked up to.

In late 1795 Cornwallis led a squadron to escort a home-bound East India convoy, and look into Cadiz, where preparations were in hand for the French. Spencer had already selected him to command on the Leeward Islands station, despite the objections of General Sir Ralph Abercromby, who was anxious to work with Admiral Christian. After Admiral

Christian's West India military convoy had twice been dispersed and driven home by gales, Cornwallis was ordered to take command and proceed with a squadron and transports in February 1796. While still in the Channel the *Royal Sovereign* collided with a transport, and was so badly damaged that Cornwallis, having seen his force safely into the Atlantic, returned to Spithead. Here he discovered that he had been promoted Vice-Admiral of England, and that the Admiralty, disapproving his return to harbour, had ordered him to hoist his flag in a frigate and proceed to Barbados with all possible speed. In reply he assured the Board that he was willing to proceed as soon as the *Royal Sovereign* was repaired, but because his health was already precarious he was obliged to decline to go in an uncomfortable frigate, which lacked the accommodation for his naval 'family'. This refusal was considered an act of disobedience and he was court-martialled. Nelson considered the whole affair 'extraordinary', finding it hard to believe that his friend could have been in error, and suspecting ill-usage by the Board.[19]

The court contained the largest number of flag officers ever assembled for such proceedings, reflecting the fact that Cornwallis had almost the entire service behind him. Their verdict had more to do with upholding the dignity of the service against the army than the details of the case.[20] He was censured for not proceeding in one of the other ships of the original squadron, but acquitted of the charge of disobedience, the court accepting his plea of ill-health. Despite this, Cornwallis had no desire to serve under such a Board of Admiralty and requested permission to strike his flag. Spencer was only too ready to grant his request. He had no further service until Spencer left the Admiralty on the fall of Pitt's ministry.[21] In 1799 Cornwallis took advantage of his considerable prize fortune, and his first long period on half pay to buy a country seat, Newlands, near Milford in Hampshire. On 14 February 1799 he became a full admiral, but there was no prospect of employment while Spencer remained in office. That year it was rumoured that he would be St Vincent's second in command in the Channel, but even in late 1800 St Vincent, who was desperate for efficient sea officers for the newly imposed close blockade of Brest, recognised that such an appointment was 'out of the question at present'.[22]

'The post of honour'[23]

When the new Addington Ministry was formed in February 1801, St Vincent replaced Spencer as First Lord and immediately selected Cornwallis to follow him in command of the Channel Fleet. St Vincent observed:

I flatter myself from the high character he bears as an officer that the choice which has been made, while it ensures the confidence of the public from the opinion universally entertained of his zeal and talents, will afford the fullest satisfaction to you and the rest of the officers now serving in the Channel Fleet.[24]

To Cornwallis he stressed, 'The French have seen, felt, and understood so much of your character, that theirs must be changed materially if they face you in preference to [me].'[25] He hoisted his flag in late February. His new flagship was the largest ship in the service, the *Ville de Paris*, a 110-gun ship named for Rodney's great prize and an enduring reminder of the great, if incomplete, victory of 12 April 1782. She would carry his flag, with little interruption, for the next five years.

Cornwallis took over a Channel Fleet that had just been overhauled by St Vincent. The Earl would appear to have adopted a close blockade as the best method of holding the French in check, and drilling his new command up to the high standards of seamanship, initiative and daring he had found in the Mediterranean.[26] Where great tacticians, notably Howe, used drill-ground close-order manoeuvres to create the fleet they required, St Vincent preferred a fleet that possessed seamanship and initiative. While Cornwallis belonged to the same 'mission analysis' school as his friend Nelson, it was his misfortune to fight all his significant actions on the defensive where 'mission analysis' could not be used. Consequently, he had to fall back on Howe's signal-driven 'directive control' style. More reliable evidence of Cornwallis's command style can be drawn from his strategic instructions to his subordinates.

As Mahan argued, St Vincent's selection of Cornwallis to carry on his work was the highest compliment to his 'nerve and tenacity'. His campaign was a masterpiece of naval operational art in the age of sail. With a large Franco-Spanish fleet in Brest harbour the position was critical. By denying the French access to stores and supplies the blockade exhausted their main fleet.[27] In contrast, the effective British victualling arrangements were critical to the success of the blockade.[28] They ensured that the only limits on the fleet were seamanship and human endurance. In fleets and squadrons led by such exemplars of seamanship and will-power as St Vincent, Cornwallis, Saumarez and Collingwood, neither quality was in short supply.

This was fortunate, for the war was reaching a new level of intensity as the political stakes steadily mounted. Following the collapse of the Second Coalition, with Britain once more effectively alone in her war with France, the blockade of Brest formed the hub around which British strategy revolved. It provided defensive cover for naval operations in the Baltic and

Mediterranean, protected shipping and prevented an invasion. St Vincent also used the Channel Fleet as a reservoir from which to draw trained and experienced officers and seamen for other tasks, notably during the formation of the Northern Armament under Hyde Parker and Nelson.[29]

Throughout this period Cornwallis's relations with the Board were excellent. Because he had their confidence he was prepared to exercise his judgement. When pressed to divide his force to reinforce the detached squadrons of Saumarez and Pellew, Cornwallis wisely objected, and the Board backed down. St Vincent had every confidence in his ability to beat the French, if they came out, and only hoped they would. For advanced warning they relied on the intelligence network run by Captain Philip d'Auvergne from the Channel Islands. This suggested the Spanish ships were too short-handed to come out. In these circumstances it was hardly surprising that both St Vincent and Cornwallis were interested in Captain Brisbane's plan to attack the ships lying in the *Goulet* with fireships. Once the preliminaries of peace had been signed, St Vincent reflected on the past season, saying he would 'always consider your having been placed at the head of the Channel fleet as an event of the greatest importance to the Country at large, and of most solid comfort to [me]'.[30] After crushing a mutinous outbreak at Berehaven in early 1802, Cornwallis came ashore in mid-April for the remaining months of the Peace of Amiens, which had been negotiated by his brother.

'the centre of the great British naval line'[31]

St Vincent re-appointed Cornwallis to the Channel Command before war resumed. He temporarily hoisted his flag on board the *Dreadnought* at Torbay on 10 May, and reached his station off Ushant on the 17th, the day before war was declared. He would retain this post, with brief respites ashore, until February 1806, when he was superseded by St Vincent. The strategic situation was famously summed up by Mahan:

> The world has never seen a more impressive demonstration of the influence of sea power upon its history. Those far distant, storm-beaten ships, upon which the Grand Army never looked, stood between it and the dominion of the world. Holding the interior positions they did, before – and therefore between – the chief dockyards and detachments of the French Navy, the latter could unite only by a concurrence of successful evasions, of which the failure of any one nullified the result. Linked together as the various British fleets were by chains of smaller vessels, chance alone could secure Bonaparte's great combination, which depended upon the covert concentration of several detachments upon a point practically within the enemy's lines. Thus, while bodily present

before Brest, Rochefort, and Toulon, strategically the British squadrons lay in the Straits of Dover, barring the way against the army of Invasion.[32]

Far from the slack and mutinous force St Vincent always perceived it to be, the Channel Fleet contained many of the outstanding officers in the service. Those selected to command a detached squadron, or a battleship in the inshore division, represented the pinnacle of seamanship. It was a task that wore out even the best officers. Among Cornwallis's subordinates off Brest, Rochefort and Lorient were such exemplars as Collingwood, Pellew, Cochrane, and Strachan. The strain told on all: Cornwallis had to go ashore occasionally for his health, being relieved by Sir Charles Cotton in July and August 1804, and Lord Gardner between April and July 1805. In 1804

Collingwood, commanding inshore, had doubted he would return: 'Nothing but a sense of its being necessary for the safety of the country could make us support such a deprivation of everything which is pleasurable.' However, when he saw the French were preparing for sea Collingwood was anxious to have the admiral back.[33] Cornwallis was now 60, of medium height, rather stout and of florid complexion. Although he and Nelson were very close, their private characters could not have been more different. Cornwallis was a modest, self-effacing, and supremely professional seaman. However, once in command afloat the two men were remarkably similar; both were highly aggressive but possessed the self-control to direct their efforts and the judgement to obtain maximum value from anything they did.

The key to the strategic situation was the ability of the Channel Fleet to defeat whatever force the French could bring into the Western Approaches. For St Vincent, and all his contemporaries, this was a matter of combat strength, not numbers of ships. As he mobilised the fleet off Brest St Vincent stressed that he wanted to concentrate the navy's three-deckers under Cornwallis.[34] In an action at close quarters three-decked ships possessed critical advantages in firepower, command and concentration over two-decked ships. For the past 150 years they had been the backbone of British tactics and strategy. A fleet based on three-deckers was a true battlefleet, sacrificing speed and endurance for firepower and strength. Until the 1780s the Royal Navy had built far more three-decked ships than her rivals; only after the American War had Spain and France began to build them in significant numbers. By concentrating his fighting power under Cornwallis, St Vincent was stressing the critical role of the Channel Fleet. While the majority of the three-deckers available in 1803 were old, cramped 90-gun ships of poor sailing performance, there were a number of large, new ships of 98 and 110 guns, like the *Temeraire* and Cornwallis's flagship the *Ville de Paris*, that combined a superior sailing performance with impressive firepower.

However, the imposition of an effective blockade required a worthwhile measure of superiority over the force to be blockaded. Down to November 1805 any 'superiority' was moral rather than material. The core strategic problem of 1803–1805 was caused by the simple fact that there were never enough ships available to the Royal Navy, because St Vincent's dockyard reforms hampered supply and the mobilisation of manpower took time, while the decision to force Spain to show her hand in October 1804, followed by her declaration of war in December, reintroduced all the problems of 1803, because it nearly doubled the available enemy force.

Nor were St Vincent and Cornwallis content simply to mass forces off Brest. Both men wanted to take the initiative. At the outbreak of war they considered a combined attack on Brest, but there were never enough troops.[35] While St Vincent tried to organise a combined operation in London, one of Cornwallis's officers revived the purely naval plans. Captain Puget planned to attack the fleet in Brest roads with fireships. However, this bold enterprise was first delayed by placing under another officer, and ultimately thwarted by Gambier, who returned as First Sea Lord under Lord Melville.

Although time has obscured the detail, it would appear that Gambier, through professional jealousy, political malice or personal spite, applied himself to frustrating Cornwallis. Gambier's hostility may have originated in one of his brief periods of sea service, as third in command in the Channel in 1801–02. There were many grounds on which a disagreement could have been founded: the two men could not have formed a more complete contrast. Cornwallis, the ultimate sea officer, spent his entire active career afloat; he never held a shore appointment. His manners were as blunt as his language, and he had no time for politicians, worldly display or posturing. He must have loathed Gambier, who lacked sea-experience, toadied his political masters at the Board, and made a public display of all the least endearing aspects of his evangelical beliefs. Lord Cochrane was not the only officer in the service to consider him 'a canting and hypocritical methodist' who owed his position to the fact that he was related to both Pitt and Middleton. His lamentable performance at the Aix Roads in 1809 certainly revealed a profound mistrust of unconventional warfare, as well as a failure of nerve, initiative and understanding.[36] The contrast between Cornwallis's relationship with St Vincent's Board of Admiralty, and with those of his two successors, can be attributed to Gambier. Gambier would make the last eighteen months of Cornwallis's sea career a sore trial of his less than perfect patience, already strained to the limit by the endless demands of blockade, and the growing realisation that he would not have the opportunity to fight.

When Pitt returned to Office in May 1804 Henry Dundas, first Lord Melville, replaced St Vincent. Fortunately, Melville and Cornwallis already knew each other well, largely through Earl Cornwallis and the Indian connection. Melville was less concerned than St Vincent had been by the French threat to invade Ireland. This reflected his wider strategic grasp, and a recognition that the French 'threat' to Ireland was little more than misinformation. By contrast, Melville stressed the threat that the French posed to key strategic possessions, notably the Cape of Good Hope, to oceanic trade, and West Indian islands: Melville recognised that the escape of one squadron could unhinge the entire blockade strategy by achieving and exploiting local superiority.[37] However, as Cornwallis heavily outnumbered a miserably manned French fleet in Brest, the 1804 campaign was not particularly difficult. Cornwallis placed his best sailing two-deckers, commanded by Rear-Admiral Edward Pellew, off Rochefort with orders to pursue the enemy if they got out. When Melville was forced to resign in May 1805 there was a groundswell of opinion in the government, which would appear to have been orchestrated by Gambier, that St Vincent should be recalled to the Channel command. However, the Earl would not serve unless Pitt apologised for the harsh words he had used in the Commons to attack St Vincent's naval administration. Consequently, Cornwallis was left to carry on. Although the new First Lord, Admiral Sir Charles Middleton, Lord Barham, provided the central direction of the 1805 campaign, he relied on his subordinates to use their initiative and take major decisions on the basis of the available intelligence. Unfortunately, he also retained Gambier, in whose house he was then living, and left him to conduct much of the business of the office.[38]

Although there is no opportunity here for a detailed discussion of the 1805 campaign, it needs to be stressed that Napoleon's plans were constantly shifting to meet each new set of circumstances, and may well have had more to do with disguising his intention of attacking Austria, and pinning down the British, than invading the British Isles. In early 1805 his plans were for a grand raid on the British West Indies, and all subsequent developments collapsed in the face of the coherence of British strategic and tactical doctrine, the superiority of British naval leadership, and his own ignorance of the peculiar problems of war at sea. Where his land campaigns relied on direct, aggressive strategies to impose battle on unwilling enemies, and then using military victory to impose a political settlement, at sea he relied on evasion, and was constantly thwarted by the principles set out by Vernon and Anson more than fifty years before.

The major French movement of 1805, Villeneuve's cruise to the West Indies, was planned as an attack on trade and colonies, only belatedly being adapted to a more ambitious purpose. When Barham divined, from the intelligence Nelson had sent back from the West Indies, and the observations of the brig *Curieux* carrying his dispatches, that Villeneuve was coming back to Europe too far to the north to be heading for the Mediterranean, he directed Cornwallis to detach Vice-Admiral Sir Robert Calder from his command, pick up the ships blockading Rochefort and Lorient and intercept Villeneuve off Cape Finisterre (Spain). This left the main fleet with twenty battleships, seven three-deckers, three powerful 80-gun two-deckers and ten 74s. In mid-July Cornwallis stretched to the south to search for Villeneuve, leaving Brest with only a frigate screen for eight days, confident Ganteaume would not come out. Despite going rather further south than Barham had intended, he did not make contact with Villeneuve and returned to his post, very much out of sorts, having once again missed the chance of a battle. As he had expected, Ganteaume evinced no inclination to come out. Calder rejoined the flag on 13 August, after his inconclusive battle with Villeneuve on 22 July. Nelson, returning from the West Indies and Cadiz, rendezvoused with Cornwallis on 15 August and placed his squadron, save only the *Victory* and *Superb* which required dockyard attention, under Cornwallis's flag. Once concentrated, Cornwallis commanded thirty-six battleships. The centre was safe, but there were now no British battleships in the Mediterranean, and precious few to the south of Brest. He was confident that Villeneuve, with at least twenty-five sail, was either at Ferrol or already moving south. Allemand's Rochefort squadron, which had gone to sea as soon as Calder lifted the blockade and was quickly lost in the Atlantic, was supposed to have joined Villeneuve. If it had not it would pose a serious threat to trade. Something had to be done. The limits of concentration of force had been reached. The initial concentration at the centre had been correct, but with Ganteaume firmly held inside Brest, and morally more than half beaten, it was time to shift to the offensive. This new strategic situation led to the most controversial decision of Cornwallis's career.

'The Western Squadron is the mainspring from which all offensive operations must proceed'[39]

On 16 August, only a day after Nelson had reinforced him, Cornwallis divided his fleet, sending half his ships under Calder to proceed off Ferrol, where he was to blockade the enemy, or to pursue them if they went to sea. Calder was given eighteen battleships, including five three-deckers, and picked up two more 74s that were already on station off Ferrol. Barham, who had anticipated the movement, was quick to approve. Mahan, the first to address the issue in detail, followed Napoleon's critical assessment that this was a stupid mistake. Mahan's obsession with concentration of force lead him to undervalue the very British principles of offensive action and economy of force. The concentration of force he advocated would have blocked up the Channel at the expense of the Mediterranean and the wider war effort, leaving the initiative with the French, who had at least thirty ships outside Brest. Mahan's views on this question must be viewed in the light of his overriding concern to educate contemporary American states-men, and his abhorrence of any division of the American fleet between the Atlantic and Pacific coasts.[40] In fact, as Philip Colomb had already pointed out, Napoleon's mistake was to think that he could fool so experienced an officer as Cornwallis by shifting his naval combinations. The discovery that he could not would explain his critical remarks. Mahan, lacking access to archival resources that would have countered the generally pro-Napoleonic interpretation of Thiers and other French historians, accepted the Em-peror's criticism at face value.[41]

In fact, Cornwallis had anticipated Barham's wishes, and had not divided his fleet quite as much as mere numbers would suggest. The seventeen ships with his flag included ten three-deckers, including the three most powerful ships in the Royal Navy, an 80-gun two-decker and only seven 74s. Corn-wallis and Nelson both rated a three-decker as the equal of two two-deckers in close combat, the only place where decisions were ever reached. Against this Villeneuve had twenty-nine ships, but only one was a three-decker, making a close combat ratio of 30 to Cornwallis's 28, while the relative combat effectiveness of the two fleets was such that Cornwallis, as St Vincent had always recognised, would not be beaten by any number of French and Spanish ships. Even Ganteaume in Brest only had three three-deckers. Consequently the degree of risk being run by dividing the Chan-nel Fleet was small, and the prize to be secured by running it was vast. After all, the fleet that Cornwallis detached under Calder was, once reinforced, the one that Nelson led at Trafalgar. Had it not been sent Villeneuve would have been able to operate against trade, as Barham feared, take a free run back to Toulon, or go on to Sicily as Napoleon desired. Once the French had begun to move their forces, the best interests of the British would be served by destroying some of their ships, wearing down their human and material resources. Between 1803 and 1805 British strategy had been complicated by the sheer number of French and Spanish battleships. Now they were at sea, offering an opportunity to apply a useful measure of attrition.

Julian Corbett stressed that Cornwallis's task was to hold the mouth of the Channel, and that the blockade of Brest was merely a method of achieving that aim, not an aim in itself. It was lifted on two occasions in 1805, when pursuing Villeneuve and later Allemand, but Ganteaume was too frightened to take advantage of the opportunity. Nor was Cornwallis's problem restricted to preventing an invasion of Britain or Ireland. The French fleets could more easily take control of the Mediterranean, which had been abandoned by Nelson, and disrupt the efforts of the Third Coalition in that theatre, or cruise against British trade – the value of the latest East and West India Convoys alone exceeded £10 million and two major military expeditions were either at sea or about to leave harbour. Cornwallis had to balance all of these conflicting priorities, and it was in this crisis that he demonstrated that his true worth was greater than that of the cool and resolute combat commander: he was a strategist of genius. This, combined with good intelligence of Villeneuve's movements, enabled him to give Calder lucid and effective instructions.[42] From this perspective Corbett argued, with the support of Laughton and contemporary naval officers, that the division was a master stroke. He expected that Mahan's view of the value of concentration might have been altered by his experience of high command in 1898.[43] In the event, Mahan persisted with his view, despite Corbett's evidence, ignoring the role of the three-decked ships as levellers, as well as the political and strategic necessities that informed Cornwallis's decision.[44]

Throughout the campaign Cornwallis, from his central rendezvous, could rely on two things that were denied to the French. Every other squadron in the Royal Navy would, in an emergency, fall back on him; in addition British cruisers kept the main fleets informed of the movements of the enemy, and the position of each British squadron. This was one of the greatest advantages provided by effective command of the sea. Consequently, Cornwallis knew that *if* Villeneuve came north to Brest, he would have Calder hot on his heels. This understanding proved critical when Ganteaume finally made his move.

On 7 August Ganteaume heard that Villeneuve was at Vigo, but only moved outside the *rade* of Brest to anchor in Bertheaume Bay on the morning of the 21st, after peremptory orders from Napoleon. He had twenty-one battleships, five frigates and three corvettes. Even as they began to clear the *Goulet* the French were sighted, and reported to Cornwallis.

Unable to get in a position to attack that evening, Cornwallis satisfied himself with a reconnaissance and anchored his seventeen battleships off the Black Rocks. At 4.30 the following morning the Channel Fleet, led by the *Ville de Paris*, weighed and stood toward Camaret in a single line. The French made sail, but when the British closed in, they went about and made for the *Goulet*, under the cover of heavy shore batteries.[45] Cornwallis tried to cut off a flagship at the rear of the French line, engaging two battleships and inflicting some casualties, but when the *Caesar* went aback within range of the shore batteries, which developed an impressive volume of fire, she lost three men and Ganteaume was able to scramble back inside the *rade*. Cornwallis himself was slightly wounded by a shell fragment. Once again he had demonstrated exemplary skill. The basic aggressive side of his nature, based on well-founded confidence, was tempered by his cool head and informed by strategic wisdom. Although Cornwallis would have preferred to let Ganteaume out to sea, where he could be defeated, the strategic situation required that he be driven back into harbour by a relentless attack. Like Nelson, Cornwallis's greatness lay in his ability to see the big picture, and adapt his tactics accordingly. Lacking the numbers required to be certain of annihilating Ganteaume, he had to be content with a partial action, the moral significance of which was as great as any fleet battle. The precipitate retreat of the French convinced Cornwallis that there was no danger of an invasion, and once he had more details of Villeneuve's movements he provided Calder with new and more detailed instructions to pursue the allied fleet if it left Ferrol, and warned Collingwood to expect it off Cadiz.

The position off Brest was complicated by the extended cruise of Allemand's squadron, which ranged from the French coast to Cape St Vincent, and then back up to the Scillies, before finally getting back to Rochefort. Allemand had five of the line and three frigates, a force sufficiently powerful to overwhelm the escort of any of the priceless commercial and military convoys then en route through the choke point. Barham wanted Cornwallis to detach an equal force to the Western Approaches to cover the convoys.[46] By detaching Rear-Admiral Stirling in early September with five sail he weakened his own force, but came very close to success. At the end of the month Allemand was reported to be lying-to in the Western Approaches, a threat too brazen to be ignored. Cornwallis took his entire fleet in pursuit, but Allemand's luck held. The Channel Fleet was back off Ushant on 8 October. Within days Barham reported Napoleon's invasion of Germany, and advised that Cornwallis should be able to detach some frigates to the west.[47]

The news of Trafalgar filled Cornwallis with a profound regret that he had not been able to speak with Nelson when his friend had passed through the fleet in the summer. Cornwallis's inshore division, under Sir Richard Strachan, detached to search for Allemand, captured Dumanoir's division, the last fugitives from Trafalgar. Allemand finally got home, unscathed, on Christmas Eve, entirely unaware of the great drama that had unfolded around him.

After Trafalgar the fleet was divided to cruise in defence of trade, satisfying Barham's dominant concern throughout the season, which had been for the defence of trade, not the insular security of Britain and Ireland. However, Cornwallis, who took a different view, resented the loss of influence this occasioned, choosing to see it as a deliberate slight. When the blockade was relaxed for the winter, to reduce the amount of damage suffered by the fleet, two battle squadrons escaped from Brest in mid-December. They achieved nothing; one was destroyed off San Domingo in January, the other, greatly reduced, got home rather later.

Deeply affected by the death of Nelson, exhausted in mind and body, and convinced there would be no more fleet actions, Cornwallis fell into a darker mood. He took an obsessive interest in the punctilio of the service, and demonstrated clear signs of paranoia. Evidently suffering from a persecution complex, he believed that the Board, in particular Admiral Gambier, whom he despised, was attempting to remove him. His suspicions of Gambier appear to have been well-founded, while elements within the Government were anxious to get rid of him, noting the limited parliamentary influence of his family. Rumours of his imminent departure were circulating by the end of 1805, when Lord Keith applied to succeed him. His state of mind was so profoundly affected that he even argued, if only briefly, with John Whitby, his closest friend and long term flag captain.[48] This only exacerbated the loneliness of high command.

With the death of Pitt in January Cornwallis must have expected a change. Fox's 'Ministry of the Talents' replaced him with St Vincent. Cornwallis did not hold the Earl to blame, and although George Canning criticised the change in the House of Commons it would appear that hauling down his flag on 22 February 1806, the death of his brother in India, followed by that of his beloved flag captain, Whitby, on 6 April 1806, marked the end of Cornwallis's earthly ambitions.

Cornwallis saw no further service, and effectively retired from public life, giving up his seat in Parliament to his nephew in early 1807. He spent his remaining years at his home in Hampshire, with his horses and parrots, latterly in the company of Mrs Whitby, the widow of his flag captain. After so long a career at sea he had few close friends, and little interest in society at large. Only the company of Mrs Whitby could stave off his loneliness. At the peace he was awarded the Grand Cross of the Bath. He died on 5 July 1819, leaving his estate to Mrs Whitby in trust for her daughter and grandson. There was also a small sum for Lieutenant William Symonds, Mrs Whitby's brother, who used the money to begin his career in naval architecture.[49] His own family, with whom he had long been out of contact, were furious, accusing Mrs Whitby of improper influence. However, the bequest stood. The admiral was, as he requested, buried in Milford churchyard, alongside Captain Whitby, in an unmarked grave. Subsequently his remains were transferred to a family vault by Whitby's daughter.

Considered by many to be eccentric, in a particularly 'naval' way, Cornwallis lacked the polish and refined manners of his elder brother, and much preferred the company of other naval men. He positively disliked society ashore, and some thought him a misogynist. He considered any form of outward show to be vulgar and disliked Indian service for this reason.[50] Although a violent partisan of the Church of England, Cornwallis loathed blood sports. Universally admired and respected by his officers, and loved by the sailors, his nicknames were all complimentary. The lower deck favoured 'Billy Blue' from his constant use of the Blue Peter to keep fleets at short notice while lying in Torbay, and 'Billy-go-tight' in mocking tribute to his *relative* abstemiousness and florid complexion. His naval contemporaries used 'Billy'.[51] His other nicknames, 'Mr Whip' and 'The Coachee', would seem to refer to his driving style of command. Given to depression and ill-humour, he was always cheered by prospect of action.

Professional to the core of his being, William Cornwallis demonstrated the highest qualities required of an admiral; his leadership, vision and determination were unsurpassed, and only the accident of history, the one that denied him a battle he could win, has kept him out of the pantheon of naval immortals. From the 1779 campaign in the West Indies it must have been obvious that Cornwallis was destined for a career of hard, unrewarding service. Although he never had the opportunity to win a great victory, unlike many lesser men who botched their battles, his pivotal role in the years of maximum danger, between 1800 and 1805, reflected leadership, judgement and professional qualities of the highest order. Like his friend Nelson he had the insight to function at the highest level, and the steadiness to do it at the one place where the war could be lost. If he lacked Nelson's genius, even his faults are that much more 'human' than Nelson's, and he made far fewer mistakes. Rather than defeating a French fleet, he secured the greatest victory, the defeat of Napoleon's strategy. His blockade of the iron-bound coast of Brittany, through all seasons and all weathers, will remain for all time the ultimate achievement of seapower in the age of sail. He should be remembered as the admiral who held the centre, around which the greatest contest between the land and the sea yet waged was played out. As John Leyland observed, 'His work in the blockade was a masterpiece of the administrative and seamanlike handling of a great naval force in operations of supreme importance to the country.'[52] Perhaps now, as we prepare for the second centenary of Trafalgar, he can receive due credit for his work.

George Keith Elphinstone, Lord Keith. Oil by William Owen

15

George Keith Elphinstone, Lord Keith

1746–1823

'Full of years and honour! He was a worthy commander'

BRIAN LAVERY

George Keith Elphinstone was born in the family tower house near Airth in Stirlingshire on 7 January 1745/6, in circumstances which have strangely poignant Jacobite links. The '45 rebellion was in progress and indeed the Jacobite army was nearby. A small rebel battery was set up near Elphinstone Tower and a minor naval battle took place in the River Forth three days after the baby's birth, when the house was attacked by the gunfire of two small warships.[1] The baby was baptised by the minister of St Ninians in Stirling on 10 February, though the church, serving as a Jacobite magazine, blew up that month leaving only the steeple.

Furthermore, the child was named after his great-uncles George, Earl Marischal and James Keith, who had taken part in the 1715 and 1719 rebellions and had been in exile ever since. Both eventually went to Prussia, where the Earl became a trusted adviser to Frederick the Great and James Keith was a field marshal. But the Jacobite cause was dead even before the final defeat of Prince Charles at Culloden in April 1746, as Marischal was one of the first to recognise. George Keith Elphinstone was to develop his career in a very different direction.

Though the family had large estates in central Scotland, it was burdened with debt and there were many children to provide for – George Keith was the fifth son of Charles, tenth Lord Elphinstone and Lady Clementina Fleming. It was necessary to find professions in which sons could make their own way. His eldest brother, John, went into the army. The second,

Charles, was killed at sea in 1758 on the way to join his regiment, while the third, William, went to sea with the East India Company, in which he became a captain and eventually a director. An uncle, James Elphinstone, had served in the *Berwick* in the 1720s but had found the Royal Navy 'very expensive to those not acquainted with it' and had died before reaching high rank. A cousin, Charles Gascoigne of the Carron Iron Company, gave reasons for George's entry to the navy:

> First, he will acquire his education and business without expense; secondly, he will, by the time he could be ready to go a second voyage to the E Indies, have served his 3 years on board a man of war, he will be as well received into that service as if he had been his first voyage in it, and he will be qualified for a lieutenant if ever there should be another naval war, for there [is] no probability of his advancement in this; thirdly, he won't clash interest with Willie, if he inclines to stay on board a man of war.

The penury of the family was underlined when his relatives refused to fund a short course in navigation: 'T'would be monstrous to throw away 5 guineas for his learning navigation for 14 days.'[2]

Early Sea Service

In later life Keith was fond of saying that he was sent to sea with only a £5 note in his pocket. He joined the 100-gun *Royal Sovereign* at Portsmouth on 4 November 1761, perhaps aided by the influence of Marischal, who had been pardoned for his Jacobite activities in 1759 and had many friends in Britain. As was common for a potential officer in his first ship, Elphinstone was mustered as an able seaman. With the French fleet already destroyed at Quiberon Bay in 1759, there was little chance of action in a First Rate ship of the line and indeed the *Sovereign* was confined to harbour service. On New Year's Day 1762 Elphinstone appeared on board the 44-gun *Gosport* under the command of John Jervis, already a promising young captain. Elphinstone was a midshipman by January 1762 and saw action in September when the French were driven out of Halifax, Nova Scotia. However, he was paid off in March 1763, with the end of the Seven Years War.

As Gascoigne had hinted, his career was more difficult in peacetime and he only stayed at sea by dropping in rank to able seaman when necessary, and with the help of his kinsmen in the navy. Probably it was the first time when a Scotsman could do this, for there had been a considerable influx of Scottish officers since 1739, and more than thirty reached the rank of captain between 1756 and 1760. He served with George Falconer in the *Juno*, Keith Stewart in the *Lively*, and Charles Douglas in the *Emerald*.

During 1764 he asked his father for money to pay the schoolmaster of the *Lively* 'for completing me in some parts of navigation, which I could not do the service without.'[3] In December 1766 he was discharged from the *Emerald* to try a different career at sea. He became third mate of the East Indiaman *Tryton*, captained by his brother William. But this was not necessarily a radical break, for service in the merchant marine counted towards the qualifying six years before becoming a lieutenant in the Royal Navy.

After his return from the East, Elphinstone considered whether to return to the navy or stay in the service of the Company. Marischal had no doubt that the royal service offered more honour, though there would be family debates about it, as he wrote from his home in Potsdam:

> . . . my lady will be of opinion to continue in the service of the Company as least dangerous; your father will say that in time of peace there is less danger in the navy as well as more honour – that you will mostly be at home; and that in time of war you will be exposed to fight in the service of the Company, and the ship not fitted for fighting.[4]

That settled, he returned to the *Emerald*, still commanded by Douglas, in August 1769. At the end of the year he became an acting lieutenant in the *Stag*, flying the broad pendant of yet another Scottish officer, Commodore Sir John Lindsay. In June 1770 he passed his examination and became a full lieutenant.

In May 1771 Elphinstone was fortunate enough to be appointed lieutenant in the *Trident*, flagship of Sir Peter Denis in peacetime command of the Mediterranean station. This post was an almost certain guarantee of promotion and he was duly made commander in September, taking charge of the sloop *Scorpion* of 14 guns. At one stage in 1773 he planned to seek leave of absence in visit his great-uncle Marischal in Germany, but with the threat of war in America it was not a good time to leave his ship. However, the *Scorpion* was sent home in 1774. In October he took part in his first parliamentary campaign, standing unsuccessfully for Dumbartonshire. In March 1775 Elphinstone took command of the *Romney* of 50 guns and two months later he received the vital promotion to post captain.

As the situation in North America deteriorated with the revolt of the colonists, Elphinstone completed one round trip to St John's, Newfoundland, carrying troops out and escorting a convoy home. In March 1776 he was transferred to the 20-gun *Perseus*, a more suitable command for a young captain. Although he found the new-built ship in poor condition, he worked hard to fit it out and later, with a captain's pride, he claimed it was 'the avowed and most compleat little ship in America and I believe the swiftest of Europe'. In July he took a convoy out from Spithead. He captured two American ships which attempted to infiltrate the convoy but soon found himself in conflict with the merchant captains, who failed to stay together. When Captain Brown of the *Dinah* brig complained that the poor sailing qualities of his ship led to her capture, Elphinstone wrote to Admiral Howe, 'with regard to Mr Brown's observations on his vessel, I do perfectly agree with him, and will venture to add she was unfit for any purpose except that of burning.'

On arrival in America, Elphinstone spent some months patrolling the coast, ranging between Newfoundland and the West Indies but mostly off the coast of Carolina. In February 1777, while in Antigua, he was transferred to the 32-gun *Pearl* on the death of Captain Wilkinson. He wrote to his sister, 'Be not on the opinion that Yanky has knocked me on the head when you see another captain in the *Perseus*.' His pride in his ship remained and after two months he preferred the *Pearl* to the *Perseus*. However, this lasted only one more month, until he went back to the *Perseus*. In the summer of 1778 he was sent to Florida, with the sloop *Otter* and the victualler *Medway* under his command, to take provisions and ordnance stores to troops under Brigadier-General Prevost, threatened by 3000 Americans. After landing the supplies, Elphinstone organised a force of fast armed boats to meet American coastal forces advancing past Nassau. The *Otter* was lost off Cape Canaveral but the Americans retreated due to sickness and discord, so the operation was judged a success.

At the end of 1779 the *Perseus* fought a brisk action with the French ship *La Thérèse*, also of 20 guns, coming out of Charleston harbour with provisions for the French fleet operating in the area. *La Thérèse* was taken after doing considerable damage to the rigging of the *Perseus*. In December Elphinstone was attached to a force which was intended to land 9000 men to take the city of Charleston. The ships were separated in bad weather and most of the army's horses and heavy artillery were lost, but in February 1780 the force finally landed on Simond's Island, 30 miles from Charleston. Elphinstone supervised the disembarkation of the transports, then led a naval brigade which advanced with the army under General Clinton, using boats to ferry the troops over the numerous creeks and passages in the area. They arrived at James Island, across the Ashley River from the town, and on 20 March the fleet passed over the difficult bar into Charleston harbour. Three weeks later Elphinstone and his seamen conveyed the army across the Ashley River and the troops took up position behind the town, which was on the end of a peninsula. The fleet moved further up the harbour, to anchor directly opposite the town and bombard it. It surrendered on 12 May.

It was a considerable victory in a war in which the British army, in particular, was starved of success. Elphinstone's share was acknowledged by Clinton. 'This gentleman's unremitted attention to us from his so ably and successfully conducting the Transports into North Edisto to this hour, with the great benefit I have derived from knowledge of the Inland Navigation of this part of the coast, merit my warmest thanks.' The Charleston campaign demonstrated Elphinstone's eye for land and sea topography, which was to remain an important asset for the rest of his career. His commander-in-chief, Marriot Arbuthnot, commented on his 'intimate knowledge of the navigation of this Country'.

In 1780, while he was absent in America, his brother William and Sir Laurence Dundas had put his name forward as the parliamentary candidate for Dumbartonshire against the powerful Argyll interest. Elphinstone arrived home with a convoy in July and went to Scotland to fight a spirited campaign during the general election of 1780. He was successful but was appointed to the command of the *Warwick* of 50 guns. While cruising in the English Channel he met a Dutch ship, the *Rotterdam*, of equal force, and captured her without losing a man. He had orders to return to America but he applied to Sandwich, the First Lord of the Admiralty, for leave of absence. Sandwich, no doubt sensing that Elphinstone was not a natural supporter of the government, was not helpful. 'The delay of the sailing of the *Warwick* is exceedingly distressful, as the service on which she is ordered is of the most pressing nature; I am every day called upon from different quarters to know why the *Warwick*'s convoy does not sail . . .'

On joining Admiral Digby's fleet off the American coast, Elphinstone was sent a new midshipman – Prince William Henry, the third son of King George III, and a future king himself. The Prince sought more action in a smaller ship and Elphinstone almost obliged him when he chased two small French frigates up the Delaware River, capturing them both. But it was not an unqualified success – the Prince was disappointed because he was below decks with an injury during the fight, while Elphinstone was no doubt grieved that the crew of one of the ships escaped ashore with a quantity of treasure. Soon after, he went home in poor health.

He arrived in Britain in November 1782 and took his seat in Parliament, voting against the preliminaries of peace in February 1783. He rarely spoke in the House, and was seen as part of the 'country' party rather than one of the main parties. He seems to have regarded his membership of the House as an aid to his naval career and family interests, rather than fostering any strong political views or ambitions. He was quite regular in his attendance after the peace of 1783, dividing his time between London and the family estates in Scotland. His acquaintance with Prince William led him to the circle of the Prince of Wales. In 1789 he was appointed treasurer and comptroller of the household of the Duke of Clarence, as Prince William was now known.

On 10 April 1787 he married Jane Mercer from Kinloss and a daughter, Margaret, was born on 12 June 1788. In December 1789 Keith and his family travelled north in a painfully slow coach journey, at a pace of 40 or 45 miles per day. At Wetherby in Yorkshire he wrote, 'We have got thus far; Jane continues to suffer prodigiously and incessantly with pain and vomiting. Margaret is getting eye-teeth and is a very bad travelling companion indeed. We are a sad set. If I were well it would be a wonder.' He was anxious about his wife, who was 'low, fretful, and changed in every respect'. But for once this was not just Elphinstone's hypochondria and Jane Elphinstone died next day at Scarthing Moor in Yorkshire.

In May 1790, as a fleet was mobilised over the Nootka Sound crisis, Elphinstone applied unsuccessfully for a command. By the autumn he was ill and asked for permission to 'withdraw into foreign parts for six months for the recovery of my health'. Having decided to go to Nice, he travelled out in the *Assistance*, 50 guns, commanded by Lord Cranstoun. Meeting Hood's squadron at Gibraltar, he was offered a post as Captain of the Fleet but declined it as 'a troublesome and not very agreeable office'. At Nice he got into an argument with a Frenchman who asserted that the English Radical Horne Tooke would soon lead a revolt; Elphinstone replied that he was 'a blackguard parson who could not get credit for £20'. From Nice he travelled to Venice and Florence, but in April 1791 he found that the fleet was being mobilised again on the threat of war with Russia. He wrote to the Admiralty, 'I shall make the best of my way home in hopes of being appointed', but arrived too late, as the crisis was settled by negotiation.[5]

The French Revolutionary War, 1793–1797

In January 1793, two days before war began with Revolutionary France, Elphinstone took command of the *Robust* of 74 guns. She was a rather aged ship of the line, but his usual pride in his ship asserted itself and in May he wrote, 'The ship sails decidedly faster than any in the fleet at present; if none of those before us clip our wings we shall be the first of the fleet.' He joined the Mediterranean Fleet under Lord Hood and the *Robust* formed part of a force of twenty-one ships of the line which arrived off the great French naval arsenal of Toulon in August. A week later, two commissioners arrived from the port, offering to surrender the base on behalf of the French royalists. Parties were soon landed and Hood at one stage planned to make

Elphinstone governor of the town. But when he landed on the 28th, he was under Rear-Admiral Goodall, with the task of protecting the eastern side of the harbour from a base in Fort La Malgue. He headed inland with a force of 600 British and Spanish troops, Marines and sailors and drove a party of French republicans out of the Ollioules Gorge, making the position much more secure.

But the republicans soon rallied and by early September they had recaptured Ollioules. In October they were close to Elphinstone's position at La Malgue. In December on the other side of the harbour a young artillery major, Napoleon Bonaparte, captured Fort Éguillette, a position which could dominate the inner and outer harbour with gunfire. On the 17th of the month Hood decided to evacuate Toulon. Sir Sidney Smith volunteered to destroy the dockyards and the French ships which could not be taken away. Meanwhile, Elphinstone supervised the re-embarkation of the troops from various nations, and the *Robust* was the last ship to leave the harbour. She carried 200 royalist refugees, of whom 80 had to be put up in Keith's own cabin.

Elphinstone was not enamoured of land service and in November he wrote to his brother:

> I have lost some thousand pounds by being sent here, and find myself affronted in the face of foreigners, all of whom have been promoted by their courts, as has all the newcomers here excepting me who had the misfortune to command the whole. . . . Why should I risk reputation in a line where common sense is my only guide without study or practice? The first general that arrives I am off.

Elphinstone returned to Britain in February 1794. He was invested with the Order of the Bath for his work at Toulon and on 15 April he was promoted to rear-admiral of the blue, the most junior grade of flag officer. He hoisted his flag in the 90-gun *Barfleur* on 24 July as part of the Channel Fleet, but of course he was too late to share in Howe's victory of the 'Glorious First of June.' He saw little service afloat for the rest of the year, but in March 1795 he was selected to head an expedition to invade the Dutch colony in the Cape of Good Hope. The Netherlands, an ally at the start of the war, was in the process of being overrun by the French and the Cape was far too important to fall into enemy hands. It was useful for ships returning from India but, more important, it would serve as a base for enemy privateers unless something was done about it. If a French force got there first, it would be disastrous for Britain's trade.

Now promoted to vice-admiral, Elphinstone sailed from Spithead on 4 April with his flag in the 74-gun *Monarch*, having organised an invasion force in little more than a month. He had four more ships of the line, two 16-gun ships and a detachment of the 78th Regiment. His ships were slow and he arrived at the Cape on 10 June, to join with Commodore Blankett and his force of three ships of the line and a sloop. The main force of troops, 3000 men under Major-General Clarke, was left behind at St Salvador (Bahia) in Brazil to await orders. The Dutch colonists in the Cape were few in number and owed little loyalty to the new government at home. However, their Governor, Abraham Sluysken, decided to temporise as he was not sure of the situation in the Netherlands. He allowed Keith's ships to anchor in False Bay and his men to come on shore for provisions, but not to take control.

Elphinstone therefore sent for Clarke's force at Bahia. Meanwhile relations with the Dutch worsened. Elphinstone took Simonstown with 450 soldiers and 350 Marines and then advanced a few miles along the coast to Muisenberg. They had some captured enemy artillery, supplemented by a few guns sent by the East India Company, and the sailors dragged them across country. They were pinned down by the Dutch and running out of supplies when, on 3 September, 'Other ships seen in the offing, they answered our signals, said to be 13 seen at 2 o'clock. They proved to be the long wished for forces from San Salvador, under General Clarke.' The joint force advanced over the 15-mile neck of land which separated them from Cape Town, going as fast as possible in view of the lack of transport facilities. The Dutch surrendered on the 16th.

Elphinstone now sailed to India, but in Madras he received intelligence that a Dutch force would be sent to recapture the colony, so he proceeded back to the Cape. A Dutch force under Rear-Admiral Lucas duly escaped the British blockade of Holland in February 1796 and arrived at Saldanha Bay, 100 miles north of Cape Town, on 6 August. But the British had identified the bay as a point where the enemy might land and troops were stationed there. Ten days later Elphinstone arrived with a vastly superior force of seven ships of the line and one 50, compared with Lucas's two of the line, a 50, a 44 and a 42. Lucas was persuaded that his position was hopeless and surrendered without a shot being fired.

Elphinstone sailed for home on 7 October in his flagship the *Monarch*, with the frigate *Daphne*. To shelter from a gale he anchored in Crookhaven, in the southwest corner of Ireland, on December 23. He found that the remnants of a French fleet of seventeen of the line and numerous smaller vessels, carrying 14,000 troops, was 15 miles away in Bantry Bay. But the French, under General Hoche, were demoralised by the bad weather and failed to land. Elphinstone sent a party ashore to help the local forces, but the French had already sailed. The *Monarch* followed them, but the French returned to Brest while Elphinstone arrived at Spithead on 3 January, where he struck his flag.

He was a public figure for the first time in his career, and a rich man. Ships technically under his command had participated in the capture of the Dutch colonies of Colombo, Banda and Amboyna, so that was added to his prize money, giving him a total of £64,000 for the expedition. Though the opposition had some criticisms of the government policy of taking the Cape, there was much praise for Elphinstone. On 16 March 1797 he was created a baron in the Irish peerage, which did not entitle him to a seat in the British House of Lords. In compliment to his great-uncles he chose the title of Baron Keith of Stonehaven Marischal and was henceforth known as Lord Keith. He was sounded out about the possibility of a new command, but he was not willing to serve abroad and all the main commands at home were filled up. He went to Bath, where he met Lady Nelson at a ball and gave her the news that her husband was to be invested with the Order of the Bath.

Meanwhile, the fleet at Spithead, including Keith's recent flagship the *Monarch*, mutinied against poor pay and bad conditions and its demands were largely met. On 12 May another revolt flared at the Nore, where eleven ships under Vice-Admiral Bruckner hoisted the red flag and refused to obey their officers. This time the government, feeling the demands were more extreme than those at Spithead, refused to give way. On 1 June Keith was ordered to assist Bruckner against the mutineers.

He arrived at Sheerness next morning, but at first his presence was not helpful; negotiations broke down largely because the mutineers accused him of withholding the Cape prize money from his men. On the 6th Keith wrote an open letter to his 'Fellow-Seamen', pointing out that so far he had received none of the money himself and he concluded in unusually populist style:

> For God's sake reflect on the happy times in which we served together, and on the advantages we brought to our country. Be not too long misled by designing men; but return to your old friends, who like myself have spent their days among you, and can defy the world to say they ever did you an injury. . . . Will you be better looked to, or more happy under a French government? Perhaps you may ruin the nation, but you will be miserable. While your respected Admiral is off the Texel unreinforced, blocking up the Dutch, you are idle at the Nore, under wicked influence. . . . I bid farewell, until we can meet as before, like men and friends, when you will find me,
>
> With true affection,
>
> Yours etc,
>
> Keith

Whether this had any effect or not, the mutineers were beginning to lose their nerve and on the 9th they rejected the more extreme authority of their delegates. By the 15th they had all surrendered and Keith began an examination to find the ringleaders on each ship.

On 26 June Keith was ordered to Portsmouth, as second in command of the Channel Fleet under Lord Bridport. Again he had to investigate mutinies, such as one in the *Saturn* at Plymouth in July. His inquiry was a mixture of threats and detective work. He addressed the crew and

> told them the ringleaders must be delivered up and I trusted the well-behaved men of the ship would bring them forth to save the lives of others for if I was obliged to select them for trial I might be led into an error – they were still silent. It then became my duty to single out particular persons which I did according to the enclosed list. The two captains of the forecastle then came forward and said they would tell me a great deal notwithstanding their lives would answer for it.

The list included the sergeant of Marines and a private who wrote out an oath for the mutineers on the sergeant's instructions, as well as several seamen and petty officers, such as the two men who came on to the forecastle and cheered first as the signal to start the mutiny.

Mediterranean Command, 1798–1802

Keith went on leave for a year at the end of 1797 and in December 1798 he was appointed to second in command of the Mediterranean Fleet under his old mentor Jervis, now Admiral the Earl of St Vincent after his victory over the Spanish fleet in February 1797. St Vincent himself had abandoned the Mediterranean in 1796 and it was only reluctantly that he had sent Nelson back into the sea in May 1798, which eventually resulted in his first great victory at the Nile in August. But St Vincent was still convinced that the most useful task for his force was to blockade the main Spanish fleet in Cadiz. Keith joined the fleet there in December 1798, with his flag in the 98-gun *Barfleur*.

St Vincent's health was failing and he spent most of his time ashore at Gibraltar, leaving Keith in command off Cadiz. On 15 April 1799 Admiral Bruix, the French minister of the marine, evaded the Channel Fleet off Brest with nineteen ships of the line. Bruix's escape caught the Mediterranean Fleet on the wrong foot, exercising the command of the sea which it believed that the Battle of the Nile had given it. Keith himself had a force of fifteen ships of the line off Cadiz, while Nelson was in Palermo with his flagship, the *Vanguard*, Troubridge was off Naples with four more, Ball was besieging Malta with three and Duckworth was at Minorca with four. When Bruix appeared off Cadiz on 3 May, Keith positioned his ships to stop the French and Spanish from joining together. Instead, Bruix headed through the Straits of Gibraltar into the Mediterranean, arriving at Toulon on 14 May. Keith followed him and was in turn followed by the Spanish fleet, which put into its base at Cartagena on 20 May.

Of the three senior British admirals in the Mediterranean, St Vincent was concerned mostly with the defence of his base at Minorca and interfered with Keith's movements to that end. Nelson considered himself committed to the defence of Naples after a promise to King Ferdinand and Queen Caroline, and flatly refused to obey orders to take his ships from the kingdom. Only Keith was committed to chasing Bruix and bringing him to battle. He missed him at Toulon and swept round the Riviera. The two fleets were only 45 miles apart before St Vincent ordered him south to protect Minorca. On 13 June Keith shifted his flag to the *Queen Charlotte*, a First Rate of 1790 and one of the finest ships in the fleet.

In the meantime Bruix had headed towards Cartagena to join the Spanish, making a huge but inefficient and unwieldy force of forty-three of the line. Unable to agree on an objective, they eventually decided to take the whole fleet to Cadiz and then to Brest, where they might take control of the English Channel. Keith remained in pursuit. He passed the Straits of Gibraltar on 30 July, eight days after the Combined Fleet left Cadiz. He made up time on the voyage north, but reached Brest one day behind the French and Spanish. The campaign was a disappointment to both sides. The French had achieved nothing after a promising start, while serious faults had appeared in the British command structure.

But Keith was now in sole command, for St Vincent had resigned due to ill health on 17 June. From Brest he took his fleet to Torbay to replenish, and serious defects in most of his ships had to be repaired. He was formally appointed Commander-in-Chief in the Mediterranean on 15 November, dashing the hopes of Nelson, who was in acting command and expected to be confirmed in the post. When Keith arrived at Gibraltar in the *Queen Charlotte* on 6 December 1799 he faced a difficult situation.

At one time or another Keith had each of the Royal Navy's wayward geniuses – Thomas Cochrane, Horatio Nelson, Sir Sidney Smith and Sir Home Popham – under his command. Since Keith was essentially a strait-laced, methodical commander, it would be surprising if there was no conflict, but indeed there was much successful co-operation. Thomas Cochrane, Earl of Dundonald, was grateful to be taken on by Keith as an officer in his flagship *Barfleur*. Keith promoted him to commander after he navigated the prize ship *Généreux* into port with an inexperienced crew, though Cochrane blamed Keith's secretary, Jackson, for the fact that he was given command of the tiny, under-gunned sloop *Speedy* instead of the much superior *Bonne Citoyenne*, which went to Jackson's brother. Nevertheless, Cochrane used the *Speedy* to capture a Spanish warship four times her size, in perhaps the most brilliant single-ship action of all time. When he was refused promotion to post captain after St Vincent took over the Admiralty, one of the possible reasons was that he had been too outspoken in criticising St Vincent's interference in the chase of Bruix.

Nelson was in a dangerous psychological condition at this time, caused by several factors – the stress and ultimate triumph of the Nile campaign and battle; the effects of a head wound; imagined slights from home over honours to himself and his officers; his increasing involvement with Emma Hamilton and in the tortuous politics of Naples. Nelson and Keith were natural opposites, who might have complemented one another in slightly better circumstances. One was dashing, the other cautious; Nelson gained his fame through great fleet battles, Keith never fought in one; Nelson was motivated by honour and glory, Keith, his critics might say, by money; Nelson's private life was scandalous, Keith's was blameless; Nelson was unsuccessful in amphibious warfare, as shown by his spectacular failures at Tenerife in 1797 and Boulogne in 1801, while Keith was its greatest exponent.

Keith was restrained in his views of Nelson, except when he wrote to his sister about Nelson's conduct in Naples, 'cutting the most absurd figure possible for folly and vanity'. Nelson was also quite restrained in his comments on Keith. He was gracious about Keith's failure to find Bruix's fleet and wrote privately, 'If he gets up with them, they will be, I am sure, annihilated.' He professed not be too surprised or disappointed when Keith took over the command of the Mediterranean Fleet, but his confidant, Sir William Hamilton, knew that he 'felt it sensibly', though he had 'wisdom enough to swallow the bitter pill for the good of the service of his King and Country'. His personal remarks on Keith were relatively guarded. His conduct was 'incomprehensible' in ordering Nelson to send ships from Naples in September 1799; he was also 'too great' to congratulate him on the capture of the *Généreux* off Malta in February 1800.[6]

As commander-in-chief in the Mediterranean at the beginning of a new century, Keith now had to take a broad strategic view. Minorca was now available as a base, but needed defence. Malta was still held by the French and besieged. The French base at Toulon still had to be watched and the remnants of Bonaparte's army in Egypt blockaded. Allies such as Naples,

Turkey, Austria-Hungary and Russia had to be supported and placated, while neutrals such as the North African states were often essential for procuring supplies for the fleet. A force of seventeen ships of the line and twenty-two smaller vessels had to be maintained and supplied, mostly in hostile conditions far away from the facilities of a full naval base. On top of that, forward action was needed against the French and their allies.

In March, Keith took the *Queen Charlotte* to Leghorn and went ashore. At 7.30 in the morning of the 17th a messenger came to his lodgings with the shattering news that the ship was on fire, apparently caused by some hay stored under the half-deck. With the help of a few officers on shore and British consular staff, he rounded up a collection of local craft and ships' boats and ordered them to the rescue, but seamen of all nations were terrified of fire above all else. As the Admiral wrote in his journal, 'I had the mortification to observe that the country boats kept at so great a distance from the ship as to leave little expectation of successful exertion. The fire increased rapidly, and at 11 o'clock the After magazine blew up and the ship immediately sunk.' As the ship burned he found time to write to his sister, 'It will give you pain to hear the *Queen Charlotte* is at this moment burning, at 10 miles distant from this place. . . . At 11 o'clock the remains of the *Charlotte* blew up. . . . *6 O'clock, AM, 18th* – the boats are returned with the sad tiding that not more than 150 will be saved.' More than 700 men were lost out of a complement of 937. It was the worst naval disaster by fire since the *Prince George* of 90 guns had burned in 1758, ironically killing Keith's elder brother. It was also a personal tragedy for Keith, for many of the deceased were personal friends and protégées. The loss of his flagship and home left the Admiral destitute for provisions and he wrote to his sister in Scotland: 'Cotton undershirts must be sent, flannel ditto, drawers flannel and cotton, gauze understockings, some socks, cotton and worsted, cotton waistcoats, nankeen breeches, neckcloths, handkerchiefs, hats, cocked and round, table and bed linen; in short I am as I stand.'

Since he had benefited from the Scottish connection during his own career, it is no surprise that Keith helped fellow Scots with theirs. Among the officers of the *Queen Charlotte* were the names of Campbell, Duff, Tod, Erskine, Vass, Douglas, Stewart, Dundas and Sutherland, while Cochrane was absent on duty at the time. A volume of 1797 gives some details on his policy on promoting officers. He received recommendations from many different people. The Admiralty Board, Lord Spencer and his fellow admirals were obvious enough patrons, but nepotism was not ruled out. George Manley was promoted to command a much larger ship on the recommendation of his father, while one officer was advanced with the support of

Mrs Moutray, presumably the wife of Commissioner John Moutray and the lady with whom Nelson had had a doomed relationship in the West Indies in 1785. Others had humbler support – Thomas Bridgenor and Charles Dickson became midshipmen because they were sons of a bosun and a gunner respectively.

Keith was constantly aware of the effects of the weather, not just on naval operations but also on his own health, and it was difficult to find a climate which pleased him. From Plymouth in July 1794 he wrote, 'we are passing our time here in wind and rain, so hot and relaxing that my stomach is all to the devil again.' In contrast, off Ireland in December 1796: 'We have had dreadful weather which bears hard on me. All is ice here.' From Sheerness in 1803 he wrote: 'Here it is cold and the wind East, and I am not so well.'

Keith hoisted his flag in the *Foudroyant* and returned to the duties of his command. Malta had been taken by Bonaparte on his way to Egypt in 1798 and the people had revolted after hearing the news of the French defeat at the Nile. The French had been besieged in Valletta ever since, though support from Britain and other allied nations was desultory and little progress was made, despite the efforts of Captain Alexander Ball, one of Nelson's 'Band of Brothers'. But the French were finally running out of resources and Keith had been present in February 1800 when Nelson took the *Généreux*, one of two French survivors of the Nile, off the island. It was Nelson's last action before he returned home to England. The *Foudroyant* helped to capture the last survivor, the *Guilliame Tell*, while she was attempting to escape from Valletta. The French surrendered in September, after two years of siege.

By this time Keith was on his way to Gibraltar in the *Foudroyant*, to join with an army force totalling 22,000 men, with orders to attack Cadiz. There was no legal way in which a naval officer could be put in charge of the land forces, or a general over an admiral, so combined operations depended on the relations between two commanders-in-chief. There had been many cases during the previous century where this had not worked, for example between Vernon and Wentworth at Cartagena in 1742-4. Keith's army colleague, Lieutenant-General Sir Ralph Abercromby, was perhaps the most promising soldier in the army. His family estate was at Tullibody, less than 15 miles away from Keith's birthplace.

The force arrived off the Spanish city on 4 October, but little had been prepared for a landing in heavy surf. Keith did not perform well. Sir John Moore, in command of the landing force, 'found him all confusion, blaming everybody and everything, but attempting to remedy nothing'. He was indecisive about whether to land or not, but ultimately it was postponed. Perhaps he was in bad health again, but more important, he had little faith in the operation, which had been imposed for political reasons. It was, as he said, 'Most sadly bitched'. Coming so soon after the failure to bring Bruix to battle, the loss of the *Queen Charlotte* and the dispute with Nelson, the criticism of Keith signalled a new low point in his career.

In the eastern Mediterranean, British sailors had enjoyed resounding success in the last few years. Apart from Nelson's great victory at the Nile, Commodore Sir Sidney Smith had stopped Bonaparte's last advance in the spring of 1799 by defending the town of Acre against him. Bonaparte himself went home later in that year. In January 1800, soon after Keith became commander-in-chief, Smith concluded an agreement with the French generals at El Arish. They were to evacuate Egypt and go home. Keith was horrified, as were most of his colleagues: 15,000 of the most experienced troops in the world were to be sent back to join the war in Europe. Smith had exceeded his authority in signing the convention and it was soon rescinded, so the French occupation of Egypt continued.

Now that Keith and Abercromby had an amphibious force at their disposal, plans were made for an invasion of Egypt. A strong amphibious force was collected in the Bay of Marmoris in southern Turkey early in 1801, consisting of 195 British and Turkish ships and 15,000 troops. This time Keith made meticulous plans for the landing and co-operation with the army was much better. Keith wrote of Abercromby, 'We meet on terms of intimacy and the duty has gone on uninterruptedly well. I have laid a shoulder to it, the army has not wanted nor been refused nothing.'

Amphibious operations were common enough in the age of sail, as Keith's own career testifies, but mostly they were opposed only by light forces. Everyone, including the French generals, knew that Aboukir Bay, the site of Nelson's victory, was the only place where such a force could be landed with any degree of safety against the sea, and indeed a Turkish force had been defeated on that spot a year earlier, so this one was certain to be fought out on the beaches. The fleet arrived at Aboukir on 1 March and the *Foudroyant* rubbed against the wreck of the French flagship, *L'Orient*, on the way in. Bad weather caused a delay of a week. Keith's journal describes the landing from his point of view.

PM [7 March] Every preparation made for beginning the debarkation of the army before the break of day tomorrow morning. At 2am [on the 8th] signals made for the boats to begin receiving the troops and at 3 to proceed to the *Mondovi*, the appointed rendezvous. At 8 the boats put off from the *Mondovi* with the reserve of the army, the Brigade of Guards and part of the First and

Second Brigade forming a corps of near 7000 men. The enemy offered a considerable resistance by which three of our boats were sunk and 97 officers and men killed and wounded, but the point was carried, and the army left in possession of the field.7

The first wave consisted of 58 flat-bottomed boats carrying 50 soldiers each, towed by ships' boats from the squadron and flanked by naval cutters. It was opposed by 2000 Frenchmen and casualties were heavy. In addition to the 97 sailors mentioned by Keith, the army lost about 500. The British pushed inland and two weeks later Abercromby was fatally wounded in battle. He might have rivalled Sir John Moore or even Wellington in fame had he lived.

Keith was only a spectator of the land campaign, though he had to protect the army's supply routes. In August he blockaded Alexandria and helped to force the surrender of the French troops. But Keith did not know that a peace treaty had been signed at Amiens, by which Egypt would be restored to Turkish rule, while the British were also to lose their conquests including Malta, Minorca and the Cape of Good Hope.

Keith did not arrive back in Britain until the middle of 1802. He had been created a Baron of the United Kingdom in December 1801 and so took up his seat in the House of Lords. In 1803 he secured a special dispensation for the title to pass to his daughter Margaret on his death. He lived mainly in his London home in Harley Street until March 1803, when he became Commander-in-Chief at Plymouth.

The North Sea Fleet, 1803-1807

By this time it was becoming obvious that the Peace of Amiens was not going to last. Keith hoped to be reappointed to the his old command in the Mediterranean, but St Vincent had already decided that it was to be given to Nelson. Keith nursed his resentment that the post should go to a junior officer and accepted the command of the North Sea Fleet instead, though it offered less independence and prize money. While this command attracted much less attention than Nelson in the Mediterranean, or even Cornwallis in the Channel, it was perhaps the most important and challenging job in the navy, with the main responsibility for preventing Bonaparte's invasion. While his more famous contemporaries blockaded the French in Toulon and Brest, Keith was in charge of a great stretch of coastline, from Selsey Bill and Barfleur in the west to the north of Scotland.

Keith arrived at Sheerness on 20 July to take up his new command. His first job was to raise the crews to man a force which would number more than 200 ships, including up to twenty-two of the line. Several 'hot presses' took place during 1803. Questionable methods often led to difficulty with local authorities. In November Keith was obliged to apologise to the Mayor of Margate after men not liable to impressment were taken up.

> On such occasions as a General Impress, it is morally impossible to carry the orders of Government into execution without incurring some risque of seizing upon Individuals who are not liable to be impressed: but I hope that there is no room to believe that on the present occasion it has been wantonly done.[8]

The defence of the United Kingdom was planned in several layers. The great fleets off Toulon and Brest were there to prevent the main French fleets from taking control of the Channel. Keith's forces had a similar role against the Dutch off the Texel, though that threat was much reduced since the previous war. At the next level, lighter forces were stationed off the possible invasion ports such as Vlissingen and Le Havre. Since enemy forces were concentrated at Boulogne, the focal point of home defence was the small squadron of frigates, sloops and gunboats that kept its station just outside the sandbanks off the port. Keith was sanguine about preventing a surprise attack across the Channel, though he recognised that in a calm the French invasion craft might be rowed across while frigates were impotent against them. He spotted the great flaw in the French plan. Boulogne was a small, drying harbour and it would take six tides, or three days, to get all the invasion craft out. It was unlikely that any calm would last that long. Even so, preparations were made in case the enemy could reach the English coast. Blockships – largely captured Dutch ships of the line – were anchored in the key channels in the Thames estuary, with gunboats attached to harass the invasion flotilla. Groups of sloops and frigates were stationed close to the likely invasion beaches along the coast. The corps of Sea Fencibles, a kind of maritime Home Guard, was organised along the coast from fishermen and boatmen under the command of naval officers.

Though he no longer had Nelson and Cochrane under him, Keith still had to deal with two more wayward geniuses. His old adversary Sir Sidney Smith was now the commodore of the force off Vlissingen. Perhaps friction was inevitable when Keith's administrative passion clashed with Smith's free spirit: 'I am again without your weekly returns, which are the only ones that do not reach me regularly on Fridays.' But on a much more serious level, Keith distrusted Smith's judgement and wrote to Lord Barham, then the First Lord, of one of Smith's schemes, 'As for attempting to burn a few vessels in that extensive Road of Boulogne, it is nonsense; we shall get our ships crippled, fail of success, and be at great expense.' Barham replied, 'There seems to me such a want of judgment in our friend Sir Sidney, that it is much safer to employ him under command than in command.'9

Keith had rather more respect for Sir Home Popham, the inventor of the first signal code in which words could be spelled out. He encouraged him to work with Robert Fulton in experiments with 'carcasses' or mines to attack Boulogne. Popham left the North Sea Fleet in 1806 and repeated Keith's feat in capturing the Cape of Good Hope. He then launched a daring and unauthorised attack on Buenos Aires, but was heavily defeated. With a number of ingenious officers, the civilian population totally engaged in preparations against invasion, and an inventive spirit in the world at large, it is not surprising that Keith was bombarded with ideas for getting at the enemy. This was augmented by political pressure after the return of the Pitt administration in May 1804. Melville, the new First Lord, wrote frankly: 'From the violence that party newspapers write and endeavour to frighten us from the further use of our new instruments of attack on the enemy fleets, large and small, Mr Pitt and I are of course more eager to admit no fair opportunity that may offer of striking such strokes as may throw themselves in our way.'

On the whole Keith was cautious and warned his subordinates 'not to suffer themselves to be drawn under the enemy's batteries on the coast, unless with a fair prospect of deriving some advantage correspondent to the risk.' To Smith he wrote:

> a very important armament is known to be preparing at Flushing, with the avowed purpose of invading HM Dominions, and that a squadron is placed under your orders for the important purpose of defeating this design, for which no other provision is, or can be, made. You will, therefore, see the high consequence of keeping your squadron in a state to meet the enemy whenever they may sail, as the most serious consequences may arise from their being disabled and rendered unserviceable in consequence of their being employed upon attacks most likely to be attended with serious loss to the enemy.

Often the proposals for attack anticipated the wars of the next century. One Charles Rogier proposed a balloon attack on the Boulogne invasion fleet, using clockwork to release combustibles over the port. Robert Fulton, the American inventor, tried to sell his idea for submarine 'plunging' boats, but Keith was sceptical. Rockets invented by William Congreve were used for the first time at Boulogne on the night of 19-20 November 1805, without success. Another idea, never tried, was to load ships with stone ballast and sink them to block the mouths of the French harbours.

Ostensibly, Keith remained detached from party politics. He had attended Parliament occasionally in peacetime but in 1804, when Melville, as First Lord of the Admiralty, solicited his support in the House of Lords, he wrote back, 'I must inform your lordship that I have not taken my seat since my last creation in fee to my daughter; and I had made it an invariable rule since the year 1792 not to engage in any political career whilst employed on service, thinking it my duty to execute the commands of my superiors faithfully without entering into their motives.' This was a little disingenuous, for he was often involved in plots with the Prince of Wales's faction. In April 1805, at the height of the invasion scare, Melville's impeachment was debated in Parliament and Keith wrote:

> The Prince thinks I am disinclined to vote against Lord Melville. I have no such feeling. Myself and my family have met with nothing in that quarter but opposition. He opposed me in Dumbartonshire and Stirlingshire. My nephew's last election cost 3000 against Lord M's son-in-law. . . . I do not pretend to say I should not have had an unpleasant sensation in giving a vote so personal against one whom I had spent pleasant days in youth and had many a hard bout with, but there was no shadow for defence in my mind.[10]

Even with his great and widespread responsibilities, Keith still found time to support young officers, especially from Scotland. Andrew Buchanan from Glasgow wrote to his mother on his arrival at Ramsgate in December 1803: 'We went to see Lord Keith, who received us very kindly and said he would send me to the Downs to join his ship the *Monarch* till I get on board a frigate which was going abroad, where he said I should be much better than on board the *Monarch*, because I should have some practice in sailing.' Keith was always in touch with his Scottish roots and was definitely known in the service as a 'Scotch officer'. Unlike Lord Barham, he had his main home in Scotland rather than England. According to Cochrane the *Queen Charlotte* under his command was known as 'the stinking Scotch ship', the first part of the epithet being caused by decaying hides stored in the hold. Yet Keith used few Scottish words or phrases, even in his intimate letters to his family. There is no sign that anyone mocked his accent, unlike Captain John Inglis of the *Belliqueux*, who took his ship into the Battle of Camperdown with the order 'Damn! Up wi' the hel-lem and gang into the middle o' it.'

Because the invasion was never launched, Keith's command was comparatively uneventful. He rarely went to sea and was never in any physical danger. His captains, however, were often engaged in skirmishes off Boulogne and the other invasion ports, in which the enemy was harassed every time he came out of port. Keith based himself at East Cliff Lodge in Ramsgate. Part of the purpose went out of the command in September 1805 when Napoleon, now crowned Emperor of France, broke up his camp at Boulogne and moved against Austria. This was reinforced the following month when Trafalgar removed any possibility of invasion for the foreseeable future. New tasks emerged during 1806, when Napoleon issued his Berlin Decrees forbidding trade with Britain. The British retaliated with a blockade on the ports of countries which implemented the Decrees. Keith now had to station forces off almost every port in the long coastline of northern Europe, not just those of naval significance, and cause them to put very complex rules into force. The command was exhausting enough and in May 1807 Keith struck his flag to begin five years of rest.

Final Service and Retirement

Keith had known Hester Maria Thrale since 1791. She was the 'Queenie' of Boswell's *Life of Johnson*, partly educated by the sage, though presumably she had not absorbed his dislike of the Scots or his lack of interest in the sea. She combined bluestocking seriousness with a juvenile whimsy, though the latter was possibly wearing thin by November 1807, when her engagement to Lord Keith was announced, for she was 45 years old. For some years she had been estranged from her mother, who had remarried to Gabriel Piozzi, an Italian musician. Nevertheless, Keith sought her approval in his most formal terms:

> [I] assure you, Madam, that the approbation of a parent is a matter of essential consequence to the General comfort of such a Union, and I shall be happy to know that it meets with yours. Our acquaintance is not of a late Date, and I hope I know and can appreciate her many Virtues as indeed I ought when I consider she condescends to become the companion of a man who has some Months past his sixtieth year, but whose study it will be to render her time as comfortable as it may be during his remaining life.

Her mother approved and wrote of him: 'A *good* man, for aught I hear; a *rich* man for aught I am told; a *brave* man, we have always heard; and a *wise* man, I trow, by his choice.' They were married in Ramsgate on 10 January 1808; Mrs Piozzi was not invited but was sent a piece of cake.

That summer Keith took his bride on a tour of Scotland and they spent the winter in his daughter Margaret's house near Coupar Angus. They returned to London in June 1809. By October it was known that Lady Keith was pregnant, despite her advanced age of 46. Mrs Piozzi, still kept at arm's length, wrote 'I suppose the Admiral is in a hurry to be giving orders to his little cabin-boy . . .'; but on 12 December in the house at Harley Street, Lady Keith was in labour for five hours, surrounded by her sisters and husband, and produced a daughter who was christened Georgiana Augusta Henrietta.[11] The family spent its time between Keith's houses at Harley Street in London, Purbrook Park near Portsmouth, and Plymouth – in 1812 he complained 'the keeping of four houses [including his ship] will ruin me'.

In February 1812 Keith was appointed Commander-in-Chief of the Channel Fleet, at the death of Sir Charles Cotton. He was in Plymouth by July, making plans to fit out his apartments on board his flagship, the *San Josef*. His wife wrote, 'the question seems more what we can leave behind him than what he is to take, for almost everything we have collected belongs to the ship.' Again the title of the fleet was a misnomer, for its responsibilities stretched as far as Spain and included watching two of the main French naval bases, at Brest and Rochefort.

By this time the Peninsular War had been going on for four years and Keith used Sir Home Popham, now a rear-admiral, to co-operate with the guerrillas on the north coast of Spain, using seapower to great advantage in a brilliant campaign culminating in the capture of the city of Santander. The blockade of the French ports remained tight but other events, such as the war with America which began in 1812, had a peripheral effect on the fleet.

Keith struck his flag at Plymouth in July 1814, when the defeat of Napoleon and his exile to Elba seemed to end the great wars. He was hurriedly recalled to the Channel Fleet in April 1815 when the Emperor escaped and resumed control of France. There was little time to mobilise the fleet before 18 June, when Wellington won the Battle of Waterloo and Napoleon fled south. When he decided to surrender to the British as most likely to treat him well, it was one of Keith's ships to which he offered himself. The *Bellerophon* under Captain Maitland was blockading Rochefort when a boat came out bearing a flag of truce. Napoleon was taken on board and then to Plymouth Sound, where Keith had the job of dealing with him, turning down some of his demands for royal protocol and breaking the devastating news that he would not be allowed to live in England as he had hoped, but would be exiled on a tiny, isolated island. He protested to Keith: 'In St Helena I should not live three months: with my habits and constitution it would be immediate death. I am used to ride twenty leagues a day. What am I to do on this little rock at the end of the world? The climate is too hot for me. No, I will not go to St Helena.' But he was put on board the *Northumberland* and taken there, where he lived another six years. There was a certain irony two years later when Keith's beloved daughter Margaret, now aged 29 and a confidante of Princess Charlotte, married one of Napoleon's aides, the comte de Flahault. Keith did not approve of the match.

In 1820 Keith excused himself from the coronation of George IV, formerly the Prince Regent, on account of his age. According to Madame D'Arblay, 'though fearful of the heat and crowd, he will stay the first two days to prove his loyalty, if necessary: and at all events, to fulfil his duty as a peer in attending the opening of this great and frightful cause: and then retire to his magnificent new building in Scotland.' In April 1800 Keith's agent, Jackson, had bought for him the estate of Tulliallan in a detached part of Perthshire, and he began to build a new home there. It was just across the Forth from Elphinstone Tower, where the Admiral had been born, and the contrast said much about the progress of Keith himself, and the Scottish upper classes, over the last half-century. Keith's birthplace was a tower-house built by the family in 1504, when Scotland was a savage land in which civil war, local conflict or English invasion were never far away. Its walls were 4½ feet thick, leaving a single room 19 feet by 14 feet on each floor. It had been sold in 1754 and renamed Dunmore House, while the Elphinstones had moved 13 miles to Cumbernauld. The new occupants embellished the estate with a bizarre stone pineapple.

Across the river, Keith owned the picturesque ruins of the old Tulliallan Castle, once home of the Blacader family. In 1817 he began the new castle, designed by William Atkinson, which was completed in 1820 and described by a modern critic as 'A large symmetrical castellated mansion in "toy town" style – lightly buttressed entrance tower with Gothic traceried windows, ponderous battlements and slender corner turrets with loopholes.'[12] It eventually became the Scottish Police College.

Keith was now a great lord. He was a full admiral since 1801 and had been raised to the dignity of viscount in 1814. He had disposed of Napoleon Bonaparte, the terror of every child in Britain. He had made well over £100,000 in prize money. He owned estates in Kincardine and Dumbartonshire and the old Marischal lands near Stonehaven. He invested in the improvement of the harbour at Kincardine and helped to reclaim the foreshore. He had seen much of the world, and conquered parts of it, but he settled down to a domestic routine. As he wrote in 1820:

I am better but weak still and have begun the acid bath with Bell's advice. I feel no effect yet of any sort. Our weather is warm but damp and foggy – rain last night. Servants are an eternal torment – Thomas A Wick after he left the infirmary at Edinburgh, married one of the maids at Kennet, not esteemed much by Lady K or the family. The ladies are gone to the kirk. I sent my pound. It is a man from Glasgow who is to preach – our pastor is 82 but in better health than he was at 32 he says. Three of the elders have died since I was here, their average age is 84.

He died on 10 March 1823 and was buried in a local church.

Though he had held command of all three of the main fleets, in the Channel, North Sea and Mediterranean, Keith never fought in a fleet battle, and that was regarded as the supreme test of a naval officer by contemporaries and, until quite recently, by historians. He was a humane man, but he had no great reputation as a reformer. He never held political office on the Board of Admiralty. He made a few enemies in his career, including Nelson and Abercromby for a time. His avarice was legendary, and slightly unattractive. Instead, his historical reputation rests on his meticulous organisation of complex fleets, such as the North Sea Fleet in 1803-7, and in his expertise on amphibious warfare. As the joint conqueror of the Cape of Good Hope and Egypt, a considerable part of the world bears the stamp of his activities, though even here he was as unfortunate in that these territories were given back by diplomats, to be reconquered later by other British officers.

Notes

Abbreviations used in the notes

Add MS: Additional Manuscripts at the British Library

Adm: Admiralty papers at the Public Record Office, Kew

BIHR: *Bulletin of the Institute of Historical Research*, London

BL: British Library, London

Bodl: Bodleian Library, Oxford

CSP: *Calendar of State Papers*

CSPD: *Calendar of State Papers Domestic*

DNB: *Dictionary of National Biography*

CO: Colonial Office papers at the Public Record Office

HLbk: The Letterbook of Arthur Herbert, 1678-1683, Yale University Library, The James Marshall and Marie Louise Osborn Collection, shelf no. fb 96.

HP: R Mackay (ed), *The Hawke Papers*: A Selection 1743-1771 (NRS 1990)

HMC: Historical Manuscripts Commission

MM: *The Mariner's Mirror*

NB: Navy Board

NMM: National Maritime Museum, Greenwich

NRS: The Navy Records Society (published in Greenwich and, latterly, in Aldershot & Greenwich)

NS: (New Style); ns (new series)

PRO: Public Record Office, Kew

SP: State Papers at the Public Record Office

Introduction

1. O Warner, *A Portrait of Lord Nelson* (London 1958) 308.

2. D and S Howarth, *Nelson: The Immortal Memory* (London 1988) 341.

3. C T Atkinson and S R Gardiner (eds), *The Letters and Papers of the First Dutch War* (6 vols NRS 1893-1930) v, 14.

4. NMM Adm/L/P132.

5. For the significance of Nelson to the emergence of professional naval history, see A D Lambert, *The Foundations of Naval History: John Knox Laughton, the Royal Navy and the historical profession* (London 1998) 172-193. For a good series of essays on how Nelson's memory was embedded in British culture, see C White (ed), *The Nelson Companion* (Stroud 1995).

6. For example, see S Howarth, 'Leadership – Fleets ahead of its time', *Financial Times*, 1 Aug 1998. For fuller account of Nelson and leadership, see J

Horsfield, *The Art of Leadership in War: the Royal Navy from the age of Nelson to the end of World War Two* (Westport, Connecticut 1980) 62-74.

7. J Ross, *Memoirs and Correspondence of Admiral Lord de Saumarez* (London 1938) i, 229, quoted in N Tracy, *Nelson's Battles: the art of victory in the age of sail* (London 1996) 116.

8. G Rawson (ed), *Nelson Letters* (London 1960) 457, Nelson to Lady Hamilton, 1 Oct 1805. The original plan had been for three lines, but was modified before the final fighting memorandum of 9 Oct written off Cadiz.

9. The naval novel is often the link between the public and their understanding of naval history. Whether the hero rises to flag rank, such as Aubrey, Hornblower or Bolitho or struggles in more lowly stations such as Drinkwater, issues of command and action dominate their lives. The novels of Patrick O'Brian are currently so popular that they warrant additional books by naval historians to explain to the public the places and nautical language found in the works. Scholarly reflections on O'Brian's work, albeit from an historical rather than a literary perspective, are now beginning to appear: see D King, J B Hattendorf and J Worth Estes, *A Sea of Words: a lexicon and companion for Patrick O'Brian's seafaring tales* (New York 1995); A E Cunningham (ed), *Patrick O'Brian: appreciations and bibliography* (Boston Spa 1994).

10. B Lavery, *Nelson's Navy: the ships, men and organisation* (London 1989); M Lewis, *The Navy of Britain: a historical portrait* (London 1948); N A M Rodger, *Wooden World: an anatomy of the Georgian navy* (London 1986).

11. C Northcote Parkinson, *Edward Pellew, Viscount Exmouth* (London 1934); L Kennedy, *Nelson and his Captains* (London 1951); R Mackay, *Admiral Hawke* (Oxford 1965); D Spinney, *Rodney* (London 1969); T Pocock, *Remember Nelson: the life of Captain Sir William Hoste* (London 1977); I Grimble, *Seawolf: the life of Admiral Cochrane* (London 1978).

12. D A Baugh, *British Naval Administration in the Age of Walpole* (Princeton 1965).

13. Bibliographies of Nelson literature rapidly become outdated, particularly as the bicentenary of Trafalgar approaches. With this *caveat* good examples of these bibliographies are: O Warner, *Lord Nelson: a guide to reading with notes on contemporary portraits* (London, 1955) and L W Cowie, *Lord Nelson, 1758-1805: a bibliography* (London 1990); the authoritative guide to the Nelson portraits is R J B Walker, *The Nelson Portraits: an iconography of Horatio, Viscount*

Nelson, KB, Vice Admiral of the White (Portsmouth 1998).

14. J Glete, *Navies and Nations: Warships, Navies and State Building, 1500–1860* (2 vols Stockholm 1993) ii, 554, 580, 631.

15. B Capp, *Cromwell's Navy: the fleet and the English Revolution, 1648–1660* (Cambridge 1989).

16. D A Baugh, 'Great Britain and "Blue Water Policy" 1689–1815', *International History Review* 10 (1988) 33–58; 'Maritime Strength and Atlantic Commerce: The uses of a grand marine empire', in L Stone (ed), *An Imperial State at War: Britain from 1689 to 1815* (London 1994) 185–223; T J Denman, 'The Political Debate over Strategy, 1689–1712', unpublished PhD (Cambridge 1985).

17. K Wilson, *The Sense of the People: politics, culture and imperialism in England, 1715–1785* (Cambridge 1998) 137–205.

18. J D Davies, *Gentlemen and Tarpaulins: the officers and men of the restoration navy* (Oxford 1991) 99–101; PRO Adm 106/355, fo 471.

19. PRO Adm 1/2215, Norris to Burchett, 3 July 1703.

20. PRO Adm 106/408, Leake to the Navy Board, 31 Oct 1691.

21. N A M Rodger, ' "A little navy of your own making": Admiral Boscawen and the Cornish Connection in the Royal Navy', in M Duffy (ed), *The Parameters of British Naval Power, 1650–1850* (Exeter 1992) 82–92.

22. PRO Adm 1/2385, Rodney to Clevland, 13 Sept 1756, quoted in D Spinney, *Rodney* (London 1969) 127.

23. PRO Adm 51/4135/1, *Defiance*; Adm 3/24, Board Minutes, 19 Nov 1709.

24. Rodger, *Wooden World* 98–112.

25. C Lloyd, *The Health of Seamen: selections from the works of Dr James Lind, Sir Gilbert Blane and Dr Thomas Trotter* (London 1965).

26. C Buchet, *La Lutte pour l'Espace Carribe et la Façade Atlantique de l'Amerique Centrale du Sud, 1678–1763* (2 vols Paris 1991) i, 74–5.

27. See St Vincent to Man, 13 Oct 1800, quoted in J S Corbett and H W Richmond (eds), *Private Papers of George second Earl Spencer, First Lord of the Admiralty 1794–1801* (4 vols NRS 1913–24) iv, 14.

28. G A R Callender (ed), *The Life of Admiral Leake* (2 vols NRS 1920–1) i, 1–12; PRO Adm 106/52, 22 Aug 1682; J H Owen, *The War at Sea Under Queen Anne* (Cambridge 1938) 30; D Sobel, *Longitude* (London 1995) 17.

29. D A Baugh (ed), *Naval Administration 1715–1750* (NRS 1977) 223, Vernon to the Secretary of the Admiralty Board, 18 June 1744; *idem*, 227, Ad Hoc Committee of Senior Officers to the Admiralty Board, 27 Nov 1745.

30. R Gardiner, *The First Frigates: nine-pounder and twelve-pounder frigates, 1748–1815* (London 1992) 10–35; B Lavery, *The Ship of the Line* (2 vols, 1983–4) i, 96–102.

31. PRO Adm 1/578, Howe to Stephens, 17 Dec 1770.

32. J B Hattendorf, 'Benbow's Last Fight', in N A M Rodger (ed), *Naval Miscellany V* (NRS 1984) 143–206.

33. NMM JOD 24, fo 145v.

34. J S Corbett, *Fighting Instructions, 1530–1816* (NRS 1905); *Signals and Instructions, 1776–1794* (NRS 1908); B Tunstall (N Tracy ed), *Naval Warfare in the Age of Sail: the evolution of fighting tactics, 1650–1815* (London 1990).

35. Tunstall and Tracy, *Naval Warfare in the Age of Sail, passim*; PRO Adm 20/54; Adm 51/3954, *Richard and John*.

36. N Tracy, *Nelson's Battles* 92–3.

37. PRO Adm 66/152, to Thomas Cole at Cowes, 1 July 1690; *Great News from the Isle of Wight giving a full and true relation of the English and French fleets there, and of the intended engagement of the English with the French* (London 1690).

38. W A Blackley (ed), *The Diplomatic Correspondence of the Right Hon Richard Hill*, (London 1845) i, 394.

39. Quoted in P Le Fevre, 'There seems not to have been much mischeif done: Sir George Rooke, Gibraltar and the Battle of Malaga, 1704', unpublished paper.

40. Quoted in D Spinney, *Rodney* (London 1969) 321.

41. M Depeyre, *Tactiques et Strategies Navales de la France et du Royaume-Uni de 1690–1815* (Paris 1998).

42. PRO Adm 106/353, fo 548.

43. PRO SP42/92, fo 274.

44. For example, see N Tracy, *Nelson's Battles* 180.

45. P Le Fevre, 'Tangier, the Navy and its Connection with the Glorious Revolution of 1688', *MM* lxviii (1987) 187–190.

46. Le Fevre, 'Tangier'; PRO Adm 33/119 (*Sapphire* paybook).

47. J S Corbett, *England in the Mediterranean, 1603–1713* (2 vols London 1907) ii, 135; E Chappell (ed), *The Tangier Papers of Samuel Pepys* (NRS 1935) 138, 152; PRO Adm 51/3863/1 (*Henrietta*), 10 April 1683.

48. Adm 52/35/1 (*Foresight*), 27 Oct 1688.

49. See for example: Russell's conversations with Benbow and Mitchell, PRO Adm 51/138/1 (*Britannia*), 4 July 1691; Dartmouth's conversations, PRO Adm 51/4322/2 (*Ruby*), and NMM DAR 16, 85.

50. Davies, *Gentlemen and Tarpaulins* 185, 187; PRO Adm 2/378, p 358, *Lords Journal*, xvi, 616. On the nature of the local network around Nelson, see C Wilkinson, 'The Nelson Network: A Social Anthropology of Nelson's Fleet', *The Nelson Despatch* (Journal of the Nelson Society) vi (pt 12), Oct 1993, 231–4 and v (pt 2), April 1994, 37–42. Also, for a different view of naval courts martial, see R E Glass, 'Naval Courts Martial in Seventeenth Century England', in W E Cogar (ed), *New Interpretations in Naval History: Selected Papers from the Twelfth Naval History Symposium* (Annapolis 1997) 53–64.

Arthur Herbert, Earl of Torrington

1. I would like to thank Dr J D Davies, Mr Richard Endsor and Professor Emeritus J R Jones for reading and commenting upon an earlier draft of this essay.

2. E Chappell (ed), *Tangier Papers of Samuel Pepys* (NRS 1935) 224 [hereafter *Tangier Papers*]; J Ehrman,

The Navy in the War of William III 1689-1697 (Cambridge 1953) 275.

3. Most of the evidence for the date of birth is to be found in P Le Fevre, *All the Vices: Arthur Herbert Earl of Torrington 1648-1716*, Chapter 2. In preparation.

4. H C Foxcroft (ed), *A Supplement to Burnet's History of My Own Time* (Oxford 1902) 280; HLbk p 115; BL Egerton MS 2621 fos 17, 19.

5. E S De Beer (ed), *The Diary of John Evelyn* (6 vols Oxford 1953) iii, 1; BL M636/10, Margaret Herbert to Sir Ralph Verney, Paris 14 Dec 1649, Sir Ralph Verney to Margaret Herbert, Blois 30 Dec 1650.

6. Edward, Earl of Clarendon (W D Macray ed), *History of the Rebellion* (6 vols Oxford 1888) v, 321-2; PRO SP 78/113 fo 361; Longleat Coventry MS 104 fo 63v.

7. HLbk p 115; *An Impartial Account of Some Remarkable Passages in the Life of Arthur Herbert Earl of Torrington together with some Modest Remarks on his Tryal and Acquitment* (1691) p 2 [hereafter *Impartial Account*].

8. R Ollard, *Man of War: Sir Robert Holmes and the Restoration Navy* (London 1969) 20, 87; P Le Fevre 'Arthur Herbert's Early Career in the Navy', *MM* lxix (1983) 91; HLbk p 115.

9. Le Fevre, 'Arthur Herbert's Early Career' 91.

10. F Fox, *A Distant Storm: The Four Days Battle of 1666* (Rotherfield 1996) 242, 372; Ollard, *Man of War* 140-1.

11. NMM ACG 6/31; PRO Adm 10/15 p 39.

12. *Impartial Account* 2; PRO Adm 2/1745 fo 138v; BL Add MS 9336 fo 87.

13. J R Powell and E K Timings (eds), *The Rupert and Monck Letter Book 1666* (NRS 1969) 148; PRO Adm 10/15 p 64.

14. PRO SP 94/52 fos 141-2; *Impartial Account* p 3; P Le Fevre, 'Another false misrepresentation', *MM* 69 (1983) 299-300.

15. PRO Adm 10/15 p 64; SP 29/298 fo 48v; SP 71/2 Part 1 fos 1-4.

16. PRO Adm 10/15 p 63; Adm 33/94/500, 515 (*Dreadnought* paybook); BL Egerton MS 928 fo 90v.

17. Bodl Carte MS 38 fo 35; PRO Adm 106/285 fos 356v, 358.

18. PRO Adm 2/1737 fo 62v; Adm 51/3817/1 *Crown*, 20-26 Feb 1674; PRO HCA 24/147 no 23.

19. PRO Adm 2/1737 fos 84v-5.

20. Bodl MS Rawl C353 fo 28v; J B Labatt (ed), *Memoires du Chevalier d'Arvieux Envoye Extraordinaire du Roy a la Porte, Consul d'Aleppo, d'Alger, de Tripoli* (7 vols Paris 1735) v, 161-2.

21. PRO Adm 7/771 pp 111-2; SP 98/16, Robert Ball to Sir Joseph Williamson, Livorne 26 June/6 July 1675; Longleat Coventry Papers xiv fo 303.

22. J R Tanner (ed), *A Descriptive Catalogue of the Naval Manuscripts in the Pepysian Library at Magdalene College, Cambridge* (4 vols NRS 1903-1923) iii, 182-3, 186; PRO Adm 106/33 Adm to NB, 13 May 1676; D C Coleman, *Sir John Banks, Baronet and Businessman* (Oxford 1963) 83.

23. A Bryant, *Samuel Pepys: the years of peril* (London 1967) 174.

24. J R Tanner (ed), *A Descriptive Catalogue of the Naval Manuscripts in the Pepysian Library at Magdalene College, Cambridge* (4 vols NRS 1903-1923) iv, 191, 425, 474, 543-4.

25. Bodl MS Rawl A 228 p 44; PRO Adm 1/3548 p 637; Adm 106/37, S Pepys to Navy Board, 12 Nov 1677.

26. PRO Adm 2/1738 fos 162v-163v, 166v.

27. PRO Adm 18/17; Adm 51/582/1 *Mary*, 20 Mar 1678; Adm 106/352 fo 66.

28. HLbk pp 5, 6; S Hornstein, *The Restoration Navy and British Foreign Trade 1674-1688* (Aldershot 1991) 180.

29. National Library of Wales MS 9346B, Lord Herbert of Cherbury to Vice-Admiral Herbert, 22 Dec 1679.

30. *Tangier Papers*; J D Davies, *Gentlemen and Tarpaulins: the officers and men of the Restoration navy* (Oxford 1991) 187-9, 194-5.

31. *Tangier Papers* 168, 216; G Taylor, *The Sea Chaplains* (Oxford 1978) 104; P Le Fevre, 'Sea Chaplains as Judge Advocates', *MM* lxvii (1981) 290.

32. HLbk p 91; D Hannay, *Naval Courts Martial* (Cambridge 1914) 2; Ehrman, *War of William III* 276.

33. PRO Adm 2/1749 p 310; Adm 112/7, 65, 77; CO 279/25 fo 191v.

34. PRO Adm 51/4131/3 *Bristol*, 17 Sept 1680; Adm 51/244/1 *Diamond*, 17 Sept 1680; Adm 106/3540 Pt 2, brown folder, petitions; Adm 112/80, 589-593; CO 279/26 fo 86v.

35. PRO CO 279/26 fos 86v-87; John Ross, *Tangiers Rescue* (London 1680) 5.

36. PRO CO 279/25 fo 268; Hornstein, *Restoration Navy* 140-6; Ross, *Tangiers Rescue* 5.

37. Hornstein, *Restoration Navy* 185-6; HLbk p 141; PRO Adm 51/4201/1 *Newcastle*, 12 Dec 1680.

38. Hornstein, *Restoration Navy* 186-193, 200-4; *Tangier Papers* 231-2.

39. Davies, *Gentlemen and Tarpaulins* 187-8; A Bryant, *Samuel Pepys: the saviour of the navy* (London 1967) 163; P Le Fevre, ' "There seems not to have been much mischief done": Sir George Rooke, Gibraltar and the Battle of Malaga', unpublished paper.

40. *Tangier Papers* 138, 152; Sir Julian Corbett, *England in the Mediterranean* (2 vols London 1904) ii, 134-5 and index for Herbert's school of captains.

41. PRO Adm 3/278 pt 3 p 164; J B Hattendorf, et al (eds), *British Naval Documents 1204-1960* (NRS 1993) 244-5; Davies, *Gentlemen and Tarpaulins* 196-8.

42. Davies, *Gentlemen and Tarpaulins* 198-9; BL Add MS 38569 fo 54; *Calendar of Treasury Books* viii (i), 69; Francis Sandford, *The History of the Coronation of the Most High, Most Mighty and Excellent Monarch, James II. By the Grace of God, King of England, Scotland, France and Ireland, Defender Of the Faith, And of His Royal Concert, Queen Mary: Solemnized in the Collegiate Church of St Peter in the City of Westminster, on Thursday 23 April* (London 1687).

43. PRO Adm 2/1727 fos 59, 60v; Adm 8/1 fo 190; Magdalene College Cambridge PL 2858, 104, 138; *CSPD* 1685, 221.

44. Dr Williams Library Morrice MS Q p 81; J S Clarke, *The Life of King James II* (2 vols London 1816) ii, 204; M J Routh (ed), *Burnet's History of My Own Times* (6 vols Oxford 1833) iii, 100-1; G F De Lord (gen ed), *Poems on Affairs of State: Augustan satirical verse 1660-1714* (7 vols Yale 1962-75) iv, 167.

45. PRO PRO 30/53/8 fos 42, 47; PRO 31/3/168 fos 51v-3; BL Sloane MS 3929 fo 17.

46. PRO SP 8/1 Part 2 fos 217-8; PRO 30/53/8 fo 51; Davies, *Gentlemen and Tarpaulins* 204.

47. *Memoirs of Sir John Reresby* (A Browning ed, Glasgow 1936; 2nd edition M Geiter and W A Speck eds, London 1991) 503-4; *Negociations De Monsieur Le Comte D'Avaux En Hollande 1685 to 1688* (6 vols Paris 1753) vi, 169; PRO PRO 30/53/8 fos 66v, 67; BL Add MS 41816 fos 104, 129.

48. N Jaipske (ed), *Correspondentie van Willem III en van Hans Willem Bentinck* (4 vols The Hague 1927-37) I(ii), 610-13; J I Israel and G Parker, 'Of Providence and Protestant Winds: the Spanish Armada of 1588 and the Dutch Armada of 1688', in J I Israel (ed), *The Anglo-Dutch Moment: essays on the Glorious Revolution and its world impact* (Cambridge 1991) 354-5; for a different view see David Davies, 'James II, William of Orange and the Admirals', in E Cruickshanks (ed), *By Force or By Default: the Revolution of 1688-9'* (Edinburgh 1989) 97.

49. Israel and Parker, 'Of Providence and Protestant Winds' 358, 362; NMM MS 9157; *Revolution Politicks: Being a compleat collection of all the Reports, Lyes and Stories which were the Forerunners of the Great Revolution in 1688* (London 1733) pt vii, 72, 74.

50. Davies, 'James II, William of Orange and the Admirals' 93-5; Davies, *Gentlemen and Tarpaulins* 211.

51. PRO Adm 52/75/1 *Newcastle*, 16 Dec 1688; Davies, 'James II, William of Orange and the Admirals' 97; E B Powley, *The Naval Side of King William's War* (London 1972), 30; J P Kenyon, *Robert Spencer Earl of Sunderland 1641-1703* (London 1958) 230-2.

52. Ehrman, *War of William III* 277-9, 290-5; PRO Adm 2/1743 for orders issued by Herbert to 8 Mar 1689; Adm 3/1, 3/2 (attendances).

53. P Le Fevre, 'The battle of Bantry Bay 1 May 1689', *The Irish Sword* 18 (1990) 1-16; *Commons Journal* x, 142-3; Guildhall Library MS 30302, 1.

54. R Gardiner (ed), *The Line of Battle: The Sailing Warship 1650-1840* (London 1992) 32, 34; PRO Adm 1/3558, 669-670; Adm 95/13 p 24; Prob 3/24/ 4; this may be the model that is now at Annapolis. I am grateful to Grant Walker for providing with me with photos of the ship.

55. HMC, *House of Lords MSS 1693-5*, 96; PRO Adm 51/3875/1 *Kingfisher*; Adm 52/45/3 *Hampshire*, 11-18 July 1689.

56. PRO ADM 52/45/3 *Hampshire*, 22-25 July 1689; Powley, *Naval Side* 180; BL Add MS 40839 fo 126v.

57. Powley, *Naval Side* 180-181; A N Ryan, 'William III and the Brest Fleet in the Nine Years War', in R Hatton and J S Bromley (eds), *William III and Louis XIV: essays 1680-1720 by and for Mark A Thomson* (Liverpool 1968) 49-67.

58. BL Add MS 22183 fos 55-55v; Add 40839 fo 126 v; Lansdowne MS 1013 fo 15; PRO Adm 52/82/2 *Oxford*; Adm 106/385 fo 23.

59. HMC, *14th Rep Appendix Part ix The Manuscripts of The Earl of Buckinghamshire . . . The Earl of Onslow* 88-9; PRO Adm 1/3563, 18 June 1691; SP 44/188 p 70; T 48/12 (uniforms).

60. PRO WO 51/40 fos 99, 213; PRO Adm 3/3 fo 88; NMM CHA/L/2, 16, 24 Feb, 10, 14, 20, 23, 30 Mar, 2 Apr 1690.

61. J S Corbett (ed), *Fighting Instructions 1530-1816* (NRS 1905) 187; B Tunstall (N Tracy ed), *Naval Warfare in the Age of Sail: The Evolution of Fighting Tactics 1650-1815* (London 1990) 50-51; PRO Adm 52/85/5 *Pearl* 11 July 1690.

62. P Le Fevre, ' "Meer Laziness or Incompetence": The Earl of Torrington and the Battle of Beachy Head', *MM* 80 (1994) 290-8; PRO Adm 106/402 fo 180; WO 49/115.

63. PRO Adm 36/3078; Adm 106/401 fo 19; Adm 106/3069.

64. Ehrman, *War of William III* 354-365; *Poems on Affairs of State* v, 231-4.

65. *The Earl of Torrington's speech to the House of Commons in November 1690* (London 1710) 29; J Leyland (ed), *The Blockade of Brest 1803-5* (2 vols NRS 1898-9) I, xxxi, 190.

66. P Le Fevre, 'The Earl of Torrington's court-martial 10 December 1690', *MM* 76 (1990) 243-9; P Le Fevre, 'Lord Torrington's Trial: A Rejoinder', *MM* 78 (1992) 7-16; Ehrman, *War of William III* 366.

67. *Lords Journal* xiv-xx; *cf* C Jones and G Holmes (eds), *The London Diaries of William Nicolson Bishop of Carlisle 1702-1718* (Oxford 1985) 28-9; HMC, *House of Lords MSS 1693-5*, 539.

68. *Lords Journal* xvi, 616; *London Diaries of William Nicolson* 196; O Browning (ed), *Journal of Sir George Rooke* (NRS 1897) 254-5.

69. C Jones, 'The Parliamentary Organization of the Whig Junto in the Reign of Queen Anne: The Evidence of Lord Ossulston's Diary', *Parliamentary History* X (1991) 164-182: Torrington's attendance's are at pp 170-2.

70. G Holmes, *British Politics in the Age of Anne* (London 1967) 433; C Jones, ' "The Scheme Lords, the Necessitous Lords, and the Scots Lords": the Earl of Oxford's management and the "Party of the Crown" in the House of Lords, 1711-14', in C Jones (ed), *Party and Management in Parliament 1660-1784* (Leicester 1984) 123-163: Torrington is at p 158.

71. Westminster Cathedral, Westminster Diocesan Archives, Browne MS 101; P A Hopkins, 'James Montgomeries of Skelmorlie', in E Cruickshanks and E Corp (eds), *The Stuart Court in Exile and the Jacobites* (London 1995) 57.

72. Narcissus Luttrell, *A Brief Historical Relations of State Affairs from September 1678 to April 1714* (6 vols Oxford 1857) v, 123; BL Add MS 17677XX fo 197v.

73. *London Diaries of William Nicolson* 331; Luttrell, *Brief Historical Relations* v, 505.

74. A J Veenandael and C Hagenkamp (eds), *Die Briefwisseling Van Anthonie Heinsius 1702-1720* (11 vols to date Gravenhaage 1976 on) xi, 122; BL Add MS 70333.

75. PRO Prob 11/553/152-3; J L Chester (ed), *The Marriages, Baptismal and Burial Registers of the Collegiate Church or Abbey of St Peter Westminster* (London 1876) 286.

76. John Macky, *Memoirs of the Secret Service of John Macky* (London 1735) 16; I have discussed this further in Chapter 1 'Almost a Professional Badman' of *All the Vices*.

77. The Van Dyck portrait was shown at the Van Dyck exhibition in the Tate Gallery, London in 1985;

Bodl MS Rawl A 228 pp 122, 150; HLbk p 115; Cumbria RO D/Lons/L/ADM Box 6, Arthur Earl of Torrington to Admiralty, 15 July 1689.

78. H Horwitz, *Revolution Politicks: the career of Daniel Finch, Second Earl of Nottingham 1647-1730* (Oxford 1968) 27; PRO Adm 106/387 fo 275; NMM CHA/L/2, Edward Gregory to Navy Board, 16 Feb 1690.

79. Davies, *Gentlemen and Tarpaulins* 187; PRO Adm 8/2; Adm 6/428; Surrey History Centre, Woking (formerly Surrey Record Office) 1248/3.

80. PRO Adm 6/425/2 pp 158-159; Adm 106/371 fo 717; *cf* Adm 6/425 and 428 for other examples of Herbert's appointments.

81. Bodl MS Rawl A 228 p 68; PRO ADM 51/4135/1 *Cambridge*, 10 Sept 1689; ADM 52/88/3 *Plymouth*, 12 Sept 1689.

Sir George Rooke and Sir Cloudesley Shovell

1. This is based on Sir Cloudesley Shovell's 1692 recollection in Shovell to Nottingham, 12 Aug 1692. HMC, *Finch* iv, 387-88.

2. Unless otherwise noted, the dates for naval and military appointments and for ship commands in this essay are based on the following sources: Samuel Pepys, 'Register of Sea Officers', in J R Tanner (ed), *A Descriptive Catalogue of the Naval Manuscripts in the Pepysian Library at Magdalene College, Cambridge* (4 vols NRS 1903-1923) i, 307-455; NMM, 'Sergison's List of Captains,' SER/136 and Pitcairn Jones, 'Ships' Cards' and manuscript annotations to 'List of Commissioned Sea Officers, 1660-1815'; PRO Adm 6 series: Commissions and Warrants; *CSPD*; David Syrett and R L DiNardo (eds), *The Commissioned Sea Officers of the Royal Navy, 1660-1815* (NRS 1994); J C Sainty, *Admiralty Officials, 1660-1870* (Office-Holders in Modern Britain, Vol 4 London 1975), J M Collinge, *Navy Board Officials, 1660-1832* (Office-Holders in Modern Britain, Vol 7 London 1978); 'Flag Officers and Commanders of Squadrons and Stations, 1689-1697,' Appendix X to John Ehrman, *The Navy in the War of William III, 1689-1697: its state and direction* (Cambridge 1953).

3. Peter Le Fevre, 'Sir Cloudesley Shovell's Early Career', *MM* 70 (1984) 92.

4. For discussion of this term, see J D Davies, *Gentlemen and Tarpaulins: the officers and men of the Restoration navy* (Oxford 1991) 5-6, and index entries under the terms.

5. PRO Adm 33/111, *Revenge* 379, 4 July 1669.

6. Pepys to Rooke, 30 August 1673. J R Tanner, *A Descriptive Catalogue of the Naval Manuscripts in the Pepysian Library at Magdalene College, Cambridge* (4 vols NRS 1903-9) ii, 40.

7. *London Gazette*, no A 1080, 21 July 1676.

8. J R Tanner, *A Descriptive Catalogue* iii, 179; iv, 295.

9. See the various reports on this subject in HMC, *Dartmouth* iii, 40-43.

10. Quoted in Davies, *Gentlemen and Tarpaulins* 186.

11. PRO Adm 1/5253, fo 12. Court Martial of Lieutenant Thomas Rooke, 10 Aug 1681.

12. Broadside: *An Exact and Faithful Account of the late Bloody Fight between Captain Hastings Commander of the Saphire, Captain Shovel, Commander of the James Galley* (London 1681).

13. E Chappell (ed), *The Tangier Papers of Samuel Pepys* (NRS 1935) xxxviii, xliv, xlviii, 74, 114, 151, 167, 186, 189, 191-197, 203, 205-206, 212, 236, 273.

14. Chappell (ed), *Tangier Papers* 287.

15. Sari Hornstein, *The Restoration Navy and English Foreign Trade, 1674-1688* (Aldershot 1991) 194 note 1.

16. Warrant of King James II, 25 Sept 1688, to seven captains, including Rooke. HMC, *Dartmouth* i, 138.

17. David Lyon, *The Sailing Navy List* (London 1993) 13.

18. BL MS Egerton 2621, fo 47.

19. Quoted in E B Powley, *The English Navy in the Revolution of 1688* (Cambridge 1928) 135.

20. Rooke to Dartmouth, 4 Dec 1688. HMC, *Dartmouth* i, 223.

21. John Knox Laughton (ed), *Memoirs Relating to Lord Torrington* (Camden Society, New Series, xlvi London 1889) 33.

22. Quoted in Powley, *The English Navy* 143-144.

23. William III to Dartmouth, 16 Dec 1688. HMC, *Dartmouth* i, 284.

24. E B Powley, *The Naval Side of King William's War* (Hamden, Conn 1972) 31-32.

25. P Le Fevre, 'The Battle of Bantry Bay, 1 May 1689', *The Irish Sword* xviii (1990) 14, 16.

26. HMC, *Finch* ii, 207.

27. PRO HCA 26/1, fo 35.

28. *The New Proceedings of English Affairs in Ireland as they Come in an Account. . . . Relating what past with the Fleet under that Valiant commander Sir Cloudsley Shovell before Dublin, and the great Conduct against the Irish there* (London 1690).

29. C H Firth (ed), *Naval Songs and Ballads* (NRS 1908) 106-107.

30. William III to Heinsius, 14 May 1691. F J L Krämer (ed), *Archives ou Correspondence inédite de la Maison d'Orange-Nassau*. Third Series (Leyden 1907), vol i, lettre CXXX, 177.

31. The Queen to the King, 6/16 July 1690, PRO SP 8/7 fo 169; also quoted in John Dalrymple, *Memoirs of Great Britain and Ireland* (2nd edition, 1771-88) ii, appendix 2, 144.

32. [John Tutchin], *A True and Impartial Account of a Great and Bloody Fight Between part of the English Fleet commanded by Sir Clovesly Shovel, and the French at sea. . . .* (London 1690).

33. F E Dyer, *The Life of Sir John Narbrough* (London 1931) 231-233, 241-242.

34. Shovell to Nottingham, 8 Sept 1691. HMC, *Finch* iii, 25.

35. Sir Bernard Burke, *The General Armoury* (London 1878) 925. Granted 6 January 1692: 'Gu. a chev. erm. betw. two crescents in chief ar. and a fleur-de-lis in base or. Crest – out of a naval coronet or, 2 demi lion gu. holding a sail ar. charged with an anchor or.'

36. Hill served as an Extra Commissioner from 27 Jan 1692 to 18 June 1702. On his death in 1706, he left £100,000 to Shovell. Dyer, *Narbrough*, 207, 232.

37. Stephen Baxter, *William III and the Defence of European Liberty, 1688-1702* (New York 1966) 306-7.

38. Baxter, *William III* and John Ehrman, 'William III and the Emergence of a Mediterranean Naval

Policy, 1692–94', *Cambridge Historical Journal* ix (1949) 269–273, and *The Navy in the War of William III* 403, 493. The relative degree of William's direction in English naval affairs is a matter of some recent discussion. He was clearly interested in the general performance of both the English and Dutch navies, as J R Bruijn suggests in *The Dutch Navy of the Seventeenth and Eighteenth Centuries* (Charleston 1984) 11, and in 'William III and his Two Navies', *Notes Rec R Soc Lond* 43 (1989) 117–132, (p 121 in particular). William was involved in regular Admiralty business, as J David Davies has shown in his study of Admiralty Board minutes in the first year of the war, 'The English Navy on the Eve of War 1689', *Guerres Maritime 1688–1713: IVes Journées franco-britanniques d'historie de la Marine* (Paris 1996) 6–7. Nevertheless, while he was clearly interested, it still does not seem that William attempted to impose any major change of course on the Admiralty's direction of affairs until early 1693.

39. HMC, *Downshire* i; now in BL Addit MS 72572.

40. Baxter, *William III* 312.

41. Ehrman, 'Mediterranean', 282.

42. E W H Fryers, 'The Story of the Machine Vessels', *MM* xi (1912) 57–78.

43. Shovell to Nottingham, 26 August 1692. HMC, *Finch Hatton* iv, 420.

44. PRO Adm 6/3, fo 59: Commission to command *Cambridge*, 3 June 1695.

45. PRO Adm 6/3, fos 107, 109: Commission as vice-admiral of the red, 26 Dec 1695; in this he was two days junior to Aylmer who was also appointed vice-admiral of the red at the same time; commission to command *Duchess*, 8 Dec 1695.

46. PRO Adm 6/3, fo 147: commission to command *Victory*, 22 April 1696; fo 150, commission as admiral of the blue, 28 April 1696.

47. PRO Adm 6/4, fo 19: commission as Commander-in-Chief, Mediterranean, 25 Aug 1696.

48. Sir George Rooke to Sir William Trumbull, 9 May 1696. HMC, *Downshire* i, 660–661.

49. PRO Adm 6/5, fo 24: appointment as admiral of the blue, 9 July 1698; commission as Commander-in-Chief of HM ships and vessels in the Rivers Thames and Medway, 25 Aug 1698.

50. Robert Walcott, *English Politics in the Early Eighteenth Century* (Oxford 1956) 53–58.

51. David W Hayton (ed), *The Parliamentary Diary of Sir Richard Cocks, 1698–1702* (Oxford 1996) footnote p 5; quote from Harley's notes on the debate, BL Loan 29/35/(1).

52. R D Merriman, *The Sergison Papers, 1689–1702* (NRS 1950) 7, 14, 56.

53. *CSP, Dom, 1699–1701*, 320, 351.

54. BL Add MS 40796, fo 167v.

55. *Memoirs of the Secret Services of John Macky, Esq* (London 1733) 121

56. *Secret Services of John Macky* 120–21.

57. *CSP, Dom, 1701–02*, 108

58. 'The Pattern of Orders to Intercept the Spanish Galleons, 1702', in Hattendorf, Knight, *et al* (eds), *British Naval Documents, 1204–1960* (NRS 1993) 204–208.

59. Shovell to Nottingham, 18 July 1702, PRO SP 42/67, fo 28; quoted in Hattendorf, *England in the War of the Spanish Succession* (New York and London 1987) 144.

60. Shovell to Nottingham, 28 July 1702, *CSP Dom, 1702–1703*, 200.

61. H A F Kamen, 'The Destruction of the Spanish Silver Fleet at Vigo in 1702', *Bulletin of the Institute of Historical Research* 39 (1966) 165–73.

62. William Cobbett, *Parliamentary History of England* (London 1806–1820) vi, 94–5.

63. Clyve Jones and Geoffrey Holmes (eds), *The London Diaries of William Nicolson, Bishop of Carlisle, 1702–1718* (Oxford 1985) 186–187, 196.

64. Admiralty Board Minutes, 7 Dec 1702. PRO Adm 3/17.

65. Daniel Defoe to Robert Harley [*circa* June 1704], enclosing his essay 'Of the Fleet and Sir George Rooke', in George Harris Healey (ed), *The Letters of Daniel Defoe* (Oxford 1955) 20–25.

66. *Defoe's* Review *in 22 Facsimile Volumes*. Publications of the Facsimile Text Society (New York 1938) vol i, 103: 20 May 1704; Paula R Backscheider, *Daniel Defoe: His Life* (Baltimore 1989) 158, 174–78, 188, 197. See also William Colepepper, *A True State of the difference between Sir George Rooke, Knt, and William Colpepper, Esq* (London 1704).

67. Godolphin to Hill, 15 Aug 1704. BL Add MS 37, 529, fo 57.

68. Among Tory publications, see William Pittis, *A Hymn to Neptune; occasioned by the late glorious victory obtain'd in the height of Malaga by her Majesty's royal navy, under the command of Sir George Rooke, vice-admiral of England . . .* (London 1705).

69. Healey (ed), *The Letters of Daniel Defoe*, 28 Sept 1704, 60–61.

70. Firth (ed), *Naval Songs and Ballads* 153–154; see also *Reflections on the Management of Sir George Rooke, Knight, vice-admiral of England, &c in the late fight in the Mediterranean* (London 1704).

71. H L Snyder (ed), *The Marlborough-Godolphin Correspondence* (Oxford 1975) vol i, 180 fn 3.

72. NMM MS JOD 24, fo 153, 8 Jan 1705.

73. Queen Anne to Godolphin, 6 June 1705. B C Brown (ed), *The Letters and Diplomatic Instructions of Queen Anne* (London 1968) 159–60. See also *Marlborough-Godolphin Correspondence* vol ii, 624, 788.

74. PRO Adm 6/8, fos 129–130: Lord High Admiral's appointment of Shovell as Rear-Admiral of England, 26 Dec 1704.

75. PRO Adm 6/8, fos 172v–173.

76. Peter McBride and Richard Larn, *Admiral Shovell's Treasure and Shipwreck in the Isles of Scilly* (Penryn 1999).

77. John Molesworth to his Mother, 28 Oct 1706, HMC, *Var Coll* viii, 240.

78. William J H Andrews (ed), *The Quest for Longitude* (Cambridge, Mass: Harvard University Collection of Historical Scientific Instruments, 1996) 81, 142–145, 207.

79. Will of Sir Cloudesley Shovell, PRO Prob 11/499, fos 166v–169v.

80. Lady Marow to her daughter, Lady Kay, 26 Aug 1708. HMC, *Dartmouth* iii, 146–147.

81. Will of Sir George Rooke, PRO Prob 11/506, fos 16–19.

82. Rev Gilbert Crokkat, *A Consolatory Letter to Lady Shovell* (1707); *The Life and Glorious Actions of Sir Cloudesly Shovel, Kt, Admiral of the Confederate Fleet in the Mediterranean Sea, who was unfortunately Drown'd upon the 22nd of October 1707, through the ship* Association *splitting on the Rocks near Scilly, in her passage from the* Streights *for England* (London 1707); *Secret Memoirs of the Life of the Honourable Sr Cloudsley Shovel, Kt, Admiral of Great Britain, containing His birth, Education and Rise, with a Full Account of all the* NAVAL BATTLES *since the Revolution and other honourable Exploits perform'd for the service of his country; and a more exact Relation of the Enterprize upon* TOULON, *than any yet extant. By a Gentleman who served in that Expedition, and was several years under Command of that Admiral. With his Effigies curiously Engraven on a Copper Plate* (London 1708);
83. William Pittis, *Nereo. A funeral-poem sacred to the immortal memory of Sir George Rooke, Kt, lately deceas'd; sometime since Vice-admiral of England, Commander in chief of her Majesty's royal Navy, and one of the lords of her most honourable Privy Council, &c* (London 1709); see also the earlier volume, *The life and glorious actions of the Right Honourable Sir George Rooke, Kt, Sometime admiral of the English Fleet, vice-admiral of England, &c* (London 1707).
84. G M Trevelyan, *England Under Queen Anne: Blenheim* (London 1932) vol i, 261.

George Byng, Viscount Torrington

Unless otherwise attributed the account of Byng is from:

J K Laughton (ed), *Memoirs Relating to the Lord Torrington* (Camden Society, New Series xlvi London 1889).
B Tunstall (ed), *The Byng Papers* (3 vols NRS 1930-3).
J L Cranmer-Byng (ed), *Pattee Byng's Journal 1718-1720* (NRS 1948).

1. J Black, *Britain as a Military Power 1688-1815* (London 1999) 80 for a good example.
2. B Tunstall, *Admiral Byng and the Loss of Minorca* (London 1928); D Pope, *At Twelve Mr Byng Was Shot* (London 1962).
3. PRO Adm 2/1738 fo 223v.
4. PRO Adm 2/1738 fos 248 & v.
5. PRO Adm 8/1.
6. F Hervey, *Naval History of Great Britain* (London 1779) 67.
7. P Le Fevre, 'John Tyrrell (1646-1692)', *MM* lxx (1984) 149-60.
8. John Ehrman, *The Navy in the War of William III, 1689-1697: its state and direction* (Cambridge 1953).
9. J D Davies, 'Pepys and The Admiralty Commission of 1679-1684', *Historical Research* 62 (1989) 48-9.
10. J D Davies, *Gentlemen and Tarpaulins: the officers and men of the Restoration navy* (Oxford 1992) 199-200.
11. Longleat Thynne papers 41 fo 49v.
12. Davies, *Gentlemen and Tarpaulins* 203.
13. Davies, *Gentlemen and Tarpaulins* 202.
14. Davies, *Gentlemen and Tarpaulins* 200-214; David Davies, 'James II, William III and the Admirals', in E Cruickshanks (ed), *By Force or By Default: the Revolution of 1688-9* (Edinburgh 1989) 82-108.

15. See above, Chapter 1: Arthur Herbert, Earl of Torrington.
16. Folger Shakespeare Lib Washington X. d451(98).
17. Geoffrey Symcox, *The Crisis of French Sea Power 1688-1697: from the guerre d'escadre to the guerre de course* (The Hague 1974).
18. Gillian Hughes, 'The Act for the Increase and Encouragement of Seamen 1696-1710. Could it have solved the Royal Navy's manning problem?', in P Le Fevre (ed), *Guerres Maritimes 1688-1713* (Vincennes 1996) 25-33.
19. J H Owen, *The War at Sea Under Queen Anne* (Cambridge 1938) 80.
20. Owen, *The War at Sea* 91.
21. Owen, *The War at Sea* 172-192.
22. Owen, *The War at Sea* 192.
23. J Gibson, *Playing the Scottish card: The Franco-Jacobite invasion of 1708* (Edinburgh 1988) 131 for quotation; *Commons Journal* xv 649.
24. D Gregory, *Minorca, the Illusory Prize* (London and Toronto 1990) 15-25.
25. PRO Adm 1/376, George Byng to Josiah Burchett, 28 July 1704.
26. Henry Snyder, 'Queen Anne versus the Junto: the effort to place Orford at the head of the Admiralty in 1709', *Huntington Library Quarterly* 35 (1972) 326-339.
27. J C Sainty, *Admiralty Officials 1669-1870* (London 1975) 18, 22; PRO Adm 3/24-6 (Admiralty Board Minutes 1709-12); S Martin-Leake (G Callender ed), *The Life of Sir John Leake* (2 vols NRS 1920-1) ii, 370.
28. PRO Adm 3/28.
29. PRO Adm 1/518.
30. John Hattendorf, 'Byng: Passaro, 1718', in E Grove (ed), *Great Battles of the Royal Navy* (London 1994) 63-70; A T Mahan, *The Influence of Sea Power upon History 1660-1783* (reprint London 1965) 237.
31. PRO Adm 1/518.
32. Quoted in J Plumb, *Sir Robert Walpole* (2 vols London 1956 & 1960) ii, 170n.
33. Sainty, *Admiralty Officials* 22; PRO Adm 3/36-41 Admiralty Minute Books 1727-37.
34. PRO Adm 3/40.
35. D Baugh, *Naval Administration 1715-1750* (NRS 1977) 6; PRO Adm 3/40 13 March 1730, 26 Nov 1730; PRO Adm 3/41 Jan 1733.

Sir Charles Wager

1. I am grateful to the following persons for their generous help on particular points of research: Dr Andrew Hanham of the History of Parliament Trust, Professor Ian K Steele, Mr Bert Lippincott of the Newport (Rhode Island) Historical Society, Captain Roger Richardson-Bunbury, RN, and Mr James Derriman.
2. Basil Williams, *The Life of William Pitt, Earl of Chatham* (2 vols London 1913) 93; John Morley, *Walpole* (London 1903); J H Plumb, *Sir Robert Walpole* (2 vols London 1956-60).
3. William Coxe, *Memoirs of the Life and Administration of Sir Robert Walpole* (3 vols London 1798) iii, 116-17.
4. Wager to Mr Samuel Cooper, 27 April 1732, *Gloucestershire Notes and Queries* i (1881) 119-20.

5. Coxe, *Walpole* iii, 116.

6. Bernard Capp, *Cromwell's Navy: the fleet and the English revolution, 1648–1660* (Oxford 1989) 172. Sir Charles believed that his father was born at Chatham (*Gloucs N & Q* i, 120). For the story of George Wager, see S R Gardiner, *Letters and Papers relating to the First Dutch War* vol i (NRS 1899) 5–6.

7. Capp, *Cromwell's Navy* 391.

8. J R Tanner (ed), *A Descriptive Catalogue of the Naval Manuscripts in the Pepysian Library* (4 vols NRS 1903–9) i, 258; J D Davies, *Gentlemen and Tarpaulins: the officers and men of the Restoration navy* (Oxford 1991) 129.

9. R C Anderson (ed), *Letters and Papers of Sir Thomas Allin, 1660–1678* (2 vols NRS 1939–40) ii, 218–20. Robert Latham and William Matthews (eds), *The Diary of Samuel Pepys* (11 vols London 1970–83) vi, 286 (2 Nov 1665); ix, 137 (27 March 1668).

10. He stated in 1732: 'my Father dy'd before I was born' (*Gloucs N & Q* i, 119). For the father's date of death, see Joseph Lemuel Chester, *The Marriage, Baptismal, and Burial Registers of the Collegiate Church or Abbey of St Peter, Westminster* (London 1876) [hereafter *Westminster Abbey Registers*], 363. Family Search International Genealogical Index (Film No 1760912) reveals a record of his birth in Rochester. International Genealogical Index produced by the Church of Jesus Christ and the Latter-day Saints.

11. Capp, *Cromwell's Navy* 374, 382, 387.

12. Two sons and four daughters (*Westminster Abbey Registers* 363).

13. John O Austin, *The Genealogical Dictionary of Rhode Island* (Albany, NY 1887), 'Hull (John)'.

14. *New England Historical and Genealogical Register* [hereafter *NEH&GR*] 31 (1877) 167–69.

15. Gertrude S Kimball, *The Correspondence of the Colonial Governors of Rhode Island, 1723–1775* (2 vols Boston and New York 1902) 215; Cambridge University Library, Cholmondeley (Houghton) [hereafter Ch. (H)] MSS 1784, 1786, 1807 (Dec 1730, Jan 1731).

16. *Bishop Burnet's History of his Own Time: With Notes* (6 vols Oxford 1833) v, 390.

17. *Westminster Abbey Registers* 363.

18. PRO Adm 8/2. The Admiralty recorded the date as 24 June, and later Wager wrote two letters to get it corrected (PRO Adm 1/2637, 29 Sept 1699; 1/2638, 7 June 1700).

19. PRO Adm 8/2–3. 'Notarial Records of Portsmouth, New Hampshire,' *NEH&GR* 69 (1915) 361; 8 Nov 1693, protest by Capt Richard Martin relating to cargo on his ship bound for England under the convoy of their Majesties' Ship Samuel and Henry, Capt Charles Wager, commander; HMC, *Buccleuch* ii, pt 1 (1903) 309.

20. *CSP, Colonial Series: America and West Indies, 1696–97* (London 1904) 420, 428.

21. PRO Adm 1/2636, 2–6 June 1698; 1/2637, 17 June 1699.

22. I am indebted to Mr James Derriman and Dr Andrew Hanham for this information.

23. PRO Adm 1/2638, 7 June 1700; 1/2639, 9 Aug 1701; Josiah Burchett, *A Complete History of the Most Remarkable Transactions at Sea* (London 1720) 642.

24. J K Laughton (ed), *Memoirs Relating to the Lord Torrington* (Camden Society, New Series xlvi London

1889) 111–14, 117; S Martin-Leake (G Callender ed), *The Life of Sir John Leake* (2 vols NRS 1920–1) ii, 129–37; Thomas Lediard, *The Naval History of England* [hereafter Lediard] (London 1735) 809.

25. Lediard 835. Accounts of the battle vary in respect to details. For the composition of the Spanish fleet see BL Add MS 61643, fos 158–9.

26. PRO Adm 1/5267 (court martial records) Port Royal, 23 July 1708.

27. *Calendar of Treasury Papers, 1708–14*, 123, 255. John Campbell, *Lives of the British Admirals* (London 1744) iv, 92.

28. H Kamen, *The War of Succession in Spain 1700–15* (London 1969) 177–96.

29. Information from Mr James Derriman, based on records relating to the Trelawny estates in Cornwall.

30. Lediard 894–8; PRO SP 42/81, fos 29–156; James F Chance, *The Alliance of Hanover* (London 1923) 338–49.

31. Lediard's account of this fleet's operations, pages 901–910, is detailed (he dedicated the book to Wager); see also Wager to Walpole, 9 May 1727, Ch (H) MSS 1422. The total value of the prizes taken by ships under Wager's command amounted to £13,274; see BL Add MS 19,019, fos 339–40.

32. J Black, *The Collapse of the Anglo-French Alliance, 1727–1731* (Gloucester 1987) 9–10, 47–50; Chance, *Alliance of Hanover* 744–50.

33. L G Wickham Legg (ed), *British Diplomatic Instructions 1689–1789* (7 vols London 1922–34) vi, 51–3.

34. PRO SP 42/82, fos 137–233.

35. Lediard 914–18; PRO SP 42/82, fos 249–396.

36. Delafaye to the Earl of Waldegrave, 18 Jan 1733, quoted in Coxe, *Walpole* iii, 128.

37. Library of Congress, Vernon-Wager MSS, Wager to Sir Chaloner Ogle, 7 July 1733; D A Baugh (ed), *Naval Administration 1715–1750* (NRS 1977) 15; N A M Rodger, *The Wooden World: an anatomy of the Georgian navy* (London 1986) calls attention to the value of having a sea officer as First Lord.

38. See, for instance, PRO SP 42/82, *passim*. The main cache, however, is the body of Vernon-Wager MSS, part of the Peter Force collection of the Library of Congress, Washington, DC, to which institution I am grateful for convenient microfilm access. There is a first-rate printed guide: Library of Congress, *List of the Vernon-Wager Manuscripts*, compiled under the direction of Worthington Chauncey Ford (Washington 1904). It is fairly clear that this body of papers had been in Wager's possession rather than Vernon's.

39. Richard Lodge (ed), *The Private Correspondence of Sir Benjamin Keene, KB* (Cambridge 1933) 3–4, letter of 30 Sept 1730. Note: Wager probably wrote 'Owners', not 'Buners' on page 3.

40. That is what Jan Glete has termed the period 1720-1740 in *Navies and Nations: warships, navies and state building in Europe and America, 1500–1860* (2 vols Stockholm 1993) i, 255–7.

41. Ch (H) MS 1422, from near Cadiz, 9 May 1727.

42. [Edward Vernon] *Some Letters To An Honest Sailor* (London 1746) 19; also 46–7.

43. The causes of failure, however, remain under investigation. Richard Harding, in *Amphibious Warfare in the Eighteenth Century: the British expedition to the*

West Indies 1740-1742 (Woodbridge 1991), counters Sir Herbert Richmond's strong inclination to side with Vernon in *The Navy in the War of 1739-48* (3 vols Cambridge 1920). The brief account of the strategic decision-making in Richard Pares, *War and Trade in the West Indies, 1739-1763* (Oxford 1936) continues to deserve close attention.

44. PRO SP 42/82, fo 137; HMC, *Diary of the first Earl of Egmont (Viscount Percival)* [hereafter *Egmont Diary*] (3 vols 1920-3) ii, 15; D A Baugh, *British Naval Administration in the Age of Walpole* (Princeton 1965) 179-201, 234-40. A French squadron that sailed about the same time carried fever with it and many men died.

45. See especially Philip Woodfine, *Britannia's Glories: the Walpole Ministry and the 1739 war with Spain* (Woodbridge 1998) 210-44.

46. BL Egerton MS 2529, fo 122, letter of 27 Feb 1741.

47. *Egmont Diary* iii, 140; Wager to the Earl of Harrington, 22 Dec, 30 Dec 1736, PRO Adm 42/81, fos 188-92; Romney Sedgwick (ed), *Lord Hervey's Memoirs* (London 1952) 224-9.

48. *Egmont Diary* iii, 219-20, 233, 236, 250. John B Owen, *The Rise of the Pelhams* (London 1957) 9.

49. Charles James Fèret, *Fulham Old and New* (3 vols London 1900) ii, 90-6. In November 1728 Wager had been made chairman of the committee to build Old Fulham (or Putney) toll bridge, which was opened for traffic a year later (i, 54-9).

50. *Westminster Abbey Registers* 363-4, 375. The epitaph is printed in John Campbell, *Lives of the British Admirals* (8 vols London 1812-17) iv, 463.

Sir John Norris

1. *DNB* xiv (1909) 582; Chidwall parish register (Childwall was the parish for Speke), National Record Office, Dublin, Register of Deeds.

2. PRO Adm 33/108 no 75 (*Gloucester Hulk* paybook); David Aldridge, 'Sir John Norris 1660/1–1749', *MM* 51 (1965) 174.

3. PRO Adm 33/119 no 224 (*Sapphire* paybook); Adm 106/353 fo 555.

4. PRO Adm 33/138 no 327 (*Anne* paybook); NMM Adm/L/A 32, Lieutenant's log *Anne*.

5. E B Powley, *The Naval Side of King William's War* (London 1972); P Le Fevre, 'The battle of Bantry Bay 1 May 1689', *The Irish Sword* xviii (1990) 14.

6. P Le Fevre, 'The Earl of Torrington's Court-martial 10 December 1690', *MM* 76 (1990) 243-9.

7. P Aubrey, *The Defeat of James Stuart's Armada 1692* (Leicester 1979).

8. PRO Adm 51/3935/1, *Plymouth*, 18-19 Jan 1695; SP 42/5 fo 1.

9. PRO Adm 51/4395, Adm 33/214 for details of the voyage.

10. PRO Adm 1/2215, John Norris to Josiah Burchett, 27 Feb 1701, 28 Feb 1701.

11. PRO Adm 1/2215, John Norris to Josiah Burchett, 13 July [1701].

12. PRO Adm 1/2215, John Norris to Josiah Burchett, 1 Mar 1702.

13. O Browning (ed), *The Journal of Sir George Rooke Admiral of the Fleet 1700-1702* [hereafter *Rooke Journal*] (NRS 1897) 181-2, 188.

14. J H Owen, *War at Sea under Queen Anne, 1702-1798* (Cambridge 1938) 81; *Rooke Journal* 250; PRO Adm 52/248/6 Master's log *Orford*.

15. PRO Adm 8/8, 1 July 1704; B McL Ranft (ed), *The Vernon Papers* (NRS 1958) 448.

16. NMM JOD 24 fo 146v; PRO Adm 52/248/9 Master's log *Orford*; A Boyer, *Annals of Queen Anne* (10 vols London 1703-11) iii, 55; Owen, *War at Sea* 12.

17. A D Francis, *The First Peninsular War 1702-1713* (London 1975) 184; Owen, *War at Sea* 145; BL Add MS 28126 fos 33-9; G W Marshall (ed), *Le Neve's Pedigrees of the Knights* (Harleian Society viii 1873) 491.

18. PRO Adm 1/2215, John Norris to Josiah Burchett, 11 Mar 1707.

19. BL Add MS 28134 fos 63, 155, 159, 163; Henry Snyder (ed), *The Marlborough Godolphin Correspondence* (3 Vols Oxford 1975) iii, 1284, 1313, 1318.

20. PRO Adm 3/24 Board Minutes; BL Add MS 28153; PRO Adm 1/4095; 1/4096; B Tunstall (N Tracy ed), *Naval Warfare in the Age of Sail* (London 1990) 73.

21. PRO Prob 11/ 771 fo 96v.

22. PRO SP 42/8-11.

23. See D Aldridge, 'Swedish Privateering 1710-1718 and the Reactions of Great Britain and the United Provinces', in *Course et Piraterie* (Paris 1975) 416-440; D Aldridge, 'The Victualling of the British Naval Expeditions to the Baltic Sea between 1715 and 1727', *Scandinavian Economic History Review* 12 (1964) 1-25; D Aldridge, 'Sir John Norris and the British Naval Expeditions in the Baltic Sea, 1715-1727', unpublished PhD thesis (London 1972).

24. PRO Adm 3/29, 4 Mar 1715, 10 May 1715; Adm 8/14, 1 June 1715; Adm 51/222, Captain's log *Cumberland*.

25. BL Add MS 28143 fos 14, 19; R K Massie, *Peter the Great* (paperback ed London 1987) 729.

26. C Nordmann, *La Crise du Nord au debut du 18e siecle* (Paris 1962) 175; PRO Adm 8/14 , 1 Apr 1716; HMC, *Polwarth Papers* i & ii.

27. BL Stowe MS 229 fo 374; NMM Upc I, letter of 15 Feb 1717.

28. BL Add MS 28145 fo 229.

29. PRO Adm 8/14.

30. Guildhall Library MS 30302 p 62.

31. BL Maps 5 e 20 for Norris's book of Maps; Guildhall Library MS 30302 p 3.

32. PRO SP42/84, *passim*; D B Horn, *British Diplomatic Representatives, 1689-1789* (London 1932) 99.

33. R R Sedgwick, *The House of Commons* (2 vols London 1970) ii, 298; Dava Sobel, *Longitude* (New York 1995) 82.

34. D Baugh, *Naval Administration 1715-1750* (NRS 1977); PRO HCA 43/8; R Pares, *Colonial blockade and Neutral Rights* (Philadephia 1975) 104.

35. Baugh, *Naval Administration* 233-40.

36. PRO Adm 1/577, 19 Jan 1739/40, 31 Dec 1703, 14 Dec 1705 and 19 Jan 1709.

37. PRO SP 42/87 *passim*.

38. Sedgwick, *The House of Commons* ii, 298.

39. BL Add MS 28133, 4 Mar 1742.

40. PRO SP42/87, 418, Norris to Newcastle, 22 Mar 1743/4.

41. B Lavery, *The Ship of the Line* (2 vols London 1983-4) i, 90-2.

42. Sedgwick, *The House of Commons* ii, 298; quotation in Lavery, *The Ship of the Line* i, 91.

43. R Gardiner, *The First Frigates: nine-pounder and twelve-pounder frigates, 1748-1815* (London 1992); Sedgwick, *The House of Commons* ii, 298; epitaph quoted in Aldridge, 'Norris' 182 from F Haslewood, *History of the Parish of Benenden Kent* (Ipswich 1889) 7-8. His will is in PRO Prob 11/771 fos 91v-101v.

44. PRO SP 42/87 fo 414, Norris to Newcastle, 18 Mar 1744.

Edward Vernon

1. I would like to thank Professor Daniel Baugh for his comments upon a draft of this paper.

2. See the highly unreliable biography by D Ford, *Admiral Vernon and theNavy* (London 1907).

3. G Jordan and N Rogers, 'Admirals as Heroes: Patriotism and Liberty in Hanoverian England', *Journal of British Studies* 28 (1989) 201-224; See also K Wilson, *The Sense of the People: politics, culture and imperialism in England, 1715-1785* (Cambridge 1998) 140-165.

4. S Anderson, *An English Consul in Turkey: Paul Rycaut at Smyrna, 1667-1678* (Oxford 1989) 104.

5. P M Handover, *A History of the London Gazette, 1665-1965* (London 1965) 21, 26-31; HMC, *12th Report*, appendix vii, Manuscripts of S W le Fleming at Rydal Hall 204, Sir John Lowther to Sir D F [Daniel Fleming], 4 Oct 1678.

6. D B Henning (ed), *The History of Parliament: The House of Commons, 1660-1690*, (3 vols London 1983) iii, 639-40 ; *DNB*.

7. The inventory of Vernon's books at his house in London in 1726 is quite extensive and shows catholic tastes. They include works in French and Latin. History, geography, law, English and foreign literature, dictionaries and religion are all present. See BL Add MS 40836 (Common Place Book).

8. O Browning (ed), *Journal of Sir George Rooke* (NRS 1897) 17.

9. HMC, *The Manuscripts of the House of Lords*, New Series vol 5: 1702-1704 (London 1910) 101-124, 24 Nov 1702.

10. J Russell (ed), *The Correspondence of John, fourth Duke of Bedford* (3 vols London 1842-1846) i, 41, Vernon to Bedford, 28 Aug 1745.

11. PRO Adm 1/2624, undated enclosure, Jan 1707.

12. His father had been given the sinecure office of teller of the exchequer in 1702 and his brother had been a clerk of the exchequer since 1709.

13. PRO Adm 1/2624, Vernon to Burchett, 26 Feb 1715/6.

14. PRO Adm 1/2624, Vernon to Burchett, 18 Mar 1715/6.

15. PRO Adm 1/2634, Vernon to Burchett, 12 Feb 1716/7.

16. A H de Groot, 'The Dragomans of the Embassies in Istanbul, 1785-1834', in F Hitzel, *Istanbul et les Langues Orientales* (Paris-Montreal 1997) 129-158. I am grateful to Professor Elena Frangakis-Syrett for drawing my attention to this article and her advice on the role of the dragoman.

17. The details of this command can be found in Vernon's lengthy correspondence with the Admiralty in PRO Adm 1/2634.

18. PRO Adm 1/2634, Vernon to Burchett.

19. A N Newman (ed), *The Parliamentary Diary of Sir Edward Knatchbull, 1722-1730* (London 1963) 47.

20. PRO Adm 1/2624, Vernon to Burchett, 4 Aug 1727.

21. BL Add MS 40776 (James Vernon Papers) fo 76, Vernon to Townshend, 6 June 1726.

22. BL Add MS 40836, notes at rear of volume.

23. J Black, *The Collapse of the Anglo-French Alliance, 1727-1731* (Gloucester 1987) 90-92.

24. Newman (ed), *Knatchbull Diary* 80. HMC, *Manuscripts of the Earl of Egmont. Diary of the First Earl of Egmont* i, 339. [herafter *Egmont Diary*] Vernon was correct about the ministry editing the documents. See G C Gibbs, 'Parliament and Foreign Policy in the Age of Stanhope and Walpole', *English Historical Review* lxxvii (1962) 333. PRO SP 42/69, Instruction to Hosier, 28 June 1726.

25. *Egmont Diary* i, 43-4.

26. *Egmont Diary* i, 263.

27. Newman (ed), *Knatchbull Diary*, 78.

28. *Egmont Diary* i, 331.

29. BL Add MS 40794 fo 9, 15 July 1729.

30. Medway Archives Office, Best Manuscripts U 480/C4, Vernon to Thomas Best, 9 May 1734. I am grateful to the Trustees of the Best family, estate and business collection and the Director of the Leisure, Arts and Libraries, Medway Council, for permission to quote from this collection.

31. Best Manuscripts U480/C4, Vernon to Thomas Best, 2 Jan 1734/5.

32. BL Add MS 40794, 14 June 1739.

33. Devonshire Papers, Chatsworth, First Series 182. 10, Newcastle to Devonshire, 7 July 1739.

34. Wager to Newcastle, 7? Dec 1738, quoted in D Baugh (ed), *Naval Administration, 1715-1750* (NRS 1977) 15.

35. Best Manuscripts U480/C1/4, Vernon to Thomas Best, 23 July 1739.

36. The text of the instructions can be found in B Mc Ranft (ed), *The Vernon Papers* (NRS 1958) 289-303.

37. Vernon to Newcastle, 29 July 1739, quoted in H W Richmond, *The Navy in the War of 1739-1748* (3 vols Cambridge 1920) i, 41.

38. Ranft (ed), *The Vernon Papers* 32-34, Vernon to Brown, 7 Nov 1739.

39. Ranft (ed), *The Vernon Papers* 313, Vernon to Burchett, 30 Aug 1740.

40. Vernon's administrative correspondence can be found in the *Vernon Papers* or in PRO Adm 1/233.

41. PRO SP 42/85, fo 37-39, Vernon to Newcastle, 31 Oct 1739.

42. BL Add MS 32694, fo 238, Newcastle to Vernon, 23 July 1740; fo 242, George II to Vernon, 10 July 1740; fo 33, A Proposal to take the Island of Cuba, 5 June 1738.

43. PRO SP 42/85, fo 203, Vernon to Newcastle, 9 May 1740.

44. Vernon's correspondence on these matters can be followed in PRO SP 42/85.

45. The references for this campaign and the attacks upon Cuba and Panama can be found in R H Harding, *Amphibious Warfare in the Eighteenth Century: the British expedition in the West Indies, 1740-1742* (Woodbridge 1991).

46. BL Add MS 40794, fo 28.

47. BL Add MS 40794, fo 26.

48. *Original Papers Relating to the Expedition to Cartagena* (London 1744); *Original Papers Relating to the Expedition to the Isle of Cuba* (London 1744); *Original Papers Relating to the Expedition to Panama* (London 1744); *Adm V——n's Opinion Upon the Present State of the British Navy in a Letter to a Certain Board* (London 1744).

49. *A Letter to the Secretary of a Certain Board*, (London 1744).

50. The enquiry and Vernon's role can be traced in BL Add MS 35337 (Parliamentary Journal of Philip Yorke).

51. HMC, *Du Cane*, 51, Henshaw to Medley, 14 Mar 1744/5.

52. *An Enquiry into the Conduct of Captain M——n* (London 1745).

53. *Vernon Papers* 445-6, Vernon to Bedford, 5 Aug 1745.

54. Vernon's letters for this period are in PRO Adm 1/648 and 649.

55. *Vernon Papers* 537, Vernon to Corbett, 1 Dec 1745.

56. H Walpole (J Brooke ed), *Memoirs of King George II* (3 vols London 1847) i, 68.

57. *Memoirs of the Reign of George II* ii, 72.

58. NMM Vernon Papers, VER/1/4/A, Francis Vernon to Edward Vernon, 17 Mar 1746/7.

George, Lord Anson

1. J Barrow, *The Life of George, Lord Anson* (London 1839) 14.

2. E K Thompson, 'George Anson in the province of South Carolina', *MM* liii (1967) 279-280. F B Stitt, 'Admiral Anson at the Admiralty, 1744-62', *Staffordshire Studies* iv (1991-2) 35-76, at p 37.

3. Glyndwr Williams, ' "The Inexhaustible Fountain of Gold"; English projects and ventures in the South Seas, 1670-1750', in John E Flint and G Williams (eds), *Perspectives of Empire: essays presented to Gerald S Graham* (London 1973) 27-53, at pp 46-48. Glyndwr Williams, *The Great South Sea: English voyages and encounters 1570-1750* (London 1997) 214-218. Glyndwr Williams, *The Prize of All the Oceans: the triumph and tragedy of Anson's voyage around the world* (London 1999) 1-15. Glyndwr Williams (ed), *Documents relating to Anson's Voyage around the world, 1740-1744* (NRS 1967) 3-44.

4. An impression based on reading the ships' muster books; *cf* J R Hutchinson, *The Press-Gang Ashore and Afloat* (London 1913) 317.

5. Williams, *The Prize of All the Oceans* 16-23.

6. Williams, *Documents* 77, quoting the journal of Lawrence Millechamp, purser of the *Tryal*.

7. For the circumnavigation generally see Williams, *The Prize of All the Oceans*; Williams, *Documents*; and R Walter and B Robins (G Williams ed), *Voyage around the World . . . by George Anson* (Oxford 1974).

8. Williams, *Documents* 224.

9. J M Haas, 'The Rise of the Bedfords, 1741-1747: a study of politics in the reign of George II', unpublished PhD thesis (Illinois 1960) 35-38. John B Owen, *The Rise of the Pelhams* (London 1957) 245-249.

10. Horace Walpole (John Brooke ed), *Memoirs of the Reign of King George II* (3 vols London 1985) i, 129. Cf *The Works of the Right Honourable Sir Chas Hanbury Williams* (3 vols London 1822) ii, 271.

11. PRO Adm 3/49-51.

12. M Duffy, 'The Establishment of the Western Squadron as the Linchpin of British Naval Strategy', in M Duffy (ed), *Parameters of British Naval Power* (Exeter 1992) 60-81. H W Richmond, *The Navy in the War of 1739-48* (3 vols Cambridge 1920) iii, 6-8, 20-23, 82-84, 226-229. B McL Ranft (ed), *The Vernon Papers* (NRS 1958) 436-437, 441, 451-452, 459. J S Corbett, *Some Principles of Maritime Strategy* (London 1911) 139-141, 195-196 & 254-256. A N Ryan, 'The Royal Navy and the Blockade of Brest, 1689-1805: Theory and Practice', in Martine Acerra, José Merino and Jean Meyer (eds), *Les Marines de Guerre Européennes, XVII-XVIIIe siècles* (Paris 1985) 175-194. N A M Rodger, *Insatiable Earl: a life of John Montagu, fourth Earl Sandwich* (London 1993) 35-37.

13. Richmond, *Navy in the War of 1739-48* iii, 78-112.

14. Sausmarez Papers, Sausmarez Manor, Guernsey, Box 72, Anson's orders of 6 Nov 1746 and signals of 19 Apr 1747. Brian Tunstall (Nicholas Tracy ed), *Naval Warfare in the Age of Sail: the evolution of fighting tactics 1650-1815* (London 1990) 92-101; John Creswell, *British Admirals of the Eighteenth Century: tactics in battle* (London 1972) 82-91. Richmond, *Navy in the War of 1739-48* iii, 263-266. R F Mackay, *Admiral Hawke* (Oxford 1965) 65-88. I am indebted to Dr Mackay for guidance on these questions.

15. BL Add MS 35387 fo 36, Elizabeth Yorke to Joseph Yorke, 5 Jun 1747.

16. BL Add MS 15957 fo 195, P Warren to G Anson, 31 May 1747.

17. BL Add MS 15957 fo 188, P Warren to G Anson, 20 May 1747.

18. David Spinney, *Rodney* (London 1969) 331.

19. Walter and Robins, *Voyage* 335-6.

20. BL Add MS 15955 fos 113-114, C Barnett to G Anson, 16 Sep 1745; *cf* Barrow, *Anson* 405.

21. Sir Havilland de Sausmarez, *Captain Philip Sausmarez, 1710-1747, and his Contemporaries* (Guernsey 1936) 12-16. BL Add MS 15957 fo 16, Sandwich to Anson, 20 Jul 1747; fo 208, Sir P Warren to Anson, 3 Aug 1747; fo 260, Warren to Anson, 2 Dec 1747. Staffordshire Record Office [SRO], D615/P(S)/1/10/7, Anson to Sir P Warren, 23 Jul 1747. Sausmarez MSS, Box 74, A Keppel to P de Saumarez, 28 Aug 1747. PRO SP 42/32 fos 306-309, Admiralty draft petition to the King, 13 Nov 1747.

22. PRO SP 42/30 fos 365-367, Secretary of the Admiralty to the Advocate-General and Admiralty Counsel, 16 May 1746.

23. Woburn MSS Vol X fo 112, Sandwich to Bedford, 22 Oct 1745. My quotations from the fourth Duke of Bedford's MSS at Woburn Abbey are by

courtesy of the Marquess of Tavistock and the Trustees of the Bedford Estates.

24. J Russell (ed), *Correspondence of John, fourth Duke of Bedford* (3 vols London 1842-6) i, 107-112 & 271. David Erskine (ed), *Augustus Hervey's Journal* (2nd ed London 1954) 78-84, quoting the Prince of Wales on p 81. D Baugh, *Naval Administration 1715-1750* (NRS 1977) 86-87. P C Yorke, *The Life and Correspondence of Philip Yorke, Earl of Hardwicke* (3 vols Cambridge 1913) ii, 84-85. W S Lewis (ed), *Horace Walpole's Correspondence* (48 vols New Haven, Conn 1937-83) xx, 33 & 38. NMM SOC/1, Sea Officers' Club Minutes, fos 15-21. J M Haas, 'The Rise of the Bedfords' 77-78.

25. BL Add MS 15956 fo197, Henry Legge to G Anson, 29 May 1747. Sausmarez MSS Box 74, T Brett to P Saumarez, 15 Aug 1747. Sir John Barrow, *The Life of Richard Earl Howe* (London 1838) 180-185. William Cobbett (ed), *The Parliamentary History of England* (36 vols London 1806-20) xxvii, 17-18. Rodger, *Insatiable Earl* 33-4.

26. Barrow, *Anson* 221-224. J S Bromley (ed), *The Manning of the Royal Navy: selected public pamphlets, 1693-1873* (NRS London 1974) xxxiv.

27. J A Lowe (ed), *Records of the Portsmouth Division of Marines, 1764-1800* (Portsmouth Record Series Vol 7, Portsmouth 1990) xiv. Barrow, *Anson* 210. John B Hattendorf et al (eds), *British Naval Documents 1204-1960* (NRS 1993) nos 244 & 245. PRO SP 42/33 fos 35-57 & 59.

28. B Lavery, *The Ship of the Line* (2 vols London 1983-4) i, 75-90. R Gardiner, *The First Frigates* (London 1992) 7-10. Rif Winfield, *The 50-Gun Ship* (London 1997) 46-62.

29. PRO Adm 106/2073, 31 Dec 1744, 12 & 23 Feb 1744/5. Adm 106/2114, 6 Aug 1745. Adm 3/49 fo 244 and Adm 3/51, Admiralty Board Minutes, 8 Feb 1744/5, 7 & 20 Jun 1745. D Baugh, *British Naval Administration in the Age of Walpole* (Princeton 1965) 251-252. Baugh, *Naval Administration 1715-50* 200 & 225-235. Lavery, *Ship of the Line* i, 93-95.

30. Woburn MSS Vol XI fo 34, H Legge to Bedford, 6 Mar 1745/6.

31. Gardiner, *First Frigates* 8-13.

32. Woburn MSS Vol XVI fo 73, G Anson to Bedford, 17 Apr 1747.

33. SRO D615/P(S)/1/9/21 & 22, B Slade to G Anson, 31 May & 21 Jul 1747. BL Add MS 15955 fo 119, W Bately to Anson, 5 Jun 1747. NMM AGC/13/25, B Slade to Anson, 10 Nov 1747. Gardiner, *First Frigates* 13-16.

34. Rodger, *Insatiable Earl* 28-29.

35. PRO Adm 3/61, Board minute of 9 Jun 1749.

36. Rodger, *Insatiable Earl* 65-66. PRO Adm 7/658, Minutes of Admiralty Visitation 1749; ADM 106/2116 s d 10 Nov 1749, 10 Jun, 26 Nov & 14 Dec 1751. Richard Middleton, 'The Visitation of the Royal Dockyards, 1749', *MM* lxxvii (1991) 21-30. James M Haas, 'The Royal Dockyards: The earliest Visitations and Reform 1749-1778', *Historical Journal* xiii (1970) 191-215.

37. NMM SAN/V/49 p 65, Chesterfield to Sandwich, 20 Feb 1746/7; SAN/V/50 p 210, C Clarke to Sandwich, 4 Mar 1747/8; SAN/V/53 p 135, Newcastle to Sandwich, 27 Mar 1747; Bonamy Dobrée (ed), *The Letters of Philip Dormer Stanhope, fourth Earl of Chesterfield* (6 vols London 1932) iii, 812 no 890, Chesterfield to Sandwich, 21 Nov 1746. Baugh, *British Naval Administration* 78-80. Russell, *Bedford Correspondence* i, 282-284. BL Add MS 32807 fos 208-9 & 263, Sandwich to Newcastle, 21 Mar & 11 Apr [NS 1747]; Add MS 15957 fo 65, Sandwich to Anson, 14 Jun NS 1748.

38. Woburn MSS Vol XV fo 74, G Anson to Bedford, 13 Dec 1746.

39. Rodger, *Insatiable Earl* 60.

40. BL Add MS 15957 fo 51, Sandwich to Anson, 5 Mar NS 1748. The version in Barrow, *Anson* p 203 requires correction.

41. Yorke, *Hardwicke* ii, 155-158. SRO D615/P(S)/1/2/2 Lady Anson to Anson, 2 May-10 Jun [1758]. Th Bussemakers (ed), *Archives ou correspondance inédité de la maison d'Orange-Nassau* Leiden (1908-17) iv, 91.

42. Rodger, *Insatiable Earl* 67-68. Philip Lawson, *George Grenville, a political life* (Oxford 1984), 62-66. Haas, 'Rise of the Bedfords' 71-90. Yorke, *Hardwicke* ii,113-118.

43. Mackay, *Hawke* 136-137 & 303-307. Charles Derrick, *Memoirs of the Rise and Progress of the Royal Navy* (London 1806) 292-295. Rodger, *Insatiable Earl* 66-67.

44. J S Corbett, *England in the Seven Years' War* (2 vols London 1907) i, 30-86.

45. Mackay, *Hawke* 136-137 & 306-308.

46. Corbett, *Seven Years' War* I,96-128. B Tunstall, *Admiral Byng and the Loss of Minorca* (London 1928) 1-148. BL Add MS 35359 fo 384, Anson to Hardwicke, 6 Dec 1755. Giles Fox-Strangeways, Earl of Ilchester, *Letters to Henry Fox, Lord Holland* (London 1915) 78-79, Newcastle to H Fox, 8 May 1756.

47. Tunstall, *Byng* 168-183. BL Add MS 32865 fo 159, Anson to Newcastle, 31 May [1756]. Add MS 35359 fos 387-388, Anson to Hardwicke, 26 Jan 1756. Russell, *Bedford Correspondence* ii, 224 & 239. N A M Rodger, *The Wooden World: an anatomy of the Georgian navy* (London 1986) 247-248.

48. Paul Langford, 'William Pitt and Public Opinion, 1757', *English Historical Review* lxxxviii (1973) 54-80, at p 74. SRO D615/P(S)/1/1, Lady Anson to Anson [25 Jun 1757]. Ilchester, *Letters to Henry Fox* 105.

49. R Middleton, *The Bells of Victory* (Cambridge 1985) 108-112 & 149-150. R Middleton, 'Pitt, Anson and the Admiralty, 1756-61', *History* New Series lv (1970) 189-198.

50. D Syrett (ed), *The Siege and Capture of Havana, 1762 (NRS 1970) xiii*. Middleton, *Bells of Victory* 205.

51. PRO Adm 1/384, Anson to Sir C Saunders, 22 Oct & reply 16 Nov 1761.

52. Middleton, 'Pitt, Anson and the Admiralty' 193, quoting Anson's colleague George Hay.

53. L Namier, *The Structure of Politics at the Accession of George III* (second ed London 1957) 34.

54. NMM UPC/3/8, E Wheeler to Anson, 2 Oct 1757. PRO Adm 73/404 no 996; Adm 1/235, T Cotes to Anson, 29 Sep 1758.

55. BL Eg MS 3444 fos 46-47, Anson to Holdernesse, 25 Jul 1755.

56. Mackay, *Hawke* 194-199. Rodger, *Wooden World* 310-311.

57. BL Add MS 35359 fos 393-394, Anson to Hardwicke, 13 May 1758.
58. BL Add MS 35359 fo 410, Anson to Hardwicke, [29 Jun 1758?].
59. BL Add MS 35359 fo 413, Anson to Hardwicke, 22 Jul 1758.
60. Stephen F Gradish, *The Manning of the British Navy during the Seven Years War* (London 1980) 161 & 164. Baugh, *Naval Admininistration 1715-50* 449-450. BL Add MS 15955 fo183, Timothy Brett to G Anson, 12 Apr 1747.
61. Rodger, *Wooden World* 101. Rodger, 'The Victualling of the British Navy during the Seven Years' War', *Bulletin du Centre d'Histoire des Éspaces Atlantiques* No 2 (Bordeaux 1985) 37-53.
62. Lowe, *Records of the Portsmouth Division of Marines* xiv-xv.
63. Lavery, *Ship of the Line* i, 96-103. Gardiner, *First Frigates* 22-37.
64. Rodger, *Wooden World* 299-300.
65. Notably by Namier, *Structure of Politics* 33-34.
66. Rodger, *Wooden World* 328-343.
67. Bussemakers, *Correspondance Inédité* iv,331.
68. Rodger, *Wooden World* 301-302.
69. Mackay, *Hawke* 303-308. Rodger, *Insatiable Earl* 131-145.
70. J C D Clark (ed), *The Memoirs and Speeches of James, second Earl Waldegrave, 1742-1763* (Cambridge 1988) 186. PRO PRO 30/9/31, diary of Lord Berkeley of Stratton, s a 1756.
71. BL Add MS 35428, fo 4, second Lord Hardwicke's 'Memorial of Family Occurances, 1760-70', Jan 1771; printed in Yorke, *Hardwicke* ii, 156-157.
72. BL Add MS 15956 fo272, S Mostyn to Anson, 29 Oct 1747.
73. Glyndwr Williams, 'Anson at Canton, 1743: "A Little Secret History" ', in Cecil H Clough and P E H Hair (eds), *The European Outthrust and Encounter: essays in tribute to David Beers Quinn* (Liverpool 1994) 270-290.
74. Woburn MSS Vol XV fo 83, G Anson to Bedford, 26 Dec 1746.
75. Mackay, *Hawke* 135-136.

Edward Hawke, Lord Hawke

1. R Mackay (ed), *The Hawke Papers* (NRS 1990) 8-9.
2. Mackay (ed), *Hawke Papers* 15-16.
3. BL Add MS 15917 (Anson Papers) fo 211, 7 Aug 1747.
4. Mackay (ed), *Hawke Papers* 37-8, 50, 55.
5. Mackay (ed), *Hawke Papers* 42.
6. Mackay (ed), *Hawke Papers* 46.
7. Mackay (ed), *Hawke Papers* 51.
8. PRO Adm 51/739/5.
9. Mackay (ed), *Hawke Papers* 73.
10. Mackay (ed), *Hawke Papers* 69.
11. Mackay (ed), *Hawke Papers* 56, 62-85.
12. D Erskine (ed), *Augustus Hervey's Journal* (London 1953) 262.
13. R Mackay, *Admiral Hawke* (Oxford 1965) 180-3.
14. D Bonner-Smith (ed), *The Barrington Papers* (2 vols NRS 1937 & 1941) i, 231-2.
15. Mackay, *Admiral Hawke* 201.

16. C Lloyd (ed), *The Health of Seamen* (NRS 1965) 121-2, 132-3.
18. Mackay (ed), *Hawke Papers* 344-50.
19. O Troude, *Batailles navales de la France* (4 vols Paris 1867) i, 386-95.
20. J S Corbett and H W Richmond (eds), *Private Papers of George second Earl Spencer, First Lord of the Admiralty 1794-1801* (4 vols NRS 1913-24) 381.
21. *DNB*, 'William Locker'; E H Locker, *Memoirs* (London 1831) 32.
22. PRO Adm 3/74-8.
23. N A M Rodger, *Insatiable Earl: A life of John Montague, fourth Earl Sandwich* (London 1993) 148-9.

George Bridges Rodney, Lord Rodney

1. PRO 30/20 26 (Rodney Papers).
2. PRO 30/20 20.
3. G R Barnes and J H Owen (eds), *The Private Papers of John Earl of Sandwich, First Lord of the Admiralty 1771-1782* (4 vols NRS 1932-1928) iii, 211, Rodney to Sandwich, 26 April 1780 [hereafter *Sandwich Papers*].
4. *Sandwich Papers* iv, 165, Sandwich to Rodney, 7 July 1781.
5. HMC, *Stopford Sackville* ii, 194, Rodney to Germain, 22 Dec 1780.
6. PRO PRO 30/20 9, Rodney to Stephens, 10 Dec 1780.
7. *Sandwich Papers* iv, 156, Hood to Sandwich, 4 May 1781.
8. D Hannay (ed), *Letters written by Sir Samuel Hood in 1781-2-3* (NRS 1895) 15, Hood to Jackson, 21 May 1781 [hereafter *Hood Letters*].
9. *Hood Letters* 16, Hood to Jackson, 21 May 1781.
10. *Hood Letters* 18, Hood to Jackson, 24 June 1781.
11. *Hood Letters* 107-8, Hood to Jackson, 16 April 1782.
12. *Hood Letters* 104, Hood to Jackson, 16 April 1782.
13. PRO PRO 30/20 9 (Rodney Letter book).
14. PRO PRO 30/20 21, Sandwich to Rodney, 25 Sept 1780.
15. D Hood, *The Admirals Hood* (London 1942) 64.
16. BL Burney Collection, *Public Advertiser*, 24 Sept 1781.
17. PRO PRO 30/20 21, Sandwich to Rodney, 6 Nov 1781.
18. G Mundy, *Life of Admiral Lord Rodney* (2 vols London 1830) ii, 195.
19. *Sandwich Papers* iv, 246, Hood to Sandwich, 31 March 1782.
20. PRO ADM 1/314, Rodney to Parker, 5 March 1782.
21. PRO ADM 51/365, Captain's log, *Formidable*.
22. PRO ADM 1/314, Rodney to Sandwich, 14 April 1782.
23. PRO PRO 30/20 26, Keppel to Rodney, 2 May 1782.
24. K C Breen, 'Sir George Rodney and St Eustatius in the American War', *MM* 84 (1998) 193-203.

Samuel Hood, First Viscount Hood

1. His father was Alexander Hood, squire of Mosterton in Dorset. See Dorothy Hood, *The Admirals Hood* (London 1942) 11; *DNB* (London 1891) xxvii, 263.

2. Hood, *Admirals Hood* 11; D Baugh, 'Sir Samuel Hood: Superior Subordinate', in G A Billias (ed), *George Washington's Generals and Opponents: their exploits and leadership* (New York 1994) 292; John Beckett, *The Rise and Fall of the Grenvilles* (Manchester 1994) 9, 26.

3. Hood, *Admirals Hood* 15.

4. Hood, *Admirals Hood* 14; PRO Adm 1/801, Watson to Admiralty, 25 Aug 1752.

5. Hood, *Admirals Hood* 14–17. Some idea of the state of Portsmouth's politics can be gleaned from N W Surry and J H Thomas, *Book of Original Entries 1731–1751* (Portsmouth Record Series, Portsmouth 1976), Introduction; R Sedgwick, *History of Parliament. The House of Commons 1715–54* (London 1970) i, 252–3; A Geddes, *Portsmouth during the Great French Wars 1770–1800* (Portsmouth Papers No 9, Portsmouth 1970) 10–17; and L Namier and J Brooke, *History of Parliament. The House of Commons 1754–90* (London 1964), 297–9. For Linzee (1700–82) see Surry and Thomas, *Book of Original Entries* 105 (which omits his mayoralty of 1745–6, p 90).

6. M Wyndham, *Chronicles of the Eighteenth Century* (London 1924) ii, 102, 108.

7. *Naval Chronicle* ii (1799) 4.

8. Baugh, 'Hood: Superior Subordinate', 292–3.

9. *DNB* xxvii.

10. J Ralfe, *Naval Biography* (4 vols London 1828) i, 203, describes the episode, but follows an error in the *Naval Chronicle* i (1799) 266, in mistakenly attributing it to Hood's brother Alexander.

11. Ralfe i, 244; Hood, *Admirals Hood* 25.

12. Spinney, *Rodney* (London 1969) 151–60.

13. Hood to Admiralty, 30 April 1760.

14. Ralfe i, 244.

15. V Birdwood (ed), *So Dearly Loved, So Much Admired: Letters to Hester Pitt, Lady Chatham* (London 1994) 45; W J Smith (ed), *The Grenville Papers* (London 1852–3) iv, 335, 361. Hood's letters to the Grenvilles also described the colonial situation he found as Commodore on the North American station.

16. Smith (ed), *Grenville Papers* iv, 306–8, 332–5, 361–3, 373–9.

17. Surry and Thomas, *Portsmouth Book of Entries* 105, 107.

18. D Hannay (ed), *Letters written by Sir Samuel Hood in 1781-2-3* (NRS 1895) 155–6.

19. Hood, *Admirals Hood* 33, 48. Hood's report on the *Marlborough* accident is in NMM SAN/F/11/85, Hood to the First Lord of the Admiralty, Sandwich, 9 July 1776.

20. PRO 30/8/44, Hood's letters to Lady Chatham, 28 May, 5 Aug 1776, 12 Feb 1778; NMM SAN/F/11/85, Hood to Sandwich, 21 Nov 1777; *Naval Chronicle* ii (1799) 6.

21. Hood, *Admirals Hood* 46–7; 'Extracts from the Papers of Samuel, First Viscount Hood', in J K Laughton (ed), *The Naval Miscellany I* (NRS 1902) 225–6.

22. Sir John Fortescue, *The Correspondence of George III* (London 1928) iv, 130, 170.

23. Quoted in Geddes, *Portsmouth during the Great French Wars* 16.

24. Hood, *Admirals Hood* 47–9, 51, 54; BL Add MS 35193, Sir S Hood to A Hood, 21 April 1780.

25. G R Barnes and J H Owen (eds), *The Private Papers of John, Earl of Sandwich* (4 vols NRS 1928–38) iii, 161–2, 228–30, 232.

26. Barnes and Owen (eds), *Sandwich Papers* iii, 229; Geddes, *Portsmouth during the Great French Wars* 11–15; A M W Stirling (ed), *Pages and Portraits from the Past. Being the private papers of Sir William Hotham* (London 1919) i, 32.

27. Barnes and Owen (eds), *Sandwich Papers* iii, 217; Spinney, *Rodney* 259.

28. Hannay (ed), *Hood Letters*, 17–18, 21–2.

29. Spinney, *Rodney* 368, 372.

30. Hannay (ed), *Hood Letters* 17.

31. K Breen, 'Divided command: the West Indies and North America, 1780–1781', in J Black and P Woodfine (eds), *The British Navy and the Use of Naval Power in the Eighteenth Century* (Leicester 1988) 201; Hannay (ed), *Hood Letters* 12–13; Sir J K Laughton (ed), *Letters and Papers of Charles, Lord Barham* (3 vols NRS 1907–11) i, 108–16; J H Owen, 'Letters from Sir Samuel Hood 1780–82', *MM* 19 (1933) 81. There are accounts of this action in W L Clowes, *The Royal Navy. A history from the earliest times to 1900* (7 vols London 1897–1903) iii, 482–7, 495–501; W M James, *The British Navy in Adversity* (London 1926) 258–61.

32. As above; Spinney, *Rodney* 373.

33. For Hood's contemporary accusations see Hannay (ed), *Hood Letters* 28–38; Laughton (ed), *Barham Papers* i, 124–6. The controversy is debated by K Breen, 'Graves and Hood at the Chesapeake', *MM* 66 (1980) 53–65; J A Sulivan, 'Graves and Hood', *MM* 69 (1983) 175–94; J Creswell, *British Admirals of the Eighteenth Century: tactics in battle* (London 1972) 154–62; B Tunstall (N Tracy ed), *Naval Warfare in the Age of Sail* (London 1990), 172–7; N A M Rodger, *The Insatiable Earl: a life of John Montagu, fourth Earl of Sandwich* (London 1993) 290–1.

34. Laughton (ed), *Barham Papers* i, 126; Hannay (ed), *Hood Letters* 48–54.

35. Hannay (ed), *Hood Letters* 62. For Hood's confidence in his captains, trained up under his own eye, see Laughton (ed), *Barham Papers* i, 141, 144.

36. Hannay (ed), *Hood Letters* 64–5.

37. Laughton (ed), *Barham Papers* i, 141–4; Hannay (ed), *Hood Letters* 79. For Hood at St Kitt's see A T Mahan, *The Influence of Sea Power upon History 1660–1783* (rep London 1965) 469–78, subsequently summarised in Clowes, *Royal Navy* iii, 510–19; Tunstall (Tracy ed), *Naval Warfare* 177–9.

38. Hannay (ed), *Hood Letters* 75–6, 82, 91–2; Laughton (ed), *Barham Papers* i, 148; *Naval Chronicle* ii (1799) 18 fn 1; Tunstall (Tracy ed), *Naval Warfare* 178–9. I have followed the *Canada's* log book on the 14th rather than Captain Manners's letter of the 22nd as to whether lieutenants or captains were summoned to synchronise their watches.

39. Hannay (ed), *Hood Letters* 83.

40. Mahan, *Influence of Sea Power*, 470, see also p 475.

41. M Battesti, *La Bataille d'Aboukir 1798* (Paris 1998) 75, 99.

42. Laughton (ed), *Barham Papers* i, 160–1; Mahan, *Influence of Sea Power* 480–97, subsequently sum-

marised in Clowes, *Royal Navy* iii, 519-37; Creswell, *British Admirals of the Eighteenth Century* 163-77; Tunstall (Tracy ed), *Naval Warfare* 179-84.

43. Spinney, *Rodney* 404-5.

44. Laughton (ed), *Barham Papers* i, 159-65, 177-80; Hannay (ed), *Hood Letters* 103-8, 131-2, 136-7; Barnes and Owen (eds), *Sandwich Papers* iv, 250-3, 260-1.

45. Laughton (ed), *Barham Papers* i, 189, 194.

46. Hannay (ed), *Hood Letters* 112; Laughton (ed), *Barham Papers* i, 184, 195.

47. Hannay (ed), *Hood Letters* 140, 145, 149, 157.

48. NMM HOO/1/115, George III to Hood, 6 Aug 1782; A Aspinall, *The Later Correspondence of George III* (5 vols Cambridge 1966) i, p xviii.

49. Sir N H Nicholas (ed), *The Despatches and Letters of Vice Admiral Lord Viscount Nelson* (7 vols London 1844-6) i, 69-70, 72.

50. Nicholas (ed), *Nelson Despatches and Letters* i, 77, 97.

51. Carr Laughton (ed), *The Life of a Sea Officer. Jeffrey Baron de Raigersfeld* (London 1929) xvi, 37-9.

52. BL Add MS 35194 fo 166; HMC, *MSS of the Duke of Rutland* iii (London 1894) 134.

53. Geddes, *Portsmouth during the Great French Wars* 13.

54. Aspinall (ed), *Later Correspondence of George III* i, 116; PRO 30/8/146, to Pitt, 12 Jan 1786.

55. Hood, *Admirals Hood* 93, 95-6; Nicholas, *Nelson Despatches and Letters* i, 203-11, B McL Ranft, 'Prince William and Lt Schomberg', *The Naval Miscellany IV* (NRS 1952) 270-93. Not for nothing did Schomberg dedicate his *Naval Chronology* (London 1802) to Hood.

56. NMM HOO/2/160.

57. Duke of Buckingham (ed), *Memoirs of the Courts and Cabinets of George III* (London 1853) i, 368, W Grenville to Buckingham, 1 April 1788.

58. BL Add MS 35194 fo 166.

59. J H Rose, *Lord Hood and the Defence of Toulon* (Cambridge 1922) 96-9.

60. Rose, *Lord Hood* 6.

61. Rose, *Lord Hood* 142, Hood to Nepean, 7 Oct 1793.

62. Rose, *Lord Hood* 126, Hood to Stephens, 29 Aug; PRO HO 28/14, Dundas to Hood, 25 Sept, Hood to Dundas, 27 Oct 1793.

63. Nicholas, *Nelson Despatches and Letters* i, 324; Cambridge University Library Add MSS 6958/7, Pitt to Westmorland, 15 Sept 1793.

64. Rose, *Lord Hood* 114-15.

65. Countess of Minto (ed), *Life and Letters of Sir Gilbert Elliot, First Earl of Minto*, (London 1874) ii, 187.

66. Nicholas, *Nelson Despatches and Letters* i, 378.

67. Rose, *Lord Hood* 46-7, 130; PRO HO 28/14, Hood to Dundas, 27 Oct 1793. In fact he had anticipated orders being sent out by Dundas, see HO 55/455, Dundas to Mulgrave, 10 Sept, 10 Oct 1793.

68. Rose, *Lord Hood* 98.

69. Sir R Vesey Hamilton (ed), *Letters and Papers of Sir Thos Byam Martin* (3 vols NRS 1898-1903) i, 188, 349-52.

70. Rose, *Lord Hood* 47-9, 54.

71. Minto (ed), *Life and Letters of Elliot* i, 191; Rose, *Lord Hood* 69-75. Hood's conduct towards the mili-

tary commanders at Toulon has been defended by Rose, p 88, and attacked by J B Fortescue, *History of the British Army* (7 vols London 1899-1912) iv pt 1, 173.

72. Rose, *Lord Hood* 64-86, 140; PRO HO 55/455, Dundas to Hood, Private 23 Nov 1793; Clowes, *The Royal Navy* iv, 552.

73. J R Dull, 'Why did the French Revolutionary Navy fail?', *Proceedings of the Consortium on Revolutionary Europe* (1989) ii, 125-7.

74. PRO WO 6/54, Dundas to Elliot, 31 March 1794.

75. Minto (ed), *Life and Letters of Elliot* ii, 233. For differing views on responsibility for these dissensions see J H Godfrey (ed), 'Corsica 1794', *The Naval Miscellany IV* 359-422; D Gregory, *The Ungovernable Rock. A history of the Anglo-Corsican Kingdom and its role in Britain's Mediterranean strategy during the Revolutionary War* (Cranbury, NJ 1985) ch 4.

76. Hood, *Admirals Hood* 152-4; 'Extracts from the Papers of Samuel, First Viscount Hood', in Laughton (ed), *Naval Miscellany I* 243-6; PRO PRO30/8/146 fos 7-8, 11-12, 13-16, Hood's letters to Pitt of 18 March, 18, 28 April 1795; J S Corbett and H W Richmond (eds), *The Private Papers of George, second Earl Spencer* (4 vols NRS 1913-24) i, 1-32; Aspinall (ed), *Later Correspondence of George III* ii, 431.

77. HMC, *Report on the MSS of J B Fortescue preserved at Dropmore* vii (London 1910) 257-8.

78. John A Tilley, *The British Navy and the American Revolution* (Columbia, SC 1987) 238-9.

79. Nicholas (ed), *Nelson Despatches and Letters* i, 487.

80. Stirling (ed), *Pages and Portraits* ii, 43.

81. BL Add MS 35193, to Alexander Hood 10, 21 April, 12 May 1780; Hannay (ed), *Hood Letters* 144.

82. Hannay (ed), *Hood Letters* 63; Nicholas (ed), *Nelson Despatches and Letters* i, 348.

83. Hannay (ed), *Hood Letters* 145.

84. G P B Naish (ed), *Nelson's Letters to his Wife and other Documents 1785-1831* (NRS 1958) 5; Tunstall (Tracy ed), *Naval Warfare* 198-9; Nicholas (ed), *Nelson Despatches and Letters* i, 312-13.

85. Nicholas (ed), *Nelson Despatches and Letters* i, 143-5.

86. Baugh, 'Hood: Superior Subordinate', in Billias (ed), *George Washington's Generals and Opponents* 145; Laughton (ed), *Barham Papers* i, 196, 208; Hannay (ed), *Hood Letters* 154; Rose, *Lord Hood* 18. Hannay (ed), *Hood Letters* 151-4 provides a good example of Hood's deductive methods.

87. Laughton (ed), *Barham Papers* i, 151.

88. G Cornwallis West (ed), *Life and letters of Admiral Cornwallis* (London 1927) 111; Nicholas (ed), *Nelson Despatches and Letters* i, 339, 361, 381.

89. Hannay (ed), *Hood Letters* 145; Laughton (ed), *Barham Papers* i, 228.

90. Stirling (ed), *Pages and Portraits* ii, 43.

91. Smith (ed), *Grenville Papers* iv, 374.

92. Laughton (ed), *Barham Papers* i, 147-8.

93. Tunstall (Tracy ed), *Naval Warfare* 197-200; NMM HOO/2/162, 164.

94. Laughton (ed), *Barham Papers* i, 165; Stirling, *Pages and Portraits* ii , 43; PRO PRO30/8/146 fos 27-8, Hood to Pitt, 12 Nov 1798.

95. *The Naval Chronicle* ii (1799) 45.
96. PRO Adm 33/539 (*Jamaica* paybook); Hood, *Admirals Hood* 53.
97. Hannay (ed), *Hood Letters* 95, 143-4.
98. Stirling (ed), *Pages and Portraits* ii, 43.
99. For a brief summary of Linzee's career see Surry and Thomas, *Portsmouth Book of Entries* 105.
100. Hannay (ed), *Hood Letters* 157; Cornwallis West (ed), *Life and letters of Cornwallis* 100; Sulivan, 'Graves and Hood', 176.
101. Hannay (ed), *Hood Letters* 3-64; Laughton (ed), *Barham Papers* i, 184.
102. Hamilton (ed), *Letters and Papers of Byam Martin* i, 174, 176-8, 189-90, 247.
103. R Morriss, *Cockburn and the British Navy in Transition. Admiral Sir George Cockburn 1772-1852* (Exeter 1997) 14-17.
104. Nicholas (ed), *Nelson Despatches and Letters* ii, 146.

Richard, Earl Howe

1. G B P Naish (ed), *Nelson's Letters to his Wife and other Documents, 1735-1831* (NRS 1958) 66, 28 Dec 1794; Anne French, *The Earl and Countess Howe by Gainsborough: a bicentenary exhibition* (English Heritage 1988) 48; D Syrett, 'A check list of Admiral Lord Howe manuscripts in United States Archives and Libraries', *MM* 67 (1981) 273-84.
2. Naish (ed), *Nelson's Letters to his Wife* 213, Nelson to his wife, 22 June 1795.
3. Sir John Barrow, *The Life of Richard Earl Howe* (London 1838) 118.
4. PRO Adm 6/86.
5. Barrow, *Life of Howe* 1-5, 314-5. See Nauticus Junior [Joseph Harris], *The Naval Atlantis* (London 1788) 4; By an officer, *An address to the Right Honourable the First Lord Commissioner of the Admiralty upon the visible Decreasing Spirit, Splendour, and Discipline of the Navy* (London 1787) 4.
6. D Erskine (ed), *Augustus Hervey's Journal* (London 1953) 143, 147-8.
7. A Pearsall, 'Landings on the French Coast, 1758', in N A M Rodger (ed), *The Naval Miscellany V* (NRS 1984) 210-40; R Harding, *Amphibious Warfare in the Eighteenth Century* (Woodbridge 1991) 181-5.
8. I D Gruber, *The Howe Brothers and the American Revolution* (New York 1972); D Syrett, *The Royal Navy in American Waters, 1775-1783* (Aldershot 1969) 1-116; D Baugh, 'The Politics of British Naval Failure, 1775-1777', *American Neptune* 52 (1992) 221-46.
9. Lady Bourchier, *Memoirs of Admiral Sir Edward Codrington* (2 vols London 1873) i, 12; Barrow, *Life of Howe* 420-1.
10. Quoted in Barrow, *Life of Howe* 117.
11. *Parliamentary Register,* 1781, vol 2, 70, app 14, 26 Feb 1781.
12 F Steuart (ed), *The Last Journals of Horace Walpole* (2 vols London 1910) ii, 429.
13. J Ehrman, *The Younger Pitt: the years of acclaim* (London 1969) 313-17; J E Talbott, *The Pen and Ink Sailor: Charles Middleton and the King's Navy, 1778-1813* (London 1998) 127-9; P C Webb, 'The Rebuilding and Repair of the Fleet, 1783-1793', *Bulletin of the Institute of Historical Research* 50 (1977) 194-209; 'The Navy and British Diplomacy 1783-1793', Mphil thesis (University of Cambridge 1971) 162, 174, 207.
14. Quoted in A Aspinall, *The Later Correspondence of George III* (5 vols London 1966) i, 12-13.
15. Barrow, *Life of Howe* 182.
16. J Pritchard, *Louis XV's Navy, 1748-1762: a study of organisation and administration* (Kingston and Montreal 1987) 70.
17. Howe's orders to Captain William Chaloner Burnaby, *Merlin* sloop, printed in J S Corbett, *Signals and Instructions, 1776-1794* (NRS 1908) 88.
18. B Lavery (ed), *Shipboard Life and Organisation 1731-1815* (NRS 1998) 61-70, 74-5; the *Magnanime's* order book is printed in full on pp 82-7.
19. PRO Adm 7/744, Signal orders issued by Howe, 23 June 1756.
20. B Tunstall (N Tracy ed), *Naval Warfare in the Age of Sail: the evolution of fighting tactics, 1650-1815* (London 1990) 117.
21. Corbett, *Signals and Instructions* 18-19; also his *Fighting Instructions, 1530-1816* (NRS London 1905) 252-79.
22. Tunstall (Tracy ed), *Naval Warfare* 194; Hugh Popham, *A Damned Cunning Fellow: the eventful life of Rear-Admiral Sir Home Popham KCB,KCH,KM,FRS 1762-1820* (Tywardreath 1991) 128-132.
23. Aspinall, *Later Correspondence of George III* i, p xvii.
24. A T Mahan, *Types of Naval Officers drawn from the History of the British Navy* (London 1902) 268.
25. R F Mackay, *Admiral Hawke* (Oxford 1965) 171-2.
26. Syrett, *American Waters* 97-110.
27. D Syrett, *The Royal Navy in European Waters during the American Revolutionary War* (Columbia, SC 1998) 156-63.
28. PRO Adm 1/101, 3 June 1794, quoted in G J Marcus, *A Naval History of England, Vol 2: the Age of Nelson* (London 1971) 36.
29. E P Brenton, *The Naval History of Great Britain* (5 vols London 1823-5) i, 366; M Duffy, 'Devon and the Naval Strategy of the French Wars, 1689-1815', in M Duffy et al (eds), *The New Maritime History of Devon* (2 vols London 1992 & 1994) i, 186. For the French cruise see E H Jenkins, *A History of the French Navy* (London 1973) 216-17.
30. I R Christie, *Stress and Stability in Late Eighteenth-Century Britain* (Oxford 1984) 35, quoted in N A M Rodger, *The Wooden World: an anatomy of the Georgian Navy* (London 1986) 345.
31. W Cobbett (ed), *The Parliamentary History of England* xx, cols 202, quoted in A N Ryan, 'The Royal Navy and the Blockade of Brest, 1689-1805', in Martine Acerra et al (eds), *Les Marines de Guerre Europeennes XVII-XVIII siecles* (Paris 1985) 184.
32. Mahan, *Types of Naval Officers* 268.

Charles Middleton, Lord Barham

1. W L Clowes, *The Royal Navy: a history from the earliest times to the present* (7 vols London 1897-1903) v, 110.

2. D Syrett, *Shipping and the American War 1775-1783: a study of British transport organisation* (London 1970) 22.
3. J K Laughton (ed*)*, *Letters and Papers of Charles Lord Barham 1758-1813* [hereafter *Barham*] (3 vols NRS 1907-1911).
4. Syrett, *Shipping* 231.
5. R A Morriss, 'Samuel Bentham and the management of the Royal Dockyards 1796-1807', *BIHR* liv (1981) 226-40.
6. *Barham* iii, 56.
7. *Barham* i, p xi.
8. *Barham* i, p xiv.
9. PRO Adm 1/5296 fo 183.
10. PRO Adm 1/5299 pt 1, fo 30.
11. *Barham* i, 1-20, 27-38.
12. J E Talbot, *The Pen and Ink Sailor. Charles Middleton and the King's Navy 1778-1813* (London 1998) 13; *Barham* i, p xvii
13. Talbot, *Pen and Ink Sailor* 12
14. *Barham* i, pp xviii-xix.
15. J M Collinge, *Navy Board Officials 1660-1832* (London 1978) 122.
16. N A M Rodger, *The Insatiable Earl: a life of John Montagu, fourth Earl of Sandwich* (London 1993) 159.
17. N A M Rodger, *The Insatiable Earl* 160.
18. D Syrett and R L DiNardo, *The Commissioned Sea Officers of the Royal Navy 660-1815* (NRS 1994) 169.
19. Talbot, *Pen and Ink Sailor* 27-8.
20. D Baugh, 'Why did Britain lose command of the sea during the war for America?', in J Black and P Woodfine (eds), *The British Navy and the Use of Naval Power in the Eighteenth Century* (Leicester 1988) 149-169; and Baugh 'The Politics of British Naval Failure, 1775-1777', *American Neptune* lii (1992) 21-46.
21. J Glete, *Navies and Nations: warships, navies and state building in Europe and America, 1500-1860* (2 vols Stockholm 1993) i, 273, 276.
22. NMM Middleton Papers MID/2/1/1 enc, 'Loose observations and hints on the proposed reformation of the Navy Board'.
23. J B Hattendorf et al (eds), *British Naval Documents 1204-1960* (NRS 1993) 460-2.
24. *Barham* ii, 300-1.
25. Syrett, *Shipping* 23, 55, 89.
26. R J B Knight, 'The performance of the Royal dockyards in England during the American War of Independence', in *The American Revolution and the Sea: the Proceedings of the 14th International Commission for Maritime History* (Basildon 1974) 139-144.
27. G R Barnes and J H Owen (eds), *The Private Papers of John Earl of Sandwich, First Lord of the Admiralty 1771-1782* [hereafter *Sandwich*] (4 vols NRS 1932-7) iii, 174-5.
28. N A M Rodger, *The Insatiable Earl* 298.
29. *Sandwich* iv, 285-7.
30. For a full account of the process of coppering the fleet see R J B Knight, 'The Introduction of Copper Sheathing into the Royal Navy 1779-1786', *MM* 59 (1973) 299-309; Talbot, *Pen and Ink Sailor* 45-60.
31. R J B Knight, 'The Royal Navy's Recovery after the Early Phase of the American Revolutionary War', in G J Andreopoulis and H E Selesky (eds), *The*

Aftermath of Defeat: societies, armed forces and the challenge of recovery (New Haven, Conn 1994) 10-25; N A M Rodger, *The Insatiable Earl* 296.
32. B Lavery, *The Arming and Fitting of English Ships of War 1600-1815* (London 1987) 105-6.
33. *Barham* ii, 42-3.
34. Talbot, *Pen and Ink Sailor* 65-9.
35. Baugh, 'Why did Britain lose command of the sea?' 153.
36. Knight, 'The Royal Navy's Recovery' 202.
37. R J B Knight, 'The Building and Maintenance of the British fleet during the Anglo-French Wars 1688-1815', in M Acerra, J Merino and J Meyer (eds), *Les Marines de Guerre Europeennes XVII-XVIIIe siecles* (Paris 1985) 35-50.
38. *Barham* iii, 295.
39. NMM Middleton Papers MID/8/6-11.
40. R J B Knight, 'Sandwich, Middleton and Dockyard appointments', *MM* 57(1971) 175-192.
41. For the correspondence between the two see *Barham* ii, 8-36; *Sandwich* iv, 376-83.
42. *Barham* ii, 2-7.
43. *Barham* ii, 315-6.
44. W L Clements Lib, University of Michigan Shelburne papers vol 151 fos 40-49 for Middleton's proposals to Shelburne concerning a general reform of the Navy Office, 9 & 26 Sept 1782; and concerning fees 10 Oct, 19 Dec 1782.
45. J Norris *Shelburne and Reform* (London 1963) 208-10.
46. *Barham* ii, 150.
47. *Barham* ii, 149, 152-3, 157-8.
48. *Barham* ii, 149, 176.
49. *Barham* ii, 149, 193-231 second after Shelburne in the Treasury Board patent of July 1782, first from Dec 1783. J Ehrman, *The Younger Pitt: the years of acclaim* (London 1969) 92, 299.
50. J Breihan, 'William Pitt and the Commission on Fees 1785-1801', *The Historical Journal* xxvii pt 1 (1984) 59-81.
51. Ehrman, *The Younger Pitt* 308, 314.
52. *Barham* ii, 207, 218, 223-250.
53. *Barham* ii, 287. The reports were eventually printed in House of Commons Accounts and Papers (1806) vii.
54. *Barham* ii, 258-9.
55. *Barham* ii, 213-17; Breihan, 'Commission on Fees' 67.
56. *Barham* ii, 193-208.
57. P Webb, 'The rebuilding and repair of the fleet, 1783-93', *BIHR* 50 (1977) 194-209.
58. R Vesey Hamilton (ed), *Letters and Papers of Admiral of the Fleet Sir Thomas Byam Martin* [hereafter *Martin*] (3 vols NRS 1898-1902) iii, 381; Ehrman, *The Younger Pitt* 313.
59. NMM Middleton Papers MID/14/13 'Observations on the Estimates, given into Parliament by the Navy Board 21st March 1786, on the calculation that a Permanent Peace Establishment would take place towards the end of the year 1790', dated July 1788.
60. Collinge, *Navy Board Officials* 143.
61. *Barham* ii, 315, 321, 324-6, 328-9, 332.
62. NMM Jackson Papers JCK/7 fos 9, 11, 92-6, 101-4. *Barham* ii, 315-9, 337-47. For discussion of the

wider issues involved in the failure to implement the reports of the Commission on Fees see Breihan, 'Commission on Fees' 69–72, 76–79; and Ehrman, *The Younger Pitt* 316–17, 556–7.

63. Collinge, *Navy Board Officials* 144; J C Sainty, *Admiralty Officials 1660–1870* (London 1975) 134.

64. *Barham* ii, 351–68.

65. Sainty, *Admiralty Officials* 26.

66. J S Corbett and H W Richmond (eds), *Private Papers of George second Earl Spencer 1794–1801* [hereafter *Spencer*] (4 vols NRS 1913–24) i, 6–7.

67. *Spencer* i, 7–14.

68. *Barham* ii, 386–414.

69. BL Add MS 41,079, 26 July 1794 and undated.

70. *Spencer* i, 46–7.

71. *Barham* i, 414–18.

72. BL Add MS 41,079, Middleton to Dundas, 10 Dec 1794; *Barham* i, 418–30; M Duffy, *Soldiers, Sugar and Seapower: the British expeditions to the West Indies and the war against revolutionary France* (Oxford 1987) 160–8.

73. NMM MID 1/186/8; MID 2/13/7; Scottish RO GD51/2/220/2, 3.

74. R A Morriss, *The Royal Dockyards during the Revolutionary and Napoleonic Wars* (Leicester 1983) 201.

75. *Barham* iii, 32, 55–6.

76. I Lloyd-Philips, 'Lord Barham at the Admiralty 1805–6', *MM* 64 (1978) 217–33.

77. *Barham* iii, p xv.

78. Talbot, *Pen and Ink Sailor* 152.

79. NMM MID/1/67/19 and 20.

80. NMM ADM BP/30A, 12 Mar 1810.

John Jervis, Earl of St Vincent

1. R F Mackay, 'Lord St Vincent's early years (1735–55)', *MM* 76 (1990) 54–5.

2. Mackay, 'Lord St Vincent' 60–2.

3. Mackay, 'Lord St Vincent' 62–3. N A M Rodger, *The Wooden World: an anatomy of the Georgian navy* (London 1986) 79–80, 262.

4. See Jervis's remark in discussions of tactics after the battle of Cape St Vincent, that 'Lord Hawke, when he ran out of the line and took the *Poder,* sickened me of tactics', Mackay, 'Lord St Vincent' 54.

5. C Lloyd, *The Capture of Quebec* (London 1959) 60.

6. The William Salt Library, Stafford, Parker-Jervis Collection 49/44, Bundle 91/1, Jervis to William Jervis, 16 Feb 1769.

7. J S Tucker, *Memoirs of Admiral the Right Honourable the Earl of St Vincent* (2 vols London 1844) ii, 15.

8. Tucker, *Memoirs* i, 86, 'however the Boys of other ships are employ'd when they are in Port, mine are kept strict to their duty, and are neither subject to habits of Vice or idleness . . .' NMM MS 94/034, Letters of John Jervis, Earl St Vincent to the second Earl of Shelburne, 1778–86, Jervis to Shelburne, 25 Nov 1781.

9. Sir Lewis Namier and John Brooke (eds), *The History of Parliament. The House of Commons 1754–1790* (2 vols London 1964) i, 682. MS 94/034, Jervis to Lord Shelburne, 29 June, 11 Aug, 25 Oct 1778, 20 July 1780, 8 Aug ?1780.

10. MS 94/034, Jervis to Lord Shelburne, 1 Sept, 20 & 29 Oct 1779.

11. J Charnock, *Biographia Navalis* (6 vols London 1794–8) v, 409. The scalp wound caused a flap of skin to fall over his eye and he suffered from a violent concussion which kept him convalescent indoors for at least ten days. He was still having trouble with his sight in August, when living with Barrington at Portsmouth. MS 94/034, 1 May, 29 Aug 1781, Jervis to Shelburne. Thus he could sympathise with Nelson, who suffered a similar wound at the Battle of the Nile.

12. MS 94/034, 23 Dec(?) 1783, Jervis to Shelburne.

13. Namier and Brooke (eds), *History of Parliament: Commons 1754–1790* ii, 682.

14. Parker-Jervis Collection, 49/44, Bundle 91/1, 21 Jan 1770.

15. Namier and Brooke (eds), *History of Parliament: Commons 1754–1790* ii, 682.

16. For Brodie see *DNB* vi, 380–81; R Thorne (ed), *The History of Parliament. The House of Commons 1790–1820* (5 vols London 1986) iv, 305.

17. R Thorne (ed), *History of Parliament: Commons 1790–1820* iv, 306.

18. M Duffy, *Soldiers, Sugar and Seapower: the British expeditions to the West Indies and the war against revolutionary France* (Oxford 1987) 106–114.

19. Tucker, *Memoirs* i, 143–4.

20. J S Corbett and H W Richmond (eds), *Private Papers of George second Earl Spencer 1794–1801* [hereafter *Spencer Papers*] (4 vols NRS 1913–24) i, 54–5, Earl Spencer to George III, 23 Sept 1795.

21. Tucker, *Memoirs* i, 149. Tucker was drawing on his memory of what his father, the admiral's secretary, had told him. Tucker correctly disclaimed his memory's accuracy and a study of the admiral's journal makes the sequence of events and dates clear. BL Add MSS 31,186, Journal of Lord St Vincent commanding in the Mediterranean [hereafter Journal of St Vincent] (2 vols 1795–1799) i, 5–8, 30 Nov to 12 Dec 1795.

22. Tucker, *Memoirs* i, 153.

23. Journal of St Vincent i, 8–19, 13 Dec 1795 to 15 Jan 1796. Tucker, *Memoirs* i, 172, Standing Order 2 Feb 1796.

24. Tucker, *Memoirs* i, 177, Standing Order 5 April 1796; 178–9, Memorandum 20 April 1796.

25. Journal of St Vincent i, 136–37, 15–18 Nov 1796.

26. Tucker, *Memoirs* i, 167–8, 189, General Order 6 July 1796.

27. BL Add MSS 31,159, Official Letter Books of the Earl of St Vincent, 1795–1807 [hereafter Letter Books of St Vincent] (7 vols) i [1795–7], 163–4, Jervis to Navy Board, 10 Aug 1796.

28. Letter Books of St Vincent i, Jervis to Navy Board, 221, 20 Sept 1796; Jervis to Navy Board, 205, 220, 8 & 20 Sept 1796.

29. Journal of St Vincent i, 6, 20, 27, 30.

30. Tucker, *Memoirs* i, 168, Standing Order 1 Jan 1796.

31. Letter Books of St Vincent i, 186, Jervis to Victualling Board, 17 Aug 1796.

32. Letter Books of St Vincent i, 213, Jervis to Sick and Hurt Board, 14 Sept, about soap; 200, 224, Jervis to Navy Board, 1 & 21 Sept 1796, about flannel shirts etc.

33. Letter Books of St Vincent i, 184, Jervis to Cookworthy, 24 Aug 1796.

34. BL Add MSS 31,166, Secret Official Letters of the Earl of St Vincent [hereafter Secret Letters of St Vincent] (2 vols 1795-1799) i, pt 1, 165-6, Jervis to Francis Drake,17 Sept 1796; pt 2, 129, St Vincent to Countess Spencer, 23 Dec 1798.

35. Letter Books of St Vincent i, 284, Jervis to Victualling Board, 11 Nov 1796.

36. N H Nicolas (ed), *Dispatches and Letters of Vice-Admiral Lord Viscount Nelson* (7 vols London 1844-6) i, 290-91, *c*17 Oct 1796.

37. C Lloyd, *St Vincent and Camperdown* (London 1963) 63.

38. C Lloyd, *St Vincent and Camperdown* 62.

39. C Lloyd, *St Vincent and Camperdown* 63.

40. C White, *The Battle of St Vincent 14 February 1797* (1805 Club, 1997) 20. The details of the battle are drawn from this latest study.

41. Nicolas, *Nelson's Letters* ii, 346, 'A Few Remarks relative to myself . . . on the most glorious Valentine's Day, 1797'.

42. C Lloyd, *St Vincent and Camperdown* 85.

43. M A J Palmer, 'Sir John's Victory: The Battle of Cape St Vincent Reconsidered', *MM* 77 (1991) 45.

44. Parker-Jervis Collection 49/44, Bundle 91/2, St Vincent to William Jervis, 16 July 1797.

45. Parker-Jervis Collection 49/44, Bundle 91/2, St Vincent to William Jervis, 16 July 1797. He wrote that he had signed as St Vincent for the first time that day, Tucker *Memoirs* i, 271.

46. Tucker, *Memoirs* i, 277, General Order 22 Dec 1796, 'The Admiral will expect every ship to be quite ready for sea in a week from the date thereof.'

47. Journal of St Vincent i, 172-96, 2 April to 18 May 1797; ii, 33-9, 9-25 Feb 1798; Secret Letters of St Vincent i, pt 2, 14-15, St Vincent to Rear-Admiral Sir William Parker, 14 Dec 1797.

48. Tucker, *Memoirs* i, 325, Evan Nepean, Secretary to the Admiralty, to St Vincent, 4 July 1797.

49. Tucker, *Memoirs* i, 401, St Vincent to Lord Spencer, 5 May 1797.

50. Tucker, *Memoirs* i, 410-11, St Vincent to Lord Spencer, 9 July 1797. Nelson approved the speedy execution despite it being carried out on a Sunday, Nicolas, *Nelson Letters* ii, 408-9, Nelson to St Vincent, 9 July 1797.

51. Tucker, *Memoirs* i, 437ff. See Secret Letters of St Vincent i, pt 2, 128, St Vincent to Don Rodrigo de Souza Continho, 22 Dec 1798, 'if there is a Man on Earth, or Sea, better formed and qualified, than another for acting in concert with allied Powers, Lord Nelson is that Man!'

52. Secret Letters of St Vincent i, pt 2, 65, St Vincent to Nelson, 17 June 1798; 85, 87, St Vincent to Sir John Orde, 1 Aug, 6 Sept 1798.

53. I hope to explore these incidents involving officers' protests in a later article.

54. Tucker, *Memoirs* i, 299, 300-301.

55. Tucker, *Memoirs* i, 449, Memoranda 14 & 15 July 1798; 447, Standing Order 3 June 1798.

56. Tucker, *Memoirs* i, 427-8, Standing Order 4 Nov 1797.

57. Tucker, *Memoirs* i, 304-8.

58. Secret Letters of St Vincent i, pt 2, 94, St Vincent to Captain Duckworth, 18 July 1798.

59. Tucker, *Memoirs* i, 314-15.

60. Tucker, *Memoirs* i, 315-16.

61. Tucker, *Memoirs* i, 476-8, St Vincent to Nepean, 16 April 1799.

62. Secret Letters of St Vincent i, pt 2, 113, St Vincent to Nelson, 8 Dec 1798 ; *Spencer Papers* ii, 402-3, St Vincent to Lord Spencer.

63. Tucker, *Memoirs* i, 445-6, Memorandum 28 May 1798; 324, Memorandum 3 July 1797, 384-7, 389.

64. Tucker, *Memoirs* i, 389-90.

65. Tucker, *Memoirs* i, 244, St Vincent to Nepean, 10 Dec 1799, 368, 377-8

66. BL Add MSS 31,187, Journal of Lord St Vincent ii, 196-7, 209, 212.

67. Tucker, *Memoirs* ii, 5.

68. BL Add MSS 35,201 Bridport Papers, vol xi, General Correspondence, vol ix, 1800-1806, fos 107-08, Domett to Lord Bridport, 16 Aug 1800.

69. Tucker, *Memoirs* ii, 9; Bonner Smith (ed), *The Letters of the Earl of St Vincent 1801-1804* [hereafter *St Vincent's Letters*] (2 volumes NRS 1921 & 1926) i, 323-4.

70. Tucker, *Memoirs* ii, 70, St Vincent to Lord Spencer, 21 June 1800.

71. Tucker, *Memoirs* ii, 65, St Vincent to Lord Spencer, 15 June 1800; Bridport Papers, fos 110-11, unsigned letter to Lord Bridport, probably from the purser of the *Royal George*, 17 Aug 1800.

72. Tucker, *Memoirs* ii, 35, St Vincent to Nepean, 25 Aug 1800.

73. Tucker, *Memoirs* ii, 97-8, General Order 20 Aug 1800 ; 57 General Order 20 May 1800.

74. Tucker, *Memoirs* ii, 35-6; 97-8 General Order 20 Aug 1800 ; 37 note.

75. Tucker, *Memoirs* ii, 98, St Vincent to Lord Spencer, 25 Aug 1800.

76. Tucker, *Memoirs* ii, 12-13.

77. Tucker, *Memoirs* ii, 13, 58, St Vincent to Nepean, 21 May 1800.

78. Tucker, *Memoirs* ii, 90, General Order 28 July 1800 ; 76, General Order 2 July 1800.

79. Tucker, *Memoirs* ii, 109, General Memorandum, 13 Oct 1800; 107, General Order 4 Oct 1800.

80. Letter Books of St Vincent i, pt 1, 183, Jervis to Sick and Hurt Board, 24 Aug 1796.

81. Tucker, *Memoirs* ii, 84-85, St Vincent to Dr Blane, 24 July 1800.

82. Tucker, *Memoirs* ii, 116, St Vincent to Lord Spencer, 19 Nov 1800.

83. Tucker, *Memoirs* ii, 31.

84. Tucker, *Memoirs* ii, 74-75, St Vincent to Hon George Berkeley, 2 July 1800.

85. Tucker, *Memoirs* ii, 60-61, St Vincent to Sir Thomas Pasley,10 June 1800; Bridport Papers, fos 107-08, Captain William Domett to Lord Bridport, 16 Aug 1800, off Brest.

86. Tucker, *Memoirs* ii, 40-42.

87. G Marcus, *A Naval History of England, Vol 2: The Age of Nelson* (London 1971) 156.

88. Nicolas, *Nelson Letters* iv, 184, Nelson to St Vincent, 1 Feb 1800.

89. Tucker, *Memoirs* ii, 128-29; 175, St Vincent to Lord Keith, 21 Feb 1801.

90. *St Vincent's Letters* i, 16–17.
91. Tucker, *Memoirs* ii, 133-36; *St Vincent's Letters* ii, 167,169-70, St Vincent to Sir A S Hamond, 9 March, 19 April 1801, 172-3, St Vincent to Commissioner Fanshawe, 30 April 1801.
92. R Morriss, *The Royal Dockyards during the Revolutionary and Napoleonic Wars* (Leicester 1983) 185. Much of what follows on dockyards and the civil reforms relies on this important book.
93. Morriss, *Royal Dockyards* 193 ; *St Vincent's Letters* i, 379-80, St Vincent to Rear-Admiral Collingwood, 15 March 1801.
94. *St Vincent's Letters* ii, 193, 29 Aug 1802, 194-5, 13 Sept 1802.
95. Tucker, *Memoirs* ii, 155-56 note.
96. Morriss, *Royal Dockyards* 194-5,196.
97. Morriss, *Royal Dockyards* 187.
98. *St Vincent's Letters* ii, 202-3, St Vincent to Sir A S Hamond, 2 Jan 1803.
99. *St Vincent's Letters* ii, 189, St Vincent to Sir A S Hamond,13 June 1802, 206, St Vincent to John Larking, 23 Jan 1803, 236, St Vincent to John Larking, 19 April 1804.
100. Morriss, *Royal Dockyards* 197, 198; Tucker, *Memoirs* ii, 127, Lord Hobart's description.
101. Morriss, *Royal Dockyards* 197-98 ; Tucker, *Memoirs* ii, 208.
102. Tucker, *Memoirs* ii, 255-6.
103. Morriss, *Royal Dockyards* 198-9.
104. Tucker, *Memoirs* ii, 252.
105. Tucker, *Memoirs* ii, 390.
106. Nicolas, *Nelson Letters* iii, 378, Nelson to St Vincent, 10 June 1799. Not all naval officers held such glowing opinions. See Captain Domett's letters to Lord Bridport, (Add MSS 35,201 Bridport Papers), with their slighting references to 'the Great Earl', fos 107-8, 16 Aug 1800, and to 'the Chief as they call him', fos 123-4, 28 Oct 1800.
107. See for example the numerous letters on the problem of promotion in *St Vincent's Letters* i, 323-63.
108. Nicolas, *Nelson's Letters* iii, 344, Nelson to St Vincent, 30 April 1799.
109. Tucker, *Memoirs* i, 101, Jervis to George Purvis, 20 Nov 1790.

Sir William Cornwallis

1. A T Mahan, *The Major Operations of the Navies in the War of American Independence* (London 1911) 157.
2. F and M Wickwire, *Cornwallis and the War of Independence* (London 1971) 34-6. Earl Cornwallis to William Cornwallis, 18 Oct 1764, in HMC, *Cornwallis Wykeham-Martin* 308.
3. N A M Rodger, *The Wooden World: an anatomy of the Georgian navy* (London 1986) 288-90.
4. Rodger, *The Wooden World* 17.
5. Sir L Namier and J Brooke (eds), *The History of Parliament. House of Commons 1754-1790* (2 vols London 1964) ii, 257-8 (Members).
6. R G Thorne (ed), *The History of Parliament. House of Commons 1790-1820* (5 vols London 1986) ii, 503-4.
7. N A M Rodger *The Insatiable Earl: a life of John Montagu, fourth Earl of Sandwich* (London 1993) 183-5, 250.

8. T Pocock, *Young Nelson in the Americas* (London 1980) 37.
9. F and M Wickwire, *Cornwallis: the imperial years* (London 1980) 48.
10. C N Parkinson, *War in the Eastern Seas* (London 1954) 58-68.
11. A T Mahan, *The Influence of Seapower upon the French Revolution and Empire* (2 vols Boston 1893) i, 177.
12. The King to Earl Spencer (First Lord of the Admiralty), in A Aspinall (ed), *Later Correspondence of King George III* (Cambridge 1968) iii, 289.
13. The alternative political philosophies symbolised by the two flagships invested the action that followed with a particular significance.
14. R Saxby, 'The Blockade of Brest in the French Revolutionary War', *MM* 78 (1992) 25-35 at p 27.
15. W James, *The Naval History of Great Britain* (6 vols London 1826) i, 236-43. James criticises both Edward Brenton and Charles Ekins for imposing a 'wedge' formation on the British force, with the *Royal Sovereign* at the 'apex' of the squadron.
16. Middleton to Lord Spencer, 27 & 30 June 1795, in J S Corbett and H W Richmond (eds), *Private Papers of George second Earl Spencer, First Lord of the Admiralty 1794-1801* [hereafter *Spencer Papers*] (4 vols NRS 1913-24) i, 47-9.
17. John Laughton entry on Cornwallis in *DNB* (London 1887) 246; Mahan, *French Revolution* i, 177.
18. M Duffy, *Soldiers, Sugar and Seapower: the British expeditions to the West Indies and the war against revolutionary France* (Oxford 1987) 166-9.
19. Nelson to Collingwood, 1 May 1796, in Sir H N Nicholas (ed), *The Dispatches and Letters of Lord Nelson* (7 vols London 1844-6) ii, 163-4.
20. *Spencer Papers* i , 137.
21. Duffy, *Soldiers, Sugar and Seapower* 215: *Spencer Papers* i, 220-9.
22. D Bonner Smith (ed), *Letters of Admiral of the Fleet the Earl of St Vincent 1801-1804* [hereafter *Letters of St Vincent*] (2 vols NRS 1921 & 1926) i, 322, St Vincent to Spencer, 29 Oct 1800; Collingwood to his sister, 16 Nov 1800, in E Hughes (ed), *The Private Correspondence of Lord Collingwood* (NRS 1957) 116-7.
23. Barham to Pitt, 9 Nov 1805, in J K Laughton (ed), *Letters of Lord Barham* [hereafter *Barham Letters*] (3 vols NRS 1907-11) iii, 333.
24. St Vincent to Vice-Admiral Sir H Harvey, 20 Feb 1801, in *Letters of St Vincent* i, 238.
25. *Letters of St Vincent* i, 243, St Vincent to Cornwallis, 1 April 1801.
26. Saxby 'Blockade of Brest' 32.
27. Mahan, *French Revolution* i, 373 & ii, 148.
28. M Steer, 'The Blockade of Brest and the Victualling of the Western Squadron, 1793-1805', *MM* 76 (1990) 307-16.
29. *Letters of St Vincent* i, 240, St Vincent to Cornwallis, 9 March 1801.
30. *Letters of St Vincent* i, 254, St Vincent to Cornwallis 3 Nov 1801.
31. Mahan, *French Revolution* ii, 148.
32. Mahan, *French Revolution* ii, 118-9.
33. Collingwood to J E Blackett, 20 July 1804 & 28 Aug 1804, in G L Newnham Collingwood, *Correspon-*

dence and Memoir of Lord Collingwood (London 1827) 96-7.

34. St Vincent to Admiral Markham, 28 Dec 1803, in Sir C Markham (ed), *Selections from the Correspondence of Admiral John Markham* (NRS 1904) 34.

35. *Letters of St Vincent* ii, 308, St Vincent to Lord Hobart, 8 July 1803 and to Cornwallis, 9 July 1803.

36. John Laughton's *DNB* entry on Gambier (vol xx, London 1889) provides an astute summary.

37. HMC, *Cornwallis Wykeham Martin* 424-5, Melville to Cornwallis, 14 July 1804.

38. Aspinall, *George III* iv, 315-6.

39. Barham, 15 Aug 1805, in HMC, *Cornwallis Wykeham-Martin* 411.

40. Mahan, *French Revolution* ii, 176 As Mahan later confessed to Laughton, his main sources for this period were the letters of Napoleon and Nelson; John Leyland, who was far better informed, was ambivalent in his introduction to the *Blockade of Brest* volumes (2 vols NRS 1898 & 1901): see ii, p xxxix.

41. P Colomb, *Naval Warfare* (London 1890) 178.

42. J S Corbett, *The Campaign of Trafalgar* (London 1910) 42-6, 187-9, 251, 253, 255, 259.

43. Corbett, *Trafalgar* 245-9 & 250n.

44. A T Mahan, *Naval Strategy* (Boston 1911) 116-8. It should be noted that this book was essentially a published version of Mahan's old lectures form the early 1890s, and he was not very happy with it.

45. E Desbriere, *The Trafalgar Campaign* (2 vols Oxford 1933; edited and translated by C Eastwick, from the French original of 1907) i, 136-9.

46. Barham to Cornwallis, 28 Aug 1805, in *Barham Letters* iii , 277.

47. *Barham Letters* iii , 280, Barham to Cornwallis, 11 Oct 1805 ; Corbett, *Trafalgar* 301-313.

48. Keith to Barham, 29 Dec 1805, and anonymous to Barham, 4 Sept & 27 Dec 1805, in *Barham Letters* iii , 178-9, 203-4.

49. A D Lambert, *The Last Sailing Battlefleet: maintaining naval mastery 1815-1850* (London 1991) 68.

50. Parkinson, *War in the Eastern Seas* 56 & 64.

51. Keith to Markham, 24 Dec 1803, in Sir C Markham (ed), *Correspondence of Admiral John Markham* 125.

52. Leyland, *Blockade of Brest* ii, introduction p xliv.

George Keith Elphinstone, Lord Keith

Uncredited quotations on operational matters are from W G Perrin (Vol i) and Christopher Lloyd (eds), *The Keith Papers* (3 vols NRS 1927, 1950, 1955). Quotations on personal matters are from the transcriptions of Keith's letters to his sister in NMM KEI/146. The originals are in Bowood House.

1. Scottish Historical Society Jacobite papers 354-8, PRO SP 54/27 fos 1d, 18b, 18c, 57.

2. Sir William Frazer, *The Elphinstone Family Book* (2 vols Edinburgh 1987) i, 270, 243.

3. Frazer, *The Elphinstone Family Book* i, 270.

4. Alexander Allardyce, *Admiral Lord Keith* (London 1882) 11-2.

5. PRO Adm 1/1763.

6. G B P Naish (ed), *Nelson's Letters to his Wife* (NRS 1958) 488, 493, 541-2, 512.

7. PRO Adm 50/36.

8. Peter Bloomfield (ed), *Kent and the Napoleonic Wars* (Gloucester 1987) 121.

9. J K Laughton (ed), *Letters of Lord Barham* (3 vols NRS 1907-11) iii, 155, 162.

10. A Aspinall (ed), *The Correspondence of George, Prince of Wales 1770-1812* (8 vols London 1963-71) v, 208-9.

11. A Hayward (ed), *Autobiography, Letters and Literary Remains of Mrs Piozzi* (2 vols London 1861) ii, 163 , 29, 171, 188, 191, 204, 241, 249, 262.

12. G L Pride, *The Kingdom of Fife, an Illustrated Architectural Guide* (Edinburgh 1990) 23.

Select Bibliography

Unless otherwise stated, place of publication is London.

P Aubrey, *The Defeat of James Stuart's Armada 1692* (Leicester 1979).

G R Barnes and J H Owen (eds), *The Private Papers of John, Earl of Sandwich First Lord of the Admiralty 1771-1782* (4 vols NRS 1932-8).

Daniel A Baugh, *British Naval Administration in the Age of Walpole* (Princeton 1965).

Daniel A Baugh (ed), *Naval Administration 1715-1750* (NRS 1977).

G A Bilias (ed), *George Washington's Opponents: British generals and admirals in the American Revolution* (New York 1969).

Jeremy Black and P Woodfine (eds), *The British Navy and the Use of Naval Power in the Eighteenth Century* (Leicester 1988).

Jeremy Black, *Britain as a Military Power 1688-1815* (1999).

D Bonner Smith (ed), *The Letters of Admiral of the Fleet the Earl of St Vincent* (2 vols NRS 1921 & 1926).

J S Bromley (ed), *The Manning of the Royal Navy: selected public pamphlets 1693-1873* (NRS 1976).

Calendar of State Papers, Domestic Series 1660-1703 (1886-1939, 1960-72).

E Chappell (ed), *The Tangier Papers of Samuel Pepys* (NRS 1935).

J M Collinge, *Navy Board Officials 1660-1832* (Office-Holders in Modern Britain vol vii 1978).

G Cornwallis-West, *The Life and Letters of Admiral Cornwallis* (1927).

Julian S Corbett, *England in the Seven Years War: a study of combined strategy* (2 vols 1907).

Julian S Corbett and Herbert W Richmond (eds), *The Private Papers of George, Second Earl Spencer, First Lord of the Admiralty* (4 vols NRS 1913-24).

Julian S Corbett (ed), *Fighting Instructions 1530-1816* (NRS 1905).

J Creswell, *British Admirals of the Eighteenth Century: tactics in battle* (1972).

D G Crewe, *Yellow Jack and the Worm; British naval administration in the West Indies 1739-1748* (Liverpool 1993).

J D Davies, *Gentlemen and Tarpaulins: the officers and men of the Restoration navy* (Oxford 1991).

J D Davies, 'James II, William of Orange and the Admirals', in E Cruickshanks (ed), *By Force or By Default: the Revolution of 1688-9* (1989).

Michael Duffy, *Soldiers, Sugar and Seapower: the British expeditions to the West Indies and the war against Revolutionary France* (Oxford 1987).

Michael Duffy (ed), *Parameters of British Naval Power 1650-1850* (Exeter 1992).

John Ehrman, *The Navy in the War of William III, 1689-1697: its state and direction* (Cambridge 1953).

A D Francis, *The First Peninsular War 1702-1713* (1975).

Robert Gardiner, *The First Frigates: nine-pounder and twelve-pounder frigates 1748-1815* (1992).

Robert Gardiner (ed), *The Line of Battle: the sailing warship 1650-1840* (1992).

Jan Glete, *Navies and Nations: warships, navies and state building in Europe and America, 1500-1860* (2 vols Stockholm 1993).

S Gradish, *The Manning of the British Navy During the Seven Years War* (1980).

Eric Grove (ed), *Great Battles of the Royal Navy as Commemorated in the Gunroom, Britannia Royal Naval College, Dartmouth* (1994).

Ira D Gruber, *The Howe Brothers and the American Revolution* (Chapel Hill, North Carolina 1972).

Richard Harding, *Amphibious Warfare in the Eighteenth Century: the British expedition to the West Indies, 1740-1742* (Woodbridge 1991).

Richard Harding, *Seapower and Naval Warfare 1650-1830* (1999).

Historical Manuscript Commission Reports: Eleventh Report appendix ii; Twelfth Report appendix vi; Thirteenth Report appendix v; Fourteenth Report appendix vi: manuscripts of the House of Lords 1678-1693 (4 vols 1887-94).

Eleventh Report appendix v; *Fifteenth Report* appendix part 1: manuscripts of the Earl of Dartmouth (3 vols 1887-1896).

Twelfth Report appendix vii: manuscripts of S W le Fleming at Rydal Hall (1890).

Fourteenth Report appendix ix: manuscripts of the Earls of Buckinghamshire, Onslow and others (1895).

Manuscripts of His Grace the Duke of Rutland, preserved at Belvoir Castle (4 vols 1888-1905).

Manuscripts of J B Fortescue Esq Preserved at Dropmore (10 vols 1892-1927).

Manuscripts of His Grace the Duke of Buccleuch and Queensbury, KG, KT preserved at Drumlanrig Castle (2 vols 1899 & 1903).

Manuscripts of the House of Lords 1693-1714 (New Series 11 vols 1900-1962).

Manuscripts in Various Collections (8 vols 1904-14).

Manuscripts of Mrs Stopford-Sackville of Drayton House, Northamptonshire (2 vols 1904 & 1910).

Manuscripts of Lady Du Cane (1905).

Manuscripts of Cornwallis Wykeham-Martin (1909).

Manuscripts of the Earls of Polwarth (3 vols 1911-31).

Manuscripts of the Late Alan George Finch, Esq of Burley-on-the-Hill, Rutland (4 vols 1913-65).

Manuscripts of the Earl of Egmont (3 vols 1920-3).

Manuscripts of the Marquess of Downshire, preserved at Easthampstead Park, Berks (2 vols 1924 & 1936).

David Hannay (ed), *Letters written by Sir Samuel Hood in 1781-3* (NRS 1895).

John B Hattendorf, *England in the War of Spanish Succession* (New York and London 1987).

John B Hattendorf et al (eds), *British Naval Documents 1204-1960* (NRS 1993).

J R Hill (ed), *The Oxford Illustrated History of The Royal Navy* (Oxford 1993).

J R Hill, *The Prizes of War: the naval prize system in the Napoleonic Wars 1793-1815* (Stroud 1998).

Sari Hornstein, *The Restoration Navy and English Foreign Trade, 1674-1688* (Aldershot 1991).

J C Hugill, *No Peace Without Spain* (1991).

Ronald Hurst, *The Golden Rock: an episode of the American War of Independence 1775-1783* (1996).

John Knox Laughton (ed), *Letters and Papers of Charles, Lord Barham 1758-1813* (3 vols NRS 1907-11).

John Knox Laughton (ed), *Memoirs Relating to the Lord Torrington* (Camden Society 1889).

Brian Lavery, *The Ship of the Line* (2 vols 1983 & 1984).

Brian Lavery (ed), *Shipboard Life and Organisation, 1731-1815* (NRS 1998).

Peter Le Fevre, 'The Battle of Bantry Bay 1 May 1689', *Irish Sword* 18 (1990).

Peter Le Fevre, ' "Sacrifice to the Allies"? the Earl of Torrington and the Battle of Beachy Head 30 June 1690', in *Guerres Maritimes 1688-1713* (IVes Journées franco-britanniques d'histoire de la marine, Vincennes 1996).

Peter Le Fevre, ' "Meer Laziness or Incompetence": the Earl of Torrington and the Battle of Beachy Head', *The Mariner's Mirror* 80 (1994).

John Leyland (ed), *The Blockade of Brest, 1803-1805* (2 vols NRS 1898 & 1901).

Lords Journal xiv-xx (1685-1718).

B McL Ranft (ed), *The Vernon Papers* (NRS 1958).

Ruddock F Mackay, *Admiral Hawke* (Oxford 1965).

Ruddock F Mackay (ed), *The Hawke Papers: a selection 1743-1771* (NRS 1990).

R D Merriman (ed), *The Sergison Papers, 1689-1702* (NRS 1950).

R D Merriman (ed), *Queen Anne's Navy* (NRS 1961).

Richard Middleton, *The Bells of Victory: the Pitt-Newcastle ministry and the conduct of the Seven Years War, 1757-1762* (Cambridge 1985).

Roger Morriss, *The Royal Dockyards during the Revolutionary and Napoleonic Wars* (Leicester 1983).

J H Owen, *War at Sea under Queen Anne* (Cambridge 1938).

Richard Pares, *War and Trade In the West Indies, 1739-1763* (Oxford 1936).

W G Perrin and C Lloyd (eds), *The Keith Papers* (3 vols NRS 1927, 1950, 1955).

E B Powley, *The English Navy and the Revolution of 1688* (Cambridge 1928).

E B Powley, *The Naval Side of King William's War* (Hamden Conn and London 1972).

Herbert W Richmond, *The Navy in the War of 1739-1748* (3 vols Cambridge 1920).

Herbert W Richmond, *The Navy as an Instrument of Policy 1558-1727* (Cambridge 1953).

N A M Rodger, *The Wooden World: an anatomy of the Georgian navy* (1986).

N A M Rodger, *The Insatiable Earl: a life of John Montagu, fourth Earl of Sandwich* (1993).

J H Rose, *Lord Hood and the Defence of Toulon* (Cambridge 1922).

J C Sainty, *Admiralty Officials 1660-1870* (Office-Holders in Modern Britain vol iv 1975).

J Sweetman (ed), *The Great Admirals: command at sea, 1587-1945* (Annapolis 1997).

D Spinney, *Rodney* (1969).

Neil Stout, *The Royal Navy in America, 1760-1775: a study of enforcement of British colonial policy in the era of the American Revolution* (Annapolis 1973).

Geoffrey Symcox, *The Crisis of French Sea Power 1688-1697: from guerre d'escadre to guerre de course* (The Hague 1974).

David Syrett, *The Royal Navy in American Waters 1775-1783* (1989).

David Syrett, *The Royal Navy in European Waters During the American Revolutionary War* (Columbia, South Carolina 1998).

David Syrett and RL DiNardo (eds), *Commissioned Sea Officers of the Royal Navy, 1660-1815* (NRS 1994).

J E Talbot, *The Pen and Ink Sailor: Charles Middleton and the King's Navy 1778-1813* (1998).

J R Tanner (ed), *A Descriptive Catalogue of the Naval Manuscripts in the Pepysian Library at Magdalene College Cambridge* (4 vols NRS 1903-1909).

John A Tilley, *The British Navy and the American Revolution* (Columbia, South Carolina 1987).

Nicholas Tracy, *Navies, Deterrence and American Independence: Britain and seapower in the 1760s and 1770s* (Vancouver, British Columbia 1988).

Nicholas Tracy, *Nelson's Battles: the art of victory in the age of sail* (1996).

Brian Tunstall (ed), *The Byng Papers* (3 vols NRS 1930-3).

Brian Tunstall (Nicholas Tracy ed), *Naval Warfare in the Age of Sail: the evolution of fighting tactics 1650-1815* (1990).

Oliver Warner, *The Glorious First of June* (1961).

Colin White, *The Battle of St Vincent 14 February 1797* (1805 Club 1997).

Glyndwr Williams (ed), *Documents relating to Anson's Voyage round the World, 1740-1744* (NRS 1967).

Glyndwr Williams, *The Prize of all the Oceans: the triumph and tragedy of Anson's voyage round the world* (London 1999).

P Woodfine, *Britannia's Glories: the Walpole ministry and the 1739 war with Spain* (Woodbridge 1998).

Index